Fifth Edition

LEADERSHIP

A Communication Perspective

Michael Z. Hackman
University of Colorado–Colorado Springs

Craig E. Johnson
George Fox University

WAVELAND

PRESS, INC.

Long Grove, Illinois

For information about this book, contact:
    Waveland Press, Inc.
    4180 IL Route 83, Suite 101
    Long Grove, IL 60047-9580
    (847) 634-0081
    info@waveland.com
    www.waveland.com

10-digit ISBN 1-57766-579-1
13-digit ISBN 978-1-57766-579-3

Printed in the United States of America

7   6   5

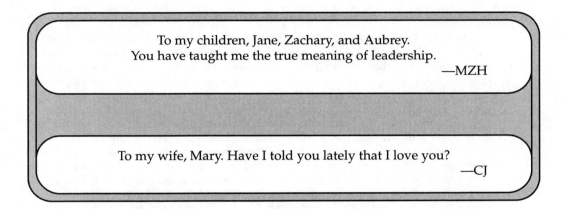

To my children, Jane, Zachary, and Aubrey.
You have taught me the true meaning of leadership.

—MZH

To my wife, Mary. Have I told you lately that I love you?

—CJ

About the Authors

Michael Z. Hackman is a Professor in the Department of Communication at the University of Colorado–Colorado Springs and an Adjunct at the Center for Creative Leadership. He teaches courses in communication at both the undergraduate and graduate levels, including courses supported by a grant from the U.S. Department of Education Fund for the Improvement of Post-Secondary Education (FIPSE) that allowed for the development of an online curriculum in organizational communication and leadership delivered to students and working professionals in the United States and Europe. In 1995, he was awarded the university-wide Outstanding Teacher Award. Dr. Hackman's research focuses on a wide range of communication issues, including: the impact of gender and culture on communication and leadership behavior, leadership succession, organizational trust, and creativity. His work has appeared in such journals as *Communication Education, Communication Quarterly, Distance Education, The Journal of Leadership Studies, Leadership, Perceptual and Motor Skills*, and the *Southern Speech Communication Journal*. Since 1991, Dr. Hackman has served as a Visiting Professor at the University of Waikato in Hamilton, New Zealand, on four separate occasions, the most recent in 2002. He also served as an adjunct Professor at the University of Siena (Italy) and the University of Vienna (Austria). Dr. Hackman has extensive experience as a consultant. He has developed and delivered training, guided organizational development initiatives, and provided executive coaching services in numerous public and private sector organizations throughout the United States and in Australia, Austria, Canada, China, Italy, Luxembourg, the Netherlands, and New Zealand. His clients have included Agilent Technologies, Bristol-Meyers Squibb, Ernst & Young, Fiat, Georgia-Pacific, Harley-Davidson, Hewlett-Packard, J.D. Edwards, Telecom New Zealand, the U.S. Air Force, the U.S. Golf Association, and Wells Fargo.

Craig E. Johnson is a Professor of Leadership Studies and Director of the Doctor of Management program at George Fox University, Newberg, Oregon. He teaches a variety of leadership, management, and ethics courses at the undergraduate and doctoral level. He also acts as faculty director of the university's interdisciplinary leadership studies minor. Previously he served as chair of the university's Department of Communication Arts.

Dr. Johnson is author of *Ethics in the Workplace: Tools and Tactics for Organizational Transformation* and *Meeting the Ethical Challenges of Leadership: Casting Light or Shadow* (3rd ed.). His articles have appeared in such journals as *Communication Quarterly, The Journal of Leadership Studies, The Journal of Leadership and Organizational Studies, The Journal of Leadership Education, Communication Education, Communication Reports*, and *The Journal of the International Listening Association*. Dr. Johnson's research interests include leadership ethics, organizational ethics, and leadership education. He has served in leadership roles in several nonprofit organizations and has participated in educational and service trips to Kenya, Honduras, Brazil, and New Zealand. Professor Johnson is a past recipient of George Fox University's distinguished teaching award.

Acknowledgments

No book makes it to a fifth edition without the help of a great many people. We are particularly grateful to readers of previous editions who demonstrated that there is a need for a text that examines leadership from a communication vantage point. Special thanks to those who have offered words of encouragement over the years.

Students and colleagues provided us with many of their own leadership stories along with encouragement, advice, and support. In particular we want to recognize Alvin Goldberg, our mentor at the University of Denver, who was instrumental in igniting our interest in the topic of leadership.

Many of our associates, past and present, have also been helpful in focusing our thoughts concerning leadership. Most notably we want to thank Ted Baartmans and Rick Koster of the Presentation Group in Bloemendaal, the Netherlands; Kevin Barge of Texas A&M University; Stephen Bowden, Neil Harnisch, and Ted Zorn of the University of Waikato, New Zealand; Jim Fleming, Shaun McNay, Scott Wade, Kristina Findley, and Mark Pothoff of George Fox University; Nadyne Guzman and Pamela Shockley-Zalabak of the University of Colorado–Colorado Springs; and Bryan Poulin of Lakehead University, Canada. Thanks also to our editor at Waveland Press, Carol Rowe, who has been a constant source of encouragement and inspiration.

Special recognition goes to the many research assistants who helped with previous editions—Almarah Belk, Karen Bisset, Marylou Berg, Carrie Brown, Chris Cooper, Joanne Desrochers, Fred Gatz, Sarah Gillespie, Gina Hallem, Hush Hancock, Peg Hutton, Misse Lampe, Ashley Lewis, Amanda Martell, Kevin O'Neill, Sandee Robinson, Melissa Rowberg, Rich Seiber, Heather Smith, and Penny Whitney—and to those who helped prepare materials for this edition—Michael Campbell, Rebeca Kerr, and Sandra Robinson. Our greatest appreciation, however, is reserved for our families who lovingly supported our journey to explore the latest developments in leadership.

Contents

3   Traits, Situational, Functional, and Relational Leadership   71

4   Transformational and Charismatic Leadership   101

12   Leader and Leadership Development   369

13   Leadership in Crisis   401

Preface

Revising a text presents a series of challenges. The first hurdle is determining what to leave in from previous editions and what to take out. Then there is the challenge of staying current with the rapidly expanding fields of leadership studies and communication. That leads to yet another dilemma—deciding just how much new material to add.

We've tried to strike a balance in answering these challenges. We have replaced a number of cases, assessment exercises, and research highlights while retaining others. We have surveyed new trends and research findings but realize we can't include them all. Instead, we have incorporated those we judged the most relevant into this fifth edition. Coverage of the text has been expanded, but within reasonable limits.

Leadership: A Communication Perspective also balances theory and practice. Each chapter blends discussion of research and theory with practical suggestions for improving leadership effectiveness. To facilitate application, chapter summaries have been replaced with chapter takeaways that highlight important concepts and action steps. There are now ten application exercises at the end of each chapter.

Readers of the previous edition of *Leadership: A Communication Perspective* will note two major additions: (1) a new chapter on crisis leadership and (2) a new feature at the end of every chapter—Spotlight on Technology—which demonstrates the impact of modern technology on the practice of leadership. There is also new material on bad leadership, shared leadership, storytelling, leadership and information processing, false agreement, organizational learning and trust, altruism, spirituality, and coaching. Discussion of a number of other topics—impression management, LMX theory, credibility, public relations, public speaking, follower ethics, and leadership development—has been expanded. We've updated examples and sources throughout the book. All of the films and documentaries highlighted in the Leadership on the Big Screen feature at the end of every chapter are new to this edition.

The first six chapters introduce the fundamentals of leadership. Chapter 1 examines the relationship between leadership and communication with an in-depth look at the nature of leadership, both good and bad, and the leader/follower relationship. Chapter 2 surveys the research on leader and follower communication styles as well as the link between information processing and style selection. Chapters 3 and 4 summarize the development of leadership theory. Chapters 5 and 6 focus on two elements—power and influence—that are essential to the practice of leadership.

The next three chapters provide an overview of leadership in specific contexts. Chapter 7 introduces group leadership, contrasts groups and teams, and describes the use of self-directed work teams. Chapter 8 is a discussion of organizational leadership with particular focus on the creation of culture and the communication of expectations. Chapter 9 examines the power of public leadership, highlighting public relations, public speaking, and persuasive campaigns.

The final four chapters look at important leadership issues. Chapter 10 describes the impact of cultural differences on leading and following, how to foster diversity, and how to narrow the gender leadership gap. Chapter 11 outlines the ethical challenges facing leaders and followers, components of ethical behavior, and ethical perspectives that can guide both leaders and followers. Chapter 12 identifies proactive leader development strategies as well as tools for managing leadership transitions. Chapter 13 examines the role of leadership in preventing and responding to crises.

As we noted in the preface to previous editions, this text is designed as an introduction to leadership from a communication vantage point, not as the final word (as if there could be one) on the topic. Please consider *Leadership: A Communication Perspective* as our part of a continuing dialogue with you on the subjects of leading and following. Throughout the book we'll invite you to disagree with our conclusions, generate additional insights of your own, debate controversial issues, and explore topics in depth through research projects, reflection papers, and small group discussions. If we've ignored issues that you think are essential to the study and practice of leadership, let us know. Send your comments and suggestions to us via e-mail or regular mail to the addresses below or in care of Waveland Press.

Michael Z. Hackman
Department of Communication
University of Colorado–Colorado Springs
1420 Austin Bluffs Parkway
Colorado Springs, CO 80918
mhackman@uccs.edu

Craig Johnson
School of Management
George Fox University
414 Meridian St.
Newberg, OR 97132
cjohnson@georgefox.edu

CHAPTER

one

Leadership and Communication

Leadership is action, not position

—Donald McGannon

OVERVIEW

Leadership: At the Core of Human Experience

Leadership attracts universal attention. Historians, philosophers, and social scientists have attempted to understand and to explain leadership for centuries. From Confucius to Plato to Machiavelli, many of the world's most renowned thinkers have theorized about how people lead one another.[1] One reason for the fascination with this subject lies in the very nature of human experience. Leadership is all around us. We get up in the morning, open the newspaper, turn on our computer, radio, or television, and discover what actions leaders all over the world have taken. We attend classes, work, and interact in social groups—all with their own distinct patterns of leadership. Our daily experiences with leadership are not that different from the experiences of individuals in other cultures. Leadership is an integral part of human life in rural tribal cultures as well as in modern industrialized nations. Looking at your past leadership efforts can help to provide a good starting point for understanding why the success of leadership often varies so significantly. Identify your own best and worst leadership moments and what you can learn from these experiences by completing the self-assessment exercise in box 1.1.

While leadership is part of every society, there are scholars who question just how much difference one leader can make. These observers argue that a leader only accounts for a small portion of a group's success or failure and gets the credit (or blame) when other forces are really at work.[2] The fate of a business, for example, may rest more on industry trends and market conditions than on the decisions of the CEO. The best school principal can't improve the academic performance of students without committed, talented teachers.

We acknowledge that the importance of leadership can be overstated. Yet, we remain convinced that leaders do make a difference. For every study that casts doubt on the importance of leadership, several more establish that leaders have a significant impact on group outcomes.[3] Attempts to devalue leadership appear to be losing their momentum. Some skeptics who earlier doubted the significance of leaders now admit that these individuals exert strong influence on organizations and the experiences of their members.[4] Followers prosper under effective leaders and suffer under ineffective leaders whatever the context: government, corporation, church or synagogue, school, athletic team, or class project group. The effects of leadership scandals in organizations such as Enron, Fannie Mae, and AIG Insurance underscore the fact that leadership does have an impact. The study of leadership, then, is more than academic. Understanding leadership has practical importance for all of us. (See the case study in box 1.2 for a dramatic example of how important leadership can be.) In this text we will examine leadership in a wide variety of situations. However, our perspective remains the same—leadership is best understood from a communication standpoint. As Gail Fairhurst and Robert Sarr explain, effective leaders use language as their most tangible tool for achieving desired outcomes.[5] Let's begin our exploration of leadership by considering the special nature of human communication and the unique qualities of leadership.

Box 1.1   Self-Assessment
Your Best and Worst Leadership Moment[6]

Everyone has enjoyed leadership success at some point. At some time—whether in high school, college, on the athletic field, in a community or religious group, or at work—we have all made things happen through other people. We have all been leaders. Looking back over your life, what is the experience that you are *most* proud of as a leader? Use the space below to capture the details of that moment.

_____

_____

_____

Just as all of us have enjoyed success, we've also experienced the pain of leadership failure. Learning to be a leader requires looking back and learning from past mistakes so that you don't repeat errors. What was your most disappointing experience as a leader? Record your thoughts in the space below.

_____

_____

_____

Given the best and worst leadership experiences you identified, consider the lessons you have learned about leadership in the past. In working through this assessment it can be very helpful to share your leadership stories with others so that you have a richer set of examples from which to compile a list of leadership lessons. The lessons learned from past leadership experiences might be things like: *It is difficult to succeed as a leader when followers are not motivated; leadership works best when you have a clear sense of direction;* or *a leader must be sure his or her message is understood to ensure followers stay involved.* Try to identify 10 leadership lessons your experiences (and, if possible, those of others) have provided.

Leadership Lessons

1.

2.

3.

4.

5.

6.

7.

8.

9.

10.

Box 1.2 Case Study

Death on Everest

Leadership in high-risk activities like white-water rafting, rappelling, and mountain climbing can literally mean the difference between life and death. In the best selling book *Into Thin Air*, writer and alpine expert Jon Krakauer describes how poor leadership decisions contributed to disaster on Mt. Everest, the highest mountain on earth at 29,038 feet.[7]

In April 1996, Krakauer joined the Adventure Consultants expedition to write an article on the Everest climb for *Outside* magazine. Several groups were on the mountain that spring, but the Adventure Consultants team was most closely allied with an expedition organized by a company called Mountain Madness. The leaders of the two teams had very different approaches to guiding. Rob Hall, 35, the New Zealander heading Adventure Consultants, was a cautious, well-organized climber. He had a "methodical, fastidious approach" to his ascents. Because of his successful experience as an Everest guide, the leaders of other parties came to him for advice. In contrast, American Scott Fischer, head of the Mountain Madness group, took a "harrowing, damn-the-torpedoes approach." The 40-year-old Fischer refused to let injuries and sickness slow him down. He was a gregarious, energetic leader who made friends quickly. This was his organization's first guided expedition up Everest. Clients, many of them novice climbers, paid $65,000 each for the trip.

Scaling Mt. Everest is a dangerous undertaking. Climbers suffer from a variety of altitude-related illnesses, including frostbite, hypothermia, severe weight loss, and lung and brain damage. Many have fallen to their deaths. At the very least, the extreme altitude (the top of the mountain is at the cruising level for commercial jet aircraft) makes reasoning difficult. In more extreme cases, trekkers hallucinate and become disoriented. Ill and injured team members must be carried halfway down the mountain to where the atmosphere thickens enough to allow evacuation by helicopter.

The Hall and Fischer expeditions (twenty climbers in all) started their final ascent around midnight on Friday, May 9. Members of both parties were told to head back to camp no later than 2 PM even if they had not reached the summit. Staying later would exhaust the climbers' bottled oxygen supply, increasing the chances of hypothermia, frostbite, and impaired thought. Tardy clients wouldn't be able to make it back to shelter before darkness fell.

The push to the top got off to a slow start due to bottlenecks of climbers at narrow places on the trail. Krakauer made it to the summit around 1 PM and headed down. However, Rob Hall and Scott Fischer ignored their own deadlines, perhaps out of competitive pressure. Hall was disappointed that most of his climbers had already turned back while Fischer's party was still on the way to the top. He wanted to make sure that a client who had failed to reach the summit the year before succeeded this time. Fischer needed a successful climb to build his business. Climbers from both groups were still on the summit well after 3 PM. Around 6 PM a blizzard struck with driving snow and winds of over 60 knots. Krakauer made it to safety but Hall and Fischer did not. Despite the rescue attempts of other climbing teams, the two leaders and three of their clients died. Another member of the Hall/Fischer party survived only to lose most of his fingers and his nose to frostbite.

A number of miscalculations contributed to the Everest tragedy. In addition to ignoring turnaround times, team leaders failed to anticipate and prevent delays during the climb. Hall had never faced severe weather conditions on previous expeditions. Perhaps he was overconfident. Fischer decided to press on to the top despite exhaustion and the flare-up of a chronic liver problem. His second in command, an experienced Russian guide, chose to return to the safety of camp instead of staying with his party. Clients also demonstrated poor judgment, continuing on when severe fatigue and altitude sickness should have convinced them to turn back. The harsh environment of Everest left no margin for error. Oxygen deprivation, frigid temperatures, and the sudden blizzard ("a fairly typical Everest squall") determined the fate of the combined expeditions, turning the miscues of leaders, guides, and clients into tragedy.

Defining Leadership

As we have noted, leadership is a fundamental element of the human condition. Wherever society exists, leadership exists. Any definition of leadership must account for its universal nature. Leadership seems to be linked to what it means to be human. As communication specialists, we believe that what makes us unique as humans is our ability to create and manipulate symbols.

> I take leadership to signify the act of making a difference.
> —Michael Useem

The Nature of Human Communication

Communication theorist Frank Dance defines symbols as abstract, arbitrary representations of reality agreed upon by human users.[8] For example, there is nothing in the physical nature of this book that mandates labeling it a "book." We have agreed to use this label, or symbol, to represent a bound collection of pages; this agreement is purely arbitrary. The meaning of a symbol, according to Leslie White, does not come from the intrinsic properties of the idea, concept, or object being represented. The value is "bestowed upon it by those who use it."[9] Words are not the only symbols we use; we attach arbitrary meanings to many nonverbal behaviors as well. Looking someone in the eye symbolizes honesty to many North Americans. However, making direct eye contact in some other cultures is considered an invasion of privacy. Meaning is generated through communication.

> [Humans] differ from the apes, and indeed all other living creatures so far as we know, in that [they are] capable of symbolic behavior. With words, [humans] create a new world, a world of ideas and philosophies.
> —Leslie White

Communication is based on the transfer of symbols, which allows individuals to create meaning. As you read this text, the words we have written are transferred to you. The meanings of these words are subject to your interpretation. It is our goal to write in a way that allows for clear understanding, but factors such as your cultural background, your previous experience, your level of interest, and our writing skills influence your perception of our message. The goal of communication is to create a shared reality between message sources and receivers.

The human ability to manipulate symbols allows for the creation of reality. Simply labeling someone as "motivated" or "lazy," for example, can lead to changes in behavior. Followers generally work hard to meet the high expectations implied in the "motivated" label; they may lower their performance to meet the low expectations of the "lazy" label. This phenomenon, discussed in detail in chapter 8, is known as the Pygmalion effect.

Symbols not only create reality but also enable us to communicate about the past, present, and future. We can evaluate our past performances, analyze current conditions, and set agendas for the future. In addition, symbolic communication is purposive and goal driven. We consciously use words, gestures, and other symbolic behaviors in order to achieve our goals. The purposeful nature of human communication differentiates it from animal communication.[10]

The communication patterns of animals are predetermined. For example, wolves normally travel in small groups known as packs. Dominance within the pack is predetermined based on such characteristics as size, physical strength, and aggressiveness. Humans, on the other hand, consciously select from an array of possibilities for achieving their goals. Human leadership is not predetermined as in the animal world; rather, it varies from situation to situation and from individual to individual.

Leadership shares all of the features of human communication described above. First, *leaders use symbols to create reality*. Leaders use language, stories, and rituals to create distinctive group cultures. Second, *leaders communicate about the past, present, and future*. They engage in evaluation, analysis, and goal setting. Effective leaders create a desirable vision outlining what the group should be like in the future. Third, *leaders make conscious use of symbols to reach their goals*. See the case study in box 1.3 for examples of the effective and ineffective use of symbols by leaders. We will have more to say about how leaders adapt their behaviors to reach their goals later in the chapter. In the meantime, let's take a closer look at the characteristics of human communication.

> Words can destroy. What we call each other ultimately becomes what we think of each other, and it matters.
>
> —Jeane Kirkpatrick

The Human Communication Process

Noted communication scholar Dean Barnlund identified five principles that reflect the basic components of human communication.[11]

Box 1.3   Case Study

The Importance of Symbols

Leadership is primarily a symbolic activity. The words and behaviors of leaders greatly influence the reactions of those who follow. Consider these examples:

Don Isley is the General Manager of Renco Manufacturing, a medium-sized manufacturing company producing precision components for the airline industry. The Renco plant is located in an office park near a commercial airport and parking is limited. Employee parking areas at the plant are divided into two lots. In one lot, managers and office staff park their vehicles near the main entrance to the Renco plant. On the other side of the building, those who work in the production area park near a side entrance to the plant. This parking arrangement is more informal than formal, but employees are consistent in their behavior and rarely park in the "wrong" lot. Isley parks in neither lot. He parks his vehicle, a new Corvette, directly in front of the building in a fire lane designated as a no parking area. Isley claims he needs to park in this location so that he can have easier access to his office. Some of the production workers who earn salaries just above minimum wage feel like Isley is "showing off." What do you think?

Peter Houghton is the CEO of a large privately owned utility company—Valley Electric. Houghton came to Valley Electric from a competitor where he was highly regarded for his successful management practices. Despite this reputation, employees at Valley Electric were nervous when Houghton was hired. He replaced a well-regarded CEO who had been at the helm during a period of rapid growth and profitability. Sensing this uneasiness, Houghton made the decision to spend his first month on the job meeting as many Valley Electric employees as he could. Houghton visited offices, power stations, and field sites. He introduced himself to employees, asked questions, and learned policies and procedures. At the end of his first month on the job, Houghton finally reported to his office. He felt ready to assume the challenge of leading Valley Electric. What do you think of this strategy?

Mark Ayala is the owner of a small T-shirt printing business. His company employs about 15 full-time staff members who are responsible for the production of a variety of custom-designed T-shirts. Most of the staff work for minimum wage, and turnover is high. The clothing produced ranges from special-order logo shirts for corporate clients to mass-produced shirts celebrating sports team championships. Ayala started the business in his garage five years ago and has built a loyal clientele by providing high-quality products that are delivered on time to his customers. Ayala and his staff must, at times, work around the clock to meet deadlines for special orders. Through his persistence and hard work, Ayala has developed a very successful business. Recently, Ayala noted that his total revenue for the year exceeded $1 million for the first time in company history. To mark this accomplishment and to thank his employees, Ayala came in late one night and printed T-shirts for his staff. The shirts featured a depiction of a $1 million dollar bill with Ayala's picture in the center. On the back each shirt read, "Thanks a Million." When Ayala announced the $1 million milestone to his employees and handed out the shirts, many of his employees were appreciative. Some, however, found the T-shirt giveaway insulting. What do you think?

Eric Littleton is the president of Bald College, a small, private, residential school in the south. Under pressure from students, Littleton recently removed the "faculty only" designation from the parking lot next to the building that houses the offices of many professors. Soon students who live in nearby dormitories occupied most of the parking spots, rarely moving their cars except on weekends. Faculty protested the loss of the parking and loading spaces to the president but to no avail. Now they routinely gripe to one another about the fact that they have to walk two or three blocks from their cars, often carrying heavy loads of books and classroom materials. Some feel that Littleton's refusal to reconsider his choice is a sign that he doesn't understand or appreciate his employees. What do you think?

(continued)

Margaret Gates is the superintendent of schools in the Elmwood Hills school district. Elmwood Hills is an affluent community located in the suburbs of a large metropolitan area. The schools in the Elmwood Hills district have an excellent reputation, and many parents choose to live in the area so their children can attend the schools. Gates was hired as superintendent after her predecessor (who had been in the district for 37 years as a teacher and administrator) retired. Gates was a well-regarded candidate; she had years of experience leading high-performing programs in school districts in another state. Within two months of her arrival at Elmwood Hills, Gates assembled all of more than 2,000 faculty and staff within the district. Although few of these teachers or staff members had met Gates yet, most were eager to hear what their new leader had to say. In the meeting, Gates unveiled a new vision statement and a set of 12 initiatives, including mandatory nightly homework assignments, a greater emphasis on core academic subjects, and revamping many of the existing programs within the district. Although many of the initiatives Gates presented had merit, most of those attending the meeting left with a very negative impression of their new leader. What do you think went wrong?

Shirley Phillips is the CEO of Hilcrest Laboratories, a multinational pharmaceutical company. As CEO, Phillips has exhibited an antipathy toward corporate perks. Like all other Hilcrest executives and managers, Phillips has a cubicle, not a private office. When Phillips travels, she flies coach class and rents a subcompact car, as do all Hilcrest executives and managers. Employees jokingly refer to the small cars they are most often given by rental agencies as "Hilcrest limousines." Phillips's efforts are viewed by some as merely an attempt to cut costs. Some senior managers feel they have earned the perks of first-class travel and full-size rental cars. Others contend that Hilcrest's profit-sharing plan is perk enough and that money shouldn't be wasted on costly airfares and rental cars. Phillips argues her actions communicate a belief that all at Hilcrest are equal in importance. What do you think?

After considering these six examples, think of some of the leaders with whom you have worked in the past. Identify examples of effective or ineffective symbolic behavior on the part of these leaders. Discuss your examples with others in class.

Communication is not a thing, it is a process. Communication is not constant; it is dynamic and ever changing. Unlike a biologist looking at a cell through a microscope, communication scholars focus on a continuous, ongoing process without a clearly defined beginning or end. Take a typical conversation, for example. Does a conversation begin when two people enter a room? When they first see each other? When they begin talking? Barnlund, and others, would suggest that a conversation actually "begins" with the experiences, skills, feelings, and other characteristics that individuals bring to an interaction.

Communication is not linear, it is circular. Models depicting the process of communication have evolved from a linear explanation, first developed by ancient Greek rhetoricians over 2,000 years ago, to a circular explanation, offered by Barnlund. In the earliest description of the communication process, a source transmitted a message to a receiver in much the same way that an archer shoots an arrow into a target. Only the source had an active role in this model; the receiver merely accepted messages. This view, known as an action model, is diagrammed below.

An Action Model of Communication

The action model provided an incomplete depiction of the communication process because the response of the receiver was ignored. Reactions to messages, known as feedback, were included in the next explanation of communication—the interaction model. The interaction model described communication as a process of sending messages back and forth from sources to receivers and receivers to sources. From this perspective, diagrammed below, communication resembles a game of tennis.

An Interaction Model of Communication

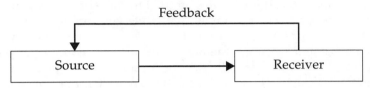

The evolution of the circular explanation of communication was completed with the development of Barnlund's transactional model. The transactional approach assumes that messages are sent and received simultaneously by source/receivers. The ongoing, continuous nature of the process of communication is implicit in this model.

A Transactional Model of Communication

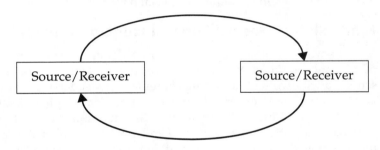

In the transactional model, communicators simultaneously transmit and receive messages. Effective communicators pay close attention to the messages being sent to them as they talk with others. The typical classroom lecture demonstrates how we act as senders and receivers at the same time. Even though only one person (the instructor) delivers the lecture, students provide important information about how the lecture is being received. If the lecture is interesting, listeners respond with smiles, head nods, and questions. If the lecture is boring, class members may fidget, fall asleep, or glance frequently at their watches. These responses are transmitted throughout the lecture. Thus, both the instructor and students simultaneously act as message source and receiver.

Communication is complex. Communication involves more than just one person sending a message to another. The process involves the negotiation of shared interpretations and understanding. Barnlund explains that when you have a conversation with another person there are, in a sense, six people involved in the conversation.

1. Who you think you are
2. Who you think the other person is
3. Who you think the other person thinks you are
4. Who the other person thinks he or she is
5. Who the other person thinks you are
6. Who the other person thinks you think he or she is

Communication is irreversible. Like a permanent ink stain, communication is indelible. If you have ever tried to "take back" something you have said to another person, you know that while you can apologize for saying something inappropriate, you cannot erase your message. Many times in the heat of an argument we say something that hurts someone. After the argument has cooled down, we generally say we are sorry for our insensitive remarks. Even though the apology is accepted and the remark is retracted, the words continue to shape the relationship. The other person may still wonder, "Did he/she really mean it?" We can never completely un-communicate.

Communication involves the total personality. A person's communication cannot be viewed separately from the person. Communication is more than a set of behaviors; it is the primary, defining characteristic of a human being. Our view of self and others is shaped, defined, and maintained through communication.

Now that you have a better understanding of the process of human communication, we will examine the special nature of leadership communication.

Leadership: A Special Form of Human Communication

One way to isolate the unique characteristics of leadership is to look at how others have defined the term. According to James MacGregor Burns, the scholar attributed with founding contemporary leadership studies, "leadership is one of the most observed and least understood phenomena on Earth."[12] Indeed, Joseph Rost found there were 221 definitions of leadership published in books and articles between 1900 and 1990—a number that given the recent interest in leadership has likely doubled since his review.[13] With so many definitions of leadership in print it is helpful to classify these conceptions into broader categories. Four primary definitional themes emerge.

Leadership is about who you are. This definitional theme focuses on leader traits and attributes and is one of the oldest ways of conceptualizing leadership. The emphasis is on identifying the characteristics that define "born leaders." Examples of such definitions of leadership published in the early part of the twentieth century are "personality in action . . . in such a way that the course of action of the many is changed by the one,"[14] and "[the] person who possesses the greatest number of desirable traits of personality and character."[15]

Leadership is about how you act. From this perspective, leadership is defined as the exercise of influence or power. To identify leaders, we need to determine who is influencing whom. For example, Paul Hersey defines leadership as "any attempt to influence the behavior of another individual or group."[16] Bernard Bass argues that "an effort to influence others is attempted leadership."[17] When others actually change, then leadership is successful. Swedish researcher Mats Alvesson focuses on the influence process from a communication perspective, arguing that leadership is a "culture-influencing activity" that involves the "management of meaning."[18]

Leadership is about what you do. This definitional thread focuses on the importance of followers. Leader influence attempts are neither random nor self-centered. Instead, leaders channel their influence and encourage change in order to meet the needs or to reach the goals of a group (task force, business organization, social movement, state legislature, military unit, nation). Note the group orientation in the following definitions:

- the behavior of an individual when he/she is involved in directing group activities;[19]
- the process (act) of influencing the activities of an organized group toward goal setting and goal achievement.[20]

Placing leadership in the context of group achievement helps to clarify the difference between leadership and persuasion. Persuasion involves changing attitudes and behavior through rational and emotional arguments. Since persuasive tactics can be used solely for personal gain, persuasion is not always a leadership activity. Persuasion, although critical to effective leadership, is only one of many influence tools available to a leader.

Leadership is about how you work with others. This definitional theme emphasizes collaboration. Leaders and followers establish mutual purposes and work together as partners to reach their goals. Success is the product of leaders' and followers' joint efforts. Joseph Rost highlights the interdependence of leaders/followers this way: "Leadership is an influence relationship among leaders and their collaborators [followers] who intend real changes that reflect their mutual purposes."[21] Others, such as Peter Block and Robert Greenleaf, discuss concepts such as "stewardship" and "servant leadership" in defining leadership as a partnership with followers.[22]

Combining our discussion of human communication with the definitional elements above, we offer the following communication-based definition of leadership: **Leadership is human (symbolic) communication, which modifies the attitudes and behaviors of others in order to meet shared group goals and needs**. (For a sampling of how some other textbooks have defined leadership, see box 1.4).

Leaders vs. Managers

Management is often equated with leadership. However, leading differs significantly from managing. Managers may act as leaders, but often they do not. Similarly, employees can take a leadership role even though they do not have a managerial position. Leadership experts James Kouzes and Barry Posner suggest the following exercise to highlight the differences between leaders and managers. Take a sheet of paper and make two columns. In the first column, identify the activities, behaviors, and actions of leaders. In the second column, list the activities, behaviors, and actions of managers. Now compare the two lists. Kouzes and Posner predict that you will associate leaders with factors such as change, crisis, and innovation and that you will associate managers with organizational stability. According to these authors, "When we think of leaders, we recall times of turbulence, conflict, innovation, and

Box 1.4

Leadership Definitions: A Textbook Sampler

"Leadership is a process whereby an individual influences a group of individuals to achieve a common goal."—Peter Northouse[23]

"Leadership is the process of influencing others to understand and agree about what needs to be done and how to do it, and the process of facilitating individual and collective efforts to accomplish shared objectives."—Gary Yukl[24]

"A leader [can be defined as] a person who influences individuals and groups within an organization, helps them in the establishment of goals, and guides them toward achievement of those goals, thereby allowing them to be effective."—Afsaneh Nahavandi[25]

"Leadership is social influence. It means leaving a mark, it is initiating and guiding, and the result is change."—George Manning and Kent Curtis[26]

"Organizational leadership behaviors emerge during interaction among individuals working toward a common goal or engaged in activity of mutual interest."—Patricia Witherspoon[27]

change. When we think of managers, we recall times of stability, harmony, maintenance, and constancy."[28]

Perhaps the key difference between a leader and a manager lies in the focus of each. While the manager is more absorbed in the status quo, the leader is more concerned with the ultimate direction of the group. Warren Bennis and Burt Nanus surveyed 90 successful corporate and public leaders in an attempt to better understand leadership. They found that *managers are people who do things right and leaders are people who do the right thing.*[29] As Bennis and Nanus further explain, managers are problem solvers who focus on physical resources. Leaders, on the other hand, are problem finders who focus on spiritual and emotional resources.

Efficiency versus effectiveness provides another contrast between management and leadership. Management is frequently concerned with efficiency. However, an organization can be efficiently run yet still fail if it does not respond to changing conditions or meet the needs of members. Bennis notes: "Leading does not mean managing; the difference between the two is crucial. There are many institutions that are very well managed and very poorly led. They may excel in the ability to handle all the routine inputs every day, yet they may never ask whether the routine should be preserved at all."[30]

> You manage things; you lead people.
>
> —Grace Murray Hopper

John Kotter uses three central activities to highlight the differences between management and leadership: creating an agenda, developing a human network for achieving the agenda, and executing the agenda (see box 1.5).

The management process for creating an agenda involves planning and budgeting. Managers at this stage tend to focus on time frames, specific details, analysis of potential risks, and resource allocation. By contrast, leaders create an agenda by establishing direction and communicating long-range views of

Box 1.5   Research Highlight

Management vs. Leadership[31]

	Managers	**Leaders**
Creating an agenda	*Planning and Budgeting*—establishing detailed steps and timetables for achieving needed results and then allocating the resources necessary to make that happen	*Establishing Direction*—developing a vision of the future, often the distant future, and strategies for producing the changes needed to achieve that vision
Developing a human network for achieving the agenda	*Organizing and Staffing*—establishing some structure for accomplishing plan requirements, staffing that structure with individuals, delegating responsibility and authority for carrying out the plan, providing policies and procedures to help guide people, and creating methods or systems to monitor implementation	*Aligning People*—communicating the direction by words and deeds to all those whose cooperation may be needed so as to influence the creation of teams and coalitions that understand the vision and strategies and accept their validity
Execution	*Controlling and Problem Solving*—monitoring results versus planning in some detail, identifying deviations, and then planning and organizing to solve these problems	*Motivating and Inspiring*—energizing people to overcome major political, bureaucratic, and resource barriers to change by satisfying very basic, but often unfulfilled, human needs
Outcomes	Produces a degree of predictability and order and has the potential of consistently producing key results expected by various stakeholders (e.g., for customers, always being on time; for stockholders, being on budget)	Produces change, often to a dramatic degree (e.g., new products that customers want, new approaches to labor relations that help make a firm more competitive)

the big picture. This process involves developing a desirable and attainable goal for the future, otherwise known as a vision. The actions of Herb Kelleher during his tenure as CEO of Southwest Airlines are examples of this type of leadership activity. In taking a fledgling airline to prominence in the U.S. airline industry, Kelleher had a clear vision of the strategy and leadership practices necessary to make Southwest Airlines a success (see the case study in box 1.6 for more about leadership at Southwest Airlines). The presence of a shared and meaningful vision is a central component of effective leadership. *Fortune* magazine's list of the "100 Best Companies to Work for in America" noted that two of the common features of great organizations are a visionary leader and a strong sense of common purpose.[32]

Once the agenda is established, people must be mobilized to achieve the plan. Managers mobilize others through organizing and staffing. The focus of this management activity involves getting individuals with the right training in the right job and then getting those individuals to carry out the agreed-upon plan. Leaders mobilize others by aligning people. Alignment focuses on integration, teamwork, and commitment. The leadership of Apple Computer

Box 1.6   Case Study
Leadership with Love at Southwest Airlines

Southwest Airlines began as a fledgling operation with four airplanes flying 18 daily round-trip flights among three cities in Texas. The early history of the airline led to the development of a unique leadership approach. Before Southwest ever had its first flight, a group of competitors filed a lawsuit to block the upstart airline from initiating its proposed service. The legal battle dragged on for three years before Southwest finally got off the ground in 1971. The early days were lean for the airline; flights often carried only a handful of passengers, and the cost of the legal battles required to establish the company drained its resources. The CEO of Southwest Airlines from its founding until his retirement in 2001 was Herb Kelleher. An attorney by training, Kelleher turned the struggling airline into a personal crusade. To survive among its hostile and much larger competitors, Kelleher worked to develop the leadership practices that would allow Southwest to prosper.

Southwest's operating strategy focuses on providing low-cost, no-frills service with frequent direct flights between cities that are an average of 400 miles, or an hour, apart. The method for achieving success in using this strategy has been to employ a revolutionary leadership approach. While many companies argue that the customer is always right, Kelleher believes employees come first. "Customers are not always right, and I think that is one of the biggest betrayals of your people you can possibly commit. The customer is frequently wrong. We don't carry those sorts of customers. We write them and say, 'Fly somebody else. Don't abuse our people.'"[33]

As Southwest's corporate philosophy explains: Employees are number one. The way you treat your employees is the way they will treat your customers. The results for customers have been exceptional. Southwest has consistently been rated by the U.S. Department of Transportation *Air Travel Consumer Report* as having the best on-time performance, best baggage handling, and fewest complaints of all major air carriers. In a highly competitive industry in which all carriers strive to get top ratings in any of the three reporting categories, Southwest is the only airline to ever be rated best in all three categories—a feat called the triple crown. Indeed, Southwest once held the triple crown for five consecutive years—an astonishing record considering no other airline has held the triple crown for even one month!

Other key corporate philosophies emphasize building relationships with suppliers, unions, and airport authorities; that work should be fun (employees are encouraged to take their jobs and the competition seriously—but not themselves); and that employees should do whatever it takes to meet the needs of customers. As former company president Colleen Barrett explains, "No employee will ever be punished for using good judgment and good old common sense when trying to accommodate a customer—no matter what our rules are."[34] Perhaps most extraordinary is Southwest's commitment to conducting its business in a loving manner. As consultants Kevin and Jackie Freiberg explain, "Southwest understands that when people feel loved they develop a greater capacity to love others. Employees bear out this belief every day in the kindness, patience, and forgiveness they extend to each other and their customers."[35] This value is so deeply ingrained in the company's culture that Southwest's stock symbol is LUV.

The results of the Southwest leadership approach have been nothing short of phenomenal. The airline has been rated as one of the nation's 10 best companies to work for.[36] Each year Southwest receives over 200,000 applications for some 4,000 available jobs. The demand for employment at the airline is so great that it is easier to get accepted at Harvard than it is to become a mechanic at Southwest![37] In an industry plagued by problems associated with excessive costs, frequent labor disputes, and the often-changing whims of travelers, Southwest has been a bastion of profitability. Southwest is the only U.S. airline to have made money every year since 1973. After the September 11 terrorist attacks caused a significant downturn in the travel industry, the 2002 stock market capitalization of Southwest exceeded the *combined* value of all 10 of the other major U.S. air carriers.[38] Certainly Southwest's well-defined operating strategy has contributed to its long-term success. The airline's major competitive advantage, however, appears to be its people and its leadership practices. Kelleher's retirement has seemingly had little impact on Southwest's ongoing culture. Under the direction of new leaders, the company appears as strong as ever.

Discussion Questions

1. How do you think an organization's past history affects leadership practices?

2. Do you agree with Herb Kelleher's contention that employees should come first? Have you ever worked somewhere where you have felt that you were particularly valued as an employee? Have you had the opposite experience?

3. Do you think people are more productive and satisfied if they have fun in the workplace? Why or why not?

4. Is there a place for "love" in organizations? How can a leader build a loving environment?

5. Southwest Airlines is noted for its outstanding customer service. What are some of the organizations you have encountered that have provided the best and the worst customer service? What do you think the relation is between customer service and leadership?

cofounder Steven Jobs exemplified this process of aligning people. During development of the Apple Macintosh computer in the early 1980s, Jobs moved his entire design team to a separate building on the Apple compound. With Jobs as project leader, and with the Jolly Roger flying over the design team's building, members of the Macintosh development team focused their attention exclusively on designing a personal computer to revolutionize the home computing industry. These "pirates" of the corporation aligned themselves to bring Jobs' compelling vision to life.[39]

The execution of the agenda from a management perspective involves controlling and problem solving. This process usually focuses on containment, control, and predictability. Leaders execute their agenda by motivating and inspiring. This process focuses on empowerment, expansion, and creativity. One organization that does an excellent job of motivating and inspiring followers is Mary Kay Cosmetics. Founded in 1963 by the late Mary Kay Ash, the company has more female employees earning over $50,000 per year than any other organization in the world. One of the most coveted awards presented to the independent agents (known as "beauty consultants") who sell Mary Kay products is a 14-carat gold brooch in the shape of a bumblebee. The bumblebee, all new recruits are reminded, has a body too big for its wings and thus should not be able to fly. But it does. Recruits are told that the ability to achieve more than seems possible is what Mary Kay Cosmetics is all about.[40]

According to Kotter, the outcomes of management and leadership differ significantly. Management produces orderly results. Leadership, on the other hand, often leads to useful change. Both these activities are important in the overall success of groups and organizations.

To be successful, organizations must consistently meet their current commitments to customers, stockholders, employees, and others, and they must also identify and adapt to the changing needs of these key constituencies over time. To do so, they must not only plan, budget, organize, staff, control, and problem solve in a competent, systematic, and rational manner, they must also establish and reestablish, when necessary, an appropriate direction for the future, align people to it, and motivate employees to create change even when painful sacrifices are required.[41]

For Kotter the key is balancing leadership and management. As he explains, not every individual is effective as both a leader and a manager. However, successful organizations nurture both. The ideal is to combine strong leadership and strong management.[42] This can be accomplished by developing both leadership and management skills within individuals or by establishing a combination of these skills among a cross-section of individuals within an organization. Despite differences in the management and leadership process, there are also some similarities. Leadership expert John Gardner observes, "Every time I encounter an utterly first-class manager he [she] turns out to have a lot of leader in him [her]."[43]

Of course, an employee may assume a leadership role even though she or he is not a manager. Consider the example of a Procter & Gamble (P&G) employee at a Jif peanut butter plant. While shopping at his neighborhood supermarket, the employee noticed that the labels on several jars of Jif peanut butter were crooked. He bought all of the stock with the poorly mounted labels, assuming that P&G would not want its image tarnished by sloppy workmanship. His leadership efforts have since become part of the folklore of P&G.[44]

The Question of "Bad" Leadership

Most of those who study and write about leadership have focused on the more positive connotations of the concept. Recently researchers, such as Barbara Kellerman at Harvard University and Jean Lipman-Blumen at Claremont University, have devoted attention to the "bad" or "toxic" side of leadership.[45] Kellerman argues that too much emphasis is placed on an idealized notion of leadership and that researchers and practitioners must embrace a more honest and holistic view that acknowledges the dark side of human nature. Similarly, Lipman-Blumen suggests that people knowingly follow, frequently prefer, and sometimes even create such leaders. These researchers argue for a broader conception of leadership that includes an exploration of those whose impact on others is destructive.

Like many leadership scholars, we believe that leaders should be ethical and serve the common good. Yet, we recognize that far too many individuals fall short of this standard, driven by personalized or harmful motives that make them more "power wielders" than leaders who serve the needs of the group.[46] These bad leaders can teach a great deal about good leadership, however. Studying examples of bad leaders can alert us to the ethical dangers of being in a leadership role (see the discussion of the ethical shadows of leadership in chapter 11); help us to prevent ethical abuses in ourselves and others; and clearly demonstrate what we DON'T want to do when our time comes to lead. To ignore such actions, according to Kellerman, is to ignore "Hitler's ghost"—to discount the impact of "bad" leaders.[47]

According to Kellerman, bad leadership falls into two categories—ineffective and unethical—and is exhibited through destructive behaviors and dysfunctional personality characteristics. Ineffective leaders are not successful in achieving desired outcomes. These "bad" leaders may be poorly skilled, may exhibit ineffective strategic or tactical planning, or may not have the requisite traits to succeed. Unethical leaders are unable to distinguish between right and wrong, often engaging in behaviors that maximize their rewards while harming others. Both types of "bad" leaders may exhibit a range of the destructive behaviors and dysfunctional personality characteristics listed in box 1.7.

Kellerman identifies seven types of "bad" leaders.[48]

Incompetent. These leaders do not have the desire or skill (or both) to sustain effective action. They may lack practical, academic, or social intelligence and can be careless, dense, distracted, lazy, or sloppy. Juan Antonio Samaranch, who presided over judging and doping scandals and rampant corruption as president of the International Olympic Committee (1981–2000), exemplifies such incompetence.

Rigid. These leaders are unyielding. Although the rigid leader may be competent, he or she is unable or unwilling to adapt to new ideas, new information, or changing times. Russian President Vladimir Putin's response to the sinking of the submarine *Kursk* in 2000 is an example. When advised of the situation, Putin showed little interest (continuing a planned vacation to the Black

---

Box 1.7

Destructive Behaviors and Dysfunctional Personality Characteristics of Toxic Leaders[49]

Destructive Behaviors
Leaving followers worse off than before
Violating basic standards of human rights
Playing to the basest fears of followers
Stifling constructive criticism
Consciously feeding followers illusions that enhance the leaders' power (e.g. suggesting followers will come to harm without their leadership)
Misleading followers with deliberate untruths
Subverting those structures and processes of the system intended to generate truth, justice, and excellence
Failing to nurture other leaders
Maliciously setting constituents against one another
Ignoring or promoting incompetence, cronyism, and corruption

Dysfunctional Personality Characteristics
Lack of integrity
Insatiable ambition
Enormous egos that blind leaders to their own shortcomings
Arrogance that prevents acknowledging mistakes and blames others instead
Amorality that makes it impossible to discern right from wrong
Avarice that drives leaders to be motivated by money and what money can buy
Reckless disregard for the costs of their actions to others
Cowardice that leads them to shrink from difficult choices
Failure to understand the nature of relevant problems
Failure to act competently and effectively in leadership situations

Sea) and initially ignored offers of assistance from other countries (particularly from the United States). Speculation was that Putin did not want to appear weak—rigidly clinging to the idea of Russia as a superpower.

Intemperate. These leaders lack self-control and are aided and abetted by followers who are unwilling or unable to intervene. Marion Barry, Jr.'s career is an example of intemperate leadership supported by followers who ignored his failings. Barry served as the mayor of Washington DC from 1979 to 1991. His arrest in 1990 on drug charges precluded him from seeking reelection. After his conviction, Barry served six months in prison, but he was elected to the DC council in 1992 and ultimately as mayor again in 1994, serving a fourth term from 1995 to 1999. Barry continues to be involved in DC politics even after pleading guilty in 2005 to charges of failing to pay federal and local taxes on more than $530,000 worth of income.

Callous. These leaders are uncaring or unkind. Corporate downsizer Al Dunlap—known as "Chainsaw Al" for zealously cutting jobs—is an example of a callous leader. Dunlap fired thousands at Crown-Zellerbach and Scott Paper in the 1980s and 1990s before becoming the CEO at Sunbeam. There he slashed 6,000 more jobs before eventually being fired himself in 1998 after just two years on the job. Dunlap walked away from CEO posts wealthy while thousands at the companies he led were left without jobs.

Corrupt. These leaders, and at least some of their followers, lie, cheat, or steal—putting self-interest ahead of the public interest. Vincent (Buddy) Cianci, Jr., who served six terms as mayor of Providence, Rhode Island, from 1975–1984 and again from 1991–2001, is an example of this type of bad leader. Over the years he, and members of his staff, were indicted on a variety of charges ranging from extortion, larceny, conspiracy, and assault to federal rack-eteering. Cianci was ultimately convicted on one count of conspiracy in 2002 and sentenced to five years in federal prison.

Insular. These leaders, and at least some followers, minimize or disregard the welfare of others outside the group or organization for which they are directly responsible. During the course of a hundred days in 1994, the Hutu government of Rwanda and its extremist allies nearly succeeded in exterminat-ing the country's Tutsi minority. Using firearms, machetes, and a variety of gar-den implements, Hutu militiamen, soldiers, and ordinary citizens murdered some 800,000 Tutsi and politically moderate Hutu. It was the fastest, most effi-cient killing spree of the twentieth century. Despite evidence that he knew about the horrible events in Rwanda, President Bill Clinton did not take action to stop the genocide, thus exemplifying insular leadership. Although Clinton later trav-eled to Africa to apologize for his inaction, the question remains as to why the U.S. government failed to intervene. (Turn to Leadership on the Big Screen in chapter 3 for a description of a film version of the Rwandan genocide.)

Evil. These leaders, and at least some followers, commit atrocities that inflict physical and/or psychological harm on others. Pol Pot, the Cambodian leader from 1975 to 1979, is a chilling example of evil leadership. His Khmer Rouge army was one of the most brutal in history. During his time as leader, violent deaths in his country were more common than deaths by natural causes. More than 1.7 million Cambodians—one-third of the population—were murdered in just four years.

The Leader/Follower Relationship

Clarifying the relationship between leading and following is the final step in defining leadership. Earlier we noted that leaders and followers function collaboratively. Recognizing that leaders and followers work together toward shared objectives should keep us from overemphasizing the importance of leaders or ignoring the contributions of followers. Unfortunately, we generally pay a lot more attention to leaders than to followers. The revival of the Chrysler Corporation in the early 1980s is a case in point. Press accounts and business texts typically credit Lee Iacocca with saving Chrysler from bankruptcy. The company would not have returned to profitability, however, without the hard work of thousands of assembly line workers, supervisors, truck drivers, warehouse workers, administrative assistants, and other followers.

Shifting some of the spotlight from leadership to followership is one way to assure that followers get the credit they deserve; recognizing that leadership duties can be widely distributed is another. In *shared leadership*, group and organizational members share the responsibility for achieving collective goals.[50] Shared leadership can take several different forms. Two individuals might function as coleaders by jointly occupying a leadership position, as in the case of William Hewlett and David Packard, cofounders of the technology giant. (See box 1.8 for more examples of coleadership.) In another form of shared leadership, group members divide up leadership functions or take turns rotating in and out of leadership roles. For instance, members of a firm's executive team may each take responsibility for one component of a merger plan (finance, operations, products, personnel). Or different team members may take the lead depending on the plan's stage of development. The chief financial officer (CFO) might be in charge as the company determines if a proposed merger will be profitable. The human resource director will likely coordinate salary and benefits when the two groups of employees are brought together after the merger is approved. In yet another form of shared leadership, leadership duties are disbursed throughout the organization rather than concentrated in the hands of a few individuals at the top of the hierarchy. Frontline supervisors and their teams are empowered to make hiring and firing decisions (see chapter 5), for example, or to shut down the production line.

Describing leaders and followers as relational partners who play complementary roles is the best way to capture what followership means.[51] Leaders exert a greater degree of influence and take more responsibility for the overall direction of the group. Followers, on the other hand, are more involved in implementing plans and carrying out the work. Most people routinely shift between leader and follower functions during the course of the day. As a student you must follow in the classroom, but you may also lead a class project group or an intramural sports team. In recognition of this fact, we suggest that you make a mental note to think of yourself not as a leader or a follower, but as a *leader-follower*. Recognize, too, that you can learn to lead by following and learn to follow by leading.

Training at West Point provides one example of followership as leadership training.[52] Submission to authority is the cornerstone of leadership development at the military academy. New cadets must obey everyone else, including upper-

Box 1.8   Research Highlight

Coleadership

Wise leaders create strong bonds with their key subordinates by sharing power and credit. David Heenan and Warren Bennis use the term "coleadership" to describe these alliances. They "make the case for coleadership" with the stories of a dozen leaders and key adjuncts from business, government, athletics, and other settings.[53] Some of these notable leader/coleader partnerships include: Intel cofounder Andy Grove and his successor Craig Barrett; humanitarian Helen Keller and her teacher Ann Sullivan Macy; Mao Tse-Tung and his deputy Chou En-lai; and Stanford women's head basketball coach Tara VanDerveer and her assistant Amy Tucker.

The researchers' first suggestion to prospective coleaders is: "Know thyself." Coleaders define success in their own terms and realize that not everyone has the talent or desire to function in the top spot. Further, they recognize that being No. 2 may be tougher than being No. 1. Coleaders may labor in obscurity, receiving little recognition when things go right but getting more than their share of the blame when things go wrong. In some cases top lieutenants are more, not less, talented than those who get more attention. General George Marshall, for example, was Army chief of staff during World War II. He directed recovery efforts in Europe after the war and served as Secretary of Defense and Secretary of State under President Truman. Winston Churchill, Dwight Eisenhower, and Harry Truman are more famous than General Marshall. Yet, all three of these leaders called Marshall "the greatest man they had ever known."[54]

Other lessons for coleaders build on the foundation of self-knowledge. According to Heenan and Bennis, prospective coleaders should also understand their superiors and their organizations. Partnerships won't work if leaders aren't willing to share power and if coleaders break the rules or assumptions of the organization's culture. Effective coleaders know when to challenge their bosses, how to cope with pressures, and when to leave an organization. Finally, coleaders recognize their dual role as leaders/followers. Top adjuncts are leaders in their own right. They are generally experts in some important organizational task and may oversee the work of thousands of followers. Craig Barrett, for instance, directed Intel's manufacturing division before replacing Andy Grove as CEO.

Heenan and Bennis believe that organizations can create cultures that foster coleadership. Among the more important steps to a coleadership culture: (1) celebrate the enterprise, not celebrity, by putting the emphasis on the collective work of the group rather than on one individual; (2) encourage togetherness through teamwork; (3) cultivate equalitarianism by keeping status distinctions to a minimum; (4) nurture trust and communicate hope in the future; (5) solicit dissent and put allegiance to group values above loyalty to the individual leader; and (6) share power and authority.

classmen. Leadership can prepare us for followership in the same way that following prepares us for leading. By observing our followers we can gain insights into what we should (and shouldn't) do when we serve in a follower role.

> A good leader can't get too far ahead of his [her] followers.
> —Franklin D. Roosevelt

As you can see, followers play an active, vital role in the success of any group, organization, or society. They are neither passive nor subservient.

Throughout this text we will use alternative terms like "constituents," "stakeholders," or "collaborators" along with "followers" to help drive home this point. We also believe that effective leadership is based on service, not hierarchy. In our discussions of transformational leadership in chapter 4 and ethical leadership in chapter 11, we suggest that truly great leaders serve rather than rule because they recognize that those whom they lead entrust them with leadership responsibilities.

Followership expert Robert Kelley sums up the work of followers and leaders this way:

> In reality followership and leadership are two separate concepts, two separate roles. . . . Neither role corners the market on brains, motivation, talent, or action. Either role can result in an award-winning performance or a flop. The greatest successes require that the people in both roles turn in top-rate performances. We must have great leaders and great followers.[55]

Viewing Leadership from a Communication Perspective

From our perspective leadership is first, and foremost, a communication-based activity. Leaders spend much of their time shaping messages that are then presented to a variety of follower, constituent, and stakeholder groups. It is also true that the more leadership responsibility one has, the more one's job focuses on communication. Certainly political leaders, executives, coaches, educators, and religious figures alike all share this common characteristic—the higher the level of leadership, the higher the demand for communication competence.

Willingness to Communicate

Leadership effectiveness depends on our willingness to interact with others and on developing effective communication skills. Those who engage in skillful communication are more likely to influence others. Communication professors James McCroskey and Virginia Richmond developed the Willingness to Communicate (WTC) scale to measure the predisposition to talk in a variety of situations.[56] Take a few minutes to complete the WTC instrument in box 1.9, and then compute your total score as well as your scores for each of the subscales.

McCroskey, Richmond, and their colleagues report that overall scores on the WTC scale are directly related to communication behavior. Individuals with high WTC scores communicate more frequently and for longer periods of time than people with low WTC scores. Increased communication activity, in turn, leads to a number of positive outcomes in the United States, a society that values individualism and assertiveness (see chapter 10). Speaking up is not viewed as favorably in other cultures, such as some Asian societies, that put more emphasis on the needs of the group as a whole.[57] In the United States:

- High WTCs are viewed as more credible and attractive and are more often identified as opinion leaders.

- People who speak frequently in small groups are more likely to hold leadership positions (see chapter 7).

Box 1.9   Self-Assessment
Willingness to Communicate Scale (WTC)[58]

Directions: Below are 20 situations in which a person might choose to communicate or not to communicate. Presume you have completely free choice. Indicate in the space at the left what percentage of the time you would choose to communicate in each type of situation. You can choose any percentage ranging from 0% (never communicating) to 100% (always communicating).

_____   1. Talk with a service station attendant.

_____   2. Talk with a physician.

_____   3. Present a talk to a group of strangers.

_____   4. Talk with an acquaintance while standing in line.

_____   5. Talk with a salesperson in a store.

_____   6. Talk in a large meeting of friends.

_____   7. Talk with a police officer.

_____   8. Talk in a small group of strangers.

_____   9. Talk with a friend while standing in line.

_____   10. Talk with a waiter/waitress in a restaurant.

_____   11. Talk in a large meeting of acquaintances.

_____   12. Talk with a stranger while standing in line.

_____   13. Talk with a secretary.

_____   14. Present a talk to a group of friends.

_____   15. Talk in a small group of acquaintances.

_____   16. Talk with a garbage collector.

_____   17. Talk in a large meeting of strangers.

_____   18. Talk with a spouse (or girl/boy friend).

_____   19. Talk in a small group of friends.

_____   20. Present a talk to a group of acquaintances.

The WTC is designed to indicate how willing you are to communicate in a variety of contexts, with different types of receivers. The higher your WTC total score, the more willing you are to communicate in general. Similarly, the higher your given subscore for a type of context or audience, the more willing you are to communicate in that type of context or with that type of audience.

Scoring: The WTC permits computation of one total score and seven subscores. The subscores relate to willingness to communicate in each of four common communication contexts and with three types of audiences. To compute your scores, merely add your scores for each item and divide by the number indicated below.

Subscore Desired	**Scoring Formula**
Group discussion	Add scores for items 8, 15, and 19; then divide by 3.
Meetings	Add scores for items 6, 11, and 17; then divide by 3.
Interpersonal conversations	Add scores for items 4, 9, and 12; then divide by 3.
Public speaking	Add scores for items 3, 14, and 20; then divide by 3.
Stranger	Add scores for items 3, 8, 12, and 17; then divide by 4.
Acquaintance	Add scores for items 4, 11, 15, and 20; then divide by 4.
Friend	Add scores for items 6, 9, 14, and 19; then divide by 4.

To compute the total WTC scores, add the subscores for stranger, acquaintance, and friend. Then divide by 3.

Norms for WTC Scores	
Group discussion	> 89 High WTC, < 57 Low WTC
Meetings	> 80 High WTC, < 39 Low WTC
Interpersonal conversations	> 94 High WTC, < 64 Low WTC
Public speaking	> 78 High WTC, < 33 Low WTC
Stranger	> 63 High WTC, < 18 Low WTC
Acquaintance	> 92 High WTC, < 57 Low WTC
Friend	> 99 High WTC, < 71 Low WTC
Total WTC	> 82 High Overall WTC, < 52 Low Overall WTC

- Talkative people are more likely to be hired and promoted. They also stay with organizations longer than their quiet colleagues.
- High WTCs are rated as more socially and sexually attractive by members of the opposite sex.
- Those who are more willing to communicate are also more open to change and enjoy tasks that require thought.[59]

There are a number of reasons why we may be reluctant to interact with others: we may have inherited a tendency to be shy, introverted, and anxious about communication; put a low value on talk; feel alienated from other people; suffer from low self-esteem; or experience fear or anxiety about specific communication situations. In some cases, we're reluctant to communicate because of a skill deficiency. We don't know how (or think we don't know how) to communicate effectively. This perceived deficiency becomes a vicious cycle. Thinking we can't communicate successfully, we avoid interaction. As a consequence, we don't get the practice we need and therefore can't communicate as well.

We can reverse the cycle by developing our skills. Skill development builds confidence and encourages us to talk. When we communicate, we practice our skills and increase our effectiveness. This results in greater self-assurance, making it even more likely that we'll participate in future interactions.

Storytelling as Leadership

One of the primary ways in which leaders shape reality is through storytelling. As Washington College professor Michael Harvey explains, "leaders frame stories and events to help [followers] understand the world, themselves, and other groups, as well as to identify or solve problems."[60] Stephen Denning suggests that leadership is an "interactive" endeavor largely shaped by narrative.[61] This is not to suggest that abstract reasoning and analysis are not important to leadership, but rather that storytelling is a valuable supplement to these generally recognized aspects of leadership. Leaders tell their stories in a variety of informal and formal contexts, from conversations over a cup of coffee to formal presentations. Through stories leaders can connect themselves with others, building strong relationships and a sense of affiliation. Stories carry multiple messages. Among other functions, they reflect important values, inspire, and describe appropriate behavior. Further, when leaders tell compelling stories they influence others to pick up the same story line, thus extending the narrative.

This process of retelling stories (often in a revised form by those who follow) is part of the cocreation of meaning that is central to storytelling. Royal Dutch Shell Group offers a good example. The group's managing directors first developed their own story lines about needed change and the future and then engaged the next layers of management in crafting their versions. Tales were told for years of profitable growth and technical leadership. These stories were then retold throughout the company across sites in more than 100 countries. As a result, all those concerned understood the case for change and told each other what they would have to do to bring the "new reality" into being.[62]

> The right anecdote can be worth a thousand theories.
>
> —Warren Bennis

Denning proposes that there are eight general categories of stories that leaders can use to assist in achieving their goals.[63]

Sparking action. These stories describe how a successful change was implemented in the past, allowing listeners to imagine how such a change might work in their situation. These "springboard" stories enable listeners to visualize the large-scale transformation required. For example, as program director of knowledge management for the World Bank in the mid-1990s, Denning struggled to get his colleagues to see the importance of the need for a central repository for the information scattered throughout the organization. The message was falling on deaf ears until Denning found a "springboard" story. He framed the need for collecting and sharing information at the World Bank by describing how technology was changing the landscape of our planet. The story he told involved a health worker in 1995 in a remote village in Zambia who logged on to the Web site of the Centers for Disease Control and Prevention in Atlanta, Georgia, and got an answer to a question on how to treat malaria. When this story was added to the presentation, audience members were able to visualize how the information collected in their organization might be used.

Communicating who you are. These stories reveal your identity to an audience, building trust and creating a connection. Political leaders such as Barack Obama, for example, write books, maintain Web sites, and give speeches designed to present a desired image of themselves to the electorate.

> Leadership is personal. Do the people you lead know who you are, what you care about, and why they ought to be following you?
>
> —Ron Sugar

Communicating the brand. These organizational stories are designed to communicate brand image to customers. Cosmetic retailer The Body Shop created a global brand without using conventional advertising. Brand identity was communicated through the stories of the company founder, the late Anita Roddick, and through commitment to a model of commerce-with-a-conscience.

Transmitting values. These stories reflect and reinforce organizational values by telling audience members "how things are done around here." Jim Sinegal, the CEO of Costco, is an example of a leader who uses stories (and his very presence) as a means for transmitting organizational values. Costco, the fourth largest retailer in the United States, is a $65 billion business. Sinegal, the founder of the company, takes only a modest salary and spends much of his time on the road. While visiting up to half a dozen Costco stores a day, he preaches his philosophy of loyalty to his customers and to his employees. (Read the case study in box 1.10 for more on Costco.)

Fostering collaboration. These stories encourage people to work together by generating a narrative to illustrate common concerns and goals. As exemplified in the case in box 1.6, Southwest Airlines is an organization with a clear set of common concerns and goals. Stories are frequently used to reinforce this collaborative culture. One such story is that of a Southwest Airlines pilot who quickly exited his flight after arrival only to return a short time later for pre-flight checks for his return trip. Where had he been? Getting a quick cup of coffee? No, he had climbed in the front bin of the aircraft on a cold and windy day to unload all of the mail and freight—with no gloves, knee pads, or coat—while the other agents off-loaded the bags in the back.[64]

Taming the grapevine. These stories highlight the incongruity between rumors and reality. For example, one might deal with a false rumor of imminent corporate-wide reorganization by jokingly recounting how difficult it is to work out the seating chart at the executive committee meetings. It is important to be careful with these types of stories as mean-spirited humor can generate a well-deserved backlash and the denial of a rumor that turns out to be true can have a devastating impact on credibility.

Sharing knowledge. These stories focus on problems and show, in detail, how corrections were made and why the solution worked. Many organizations use an after-action review (AAR) in this manner. AARs are assessments conducted after a project or major activity that allow employees and leaders to explore what happened and why. They may be thought of as a professional discussion of an event that enables employees to understand why things happened during the progression of the process and to learn from that experience. AARs can be useful in a variety of situations, including: following the introduction of a new product line or computer system upgrade, after a busy holiday

---

Box 1.10   Case Study

It's All About the Message: Leadership Communication at Costco[65]

Jim Sinegal, cofounder and the current CEO at Costco, began his career at age 18 unloading mattresses in a month-old venture called Fed-Mart. After several acquisitions and start-ups Fed-Mart morphed into Costco in the early 1980s. Today Costco is the fourth largest retailer in the United States with some 500 stores in 37 states and eight countries and sales exceeding $65 billion a year. Costco is a warehouse merchandiser in the mold of Sam's Club or Wal-Mart and sells everything from wine (more than any other single retailer in the world) and salmon fillets to flat-screen TVs and leather sofas. But while Sam's Club and Wal-Mart have been criticized for being driven strictly by profit, Costco has adopted a values-driven approach that is firmly anchored by Sinegal.

(continued)

Sinegal believes that employees should be paid fair wages for their valuable contributions to the organization. The average Costco warehouse employee earns $17.60 per hour—40% more than amounts paid by the other warehouse merchandisers. Costco also offers better than average benefits, including health care coverage to more than 90% of its workforce. As Sinegal explains, there is a real business advantage in treating employees well. He calls his 120,000 loyal employees "ambassadors." These employees tell the company's story to the more than 45 million shoppers who visit a Costco store, and they often stay with the company (Costco has the lowest employee turnover rate in retailing). Sinegal also takes an unorthodox view on his own compensation. While the average annual salary for CEOs in the United States is measured in the millions, Sinegal's salary is just $350,000 plus additional bonuses that still leave his total salary well below the $1 million mark. "I figured that if I was making something like twelve times more than the typical person working on the floor, that's a fair salary," he explains. Further, Sinegal's CEO employment contract with Costco is the shortest of more than 2,000 such contracts reviewed by the corporate governance organization, The Corporate Library—and the only one that specifically states that he can be "terminated for cause" if he doesn't perform.

As unique as all of this is, perhaps the most exceptional element of Sinegal's leadership is his presence within the company. He leads from the road, hopping on the corporate jet, and visiting up to half a dozen Costco stores a day, including the grand openings of all new store locations. During these visits he interacts with his 120,000 "ambassadors," meets with customers and, quite simply, pitches in where he can help—always wearing his Costco employee name tag that simply reads, Jim. When he is at his corporate office he answers his own telephone ("if a customer's calling and they have a gripe, don't you think they enjoy the fact that I picked up the phone and talked to them?"). Costco employees gush about the family atmosphere, and why not? The company promotes almost 100 percent from within. As Sinegal explains, "we have guys who started pushing shopping carts out in the parking lot who are now vice presidents of our company." It's not just loyalty that pushes Sinegal to hire from within; those who have been with the company know the Costco story and, as such, are better able to adhere to the core philosophy of providing quality and value. Examples of adherence to the corporate philosophy are labeled "salmon" stories in honor of a particularly successful effort. In 1996 Costco sold salmon fillets at $5.99 per pound. Over a five-year period Costco buyers were able to negotiate price reductions that lowered the price to $3.99 per pound while, at the same time, substantially increasing the quality of the product by improving the trim and removing the pin bones, among other enhancements. This story is used as a teaching tool at Costco to encourage others to hold fast to the company philosophy. Even more powerful is that fact that Costco employees now approach Sinegal to tell him their version of the "salmon" story, explaining the efforts they have undertaken to reduce prices while increasing value to the customer.

Discussion Questions

1. Do you agree with Sinegal that employees will be more effective at telling the corporate story to customers if they are treated as "ambassadors"?

2. Should a CEO be paid a salary more than 12 times of that of a first-line employee? Why? Why not?

3. Have you ever been involved with an organization where the CEO had a strong (or weak) presence? What was the impact of having regular interaction (or a lack of interaction) with this individual?

4. Do you think Costco's generous pay and benefits policies and strategy of hiring from within are mostly helpful or harmful to the bottom line?

5. Have you ever been part of a group or organization that had its own version of a "salmon" story? If so, what was the impact of this story?

season in a retail store, or after a major training activity or a change in procedures. The discussion during the AAR allows leaders to use sharing knowledge stories to improve subsequent organizational responses to similar situations.

Leading people into the future. These stories evoke images of a desired future. Often such stories provide limited detail while encouraging listeners to imagine what the future might be. There are many fine historical examples of such stories, but none, perhaps, had more impact on twentieth century life in the United States than Martin Luther King, Jr.'s "I Have a Dream" speech. King had a vision of whites and blacks living in racial harmony; where his children "would be judged, not by the color of their skin, but by the content of their character."

Emotional Communication Competencies

The rational dimension of leadership is critical. In the chapters to come, we'll outline ways that leaders use thinking and reasoning skills to solve problems, set goals, negotiate, argue, shape public opinion, adapt to cultural differences, and organize and deliver effective presentations. Forgetting the emotional side of leadership, however, would be a mistake. Effective leaders are also skilled at sharing and responding to emotions. For example, they know how to communicate affection, liking, and excitement to followers. In addition, they know how to channel their emotions in order to achieve their objectives and to maintain friendly group relations.

Growing recognition of the importance of emotional leadership is due in large part to the emotional intelligence (EI) movement.[66] Psychologist Daniel Goleman and others argue that emotional intelligence (the ability to recognize, control, and express emotions) is more important to success in life than is traditional IQ.[67] This is particularly apparent in the workplace where emotional sensitivity sets excellent performers apart from ordinary ones.[68] For example, store managers who are better at managing stress have higher sales per square foot of floor space. More effective counselors respond calmly to emotional attacks from clients, and the best sales people are sensitive to the emotional desires of their customers.

Emotional intelligence becomes increasingly important with every step up the organizational ladder. Higher-level positions are generally more complex, involve more communication, and have a greater impact on the bottom line. Not surprisingly, then, emotional competence is critical to top executives. They carry out a series of sophisticated tasks, most of which involve interaction with subordinates and other leaders, and are responsible for the performance of the entire group. Their ability to manage emotions is integral to both their personal success and the success of their organizations.

The most significant task of senior leaders, according to Goleman and his colleagues, is to foster a positive emotional climate. They introduce the term "primal leadership" to describe how effective leaders create or "prime" good feelings in followers. Creating a positive emotional climate brings out the best in leaders and followers alike, an effect called *resonance*.[69] The benefits of resonance include more optimism about reaching objectives, increased creativity, greater cooperation, and sustained focus on the task, all of which contribute to higher profits and growth.

Unfortunately, proponents of emotional intelligence appear to overstate its importance to leaders. They go so far as to argue that nearly 90 percent of the competencies that account for executive success are emotional rather than cognitive in nature.[70] They also label some competencies as "emotional" that seem to have more to do with thinking than feeling. For instance, EI researchers identify conflict management and influence as emotional skills, but we consider them to be rational leadership communication abilities.

Striking a balance between logic and emotion is safer than making one more important than the other. When it comes to leadership, *both* are essential.[71] An example of the importance of both cognitive and emotional competencies is provided by looking at crisis decision making (see chapter 13). To avoid making a hasty decision in a crisis, leaders must use a variety of cognitive skills, such as rejecting their faulty beliefs and assumptions, gathering facts, identifying stakeholders, soliciting a broad range of opinions, keeping records, and perspective taking. At the same time, they must employ such emotional skills as managing stress, overcoming mental and physical fatigue, and resisting group pressures.

The following set of emotional competencies demonstrates that the success of followers and leaders depends on how well are they able to integrate emotion and cognition. Skillfully blending feeling and thinking requires the five skills listed below.[72]

1. *Perception, appraisal, and expression of emotion.* Emotional intelligence begins with the ability to identify, evaluate, and then express emotional states. These skills may seem rudimentary, but some people are "emotionally illiterate." For example, people can be oblivious to the fact that they are irritating everyone else in the group. While most of us are not this insensitive, we frequently suffer from emotional blind spots. There are times when we feel uneasy but can't identify our emotions or when we don't know exactly how to express our affection for friends or loved ones.

2. *Attending to the emotions of others.* Those in a leadership role must understand the feelings of followers in order to connect with them. Consider the case of a CEO who doesn't understand that his employees are feeling overworked and discouraged. If he fails to acknowledge their frustration and tries to inspire them to work harder, they aren't likely to put forth additional effort. Instead, he will appear out of touch.

3. *Emotional facilitation of thinking.* Emotional states impact decision-making styles. Good moods facilitate creative thinking while sad moods slow the decision-making process and encourage more attention to detail. Both emotional states have a role to play in problem solving. Some problems require intuitive, broad thinking; others demand a more linear, logical approach. Emotionally intelligent leaders know how to match the mood with the problem. Further, they recognize the dangers of ignoring risks when in an optimistic frame of mind, or of being too critical when feeling pessimistic. Using emotions to facilitate thinking also means channeling feelings in order to reach goals. For example, moderate fear of failure can spur us to prepare before making a presentation. Remembering past successes can reduce our anxiety before we deliver the speech.

4. *Understanding and analyzing emotional information and employing emotional knowledge.* This cluster of competencies links symbols to emotions. Leaders must be able to label what they feel and recognize the relationship between that label and other related terms. For example, "anger" belongs to a family of words that includes "irritation," "rage," "hostility," and "annoyance." The internal states identified by these labels are connected in specific ways. Irritation and annoyance lead to anger and rage, not the other way around. Understanding this fact can empower leaders. A supervisor may decide to postpone a meeting with a disagreeable employee, for instance, when she senses that her irritation with this individual could escalate into unwanted anger. Recognizing how emotions blend together is also important. Surprise is one example of an emotion that rarely stands alone. When we feel surprised, we generally experience some other emotion, perhaps happiness, disappointment, or anger, at the same time.

5. *Regulation of emotion.* The last component of emotional intelligence puts knowledge into action. This set of competencies enables leaders to create the feelings they desire in themselves and in others. Emotionally skilled leaders know how to maintain positive moods and how to repair negative ones. To do so, they employ such tactics as avoiding unpleasant situations, engaging in rewarding tasks, and creating a comfortable work environment. In addition, they can step back and evaluate their feelings to determine if their responses in a situation were appropriate. Such evaluation can encourage them to remain calm instead of getting upset and to be more supportive instead of only focusing on the task. Effective leaders also help others maintain and improve their moods. They use these skills to create cohesive groups and to inspire and motivate followers.

> Humans are not, in any practical sense, predominantly rational beings, nor are they predominantly emotional beings. They are both.
> —Peter Salovey

Playing to a Packed House: Leaders as Impression Managers

From a communication standpoint, leaders are made, not born. We increase our leadership competence as we increase our communication skills. We can compare the leadership role to a part played on stage to illustrate how effective communication skills translate into effective leadership.

Sociologist Erving Goffman and others have adapted Shakespeare's adage that life is a stage to develop what is called the dramaturgical approach to human interaction. Proponents of this perspective argue that, like actors in a drama, people create meaning and influence others through their performances.[73] Let's look at a typical date, for example. The date is a performance that may take place on any number of stages: the dance floor, the living room, the movie theater, the football game. The actors (the couple) prepare in their dressing rooms at home before the performance and may return to the same locations for a critique session after the date ends. Particularly on the first date, the interactants may work very hard to create desired impressions—they engage in "impression management." Each dating partner tries to manage the perceptions of the other person by using appropriate behaviors, which might include dressing in the latest fashions, acting in a courteous manner, engaging in polite conversation, and paying for meals and other activities.

To see how impression management works, change one aspect of your usual communication and watch how others respond. If friends have told you that you seem unfriendly because you are quiet when meeting new people, try being more assertive the next time you meet strangers at a party. If you make a conscious effort to greet others, introduce yourself, and learn more about the others at the gathering, you may shake your cool, unfriendly image.

Leaders also engage in impression management to achieve their goals. Remember that as a leader you'll play to a packed house. People in organizations carefully watch the behavior of the CEO for information about the executive officer's character and for clues as to organizational priorities, values, and future directions. They seek answers to such questions as: "Can I trust him/her?" "What kind of behavior gets rewarded around here?" "Is she or he really interested in my welfare?" "Is dishonesty tolerated?" "Are we going to survive the next five years?" "Is this an enjoyable, exciting place to work?"

Important clues to how we can shape the impressions others have of us can be gleaned from the examples of outstanding leaders. (See box 1.11 to see how successful military leaders use impression management.) Charismatic or transformational leaders (see chapter 4) are skilled actors who create the impression that they are trustworthy, effective, morally worthy, innovative, and skilled. To create these and other favorable images, they make effective use of the following dramatic elements.[74]

Framing. Successful leaders help followers interpret the meaning of events. A CEO, for example, might explain that layoffs are only a temporary measure that will guarantee the long-term health of the company or that market trends point to a bright future for the firm's products. Notable leaders also frame the organization's purpose in a way that inspires followers by tying into audience values and stressing the vision's importance and feasibility. (We'll take a closer look at framing in chapter 8.)

Scripting. Scripts are directions or guidelines for behavior. While frames define the situation, scripts outline the roles of players, what they are to say, and how they are to act. Scripting begins with *casting*, the process of identifying and then defining the roles of the main performers, supporting players, audiences, and enemies. Effective leaders outline their role in the drama, convince followers that they have a significant part to play in achieving shared goals, and identify outside groups that need to be approached for support. They then script the *dialogue* or interaction with followers. Powerful dialogue techniques include storytelling, which was discussed earlier, as well as creating metaphors, drawing analogies, and communicating overarching goals. Successful leaders provide *direction* to guide performances, with specific attention to nonverbal behaviors and emotional displays. When they want to be perceived as

Box 1.11   Research Highlight

Impression Management in the Military

British military historian John Keegan believes that impression management is the key to successful military leadership.[75] All commanders are actors who perform before their troops. However, only those who create the right image or "mask of command" will consistently lead their armies to victory. According to Keegan, "The theatrical impulse will be strong in the successful politician, teacher, entrepreneur, athlete, or divine, and will be both expected and reinforced by the audiences to which they perform."[76] Men and women who must lead others into battle show themselves to followers only through a mask. The mask reveals what followers hope and require; it conceals what they should not know. The mask the leader constructs marks him or her as the leader wanted and needed at a particular time and place.

Keegan examines the careers of Alexander the Great, Wellington, Ulysses S. Grant, and Adolph Hitler to determine the elements that make up the desired mask of command.

1. **Kinship.** Effective commanders select staff members who help them create a bond with their troops. These officers simultaneously carry out two functions. They relay the message that the commander cares about the needs of his/her soldiers; simultaneously they bring the concerns of those on the front line to the leader's attention. Hitler didn't establish kinship with his soldiers because he surrounded himself with advisors who echoed his opinions and had no empathy for the misery of the German army.

2. **Public speaking.** No commander can rely entirely on his/her staff, no matter how effective those officers might be. There are times when he/she must directly address the troops, "raising their spirits in times of trouble, inspiring them at moments of crisis and thanking them in victory."[77] This makes public speaking one of the most important skills of military leadership. Contemporaries of Alexander the Great were so impressed by his battlefield addresses that they recorded his words for future generations.

3. **Sanction.** To maintain an aura of authority, every commander needs to punish those who desert, pillage, or otherwise disobey orders. Yet, physical force should be used sparingly lest the leader become as much an enemy to his/her soldiers as the opposing army. Rewards reduce the need for coercion. Over the centuries military leaders have encouraged obedience by rewarding followers with money, material goods, vacation leaves, medals, and war memorials.

4. **Action.** The images of military commanders rest heavily on what they accomplish on the battlefield. Winning generals combine what Keegan calls *knowing* and *seeing*. Wellington and Grant triumphed because they learned everything they could about the terrain and their enemies before the battle started (knowing). When the fighting began, they periodically visited the front lines to witness developments firsthand (seeing). Hitler, while he knew a great deal about military matters, stayed in his bunker. As a result, he didn't really understand (see) battlefield conditions and ended up as one of history's most notable military failures.

5. **Example.** Keegan contends that the greatest imperative of command is to share risks with followers. Military leaders must stay alive to direct the fight but can't completely insulate themselves from danger and discomfort if they hope to earn the respect of their followers. Staying in a luxurious headquarters far from the chaos of the front lines is a prescription for disaster. In World War I, for example, the morale of the French, German, Russian, Italian, and British armies all collapsed when soldiers suffering in the trenches rebelled against elite officers who lived like country gentlemen in comfortable chateaux. With the dangers of "chateau generalship" in mind, the modern Israeli, Vietnamese, and Chinese armies insist that their commanders live with their troops and lead by example.

dynamic, for example, they exhibit more eye contact, vocal variety, relaxed posture, and animated facial expressions. When they want to be seen as considerate, they are less animated and expressive.

Staging. Effective leaders pay close attention to how performances are staged, making sure that their personal appearance, the setting, and props support the image they want to project. For instance, when addressing the nation in times of crisis, presidents dress formally in dark colors and speak from the Oval Office surrounded by such props as the American flag and the presidential seal.

Performing. Performing is carrying out the behaviors outlined in the script. Outstanding leaders make effective use of four types of impression management. The first type is *exemplification*, which refers to living out or role modeling desired values and behaviors. For example: engaging in self-sacrificing or risky behavior like working extra hours or investing in a new venture; helping others; or demonstrating personal integrity. The second type is *promotion*—the communication of favorable information. The leader can promote (a) him- or herself (skills and accomplishments), (b) the vision (selling its merits and the leader's ability to bring it to pass), and (c) the organization (highlighting the success of the collective, which reflects well on the leader). Effective leaders are careful not to overstate their accomplishments, the vision, or the group's success. Overpromoting the self can backfire, generating skepticism and resentment; overpromoting the vision and organization can be seen as overzealous and unrealistic.

The third type of impression management used by notable leaders consists of *facework*, communication designed to protect or repair damage done to personal or collective images. Charismatic leaders know how to account for their missteps in ways that reduce their negative impact. They may deny responsibility for what happened, excuse their behavior, or justify their actions based on the fact that they were right to act as they did. Ronald Reagan successfully used accounting tactics to protect his image during the Iran-Contra scandal, when his administration was accused of trading weapons for hostages. He took "full responsibility" but yet blamed others for acting without his knowledge.[78]

The fourth type of impression management is *ingratiation*. Effective leaders make themselves appear more attractive and likeable to others through complements, praise, agreeing, and offering to do things for others. They create the impression that they are warm and friendly. They take care to avoid intimidating behaviors that make them appear dangerous and threatening.

Many people are uncomfortable with the idea of impression management. They equate playing a role with being insincere, since true feelings and beliefs might be hidden. They note that far too often fellow students and coworkers get ahead by acting like chameleons, changing their behaviors to conform to the wishes of whatever group they find themselves in. These are very real dangers. Self-promotion and ingratiation can trump competence and hard work. However, research suggests that individuals typically use impression management to project a public image that is congruent with their self-concepts. Followers continually watch for inconsistencies and often "see through" insincere performances of leaders. Further, impression management is part of every human interaction. Others form impressions of us, whether we are intentional about our behaviors or not. Frequently, we have no choice but to play many roles. We are forced into performances as job applicants, students, dating partners, and leaders each day. The real problem is that we often mismanage the impressions we make. Our behaviors may make us appear dull or untrustworthy when we really are interesting and honest.

Some fear that leaders can manipulate impressions to mislead the group. This is a legitimate concern (we'll discuss the ethical dimension of leadership in greater detail in chapter 11). Yet, impression management is essential for achieving worthy objectives. The state human services director who inspires her employees to meet the needs of more clients through exemplification and ingratiation is helping the disadvantaged, making better use of state funds, and boosting the morale of her organization.

Because impression management can be used to further group goals or to subvert them, it should be judged by its end products. Ethical impression management meets group wants and needs and, in the ideal, spurs the group to reach higher goals. Organizational impression experts Paul Rosenfeld, Robert Giacalone, and Catherine Riordan offer the following guidelines for determining if impression management is beneficial or detrimental to an organization.[79] Beneficial impression management helps the organization achieve its objectives by: (1) promoting positive interpersonal relationships and increasing cooperation with both those inside and outside the organization; (2) accurately portraying positive persons, events, or products to insiders and outsiders; and (3) facilitating decision making, helping management and consumers make the right choices. Detrimental or dysfunctional impression management damages the organization by (1) blocking or undermining relationships with those who work with or do business with the organization; (2) incorrectly casting people, events, or products in a negative light to insiders and outsiders; and (3) distorting information that results in managers and consumers reaching the wrong conclusions and/or decisions.

> In this theater of man's [woman's] life it is reserved only for God and the angels to be lookers on.
>
> —Francis Bacon

CHAPTER TAKEAWAYS

- Leadership attracts universal attention. Historians, philosophers, and social scientists have attempted to understand and to explain leadership for centuries.

- Leadership is a fundamental element of the human condition. Wherever society exists, leadership exists. Any definition of leadership must account for its universal nature. Leadership seems to be linked to what it means to be human. What makes us unique as humans is our ability to create and manipulate symbols—abstract, arbitrary representations of reality.

- One way to isolate the unique characteristics of leadership is to look at how others have defined the term. Four primary definitional themes have emerged in the leadership literature: (1) leadership is about who you are; (2) leadership is about how you act; (3) leadership is about what you do; and (4) leadership is about how you work with others. We offer the following communication-based definition of leadership: Leadership is human (symbolic) communication, which modifies the attitudes and behaviors of others in order to meet shared group goals and needs.

- Management is often equated with leadership. However, leading differs significantly from managing. Perhaps the key difference between a leader and a manager lies in the focus of each. While the manager is more absorbed in the status quo, the leader is more concerned with the ultimate direction of the group.

- Most of those who study and write about leadership have focused on the more positive connotations of the concept. Recently researchers have devoted attention to the "bad" or "toxic" side of leadership. Bad leaders can be classified as incompetent, rigid, intemperate, callous, corrupt, insular, or evil.

- Leaders and followers are relational partners who play complementary roles. Leaders exert a greater degree of influence and followers have more responsibility for carrying out the work. In shared leadership, responsibility for achieving shared goals is distributed throughout the group. Think of yourself as a leader-follower, routinely shifting between leader and follower functions. Following is excellent preparation for leadership, and leading can prepare you for the follower role.

- Leaders spend much of their time shaping messages that are then presented to a variety of follower, constituent, and stakeholder groups. It is also true that the more leadership responsibility you have, the more your job will focus on communication.

- Viewing leadership from a communication perspective recognizes that your leadership effectiveness depends on your willingness to interact with others (the willingness to communicate) and on making skillful use of storytelling, emotional communication competencies, and impression management.

- Leadership is an "interactive" endeavor largely shaped by narrative. Storytelling is a valuable supplement to abstract reasoning and analysis. Important types of stories include those that: (a) spark action, (b) communicate who you are, (c) communicate the brand image to customers, (d) transmit organizational values, (e) foster collaboration, (f) tame the grapevine by pointing out the disconnect between rumors and reality, (g) share knowledge about problem solving, and (h) lead people into the future.

- Effective leaders are skilled at sharing and responding to emotions. For example, they know how to communicate affection, liking, and excitement to followers. In addition, they know how to channel their emotions in order to achieve their objectives and to maintain friendly group relations.

- To achieve your goals as a leader, you'll need to manage the impressions others have of you. Generate positive images through the use of framing, scripting, staging, and performing (exemplification, promotion, facework, and ingratiation).

- Ethical leaders use impression management to reach group objectives rather than to satisfy selfish, personal goals. Beneficial impression management promotes positive interpersonal relationships and cooperation; accurately portrays people, events, or products; and facilitates effective decision making.

APPLICATION EXERCISES

1. Take a trip to a local bookstore and check to see how many books you can find on leadership. Did you find more or fewer titles than you expected? Report your findings in class.

2. Conduct a debate regarding the importance of leaders. Have one-half of your class argue that leaders are more important than ever and have the other half argue that leaders are less necessary than in the past. As an alternative, debate the concept of "bad" leadership. Should we consider people like Hitler, Stalin, Pol Pot, and Osama bin Laden leaders or are they merely "power wielders"?

3. Develop your own definition of leadership. How does it compare to the ones given in the chapter?

4. Make a list of the characteristics of leaders and managers. Are your characteristics the same as those described by Kouzes, Posner, and Kotter? To clarify the differences between leaders and managers, describe someone who is an effective leader and then someone who is an effective manager. How do these two people differ? Share your descriptions with others in class.

5. Select one of your follower roles (student, employee, team member, etc.) and then select one of your leadership roles (team captain, project group leader, coach). Consider the behaviors and qualities you appreciate or dislike in those who lead or follow you. What can you learn from those strengths and weaknesses that you can apply as a leader-follower? What conclusions can you draw about being an effective leader or follower? Write up your findings.

6. In a group, determine the advantages and disadvantages of sharing leadership responsibilities in a group or organization. Based on your discussion, what conclusions do you reach about shared leadership?

7. Pair off with someone and compare your overall Willingness to Communicate (WTC) scores as well as your seven subscores. What factors make you and your partner reluctant to communicate in all situations or in particular contexts? What can each of you do to increase your willingness to communicate? What communication skills do you need to sharpen?

8. Consider the stories you have heard from leaders in the past. Discuss with others in class which stories you found to be most/least effective and why.

9. Identify individuals you believe have low or high emotional intelligence. Discuss what you feel the impact of these ratings are on leadership effectiveness.

10. Analyze the impression management strategies of a well-known leader. What image does this individual create? How effectively does he/she use the dramatic elements described in the chapter? Write up your findings.

CULTURAL CONNECTIONS:
DEVELOPING INTERCULTURAL EMOTIONAL COMPETENCE

Dealing with groups of followers from a variety of cultural backgrounds is a fact of life for modern leaders. Leadership effectiveness increasingly depends on intercultural emotional competency—the ability to accurately send and receive emotional messages across cultural boundaries. Consider, for instance, the importance of correctly interpreting the mood of a Japanese negotiator when setting up a trade agreement or of knowing how enthusiastic to be when presenting a new company initiative to a group of German employees.

Transferring emotional intelligence to other cultures is difficult because the rules governing the understanding and expression of emotion vary from society to society. Sally Planalp, a communication professor at both the University of Utah and the University of Waikato in New Zealand, offers a number of examples of cultural differences in her book *Communicating Emotion: Social, Moral, and Cultural Processes*.[80] Here are just a few of the ways that emotional communication differs between cultures.

- Utku Eskimos, who live in extreme hardship, are more likely to tolerate negative events and rarely express anger or aggression.

- The Ifaluk of Micronesia believe that unwanted feelings must be expressed or physical or mental illness will result; the Chinese believe that too much expression of emotion produces sickness.

- European-Americans value emotional self-restraint; African Americans value emotional expressiveness.

- Among the Wolof people of Senegal, members of the griot (lower) caste act as emotional spokespeople for their noble patrons, sharing the feelings of the nobility in public meetings.

- The Maori of New Zealand value spontaneous, heart-felt speech over carefully prepared remarks.

- The Balinese both laugh and cry in response to death and fall asleep in the face of frightening events.

- In Malaysia, peasants would "run amok," engaging in random attacks as a way of controlling the power of the ruling class.

In the face of such differences, making assumptions about the likely emotional responses of the members of other groups will probably end in cross-cultural disaster. Most people in the United States trust that "a smile coupled with a friendly and enthusiastic attitude can provide the transcultural social lubricant" to make it through any cross-cultural interaction.[81] However, many foreigners find U.S. friendliness shallow and insulting. Even asking questions about others can backfire. Native Hawaiians view such behavior as invasive and rude.

Effective leaders (and followers) set aside their preconceived notions about how to send and interpret emotional messages and seek instead to learn as much as they can about the feeling rules of other cultures. Only then can they begin to develop the intercultural emotional intelligence they need to succeed in a multicultural world.

SPOTLIGHT ON TECHNOLOGY:
GETTING THE WIRES CROSSED AT AIRBUS

In late 2006, the new Airbus A380, the world's largest passenger jet, took to the sky for the first time with a full load of passengers. The seven-hour test flight of the 308-ton super jumbo jet that can carry up to 555 passengers was an aeronautical triumph. But when the plane (larger than a Boeing 747) touched down near the Airbus factory in southern France, questions began to surface about the viability of the aircraft in the wake of massive delivery delays to customers around the world. What had originally been announced as a six-month delay in the manufacture of the aircraft will ultimately push back delivery dates two full years, leading major customers such as the United Arab Emirates and FedEx to cancel orders and resulting in the potential loss of billions of dollars in revenue for Airbus.[82] The reasons for the delay are complex—the result of the intricacies of leading a multinational operation that has manufacturing sites across Europe, with French, German, British, and Spanish stakeholders.

When the problems with the A380 were investigated, Airbus executives acknowledged the primary reason for the delay was that the design software used in factories in France and Germany was not compatible.[83] The A380 has more than 300 miles of internal electrical wiring, and the wiring built in Hamburg, Germany, did not fit properly into the plane on the assembly line in Toulouse, France. As inconceivable as it sounds, engineers in Germany and France were using different versions of the CAD-CAM software critical to allowing design specs to be transferred easily back and forth between the two locations. When the bundles of cabin wire arrived in France, workers had difficulty fitting the wires into the airplane fuselage. They tried to pull the wires apart and rethread them through the aircraft, but that proved to be impractical. Ultimately, Airbus was forced to invest in new software to correct the wiring design. Delays for the A380 mounted while Airbus engineers learned the new software. To further complicate matters, Airbus had not designed a full 3-D digital mock-up of the A380. Such models, which are common in airplane manufacturing, are particularly useful for electrical wires that are difficult to track in two dimensions as they twist through the plane. Airbus only signed a contract for such mock-up software in 2005, well after the A380 was into production. The blunder has already cost two Airbus CEOs their jobs, and the fallout will likely linger at least until the long-term viability of the A380 is determined.

LEADERSHIP ON THE BIG SCREEN: *ELIZABETH*

Starring: Cate Blanchett, Geoffrey Rush, Joseph Fiennes, Richard Attenborough

Rating: R for sexual content and violence

Synopsis: Blanchett stars as England's Queen Elizabeth I, at the beginning of her 40-year reign that would transform the nation into a world power. The young monarch must overcome the opposition of her half sister (Queen Mary of Scotland), traitors in the royal court, as well as the Catholic Church to consolidate her power and to establish the Church of England. She succeeds (in a male-dominated culture) through the skillful use of impression management and power, assisted by her loyal counselor Walsingham (played by Rush).

Chapter Links: impression management, leadership communication, leader/follower relationships, emotional intelligence

Leadership and Followership Communication Styles

Proper words in proper places, make the true definition of a style.
—Jonathan Swift

OVERVIEW

- The Dimensions of Leadership Communication Style
- Authoritarian, Democratic, and Laissez-Faire Leadership
- Task and Interpersonal Leadership
  The Michigan Leadership Studies
  The Ohio State Leadership Studies
  McGregor's Theory X and Theory Y
  Blake and McCanse's Leadership Grid®
- Follower Communication Styles
- Communication Styles and Information Processing

The Dimensions of Leadership Communication Style

Think of the leaders with whom you have worked in the past. Chances are you enjoyed interacting with some of these people more than others. The leaders you enjoyed working with were most likely those who created a productive and satisfying work climate. Under their guidance, you probably accomplished a great deal and had a pleasant and memorable experience.

One factor that contributes to variations in leader effectiveness is communication style. Leadership communication style is a relatively enduring set of communicative behaviors in which a leader engages when interacting with followers. A leader's communication style may reflect a philosophical belief about human nature, or it may simply be a strategy designed to maximize outcomes in a given situation. The communication style a leader selects contributes to the success or failure of any attempt to exert influence. To explore your own leadership style preferences, complete the self-assessment in box 2.1.

Researchers have identified a number of leadership communication styles in the past half-century. These varying styles can be pared down to two primary models of communication: one model compares *authoritarian, democratic,* and *laissez-faire* styles of leadership communication; a second model contrasts *task* and *interpersonal* leadership communication. Let's look more closely at these two models of communication.

Box 2.1   Self-Assessment
Leadership Communication Style Preferences Inventory[1]

Directions: Read the twelve statements below. For each statement indicate your level of agreement.

	Strongly Disagree	Disagree	Unsure	Agree	Strongly Agree
1. A leader should set direction without input from followers.	1	2	3	4	5
2. A leader should set direction with input and consultation with followers.	1	2	3	4	5
3. A leader should set direction based on the wishes of followers.	1	2	3	4	5
4. A leader should use a task force or committee rather than making a decision alone.	1	2	3	4	5
5. A leader should evaluate the progress of work with little input from followers.	1	2	3	4	5

	Strongly Disagree	Disagree	Unsure	Agree	Strongly Agree
6. A leader should leave it up to followers to initiate informal, day-to-day communication.	1	2	3	4	5
7. A leader should encourage followers to initiate decision making without first seeking approval.	1	2	3	4	5
8. A leader should closely monitor rules and regulations—punishing those who break the rules.	1	2	3	4	5
9. A leader should keep followers up to date on issues affecting the work group.	1	2	3	4	5
10. A leader should explain the reasons for making a decision to his/her followers.	1	2	3	4	5
11. A leader should remain aloof and not get too friendly with his/her followers.	1	2	3	4	5
12. A leader should provide broad goals and leave decisions regarding the methods for achieving the goals to followers.	1	2	3	4	5

Scoring: Tally your score on each of the leadership communication styles listed below by totaling your points as indicated.

Authoritarian	**Democratic**	**Laissez-Faire**
Question 1 _____	Question 2 _____	Question 3 _____
Question 5 _____	Question 4 _____	Question 6 _____
Question 8 _____	Question 9 _____	Question 7 _____
Question 11 _____	Question 10 _____	Question 12 _____
TOTAL _____	TOTAL _____	TOTAL _____

The higher your score, the greater your preference for a given leadership communication style. An unequal distribution of scores generally indicates a stronger preference for a certain style. Relatively equal scores indicate a more balanced preference of styles. This likely indicates a blended approach in which styles are based on situational factors.

Authoritarian, Democratic, and Laissez-Faire Leadership

Kurt Lewin, Ronald Lippitt, and Ralph White undertook one of the earliest investigations of leadership communication style.[2] They studied the impact of authoritarian, democratic, and laissez-faire leadership communication styles on group outcomes.

Each of these styles of communication has unique features that affect how leaders interact with followers. The authoritarian leader maintains strict control over followers by directly regulating policy, procedures, and behavior. Authoritarian leaders create distance between themselves and their followers as a means of emphasizing role distinctions. Many authoritarian leaders believe that followers would not function effectively without direct supervision. The authoritarian leader generally feels that people left to complete work on their own will be unproductive. Examples of authoritarian communicative behavior include a police officer directing traffic, a teacher ordering a student to do his or her assignment, and a supervisor instructing a subordinate to clean a workstation.

Democratic leaders engage in supportive communication that facilitates interaction between leaders and followers. The leader adopting the democratic communication style encourages follower involvement and participation in the determination of goals and procedures. Democratic leaders assume that followers are capable of making informed decisions. The democratic leader does not feel intimidated by the suggestions provided by followers but believes that the contributions of others improve the overall quality of decision making. The adage that "two heads are better than one" is the motto of the democratic leader. A group leader soliciting ideas from group members, a teacher asking students to suggest the due date for an assignment, and a district manager asking a salesperson for recommendations regarding the display of a new product are examples of democratic communicative behavior.

> I not only use all the brains that I have, but all that I can borrow.
> —Woodrow Wilson

Laissez-faire, a French word roughly translated as "leave them alone," refers to a form of leader communication that has been called *nonleadership* by some.[3] An ineffective version of this leadership communication style involves *abdication* of responsibility on the part of the leader; leaders withdraw from followers and offer little guidance or support. As a result, productivity, cohesiveness, and satisfaction often suffer. A supervisor who is incompetent, nearing retirement, or in jeopardy of being laid off or fired may exhibit the abdicating form of the laissez-faire leadership communication style. A more positive form of the laissez-faire leadership communication style affords followers a high degree of autonomy and self-rule while, at the same time, offering guidance and support when asked. The laissez-faire leader providing *guided freedom* does not directly participate in decision making unless requested to do so by followers or if such intervention is deemed necessary to facilitate task completion.[4] Examples of guided-freedom communicative behavior include a leader quietly observing group deliberations (providing information and ideas only when asked), a teacher allowing students to create their own assignments, and a research and development manager allowing his or her subordinates to work on product designs without intervention. Take a look at box 2.2 on p. 44 and see if you believe the behavior exhibited by Roland Ortmayer is an effective or ineffective use of the laissez-faire leadership communication style.

How can you tell if a leader is using an authoritarian, democratic, or laissez-faire style? Pay close attention to the leader's communication. The following communication patterns will help you recognize the style of leadership:

Democratic	Authoritarian	Laissez-Faire
Involves followers in setting goals	Sets goals individually	Allows followers free rein to set their own goals
Engages in two-way, open communication	Engages primarily in one-way, downward communication	Engages in noncommittal, superficial communication
Facilitates discussion with followers	Controls discussion with followers	Avoids discussion with followers
Solicits input regarding determination of policy and procedures	Sets policy and procedures unilaterally	Allows followers to set policy and procedures
Focuses interaction	Dominates interaction	Avoids interaction
Provides suggestions and alternatives for the completion of tasks	Personally directs the completion of tasks	Provides suggestions and alternatives for the completion of tasks only when asked to do so by followers
Provides frequent positive feedback	Provides infrequent positive feedback	Provides infrequent feedback of any kind
Rewards good work and uses punishment only as a last resort	Rewards obedience and punishes mistakes	Avoids offering rewards or punishments
Exhibits effective listening skills	Exhibits poor listening skills	May exhibit either poor or effective listening skills
Mediates conflict for group gain	Uses conflict for personal gain	Avoids conflict

Lewin and his colleagues taught these communication styles to adult leaders who supervised groups of 10-year-old children working on hobby projects at a YMCA. The authoritarian leader was instructed to establish and to maintain policy and procedures unilaterally, to supervise the completion of task assignments directly, and to dictate follower behavior in all situations. The democratic leader was told to encourage the participation of followers in the

Box 2.2   Case Study

The Laid-Back Leader[5]

Roland Ortmayer is a most unusual leader. Ort—as he is known to his friends—was head football coach at a small southern California school, the University of La Verne, for 43 years. In a profession in which winning is the measure of success, Ort's teams won only slightly more games than they lost during his coaching career (190 wins, 186 losses, 6 ties). That does not trouble Ort; he truly believes the adage let the better team win, even if that team is the opposition. If Ort's view of competition seems unusual, consider the following:

Ort never required his players to attend practices. "I think there is something wrong with a player if he practices every day," says Ort. When players did attend his practices, Ort offered his own homespun brand of logic. For example, Ort cut short passing drills after eight consecutive incompletions. Conventional wisdom suggests eight missed passes in a row would demand more, not less, practice. Explains Ort, "The problem was all we were practicing was incompletions."

Ort never recruited a player. He believed that athletes should attend La Verne because of its academic programs, not because of the football team. "I don't like recruiting. If you can out-recruit a school you can outplay them. Sports should be fun and play." Ort taught 10 physical education courses per year while at La Verne and considered himself, first and foremost, a teacher. Football is an "educational adjunct," explains Ort. Besides, he adds, there are many different ways to win. Some years Ort had "a miserable football season but a great archery class." He did not measure his success on his win-loss record on the football field.

Ort does not believe that football players should lift weights. There is too much physical work that needs to be done to waste time lifting useless weight. "I don't care if a player can bench press the world," the coach explains. "I just want my players to become the best they can be."

Ort didn't have a playbook. According to Ort, if he scripted all of the plays in advance there would be no incentive to be creative. "If players would rather run something out of the I formation than out of split backs, that's okay with me. I teach that it's all right to use your brains."

Ort had no team meetings and never kicked a player off any of his teams. Practice lasted from 3:45 to 5:30 P.M. Beyond that, a player's time was his own. "Relationships without punishment are most likely to gain in the long run," Ort contends. "I always feel that everyone who wants to play should play. Sometimes I lost because I tried to play too many players."

Ort lined the field before each game and washed the team's uniforms each Sunday. According to Ort, these activities made him "feel closer to the guys." As Ort explains, "I always carry the balls onto the field and off the field. I am interested in all aspects of the game; that is my responsibility and commitment."

Ort's laid-back style of leadership might not be effective at a larger institution where there is pressure to recruit top-notch athletes and to win big games. But at tiny La Verne, Ort was respected by administrators, faculty, and students alike, although he concedes that "sometimes the university president wanted us to win more games." He coached with compassion and understanding and helped his young men learn the value of competing and trying to be the best they could be. Asked to sum up the contribution he made in 43 years of coaching at La Verne, Ort replied: "None of my players ever quit college to my knowledge. Some fellas are lawyers today, but I don't like lawyers. I think a culture with more lawyers than farmers is sick. I still have real pride in my former players. We all have responsibilities in society, and I just tried to take care of mine."

Discussion Questions

1. Under what conditions is the laissez-faire style of leadership communication most effective?

2. Do you think Ort used the abdication or guided-freedom approach to laissez-faire leadership?

3. How should a leader's success be measured? Does it matter that Ort's teams won only slightly more games than they lost over the years?

4. Do you agree with the definition of leadership presented in chapter 1, which claims that leaders help followers achieve their goals and meet their needs? Did Ort do this?

5. How would you rate Ort as a leader? Would you like to play on his team?

determination of policy and procedures related to task completion and follower behavior. The laissez-faire leader was instructed to avoid direct involvement in the establishment of policy and procedures by supplying ideas and information only when asked to do so by followers.[6]

The responses of the children in these experiments led to the formation of six generalizations regarding the impact of leadership communication style on group effectiveness.[7]

1. *Laissez-faire and democratic leadership communication styles are not the same.* Groups with laissez-faire leaders are not as productive and satisfying as groups with democratic leaders. The amount and quality of work done by children in laissez-faire groups was less than that of democratic groups. Additionally, the majority of children in laissez-faire groups expressed dissatisfaction despite the fact that more than twice as much play occurred in these groups.

2. *Although groups headed by authoritarian leaders are often most efficient, democratic leaders also achieve high efficiency.* The greatest number of tasks were completed under authoritarian leadership. This productivity depended on the leader's direct supervision. When the authoritarian leader left the room, productivity dropped by nearly 40 percent in some groups. Democratic groups were only slightly less productive. Further, productivity in these groups remained steady with or without direct adult supervision.

3. *Groups with authoritarian leadership experience more hostility and aggression than groups with democratic or laissez-faire leaders.* Hostile and aggressive behavior in the form of arguing, property damage, and blaming occurred much more frequently in authoritarian groups than in other groups.

4. *Authoritarian-led groups may experience discontent that is not evident on the surface.* Even in authoritarian-led groups with high levels of productivity and little evidence of hostility and aggression, absenteeism and turnover were greater than in democratic and laissez-faire groups. Further, children who switched from authoritarian groups to more permissive groups exhibited tension-release behavior in the form of energetic and aggressive play.

5. *Followers exhibit more dependence and less individuality under authoritarian leaders.* Children in authoritarian groups were more submissive than those in other groups. These children were less likely to initiate action without the approval of the leader and less likely to express their opinions and ideas than children in the democratic and laissez-faire groups.

6. *Followers exhibit more commitment and cohesiveness under democratic leaders.* Children in democratic groups demonstrated a higher degree of commitment to group outcomes. The climate in democratic groups was generally supportive and friendly.

A number of follow-up studies to the work of Lewin, Lippitt, and White have provided additional information about the effects of authoritarian, democratic, and laissez-faire leader communication. Box 2.3 summarizes these findings.

The findings related to leadership communication style suggest the leader adopting authoritarian communication can expect: high productivity (particu-

---

Box 2.3   Research Highlight

The Effects of Authoritarian, Democratic, and Laissez-Faire Leadership Communication Styles

Authoritarian Leadership	**Democratic Leadership**	**Laissez-Faire Leadership**
Increases productivity when the leader is present[8]	Lowers turnover and absenteeism rates[14]	Decreases innovation when leaders abdicate, but increases innovation when leaders provide guidance as requested[20]
Produces more accurate solutions when leader is knowledgeable[9]	Increases follower satisfaction[15]	Decreases follower motivation and satisfaction when leaders abdicate[21]
Is more positively accepted in larger groups[10]	Increases follower participation[16]	Results in feelings of isolation and a decrease in participation when leaders abdicate[22]
Enhances performance on simple tasks and decreases performance on complex tasks[11]	Increases follower commitment to decisions[17]	Decreases quality and quantity of output when leaders abdicate[23]
Increases aggression levels among followers[12]	Increases innovation[18]	Increases productivity and satisfaction for highly motivated experts[24]
Increases turnover rates[13]	Increases a follower's perceived responsibility to a group or organization[19]	

---

larly under optimal conditions: a simple task completed over a short period of time with direct supervision by the leader); increased hostility, aggression, and discontent; and decreased commitment, independence, and creativity among followers. This style of communication would seem best suited for tasks requiring specific compliance procedures and minimal commitment or initiative. Routinized, highly structured, or simple tasks are often effectively accomplished under authoritarian leadership. Authoritarian leadership is also recommended when a leader is much more knowledgeable than his or her followers, when groups of followers are extremely large, or when there is insufficient time to engage in democratic decision making. Certainly a military combat leader (see Leadership on the Big Screen at the end of the chapter) would not stop to discuss the possibilities of advancing or retreating while under enemy fire.

Democratic leadership communication contributes to relatively high productivity (whether or not the leader directly supervises followers) and to increased satisfaction, commitment, and cohesiveness. This style of communication is best suited for tasks that require participation and involvement, creativity, and commitment to a decision. The only significant drawbacks to democratic leadership are that democratic techniques are time consuming and can be cumbersome with larger groups. (See the case study in box 2.4 to see how democratic leadership has been used at one successful company.)

The leader adopting the laissez-faire communication style may be accused of leadership avoidance. This communication style results in decreased productivity and less satisfaction for most followers. A number of variables, including

Box 2.4   Case Study
The Reluctant Executive: Sustainability, Surfing, and Leadership Style at Patagonia[25]

Yvon Chouinard was an accomplished mountain climber in the 1960s, successfully ascending peaks throughout the world. To support his climbing activities, he began selling mountaineering equipment out of the back of his car. This endeavor evolved into Chouinard Equipment, a full-service climbing gear manufacturing and sales operation located in Ventura, California. Chouinard increased sales volume by importing rugby shirts, gloves, hats, and other clothing from Europe and New Zealand. Soon, the focus turned to manufacturing clothing, and in 1973 the Patagonia clothing company was born. The business struggled at first, but by the mid-1980s sales began to increase, growing from $20 million to over $100 million by 1990. Today, sales volume at Patagonia is around $250 million per year, and the company makes a wide range of products from outdoor clothing and travel gear to fishing equipment.

Chouinard never aspired to be an executive, but he soon found himself facing business challenges as the founder and owner of an expanding company. Despite the growth, he held fast to the values of teamwork and camaraderie he had enjoyed as a mountaineer. Employees at Patagonia dress as they please (often in t-shirts and shorts, sitting barefoot at their desks); surf when the conditions at nearby beaches are good (the daily surf report is prominently displayed in the lobby of the corporate headquarters, and employees can take advantage of liberal flextime policies); and enjoy company-sponsored ski and climbing trips; a cafeteria serving high quality, healthy food (including a wide range of vegetarian options); a subsidized on-site day care center; and the option to take a leave of absence from work for up to two months at a nonprofit of their choice, while still receiving their full pay from Patagonia. These benefits make the company a highly desirable place of employment—on average some 900 people apply for every open position.

The company is highly committed to environmental causes and a corporate philosophy to "do no harm." Chouinard and each of Patagonia's 1,200 employees try to make decisions based on the impact that will be felt 100 years from now. That approach requires asking tough questions about manufacturing processes and making the right choices, even if production costs increase. In the early 1990s, for example, an environmental audit revealed that the chemicals commonly used for growing and harvesting cotton made it one of the most damaging fibers used by Patagonia. Cotton farming, Chouinard discovered, consumes 25 percent of the world's pesticides on just 3 percent of the world's farmland. As a result, the company switched its entire product line to organic cotton, a decision that ultimately improved profitability. More recently Patagonia decided to shift from the traditional kind of polyester used to make its fleece jackets to a new type of polyester made from recycled soda pop bottles. It takes 25 soda bottles from landfills to make a jacket; between 1993 and 2003 Patagonia diverted 86 million soda bottles from landfills.

How does Chouinard lead the company and drive this environmental mission? Through a hands-on, directive approach? No, he uses what he calls his MBA theory—management by absence. Chouinard travels the globe developing and testing Patagonia products and serving as a crusader for environmental issues. To run his business, he hires employees who will question authority—challenging bad decisions and working with others to seek out the best solutions. As he explains, "the best democracy exists when decisions are made through consensus . . . decisions based on compromise often leave the problem not completely solved, with both sides feeling cheated or unimportant."[26] And the most effective leaders, Chouinard argues, are those who can communicate their ideas to others, not via e-mail, but by talking face-to-face to work out collaborative agreements. To support this democratic approach, there are no private offices at Patagonia—everyone works in open rooms with no doors or separations. When Chouinard is at the Patagonia headquarters, he does not have a reserved parking spot (such spots are reserved for those who drive fuel-efficient cars) or special perks or office space; he considers himself no more important than others in the organization. Such treatment would only damage the democratic spirit of the company. Chouinard believes: "finding the right balance between the management

(continued)

problems that come with growth and maintaining our philosophy of hiring independent-minded people and trusting them with responsibility is the key to Patagonia's success."[27]

Discussion Questions

1. What is your opinion regarding the corporate policies at Patagonia? Would you like to work for a company like this?

2. Do you believe that focusing on sustainability and environmental issues is important for leaders?

3. How effectively do you think Chouinard's MBA philosophy might work in other organizations?

4. Do you agree that consensus is critical in organizational decision making?

5. What advantages/disadvantages do you see in leading the way that Chouinard does?

the personality, age, and job experience of followers, impact the effectiveness of laissez-faire leadership (see box 2.5 on p. 49 for the impact of age on leadership style preferences). A group led by a laissez-faire leader, particularly when the leader engages in abdication, may be less innovative than groups with leaders employing authoritarian or democratic communication styles. However, laissez-faire leadership can be highly effective with groups of motivated and knowledgeable experts. These groups often do not require direct guidance and produce better results when left alone. A group of medical researchers, for example, might function very effectively when provided with the necessary information and materials without any direct guidance or intervention by a leader (see box 2.6 on p. 50 for an example of what happens when highly motivated and knowledgeable followers are supervised too closely).

> Treat people as if they were what they ought to be and you may help them to become what they are capable of being.
> —Johann Wolfgang von Goethe

Researchers have concluded that the democratic style of leadership communication is often most effective. Generally, the benefits derived from democratic communication far outweigh any potential costs. Democratic leadership is associated with increased follower productivity, satisfaction, and involvement/commitment. A negative element is that democratic leadership can become mired in lengthy debate over policy, procedures, and strategies. In most cases, the increase in follower involvement and commitment more than make up for any such delays. Authoritarian leadership is effective in terms of output (particularly when the leader directly supervises behavior) but is generally ineffective in enhancing follower satisfaction and commitment. The abdication factor in laissez-faire leadership often damages productivity, satisfaction, and commitment. The laissez-faire style can be effective when it represents guided freedom or when it is used with highly knowledgeable and motivated experts. In many situations, the costs associated with the authoritarian and laissez-faire styles of leadership can seriously hamper a leader's effectiveness.

Box 2.5   Research Highlight
Leadership Style Across Generations[28]

In their book, *Generations at Work*, management consultants Ron Zemke, Claire Raines, and Bob Filipczak suggest that four primary generational groups exist in the United States: veterans (52 million people born between 1922 and 1943), baby boomers (73 million people born between 1944 and 1960), generation Xers (70 million people born between 1961 and 1980), and generation nexters (70 million people and counting born between 1981 and today). Each generation, they suggest, exhibits unique leadership style preferences.

Veterans. The hard work and vision of this generation shaped the United States as we know it today. Veterans built a space program and landed a man on the moon, revolutionized modern medicine, and helped pave the road for U.S. financial supremacy. Veterans are generally thought to be solid, reliable, no-nonsense employees. In leadership roles, veterans tend toward a directive style that was the norm when they entered the world of work. It is not unusual for veterans to lead by taking charge, making most decisions on their own, and delegating tasks to followers.

Baby Boomers. This group grew up in a time of unprecedented expansion and economic growth. Their generation tends to be optimistic, believing they can positively impact the world. Baby boomers live for the present—working long hours to obtain the material goods they desire while saving less and charging more on credit cards than other generations. As leaders, baby boomers tend toward a collegial and consensual style and are genuinely concerned about the welfare of others. Baby boomers work at encouraging participation in the workplace but (having worked for veterans in their formative years) are not always skilled at achieving these ends.

Generation Xers. This generation came of age in an era when political scandal, a struggling economy, soaring divorce rates, and increasing reliance on technology fundamentally changed society. Many generation Xers became disillusioned, withholding their optimism and excitement as a means for avoiding disappointment. This tendency led some in other generations to label the Xers as "slackers." In fact, the tendency to challenge authority and question the methods of past generations has been a distinct advantage for this group. Like no previous time in history, the leader of today must be adept at dealing with change and uncertainty. As leaders, generation Xers tend to be fair, competent, and honest (sometimes painfully so). They tend to be supportive of diversity in work habits and believe that allowing workers freedom in their jobs helps produce better overall results.

Generation Nexters. These people are multiculturalists comfortable with diversity of race, religion, and social background. They have lived in a world permeated by the home computer and the Internet, affording them the opportunity to develop a comfort with technology and an appreciation for other cultures and viewpoints. The global mind-set of the generation nexters has made them the most tolerant of all generational groups. They are also highly organized and rule oriented. Indeed, they seem to have more in common with their grandparents and great-grandparents, the veterans, than with the baby boomers or generation Xers. Generation nexters put a premium on ethics and manners and are highly committed to their work. As a group, they exhibit the dedication to teamwork of the baby boomers, the can-do attitude of the veterans, and the technological skill of the generation Xers, suggesting their leadership will exemplify a strong commitment to both the value of the individual and to the quality of the task.

Of course, generational differences are not always cut and dried, particularly among those who were born near the generational transition years. Despite this admonition, Zemke, Raines, and Filipczak offer an interesting argument for the impact of age on leadership style preferences.

Box 2.6   Case Study

The Importance of Leadership Communication Style: SuperNova Microcomputer

Jay Brooks is the project director of a product development team at SuperNova Microcomputer. His team of 30 employees has been charged with the task of developing a new "highly user friendly" computer system for the home market. This group of 30 consists of the best technicians within the organization.

Unfortunately, Jay's team has been experiencing numerous difficulties and delays in the development of the new computer system. A number of team members have complained to the president of SuperNova, Sam Lowell, that Brooks is stifling creativity within the team and that Laura Martin, the project assistant, would be a much more effective leader. "We could get this project moving if Laura were in charge," claims one team member.

Brooks, who was hired from a major competitor six months ago, is a very directive leader. He holds a daily meeting from 8 to 10 A.M. in which every unit of the entire team presents their latest innovations. All new ideas must be cleared through Brooks. Many team members have complained about these meetings, claiming that "Brooks might as well build this system by himself if he is going to approve every chip." In addition, all team members must complete a worksheet isolating the specific tasks they have undertaken each day. This worksheet, wryly called "form 1984" by members of the team, is a major source of dissatisfaction among team members.

Laura Martin has been with the company since its inception a decade ago. Laura was passed over for the job as project director because Sam Lowell felt that she was not as technically competent as she needed to be. Laura was disappointed, but she accepted the decision because, overall, she has been very happy at SuperNova. Indeed, Laura has been instrumental in promoting the open, democratic, employee-oriented management style that is characteristic of SuperNova. As project assistant she interacts frequently with all members of the team. She has discovered that many of the members feel unappreciated. One team member complains, "We are expected to create one of the most advanced home computer systems in existence, but we are treated like a bunch of rebellious third graders."

Sam Lowell is disturbed because the project is falling way behind schedule. After only six months, major delays have pushed back the target date for the project by a full year. The team members themselves don't seem to be aware that they are falling behind any projected schedule; they only realize that the project is bogging down.

Things have gotten to the point that a number of team members are threatening to quit. If they leave, the entire project will be jeopardized. Further, rumors are spreading through the team that upper management is disappointed with productivity and may replace several key members. All in all, members of the team seem very frustrated. "We just want to build the best product that we can," says one team member, adding, "I only wish they would let us."

Discussion Questions

1. What problems can you identify at SuperNova Microcomputer?

2. Which leadership (s) would be most effective in working with the product development team? Why?

3. How would you suggest a leader might get the product development team back on schedule? What policy and/or personnel changes would you recommend?

4. What recommendations would you make concerning the overall operation at SuperNova Microcomputer?

5. How might the leaders at SuperNova Microcomputer assure their employees that problems like this can be avoided in the future?

Task and Interpersonal Leadership

Closely related to the authoritarian, democratic, and laissez-faire model of leadership style is the task and interpersonal model. From the late 1940s until the early 1960s, several groups of researchers worked to identify and to label the dimensions of leadership communication. These researchers used different methodologies and measurement techniques but came to similar conclusions. Each of the research teams suggested that leadership consists of two primary communication dimensions: task and interpersonal. Although each group of researchers applied its own unique label to the communication styles discovered, the groups were essentially talking about the same set of communicative behaviors.

Task-oriented communication has been referred to as: *production oriented; initiating structure; Theory X management; concern for production.* **Interpersonal-oriented communication** has been called: *employee oriented; consideration; Theory Y management; concern for people.*

The similarity in findings among these researchers is not surprising. Leadership boils down to two primary ingredients: work that needs to be done and the people who do the work. Without these ingredients there is no need for leadership!

The leader employing the task style is primarily concerned with the successful completion of task assignments. The task-oriented leader demonstrates a much greater concern for getting work done than for the people doing the work. The task leader is often highly authoritarian. In contrast, the interpersonal leader is concerned with relationships. This style, similar to the democratic style, emphasizes teamwork, cooperation, and supportive communication.

Ernest Stech describes the typical communication patterns of task- and interpersonal-oriented leaders in his book, *Leadership Communication.*[29] He lists the following distinctions between these two styles of leadership.

Task Orientation	Interpersonal Orientation
Disseminates information	Solicits opinions
Ignores the positions, ideas, and feelings of others	Recognizes the positions, ideas, and feelings of others
Engages in rigid, stylized communication	Engages in flexible, open communication
Interrupts others	Listens carefully to others
Makes demands	Makes requests
Focuses on facts, data, and information as they relate to tasks	Focuses on feelings, emotions, and attitudes as they relate to personal needs
Emphasizes productivity through the acquisition of technical skills	Emphasizes productivity through the acquisition of personal skills
Most often communicates in writing	Most often communicates orally
Maintains a "closed door" policy	Maintains an "open door" policy

In the next sections, we will focus on four of the most significant attempts to identify the communication patterns of leaders: (1) the Michigan leadership studies, (2) the Ohio State leadership studies, (3) McGregor's Theory X and Theory Y, and (4) Blake and McCanse's Leadership Grid.®

The Michigan Leadership Studies

Shortly after World War II, a team of researchers at the University of Michigan set out to discover which leadership practices contributed to effective group performance. To determine the characteristics of effective leaders, the Michigan researchers looked at both high- and low-performing teams within two organizations. Twenty-four groups of clerical workers in a life insurance company and 72 groups of railroad workers were studied in an attempt to identify the factors contributing to satisfactory and unsatisfactory group leadership.[30]

From their observations of these work groups, the Michigan researchers noted a distinction between what they called "production-oriented" and "employee-oriented" styles of leadership communication. Production-oriented leaders focus on accomplishing tasks by emphasizing technical procedures, planning, and organization. The production-oriented leader is primarily concerned with getting work done. Employee-oriented leaders focus on relationships between people and are particularly interested in motivating and training followers. Employee-oriented leaders demonstrate a genuine interest in the well-being of followers both on and off the job.

The Michigan researchers believed that the production-oriented and employee-oriented styles were opposing sets of communicative behaviors. They suggested these leadership communication styles could be described along a continuum as illustrated in figure 2.1. A leader could choose either a production-oriented style, an employee-oriented style, or a neutral style of communication. According to the Michigan research, leaders who exhibited employee oriented styles had more productive and satisfied work groups.

This one-dimensional view of leadership communication style was short lived.[31] Follow-up studies performed by the University of Michigan researchers suggested that it was possible for leaders to adopt both production-oriented *and* employee-oriented styles. Further, leaders who demonstrated high concern for both production and people were found to be more effective than leaders who exhibited only employee-oriented or production-oriented communication.[32] Production-oriented and employee-oriented leadership styles were not polar opposites but rather two distinct dimensions of leadership communication style.

Figure 2.1   Employee- versus Production-Oriented Leadership Communication Styles

Neutral

[———————————————————————————————]

Employee-Oriented   Production-Oriented

The Ohio State Leadership Studies

At the same time that the Michigan researchers were involved in their observations of work groups, an interdisciplinary team of researchers at The

Ohio State University attempted to identify the factors associated with leadership communication.[33] The Ohio State researchers developed a questionnaire they called the Leader Behavior Description Questionnaire (LBDQ). The LBDQ was administered to groups of military personnel who were asked to rate their commanders.

Statistical analysis of the LBDQ indicated two primary dimensions of leadership. These dimensions were labeled *consideration* and *initiating structure.* Consideration consisted of interpersonal-oriented communication designed to express affection and liking for followers; the consideration of followers' feelings, opinions, and ideas; and the maintenance of an amiable working environment. Inconsiderate leaders criticized followers in front of others, made threats, and refused to accept followers' suggestions or explanations. Initiating structure referred to task-related behaviors involved in the initiation of action, the organization and assignment of tasks, and the determination of clear-cut standards of performance.

Consideration and initiating structure were believed to be two separate dimensions of leadership. As a result, a leader could rate high or low on either dimension. This representation of leader communication style allowed for the development of a two-dimensional view of leadership. As depicted in figure 2.2, the Ohio State researchers believed that it was possible for a leader to demonstrate varying amounts of task (initiating structure) or interpersonal (consideration) communication.

Conclusions drawn from the Ohio State research focusing on the use of task and interpersonal styles of leadership communication are complicated by variations in methodology and instrumentation. Over the years, several different versions of the LBDQ have been used to measure task (initiating structure) and interpersonal (consideration) related messages. As a result, the findings of the Ohio State team are inconsistent. In general, both consideration and initiat-

Figure 2.2   A Two-Dimensional View of Leadership

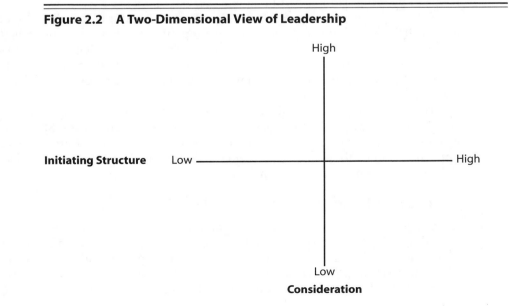

ing structure are important to effective leadership. Considerate leadership communication seems to increase follower satisfaction while decreasing hostility and strife. Initiating structure appears important in guiding and organizing the completion of tasks.[34]

McGregor's Theory X and Theory Y

In the late 1950s, Douglas McGregor, a professor of management at the Massachusetts Institute of Technology, attempted to isolate the ways in which attitudes and behaviors influence organizational management. The result of this investigation was McGregor's classic work, *The Human Side of Enterprise.*[35] In his book, McGregor identifies two basic approaches to supervision—Theory X management and Theory Y management.

Theory X and Theory Y represent basic approaches for dealing with followers. Both approaches are based on a set of assumptions regarding human nature. Theory X managers believe that the average person has an inherent dislike for work and will avoid engaging in productive activities whenever possible. Managers must coerce, control, direct, and threaten workers in order to ensure performance. Indeed, Theory X management assumes that most people actually desire strict supervision as a means of insuring security. If workers are told what to do, they can have little doubt that they are performing as expected. This approach emphasizes task supervision with little or no concern for individual needs.

Theory Y managers work to integrate organizational and individual goals. Theory Y assumes that work is as natural as play or rest. Work is not viewed as inherently unpleasant but rather as a source of satisfaction. Therefore, threats, punishment, and direct supervision are not necessary to ensure productivity. Personal commitment and pride are sufficient to ensure quality workmanship. Further, Theory Y argues that the average person seeks responsibility as an outlet for imagination and creativity. This approach emphasizes individual commitment by recognizing individual needs as well as organizational needs.

The leader employing a Theory X orientation adopts a task-oriented approach. This leader focuses on methods for getting work done. Little consideration is given to those doing the work. The Theory Y leader, on the other hand, focuses on the unique characteristics of the individuals performing the tasks. The tasks themselves are not ignored but are viewed in terms of the people involved.

The Theory X–Theory Y dichotomy has been criticized for being an overly simplistic attempt to identify polarized extremes of human nature. McGregor responded to his critics by explaining that Theory X and Theory Y are not polar opposites. Rather, they are independent options from which a leader can select, depending on the situation and the people involved.

Blake and McCanse's Leadership Grid®

One of the most commonly cited examples of the task and interpersonal approach to leadership communication styles is the Leadership Grid by Robert Blake and Anne Adams McCanse (formerly the Managerial Grid developed by Blake and Mouton).[36] Blake and McCanse identify communication styles based on the degree of concern for production (task orientation) and concern for people (interpersonal orientation) exhibited by a leader. These communication styles are plotted on a graph with axes ranging from one to nine. (See figure 2.3.)

The five plotted leader communication styles are:

1,1 Impoverished Management. The impoverished leader demonstrates a low concern for tasks and a low concern for relationships. The leader with a 1,1 orientation does not actively attempt to influence others but rather assigns responsibilities and leaves followers to complete tasks on their own.

9,1 Authority Compliance. This leader is highly concerned with the completion of task assignments but demonstrates little concern for personal relationships. The primary function of the 9,1 oriented leader is to plan, direct, and control behavior. Followers are viewed as human resources who facilitate the completion of tasks. Input from followers is not encouraged; the 9,1 oriented leader attempts to dominate decision making.

5,5 Middle-of-the-Road Management. This middle-of-the-road leader is adequately concerned with both production and people. In an attempt to involve followers, the 5,5 leader engages in compromise. Middle-of-the-road leaders do not rock the boat—they push enough to achieve adequate productivity but yield if they believe increasing the workload will strain interpersonal relationships. As a result, the 5,5 leader often achieves mediocre results.

Figure 2.3[37]   The Leadership Grid®

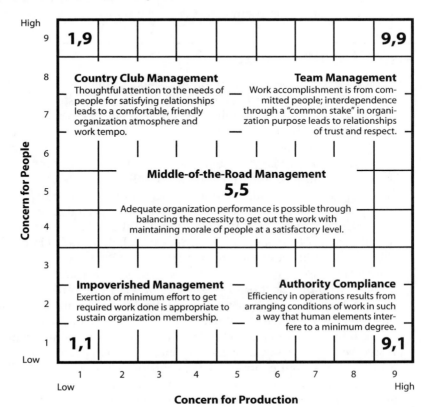

1,9 Country Club Management. The country club leader is more concerned with interpersonal relationships than with the completion of tasks. The 1,9 leader seeks to establish a supportive, friendly environment. Although country club leaders may want tasks to be completed effectively, they will emphasize factors that contribute to the personal satisfaction and happiness of followers. The 1,9 leader believes his or her primary responsibility is to provide a positive working environment.

9,9 Team Management. Team leadership involves a high concern for both production and people. The 9,9 leadership style is the ideal in which the successful execution of task assignments as well as individual support and caring are emphasized. The 9,9 leader nurtures followers so that they are able to achieve excellence in both personal and team goals. Under team leadership, both leaders and followers work together to achieve the highest level of productivity and personal accomplishment.

Leaders generally adopt one leadership communication style, which they use in most situations. This is called a *dominant style.* A second orientation from the model may be used as a backup style. For example, a leader might generally adopt a 5,5 leadership communication style but might shift to a 9,1 style when pressured to get orders out to an important customer.

The most effective leadership communication style, according to Blake and McCanse, is team management (9,9). Implementation of the 9,9 style in organizational contexts is associated with increased productivity and profitability, increased frequency of communication, and improved leader-follower relations.[38]

Follower Communication Styles

Robert Kelley believes that followers, like leaders, need to understand their communication styles to carry out their roles successfully.[39] To identify the components that make up follower styles, Kelley asked individuals and focus groups to describe the best, worst, and typical followers in their organizations. He found that followers differ on two dimensions—independent/critical thinking and active engagement. The best followers are people who think for themselves and take initiative. The worst followers have to be told what to do and require constant supervision. Typical followers take direction and complete jobs on their own after being told what is expected of them.

Once he had isolated the key characteristics of followership, Kelley then developed the questionnaire found in box 2.7. Followers fall into one of five categories based on how they respond to the independent thinking and active engagement sections of this test. *Alienated followers* are highly independent thinkers who put most of their energies into fighting rather than serving their organizations because they've become disillusioned with their leaders or feel unappreciated. Alienated followers provide a dose of healthy skepticism for the group but generally come off as cynical. An example of an alienated follower would be Dr. Luka Kovac on *ER*. In contrast, *conformists* are committed to organizational goals but express few thoughts of their own. These followers (often referred to as "yes men/women" in popular culture) may hold back their ideas out of fear or deference to authority. *Pragmatists* are moderately independent

Box 2.7   Self-Assessment
Followership Style Questionnaire[40]

For each statement, think of a followership situation and how you acted. Choose a number from 0 to 6 to indicate the extent to which the statement describes you. 0 indicates rarely applies and 6 indicates almost always.

_____ 1. Does your work help you fulfill some societal goal or personal dream that is important to you?

_____ 2. Are your personal work goals aligned with the organization's priority goals?

_____ 3. Are you highly committed to and energized by your work and organization, giving them your best ideas and performance?

_____ 4. Does your enthusiasm also spread to and energize your coworkers?

_____ 5. Instead of waiting for or merely accepting what the leader tells you, do you personally identify which organizational activities are most critical for achieving the organization's priority goals?

_____ 6. Do you actively develop a distinctive competence in those critical activities so that you become more valuable to the leader and the organization?

_____ 7. When starting a new job or assignment, do you promptly build a record of successes in tasks that are important to the leader?

_____ 8. Can the leader give you a difficult assignment without the benefit of much supervision, knowing that you will meet your deadline with highest-quality work and that you will "fill in the cracks" if need be?

_____ 9. Do you take the initiative to seek out and successfully complete assignments that go above and beyond your job?

_____ 10. When you are not the leader of a group project, do you still contribute at a high level, often doing more than your share?

_____ 11. Do you independently think up and champion new ideas that will contribute significantly to the leader's or the organization's goals?

_____ 12. Do you try to solve the tough problems (technical or organizational), rather than look to the leader to do it for you?

_____ 13. Do you help out other coworkers, making them look good, even when you don't get any credit?

_____ 14. Do you help the leader or group see both the upside potential and downside risks of idea or plans, playing the devil's advocate if need be?

_____ 15. Do you understand the leader's needs, goals, and constraints, and work hard to help meet them?

_____ 16. Do you actively and honestly own up to your strengths and weaknesses rather than put off evaluation?

_____ 17. Do you make a habit of internally questioning the wisdom of the leader's decision rather than just doing what you are told?

_____ 18. When the leader asks you to do something that runs contrary to your professional or personal preferences, do you say "no" rather than "yes"?

_____ 19. Do you act on your own ethical standards rather than the leader's or the group's standards?

_____ 20. Do you assert your views on important issues, even though it might mean conflict with your group or reprisals from the leader?

(continued)

Finding Your Followership Style
Use the scoring key below to score your answers to the questions.

Independent Thinking Items	Active Engagement Items
Question 1. ____	Question 2. ____
5. ____	3. ____
11. ____	4. ____
12. ____	6. ____
14. ____	7. ____
16. ____	8. ____
17. ____	9. ____
18. ____	10. ____
19. ____	13. ____
20. ____	15. ____
Total Score ____	Total Score ____

Add up your scores on the independent thinking items. Record the total on a vertical axis, as in the graph below. Repeat the procedure for the active engagement items and mark the total on a horizontal axis. Now plot your scores on the graph by drawing perpendicular lines connecting your two scores.

The juxtaposition of these two dimensions forms the basis on which people classify followership styles.

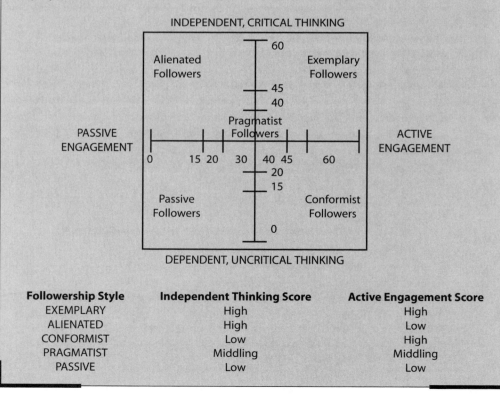

Followership Style	Independent Thinking Score	Active Engagement Score
EXEMPLARY	High	High
ALIENATED	High	Low
CONFORMIST	Low	High
PRAGMATIST	Middling	Middling
PASSIVE	Low	Low

and engaged. Pragmatism is a way of coping with organizational uncertainty caused by frequent changes of leadership, layoffs, and restructuring. These organizational survivors hold on to their jobs but are not likely to be promoted. *Passive followers* demonstrate little original thought or commitment. They rely heavily on the leader's direction and meet only minimal expectations. Their passivity may stem from a lack of skills or be a response to serving under authoritarian leaders. Passive followers can be found at many fast-food restaurants where teenagers with limited job experience work under highly directive supervisors. *Exemplary followers* rate highly as both critical thinkers and active participants, contributing innovative ideas and going beyond what is required.

Kelley outlines three sets of skills and values that characterize exemplary followership. Utilizing these skills can help us shift from the alienated, conformist, pragmatist, and passive styles to the exemplary category. First, exemplary followers add value to the organization by helping it reach its objectives. They know what they want to achieve in life and commit themselves to organizations that share the same purposes. They understand what tasks are most important to achieving an organization's vision and develop the skills necessary to carry out these critical path activities. Second, outstanding followers "weave a web of relationships" through joining teams, building bridges to others throughout the organization, and working as partners with leaders. Third, exemplary followers cultivate a courageous conscience by making the right ethical judgments and then following through on those choices. They anticipate and eliminate ethical problems before they pose a significant threat and disobey leaders who issue directives that put the organization at risk. (For an in-depth discussion of courageous followership, see chapter 11.)

Kelley's typology provides a useful framework for understanding follower communication styles, but there may be other dimensions of followership that he overlooks. Like leaders, some followers may be oriented toward completing the task while others are more concerned about maintaining relationships. Exemplary followership is probably the best approach in most situations, as Kelley suggests. However, other attributes might be necessary if the group faces a dangerous task or an unreasonable leader. (See box 2.8 for an example of how followers can impact a leader.) We'll have more to say about the relationship between situational variables and leading/following in chapter 3.

Max DePree, the former chairman of the board of the Herman Miller Company and the author of several best-selling books on leadership, suggests that leaders play an important role in enabling followers to maximize their effectiveness.[41] To allow followers the best opportunity to develop the exemplary follower style, DePree suggests leaders must remember the following:

- When leaders exhibit cynicism, destructive criticism, unnecessary conflict, personal animosity, or gossip, they create an environment where followers cannot flourish.
- Leaders must supply good training and access to all relevant information to enable followers to succeed.
- Leaders must make followers feel needed.
- Change is essential to survival. Followers are good at change when leaders are good at managing change.

- Leaders must listen and be available to help, especially when they don't like what they hear.
- Leaders must be fair with both the division of resources and the evaluation of followers.

Box 2.8   Case Study

When Followers Dare

National Insurance Company is a full-service insurance provider with corporate divisions in 15 locations in the United States. Each division is responsible for writing and servicing policies within its geographic area. For several years the general manager of the Western Division was Fred Jackson. Under Jackson's leadership, the Western Division became the most successful division in the company, achieving a goal of policy sales of $100 million a full 18 months ahead of projections. The success of the Western Division was directly attributable to Jackson's open, democratic leadership style. Jackson knew all of his 250 employees by their first names and was always willing to talk with an employee who had a question or concern. Jackson, who had worked his way up from an entry-level position in the company, was a tireless cheerleader for his staff and never failed to recognize his employees' achievements. When his division reached its goal of $100 million in policy sales, Jackson hired a local high school band to march through the parking lot and then invited all of his employees to join him for a catered lunch-hour barbecue. Senior management at National recognized Jackson's leadership prowess, and he was promoted to the corporate headquarters in New York.

Jackson's replacement in the Western Division was a recent Stanford MBA graduate named Jason Hirsch. Hirsch's leadership style was very different than his predecessor's. Where Jackson had been open and interactive, Hirsch was closed and private. He spent most of his time alone in his office and made only token appearances at company meetings and functions. Most of Hirsch's communication consisted of directives handed to the senior management team. Within a few months of Hirsch's arrival, the mood at the Western Division began to change. The energy and team spirit that had been so prevalent under Jackson's leadership was significantly diminished. Sales declined dramatically, and rumors surfaced suggesting the Western Division would be closed with its business moving to other National Insurance Company divisions.

These rumors were the catalyst for a plan among the senior management team in the Western Division. These managers felt that it was their responsibility to communicate their dissatisfaction to Hirsch to save jobs in the Western Division. One morning when Hirsch entered the building, he was greeted by his 12 senior managers dressed in military fatigues. Hirsch was informed that his managers had "taken over the office," and he was escorted to a meeting room. The managers explained to Hirsch that the military uniforms were a joke and that their "coup" was only an attempt to sit down with Hirsch and discuss how to improve the Western Division. Surprisingly (some of the managers fully expected they might be fired for their actions), Hirsch was very open to discussing the situation. As a newcomer to the Western Division, he had felt like an outsider. This bold move by his followers offered an opportunity for communication. Hirsch admitted that he was very nervous about taking charge of the division after the departure of the very popular and successful Fred Jackson. Once Hirsch and his managers began to communicate, they were able to identify strategies for improving the situation in the Western Division. Although it took time, the managers' coup helped to develop a much improved relationship between Hirsch and his staff. Within six months the Western Division was, once again, among the most successful divisions within National Insurance Company.

Ultimately, the follower styles exhibited within a group, team, or organization are a reflection of the behaviors that are expected, demanded, promoted, or discouraged by formal leaders.[42] Although some followers may thrive when working with almost any leader or in almost any context or situation, most followers are powerfully impacted, for better or for worse, by the leaders with whom they work.

> This business of making another person feel good in the unspectacular course of his [her] daily comings and goings is, in my view, the very essence of leadership.
>
> —Irwin Federman

Communication Styles and Information Processing

So far in this chapter we have focused on the observable behaviors of leaders and followers and explored the link between communication styles and performance. However, this approach leaves a number of important questions unanswered. For example: Why do leaders choose one style over another? How do constituents decide if someone is a leader? What factors make leaders and followers more receptive or resistant to influence from the other party? Information processing scholars Douglas Brown, Kristyn Scott, and Hayden Lewis argue that we must look inside the minds of leaders and followers to answer questions like these.[43] They focus on cognitive processes that determine behavior, "attempting to discern how individuals acquire, store, retrieve, and use information to better understand how those individuals (i.e., leaders and followers) function and adapt to the current context."[44]

Three concepts are crucial to understanding the information processing perspective. First, the basic building blocks of knowledge are symbols and categories of symbols. These symbols (generally words) are stored in long-term memory and allow us to engage in conceptual thinking. We draw on language whenever we think, problem solve, plan, and remember.[45] Second, these symbolic bits of knowledge form interconnected networks called *schemas* or *schemata*, which assist us in interpreting and making sense of the world around us. Imagine, for example, how confusing it would be to attend a wedding for the first time without any schema for figuring out what is going on. You would have no idea how to dress, where to sit, how to behave during the ceremony, the roles of the wedding party, and so forth. Leaders and followers, too, have schemata that guide their behaviors, helping them to determine who is a "motivated" or "unmotivated" follower or a "successful" or "unsuccessful" leader, for example. Third, schemas must be activated in order to influence perceptions, attitudes, and behavior. The large volume of schemata in long-term memory and the limited capacity of working memory mean that only a small subset of schemas can be activated at a given time.

A leader's selection of a particular behavioral style depends in part on the schemata that she or he has stored in long-term memory. The leader who thinks of followers as generally incompetent, for instance, is much more likely to engage in authoritarian leadership that calls for strict supervision and direction on his or her part. If the leader's schema holds that followers perform better when they like their supervisors, she or he will adopt a relationally oriented style. Not surprisingly, leaders can't utilize an alternative style unless they have established a schemata for the beliefs, attitudes, and behaviors of that style. In the case of our authoritarian leader, it would be difficult for this individual (perhaps someone raised by authoritative parents) to adopt a more democratic approach unless he or she understands what this style entails.

Researchers report that leaders with a broader variety of schemata are better able to adjust their behavior to the situation and to generate superior solutions more quickly. Experience plays an important role in developing expert knowledge that leads to improved performance. For example, when compared to junior officers, senior military officers have schemata that are better organized and that are based on principles that can be applied to a variety of situations.[46] Experience isn't the only way to develop new schemata, however. New symbolic networks can be created through training programs, books, and videos as well.

Leaders also respond to the situation when choosing which communication style to use. In particular, they must "make sense" of their followers through categorization. How they categorize followers determines their style that, in turn, has a direct impact on the performance of subordinates as well as the organization as a whole. As we'll see in our discussion of leader-member exchange theory in chapter 3, followers selected to be members of the leader's "in-group" have more flexibility when it comes to completing their tasks and exert more influence in decision making. In contrast, leaders are more dominant in interactions with followers who make up the "out-group." In-group members are more productive and satisfied than their out-group counterparts as a result.

Categorization extends to attributions about the causes of the followers' behaviors. Superiors are more likely to punish poor performance (e.g., a delayed shipment) if they perceive it is the product of internal forces (lack of motivation) rather than external forces (unexpected delays caused by the weather). Such attributions are often biased. Leaders will protect themselves by blaming failure on internal forces, such as the shortcomings of followers, rather than on external factors, such as the leaders' failure to provide adequate guidance and resources. Supervisors are generally more tolerant of the failings of subordinates they like.

Followers, like leaders, are guided by schemas. In fact, the impact of a leader's style rests on how subordinates interpret his/her actions. Consider who gets selected for a leadership role, for example. Judgments of who is suitable to lead are largely based on implicit leadership theory—our beliefs about what distinguishes a leader from a nonleader.[47] The ideal small-group leader takes an active role in the discussion through setting goals, giving directions, managing conflict, and summarizing the group's deliberations (see chapter 7). The group member who engages in these prototypical behaviors is most likely to emerge as leader when one has not been appointed ahead of time. In a similar fashion, presidential candidates who create the impression that they are decisive, informed, responsible, dignified, and intelligent (characteristics associated with the prototypical president) are most likely to get elected. It should be noted that a leader candidate doesn't have to have all the prototypical characteristics to be selected for the role and that the ideal leader will vary between situations. We have different expectations of a military leader than of a religious one or of a frontline supervisor and the CEO in the same organization. However, the more a follower identifies with the group, the more important it is for the leader candidate to fit the group leader prototype. (Turn to box 2.9 to see how the prototypical leader in the United States compares to those in other countries.)

Performance outcomes serve as indirect cues for evaluating those in leadership roles. Observers make judgments about a leader's effectiveness based on how well the group performs and on whether or not they believe the leader is responsible for its successes or failures. We generally infer, for example, that the CEO of a highly profitable company is effective due to the success of the corporation and our belief that she or he plays a critical role in the organization's high performance.[48]

In recent years, social psychologists have increasingly focused on how leaders achieve their goals by influencing the ways that followers think of themselves.[49] The self-concept is made up of many different self-schemas, which are activated at different times. When you are sitting in class, your student script is active. If you call your mother on your cell phone after class, your son or daughter schema takes center stage. Levels of self-identity range from individual (defining the self as different from others), to the interpersonal or relational (defining the self in terms of relationships with others), to the collective (identifying with the group or larger organization).

To be effective, leaders must both tailor their communication styles to the self-identification level of their followers and, at the same time, help followers change how they view themselves. Those followers who think of themselves as individuals will be more open to personal performance feedback and rewards. Those operating at the interpersonal level will be looking to establish a positive emotional relationship with their leaders. Followers who define themselves at the collective level will be more motivated by messages that emphasize teamwork and organizational goals. Outstanding leaders encourage followers to shift their focus from personal concerns to the group as a whole, which

---

Box 2.9

National Differences in Leadership Prototypes[50]

Nation	Prototype
United States	*Free Agent Star.* A winner who gets short-term results; sees money as an indicator of worth
Latin America	*General.* Strong man in charge, keeps order, promotes change, controls
France	*Genius.* Smartest one, best exam score, member of intellectual elite, graduate of the best school
United Kingdom	*Diplomat.* Big thinker, well-educated, well-traveled, good social skills
Germany	*Master.* Most respected by peers, expert in field, has in-depth knowledge
Italy	*Godfather.* Holds together conflicting factions, punishes and favors, paternalistic
Holland	*Marathon Winner.* Outworks the rest, runs hard, trains well, endures, at head of pack
Poland	*Baron.* Protects castle and fiefdom, exercises power for self and close associates
Japan	*Senior Statesman.* Older, wiser; from the group; survivor, consensus builder
China	*Warlord.* Local power; uses *quanxi* (favors) for loyal supporters; rich
Vietnam	*Communist Party Boss.* Wears numerous hats; favors to family and friends; ideological
Israel	*Field Commander.* Smart, energetic, creative, tactical, self-made
Africa	*Tribal Chief.* Older, wiser, consultative; orchestrates various networks, builds factions

---

increases individual commitment and collective performance. Often this shift begins with establishing good relationships with new followers. Over time, these followers develop schemas that highlight their group membership. They adopt the values and standards communicated by the leader and begin to regulate their own behavior according to these guidelines. Their personal goals (their images of what they would like to be in the future) become linked to the vision of the organization.

Information processing theory deepens our understanding of leader and follower styles by shifting the focus to intrapersonal communication—communication that occurs within the individual. The selection and effectiveness of leadership styles depends on the storage and activation of symbols and symbolic networks. Here are some implications of this approach for aspiring leaders.

1. *Develop your knowledge and experience base.* The more you learn about leadership and get firsthand experience serving as a leader, the greater your ability to meet the demands of the situation and to generate good solutions.

2. *Acknowledge the power of categorization.* How you categorize others will determine how you respond to those individuals, how they respond to you, how well they perform, and how well the group as a whole performs. Beware of possible perceptual biases that unfairly categorize followers or protect you at the expense of others.

3. *Know your audience.* Determine the leadership prototypes held by the group and act in a way that fulfills those expectations. What followers expect of you, as a leader, will depend on a variety of factors, including organizational and national culture, group history, and elements of the situation. Not fulfilling leadership prototypes is a major cause of failure when leaders are placed in other cultures. Know, too, how your followers define themselves and direct messages to their level of identity—self, relational, or organization centered.

4. *Performance counts.* Recognize that performance counts or, rather, your connection with performance counts. To emerge as a leader and to be effective in a leadership role, you'll need to be perceived as contributing to the group's success. Increase your power or discretion to influence events through your knowledge and example (see chapter 5) while establishing coalitions with others in the organization.

5. *Be flexible.* Different audiences and situations will call for a variety of responses. A style that works in one setting may not work in another. Seek feedback about how followers are responding to your behavior and adjust accordingly.

6. *Focus attention on the "we" not the "me."* Emphasize the importance of the group or organization's shared mission and goals to encourage followers to activate their collective identities. Such shared focus can boost individual motivation and performance, which, in turn, helps the group become more productive. One simple way to start this process is through your choice of words. Use more inclusive language like "us" and "we" instead of "I" and "you." Frequently communicate shared values and reward behavior that serves common goals.

CHAPTER TAKEAWAYS

- One factor that contributes to variations in leader effectiveness is communication style. Leadership communication style is a relatively enduring set of communicative behaviors that a leader engages in when interacting with followers. A leader's communication style may reflect a philosophical belief about human nature or may simply be a strategy designed to maximize outcomes in a given situation.

- Authoritarian leaders maintain strict control over followers by directly regulating policy, procedures, and behavior. Authoritarian leaders create distance between themselves and their followers as a means of emphasizing role distinctions. Many authoritarian leaders believe that followers would not function effectively without direct supervision. The authoritarian leader generally feels that people left to complete work on their own will be unproductive. Authoritarian leadership can boost output, but it reduces follower satisfaction and commitment.

- Democratic leaders engage in supportive communication that facilitates interaction between leaders and followers. The leader adopting the democratic communication style encourages follower involvement and participation in the determination of goals and procedures. Democratic leaders assume that followers are capable of making informed decisions. The democratic style of leadership is often most effective, being associated with increased follower productivity, satisfaction, and involvement/commitment.

- Laissez-faire refers to a form of leader communication that has been called *nonleadership* by some. An ineffective version of this leadership communication style involves *abdication* of responsibility on the part of the leader; leaders withdraw from followers and offer little guidance or support. As a result, productivity, cohesiveness, and satisfaction often suffer. A more positive form of the laissez-faire leadership communication style affords followers a high degree of autonomy and self-rule while, at the same time, offering guidance and support when requested. The laissez-faire leader providing *guided freedom* does not directly participate in decision making unless requested to do so by followers or if such intervention is deemed necessary to facilitate task completion. The laissez-faire approach works best when used with highly knowledgeable and motivated experts.

- A number of researchers have concluded that leadership consists of two primary communication dimensions: task and interpersonal, which focus on work that needs to be done and the people who do the work.

- Several models focusing on the task and interpersonal dimensions of leadership have been developed. Most notable are: (1) the Michigan leadership studies, (2) the Ohio State leadership studies, (3) McGregor's Theory X and Theory Y, and (4) Blake and McCanse's Leadership Grid.®

- Followers, like leaders, need to understand their communication styles to carry out their roles successfully. The best followers are people who think for themselves and take initiative. The worst followers have to be told what to do and require constant supervision. Typical followers take direction and complete jobs on their own after being told what is expected of them.

- Ultimately, the follower styles exhibited within a group, team, or organization are a reflection of the behaviors that are expected, demanded, promoted, or discouraged by formal leaders.

- Information processing theory looks inside the minds of leaders and followers to determine how they select and respond to communication styles. A leader's selection of a particular style depends (1) on schemata (interconnected bits of symbolic knowledge) stored in memory, and (2) on the categorization of followers and other elements of the situation.

- Followers employ schemas when selecting leaders. Those who most closely resemble the image of the ideal or prototypical leader generally get selected for the leadership role. Followers also make inferences about a leader's effectiveness based on performance outcomes or cues.

- Leaders achieve their goals by influencing how followers think of themselves. They tailor their styles to the self-concepts of followers, who may be individually, relationally, or organizationally focused, and, at the same time, encourage followers to identify with collective values and goals.

• Important implications of the information processing approach include: (1) develop your knowledge and experience base as a leader; (2) acknowledge the power of categorization, (3) know your audience, (4) performance counts, (5) be flexible, and (6) focus attention on the "we," not the "me."

APPLICATION EXERCISES

1. Make a list of the qualities that you believe are important for effective leadership. Compare your list with the communicative behaviors listed on p. 43. Do effective leaders seem to adopt one leadership communication style more than others?

2. In what types of situations do you believe each of the leadership communication styles identified in this chapter would be most effective? Least effective?

3. Try to think of historical examples of leaders who adopted one of the five grid positions identified by Blake and McCanse. Which of these leaders was most effective? Why?

4. Identify as many alternatives to the styles of leadership communication outlined in this chapter as you can. Discuss with others in class the various styles you identify.

5. In a group, brainstorm examples for each of the five follower categories described in the chapter. Are there other dimensions that categorize follower communication styles besides independent/critical thinking and active engagement? Is exemplary followership always the best approach? Why or why not? Report your conclusions to the rest of the class.

6. Identify your follower communication style using the self-assessment questionnaire found in box 2.7. Why do you think you have adopted this style? What are your strengths and weaknesses as a follower? If you're not an exemplary follower, develop a strategy for becoming one. If you categorized yourself as exemplary, what can you do to become even more effective? Write up your findings.

7. In a group, discuss the relationship between leadership and followership styles. Based on your past experience, identify how leader communication styles have affected your performance as a follower. Try to pinpoint the leadership behaviors you think are most important in promoting exemplary followership.

8. Thinking back on your past experiences with leadership, try to identify how your view of the most/least desirable leadership communication styles has been affected. What have been the primary influences on your view (home, work, school, other)?

9. Describe your prototypical political leader, student body president, professor, and supervisor at work. How are these images similar? Different? Why? As an alternative, select a group that you might want to lead. Describe the prototypical leader for this group. What leadership communication style would you need to use to be selected for this role?

10. Keep a record of your leadership activities over a period of one to two weeks. Evaluate your efforts in terms of the information processing approach outlined in this chapter. How well did you: (1) develop your knowledge and experience base as a leader, (2) acknowledge the power of categorization, (3) know your audience, (4) perform as a leader, (5) exhibit flexibility, and (6) focus attention on the "we," not the "me"?

CULTURAL CONNECTIONS: LEADERSHIP COMMUNICATION STYLES IN EUROPE[51]

Leaders often exhibit preferences for particular leadership communication styles. These preferences may be based on past successes or failures, the work environment, or the perception that one style may be more effective than another in dealing with a given situation. One factor that appears to impact the selection of leadership communication styles is national culture.

Researchers at the Cranfield School of Management in the United Kingdom surveyed over 2,500 top executives in eight European countries in an attempt to determine if there was a unified leadership communication style that would enable managers to "act European" in their business dealings. The Cranfield results suggested no singular European leadership communication style exists. Indeed, the researchers found distinct cultural differences among leadership communication style preferences across the countries in their study. They labeled the styles used within Europe as (1) *consensus*, (2) *towards a common goal*, (3) *managing from a distance*, and (4) *leading from the front*. Although the names used by the Cranfield researchers are different, the communication styles identified in the European study are strikingly similar to the authoritarian, democratic, and laissez-faire styles that have been a part of the leadership literature for more than 60 years.

The consensus style emphasizes open discussion and frequent team meetings, allowing everyone in the organization to be aware of important decisions and developments. Leaders using this style place a high value on effective communication and encourage shared decision making. The consensus style, which has much in common with the democratic approach discussed in this chapter, is most preferred by top managers in Sweden and Finland.

Towards a common goal is based on a strong display of authority. Like those using the authoritarian style, leaders using the common goal style employ strict controls and provide a clear description of roles and responsibilities. The implementation of systems, controls, and procedures is seen as a vehicle for promoting success. The executives in the Cranfield study using this style were more likely to rate themselves and their subordinates as highly disciplined in carrying out their duties. The majority of German and Austrian executives fit into this classification.

The managing-from-a-distance style is similar to the laissez-faire abdication style outlined in this chapter. This style is characterized by the inconsistent communication of key messages and strategies, a lack of discipline, high levels of uncertainty and ambiguity, and the frequent pursuit of personal, rather than group, agendas. This particular classification was unique in the Cranfield study in that only executives from France noted a preference for this style.

Indeed, the preference for this style was very strong among French executives, with 83 percent identifying this approach as their primary leadership communication style.

The leading-from-the-front style is centered primarily on an individual's performance. Leaders exhibiting this style are reluctant to create rules or procedures that might hinder individual performance. This style, like the laissez-faire guided freedom approach, is based on the belief that people are self-motivated and skilled and can perform at the highest levels only when organizational structures do not inhibit performance. Among the Cranfield sample, top executives from Spain, Ireland, and the United Kingdom showed the strongest preference for this style.

Although many factors may impact leadership communication style choices, the Cranfield research provides evidence that national culture may be of central importance. Leaders and followers must consider this important factor when assessing the appropriate uses of leadership communication styles around the globe.

SPOTLIGHT ON TECHNOLOGY:
SELECTING THE MOST EFFECTIVE STYLE FOR VIRTUAL LEADERSHIP

One of the difficult challenges many leaders face is directing the actions of those at remote sites. This distributed leadership is often accomplished virtually and mediated through a variety of technologies ranging from e-mail to teleconferencing. Of the Fortune 1000 companies, 950 have formally implemented virtual work, often in the form of telecommuting.[52] To be successful at leading from a distance, it is vital to select the appropriate leadership style. Kimball Fisher and Mareen Duncan Fisher argue that the authoritarian and laissez-faire abdication styles of leadership are least effective when leading virtually.[53] As Fisher and Fisher point out, authoritarian leaders are rarely successful with virtual teams, which depend on individuals willingly contributing their fullest effort. Even the perception of authoritarian leadership can undermine remote workers who may believe their participation is not valued. There are many ways that a leader can appear to be too authoritarian, but focusing too much attention on the means for accomplishing tasks rather than on the end product is one of the most common. Certainly there are times when the process needs to be monitored, but when a virtual leader regulates work process solely out of the fear that tasks may not be completed in his or her absence, problems tend to arise. Indeed, research suggests the process of submitting electronic status reports to virtual leaders costs significantly more in lost time and salaries than the value of the improvements that result from such activities.[54] Virtual leaders must also be careful not to abdicate their responsibilities. Some well-intended leaders have left their teams alone, even when the team appeared to be having difficulty, assuming that such actions encourage the team to accept responsibility and take more ownership for problems. Quite the contrary, this approach often leads to frustration and alienation.

What style of leadership is most effective for the virtual leader? A style that emphasizes coordination over control encourages follower commitment; manages to principles and objectives rather than policy and processes; empowers followers; rewards continuous improvement; and encourages thoughtful disagreement.[55] The virtual leader must accept a less controlled environment by sharing responsibility with his or her followers. Finally, an effective virtual leader must realize that leadership is about connection, not just physical presence.[56] Regardless of the physical distance, virtual leaders must reach out and build rapport by listening, supporting, appreciating, valuing, and respecting their remote followers. Virtual relationships can be enhanced by face-to-face interaction but must be established primarily through mediated communication where such relationships can be managed on a day-to-day basis. (We'll look at some additional keys to leading virtual teams in chapter 7.)

LEADERSHIP ON THE BIG SCREEN: *PATTON*

Starring: George C. Scott, Karl Malden, Stephen Young, Michael Strong, Frank Lattimore

Rating: PG for language and violence

Synopsis: This film classic won seven Academy Awards, including a Best Actor Oscar for George C. Scott who plays General George Patton, one of the most controversial figures of World War II. The highly autocratic Patton used threats and strict discipline to make his troops battle ready. An avid student of military history (he viewed himself as a reincarnated ancient warrior), Patton anticipated the strategic moves of the German army and led his troops to stunning victories in North Africa, Italy, France, and Germany. His military brilliance was undermined by his ego, temper, and political insensitivity, however. He sometimes put his troops in harm's way so that he could claim the glory. Patton was relieved of command for slapping a sick soldier and later for refusing to cooperate with the Russians. General Omar Bradley (played by Malden) provides a sharp contrast to Patton. Known as the "GI's General," Bradley shunned the limelight and established a close bond with the soldiers under his command.

Chapter Links: authoritarian and democratic leadership communication styles, task versus interpersonal orientations

Traits, Situational, Functional, and Relational Leadership

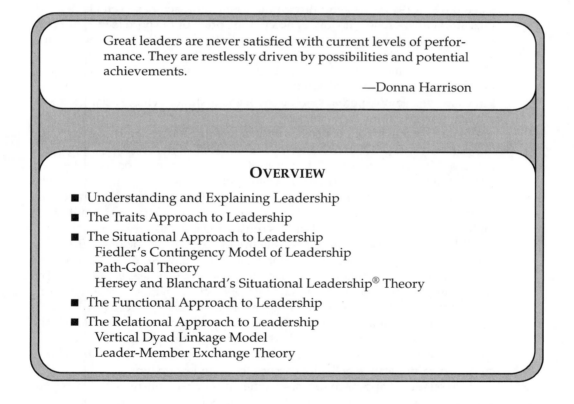

Great leaders are never satisfied with current levels of performance. They are restlessly driven by possibilities and potential achievements.

—Donna Harrison

OVERVIEW

- Understanding and Explaining Leadership
- The Traits Approach to Leadership
- The Situational Approach to Leadership
  Fiedler's Contingency Model of Leadership
  Path-Goal Theory
  Hersey and Blanchard's Situational Leadership® Theory
- The Functional Approach to Leadership
- The Relational Approach to Leadership
  Vertical Dyad Linkage Model
  Leader-Member Exchange Theory

Understanding and Explaining Leadership

Much of what was written about leadership prior to 1900 was based on observation, commentary, and moralization. The increasing use of "scientific" procedures and techniques to measure human behavior, which blossomed in the early twentieth century, changed the way scholars looked at leadership. Over the past 100 years, five primary approaches for understanding and explaining leadership have evolved: the *traits approach*, the *situational approach*, the *functional approach*, the *relational approach*, and the *transformational approach*.

Early social scientists believed that leadership qualities were innate; an individual was either born with the traits needed to be a leader, or he or she lacked the physiological and psychological characteristics necessary for successful leadership. This approach to leadership, known as the traits approach, suggested that nature played a key role in determining leadership potential. The idea that inherent leadership traits could be identified served as the impetus for hundreds of research studies in the early part of the twentieth century. Since the late 1940s, the centrality of the traits approach has been challenged. Present-day researchers no longer accept the notion of the born leader, but continue to be interested in the significance of traits in shaping performance and the perceptions of leadership effectiveness.

The situational approach argues that the traits, skills, and behaviors necessary for effective leadership vary from situation to situation. Think of a successful leader you know; perhaps he or she leads a student club, social group, or religious congregation. Now imagine this leader as a union boss, school principal, football coach, lab supervisor, or military commander. Is it difficult to picture this person playing different leadership roles effectively? A leader is not always successful in every situation. A leader's effectiveness depends on his or her personality, the behavior of followers, the nature of the task, and many other contextual factors. The eighteenth president of the United States, Ulysses S. Grant, is an example of how a leader's effectiveness varies between situations. Grant was a highly effective military leader but was considered inept as president.

While many researchers have attempted to identify factors influencing leadership effectiveness in various contexts, others have studied the functions of leadership. The functional approach looks at the way leaders behave. The underlying assumption of the functional approach is that leaders perform certain functions that allow a group or organization to operate effectively. An individual is considered a leader if he or she performs these functions. The functional approach has been applied primarily to group leadership. The perspective is important to communication scholars because it attempts to identify specific communicative behaviors associated with leadership.

The relational approach focuses on the links or relationships between leaders and followers. This approach to leadership explores the unique interactions a leader has with each of her or his followers. These interactions are critical in developing leader-follower relationships, which, in turn, impact effectiveness. Those who have positive relationships with their leaders are generally more satisfied and productive. Effective leaders try to establish high-quality relationships with as many followers as possible.

In this chapter we will explore the traits, situational, functional, and relational approaches to leadership. Another approach to leadership, known as the transformational approach, will be discussed in the next chapter. All five approaches provide perspectives for understanding and explaining leadership—frameworks that guide leadership theory, research, and practice. Sometimes the approaches overlap; other times they contradict one another. No single approach provides a universal explanation of leadership behavior, but each provides useful insights. As you read, try to identify at least one concept from each approach that you can use to become a more effective leader (see application exercise 10 on p. 97).

The Traits Approach to Leadership

In the early part of the twentieth century, it was widely believed that leaders possessed unique physical and psychological characteristics that predisposed them to positions of influence. Researchers were not completely sure which characteristics were most important, but they assumed that an individual's physical and psychological features were the best indicators of leadership potential. Scores of leadership studies focused on factors such as height, weight, appearance, intelligence, and disposition. Other studies looked at status, social skill, mobility, popularity and other social traits in order to determine which of these characteristics were most strongly associated with leadership. Researchers wanted to know, for example, were leaders: tall or short? bright or dull? outgoing or shy?

In 1948, Ralph Stogdill published a review of 124 studies that had appeared in print between 1904 and 1947 with a focus on traits and personal factors related to leadership.[1] Stogdill's review uncovered a number of inconsistent findings. Leaders were found to be both young and old, tall and short, heavy and thin, extroverted and introverted, and physically attractive as well as physically unattractive. Further, the strength of the relationship between a given trait and leadership prowess varied significantly from study to study. Stogdill concluded, "A person does not become a leader by virtue of the possession of some combination of traits, but the pattern of personal characteristics of the leader must bear some relevant relationship to the characteristics, activities, and goals of the followers."[2]

In 1974, Stogdill again published an exhaustive review of traits research. This time he analyzed 163 traits studies published between 1949 and 1970.[3] Fewer inconsistencies were uncovered in this research, but Stogdill remained convinced that personality traits *alone* did not adequately explain leadership. Once again, Stogdill concluded that *both* personal traits and situational factors influenced leadership.

> Leaders are made, they are not born. They are made by hard effort, which is the price which all of us must pay to achieve any goal that is worthwhile.
>
> —Vince Lombardi

Stogdill's work has sometimes been cited as evidence that personal traits have no bearing on leadership. Stogdill himself did not hold this view. In 1974, he wrote:

> [I] have been cited frequently as evidence in support of the view that leadership is entirely situational in origin and that no personal characteristics are predictive of leadership. This view seems to overemphasize the situational and underemphasize the personal nature of leadership. Strong evidence indicates that different leadership skills and traits are required in different situations. The behaviors and traits enabling a mobster to gain and maintain control over a criminal gang are not the same as those enabling a religious leader to gain and maintain a large following. Yet certain general qualities—such as courage, fortitude, and conviction—appear to characterize both.[4]

Later researchers used advanced statistical techniques to reanalyze previous reviews of trait research.[5] The updated analyses suggest that personal characteristics do have an influence on leadership behavior and perceptions. Certain traits may be important in explaining leadership effectiveness and who is *perceived* as a leader (see box 3.1 for a discussion of the five sets of traits that are most closely related to leadership). Such perceptions seem particularly important in gauging political leadership. Research indicates that characteristics such as intelligence, honesty, altruism, and foresight are commonly perceived as qualities of effective political leaders.[6]

Minimal levels of some traits may be required to function as a leader. It is hard to imagine someone with an extremely low level of intelligence or motivation assuming a leadership role, for example. However, the notion that certain personal traits *guarantee* leadership effectiveness has never been satisfactorily supported. Certain traits do seem to be advantageous in certain situations, but personal traits alone do not predispose individuals to success as a leader. Every tall person will not become a great basketball player, and every outgoing and intelligent person will not become a great leader. While many people possessing desirable personal traits have risen to positions of influence, just as many who lacked the personal characteristics deemed necessary for leadership have been successful leaders (see box 3.2). The assumption that leaders are *born* is not accurate. A more reasonable assumption is that leaders are *made* through training and experience.

Box 3.1   Research Highlight

Traits of Successful Leaders[7]

Research on the traits of leaders has not been able to demonstrate that any combination of physical and psychological characteristics **guarantee** an individual will be an effective leader in all situations. There does, however, seem to be a set of traits (*competencies* or *skills*, as they have been labeled by some researchers) that appear to differentiate successful leaders from their less successful counterparts. Five sets of traits, in particular, appear to be critical to leadership. These traits are not evident in all successful leaders, but the following attributes do appear to **enhance leadership effectiveness** (and follower perceptions of leaders) in a variety of contexts.

1. **Interpersonal factors:** A number of interpersonal competencies appear to be related to leadership effectiveness. These interpersonal factors range from skill-based behaviors, such as the ability to present an effective oral presentation or to manage conflict, to more individual-based factors, such as emotional stability and self-confidence. Among the most common defi-

ciencies of unsuccessful leaders are interpersonal insensitivity and a lack of personal integrity. Successful leaders are highly consistent in their behavior and, therefore, easy to trust. Interpersonal competencies allow leaders to communicate their message and to build relationships with their constituents.

2. **Cognitive factors:** Intelligence appears to be positively related to leadership effectiveness. Traits researchers argue that more intelligent leaders are generally more effective at problem solving and decision making. Intelligent leaders may be better at critical thinking and may also be more creative than leaders with less cognitive ability. It should be noted, however, that some researchers argue there is not a strong correlation between intelligence and creativity.[8] Highly intelligent leaders may have difficulty relating to less intelligent followers or may find they get bogged down in the details of a problem. Further, gifted individuals may be unproductive because they have poor work habits. Generally, though, traits research suggests intelligence contributes to leadership effectiveness, particularly at higher levels where problems are usually more complex and require more creative solutions.

3. **Personality factors:** In the past few years, the most widely investigated set of traits have been those related to leader personality. This focus on personality has coincided with a breakthrough in research suggesting that personality traits can be broadly organized into five major categories. These personality factors, known as the *Big Five*, are: **n**euroticism (emotional stability), **e**xtraversion (sociability), **o**penness to experience (creative and curious), **a**greeableness (trusting and nurturing), and **c**onscientiousness (organized and dependable).[9] Meta-analysis of 78 leadership and personality studies has linked the Big Five personality factors (often referred to by the acronym NEOAC) to leadership effectiveness. Extraversion was found to have the strongest relationship to leadership, followed by conscientiousness, neuroticism, and openness. Agreeableness was found to have only a weak association with leadership.[10] In practical terms, those with higher or lower ranges within these personality dimensions can be expected to experience work differently. Those who are higher on neuroticism tend to be more reactive and affected by stress while those scoring lower on this dimension are generally calm and less impacted by stress. High extraverts like to be around people, while those scoring lower on this dimension are more energized by working alone. Those with a higher openness to experience are intrigued by new ideas and activities, while workers scoring lower on this dimension prefer the familiar and tend to be more practical. Highly agreeable people have a tendency to accommodate to the needs of others, while those scoring lower on this dimension are more inclined to focus on their own personal needs. Those with high conscientiousness scores tend to be more focused and organized, while those scoring lower on this dimension are more spontaneous and tend to be more comfortable with multitasking.[11]

4. **Motivational factors:** Those leaders who are more motivated and have higher needs for power and influence may be more successful in their leadership efforts. Motivation has been found to be positively associated with ratings of leadership potential, career achievement, and promotion. Not all motivated leaders succeed, but motivation levels may impact followers' perceptions of a leader's potential and the leader's overall effectiveness.

5. **Expertise and knowledge factors:** Various administrative or technical factors also contribute to leadership effectiveness. According to scholars adopting a traits perspective, successful leaders are better at planning and organizing and are generally well versed in the methods, processes, procedures, and techniques required for the completion of tasks performed by their followers. Although it is not necessary to be able to complete every task performed by followers, traits researchers believe the most successful leaders have an extensive integrated functional knowledge of the work performed within the group or organization they lead.

Strong interpersonal, cognitive, personality, motivational, and expertise and knowledge abilities do not assure leadership effectiveness, but leaders who possess these traits may be more successful over time.

Box 3.2   Case Study

Eleanor Roosevelt: The Timid Child Who Became the World's First Lady[12]

Eleanor Roosevelt was one of the most important leaders of the twentieth century. While her husband Franklin Delano Roosevelt was president, she devoted herself to promoting social issues like civil rights, better treatment for the poor, workers rights, and equality for women. She had a hand in creating the National Youth Administration (a work training program for young people) and keeping other New Deal programs operating during World War II. Eleanor served as Franklin's "eyes and ears," traveling extensively as his representative to visit combat troops, coal miners, farmers, housewives, school children, and other groups. Franklin supported her efforts, even though he didn't always know what she was up to. In one case, she left early to visit a prison without saying goodbye to her husband. When he asked Eleanor's secretary where she was, the secretary replied, "She's in prison, Mr. President." "I'm not surprised," Franklin replied, "but what for?"[13]

Mrs. Roosevelt continued her activism after FDR died. President Truman asked her to be a delegate to the first session of the United Nations after World War II. There she chaired the UN committee that drafted the Universal Declaration of Human Rights. She made a number of international trips promoting understanding between cultures. At her death many considered her to be the "First Lady of the World."

Mrs. Roosevelt's emergence as a world figure is surprising given that she had few of the qualities typically associated with leaders. She began life as a shy and unattractive child who earned the family nickname "Granny" because she was so somber. In Eleanor's words, "I was a solemn child, without beauty and painfully shy and I seemed like a little old woman entirely lacking in the spontaneous joy and mirth of youth."[14] Her insecurity grew when she was orphaned (her mother died of diphtheria and her father of alcoholism). After her marriage to FDR, her timidity kept her out of the limelight as she gave birth to six children. Her fear made her a poor public speaker when she finally did start campaigning on behalf of her husband. Through diligent preparation, she overcame her fears and changed her speaking voice, eliminated her nervous giggle, and learned to make eye contact. She also had to learn to deal with the media. (In one bold step, Mrs. Roosevelt began to hold press conferences for women reporters only.) Once she found her voice, she had to endure verbal assaults that would shake the confidence of even the most assured leader. She became the brunt of jokes and vicious attacks, particularly in the South, for her efforts to end lynching and for her friendship with black leaders. Eleanor summed up her evolution as a leader this way:

> [O]ne can, even without any particular gifts, overcome obstacles that seem insurmountable if one is willing to face the fact that they must be overcome; that, in spite of timidity and fear, in spite of a lack of special talents, one can find a way to live widely and fully.[15]

What enabled Mrs. Roosevelt to overcome personal and societal obstacles? To begin, it is clear that she did have some "special talents"—the ability to write, to empathize with the needs of others, to persevere. She also had a learning attitude, which enabled her to reflect on her childhood, grow from mistakes, accept help from mentors, listen to others, and respect people from other cultures. Eleanor didn't appear to have a strong achievement orientation but was motivated instead by her passion: to help others. To pursue her vision, she took risks, endured criticism, and created networks of friends and supporters.

Discussion Questions

1. What do you know about Eleanor Roosevelt from prior courses and study? How would you evaluate her as a leader?

2. What leadership traits did Eleanor Roosevelt appear to lack? What traits, if any, did she have?

3. Does Mrs. Roosevelt demonstrate that leaders are made rather than born? Why or why not?

4. Can you think of other leaders who succeeded even though they lacked important characteristics that we associate with effective leadership? What accounts for their success?

5. What principles do you see in the life of Eleanor Roosevelt that can help you become a better leader?

The Situational Approach to Leadership

As the traits approach became less accepted as an explanation of leadership behavior, many researchers began to pursue situational explanations for leadership. These approaches, often called contingency approaches, assume that leadership behavior is contingent on variations in the situation.[16] For example, the strategy for effectively leading a high-tech research and development team is much different from the strategy for effectively leading a military combat unit. The differences in leadership style might be attributed to task and relational structure, superior-subordinate interactions, the motivation of followers, or any one of a number of other situational factors. (See box 3.3 for an example of the importance of response to situational factors outside the organization.) The most commonly studied situational approaches are Fiedler's contingency model of leadership, path-goal theory, and Hersey and Blanchard's Situational Leadership® theory.

Box 3.3   Research Highlight
The Importance of Contextual Intelligence[17]

Harvard professors Anthony Mayo and Nitin Nohira believe that great leadership is based on contextual intelligence, which they define as sensitivity to the opportunities and threats posed by important societal and historical trends. They reached this conclusion while developing a list of the top business leaders of the twentieth century. Mayo and Nohira found that these business legends were "first class noticers." Highly successful founders and CEOs paid attention to events and trends around them and then took advantage of emerging opportunities by acting as ***entrepreneurs, managers,*** or ***leaders***. Entrepreneurs like Cyrus Curtis (*Saturday Evening Post*), Sam Walton (Wal-Mart), Henry and Richard Bloch (H&R Block), Dee Ward Hock (Visa International), and Pierre Omidyear (eBay) overcame barriers to create something new. Managers such as Clarence Wooley (American Standard plumbing fixtures), Robert Woodruff (Coca-Cola), Howard Morgens (Proctor & Gamble), Max DePree (Herman Miller furniture), and Alfred Zein (Gillette Company) brought discipline, structure, and organization to their companies. Leaders injected new life into deteriorating firms. Prominent business leaders of the past century include Frank Ball (Ball jars, cans, and bottles), William Fairburn (Diamond Match Company), Malcolm MacLean (SeaLand shipping), Lee Iococca (Chrysler), and Lou Gerstner (IBM).

The researchers identify six contextual factors that are key to determining the success or failure of a business venture: government intervention, global affairs, demography, social mores, technology, and labor relations. For example, Henry Ford lost market share to General Motors (led by Alfred Sloan) when he didn't respond to the growing market for consumer products and services following World War I. Ford ignored consumer tastes and offered the same car (the Model T) in the same color (black). Sloan understood that social values were changing. Americans wanted to express their individuality and status through their cars. He offered a variety of models designed for different markets along with an installment credit plan. Louis Neumiller of Caterpillar tractors expanded his company by supplying products to the military during World War II. Edward DeBartolo realized that consumers were moving out from the central city after the war and made a fortune by building shopping malls in the suburbs. Conversely, Juan Trippe's Pan Am Airways prospered from the 1920s until the 1960s, when Trippe was unable to adapt to increasing competition from other airlines.

(continued)

Mayo and Nohira argue that contemporary business leaders can learn a great deal from the business legends of the past century. They contend that great leadership is the product of context plus the personal characteristics of the leader plus the leader's ability to adapt to a changing environment. Further, past success is no guarantee of future success. Just because a leader was effective in one setting does not mean that he or she will be successful in another. The Harvard professors offer several suggestions for boosting contextual intelligence. (1) Develop an appreciation of history (learn from the past). (2) Keep up on current trends in technology, global politics, government regulations, and other fields. (3) Break out of current ways of thinking by traveling to other countries and experiencing their cultures and economies and by participating in conferences and trade associations. (4) Systematically envision the future through creating possible scenarios, strategic planning, and other means. Equip the organization to take advantage of opportunities while preparing for possible threats. (5) Make the development of contextual intelligence an ongoing process. Pay constant attention to outside forces and be willing to act on cues from the environment.

Fiedler's Contingency Model of Leadership

One of the earliest, and most often cited, situational models is Fred Fiedler's contingency model of leadership.[18] In the early 1950s, Fiedler became interested in the interpersonal communication in therapeutic relationships. He discovered that competent therapists viewed themselves as more similar to their patients than less competent therapists did. Fiedler wondered how these findings related to group performance and leadership. He decided to assess how workers perceived their coworkers. He developed a measure of assumed similarity between opposites (ASo) to score differences in ratings of most and least-preferred coworkers.

Ratings of least-preferred coworkers (LPC) became the primary element in Fiedler's contingency model of leadership. Fiedler claims that our ratings of others with whom we do not like to work provide us with valuable information about our leadership behavior. This information can help us identify the situations in which we might most effectively lead others. Before continuing with this chapter, take a moment to complete the LPC scale in box 3.4.

Highly negative evaluations of a least preferred coworker result in low LPC scores; favorable evaluations result in higher LPC scores. According to Fiedler, low-LPC leaders are more concerned with tasks, and high-LPC leaders demonstrate greater concern for relationships. The effectiveness of a leader in a given situation is influenced by three primary factors that control the amount of influence a leader has over followers. These are: (1) the leader's position power, (2) task structure, and (3) the interpersonal relationship between leader and members.

Position Power. A leader gains power by virtue of his or her position within a group or organization. Positions that afford a leader the ability to reward and punish provide substantial position power. The leader of a classroom problem-solving group has little power to reward or punish group members as compared to an employer who can offer a raise or a bonus, a more appealing work schedule, or long-term job security.

Task Structure. Some tasks are highly structured. These tasks have very specific procedures, agreed-upon outcomes, and are generally easy for leaders

Box 3.4   Self-Assessment

Least Preferred Coworker (LPC) Scale[19]

										Score
Pleasant	8	7	6	5	4	3	2	1	Unpleasant	___
Friendly	8	7	6	5	4	3	2	1	Unfriendly	___
Rejecting	1	2	3	4	5	6	7	8	Accepting	___
Tense	1	2	3	4	5	6	7	8	Relaxed	___
Distant	1	2	3	4	5	6	7	8	Close	___
Cold	1	2	3	4	5	6	7	8	Warm	___
Supportive	8	7	6	5	4	3	2	1	Hostile	___
Boring	1	2	3	4	5	6	7	8	Interesting	___
Quarrelsome	1	2	3	4	5	6	7	8	Harmonious	___
Gloomy	1	2	3	4	5	6	7	8	Cheerful	___
Open	8	7	6	5	4	3	2	1	Guarded	___
Backbiting	1	2	3	4	5	6	7	8	Loyal	___
Untrustworthy	1	2	3	4	5	6	7	8	Trustworthy	___
Considerate	8	7	6	5	4	3	2	1	Inconsiderate	___
Nasty	1	2	3	4	5	6	7	8	Nice	___
Agreeable	8	7	6	5	4	3	2	1	Disagreeable	___
Insincere	1	2	3	4	5	6	7	8	Sincere	___
Kind	8	7	6	5	4	3	2	1	Unkind	___
									Total	___

Scoring of the LPC

The LPC score is obtained by adding your responses on the item ratings. Your total score should range between 18 and 144. Scores on the LPC are used to identify two types of leadership styles. If your score is **64 or above**, you are a **high LPC leader.** *High LPC leaders tend to be more relationship-oriented.* If your score is **57 or below**, you are a **low LPC leader.** *Low LPC leaders tend to be more task-oriented.* If your score falls **between 58 and 63**, you likely have **both low LPC and high LPC tendencies**; therefore, you *may be either relationship- or task-oriented.*

to evaluate. The production of a circuit board on an assembly line is an example of a structured task. Other tasks are largely unstructured. These tasks may be accomplished in a number of different ways. In these situations, it is very difficult for a leader to determine the best method of task completion, and evaluations of performance are extremely difficult to make. The writing of a television or movie script would be an example of an unstructured task.

Leader-Member Relations. A leader builds a relationship with his or her followers through interaction. A good relationship is characterized by loyalty, affection, trust, and respect. Poor relationships result in lower motivation and commitment.

Fiedler plotted each of the three situational variables for leaders on a continuum from favorable to unfavorable to create his contingency model (see figure 3.1). The most favorable conditions for leaders exist when the relationship between the leader and followers is good, the task is highly structured, and the leader's position power is strong. The least favorable conditions exist when the relationship between the leader and followers is poor, the task is highly unstructured, and the leader's position power is weak. According to Fiedler, the effectiveness of a leader in a given situation is influenced by LPC scores. Leaders with low LPC scores (task orientation) are most effective when conditions are either highly favorable or unfavorable for the leader. Notice that in figure 3.1 the tails on each end of the graph represent the correlation between group performance and low leader LPC scores. The hump in the center of the graph indicates a relationship between high LPC scores (relational orientation) and group performance. High-LPC leaders are most effective when situational variables are neither extremely favorable nor unfavorable.

Criticism of Fiedler's contingency model has been fierce.[20] Most of the criticism has focused on the development of the LPC measure and the methods used to distinguish the effect of position power, task structure, and leader-member relations on leader effectiveness. Additional concerns have been expressed regarding the utility of the contingency model. Since LPC scores are relatively consistent personality measures, situations must be adapted to fit leaders, as opposed to leaders modifying behavior to fit situations.

Path-Goal Theory

Path-goal theory is based on a theory of organizational motivation called expectancy theory. Expectancy theory claims that followers are more motivated to be productive when they believe that successful task completion will provide a path to a valuable goal. According to Robert House and his associates, leaders play an important role in influencing follower perceptions of task paths and goal desirability.[21] It is a leader's responsibility to communicate clearly what is expected of followers and what rewards can be anticipated when tasks are successfully completed. Take, for example, a group of students assigned to give a classroom presentation. How might the leader of such a group apply expectancy theory? By providing specific expectations for individual task assignments and reinforcing the group goal (a quality product that will receive a good grade), the group leader can increase the motivation and satisfaction level of followers.

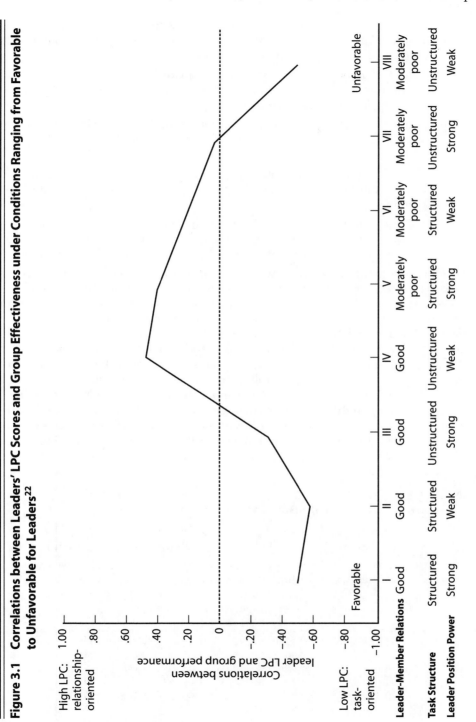

Figure 3.1   Correlations between Leaders' LPC Scores and Group Effectiveness under Conditions Ranging from Favorable to Unfavorable for Leaders[22]

According to House and Terence Mitchell, the ability to motivate followers is influenced by a leader's communication style as well as by certain situational factors. Four communication styles are identified.

1. *Directive leadership.* procedure-related communication behavior that includes planning and organizing, task coordination, policy setting, and other forms of specific guidance.

2. *Supportive leadership.* interpersonal communication focusing on concerns for the needs and well-being of followers and the facilitation of a desirable climate for interaction.

3. *Participative leadership.* communication designed to solicit opinions and ideas from followers for the purpose of involving followers in decision making.

4. *Achievement-oriented leadership.* communication focusing on goal attainment and accomplishment, emphasizing the achievement of excellence by demonstrating confidence in the ability of followers to achieve their goals.

In path-goal theory, two situational variables are most influential in the selection of an appropriate leadership communication style: the nature of followers and the nature of the task. Follower characteristics thought to be important include follower needs, abilities, values, and personality. Important task factors include task structure and clarity. These factors influence motivation and satisfaction levels among followers and determine the most effective leader communication style. Box 3.5 diagrams the use of particular leader communication styles depending on follower abilities and task structure.

Directive leader communication is most effective when followers are inexperienced or when the task is unstructured. In these situations, followers might have a low expectation of their ability to perform satisfactorily. This expectation can lead to decreased motivation and satisfaction. In general, when

---

Box 3.5

Path-Goal Theory Factors

Communication Style	Achievement-Oriented	Participative	Supportive	Directive
Nature of Followers	Followers possess necessary skills.	Followers are unsure (particularly if uncertainty prompts apprehension).	Followers are skilled, but lack confidence or commitment.	Followers are inexperienced or unsure.
Nature of Task	Task is unstructured.	Task is unstructured.	Task is structured (particularly if task is stressful, tedious, frustrating, difficult, or dissatisfying).	Task is unstructured.

expected behavior and task assignments are ambiguous, such as in a new position or job function, followers need directive leadership. On the other hand, if behavioral expectations are clearly understood and followers are competent in performing tasks, directive leadership lowers motivation and satisfaction. Nobody likes to have someone looking over her or his shoulder when the task is clear and performance is not problematic.

When followers confront structured tasks that are stressful, tedious, frustrating, difficult, or dissatisfying (such as working on an assembly line), a leader can make the situation more tolerable by engaging in supportive leader communication. In situations such as these, followers might have the necessary skills to complete tasks effectively, but they may lack confidence or commitment. This lack of confidence or commitment can produce a low self-expectation, resulting in poor performance. Supportive communication bolsters confidence and commitment and offers social rewards that can enhance motivation and satisfaction. Simply recognizing the difficulty of a task and expressing your appreciation for a follower's efforts can increase motivation and satisfaction levels. Supportive communication will contribute less to motivation and satisfaction when tasks are already stimulating and enjoyable.

> Good leadership consists of showing average people how to do the work of superior people.
>
> —John D. Rockefeller

Situations in which tasks are unstructured and behavior expectations are ambiguous are good opportunities for participative leader communication. Participating in decision making allows followers to think critically about expected behavior and task performance. Becoming more intimately involved with an unclear task can increase understanding and motivation. A follower struggling to develop a program to simplify a new computerized accounting system might benefit from participative communication. When uncertainty is uncomfortable for followers, participative communication stimulates understanding and clarity and can increase satisfaction. In situations where the task is highly structured and followers are aware of behavior expectations, participative leadership will have a minimal effect on motivation and satisfaction, according to path-goal theory.

Achievement-oriented leader communication increases a follower's confidence in his or her ability to realize challenging goals. By emphasizing excellence and demonstrating confidence in a follower's abilities, a leader can create a positive performance expectation. We are more likely to produce excellent results when others have expressed confidence in our ability to excel. The expectations of his coach and teammates might offer a partial explanation for the incredible success of Michael Jordan when he played for the Chicago Bulls. When the coach was asked what his game plan was, he claimed, "We give the ball to Michael and get out of his way." Achievement-oriented communication is most effective in unstructured situations. Followers performing highly structured tasks will not be as effectively motivated by achievement-oriented messages.

Path-goal theory attempts to explain follower motivation and satisfaction in terms of leader behavior and task structure. Although the theory neglects many situational variables that might potentially be important (such as power, organizational climate, and group cohesiveness), path-goal theory provides a viable explanation of the relationship among leaders, followers, and tasks.

Hersey and Blanchard's Situational Leadership® Theory

Paul Hersey and Kenneth Blanchard suggest that the readiness level of followers plays an important role in selecting appropriate leadership behavior.[23] As do the Fiedler model and path-goal theory, Hersey and Blanchard divide leader behavior into task and relationship dimensions. The appropriate degree of task and relationship behavior exhibited by a leader depends on the readiness of followers.

According to Hersey and Blanchard, follower readiness consists of two major components that can be plotted along a continuum: ability and willingness. Ability refers to skills, knowledge, and experience. A medical intern making rounds for the first time has low ability. A budget officer preparing a yearly financial statement for the twentieth consecutive year has high ability. Willingness relates to feelings of confidence, commitment, and motivation. A factory worker who is bored and unchallenged by a repetitive task has low willingness, while a teacher committed to excellence in the classroom has high willingness. Readiness levels can fluctuate as a follower moves from task to task or from one situation to another.

Four combinations of ability and willingness indicate follower readiness:

Readiness Level 1: Low ability and low willingness (follower lacks skills and motivation)

Readiness Level 2: Low ability and high willingness (follower lacks skills but is committed)

Readiness Level 3: High ability and low willingness (follower is skilled but lacks motivation)

Readiness Level 4: High ability and high willingness (follower is skilled and motivated)

According to Situational Leadership® theory, the readiness level of followers dictates effective leader behavior (see figure 3.2). By adapting the Blake and McCanse Leadership Grid® discussed in chapter 2, Hersey and Blanchard suggest appropriate task and relational orientations for each of the four levels of follower readiness. R1 followers require specific guidance. The most effective leader behavior with R1 followers is high task-directed communication and low relationship-directed communication. Task-related messages direct and guide follower behavior. The use of supportive, relationship-directed communication should be avoided at this level, as such messages might be interpreted as a reward for poor performance.

R2 followers lack skills but are willing. Because they do not possess necessary task skills, they need direct guidance. Because they are putting forth effort, they need support. Thus, the most effective leader behavior with R2 followers is high task/high relationship. At this level, the leader is "selling" the belief

Figure 3.2   Hersey and Blanchard's Situational Leadership® Theory[24]

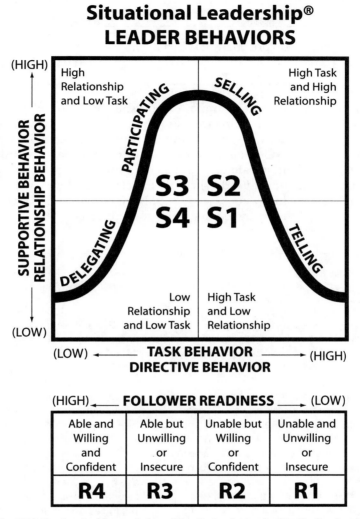

Situational Leadership®
LEADER BEHAVIORS

that the necessary skills can be acquired. R3 followers are skilled but lack the willingness to perform. Leaders need to promote follower participation in decision making. Task guidance is not necessary since performance has been demonstrated, but leaders must encourage R3 followers to discuss problems or fears hampering commitment or confidence. The most effective leader behavior facilitates involvement by using low task and high relationship behavior.

R4 followers are skilled and willing. Delegating authority to these performers is the best strategy. Since task skills are well developed, task guidance is not necessary. Relationship behavior is not required because commitment and confidence are not a problem. This does not mean that relationship behavior should be completely ignored. Certainly a leader needs to offer support and recognition periodically to maintain the level of excellence of the R4 follower.

> Things do not change, we change.
>
> —Henry David Thoreau

By engaging in appropriate leadership behavior, Hersey and Blanchard suggest a leader can influence follower behavior. The manipulation of task and relationship behaviors in accordance with follower readiness can facilitate growth and development among followers. If leaders carefully diagnose the situation, communicate accordingly, and maintain flexibility as the situation changes, Situational Leadership® theory claims that they will be more effective in influencing followers. (Practice applying Hersey and Blanchard's Situational Leadership® theory by reading the case study in box 3.6.)

Box 3.6   Case Study

Leadership at *The Campus News*

Maryanne Norton is the faculty advisor to *The Campus News*, the student newspaper at Algonquian University. She oversees production of the weekly publication and advises the newspaper's editor, Mark Lee, and his staff. Mark is a junior political science major with little experience in journalism. He is, however, enthusiastic and excited about his role as editor of *The Campus News*. Mark is typical of many of the staff in his lack of journalistic skills. In fact, many of *The Campus News* reporters have no background in news writing. As a faculty member in the Department of Communication, Maryanne teaches four courses per semester and is responsible for several other projects, including supervision of the internship program. Maryanne has a keen interest in student journalism and has long been an advocate of the rights of student reporters. Although Maryanne is very busy, she takes time to meet with the staff of *The Campus News* each week prior to publication and often hosts social gatherings for the students at her home. Although the staff of *The Campus News* is comprised of students, Maryanne believes the most effective approach to leading is to treat followers as peers and colleagues; she is most comfortable serving as a confidant and a friend to her advisees. She rarely criticizes a story and feels it is not her place to correct the work of the student reporters. She is quick to offer suggestions or guidance when asked for advice, but mainly she tries to make the experience of working for *The Campus News* enjoyable and rewarding for students.

Although there have been minor problems in the past during Maryanne's term as advisor, *The Campus News* has been heavily criticized recently. The inexperience of Mark and his staff have been evident in the last few issues of the student newspaper. In one headline, the name of the Dean of Engineering was misspelled, and details have been inaccurately reported in several stories. The most troubling error occurred in a story about Algonquian's attempt to settle a dispute with a faculty member who had been denied tenure. The story did not present the situation accurately and contained several quotes attributed to administrators at Algonquian that were later determined to have been taken out of context. One of the statements was so inflammatory that the administrator quoted was subpoenaed and asked to explain his comments in a deposition.

Shortly after that incident Maryanne was called into the university president's office to discuss the situation at *The Campus News*.

Discussion Questions

1. What is the problem at *The Campus News*?

2. How would you rate Maryanne Norton as a leader? How would you rate Mark Lee as a follower?

3. Which leadership style discussed in the Hersey and Blanchard Situational Leadership® theory does Maryanne exhibit? How would you rate the readiness level of the student followers at *The Campus News*?

4. What Hersey and Blanchard Situational Leadership® style would be most effective with the students working for *The Campus News*? Why?

5. What would you advise Maryanne to tell the president of Algonquian University she will do to improve the situation at *The Campus News*?

The Functional Approach to Leadership

Traits and situational approaches focus primarily on the individual characteristics of leaders and followers. The functional approach looks at the communicative *behavior* of leaders. The functional approach suggests that it is the ability to communicate like a leader that determines leadership. Imagine that while driving you witness an accident. Several motorists, including you, stop to offer assistance. Who will become the leader in this emergency situation? Will the leader be the person with the most knowledge regarding first aid? Perhaps. Will the leader be the person with the right combination of motivation and willingness for the situation? Maybe. Most likely the leader will be the person who starts behaving like a leader. Leadership functions in this situation might include assigning tasks ("You call 911"), initiating action ("I'll put my jacket on him so he'll be warm"), giving support ("The ambulance will be here in just a few minutes"), and mediating conflict ("Let's not worry about whose fault it was until everyone is feeling better"). By performing the functions of leadership, an individual will be viewed as a leader by others.

Many ordinary people took on leadership functions during the horrific events of September 11, 2001. Office workers carried injured colleagues down the stairs of the World Trade Center, while firefighters rushed up to help victims. Those in buildings near Ground Zero pulled pedestrians off the street and out of harm's way. Staff at Starbucks and other businesses organized to provide food to relief workers. Employees at many firms in Manhattan refused to be cut off from their jobs, finding new ways to get to work by kayaking the East River, renting buses, and hiking. (Turn to chapter 13 for more information on the leadership lessons of 9/11.)

One of the earliest contributions to the functional approach was Chester Barnard's 1938 classic, *The Functions of the Executive*.[25] Barnard's work isolated communication as the central function of organizational leadership. Since then, a number of researchers have attempted to identify the various behaviors associated with leadership in organizations and groups. Kenneth Benne and Paul Sheats were pioneers in the classification of functional roles in groups.[26] After analyzing group communication patterns, they identified three types of group roles: *task-related, group building and maintenance,* and *individual.*

Task-related roles contribute to the organization and completion of group tasks. Six task-related roles are listed below.

The initiator defines the problem, establishes the agenda and procedures, and proposes innovative strategies and solutions. The initiator makes statements such as: "I see our problem as maintaining our market share," or "Let's begin by just throwing out some possible ways to approach this problem."

The information/opinion seeker solicits ideas, asks questions about information provided by others, and asks for evaluations of information and procedure. The information/opinion seeker makes statements such as: "Why do you think our production costs will increase in the next quarter?" or "Do you think we are spending enough time discussing possible solutions?"

The information/opinion giver presents and evaluates facts and information and evaluates procedure. The information/opinion giver makes statements such as: "I think we will serve our students better by offering more night courses next semester," or "I learned in my group communication course that we shouldn't offer solutions until we have thoroughly analyzed the problem."

The elaborator provides examples and background as a means for clarifying ideas and speculates how proposed solutions might work. The elaborator makes statements such as: "A raffle may be an effective way to raise money. Last year, the Ski Club made $1,000 from its raffle."

The orienter/coordinator summarizes interaction, looks for relationships among ideas and suggestions, and focuses group members on specific issues and tasks. The orienter/coordinator makes statements such as: "That suggestion seems to fit with Glenn's idea about training," or "Maybe if we all come to the next meeting with a few pages of notes we could put together an outline for our presentation."

The energizer stimulates or arouses the group to achieve excellence and promotes activity and excitement. The energizer makes statements such as: "If we can get this product out on schedule, I think it will revolutionize the industry."

Group building and maintenance roles contribute to the development and maintenance of open, supportive, and healthy interpersonal relationships among group members. Four group building and maintenance roles appear below.

The encourager supports and praises the contributions of others, communicates a sense of belonging and solidarity among group members, and accepts and appreciates divergent viewpoints. The encourager makes statements such as: "I agree with Susan," or "I am confident that our group will do a great job next week," or "I can appreciate your concern about reaching a decision too quickly. We must be careful not to jump to premature conclusions."

The harmonizer/compromiser mediates conflict, reduces tension through joking, and attempts to bring group members with opposing points of view closer together. The harmonizer/compromiser makes statements such as: "What's the worst thing that could happen if we don't get this project done on time? Okay, what's the second worst thing that could happen?" or "Is there any way both you and Brett can get what you want from this decision?"

The gatekeeper encourages the involvement of shy or uninvolved group members and proposes regulations of the flow of communication through means such as time and topic limitation. The gatekeeper makes statements such as: "I'd be interested to hear what Luisa has to say about this," or "Why don't we limit our discussion of the budget to twenty minutes."

The standard-setter expresses group values and standards and applies standards to the evaluation of the group process. The standard-setter makes statements such as: "Our goal has always been to develop user-friendly products," or "Let's try to be critical of ideas, not people. That has always been our policy in the past."

Individual roles not supportive of task or group relationships can minimize group effectiveness. Although a certain degree of individuality is healthy, individual-centered behaviors do not contribute to task completion or relationship development and maintenance. Five possible disruptive individual roles are included here.

The aggressor attacks the ideas, opinions, and values of others; uses aggressive humor; and makes personal judgments. The aggressor makes statements such as: "It is better to keep your mouth shut and appear stupid than to open it and remove all doubt," or "Pete's concern for equal workloads is the reason this group is so unproductive."

The blocker resists the ideas and opinions of others and brings up "dead" issues after the group has rejected them. The blocker makes statements such as: "I don't care if we already voted on it; I still think that we ought to go ahead with the project."

The recognition-seeker relates personal accomplishments to the group and claims to be more expert and knowledgeable than other group members on virtually every topic. The recognition-seeker makes statements such as: "I know I am not a nurse, but I might as well be, considering how much time I spent with my husband when he was ill."

The player maintains a noncaring or cynical attitude and makes jokes at inappropriate times. The player makes statements such as: "We can't get much accomplished in one hour. Let's knock off early and get a beer."

The dominator lacks respect for the views of others, disconfirms the ideas and opinions of others, and frequently interrupts. The dominator makes statements such as: "Steve's idea doesn't seem worthwhile to me. The way to get this program to run is to do what I have suggested."

Roles associated with the successful completion of the task and the development and maintenance of group interaction help facilitate goal achievement and the satisfaction of group needs. These roles serve a leadership function. Roles associated with the satisfaction of individual needs do not contribute to the goals of the group as a whole and are usually not associated with leadership. By engaging in task-related and group-building/maintenance role behaviors (and avoiding individual role behavior), a group member can perform leadership functions and increase the likelihood that he or she will achieve leadership status within the group. (For an in-depth look at group leadership, see chapter 7.)

In addition to the Benne and Sheats categories, several other communicative behaviors associated with leadership have been identified. Box 3.7 provides a listing of three sets of proposed leadership functions.

The functional approach provides guidelines for the behavior of leaders by suggesting the necessary functions that a leader should perform. In its present

---

Box 3.7   Research Highlight

The Functions of Leadership

Krech and Crutchfield (1948)[27]

- executive
- planner
- policy maker
- expert
- external group representative
- facilitator of internal relationships
- supplier of rewards and punishments

- arbitrator
- role model
- group symbol
- surrogate for individual responsibility
- ideologist
- parental figure
- scapegoat

Bowers and Seashore (1966)[28]

- supporter of others
- interaction facilitator

- goal emphasizer
- work facilitator

Cartwright and Zander (1968)[29]

- goal achievement (including: initiating action, focusing on goals, clarifying issues, developing procedural plans, and evaluating outcomes)

- maintenance behavior (including: keeping interpersonal relationships pleasant, mediating disputes, providing encouragement, involving reticent followers, and increasing interdependence among members)

---

form, the functional approach does not provide a clear, well-developed prescription for leader behavior. Many of the identified leader behaviors are vague, and some are contradictory. How, for example, can a leader increase interdependence among group members? What specific leader behaviors facilitate work? Still, the functional approach does provide a useful framework for identifying communication behaviors that contribute to the exercise of leadership.

The Relational Approach to Leadership

The relational approach to leadership shifts the focus from the characteristics of leaders and followers (traits and situational) and leadership behaviors (functional) to the relationships among leaders and followers. The relational approach has progressed through an early phase focusing on vertical dyadic relationships to the notion of leader-member exchange.

Vertical Dyad Linkage Model

The most significant early relational approach to leadership was the vertical dyad linkage (VDL) model developed by George Graen and his associates.[30] Until the development of VDL theory, researchers believed that leaders used the same style, on average, with all the members of the group. Graen and his colleagues discovered that this was not the case. They found that leaders treat individual followers differently and that followers offered differing descriptions of the same leader. Some followers reported their relationship with a leader to be very positive. These followers indicated they felt high levels of trust and respect for the leader. In such relationships followers felt a sense of duty and obligation to the leader and the tasks of the group or organization. Other followers perceived their relationship with the leader to be strained. In these cases, the perception of the leader and the importance of the work being done were lower. These variations in linkage patterns resulted in two types of relationships: in-group and out-group. Members of the "in-group" play the role of assistant, lieutenant, or advisor to a leader. The remaining followers will be members of the "out-group." Leader-follower exchanges differ in each group. *High levels of trust, mutual influence, and support characterize in-group exchanges.* In-group exchanges allow for wider latitude in task development; followers are granted more responsibility and influence in decision making. *Low levels of trust and support characterize out-group exchanges.* Authoritarian and task-oriented leadership communication is often evident in out-group exchanges.

Leaders make choices regarding the inclusion of followers in both the in-group and the out-group. Such factors as compatibility, liking, similarity in values, and personality may influence in-group/out-group determinations. Leaders and followers also negotiate their respective roles. The leader might offer a follower more responsibility. If the follower accepts these additional duties and performs well, he or she may become a member of the in-group. Conversely, a follower may volunteer to work extra hours and move from the out-group to the in-group. (To consider how in-groups and out-groups develop in the classroom, see box 3.8.)

Box 3.8   Case Study

In-Groups and Out-Groups in the Classroom

Todd Higuera recently joined the faculty of Belmont University after earning his PhD. This is his first full-time teaching position. Belmont, a branch of the larger state university system, is known primarily as a teaching institution. Professor Higuera is expected to publish the occasional book or article, but most of his success will depend on his performance in the classroom. So far Todd is off to a good start. His evaluations are high, with students reporting that he is both enthusiastic and knowledgeable about his subject.

There is one consistent negative thread in the feedback that Todd receives that might cause him difficulty when he comes up for promotion and tenure. A number of students rate him low on the item on the instructor evaluation form that reads "Treats all students fairly." Written comments on the form include such remarks as: "The instructor plays favorites"; "I felt ignored in the class"; and "I am concerned that some students are given second chances while others are not." Todd finds these comments particularly troubling since he believes that it is unethical to treat people unfairly and, coming from a Hispanic background, he has experienced discrimination firsthand. Yet, as the primary instructor in a small major, he knows some students better than others since he has taught them in several classes. He can see how students he meets for the first time could think that they were at a disadvantage.

The beginning of the semester is approaching, and Todd wants to address the fairness issue before he creates his syllabi for the upcoming term. He is open to advice from both students and his fellow professors.

(continued)

Discussion Questions

1. What instructor behaviors create in-groups and out-groups in the classroom? How do these behaviors influence student performance?

2. Which of the behaviors you identified might be occurring in this case?

3. What advice would you give to Dr. Higuera for building high-quality relationships with his students?

4. Should Dr. Higuera expect that he can establish in-group relationships with all of his students? A majority of them? Can he still be perceived as fair if he doesn't?

5. What responsibilities do students have for creating high-quality relationships with their instructors? What steps should they take to help this happen?

To fulfill leader expectations, members of the out-group must meet formal role expectations, such as following company procedures, meeting deadlines, or submitting work containing few errors. In-group members are expected to work harder, be more committed, take on more administrative duties, and be more loyal to the leader than out-group members. The assistance of committed followers can be very useful to a leader. Nonetheless, the leader must be mindful of maintaining the in-group relationship by paying attention to the needs of in-group followers. An in-group relationship is reciprocal; both the leader and the follower must maintain it.

Leader-Member Exchange Theory

Vertical dyad linkage marked the first stage of what was to become leader-member exchange (LMX) theory. LMX theory focuses on the quality of the relationship between an individual leader and follower rather than on categorizing followers as either a member of the in-group or the out-group.[31] The quality of a leader-follower relationship (which ranges from low LMX to high LMX) can be plotted along a continuum using the scale found in the self-assessment in box 3.9.

LMX researchers report that there is a link between relational quality and personal and organizational effectiveness. Followers who have high LMX relationships with their leaders are:[32]

- more productive (produce a higher quality and quantity of work)
- more satisfied with their jobs
- less likely to quit
- more satisfied with their supervisors
- more committed to the organization
- more satisfied with the communication practices of the group and organization
- clearer about their roles in the organization
- more likely to go beyond their job duties to help other employees
- more successful in their careers
- likely to provide honest feedback

- highly motivated
- more influential in their organizations

While Graen and his colleagues initially believed that leaders could only maintain a few high-quality relationships with trusted assistants due to limited time and resources, they later became convinced that leaders should attempt to build high-quality partnerships with *all* their followers, not just a chosen few. This marked a shift to the third stage of LMX theory—leadership making. Leadership making focuses on how leaders can establish partnerships with followers. Not all relationships will become partnerships, but leaders have a duty

---

Box 3.9   Self-Assessment
Recommended Measure of Leader-Member Exchange (LMX-7)[33]

Directions: Rate your relationship as a follower with a leader of your choice by circling the numbers preceding your responses to these seven items. You can also rate your relationship as a leader with a follower of your choice (leader items are in parentheses).

1. Do you know where you stand with your leader; that is, do you usually know how satisfied your leader is with what you do? (Does your member usually know?)

   (1) Rarely   (2) Occasionally   (3) Sometimes   (4) Fairly Often   (5) Very Often

2. How well does your leader understand your job problems and needs? (How well do you understand the problems and needs of your member?)

   (1) Not a Bit   (2) A Little   (3) A Fair Amount   (4) Quite a Bit   (5) A Great Deal

3. How well does your leader recognize your potential? (How well do you recognize member potential?)

   (1) Not at All   (2) A Little   (3) Moderately   (4) Mostly   (5) Fully

4. Regardless of how much formal authority he/she has built into his/her position, what are the chances that your leader would use his/her power to help you solve problems in your work? (What are the chances that you would use your power to help a member solve problems?)

   (1) None   (2) Small   (3) Moderate   (4) High   (5) Very High

5. Again, regardless of the amount of formal authority your leader has, what are the chances that he/she would "bail you out," at his/her expense? (What are the chances that you would use your power to cover a member's shortcomings?)

   (1) None   (2) Small   (3) Moderate   (4) High   (5) Very High

6. I have enough confidence in my leader that I would defend and justify his/her decision if he/she were not present to do so. (Your member would support your decisions.)

   (1) Strongly Disagree   (2) Disagree   (3) Neutral   (4) Agree   (5) Strongly Agree

7. How would you characterize your working relationship with your leader? (How would your member characterize your working relationship?)

   (1) Extremely Ineffective   (2) Worse Than Average   (3) Average   (4) Better Than Average
   (5) Extremely Effective

Total the numbers preceding your responses. The higher the score, the better your perceived relationship with your leader. To determine if your view matches that of your relational partner, compare your rankings with those of your leader or follower.

to make the offer of partnership to all of their followers. Doing so will increase the number of high-quality relationships and improve the performance of the organizational unit.

Graen and Mary Uhl-Bien offer a three-phase model of the leadership-making process.[34] In the first phase—stranger—leaders and followers are essentially strangers who occupy their respective roles. The rules and the organizational hierarchy determine their interactions, which are largely formal in nature. The leader makes requests, and the follower complies based on self-interest. In the second phase—acquaintanceship—the parties begin to build more productive working relationships. They begin to share social as well as task information. This is a testing phase, though, and the relationship could return to phase one. The third and final phase—partnership—marks the highest level of relational maturity. Leaders and followers exert mutual influence on one another, sharing a wide range of task and social information. They enjoy a high level of mutual trust, respect, and sense of obligation. Each feels empowered to provide criticism and support to the other. Their relationship has expanded well beyond the formal work contract and work rules that define the stranger phase.

Interest in LMX theory has not waned, even though it was first developed over 30 years ago. There are several possible reasons for the enduring popularity of the relational approach to leadership. First, it is confirmed by our personal experiences. We have all experienced in-group and out-group relationships. Teachers, coaches, and bosses, among others in leadership roles, may spend more time with and give more attention to those students, team members, and employees they prefer. We know firsthand the costs of being in low-LMX relationships and the benefits of high-LMX relationships. Second, there is a strong link between relational quality and important individual and organizational outcomes. Developing relational partnerships pays off for the individual and the group. Third, LMX theory has matured, moving from descriptive to prescriptive while becoming more equitable. In its early stages, the model described differences in leader-follower relationships and appeared to promote inequality. Leaders could only develop quality exchanges with a few followers and the rest of the group suffered as a result. Now theorists offer prescriptive advice to leaders, urging them to develop high-LMX relationships with as many followers as possible. Following this advice fosters justice and fairness. Fourth, the theory highlights the importance of communication. Communication patterns differ between in- and out-groups. Partnerships are built and maintained through communication.

While influential, LMX theory has not escaped criticism.[35] Critics point out that a variety of measures have been used to measure leader-member exchanges, generating confusion and making it hard to compare the results of different studies. They complain that LMX theorists provide little practical advice to leaders who want to develop relational partnerships. Some observers believe that the LMX model, despite its evolution, still promotes inequality. These appear to be valid criticisms, but the relational approach will likely continue to provide unique and valuable insights into the study and practice of leadership for decades to come.

Chapter Takeaways

- Over the past 100 years, five primary approaches for understanding and explaining leadership have evolved: the *traits approach*, the *situational approach*, the *functional approach*, the *relational approach*, and the *transformational approach*.

- Early social scientists believed that leadership qualities were innate; an individual was either born with the traits needed to be a leader, or he or she lacked the physiological and psychological characteristics necessary for successful leadership. This approach to leadership, known as the traits approach, suggested that nature played a key role in determining leadership potential. Present-day researchers no longer accept the notion of the born leader but continue to be interested in the significance of interpersonal competency, intelligence, personality, motivation, expertise, and other factors in shaping performance and the perceptions of leadership effectiveness.

- The situational approach argues that the traits, skills, and behaviors necessary for effective leadership vary from situation to situation. The most commonly studied situational approaches are Fiedler's contingency model of leadership, path-goal theory, and Hersey and Blanchard's Situational Leadership® theory.

- According to the contingency model of leadership, our ratings of those with whom we do not want to work (LPC scores) can help us identify situations in which we would work most effectively. Task-oriented leaders (those with low LPC scores) are more likely to succeed when conditions are highly favorable or unfavorable. The most favorable conditions exist when the relationship between leaders and followers is good, the task is highly structured, and the leader's position power is strong. The least favorable conditions are when the leader-follower relationship is poor, the job is highly unstructured, and the leader's position power is weak. Interpersonally oriented leaders (those with high LPC scores) are more likely to succeed when situational factors are neither extremely favorable nor unfavorable.

- According to path-goal theory, leaders influence followers' perceptions of the task and the goal. Two factors are key when choosing a communication style: the nature of the followers and the nature of the task. Directive leader communication is most effective when followers are inexperienced or when the task is unstructured. Supportive leadership is appropriate when the task is stressful and dissatisfying and followers lack confidence and commitment. Participative leader communication is best when tasks are unstructured and followers feel uncertain as a result. Achievement-oriented leadership boosts follower's confidence that they can reach challenging goals and is most effective when performing unstructured tasks.

- According to Situational Leadership® theory, you should focus on the job maturity and psychological maturity of followers. A telling style (high task/low relationship) succeeds with followers who are both unskilled at the tasks and unwilling to do the job. A selling style (high task/high relationship) should be used with followers who lack skills but are willing. A participating style (low task/high relationship) should be employed when dealing with skilled followers who are unwilling. A delegating style (low task/low relationship) generates the best results with followers who are both skilled and willing.

- The underlying assumption of the functional approach is that leaders perform certain functions that allow a group or organization to operate effectively. You will likely be considered a leader if you perform (a) task-related roles that contribute to the organization and completion of group tasks and/or (b) group building and maintenance roles that develop and maintain supportive and healthy interpersonal relationships. However, you will undermine your group's effectiveness if you play selfish individual roles that are disruptive.

- The relational approach to leadership shifts the focus from the characteristics of leaders and followers (traits and situational) and leadership behaviors (functional) to the relationships between leaders and followers. According to vertical dyad linkage (VDL) theory, some followers (in-group members) enjoy a closer relationship or linkage with their leaders than other followers (members of the out-group). In-group leader-follower exchanges are marked by higher levels of trust, mutual influence, and support than out-group exchanges.

- Leader-member (LMX) theory focuses on the quality of the relationship between an individual leader and follower. Followers in high-quality (high-LMX) relationships are generally more productive and satisfied. You should try to establish partnerships with all of your followers, not just a few. The greater the number of high-quality relationships you build with followers, the higher the likely performance of your work group or organization.

APPLICATION EXERCISES

1. Make a list of traits that might be perceived as characteristics of leadership. Determine the accuracy of your list by comparing it with the actual traits of some of the effective leaders you have seen.

2. Review the five traits of successful leaders outlined in box 3.1 on pp. 74–75. Discuss with others in class whether or not you think these traits contribute to leadership effectiveness. Which trait or traits do you feel are most important for leaders?

3. Complete the LPC scale on p. 79. See if your LPC score is indicative of a task or relational orientation. Do you agree with Fiedler's assertions?

4. Discuss the Hersey and Blanchard Situational Leadership® theory model (on p. 85) with someone who is currently in a management position. Ask the person to evaluate this model's effectiveness given his/her past experiences. Share your findings with others in class.

5. Either alone, or in a group, make a list of leadership functions. Try to engage in these behaviors the next time you participate in a group. See if others look to you for leadership.

6. Next time you are in a problem-solving group, make a list of positive and negative leadership actions you observe from other group members. Compare your list with the Benne and Sheats typology on pp. 88–89. Compare the similarities and differences in the two lists.

7. Describe a time when you or someone you know became a leader by communicating like a leader. Identify the specific behaviors that led to you or the person you observed becoming the leader. What can you learn from the situation to apply to other leadership situations? Write up your analysis and conclusions.

8. Complete the LMX scale on p. 93. What factors contribute to your ratings on each of the items? What can you do to improve your relationship with this leader or follower?

9. Conduct interviews with several effective leaders. Try to identify which approach to leadership provides the best explanation for their success. Share your results with your classmates.

10. Create a list of concepts from the chapter that can help you become a more effective leader. Gather with others and create a group list. Share your list along with those of other groups and then create a master list for the class.

Cultural Connections:
Are Leadership Theories Culturally Bound?

Nearly all the leadership theories discussed in the first section of this text were developed in the United States. U.S. teachers and consultants frequently export these ideas to Europe, Africa, Asia, Latin America, and other regions. According to cross-cultural expert Geert Hofstede, the transfer of organizational theories across boundaries, whether from the United States or any other culture, is dangerous.[36] Ideas about how to plan, motivate, evaluate, and reach goals are culture specific, reflecting the particular value system of the country of origin. As a result, what works in one region may not work in another. Transfer is possible but demands "prudence and judgment."[37]

Hofstede offers the following examples of U.S. leadership theories that are culturally bound.

• Expectancy theories of motivation are based on the premise that individuals operate according to their self-interest. In more collectivist or group-oriented cultures, the relationship between workers and organizations is moral in nature. For example, layoffs are a common way to cut costs in the United States. In Japan, companies have an ethical obligation to retain their employees no matter what the economic climate.

• In Maslow's hierarchy (see figure 4.1), self-actualization (a very individualistic motive) is the ultimate human need. Only U.S. participants seem to follow the hierarchy (security, social needs, esteem, self-actualization) outlined by Maslow.

- Both Theory X and Theory Y are based on the assumption that work is good and desirable and should serve the goals of the organization. Southeast Asian societies view work as a necessity and are more concerned with tradition and their place in society.

- U.S. researchers and writers focus on the deeds of the individual leader who makes important decisions. The Dutch expect to be involved in consensus decision making.

- The Leadership Grid® (see chapter 2) and related theories promote participative management but assume that the leader will take the initiative to solicit employee input. In Sweden, Norway, Germany, and Israel, subordinates take the initiative, expecting to participate in the decision process. In societies that accept large differences in power and status, such as Greece, workers don't expect leaders to ask them for feedback; they expect leaders to tell them what to do.

SPOTLIGHT ON TECHNOLOGY: E-MAIL OVERLOAD

One of the most ever-present forms of communication that leaders and followers must manage is e-mail. A recent survey of communication technology usage in over 1,000 organizations indicated that employees receive an average of 75 e-mails each day. These messages come via computer (both at home and at the office), Blackberry, and PDA—tying up about one-third of the respondent's workdays.[38] Although e-mail can be an effective leadership tool for certain types of messages (such as giving directions, monitoring or assessing progress on tasks, exchanging information, or giving recognition), such messages are less effective in reviewing performance, building trust and rapport, and managing conflict.[39] The limits of e-mail may be even greater; research suggests that as few as 50 percent of users grasp the true tone or intent of an e-mail message and that most people vastly overestimate their ability to accurately comprehend messages.[40] Some organizations are attempting to halt e-mail overload by asking employees to send e-mails only when absolutely necessary (for example, to send large documents or when written communication enhances message clarity) or by initiatives such as "no e-mail Fridays" in which employees are asked (at least one day a week) to pick up the telephone or schedule meetings instead of using e-mail to communicate.[41] It is unlikely that e-mail will be eliminated from the organizational landscape any time soon, so it is imperative that leaders utilize strategies for minimizing the negative consequences of e-mail overload and to maximize the effectiveness of the messages that are sent and received. The following e-mail tips can be helpful:

Tip 1. Limit e-mail messages to one page. Procter & Gamble has a one-page rule for memos—if you send a memo longer than one page, only the first page will be read. Similar rules for e-mail (called no-scrolling rules) are used in a variety of organizations.

Tip 2. Avoid group replies. Replies should only be sent to all the recipients on an e-mail list when all of those on the list need the information in the message. The routine use of the "reply all" function is akin to spamming workmates when messages are sent to those with little interest or personal stake in the reply.

Tip 3. Use the subject line well. Provide a clear description of message content in the subject line and only label e-mails as "urgent" when they truly are.

Tip 4. Establish e-mail protocols. Work units should establish agreements regarding the use of e-mail. Such protocols might address issues such as the appropriate length and content of e-mail messages, e-mail distribution guidelines, e-mail etiquette, content restrictions, and expectations for the timeliness of responses to e-mails.

Tip 5. Remember the limitations of e-mail. There are a variety of message types that should be avoided on e-mail. Never write anything that is private or confidential in an e-mail, do not send inappropriate e-mails (many organizations have explicit e-mail policies regarding what is deemed inappropriate), avoid using e-mail to address behavioral or interpersonal issues such as performance appraisal or corrective action, and remember that emotional content can be easily misinterpreted in e-mail messages. If you are sending an emotionally charged e-mail, the best advice is to wait at least 24 hours before hitting the send button to ensure that the message is truly the one you want to deliver.[46]

LEADERSHIP ON THE BIG SCREEN: *HOTEL RWANDA*

Starring: Don Cheadle, Sophie Okonedo, Nick Nolte, Joaquin Phoenix, Desmond Dube

Rating: PG-13 for graphic violence, language and subject matter

Synopsis: Dramatizes the true story of Paul Rusesabagina (played by Cheadle), who emerges as an unlikely hero during the Rwandan genocide in 1994. A million Tutsis were slaughtered by their machete wielding Hutu neighbors as the rest of the world looked on. In the midst of the carnage, Rusesabagina uses his personal connections, bribes, and bargaining skills to shelter over a thousand innocent people (including his wife and children) in the five-star hotel he manages. Nick Nolte plays the commander of the UN peacekeeping force who is unable to stop the murders.

Chapter Links: situational and functional leadership approaches

Transformational and Charismatic Leadership

> The new leader is one who commits people to action, who converts followers into leaders, and who may convert leaders into agents of change.
>
> —Warren Bennis

OVERVIEW

- The Transformational Approach to Leadership
- The Characteristics of Transformational Leadership
    Creative
    Interactive
    Visionary
    Empowering
    Passionate
- Perspectives on Charisma
    The Sociological Approach
    The Behavioral/Attribution Approach
    The Communication Approach

The Transformational Approach to Leadership

Beginning in the late 1970s, the transformational approach emerged as a new perspective for understanding and explaining leadership. The transformational approach was first outlined by James MacGregor Burns. He compared traditional leadership, which he labeled as *transactional*, with a more "complex" and "potent" type of leadership he called *transformational*.[1] The motivational appeals of the transactional leader are designed to satisfy basic human needs; the appeals of the transformational leader go beyond those basic needs to satisfy a follower's higher-level needs.

According to Abraham Maslow, five hierarchically arranged human needs exist: physiological, safety, belonging and love, self-esteem, and self-actualization.[2] (See figure 4.1.) The most basic human needs are physiological. Before we can concern ourselves with other needs, we must secure the basic necessities: oxygen, food, water, and sleep. If you study for several days without sleeping, the need for sleep takes precedence over any other concern. Once physiological needs are satisfied, we can turn our attention to the second level of the hierarchy, safety needs. Humans seek predictability and protection. We are generally most comfortable in environments that are familiar and free from danger. If you become lost in the desert in the heat of the day, one of your first priorities

Figure 4.1   Maslow's Hierarchy of Needs

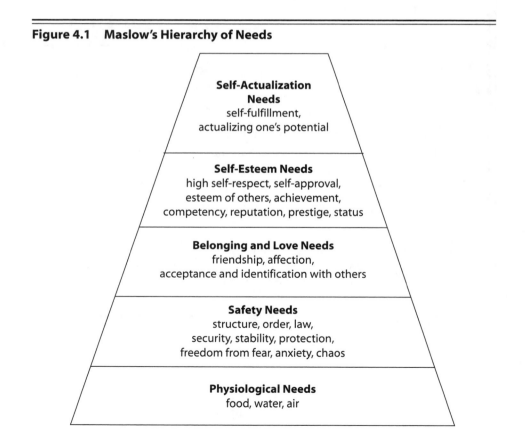

will be finding a safer, cooler environment. After environmental factors are satisfied, social belonging and love needs surface. Humans desire affiliation with others. Whether you are a member of a group or an organization, involved in a friendship or an intimate relationship, all these situations involve seeking social connections with others.

Self-esteem needs become important after the first three levels have been reasonably well satisfied. Self-esteem needs relate to our desire to feel good about ourselves. Self-esteem consists of internal feelings of competence, respect, and self-worth as well as external feedback and recognition that support positive esteem. The feeling of satisfaction you get when you finish a difficult assignment, and the "A" your instructor gives you for your hard work, help to satisfy your self-esteem needs.

When all other needs are satisfied, we can turn our attention to self-actualization needs. Self-actualization is the process of applying your own unique set of interests and abilities to become the best person you can possibly become. If you are self-actualized, Maslow claims you will feel a sense of fulfillment and purpose. He also suggests those who achieve self-actualization have a strong urge to help others satisfy their self-actualization needs.

For Burns, the distinction between transactional and transformational leadership is dichotomous—leaders are either transactional or they are transformational. Subsequent research proposed that transformational leadership augments the effects of transactional leadership.[3] Similar to the hierarchy Maslow described, lower-level transactional leadership is the foundation for higher-level transformational leadership. As leadership expert Bernard Bass explains: "Many of the great transformational leaders, including Abraham Lincoln, Franklin Delano Roosevelt, and John F. Kennedy, did not shy away from being transactional. They were able to move the nation as well as play petty politics."[4]

The transactional leader is most concerned with the satisfaction of physiological, safety, and belonging needs. To meet these needs, a transactional leader exchanges rewards or privileges for desirable outcomes—much the way a Marine drill sergeant would trade a weekend pass for a clean barracks. Transformational leaders also attempt to satisfy the basic needs of followers, but they go beyond mere exchange by engaging the total person in an attempt to satisfy the higher-level needs of self-esteem and self-actualization. Transformational leadership is empowering and inspirational; it elevates leaders and followers to higher levels of motivation and morality. According to Burns, "The result of transforming leadership is a relationship of mutual stimulation and elevation that converts followers into leaders and may convert leaders into moral agents."[5]

> The function of leadership is to produce more leaders, not more followers.
>
> —Ralph Nader

In a series of research studies involving groups of military leaders, university students, corporate managers, and educators, Bernard Bass and his associates looked at the factors of transactional and transformational leadership.[6]

These researchers identified seven leadership factors: two dimensions of transactional leadership, four dimensions of transformational leadership, and one non-leadership dimension (see box 4.1). Transactional leadership is primarily passive. The behaviors most often associated with transactional leadership are establishing the criteria for rewarding followers and maintaining the status quo. Those leaders who went beyond transaction and engaged in transformational leadership demonstrated active behaviors that included providing a sense of mission, inspiration, emotional support, and intellectual stimulation. As Bass explains:

> Unlike the transactional leader who indicates how current needs of followers can be fulfilled, the transformational leader sharply arouses or alters the strength of needs that may have lain dormant. . . . It is leadership that is transformational that can bring about the big differences and big changes in groups, organizations, and societies.[7]

Box 4.1

Dimensions of Transactional and Transformational Leadership[8]

Transactional Leadership Factors

Contingent reward: Provide rewards for effort; recognize good performance.

Management-by-exception: Maintain the status quo; intervene when subordinates do not meet acceptable performance levels; initiate corrective action to improve performance.

Transformational Leadership Factors

Charisma: Provide vision and a sense of mission; inspire; build trust and respect.

Individualized consideration: Exhibit considerate and supportive behavior directed toward each individual subordinate; coach and advise.

Inspiration: Communicate high expectations; use symbols to focus efforts and enhance understanding of goals.

Intellectual stimulation: Promote innovative ways of viewing situations; stimulate intelligent problem solving and decision making.

Nonleadership Factor

Laissez-faire (abdication): Abdicate leadership responsibility; avoid problem solving and decision making.

Whether or not a leader exhibits transformational behavior may be directly related to his or her communication skills. Ted Zorn discovered a relationship between the complexity of a leader's communication system and the tendency to exhibit transformational leadership behavior.[9] Zorn found those leaders with the most developed cognitive and communicative abilities were the most likely to be perceived as transformational by their followers. This is important as an increasing number of studies suggest that transformational leadership improves outcomes in a variety of contexts.[10]

The Characteristics of Transformational Leadership

Many researchers have attempted to describe the characteristics of transformational leaders. Tom Peters and Robert Waterman studied 62 successful American companies. They discovered that excellent companies were most often blessed with extraordinary leadership.[11] Later, Peters and Nancy Austin extended the exploration of the phenomenon of extraordinary leadership in *A Passion for Excellence*.[12] Peters expanded his discussion of transformational leadership in *Liberation Management*, in which he described the adaptable and flexible leadership practices required to deal with the necessary disorganization of the rapidly changing business environment.[13] Warren Bennis and Burt Nanus studied 90 successful leaders from business, government, education, and sports in an attempt to identify the strategies used by transformational leaders.[14] James Kouzes and Barry Posner surveyed over 1,300 managers in order to discover practices common to successful transformational leaders.[15] Thomas Neff and James Citrin attempted to identify the best business leaders in the United States, and Bruce Avolio and Bernard Bass developed a series of leadership case studies suggesting the most successful leaders exhibit transformational leadership behaviors.[16]

The characteristics of transformational leaders identified by all of these researchers are strikingly similar. Five primary characteristics appear, in one form or another, in all of the classification systems dealing with extraordinary leaders. Transformational leaders are *creative, interactive, visionary, empowering*, and *passionate*. Further, since transformational leadership can convert followers into leaders themselves, these characteristics are often filtered throughout transformed groups and organizations.

Creative

Transformational leaders are innovative and foresighted. They constantly challenge the status quo by seeking out new ideas, products, and ways of performing tasks. Transformational leaders recognize that satisfaction with the status quo poses a serious threat to group or organization survival. Resting on past achievements can blind members to new opportunities and potential problems. As organizations such as Ford, AOL TimeWarner, and Merrill Lynch have discovered, the most successful organizations are often in the most danger. Transformational leaders ignore the adage, "If it ain't broke, don't fix it." Instead, the transformational leader adopts the attitude, "If it ain't broke, you're not looking hard enough."[17] As Toyota executive Iwao Isomura explains, "Success is the best reason to change."[18]

The Process of Creativity

To clarify the relationship between creativity and leadership, we first need to understand how the creative process works. Creativity, like leadership, is based on our capacity for creating and manipulating symbols. Not only does creative problem solving involve abstract thought (which is made possible by language), but creative ideas nearly always take a particular symbolic form—as chemical formulas, sentences, drawings, ad slogans, and so on.

Experts suggest that creativity involves making new combinations or associations with existing elements. Educator Sidney Parnes, for example, describes creating as "the fresh and relevant association of thoughts, facts, ideas, etc. in a new configuration."[19] Psychologist Sarnoff Mednick defines creativity as "the forming of associative elements into new combinations which either meet specified requirements or are in some way useful."[20]

Creative thinking is frequently referred to as divergent or lateral thinking because it requires looking at problems from a number of different perspectives, thinking in broad categories, and producing a variety of solutions. Once a creative idea is generated through lateral thinking, however, the concept is refined through analysis, evaluation, and other convergent (vertical) thinking strategies. For example, to develop his theory of relativity, Einstein used lateral thinking to visualize himself as a passenger holding a mirror as he rode on a ray of light. He determined that his image would never reach the mirror because both he and the glass would move at the speed of light. In contrast, a stationary observer could catch Einstein's reflection in a mirror as the scientist passed by. Einstein started work on his theory of relativity as a result of this visualization. In order to complete the task, he worked for a decade using such vertical thought processes as calculation and reasoning.

One widely used description of creative problem solving was developed by George Graham Wallas. Based on research done with problem solvers, Wallas claimed that there are four steps to the creative process.[21]

1. *Preparation.* Creativity often begins with a conscious attempt to define and solve a problem. The preparation stage involves days, months, and even years of reading, gathering information, and repeated experiments. Composers, for example, may spend over 10 years in study before their first important compositions are finished. The more extensive the preparation, the more likely the creative solution. As two-time Nobel Prize winner Linus Pauling once pointed out: "The best way to get a good idea is to get lots of ideas." In addition, valuable new insights often come from unrelated fields of study. Take the case of Steven Jobs, who codeveloped the Apple computer. Before starting Apple, Jobs designed video games at Atari. He attributes his success in developing the game Breakout to what he learned about movement and perception in a college dance class.[22]

2. *Incubation.* During the incubation period, the conscious mind shifts to other interests and the subconscious has an opportunity to make new associations, which lead to creative problem solving. To see how the incubation process works, build in an incubation period as you write your next major paper. Work as hard as you can for a few hours, and then turn your attention to other matters. When you return to write, you may find that ideas come more easily.

3. *Illumination.* Ideas may appear as sudden inspirations during the creative process. These flashes of insight come during the illumination stage, often when a person is alone and more sensitive to intuitive messages. Carol Orsag Madigan and Ann Elwood compiled the stories of many such inspirational moments in a book called *Brainstorms and Thunderbolts.*[23] Here are a few examples of famous flashes of illumination:

   • While in the bathtub, the ancient Greek scientist Archimedes discovered the principle that "a body immersed in liquid loses as much in weight as the weight of the fluid it displaces." Afterwards he celebrated his discovery by running naked through the streets, shouting "Eureka!" ("I have found it!")

- The formula for the structure of benzene came to German chemist Friedrich August Kekule (1847) in a dream. Dreams were also a source of story plots for Robert Louis Stevenson. Mary Shelley, on the other hand, got her inspiration for the novel *Frankenstein* during a sleepless night.

- William Booth, the founder of the Salvation Army, came home after a walk through the slums of London to announce to his wife, "Darling, I have found my destiny."

- Mary Baker Eddy used her recovery from a fall on the ice to launch a new faith—Christian Science.

4. *Verification.* In this last stage, the creator develops the ideas that have come through preparation, incubation, and illumination. Verification can include writing poetry and novels, testing mathematical theorems, or checking with suppliers and running cost data.

Creative Roadblocks

One common misconception about creativity is the belief that only a few people are blessed with creative ability. According to this view, some outstanding individuals like William Shakespeare, Marie Pasteur, Bill Gates, or artist Georgia O'Keefe have large amounts of creative talent while most people have little or none. Research suggests, however, that everyone can think creatively—not just a few creative superstars. Studies of creative people reveal that they do not fit a single profile. Creative individuals are both aggressive and passive, introverted and extroverted, unstable and adjusted. Creative people share only three characteristics: (1) they are hardworking and persevering; (2) they are independent and nonconformist in their thinking; and (3) they are comfortable with complexity and ambiguity.[24] If we all have creative potential, then we need to identify those factors that keep us from being effective as creative problem solvers. James Adams identifies four types of creative blocks in his book *Conceptual Blockbusting.*[25]

1. *Perceptual blocks.* According to Adams, "Perceptual blocks are obstacles that prevent the problem solver from clearly perceiving either the problem itself or the information needed to solve the problem." Such blocks can include seeing what you expect to see (stereotyping), difficulty in isolating the problem, putting too many constraints on the problem, being unable to see the problem from many different viewpoints, being too close to the problem (saturation), and failure to use all the senses to understand the problem.

2. *Emotional blocks.* Our fears and emotions can also keep us from using our creative potential. We may fear risk, failure, or uncertainty; we might be unenthusiastic and too quick to judge new ideas; or we might confuse fantasy with reality.

3. *Cultural and environmental blocks.* Not all blocks to creativity come from within. Society often imposes stringent guidelines that inhibit the creative process. Cultural taboos eliminate certain solutions, and societal norms frequently emphasize reason to the exclusion of other methods of problem solving. Reliance on tradition ("We never did it that way before") also inhibits creative thinking. Ours is a rational society that

emphasizes vertical thinking. When was the last time you took a course in creativity, for example, or talked about intuition in class? The result of a study of Oregon teachers demonstrates how little time is devoted to creative activities in the classroom. The teachers spent 67 percent of their time teaching cognitive learning skills (such as reading, writing, and math), while another 15 percent of their school day was devoted to administrative tasks. Most of their instructional methods were analytical, centering on lecture, discussion, recitation, and drill/practice.[26]

4. *Intellectual and expressive blocks.* Intellectual blocks come from using the wrong strategies to solve problems, from being inflexible, or from not having enough (or correct) information. Expressive blocks keep us from communicating ideas effectively. Using words, for instance, is not always the best way to share ideas with others. To demonstrate the limitations of language, Adams suggests that you have someone place an unfamiliar object in a bag so that you can feel the item but not see it. Describe the object while others try to draw a picture based on your description. You will find this task to be extremely difficult if you rely on common verbal symbols ("the top is circular with a piece cut out, and the longest side comes down from this cut off area"). You will be more successful if you describe the object in coordinates or geometric terms.

Becoming a Creative Leader

Becoming a creative leader means thinking more creatively yourself, while at the same time helping followers develop their creative abilities. To achieve these goals, leaders need to adopt a problem-finding perspective, learn to tolerate failure, and focus collective attention on innovation.

Identifying new problems is called the **problem-finding orientation** to creativity.[27] In order to develop a problem-finding orientation, keep in constant touch with sources both inside and outside the organization or group—employees, members of other task forces, customers, stockholders, government officials, media outlets, industry officials, and others. These linkages will reveal gaps between what the organization is and should be doing, shifts in the political or social climate, and so on. In addition, go looking for "trouble" by posing questions that challenge current products, practices, procedures, and beliefs. Psychologists Robert Kriegel and David Brandt call this process hunting for sacred cows.[28] Sacred cows are outmoded, usually invisible ways of doing things that blind organizations to new opportunities. For example, many reports, proposals, and publications could be eliminated because nobody reads them. To round up sacred cows, listen to complaints, identify and analyze basic assumptions, and form cow-hunting groups. Pay particular attention to the way you spend your time. Keep a daily log for an average week and then eliminate the sacred cows by asking yourself: (1) Why am I doing this activity, and what would happen if it didn't exist? (2) Is someone else doing this task? (3) How and when did this practice come into being, and who started it? and (4) Can another person, department, or company do it faster, better, or more easily?

> A leader is someone who can take a group of people to a place they don't think they can go.
>
> —Bob Eaton

Because every creative idea carries with it the risk of failure, we need to tolerate mistakes if we hope to foster creativity in ourselves and those we lead. Creative leaders concentrate on the task rather than on what can go wrong. They recognize that failure is a significant learning tool; the only people who don't fail are those who don't try. The founder of the Johnson & Johnson company once declared: "If I wasn't making mistakes, I wasn't making decisions."[29] IBM's first president, Thomas Watson, took this philosophy to heart. After making a $10 million blunder, a young executive walked into his office and began the conversation by saying, "I guess you want my resignation." Watson replied: "You can't be serious. We've just spent $10 million educating you!"[30] Microsoft's Bill Gates likes to hire people who have made mistakes: "It shows they take risks. The way people deal with things that go wrong is an indicator of how they deal with change."[31] (See box 4.2 for a discussion of how the transformational leader approaches failure.)

If you want to encourage creativity, you need to help your group focus on generating new products, ideas, and procedures. In an organizational setting, invest your own time in project start-ups and other innovative activities. Encourage creativity by measuring and rewarding creative efforts. At 3M, for instance, 30 percent of each division's profits must be generated by products developed in the past four years (see the case study in box 4.3).

Box 4.2   Research Highlight

The Wallenda Factor[32]

Warren Bennis and Burt Nanus interviewed 90 successful public and private leaders. Although the leaders Bennis and Nanus studied were different in many respects, they were similar in the way they responded to failure. They simply didn't concern themselves with failing. Indeed, many of these extraordinary leaders created euphemisms such as "glitch," "bollix," and "setback" to refer to their mistakes. As far as these leaders were concerned, their mistakes served as a learning tool. Bennis and Nanus called this positive approach to failure the "Wallenda factor."

The Wallenda factor originates from the famed tightrope aerialist, Karl Wallenda. Wallenda fell to his death in 1978 traversing a 75-foot high wire in downtown San Juan, Puerto Rico. The walk was among the most dangerous Wallenda had ever attempted. For months prior to the walk he worried about failing. He was so concerned about his safety that he personally supervised the installation of the tightrope for the first time in his career. Wallenda focused all of his energies on not falling, rather than on walking.

Focusing on what can go wrong virtually guarantees failure. Transformational leaders put their energies into the task and don't concern themselves with potential failures. Although these leaders do not ignore possible failure, they also don't fear failure. As one leader quoted by Bennis and Nanus explained: "There isn't a senior manager in this company who hasn't been associated with a product that flopped. That includes me. It's like learning to ski. If you're not falling down, you're not learning."

Box 4.3   Case Study

Encouraging Innovation at 3M[33]

Many of us associate innovation with computer manufacturers, software developers, robotics, and other high-tech industries. Yet one of the most innovative companies in the United States manufactures products as mundane as tape and sandpaper. At the Minnesota Mining and Manufacturing Company (3M), innovation has been essential to the company's success since its earliest days. 3M started when a group of investors bought a piece of land so they could mine corundum, the abrasive that makes sandpaper scratchy. When the investors discovered the land didn't hold any corundum, they had to create new products or quit. The firm's first successful inventions were an abrasive cloth for metal finishing and waterproof sandpaper used for polishing exterior auto finishes. From the outset, innovators at 3M learned from their mistakes. Early inventor Francis Okie initially suggested that sandpaper could be sold to men as a replacement for razor blades! Despite this dubious suggestion, Okie kept his job and went on to invent the waterproof sandpaper that helped the company survive. Today, 3M is a $23 billion manufacturing company with over 70,000 employees worldwide and more than 60,000 products, including Post-it notes, Scotchgard fabric protector, overhead projectors, heart-lung machines, insulating materials, and light fixtures. Innovation is so important at 3M that it is central to the company's vision—*to be the most innovative company in the markets it serves*. How does a company as diverse as 3M maintain its creative edge?

1. ***Challenging People.*** The goal at 3M is for 30 percent of sales to come from products introduced within the past four years. Not every 3M division achieves this target, but managers are judged on the number of new products as well as on the expansion of existing product lines. To support creativity, current CEO George Buckley increased the R&D budget 20 percent—to a total of $1.5 billion.

2. ***Using Sponsors.*** Most successful creators have a sponsor in upper management. Senior executives must be willing to help innovators gain access to resources and offer protection when projects fail.

3. ***Providing Rewards.*** Rewarding innovation is a tricky matter. Most successful innovators find gratification in seeing their ideas turned into reality and are less motivated by financial rewards and promotions. The best reward for a successful idea is most often the freedom to work on other projects. At 3M, being a successful innovator is like playing a video game—if you win you get to play again!

4. ***Guaranteeing Time.*** Creative staff at 3M are encouraged to spend up to 15 percent of their time on projects of their own choosing. Known as "bootlegging," this concept enables innovators to work on pet projects without first gaining management approval.

5. ***Communicating.*** 3M doesn't allow creative personnel to work in isolation. The company requires its scientists to attend seminars where they meet their counterparts in other departments and discuss applications for new research. Annual private trade shows encourage technology sharing by showcasing new ideas being developed in every laboratory in the company. Communication is facilitated by sending engineers to 3M labs in other countries and through the use of computer-mediated forums, teleconferences, and an internal television network.

6. ***Recognizing Outstanding Performance.*** When a product is successful, leaders at 3M recognize those responsible. The Carlton Society, a company hall of fame, honors the achievements of outstanding scientists; the Golden Step Award honors teams of people who have successfully developed and marketed new products.

7. ***Accepting (Original) Mistakes.*** Failure is a major concern for innovators, since it will happen to most of them at one time or another. 3M is very insightful in realizing that nothing inhibits creativity like the fear of punishment for failure. More than 60 percent of new product ideas

developed at 3M ultimately fail. This figure does not include the countless failures occurring on a daily basis in 3M research and development labs. However, successes like the Post-it note (found in virtually every office in the world) more than compensate for 3M's product failures. Post-its were developed by adapting materials from a failed venture. The compound used for the adhesive on the back of the Post-it note was initially deemed useless because of its limited adherence to other objects—the very quality that made Post-it notes a success! Today, there are more than 400 Post-it products sold in over 100 countries around the world, and a product born from failure is the centerpiece of 3M's $3.2 billion business products division.

Discussion Questions

1. Does a company have to have a history of innovation like 3M in order to be highly creative? If not, how can an innovative climate be fostered?

2. What type of reward do you feel is most effective in motivating creative people? Are financial rewards important?

3. What advantages/disadvantages do you see in the 3M policy of "bootlegging"?

4. Do you agree with the 3M philosophy that all original mistakes should be accepted without punishment? Under what conditions should people be punished for failure?

5. How could the seven methods for fostering creativity employed at 3M be used in an organization with which you are familiar?

> Creative activity is one of the few self-rewarding activities. Being creative is like being in love!
>
> —Woody Flowers

Interactive

Transformational leaders are masterful communicators able to articulate and define ideas and concepts that escape others. As suggested earlier, the process of leadership depends on the existence of symbols that facilitate coordinated action. Transformational leaders transmit their ideas through images, metaphors, and models that organize meanings for followers. Extraordinary leadership is first, and foremost, a product of extraordinary communication. To communicate successfully, a transformational leader must be aware of the needs and motivations of his or her followers. Only when a leader is involved with followers can he or she find ways to do things better. Tom Peters and Nancy Austin suggest that "managing by wandering around" (MBWA) is one way to become involved with followers.[34] MBWA involves walking the floor, interacting with followers on a regular basis. The transformational leader engaging in MBWA does not play the role of a cop on patrol but acts as a coach whose primary activities are listening, teaching, and helping followers with problems.

One organization that embodies the transformational philosophy is Johnsonville Foods of Sheboygan, Wisconsin. At Johnsonville, traditional organizational structure was replaced in the early 1980s by self-directed work teams. Middle managers adopted the leadership roles of coordinators and coaches rather than the traditional roles of supervisors and disciplinarians. Leaders were responsible for teaching team members how to lead themselves more effectively. In short, the primary job responsibility of organizational leaders at Johnsonville Foods became one of interacting with team members (see box 4.4).

Thomas Neff and James Citrin, senior executives at Spencer Stuart, one of the most well regarded executive search firms in the world, surveyed over 500 leaders in business and education to identify the 50 best public and private sector business leaders in the United States. One common trait among the 50 top-rated business leaders was the ability to communicate effectively. As Neff and Citrin explain, "Nowhere is it more critical to be a strong communicator than in leading people." [35] One of their most powerful examples is Mike Armstrong, the former CEO of AT&T. Every Monday, Armstrong brought together the company's top executives—eight to 10 people—who met for the entire day to make sure the company was on track. Armstrong said the key was to "communicate, communicate, communicate. You cannot be a remote image. You've got to be touched, felt, heard, and believed."[36] This is particularly important in times of change. In the days following the September 11, 2001, terrorist attacks, Continental Airlines CEO Gordon Bethune recorded a daily voice-mail message to keep all of his employees fully informed about the rapidly changing situation in their industry.[37] These examples illustrate the importance of communication to successful leadership. Indeed, the more leadership responsibility an individual has, the more likely it is there will be a significant communication component to his or her job. Political and social leaders, CEOs, and senior executives all devote a great deal of energy to clearly communicating their message to followers.

By encouraging open communication, a leader allows followers to share their ideas and insights. The experience of the U.S. Forest Service provides a good example of how simplifying the communication process can help foster employee participation. The Eastern Region of the U.S. Forest Service had a sys-

---

Box 4.4   Case Study

The Revolution at Johnsonville Foods[38]

Ralph Stayer joined his family's sausage-making business in Sheboygan, Wisconsin, after graduating from Notre Dame in 1965. In 1978, he replaced his father as president of Johnsonville Foods. Stayer inherited a stable company with annual growth averaging around 20 percent. Johnsonville was a successful company by all accounts, yet Stayer sensed problems. He noticed workers were operating far below their potential. Employees were disinterested. Most who worked at Johnsonville Foods appeared to be doing no more than meeting minimum performance expectations. Few seemed concerned with excelling in their work. Stayer felt there had to "be a better way."

After attending a series of seminars by University of Wisconsin communication professor Lee Thayer, Stayer became inspired to revolutionize leadership practices at Johnsonville Foods. In 1982, Stayer wrote a six-page letter to his employees. Leadership at Johnsonville Foods was going to change. Employees would be asked to take far more responsibility for the work they performed. Further, the compensation system would be overhauled. Instead of across-the-board annual raises, employees would be paid for performance. Those who learned new skills and developed their talents would receive the largest salary increases and profit-sharing bonuses.

The traditional organizational structure was dismantled. First-line employees were organized into self-directed work teams. These employees, known as members, were given a wide array of responsibilities ranging from budgeting, scheduling, quality control, and marketing to strategic planning and personnel, including the hiring *and* firing of their fellow team members. Middle managers, formerly responsible for the tasks turned over to the first-line workers, now focused their efforts on teaching and on coaching members to lead themselves. Meanwhile, Ralph Stayer turned his attention away from the day-to-day operation of Johnsonville Foods and began to focus more energy on maintaining his philosophy of transformational leadership. Slowly, members working on the production line began to take over more of the responsibility for operating Johnsonville Foods.

The watershed moment came in 1985 when Johnsonville was asked to produce a new line of meats for another manufacturer. To make the venture work successfully, employees at Johnsonville would have to make tremendous sacrifices. During the start-up phase, members would have to work six- and seven-day workweeks for months on end. Further, quality would have to be maintained at the highest level to ensure that the contract continued. In the past, Stayer would have consulted with his senior management team before making a decision of this importance. This time, however, Stayer continued with his plan to revolutionize leadership practices at Johnsonville Foods. He conducted a forum with all members in the plant and presented the problem to them. Two weeks later the members decided, almost unanimously, to take the business.

The venture was a great success! Quality rose on the new product line as well as on the original Johnsonville product line. The reject rate dropped from 5 percent to less than one-half of 1 percent. Revenues increased nineteenfold in a 10-year period. All this occurred at a time when people were eating healthier and most other sausage products were experiencing declining sales.

Today, transformational leadership has fully taken root at Johnsonville Foods. Members have assumed so much responsibility that Stayer has moved away from the day-to-day leadership of Johnsonville. He now works primarily on other projects, including the development of a line of pasta products and a successful leadership consulting business. To maintain the leadership approach, every new employee attends a series of courses at "Johnsonville University" beginning with an overview of the company culture and continuing with courses in teamwork, diversity, and financial operations. The company supports a philosophy of worker involvement. Production line employees hold meetings before each shift to discuss the operation and address any problems. Further, all members are authorized to shut down the production line at any time if they believe something isn't right. Johnsonville was recently recognized by *HR Magazine* as one of the 50 best places to work, and employees seem to agree. In an industry with turnover rates approaching 20 percent, the turnover rate at Johnsonville is a mere 8 percent. Although it took over a decade to fulfill his promise, Ralph Stayer did revolutionize leadership practices at Johnsonville Foods, and the changes he implemented in the 1980s are still reaping rewards today.

Discussion Questions

1. Is it fair to ask employees to take more responsibility for their work without offering a significant increase in pay? What should Johnsonville Foods do about employees who don't want more responsibility?

2. Are there some responsibilities that should not be given to first-line workers?

3. What are the advantages/disadvantages of having members hire and fire (if necessary) their own teammates?

4. Why do you think Johnsonville Foods was so successful in producing a new line of meats in 1985? Do you think this venture would have been as successful if the senior management team had made the decision to take on this project?

5. What conditions do you believe are necessary for this revolutionary approach to leadership to work elsewhere?

tem for suggestions that required employees to fill out a four-page form each time they had an idea. In a four-year period the region's 2,500 employees submitted 252 ideas for consideration, or about one idea per person every forty years. To see if they could improve participation, the Forest Service officials changed the process to make it easier for employees to communicate with their superiors. The new system allows anyone with an idea to submit a brief description by e-mail. Under the new system, employees sent in 6,000 new ideas in the first year, an average of more than two ideas per employee each year![39]

Openness to interaction and feedback extends beyond the leader/follower relationship. Transformational leaders also engage in frequent communication with suppliers, customers, and even with industry competitors. In 2002, executives from the aircraft manufacturer Boeing met with a group of global airline representatives. Leaders at Boeing scheduled the meeting to determine customer needs in the face of increasing competition from rival manufacturer Airbus. The feedback from the airline industry was clear—Boeing's customers were much more interested in fuel efficiency than the speed of an aircraft or the number of passengers that could be carried. Based on this information, Boeing scrapped its plans for a high-speed, high-cost jetliner and began work on a new fuel-efficient airplane, the 787 Dreamliner. Five years after that meeting Boeing had orders for nearly 700 Dreamliners totaling some $114 billion in sales.[40]

The manufacturing process for BMW automobiles built in Leipzig, Germany, has been streamlined by including suppliers on-site. The French auto-parts company Faurecia assembles cockpits and seats for the BMW in the plant, not at an off-site location as is generally the norm. As a result of the frequent interaction among employees from the two companies (workers from both companies even share the same cafeteria), custom vehicle orders can be filled in just 20 minutes, a process improvement that is central to BMW's goal of improving efficiency by 5 percent each year. One of the strategies for cutting costs is to solicit creative ideas from suppliers, like Faurecia. Over a three-year period some 10,000 suggestions have been offered—and about a third have been put into practice.[41]

Visionary

Communicating a vision to followers may well be the most important act of the transformational leader. A vision is a concise statement or description of the direction in which an individual, group, or organization is headed. Compelling visions provide people with a sense of purpose and encourage commitment. Followers achieve more and make more ethical decisions when they pursue a worthy goal. To be compelling, a vision must be both desirable and attainable. Uninspiring or unachievable visions are ineffective and may demoralize followers.

Warren Bennis and Burt Nanus found that transformational leaders spend a good deal of time talking with employees, clients, other leaders, and consultants before developing a vision for their organization.[42] They study the history of their organization to determine the reasons for past successes and failures; they study the present to determine current strengths, weaknesses, and resources; and they look to the future to identify possible long-term social, political, and environmental changes. The leaders then interpret the information and construct a realistic vision that fits the norms of the group and inspires followers to put forth more effort.

Burt Nanus lists four characteristics of effective visions.[43]

1. *An effective vision attracts commitment and energizes people.* People are willing, even eager, to commit to worthwhile projects. An effective vision inspires people by transcending the bottom line. Whether it involves something that improves conditions for others (such as the development of new medical technology) or something that allows for growth and development on the part of the follower (such as increased autonomy), people are motivated to meet challenges that make life better.

2. *An effective vision creates meaning for followers.* People find meaning in their work lives. When groups and organizations share a vision, individuals see themselves not just as sales clerks or assembly workers or whatever their job description names, but as part of a team providing a valuable product or service.

3. *An effective vision establishes a standard of excellence.* Most people want to do a good job. A shared commitment to excellence provides a standard for measuring performance. Establishing a standard of excellence helps followers identify expectations and provides a model for the distinctive competence of a group or organization.

4. *An effective vision bridges the present and the future.* A vision is a mental model of a desirable and idealistic future. By bridging the present and the future, an effective vision transcends the status quo by linking what is happening now with what should happen in the future.

Extraordinary leaders at every level communicate compelling visions. Whether the vision is to have the best customer service in the industry or the fewest defects on an assembly line, a sense of direction and purpose is essential to inspired leadership. The behavior exhibited by a transformational leader provides the basis for reinforcing a vision. When the plant manager jumps into a delivery truck to rush an order to an important customer, people notice. This kind of dramatic behavior reinforces priorities and values and sets a standard for follower behavior. As James Collins and Jerry Porras explain in their book *Built to Last*, organizations with a well-articulated vision that permeates the company are most likely to prosper and have long-term success.[44] Visionary companies such as Boeing, General Electric, Hewlett-Packard, Nordstrom, Sony, and Walt Disney tend to be the premier market leaders in their industries. Collins and Porras found that visionary companies were more likely to prosper over long periods of time—even through multiple product cycles and changes in corporate leadership.

According to John Kotter, an effective vision is specific enough to provide real guidance to people, yet vague enough to encourage initiative and remain relevant under a variety of conditions.[45] If a vision is too specific, it may leave followers floundering once the goals it articulates are achieved. An example of an overly narrow vision statement was President John F. Kennedy's vision for NASA. In 1962, Kennedy defined NASA's vision as "landing a man on the moon and returning him safely to earth before this decade is out." When a vision this specific is achieved (as it was in 1969), followers may feel a sense of confusion regarding what to do next (as NASA did in the 1970s and 1980s).[46]

> If you do not know where you are going, every road will get you nowhere.
>
> —Henry Kissinger

More effective vision statements offer general guiding philosophies without detailing specific end results. The following vision statements are examples of well-conceived organizational visions:

Amazon.com	To be Earth's most customer-centered company.
American Medical Association (AMA)	To promote the art and science of medicine and the betterment of public health.
AT&T	We are dedicated to being the world's best at bringing people together—giving them easy access to each other and to information and services they want and need—anytime, anywhere.
Bristol-Myers Squibb	To extend and enhance human life by providing the highest-quality health and personal care products.
British Airways	To be the world's favorite airline.
Celestial Seasonings	To create and sell healthful, naturally oriented products that nurture people's bodies and uplift their souls.
Google	To organize the world's information and make it universally accessible and useful.
McDonald's	To provide the world's best quick service restaurant experience consistently satisfying customers better than anyone else through outstanding quality, service, cleanliness, and value.
Microsoft	To help people and businesses throughout the world realize their full potential.
Unilever	To add vitality to life. We meet the everyday needs for nutrition, hygiene, and personal care with brands that help people feel good, look good, and get more out of life.
Walt Disney	We create happiness by providing the finest in entertainment for people of all ages, everywhere.[47]

These vision statements provide a general philosophy that guides the actions of members of the organization while simultaneously reflecting key organizational values. Well-conceived vision statements evolve directly from the core values shared by members of a group or organization. (To see how the process of developing a personal vision statement works, try the self-assessment activity in box 4.5.)

A company's vision is not the same as its mission. While the vision provides a sense of direction and an idea or image of a desirable future, the mission

Box 4.5   Self-Assessment
Developing a Personal Vision Statement[48]

Values are at the core of individual, group, and organizational identity. Values are relatively enduring conceptions or judgments about what we consider to be important. According to Milton Rokeach, there are two types of personal values.

Terminal values   Lifelong goals (e.g., freedom, inner harmony, salvation)
Instrumental values Behaviors that help people achieve lifelong goals (e.g., independence, ambition, obedience)

Values guide and direct behavior. There is substantial research suggesting that a number of positive effects result from agreement between personal values and the values most prized in the organization at which we work. Agreement between personal and organizational values result in increased personal identification with the organization, higher levels of job satisfaction, greater team effectiveness, and lower turnover rates. Values play a key role in the development of vision. Try to identify your own personal vision by ranking the values on the lists below. These two lists represent key terminal and instrumental values as identified by Rokeach. There are 18 values on each list. Rank order each from 1 (most important) to 18 (least important). Remember to consider the values on each list separately. You are to create two rank-ordered lists. Many people find this to be a very difficult process. Remember, you are ranking values from most important to least important—not from important to unimportant. Because values are so central to our personality, there are few unimportant values.

Terminal Values

____ **Freedom** (independence, free choice)

____ **Self-respect** (self-esteem)

____ **Mature love** (sexual and spiritual intimacy)

____ **An exciting life** (activity)

____ **A comfortable life** (prosperity)

____ **Family security** (taking care of loved ones)

____ **True friendship** (close companionship)

____ **Social recognition** (respect, admiration)

____ **Wisdom** (an understanding of life)

____ **Happiness** (contentedness)

____ **A world at peace** (free of war and conflict)

____ **A world of beauty** (beauty of nature and art)

____ **Pleasure** (an enjoyable, leisurely life)

____ **Equality** (brotherhood, equal opportunity for all)

____ **A sense of accomplishment** (lasting contribution)

____ **Inner harmony** (freedom from inner conflict)

____ **National security** (protection from attack)

____ **Salvation** (saved, eternal life)

Instrumental Values

____ **Loving** (affection, tenderness)

____ **Independent** (self-reliant, self-sufficient)

____ **Capable** (competent, effective)

____ **Broad minded** (open minded)

____ **Intellectual** (intelligent, reflective)

____ **Honest** (sincere, truthful)

____ **Responsible** (dependable, reliable)

____ **Ambitious** (hardworking, aspiring)

____ **Imaginative** (daring, creative)

____ **Helpful** (working for the welfare of others)

____ **Forgiving** (willing to pardon others)

____ **Logical** (consistent, rational)

____ **Cheerful** (lighthearted, joyful)

____ **Self-controlled** (restrained, self-disciplined)

____ **Courageous** (standing up for your own beliefs)

____ **Polite** (courteous, well-mannered)

____ **Obedient** (dutiful, respectful)

____ **Clean** (neat, tidy)

(continued)

When you complete your rankings, write down six of the top-rated values from each of your lists in the space below.

Terminal Values

1.
2.
3.
4.
5.
6.

Instrumental Values

1.
2.
3.
4.
5.
6.

Carefully examine the list of your top-rated terminal and instrumental values. Look for similarities, patterns, and themes. Using this as a starting point, try to create your own personal vision statement. Remember, this vision statement should emerge from the top-rated core values you identified. Your vision statement should be concise (usually a single sentence). Look back at the examples of well-conceived organizational vision statements on p. 116 if you need a reminder of what a vision statement looks like.

My Personal Vision Statement:

_____
_____
_____
_____
_____
_____

Once you have developed your personal vision statement, try to shorten your statement into a slogan. A slogan is a shorter version of the vision statement you previously created. Slogans are most often associated with corporate advertising (e.g., Just Do it—Nike; Because I'm Worth It—L'Oreal; We Try Harder—Avis). Write your slogan below and share it with others in your class.

My Personal Slogan:

_____
_____
_____
_____

Discussion Questions

1. How does your personal vision statement and slogan match that of your present or past employer? How do think your personal vision statement might impact your job satisfaction?

2. Based on the slogans presented, what values do you perceive to be most prized in your class?

3. How can learning what is important to us (as well as to others) help organizations operate more effectively?

4. What is the most significant thing you learned about yourself in this exercise?

is a description of the organization and how it is aligned to achieve its vision. As author and consultant Laurie Beth Jones explains, "The mission statement is centered on the process of what you need to be doing."[49] Ernst & Young consultant Ira Levin goes on to add, "Mission describes who the organization is and what it does. It is a statement of purpose, not direction."[50] Simply stated, a mission is a statement that identifies the scope of an organization's operations—it defines a company's core values and reason for being, while a vision mobilizes people into action by presenting an image of the desired future. It can be confusing when looking at organizational vision and mission statements as the terms are often used interchangeably in practice. Whatever label is used, the research is consistent in regard to the importance of having a unifying vision. Well-articulated visions have the potential to inspire and guide organizational behavior; they are associated with higher levels of performance.[51]

Empowering

Transformational leaders empower others. Even an extraordinary leader cannot accomplish a great deal without capable followers. Transformational leaders encourage participation and involvement. The exchange of ideas between leader and follower does not pose a threat to the transformational leader. Extraordinary leaders realize that individual achievement and success is the basis for team achievement and success. Transformational leaders know how to give power away and how to make others feel powerful. Transformational leaders give followers access to the funds, materials, authority, and information needed to complete tasks and to develop new ideas (see chapter 5 for an in-depth discussion of empowerment). These leaders allow others to make decisions rather than insisting on making all the decisions themselves. Implicit in the concept of empowerment is the fact that such autonomy encourages employees to take ownership of their work. Disney exemplifies this type of ownership. It encourages employees to treat every customer like a guest in their own home. To provide such service, employees must be empowered to make decisions without management approval. An astonishing indication of the depth of employee empowerment at Disney is the fact that customer service representatives, the people who take the tickets at the theme park entrances, have $500,000 in tickets and cash at their disposal to give out to guests who lose or forget their tickets, run out of money, or encounter any other problem.[52]

> The growth and development of people is the highest calling of leadership.
>
> —Harvey S. Firestone

Followers will only take ownership of their jobs when there is sufficient trust within the organization. Without such trust, followers will be reluctant to make decisions for fear of possible reprisals. Researchers Pam Shockley-Zalabak, Kathy Ellis, and Ruggero Cesaria suggest that product and service quality critically depend on employees' trust in their organization and its leaders.[53]

Collecting data from around the world, the researchers identified five key dimensions of organizational trust.

- *Competence.* The extent to which leaders, coworkers, and the organization as a whole are viewed as effective
- *Openness and Honesty.* The extent to which the amount, accuracy, and sincerity of communication is perceived as appropriate
- *Concern for Employees.* The extent to which feelings of caring, empathy, tolerance, and concern for safety are exhibited
- *Reliability.* The extent to which leaders, coworkers, and the organization as a whole is perceived as consistent and dependable
- *Identification.* The extent to which we share common goals, norms, values, and beliefs with those associated with the organization's culture

Leaders hoping to empower their followers need to be aware of perceptions of trust and should work to enhance overall trust levels (for more information on this approach to trust see chapter 8).

> Many hands, and hearts, and minds generally contribute to anyone's notable achievements.
>
> —Walt Disney

Max DePree (former chairman of the board of the Herman Miller furniture company) goes so far as to suggest that leaders act as "servants" to their followers.[54] The leader serves followers by providing necessary resources and encouragement, empowering followers to complete assignments in the most productive manner. (See the case study in box 4.6 for an example of how empowerment and servant leadership can contribute to outstanding customer service.) In the words of Jan Carlzon, the former CEO of Scandinavian Airline Systems, "If you're not serving the customer, you'd better be serving someone who is."[55] This philosophy is exemplified by another retired airline CEO, Herb Kelleher of Southwest Airlines. Since Thanksgiving is a popular travel day, the staff at Southwest Airlines often has to be away from their families on this holiday. Kelleher made it a tradition to work along with his staff on Thanksgiving Day—taking tickets and handling bags along with his rank-and-file employees. As Kelleher explains, "You have to be willing to subjugate your ego to the needs of your business . . . and your people."[56] (For more information on servant leadership turn to chapter 11.)

Passionate

Transformational leaders are passionately committed to their work. They love their jobs and have a great deal of affection for the people with whom they work. This passion and personal enthusiasm motivates others to perform at their highest levels as well. Transformational leaders are able to encourage others because they, first and foremost, encourage themselves.

One organization that has received cult-like recognition for the passion exhibited by its employees is the Pike Place Fish Market in Seattle. Books and

Box 4.6   Case Study
Working by the Rule Book at Nordstrom

Nordstrom began as a small shoe store in Seattle in 1901 and has grown into a retail giant with more than 100 large department stores and 50 outlet clearance centers (Nordstrom Rack) in the United States, 30 boutiques in Europe (Faconnable), and one of the top-rated online customer apparel companies (Nordstrom.com). Together they generate some $8 billion per year in sales. Although other retailers may be larger, few engender so much enthusiasm and loyalty from both customers and employees.

From the beginning, Nordstrom incorporated the idea that outstanding customer service offers a competitive advantage. Stories abound concerning the almost mythic levels of assistance offered by Nordstrom staff. This (well deserved) reputation has turned the opening of new Nordstrom stores into civic events. When the first Nordstrom was built in Denver in the 1990s, hundreds of shoppers camped overnight in the parking lot in anticipation of the store's grand opening. Nordstrom capitalizes on this customer devotion, producing sales of about $400 per square foot—nearly double the sales for an average department store.

The key to Nordstrom's success is its leadership philosophy based on empowering employees to do whatever it takes to satisfy customers. As in many companies, new hires at Nordstrom attend a day-long employee orientation before they begin work on the sales floor. Unlike other companies, however, the training focuses almost exclusively on customer service. Each new hire is given a 5″ × 7″ card entitled Nordstrom Rule Book, which reads:

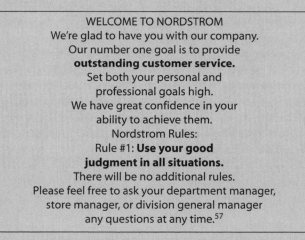

WELCOME TO NORDSTROM
We're glad to have you with our company.
Our number one goal is to provide
outstanding customer service.
Set both your personal and
professional goals high.
We have great confidence in your
ability to achieve them.
Nordstrom Rules:
Rule #1: **Use your good
judgment in all situations.**
There will be no additional rules.
Please feel free to ask your department manager,
store manager, or division general manager
any questions at any time.[57]

This entrepreneurial spirit allows Nordstrom sales associates to perform at levels that often exceed customers' expectations. For example, a Nordstrom sales associate in suburban Washington DC received a letter from a Swedish business executive who had purchased $2,000 worth of shirts and ties from Nordstrom while in the United States. After returning to Sweden, he washed the shirts in hot water; they shrank. He wrote to Nordstrom to ask for advice on how he might deal with his problem. The Nordstrom sales associate immediately put through a call to Sweden and told the customer he would replace the shirts with new ones at no charge. He asked the customer to mail the damaged shirts to the store—at Nordstrom's expense—so he could send back the appropriate replacements. Such a move would likely require several levels of approval—if it would happen at all—at most stores, but as the Nordstrom sales associate explained, he "didn't have to ask for anyone's permission. . . . Nordstrom would rather leave it up to me to decide what's best."[58] In another example, a woman brought a pair of shoes purchased at Bloom-

(continued)

ingdale's into a New York area Nordstrom. The customer explained the shoes were too small. She had purchased them because she liked the style, but Bloomingdale's didn't have her size. After being fitted with the same shoe in the proper size (the average Nordstrom store carries over 150,000 pairs of shoes), the customer started to pay for the shoes. The salesperson suggested the customer simply exchange the too-small shoes and take the correctly fitting pair for free. When the customer reminded the sales associate she had purchased the shoes at Bloomingdale's, the Nordstrom salesperson explained, "If I take these shoes for you, you won't have any reason to return to Bloomingdale's."[59] These liberal return and exchange policies might invite abuse, but the company's unconditional money-back guarantee is designed for the 98 percent of customers that Nordstrom finds to be honestly seeking fair treatment.

Developing this level of customer service can be challenging. Nordstrom prefers to hire people without previous sales experience. As Jim Nordstrom, the late cochairman of the company once explained, those with little sales experience "haven't learned to say 'no' to customers, because they haven't worked for anybody else."[60] Nordstrom expects its sales staff to exhibit high levels of professionalism and initiative and pays its sales associates about 20 percent above industry standards. Most exceed their base pay rate by earning a higher commission-based pay of approximately 6.75 percent of their sales volume. In 2005, the company reported that 76 employees exceeded $1 million in sales. This allows Nordstrom staff the opportunity to earn exceptional salaries as their sales increase, benefiting both the employee and the bottom line at Nordstrom. Salespeople also receive full benefits, including retirement, medical and dental insurance, plus a variety of incentives supporting work and life balance. As Nordstrom has learned, financial outcomes are best for the staff and for the company when employees are empowered to offer the highest imaginable levels of customer service and attention.

Discussion Questions

1. What constitutes outstanding customer service? What are the best and worst customer service experiences you have had?

2. What is the relationship between empowerment and customer service?

3. What do you think of the Nordstrom Rule Book? Would you like to work for a company like this? Why? Why not?

4. Do you think the Nordstrom return and exchange policies might be abused by more than the estimated 2 percent of its customers?

5. If a company expects people to take on more responsibility at work, what, if anything, should an employer be expected to offer in return?

training videos have documented the popularity of the seafood store as a tourist attraction. Thousands flock each day to watch the employees perform their jobs. The onlookers are treated to a spectacle that includes constant banter with customers, fish flying through the air to the cashier, and countless other zany antics.[61] Another example is the 2007 FedEx advertising campaign that highlighted the passion of company employees around the globe. The focal point of the advertisement was a Web site, fedexstories.com, that chronicled the exploits of workers who went above and beyond for their customers. Examples included an Italian courier who drove 300 miles in his own vehicle to deliver a late package, an Australian FedEx Kinko's manager who came to work at 3:00 AM to assist his employees with a malfunctioning copier machine, and a delivery manager in Michigan who went to extraordinary lengths to deliver a mobility scooter to a customer with a ruptured tendon. The scooter arrived too late for delivery at the customer's home address in Michigan. When the delivery manager found out the customer was limping around on crutches in New York where he was visiting his children at summer camp, the manager mobilized a team of FedEx employees who assembled the vehicle, charged the battery, and shipped the fully constructed scooter at no additional charge to New York for the man to use on his trip.

Organizational consultant Richard Chang suggests that passion is the single most important competitive advantage an organization can have.[62] Passion is a reflection of the organization and its leaders. In the book *Good to Great*, Jim Collins investigated elite companies that exhibited sustained greatness over a period of at least 15 years, such as Circuit City, Gillette, Walgreens, and Wells Fargo.[63] One of his key findings was that great companies focus their energies on what they can get passionate about. For example, when Gillette executives made the choice to build sophisticated and more expensive shaving systems rather than expand in the low-margin disposable market, they did so in large part because they had little enthusiasm for developing cheap disposable razors. For executives at Gillette, the technical design of shaving systems sparks the same type of excitement that might be expected from an aeronautical engineer working on the latest advancements in aviation. People who aren't passionate about Gillette are not welcome in the organization. One top business school graduate wasn't hired by the company because she simply didn't show enough passion for deodorant.

> Nothing great in the world has ever been accomplished without passion.
>
> —Georg Friedrich Wilhelm Hegel

By demonstrating the characteristics of transformational leaders, individuals can begin to transform themselves and their organizations. By encouraging creativity, fostering open communication, demonstrating forward thinking, sharing responsibility, and exhibiting commitment, leaders can help construct organizations that are prepared to meet the challenges of the future.

Most of the observations of transformational leaders have been made in organizational settings. Many questions remain to be answered concerning the viability of transforming leadership in less permanent contexts (such as a group that meets only once). Further, as was noted in our discussion of "bad" leadership in chapter 1, there is controversy regarding the motives of leaders. Can a leader be transformational if his or her intentions are selfish, exploitative, or motivated merely by a desire for personal power or wealth? Although such leaders may exhibit transformational characteristics, these self-interested individuals have been labeled as pseudotransformational.[64] The question as to what constitutes authentic transformational leadership remains to be answered, but there are a number of recent studies that suggest a link between transformational leadership and ethical leadership behavior.[65] Jane Howell and Bruce Avolio offer the following guidelines for distinguishing between ethical and unethical leadership.[66]

The ethical leader	The unethical leader
uses power to serve others	uses power only for personal gain
aligns vision with the needs and aspirations of followers	promotes his/her own personal vision
considers and learns from criticism	censures critical or opposing views
stimulates followers to think independently and to question the leader's view	demands that his or her own decisions be accepted without question
engages in open, two-way communication	engages in one-way communication
coaches, develops, and supports followers	is insensitive to the needs of followers
relies on internal moral standards to satisfy organizational and societal interests	relies on convenient external moral standards to satisfy self-interests

The behavior of authentic transformational leaders is aligned with those actions in the first column, while pseudotransformationals exhibit the unethical behaviors in the second column. Regardless of the ongoing debate, the transformational approach represents a bold and exciting perspective for understanding and explaining leadership.

Perspectives on Charisma

Charismatic leaders are the "superstars" of leadership. We usually reserve the label "charismatic" for well-known political, social, and business leaders who have had significant impact on the lives of others. Notable historical figures such as Joan of Arc, Queen Elizabeth I, Henry Ford, John F. Kennedy, Martin Luther King, Jr., and Walt Disney likely come to mind when we think of charisma. More recent conceptions of charisma, however, suggest that charismatic leadership can be found at all levels—not just among those in senior positions. By discovering how charismatics communicate, we can increase our effectiveness as leaders. In this section of the chapter, we'll summarize some of the most significant approaches to the study of charismatic leadership.

The Sociological Approach

German sociologist Max Weber, writing in the early twentieth century, was one of the first scholars to use the term charisma to describe secular leaders. The word charisma, which Weber borrowed from theology, means "gift" in Greek. Early Christians believed that God gave special gifts or abilities to church leaders.[67] Weber expanded the definition of gifted leadership to include all leaders, both religious and nonreligious, who attracted devoted followers through their extraordinary powers. In summarizing the nature of the charismatic leader, Weber wrote:

[H]e [she] is set apart from ordinary men [women] and treated as endowed with supernatural, superhuman, or at least specifically exceptional powers or qualities. These [powers] are such as are not accessible to the ordinary person, but are regarded as of divine origin or as exemplary and on the basis of them the individual concerned is treated as a leader.[68]

According to Weber, a leader retains charismatic status as long as he or she is seen as charismatic. A charismatic must periodically demonstrate his or her exceptional personal gifts in order to maintain power over followers. Harrison Trice and Janice Beyer found five key components in Weber's foundational conception of charisma.[69]

1. A leader with extraordinary, almost magical, talents

2. An unstable or crisis situation

3. A radical vision for providing a solution to the crisis

4. A group of followers attracted to the extraordinary leader because they believe they are linked through the leader to powers that exceed usual limits

5. A validation, through repeated success, of the extraordinary leader's talents and power

> Great crises produce great deeds of courage.
>
> —John F. Kennedy

A number of important details are missing from Weber's pioneering theory of charismatic leadership. Weber never describes the origin or exact nature of the charismatic leader's extraordinary powers, nor does he clarify how charismatic authority rests both on the traits of the leader and on the perceptions of followers. Much debate is also generated by the claim that instability or crisis is a necessary condition for charismatic leadership. Many scholars argue that charisma can be demonstrated in the absence of crisis, noting that charismatic leaders with compelling visions often appear in the business world in times of stability and calm.[70]

The Behavioral/Attribution Approach

Behavioral scientists argue that organizational leaders, like Thomas Watson of IBM and George Johnson of Endicott-Johnson Shoes, can also be described as charismatic. Behavioralists try to quantify the differences between charismatic and noncharismatic leaders. By describing charisma as a set of behaviors, they hope to clarify what charisma is and to predict the effects of charismatic leadership.[71]

> Do what you can, with what you have, where you are.
>
> —Theodore Roosevelt

Based on a behavioral model of charisma, Robert House and Bernard Bass developed a set of propositions or conclusions about charismatic leaders.[72] These propositions fall into three major categories:

- *Leader behaviors.* Charismatic leaders have strong power needs, display high self-confidence, demonstrate competence, serve as role models, communicate high expectations, engage in effective argumentation, and create transcendent goals.

- *Leader/follower relations.* Charismatics serve as targets for follower hopes, frustrations, and fears. They also create a sense of excitement and adventure. While charismatics lead groups toward new visions, they build their appeals to followers on widely shared beliefs, values, and goals.

- *Elements of the charismatic situation.* Charismatic leaders are most likely to appear when groups are under stress. For a corporation, stress might involve bankruptcy or the loss of a major market. Chrysler's financial problems, for example, set the stage for Lee Iacocca's emergence as a charismatic figure. Societies experience tension when they move from an agricultural to an industrial economic base, fight a war, or face a depression. Ironically, the charismatic's success in rallying support in response to an emergency may also explain the strong resistance she or he faces. Charismatic leaders generate intense feelings of love or hate. Charismatic movie czar Louis B. Mayer convinced members of the financial community to back his movies at a time when the future of the film industry was in doubt, yet many considered him to be a vain tyrant. In fact, Samuel Goldwyn claimed that the reason so many people came to Mayer's funeral was to make sure he was really dead.[73]

Closely linked to the behavioral approach is the attribution approach. Jay Conger and Rabindra Kanungo view charismatic leadership as an attributional process.[74] Charisma is defined in terms of the perceptions of followers. Conger and Kanungo claim certain leader behaviors motivate followers to regard individuals as charismatic. Five behaviors that encourage followers to attribute charismatic characteristics to leaders are:

- *Possess a vision that is unique, yet attainable.* A charismatic leader's vision differs markedly from the status quo. It is unique, innovative, and energizing. At the same time, the charismatic leader's vision is not too radical. A vision that challenges conventional wisdom too greatly (for example, a presidential candidate claiming it is possible to balance the federal budget in one year) will promote distrust. Followers attribute powers of observation and insight to a leader who communicates a singular, achievable vision.

- *Act in an unconventional, counternormative manner.* By engaging in behaviors that are outside traditional normative bounds, a charismatic demonstrates he or she is different from other leaders. When such behaviors produce successful outcomes, a leader appears to transcend the existing societal, organizational, or group order.

- *Demonstrate personal commitment and risk taking.* Trust is an important component of charisma, and followers have greater trust for a leader who is personally committed to his or her own vision. Most impressive is a leader who is willing to risk losing such things as power, status, or money.

- *Demonstrate confidence and expertise.* Leaders who appear confident and knowledgeable are far more likely to be viewed as charismatic than those who seem unsure and confused. A leader's confidence can be infectious. When a leader believes in his or her decision making, followers are likely to be more confident in their judgments as well. This shared confidence increases the likelihood of success for both leaders and followers and enhances the status of a leader among his or her followers. At the same time, when a leader demonstrates a high level of expertise, followers may believe the leader has privileged knowledge. The leader's successes will be attributed to expert decision making as opposed to chance.

- *Demonstrate personal power.* Followers are more likely to attribute charisma to leaders who use personal power to meet the objectives of their vision than to those who use authoritarian or democratic approaches. Leaders who use authoritarian means based on position power when implementing a vision are not likely to be perceived as charismatic. Likewise, leaders who delegate responsibility by asking followers to develop their own strategies for achieving a vision are unlikely to be seen as charismatic. Although these democratic leaders are generally well-liked, they usually are not considered extraordinary by followers. Those leaders who demonstrate their personal power through the use of compelling oratory or persuasive appeals, however, are likely to be viewed by followers as possessing charismatic characteristics.

The Communication Approach

None of the perspectives on charisma that we have discussed so far view the topic specifically from a communication vantage point. Nonetheless, sociologist Weber emphasized that charisma is perceived by followers who look to the leader to illustrate his or her charismatic standing through communication. Behaviorists recognize the importance of (1) the charismatic leader's command of rhetoric and persuasion, (2) the charismatic's creation of a self-confident, competent image, and (3) the link between symbolic myths and goals and charismatic emergence. Attribution researchers Conger and Kanungo emphasize the importance of articulating a compelling vision through personal communication.

We think that communication is more than an important element of charismatic leadership, however. We believe that ***charisma is the product of communication.*** We agree with Robert Richardson and Katherine Thayer who point out that "charisma isn't so much a gift as it is a specific form of communication."[75] Richardson and Thayer argue that we can exert charismatic influence by working to improve our communication skills.

Charismatic leaders excel in three core functions of communication.

Charismatics as Relationship Builders

Charismatic leaders are skilled at linking with others. Their relationships with followers are characterized by strong feelings. As we've seen, such terms as excitement, adventure, loyalty, and devotion are frequently used to describe charismatic leader/follower relations. In addition, charismatics convince followers that as leaders they have a significant impact on the course of events—that they are "at the center of things."[76]

Charismatics as Visionaries

Charismatic leaders can also be defined in terms of their ability to create symbolic visions. Above all, charismatics emphasize the transcendent. According to one scholar, "They provide in themselves and in their visions an opportunity for the follower to imagine himself and his society transformed into something entirely new."[77]

Although the visions of charismatic leaders are new images of the group's future, they are built on the foundation of previous myths and values. The power of the charismatic grows as larger and larger numbers of people accept his/her symbolic focus. Stressful events like unemployment, war, fear for the future, and racial strife discredit current definitions of reality. This creates a more receptive audience for the charismatic leader's new vision. For example, the civil rights movement of the 1960s made many white Americans aware of the extent of racial injustice. Martin Luther King, Jr.'s nonviolent message gained wide acceptance because people of all racial groups could accept King's vision of a world united by love.[78]

Charismatics as Influence Agents

Charismatics are masters at influence and inspiration. In some instances, their influence is so great that followers never question their decisions or directives. Charismatic leaders project an image of confidence, competence, and trustworthiness. They utilize the power of positive expectations to generate high productivity, and they make effective use of language and persuasion to achieve their goals. Such leaders rely heavily on referent power (their influence as role models) to encourage others to sacrifice on behalf of the group.

If the perception of charisma is the result of communication behaviors, then we all have the potential to act as charismatic leaders. We can generate charismatic effects as small group, organizational, and public leaders. Though we may never influence millions as did Mahatma Gandhi or Martin Luther King, Jr., we can have a strong impact on the lives of others through shaping the symbolic focus of the group, generating perceptions of confidence and competence, communicating high expectations, and inspiring others.

CHAPTER TAKEAWAYS

- Beginning in the late 1970s, the transformational approach emerged as a new perspective for understanding and explaining leadership.

- The transformational approach contrasts traditional leadership, labeled as *transactional*, with a more "complex" and "potent" type of leadership known as *transformational.*

- The motivational appeals of the transactional leader are designed to satisfy basic human needs; the appeals of the transformational leader go beyond those basic needs to satisfy a follower's higher-level needs.

- Transformational leaders are *creative, interactive, visionary, empowering,* and *passionate.* Further, since transformational leadership can convert followers into leaders in their own right, these five primary characteristics are often filtered throughout transformed groups and organizations.

- Transformational leaders are innovative and foresighted. They constantly challenge the status quo by seeking out new ideas, products, and ways of performing tasks.

- Transformational leaders are masterful communicators able to articulate and define ideas and concepts that escape others.

- Communicating a vision to followers may well be the most important act of the transformational leader. A vision is a concise statement or description of the direction in which an individual, group, or organization is headed. Compelling visions provide people with a sense of purpose and encourage commitment.

- Transformational leaders empower others. These leaders encourage participation and involvement. The exchange of ideas between leader and follower does not pose a threat to the transformational leader. Extraordinary leaders realize that individual achievement and success is the basis for team achievement and success. Transformational leaders know how to give power away and how to make others feel powerful.

- Transformational leaders are passionately committed to their work. They love their jobs and have a great deal of affection for the people with whom they work. This passion and personal enthusiasm motivates others to perform to their highest levels as well. Transformational leaders are able to encourage others because they, first and foremost, encourage themselves.

- Charismatic leaders are the "superstars" of leadership. We usually reserve the label "charismatic" for well-known political, social, and business leaders who have had significant impact on the lives of others.

- Weber's sociological approach to charisma included five key components: a leader with extraordinary talents; an unstable or crisis situation; a radical vision for providing a solution to the crisis; a group of followers who believe the extraordinary leader links them to powers that exceed usual limits; and a validation of the extraordinary leader's talents and power through repeated success.

- By describing charisma as a set of behaviors, the behavioral approach attempts to clarify what charisma is and to predict the effects of charismatic leadership. The attribution approach defines charisma by the perceptions of followers.

- The communication approach suggests that charisma is a specific form of communication. Charismatic leaders excel in three core functions of communication: relationship building, visioning, and influencing.

APPLICATION EXERCISES

1. Select a particular leader discussed in one of the many books focusing on transformational leadership (*In Search of Excellence, Passion for Excel-*

lence, Leaders, The Leadership Challenge, Built to Last, Lessons From the Top, Developing Potential Across a Full Range of Leadership, or *Good to Great,* for example). Analyze how effectively the leader applies transformational techniques. Does he/she meet the higher-level needs of followers? Is he/she an effective communicator? Does he/she have a clearly stated vision?

2. Conduct a debate on the distinction between transformational and pseudotransformational leadership. Do you believe that transformational leadership has an inherent moral component? Why? Why not?

3. Think of a time when you came up with a creative solution to a major problem. Analyze your problem-solving effort based on the four stages of the creative process identified by Wallas: preparation, incubation, illumination, and verification. Did you experience each stage? Which was most difficult for you? How can you overcome creative blocks and increase your flow of creative ideas in the future? Report your findings.

4. Research the development of a product that you use. Identify the process(es) that enabled this product to be created. Present your research in class.

5. Collect vision statements from several sources. Share your examples with others in class. Identify the common characteristics of the vision statements you think are most effective.

6. Discuss your past experiences with empowerment. Identify factors that let you know that you were truly empowered. Discuss factors that undermine empowerment. Develop a set of guidelines for effective empowerment.

7. Make a list of your passions. How could these passions be used to guide your career and future leadership experiences?

8. Form a small group and generate a composite list of 10 charismatic leaders. To make the group's list, a leader must be accepted as charismatic by all the members of the group. Keep a record of those individuals who fail to receive unanimous support. Present your findings to the rest of the class. As part of your report, describe the criteria that the group used to compile its list. In addition, name those individuals who were rejected by the group. Explain why these leaders failed to make the master list.

9. Conduct a debate on Weber's notion that "crisis" is necessary for charismatic leadership.

10. Do an in-depth study of a public charismatic leader. Describe how this person's use of communication resulted in his/her emergence as a charismatic figure. Write up your findings.

CULTURAL CONNECTIONS:
IS TRANSFORMATIONAL LEADERSHIP A UNIVERSAL CONCEPT?[79]

As society becomes increasingly global in its focus, it is important to assess the universality of leadership research and theory. Bernard Bass argues that the concept of transformational leadership may be truly universal—transcending organizational and national boundaries. Evidence supporting the viability of the transformational approach has been gathered from all continents except Antarctica. The results suggest leadership, in general, and transformational leadership, in particular, are found in one form or another at all levels and in all cultures. Additional research conducted by Robert House and 170 research associates around the world as part of the Global Leadership and Organizational Behavior Effectiveness (GLOBE) project also supports the notion that transformational leadership has universal features.

Initially Bass and his colleagues believed that transformational leadership was only exhibited by leaders in senior positions. Soon it became apparent that a variety of leaders, including middle managers, community activists, students, housewives, team leaders, salespeople, and members of the clergy exhibited transformational characteristics. Based on this broad application of the approach, Bass and fellow researcher Bruce Avolio offered three corollaries, which have subsequently been supported across a variety of cultures.

1. *Transformational leaders are more effective than leaders adopting a more transactional approach.* This has been verified in research conducted in the United States, Canada, Austria, Belgium, Italy, Germany, Spain, India, Singapore, Japan, China, New Zealand, and several other countries. Based on the perceptions of followers and organizational outcomes, including performance appraisals, career advancement, and performance of the work unit, transformational leaders consistently exceeded the performance of transactional leaders.

2. *Transformational leadership adds value to transactional leadership, but the inverse is not true.* Results supporting this corollary have been obtained in the United States, Canada, the Dominican Republic, India, Singapore, and several other countries. While transformational leadership appears to augment transactional leadership, transactional leadership does not enhance transformational leadership.

3. *Whatever the country, when people think of leadership, their prototypes and ideals are transformational.* Participants in research conducted in the United States, Canada, South Africa, Spain, Austria, Sweden, Italy, Israel, Japan, Taiwan, Sri Lanka, New Zealand, and elsewhere consistently described the ideal leader as possessing the traits and characteristics of transformational leaders.

The researchers in the GLOBE project surveyed over 15,000 middle managers from 60 different cultures. Their research, like that conducted by Bass and his colleagues, suggests that attributes of transformational leadership (such as being trustworthy, skilled, encouraging, visionary, communicative, and inspiring) are universally endorsed leadership components. Bass acknowledges that there may be cultures in which transformational leadership is not found. In those cultures trust between the leader and the led would be unimportant, and followers would have to demonstrate no concern for self-esteem, intrinsic motivation, consistency in the actions of leaders, or meaningfulness in their work and lives. Based on his work and that of the GLOBE project researchers, Bass argues such cultures would be the exception rather than the rule.

SPOTLIGHT ON TECHNOLOGY: WIKINOMICS AT GEEK SQUAD

For centuries organizations have been structured as hierarchies. Subordinate relationships—manager and employee; marketer and customer; producer and supplier—placed one party above the other. While hierarchies still exist, technology is flattening out many of these historical relationships, leading to a new structure that Don Tapscott and Anthony Williams call Wikinomics.[80] Today millions around the globe use blogs, wikis, chat rooms, and personal broadcasting to create a stream of dialogue. Web sites such as MySpace, Facebook, YouTube, Flickr, and LinkedIn allow individuals to build communities, collaborate, and self-organize independent of any hierarchical control. This revolution has been called the new Web, Web 2.0, the living Web, and the read/write Web, among other designations. Whatever it is called, the era of technologically assisted mass collaboration is changing how goods and services are invented, produced, marketed, and distributed—creating wiki workplaces.

One such work environment is Geek Squad. Started in 1994 as a small computer consulting business, Geek Squad was acquired by Best Buy in 2002. At the time of the purchase, Geek Squad had 60 employees and annual revenues of $3 million. Just four years later, Geek Squad employed over 12,000 technicians (called service agents) and, located within more than 700 Best Buy stores, had nearly $1 billion in earnings. To support this explosive growth Geek Squad created a wiki workplace in which employees use wikis, video games, and other collaborative technologies to manage projects, swap service tips, and socialize. Even with all of the formal collaborative tools in place, executives at Geek Squad observed that the informal networks were often the most fruitful. Employees play online multiplayer games such as Battlefield 2. These games involve as many as 400 Geek Squad staff simultaneously playing at one time. Between virtual battles, employees discuss business ideas, share tips (like how to reset the password on a Linksys router), and build relationships.

One such dialogue produced one of the company's most successful public relations coups. Service agents predicted that Geek Squad business would increase at the time of the release of the last installment of the *Star Wars* series. The thinking was that IT workers were the people who were most likely to line up for tickets to *Star Wars*. As a result of their late hours of buying tickets and attending midnight showings of the movie, these same workers would be more inclined to call in sick to work. To help their fellow IT geeks, the agents at Geek Squad had an idea. They suggested the company post an excuse note that could be downloaded from their Web site to justify absences from work as a result of "prequelitis." They got over 800,000 downloads, and the buzz regarding the phony excuse was so great that a Geek Squad executive was asked to appear on the *Today Show*.[81]

LEADERSHIP ON THE BIG SCREEN: *TAKE THE LEAD*

Starring: Antonio Banderas, Alfre Woodard, Rob Brown, Yava DaCosta, John Ortiz

Rating: PG-13 for sexuality, violence, and language

Synopsis: This film, based on a factual story, documents dance instructor Pierre Dulaine's efforts to transform the lives of a group of inner-city New York high school students through ballroom dancing. Dulaine is the impeccably dressed, courtly gentleman who opens doors for women and rides his bike through Manhattan. His reluctant pupils (who are sentenced to the school's detention center) come from families struggling to survive and inhabit hip-hop culture. Dulaine manages to overcome these barriers. His dancers are not only able to compete with the best ballroom dancers from around the city but, in the process, learn about respect, civility, discipline, leading, and following. Twelve thousand students now participate in the "Dancing Classrooms" program started by Dulaine.

Chapter Links: transformational leadership, charisma

Leadership and Power

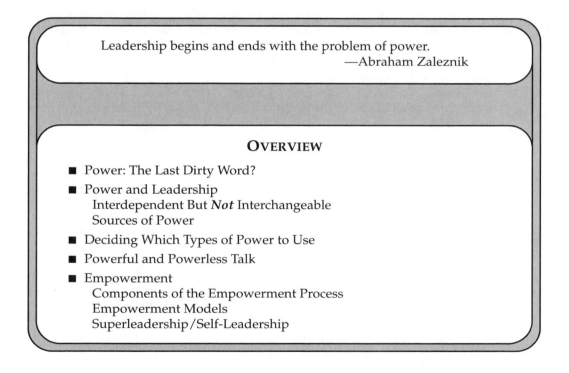

Leadership begins and ends with the problem of power.
—Abraham Zaleznik

OVERVIEW

- Power: The Last Dirty Word?
- Power and Leadership
  Interdependent But *Not* Interchangeable
  Sources of Power
- Deciding Which Types of Power to Use
- Powerful and Powerless Talk
- Empowerment
  Components of the Empowerment Process
  Empowerment Models
  Superleadership/Self-Leadership

Power: The Last Dirty Word?

Americans have contradictory feelings about power. On the one hand, we are fascinated by the power and wealth we see on television shows. We admire those with "clout," those who move quickly and decisively to get things done. We also loathe the corruption and greed that often comes with power. We're uneasy with exercising power—just discussing the topic can make us uncomfortable. According to Rosabeth Moss Kanter, "Power is America's last dirty word. It is easier to talk about money and much easier to talk about sex than it is to talk about power."[1]

As a society, we pay a high price for our ambivalence toward power. Avoiding the subject makes us more vulnerable to the misuse of power by those in authority. A chilling example is cult leader Jim Jones, who presided over the mass suicide of 800 followers in Guyana. This tragedy might have been prevented if cult members and outsiders had recognized and challenged Jones's unhealthy use of power.[2] Conversely, our discomfort with the subject of power diminishes our capacity to be successful. Leaders can only bring about change if they skillfully use power to enlist the support of followers, overcome resistance, collect resources, create alliances, and so on. If we ignore the reality of power, we won't learn how to exercise power effectively on behalf of worthy goals.

Power is a given. Treating it as a dirty word won't make it go away. Instead, we need to acknowledge the importance of power and determine how to use it appropriately. In the words of John Gardner:

> To say a leader is preoccupied with power is like saying that a tennis player is preoccupied with making shots his [her] opponent cannot return. Of course leaders are preoccupied with power! The significant questions are: What means do they use to gain it? How do they exercise it? To what ends do they exercise it?[3]

Power and Leadership

Sorting out the relationship between power and leadership can be confusing. Is using power the same as exerting leadership? Does having power automatically make you a leader? Power and leadership are obviously interdependent; however, they are not interchangeable. While power can exist without leadership, leadership cannot exist without power.

Interdependent But *Not* Interchangeable

We define power as *the ability to influence others*. Leadership is impossible without power since a leader must modify attitudes and behaviors. Yet influencing others does not automatically qualify as leadership; power must be used in pursuit of group goals to merit leadership classification. Imagine a robber armed with a semiautomatic weapon bursting into a bank, ordering everyone to lie on the floor. The group obeys. The bank robber certainly exerted power—a very negative manifestation of power. We would not label him a "leader," however. His power was exercised only on behalf of his own interests. In other instances, powerful individuals do not use their power and thus fail to take a leadership role. The small-group member who knows the most about a topic would be a natural candidate for group leadership. However, this person may refuse to participate in the group's discussion.

Leadership experts Warren Bennis and Burt Nanus summarize the relationship between power and leadership this way: "Power is . . . the *capacity to translate intention into reality and sustain it.* Leadership is the wise use of this power. . . . Vision is the commodity of leaders, and power is their currency."[4]

> Being powerful is like being a lady. If you have to tell people you are, you aren't.
>
> —Margaret Thatcher

Sources of Power

If power is the "currency of leadership," then understanding the sources and uses of power is essential to effective leadership. The ability to influence others can be based on a wide variety of factors. John French and Bertram Raven have isolated five primary sources of power.[5] Chances are you prefer to use one or two of these power bases more than the others (see the self-assessment exercise in box 5.1).

Coercive power is based on the ability to administer punishment or to give negative reinforcements. Examples of coercion range from reducing status, salary, and benefits to requiring others to do something they don't like. In the most extreme form, coercive power translates into brute physical force. Whistle-blowers (employees who have pointed out unethical practices like cost overruns and safety hazards) often experience coercion. They may be fired, assigned to distasteful jobs, or socially ostracized.

Coercion is most effective when those subject to this form of power are aware of expectations and are warned in advance about the penalties for failure to comply. Leaders using coercive power must consistently carry out threatened punishments. A parent who punishes without first establishing expectations and the consequences for failure will be less effective than a parent who clearly sets the ground rules. The effective parent says: "I expect you home by 10:00. If you're not home by then, you will be grounded for the rest of the weekend." The user of coercive power must then follow through with the announced consequence. Threatening over and over again to ground a teenager for being late without ever carrying out the punishment significantly diminishes coercive power. The same is true in organizational settings. A supervisor who threatens to take action against a subordinate must carry out the threat if coercive power is to remain a viable source of power.

Failure to execute threats can produce a cycle of negative behavior. Warnings to punish represent attention. Although humans certainly prefer positive reinforcement, they will select negative reinforcement over no reinforcement at

Box 5.1   Self-Assessment

Personal Power Profile[6]

Instructions: Below is a list of statements describing possible behaviors of leaders in work organizations. Carefully read each statement, thinking about *how you prefer to influence others.* Mark the number that most closely represents how you feel.

	Strongly Disagree	Disagree	Neither Agree nor Disagree	Agree	Strongly Agree
I prefer to influence others by					
1. increasing their pay level	1	2	3	4	5
2. making them feel valued	1	2	3	4	5
3. giving undesirable job assignments	1	2	3	4	5
4. making them feel like I approve of them	1	2	3	4	5
5. making them feel that they have commitments to meet	1	2	3	4	5
6. making them feel personally accepted	1	2	3	4	5
7. making them feel important	1	2	3	4	5
8. giving them good technical suggestions	1	2	3	4	5
9. making the work difficult for them	1	2	3	4	5
10. sharing my experience and/or training	1	2	3	4	5
11. making things unpleasant here	1	2	3	4	5
12. making work distasteful	1	2	3	4	5
13. helping them get a pay increase	1	2	3	4	5
14. making them feel they should satisfy job requirements	1	2	3	4	5
15. providing them with sound job-related advice	1	2	3	4	5
16. providing them with special benefits	1	2	3	4	5
17. helping them get a promotion	1	2	3	4	5
18. giving them the feeling that they have responsibilities to fulfill	1	2	3	4	5
19. providing them with needed technical knowledge	1	2	3	4	5
20. making them recognize that they have tasks to accomplish	1	2	3	4	5

Scoring: Record your responses to the 20 questions in the corresponding numbered blanks below. Total each column, then divide the result by 4 for each of the five types of influence.

	Reward	Coercive	Legitimate	Referent	Expert
	1 _____	3 _____	5 _____	2 _____	8 _____
	13 _____	9 _____	14 _____	4 _____	10 _____
	16 _____	11 _____	18 _____	6 _____	15 _____
	17 _____	12 _____	20 _____	7 _____	19 _____
Total	_____	_____	_____	_____	_____
Divide by 4	_____	_____	_____	_____	_____

Interpretation: A score of 4 or 5 on any of the five dimensions of power indicates that you prefer to influence others by using that particular form of power. A score of 2 or less indicates that you prefer not to employ this particular type of power to influence others. Your power profile is not a simple addition of each of the five sources. Some combinations are more synergistic than the simple sum of their parts. For example, referent power magnifies the impact of other power sources because these other influence attempts come from a "respected" person. Reward power often increases the impact of referent power because people generally tend to like those who can give them things. Some power combinations tend to produce the opposite of synergistic effects. Coercive power, for example, often negates the effects of other types of influence.

all (apathy). Humans would rather be punished than ignored. If a child is unable to attract positive attention, he or she may begin to misbehave in an attempt to attract negative attention. Employees in organizations are no different. "Problem" employees who receive warning after warning may simply need attention. Following the guidelines regarding the use of coercive power and offering positive reinforcement minimizes the negative behavior.

> I praise loudly, I blame softly.
>
> —Catherine the Great

Reward power rests on the ability to deliver something of value to others. The reward can be tangible (money, health benefits, or grades, for example) or something intangible like warmth and supportiveness (see box 5.2). Many organizations use both tangible and intangible rewards to recognize superior performance.

Any reward must be desirable and attractive to serve as a sufficient motivator. One of our students worked in a large organization that decided to change computing systems. The changeover took six months and required employees to work many hours of overtime. When the new system was finally in place, the corporation hosted a Friday afternoon party and rewarded those who had worked such long hours with T-shirts that said, "I Survived the Changeover." The student and her coworkers were insulted. More suitable rewards, like giving workers the day off after so many weeks of overtime, might have been more appreciated and more attractive to employees. This student's unhappy experience with rewards is all too common, prompting some

Box 5.2   Case Study

The Power of Pride[7]

Many leaders rely on financial incentives to motivate followers. They believe that offering pay raises and performance bonuses is the best way to retain employees and to encourage them to work harder. Organizational consultant and researcher Jon Katzenbach argues that these leaders are mistaken. It is pride, not money, that builds institutions that deliver the best products and services along with superior economic performance.

Katzenbach acknowledges that there are some advantages of monetary rewards, including the fact that they are widely accepted and easily understood. However, Katzenbach is convinced that the disadvantages of financial incentives far outweigh their advantages. That's because:

- money attracts and retains better than it motivates excellent performance;
- money is effective only as long as the leader can pay more than the competition;
- money can promote behavior (delaying investments, booking earnings prematurely) that conflicts with the goals of the organization;
- money and titles are more motivating for top-level executives than frontline employees;
- money and ego are better at motivating individuals than teams or groups; and
- materialism encourages greed and other selfish behaviors.

Financial rewards foster self-serving pride. Those motivated by this kind of pride look for the biggest paycheck and the most recognition. They are quick to leave in an economic downturn. Institution-building pride, on the other hand, is intrinsic, promoting commitment to shared goals. This type of pride comes from doing something well and, when linked to organizational goals, produces energy and commitment. Those driven by intrinsic pride focus more on the organization's performance—customer satisfaction, product quality, respect of peers—than on themselves. Such pride comes from the *results* of their work (product quality, the type of work), *how* they work (values, standards, commitment), and with *whom* they work (colleagues and the organization).

Katzenbach points to the Marines, Home Depot, Aetna insurance, Hills Pet Nutrition, and Southwest Airlines as examples of organizations that tap into the power of institution-building pride. Their leaders follow one or more paths to fostering pride. The first path focuses on mission, values, and collective pride (MVP). The Marines, for example, are proud of their history, heroes, and values ("Do the right thing, in the right way, for the right reasons"). The second path emphasizes process and metrics. High-pride organizations involve followers in designing measurement instruments and provide constant feedback. The walls of Avon manufacturing plants are covered with charts and graphs, developed with employee input, that help workers track their progress. The third path nurtures entrepreneurial spirit. Peak performers are energized by the pride they feel in doing something new—developing a product or service, redesigning a process, or reaching out to additional customers. Ski instructors at Vail, for instance, operate as entrepreneurs, booking their own clients. They take pride in the development of their students. As a result, they stay over 10 years (much longer than the norm in the skiing industry). The fourth path fosters pride by providing lots of opportunities for individual growth and development. For example, inventors at 3M are rewarded for creating new products and then taking them to market. The fifth pride-building path highlights recognition and celebration. Leaders in these cultures (such as Southwest Airlines) sponsor parties, friendly competitions, and celebrations.

Katzenbach believes that all leaders can learn to become institutional pride builders by following the example of the most effective "manager motivators." The best pride builders keep in mind that the journey is more important than the destination. They encourage followers to take pride in what they do every day and strive to create emotional commitment, not just cognitive compliance. These leaders realize that what works in one location may not work in another. They tie their efforts to local events and role models and reach outside the organization to build pride through family gatherings and community service. Finally, those who excel at pride building highlight a few key themes to link their efforts. They emphasize those themes by repeating the same important stories and keep the group focused on a few key indicators like safety, product quality, or customer service.

Discussion Questions

1. What do you see as the advantages and disadvantages of using money as a motivational tool? Do the shortfalls of monetary rewards outweigh their benefits?

2. Do financial incentives motivate you to perform your best? Why or why not?

3. Can you think of other leaders and organizations that excel at pride building? Which pride-building paths do they follow?

4. How can your employer or school better foster pride?

5. What steps can you take to become a better "manager motivator"?

experts to suggest that leaders should strictly limit their use of tangible rewards as a motivational strategy.

Legitimate power resides in the position rather than in the person. Persons with legitimate power have the right to prescribe our behavior within specified parameters (for example, judges, police officers, teachers, and parents). Although we may disagree with our supervisor at work, we go along with a decision because that person is "the boss." The amount of legitimate power someone has depends on the importance of the position she or he occupies and the willingness to grant authority to the person in that position. Individuals grant legitimate power based on particular circumstances. An assistant will comply when the boss assigns a word-processing project or requires the phone to be answered because those are legitimate requests. The assistant may not be willing to assent to tasks that are not related to work.

Expert power is based on the person, not the position, in contrast to legitimate power. Experts are influential because they supply needed information and skills. In our culture, it is particularly important to be perceived as an expert. Those with credentials are more powerful than those without appropriate certification. When visiting a new physician, do you immediately check his/her diploma? Our culture mandates that certain credentials must be obtained before an individual can be considered a professional. Demonstrating practical knowledge and skills can also build expert power. For this reason, members of an organization often have little legitimate power but a great deal of expert power. Receptionists can be extremely influential because of what they learn through talking to employees, managers, customers, and others. School janitors are often powerful because they know how to fix bulletin boards, open locked doors, and so on.

Referent power is role model power. When people admire someone, they confer on the admired person the ability to influence their behavior. Referent power depends on feelings of affection, esteem, and respect for another individual. This loyalty generally develops over an extended period of time. Since referent power takes so long to nurture, it should be used carefully. A supervisor who asks a subordinate to work overtime as "a personal favor" will succeed if the employee likes and respects the supervisor. Referent power will probably be effective the first weekend and possibly the second, but after several weeks the employee will tire of doing "favors" for his/her supervisor. Once depleted, referent power must be replenished by engaging in behavior that will produce new feelings of affection, esteem, and support.

> The measure of a [hu]man is what he [she] does with power.
> —Pittacus

Deciding Which Types of Power to Use

A useful way of determining the relative advantages and disadvantages of each source of power is to view leadership as a reciprocal relationship. While leaders exert more influence than other group members, leaders are also influenced by followers. According to social exchange theory, leaders must maintain profitable relationships with followers.[8] They do this by providing rewards like approval, information, or salary in return for such commodities as labor, compliance, and commitment. When the relationship becomes unprofitable to either party (the costs outweigh the benefits), then the relationship is redefined or ended. There are potential costs and benefits associated with using each power type. For example, coercion can be used by followers as well as by leaders. Students may punish instructors who rely heavily on threats and other coercive tactics by giving them low course evaluations. Politicians who legislate unpopular tax measures are often removed from office.

A list of the benefits and costs of each type of power is given below. The list (which incorporates the thoughts of the authors and a number of researchers) is not exhaustive.[9] In fact, we hope that you will add your own costs, benefits, and conclusions (see application exercise 2).

BENEFITS	COSTS
Coercive Power	
Effective for gaining obedience	Drains physical and emotional energy from user
Appropriate for disciplinary actions	Lowers task satisfaction of followers
Achieves quick results	Destroys trust and commitment
	Becomes less effective over time
	Followers may respond in kind
Reward Power	
Culturally sanctioned	Lower task satisfaction than with expert and referent power
Focuses attention on group priorities	Not consistently linked with high task performance

Effective for gaining obedience	Escalating financial and material costs to provide ever-greater tangible rewards
Boosts short-term performance	Some groups, like nonprofit agencies, have limited tangible rewards to give
	Ineffective or destructive if rewards are not desirable or attractive, or if the wrong individuals are rewarded
Legitimate Power	
Culturally sanctioned	Lowers follower task performance
Incorporates weight of the entire organization	Lowers follower task satisfaction
Effective for gaining obedience	May become less effective over time
Helps large organizations function efficiently	
Expert Power	
High follower task satisfaction	Takes a long time to develop
High follower task performance	Must possess the necessary knowledge and skills
Drains little, if any, emotional energy from the user	Not as effective in gaining obedience as coercion, reward, or legitimate power
	May not be effective if followers do not share the leader's goals
Referent Power	
High follower task satisfaction	Takes a long time to develop
High follower task performance	Can diminish if overused
	Must possess the necessary knowledge and interpersonal skills
	Not as effective for gaining obedience as coercion, reward, or legitimate power

The cost/benefit ratios suggest that leaders should rely heavily on expert and referent power. These forms of power have a positive effect on the performance and satisfaction of those being influenced and are less costly to use. They are most likely to maintain a profitable relationship between leader and follower. Yet, effective leaders need access to all five types of power. Taking charge may require discipline through coercion, the judicious use of rewards, and the power of position. In fact, a leader's impact is enhanced if, for example, she or he combines legitimate power with expert and referent power. A highly respected group member who is appointed the chair of a committee is in a very powerful position. (Leadership on the Big Screen at the end of the chapter describes one leader who skillfully drew on all the power sources to achieve his goals and the goals of his group.)

To summarize, group members seem to prefer leaders who rely on power associated with the unique characteristics of the person (expert and referent) rather than leaders who rely on power related to their position (coercion, reward, legitimate). Since effectiveness is more directly tied to personal performance than to official position, we can manage our communication behaviors to increase our power—which, in turn, can increase our ability to lead. Let's take a closer look at one cluster of communication behaviors—powerful forms of talk—that seem particularly well-suited to building both expert and referent power.

Powerful and Powerless Talk

Sociolinguists, anthropologists, communication specialists, and others have long been fascinated with the two-way relationship between language and power. Viewed from the perspective of society, language is a mirror reflecting power differences. Every culture has a "standard language" that is spoken by the highest socioeconomic group in that society. Nonstandard languages are dialects spoken by less advantaged people.[10] The use of language both reflects and creates power differentials.[11] Speakers are stereotyped as powerless or powerful based on their word choices.

The fact that speakers are perceived as powerless or powerful based on the way they talk means that language can be an important tool for building power bases. Conversely, inappropriate language can reduce perceived power and leadership potential. A number of language features have been identified as "powerful" or "powerless" by researchers.[12] Powerful talk makes speakers seem knowledgeable and confident; powerless talk is tentative and submissive. Most researchers have concentrated on identifying powerless speech forms, while powerful speech has been treated as speech without powerless speech features. Here are some forms of powerless types of talk:

- *Hesitations* ("uh," "ah," "well," "um," "you know") are the most frequently used form of powerless talk and the least powerful speech feature. The characteristic that is most likely to clutter our talk is also the most likely to reduce our power.

- *Hedges* ("kinda," "I think," "I guess") may occasionally be appropriate (when we truly are not sure of our facts, for example), but they greatly reduce the impact of what we say. Compare "I think you should have that report in by Friday" to "Have that report in by Friday."

- *Tag Questions* ("isn't it?"; "wouldn't it?") on the end of a sentence indicate uncertainty. These expressions make a declarative statement much less forceful. For example, "That presentation was unorganized, wasn't it?"

- *Disclaimers* ("Don't get me wrong, but"; "I know this sounds crazy, but") can be a useful conversational tool. Speakers use disclaimers when they are not sure if listeners will accept what they have to say. For instance: "I'm not trying to be critical, but your speech was way too long." They should be used with caution, however, since they can signal that we lack confidence in our statements.

- *Accounts* (excuses or justifications) deny responsibility for what happened. Speakers employ accounts after they say or do the wrong thing: "It was an accident," or "I wasn't ready for the test because I stayed up all night helping my roommate with a problem." A speaker who frequently excuses or justifies his/her behavior will be seen as inept or uncertain.
- *Side Particles* ("like," "simply," "that is") detract from a powerful image. They can be irritating for listeners.

Researchers report that the use of powerless speech in experimental settings significantly lowers source credibility. (We'll have more to say about believability—what communication experts call credibility—in the next chapter.) Listeners consistently rate the knowledge and ability (competence) of powerless speakers lower than that of powerful speakers when both deliver the same message. In addition, they find such sources less trustworthy, less dynamic, and less sure of themselves. Powerless speakers are perceived as less attractive and less persuasive. Audiences don't retain as much information from a speech or lecture if the message is delivered in a tentative style.[13]

Language choices clearly have a strong influence on the two bases of power most easily controlled by the communicator: expert and referent power. Powerless speakers often *appear* to be uninformed and unskilled even if they do, in fact, possess the necessary knowledge and abilities. On the other hand, powerful speakers are frequently seen as competent and attractive, and their messages have more persuasive and informational impact. Some evidence suggests that powerful talk can help overcome the disadvantages that come from having low legitimate power.[14] It should be noted, however, that other variables may moderate or override the influence of powerless speech. For example, students are less distracted by an instructor's use of powerless talk if they like that professor or if the information contained in the lecture is important to them.[15] Also, powerful speech is most effective when speakers are trying to be authoritative. There are times when a powerless style may be more appropriate, such as in a conversation between friends or when a superior is trying to establish common ground with a subordinate. The key is to adopt the appropriate style for the situation.

Fortunately, we can eliminate powerless language features if we choose to do so. Lawyers report that they can teach clients to avoid powerless language. Public speaking instructors help their students eliminate powerless talk by noting powerless speech features on speech evaluation forms. To become a more powerful speaker, start by monitoring your powerless speech habits. Record a conversation and count the number of powerless speech features you used, or ask a friend to give you feedback about your powerless speech patterns. Make a conscious effort to eliminate powerless language. Keep track of your progress using the recording and feedback methods described above. Another way to become a more powerful speaker is by monitoring public speakers (including instructors). Evaluating what others do can help to improve your own performance.[16]

Empowerment

Up to this point, we have emphasized how power is the essential currency of leadership. There is no leadership without power, and some forms of power are more effective for leaders than others. However, a leader will frequently want to distribute rather than to maintain power. Reducing power differentials often enhances group performance and may be the key to organizational survival. (Take a look at the case study in box 5.3 to see how empowerment can increase productivity.)

Box 5.3   Case Study
Empowerment on the Load Line at Techstar Industries

Techstar Industries is one of several companies responsible for assembling the circuit boards used in personal computers. Companies like Techstar compete with many other organizations doing the same type of work. The assembling of circuit boards is tedious and demanding; the work is often repetitive and dull. At the same time, there is tremendous pressure to assemble large numbers of boards with very few rejects. The only competitive advantage a company like Techstar can hope for is to produce a higher quality product at a lower price than its competitors.

Boards at Techstar are assembled on the load line. Parts are loaded by hand onto the board as it travels along a conveyer belt. The most recent Techstar board, the MT2000, has 27 parts that are loaded at six different stations by a team of operators. To be profitable, Techstar must manufacture 600 usable boards with fewer than 10 rejects during each eight-hour shift.

The load line team has averaged fewer than 500 usable boards with as many as 30 defective boards produced on each shift. The supervisor, Tom Friedman, decided that the only way to improve the situation was to turn the problem over to the operators. Tom called a meeting to announce his intentions. Despite his team's apprehension, he told the operators he wanted them to generate ideas for improving their productivity. To get the team started, Tom chaired the first few meetings. He told the team he would provide all the necessary support required to improve the situation. Further, Tom made it clear that he was willing to turn over control of the load line to the operators if they could meet the production goal for profitability and keep him apprised of their progress.

Over the next two months, the load line team met on a regular basis. They identified 20 ways to improve the process. Among the most important suggestions were: cross-train operators, develop a system for keeping the line stocked with parts, and reengineer the line to optimize efficiency. The team based these suggestions on several problems that they identified during their meetings. First, each operator was trained to work at only one of six stations. When an operator needed to leave the line for any reason, the entire assembly process came to a halt. Second, when an operator on the line ran out of parts, the line had to be stopped until the parts were replenished. Finally, with six stations operating at once, all members of the load line team were tied to the line. This became even more problematic when the team realized that the demands of each station were very different. Because workloads were unevenly distributed, some operators were rushing to get their parts loaded while those at other stations worked at a much slower pace.

The team presented their plan to Tom. They requested downtime to train each member of the team to work at each station. The team felt the process could be improved if there were only five stations rather than six. This would enable the team to balance the workload so that the demands of each station would be roughly equal. In addition, five workstations would allow one team member to circulate between stations. This team member would be responsible for filling in for other team members when they left the line, for stocking parts, and for troubleshooting before defective boards were produced.

Tom liked the team's ideas and, as he promised, offered his support. Within a few days the line was reconfigured and the load line team began assembling MT2000 boards on their new five-station line. With team members working together and rotating positions on the load line throughout their shift, the number of MT2000 boards produced began to climb. Within three months, the team not only met Tom's production goal, they exceeded it—producing over 700 usable boards with an average of only three defective boards per eight-hour shift.

Discussion Questions

1. How do you think the assembly process would have been affected if Tom had decided to reconfigure the load line without consulting the team?

2. What are the major advantages/disadvantages of the type of empowerment strategy Tom used?

3. What advice would you offer Tom for dealing with the load line team if their suggestions for improvement had not resulted in increased productivity?

4. Discuss a time when you have been empowered to make a decision. What were the results?

5. What kinds of tasks do you think should be among the first delegated to followers as part of a leader's empowerment effort? Why?

Paradoxically, leaders gain more power by empowering others. There are five major reasons why leaders choose to share power. In an organizational setting, distributing power *increases the job satisfaction and performance of employees.* People like their jobs more, generally experience less stress, and work harder when they feel that they have a significant voice in shaping decisions.[17] Withholding power has the opposite result. Those who feel powerless often respond by becoming cautious, defensive, and critical.[18] In extreme cases, they lash out at coworkers and damage the organization through such tactics as work slow downs and equipment sabotage.

Sharing power *fosters greater cooperation among group members.* Cooperation, in turn, increases group accomplishment. The effectiveness of any group depends in large part on the cooperation of group members. For instance, a small group cannot get an "A" on a class project if members withhold information from each other or if a number of members refuse to participate at all. The same is true for a sales team or computer project group. The genius of organizing lies in combining individual efforts in order to achieve goals that would be beyond the capability of any one person. The group advantage is lost or diluted when participation is only halfhearted. James Kouzes and Barry Posner report that enabling others is a key to leadership; accomplishment results from the efforts of many people, not just the leader. According to Kouzes and Posner: "We developed a simple test to detect whether someone is on the road to becoming a leader. That test is the frequency of the word *we.*"[19]

> There is no limit to what you can do if you don't care who gets the credit.
>
> —John Wooden

Distributing power means *collective survival*; the group endures rather than fails. One of the best ways to stay competitive in a fast-paced, global environment is to develop a "flat" organizational structure. Flat structures are decentralized and grant a great deal of decision-making authority to lower-level leaders. For instance, branch managers in flat corporations control decisions affecting their operations. They do not have to check with headquarters constantly. In these companies, project groups blur traditional lines of authority in order to develop new ideas. Flat organizations offer two advantages: (1) they can move quickly to meet changing market conditions, and (2) they foster innovation—the development of new products and processes on which a business ultimately depends.

Effective leadership helps *personal growth and learning.* Group members become more mature and productive than they were before. Empowerment is one way to stimulate growth. Sharing power with followers can help them tackle new challenges, learn new skills, and find greater fulfillment.[20] In the end, both the group member and the group are transformed when power is shared. Not only does the individual grow, but the collective gains a more committed and skilled member.

Sharing power *prevents power abuses.* Concentrating power in the hands of a few individuals is dangerous. As Britain's Lord Acton observed, "Power corrupts, and absolute power corrupts absolutely." Individuals who do not share power are free to project their insecurities, fears, and hostility on others and to further their own interests at the expense of followers. Tyrannical bosses, for example, seek to maintain their positions by (1) tracking every move of employees, (2) sending conflicting messages about what they want, (3) engaging in angry outbursts, (4) demanding absolute obedience, (5) putting followers down in public, (6) acting arbitrarily, and (7) coercing subordinates into unethical behavior.[21]

Powerful individuals often ignore the needs of others. Compared to the powerless, they typically devote less attention to finding out how other people think and feel. As a consequence, they are more likely to hold and to act on harmful stereotypes, particularly of minority group members.[22] Leaders who distribute power, on the other hand, are less likely to abuse their positions, to take advantage of followers, to ignore the needs of others, or to stereotype.

> Oh, it is excellent to have a giant's strength, but it is tyrannous to use it like a giant.
>
> —William Shakespeare

Making a case for empowering followers is easier than making empowerment happen. Many organizations continue to operate under the traditional, hierarchical model where top executives often get treated like royalty, and middle- and lower-level managers are rewarded for keeping, not sharing, their authority. Giving power away is difficult in these hostile environments. (Turn to the research highlight in box 5.4 for some vivid examples of how organizations create feelings of powerlessness.) Other organizations fail to reward followers who take on added responsibilities. Yet, empowerment efforts can and do succeed. Leaders have relinquished much of their legitimate, reward, expert, and coercive power bases at companies like Gore and Associates (mak-

Box 5.4   Research Highlight

The View from the Cubicle[23]

DILBERT: © Scott Adams/Dist. by United Feature Syndicate, Inc.

The popularity of the Dilbert cartoon strip is one indication that empowerment is more of a myth than a reality in many large organizations. Millions of white-collar workers can relate to cartoonist Scott Adams's depiction of company life. Collections of his daily strips and humorous observations about work are best sellers. Adams pokes fun at everyone—middle managers, top executives, consultants, coworkers, engineers—and nearly everything—meetings, training programs, working conditions, memos, and management fads—in corporate America.

In a very real sense, Adams is a researcher. He spent several years gathering data as an employee at a bank and at Pacific Bell before quitting to become a full-time cartoonist. Readers keep him posted on the "dark side" of organizations by e-mailing him with their workplace stories. The real-life examples he receives are often more absurd than anything he can make up. Consider the following:

From: (name withheld)
To: scottadams@aol.com
Shortly after taking my first job, I submitted a trip report and expense account only to have it returned to my desk because one item "violated company policy." Being a concerned employee, I immediately contacted the soon-to-be retired career bureaucrat in charge, expressed my contrition, and requested a copy of the company policies so as to avoid another violation. The bureaucrat informed me that company policies were secret and not for general distribution, as then "everyone would know them."[24]

Other real-world examples of how corporations confuse and humiliate their employees instead of empowering them include:

- Permanently attaching laptop computers (purchased for business trips) to desks so they won't get stolen

- Assigning "Positivity Police" to catch those displaying a "Non-Positive Attitude" (NPA)

- Editing resignation letters and making employees rewrite and resubmit them

- Requiring semi-daily progress reports or asking salaried workers to account for their time in six-minute increments

- Using meaningless technical jargon ("utilize issue clarification processes"; "act in the best interests of achieving the team")

- Consultants taking employee suggestions and presenting them to company executives as their own ideas

(continued)

- Cost cutting by turning off the down escalator or restricting workers to one donut at weekly meetings (enforced by the use of a "donut ticket")
- Putting employees about to be laid off into the "mobility pool" or enrolling them in the new "Career Transition Plan"
- Instituting a random drug testing program and "Individual Dignity Enhancement Program" at the same time
- Refusing to list the extension numbers of Human Resources representatives
- Adopting confusing slogans like "Our innovation makes us first, our quality makes us last!"

ers of Gore-Tex fabric), Johnsonville Foods, Harley-Davidson, McCormick Spice Company, and many other successful organizations. Self-directed work teams (SDWTs), as we'll see in chapter 7, are taking over many of the functions traditionally reserved for lower- and middle-level managers and are being rewarded for doing so.

Power sharing is most likely to occur when leaders understand the components of the empowerment process and are equipped with implementation strategies. With that in mind, we'll take the remainder of the chapter to outline the important elements of empowerment and to describe two models that take a systematic approach to giving power away.

Components of the Empowerment Process

Component 1: Modifying the Environment

Environment refers to the setting where work occurs. Important elements of the environment include reward systems, job tasks, organizational structure and workflow, rules, charts, and physical layout. The first step in the empowerment process is often the elimination of situational factors that create feelings of powerlessness, like inappropriate rewards, authoritarian supervision, and petty regulations (see box 5.5). Next, the environment is redesigned to shift decision-making authority to followers. Those assigned to do the work get a great deal of say in how the job gets done.

Component 2: Building Intrinsic Motivation

Empowered followers are energized to carry out tasks associated with their work roles. They take an active, not passive, approach toward their job responsibilities. Such intrinsic motivation is the product of the following four factors.[25]

Meaning.   Meaning is the value placed on a task, goal, or purpose based on personal ideals or standards. Low levels of meaning produce apathy and detachment; higher levels focus energy and produce commitment and involvement. You can foster a sense of meaning by (1) hiring those who share the group's values, (2) promoting the organization's purpose and vision, (3) clarifying work roles, (4) matching individuals with jobs they find meaningful, and (5) explaining how individual tasks support the group's mission and goals.

Choice (self-determination).   Choice reflects a sense of self-direction or control. Those who have choice about how to carry out their jobs (when to start,

---

Box 5.5   Research Highlight
Situational Factors Leading to a Potential State of Powerlessness[26]

Organizational Factors
　Significant organizational changes/transitions
　Start-up ventures
　Excessive, competitive pressures
　Impersonal, bureaucratic climate
　Poor communications and limited network-forming systems
　Highly centralized organizational resources

Supervisory Style
　Authoritarian (high control)
　Negativism (emphasis on failures)
　Lack of reasons for actions/consequences

Reward Systems
　Noncontingency (arbitrary) reward allocations
　Low incentive value of rewards
　Lack of competence-based rewards
　Lack of innovation-based rewards

Job Design
　Lack of role clarity
　Lack of training and technical support
　Unrealistic goals
　Lack of appropriate authority/discretion
　Low task variety
　Limited participation in programs, meetings, and decisions that have a direct impact on job
　　performance
　Lack of appropriate/necessary resources
　Lack of opportunities to form networks
　Highly established work routines
　Too many rules and guidelines
　Low advancement opportunities
　Lack of meaningful goals/tasks
　Limited contact with senior management

---

how fast to work, how to prioritize tasks) feel a greater sense of responsibility and are more flexible, creative, and resilient. Shifting decision-making authority to followers is one way to encourage a sense of self-determination. In addition, create a participative climate that values employees and takes their ideas seriously. Emphasize the importance of taking individual initiative and making a personal contribution. Make followers accountable for their choices and set boundaries on what they can and cannot do. Ritz-Carlton, for example, lets hotel employees spend up to $2,500 to satisfy an unhappy guest. Finally, support those who take risks. Years ago, a UPS employee ordered an extra plane to make sure that packages left behind during the Christmas rush were delivered on time. Rather than punish this individual for going above the budget, company leaders praised him. His story (still told at the company) sends the message that UPS leaders will stand behind those who take initiative.

Competence.   Competence is based on the individual's assessment that he or she can do the job required. It is a subset of what psychologist Albert Bandura refers to as self-efficacy or personal power. Self-efficacy is the sense that we can deal with events, situations, and people at work and in other environments as well. Followers who have a sense of self-efficacy or personal power are more likely to take initiative, to set and achieve higher goals, and to persist in the face of difficult circumstances. Constituents who believe that they have limited self-efficacy and feel powerless dwell on their failures. They are less inclined to offer new ideas, to set and meet challenging standards, or to continue when they encounter obstacles.[27] Leaders can build followers' perceptions of their personal power by:[28]

- providing positive emotional support, particularly during times of stress and anxiety. Stress, fear, depression, and other negative factors reduce feelings of personal efficacy. The impact of these factors can be diminished if a leader clearly defines the task, offers assistance, engages in play to create a positive emotional climate, and uses films, speakers, seminars, and other devices to build excitement and confidence.

- expressing confidence. The most effective leaders spend time every day encouraging others and expressing confidence in their abilities at meetings, during speeches, in the lunchroom, in hallways, and in offices.

- modeling successful performance themselves or providing opportunities to observe others who are successful. Knowing that someone else can handle a task makes it easier for a worker to continue to learn the same task even after repeated failures.

- structuring tasks so that followers experience initial success. Initial victories build expectations for future triumphs. Effective leaders structure tasks so that they become increasingly complex. Completing one part of the job is followed by training and then greater responsibilities. The same strategy can be used to introduce large-scale change. A new marketing strategy or billing system can be started in one plant or region and then adopted by the organization as a whole. (See chapter 8 for additional information on demonstration projects.)

Impact.   Impact describes the individual's belief that he or she can influence the environment of the organization. Followers with a high sense of impact are convinced that they can make a difference in the work group's plans, goals, and procedures. You can foster this perception by including workers in strategic planning and by involving them in setting collective rules and standards. Encourage their efforts to introduce innovations.

Component 3: Supplying Resources

Empowerment increases the demand for resources. No follower, no matter how motivated, can complete a task if she/he doesn't have adequate funds and supplies, enough time to devote to the job, and a place to work. Political support—the approval of important individuals—is essential for the completion of major projects. Leaders supply this resource when they publicly endorse the work of stakeholders and encourage other leaders to "buy in" to initiatives.[29]

Information is a particularly important resource for newly empowered followers. Consider the machine operator who has just joined a self-directed work team, for example. Under the old system, she had to know how to run a single piece of equipment. Now she's part of a group that makes decisions for an entire department: planning, scheduling, hiring, and quality control. In addition to operating her machine, she must learn how to work in a team, set objectives, measure results, read a profit-and-loss statement, conduct a hiring interview, and so forth. She can only succeed if she receives adequate training and if company management supplies the team with financial and performance data for planning and measurement.

Empowerment Models

Leaders who empower followers take on different tasks than they do under the traditional, hierarchical model. According to James Belasco and Ralph Stayer, an empowering leader acts more like a lead goose than a head buffalo.[30] As head buffalo, a leader takes charge while loyal followers look on, waiting for direction. In contrast, geese flying in a V formation on their annual migrations frequently shift leaders and roles in response to travel conditions. (See box 5.6 for an example of a highly successful organization that routinely rotates members in and out of leadership roles.)

> Buffalo are loyal to one leader; they stand around and wait for the leader to show them what to do. When the leader isn't around, they wait for him to show up. That's why the early settlers could decimate the buffalo herds so easily by killing the lead buffalo. The rest of the herd stood around, waiting for their leader to lead them, and were slaughtered.
>
> —James Belasco & Ralph Stayer

Leading the Journey

Belasco and Stayer call their model for a systematic approach to empowerment "Leading the Journey." In this model, leaders (acting as lead geese) are responsible for determining vision and direction, removing obstacles, developing ownership, and stimulating self-directed action.

- *Determining focus and direction.* Leaders at all levels of an organization are responsible for setting vision and direction. Staying in touch with customers (those who use an organization's products and services) is the key to determining direction. Your goal is to put on an outstanding performance for the end user, not just an adequate one.

- *Removing obstacles.* Eliminate obstacles that keep followers from providing outstanding performances. Help ensure that all systems (compensation, information, procedures) support this one objective. At Johnsonville Foods, product quality improved when customer complaint letters, which used to go to the marketing department, went directly to line

Box 5.6   Case Study

The Empowered Orchestra[31]

The Orpheus Chamber Orchestra is one of the country's premiere classical musical ensembles. This symphony orchestra, based at New York City's Carnegie Hall, is made up of musicians who teach at prestigious schools like Julliard and the Manhattan School of Music. What makes Orpheus unique, and its success all the more remarkable, is the fact that the orchestra has no conductor. Members have shared artistic power since the group was founded in 1972. The orchestra as a whole, not a conductor, chooses which pieces to play and how they should be performed.

Some observers refer to Orpheus as a leaderless orchestra. That would be a mistake. The group has many leaders, not just one. A leadership team of five to 10 players is chosen for each piece of music. This committee then selects a concertmaster to be in charge of the practices and the performance. During rehearsals, members of the entire orchestra offer suggestions and criticisms. Any disagreements are worked out on the spot. When a concert is complete, members suggest further refinements before presenting the program again.

Orpheus has drawn the attention of a number of large corporations and nonprofit groups for the way it utilizes the talents of its employees. Orchestra members (like engineers, software developers, and bankers) are knowledge workers. Their information and skills are critical to the group's success. Like highly trained professionals in other fields, musicians often feel stifled by top-down leadership. Orpheus actively seeks the input of its knowledge workers and is rewarded by a high level of commitment and performance. Other organizations (Morgan Stanley, The Ritz-Carlton Hotel Company, Gore Associates, the San Diego Zoo) are discovering that the same model can work for them. They are utilizing some or all of the following eight Orpheus principles.

1. Put power in the hands of the people doing the work. Orpheus disperses power throughout the organization, giving individuals the authority to make significant decisions.

2. Encourage individual responsibility. With authority comes responsibility. Each orchestra member ensures that his or her individual performance and the group's performance is the best possible. At Orpheus, there are no supervisors to take charge of fixing problems; individuals must do so on their own.

3. Create clarity of roles and functions. Orpheus is very clear about the duties of the core group, concertmaster, and support staff. Clarity reduces unnecessary conflict and makes people accountable by identifying who is responsible for each task.

4. Share and rotate leadership. Everyone must lead in Orpheus. Players in each section routinely rotate positions, for example, so that everyone in that section takes a turn as leader.

5. Foster horizontal teamwork. Core groups are made up of individuals who play a variety of instruments.

6. Learn to listen, learn to talk. Members must learn from one another. They can only do so when every player both listens to and expresses opinions. Anyone keeping silent hurts the orchestra as a whole.

7. Seek consensus. Consensus doesn't translate into total agreement among chamber members but means achieving a "critical mass" that allows the group to go forward. If Orpheus can't reach agreement, it may consult an outside expert or take a vote. However, consensus is almost always achieved. The musicians make thousands of joint decisions every year; yet only two or three issues are divisive enough to be put to a vote.

8. Dedicate passionately to your mission. The mission of Orpheus isn't imposed from above; it is continually developed and reinforced by the players.

Discussion Questions

1. Would you like to perform with Orpheus (assuming that you had the necessary skills)? What might be frustrating for you as an orchestra member? What might be particularly rewarding?

2. Why don't other large musical groups go without conductors? What factors might hold them back?

3. In what ways is an orchestra like a company? What is its "product," for example? What business decisions must it make? What competitive and other pressures does it face?

4. Would the Orpheus model transfer to the organizations of which you are a part? Why or why not?

5. Can you think of organizations that use some or all of the Orpheus principles? What have been the results?

---

workers instead. The people on the line responded to the complaints and then took responsibility for measuring product quality. Soon these measurements led to improvements in production processes.

- *Developing ownership.* Refuse to accept responsibility for problems that can be solved by followers. Use questions to coach followers instead of providing answers. Coaching questions include:
  — "In the best of all worlds, what is great performance for your customers?"
  — "What do you want to achieve in the next two or three years?"
  — "How will you measure your performance?"
  — "What things do you need to learn in order to reach your goals?"
  — "What work experience do you need to help you learn what is needed to achieve your goals?"

- *Stimulating self-directed actions.* Decide what you do best and give your other responsibilities away. Change systems and structures so that followers are rewarded for solving their own problems and not for bringing their problems to you. Hire the best performers and fire or transfer those who aren't contributing.

Belasco and Stayer argue that the only way to master the leadership tasks described above is to learn by doing. Test these behaviors and learn from your failures. Use mistakes, fear of failure, anger, terminations, and other obstacles and setbacks as teachers. In sum: "Leading requires learning. Learning requires doing. So get on with the doing. Then study how you did it."[32]

Superleadership/Self-Leadership

Management professors Henry Sims and Charles Manz argue that the ultimate goal of leadership is empowering followers to take charge of their thoughts and behaviors. Sims and Manz use the term "superleaders" to describe those who help followers learn to lead themselves. They use the label "self-leaders" to refer to followers who act on their own.[33]

Guiding followers from dependence to independence (see box 5.7) is a process that begins with the leader modeling the desired behaviors. Followers then work under the guidance of the leader who encourages and rewards ini-

Box 5.7

Shifting Followers to Self-Leadership[34]

FROM (DEPENDENT)	TO (INDEPENDENT)
External observation	Self-observation
Assigned goals	Self-set goals
External reinforcement for task performance	Internal reinforcement plus external reinforcement for self-leadership behavior
Motivation mainly based on external compensation	Motivation also based on the "natural" rewards of the work
External criticism	Self-criticism
External problem solving	Self-problem solving
External planning	Self-planning
External task design	Self-design of tasks
Obstacle thinking	Opportunity thinking
Compliance with the organization's vision	Commitment to a vision that the follower helped to create

tiative and provides the necessary resources and training. In the final stage, followers act on their own with minimal direction from the leader.

Superleaders use three strategies to create a climate that promotes independent thought and action. (1) *Changing organizational structures.* They reconfigure roles, functions, and responsibilities to reduce hierarchy and specialization; create self-managing teams; remove layers of organizational structure; and reduce job and pay classifications. (2) *Changing organizational processes.* Superleaders redesign the way that communication and materials flow in the organization. They push decisions down to the lowest possible level, encourage teams to solve their own problems, and reengineer jobs so that followers have the responsibility for the whole project, not just part of it. (3) *Changing interpersonal communication patterns.* Effective leaders use verbal and nonverbal behaviors to build follower confidence. They listen more and command less, ask followers to solve their own problems, express confidence in employees, and compliment initiative.

According to Manz and Sims, followers can learn to lead themselves without the guidance of those in authority if they become self-disciplined, find rewards in the task, and adopt positive thought patterns. We'll illustrate these self-leadership tactics by applying them to a common classroom assignment: the term paper.

The first set of self-leadership strategies involves self-behavior modification. Most of us complete jobs we enjoy, but we often miss deadlines when tackling difficult or unpleasant tasks like research papers. To succeed we need self-discipline. Self-discipline can be fostered by deliberately taking actions that enhance our performance on challenging assignments. Goal setting is one such self-behavior modification strategy. Chances are you already engage in goal setting by keeping a to-do list or a record of upcoming assignments for class. Effective goals, whether as simple as a daily list or as complicated as a five-year plan, put specific completion dates and benchmarks in writing. Goal setting for a term paper project would mean breaking the assignment into a series of smaller sections or tasks and making up a schedule of due dates.

Seeking out opportunities to observe and evaluate your actions is the best way to determine if you're reaching your goals. Don't wait for feedback from others; instead, watch your own behavior to determine what factors raise or lower your performance. Track how frequently you carry out a desired behavior, such as going to the library or completing sections of your paper. When self-observation indicates you're achieving your objectives, reward yourself (take a break, go to a movie, fix your favorite meal). Avoid self-punishment because it focuses on past failures rather than on improvement (see the discussion of the Wallenda factor in chapter 4).

Modifying the physical environment through cueing strategies is another important self-behavior modification strategy. Eliminate those cues that undermine performance. Remove the Wii or television that would distract you from your paper, for instance. Instead, determine those conditions that encourage peak performance and build those elements into the work setting. If you write best in a quiet location, take your laptop computer to the library or work when your roommates or family members are gone. Hang around those who model good study habits. Use rehearsal strategies to prepare for particularly important communication performances like speeches, interviews, sales calls, or presenting your research paper to the rest of the class. Identify the key elements of the situation and rehearse by visualizing the setting and a successful performance. Practice out loud whenever possible.

The second set of self-leadership strategies focuses on the task itself. We achieve more when we are pulled or attracted to a project. The key is in finding enjoyment or pleasure in the job itself. Naturally rewarding activities make us feel competent and in control and contribute to our sense of purpose. When it comes to term papers, you may enjoy mastering a difficult subject, setting your own work pace for a project, or learning material that will further your career and benefit others. Focus on the rewards, not the unpleasant aspects of the task (the investment of time and energy, the difficulty of writing). The setting also plays an important role in how we feel about a task. Whenever possible, pleasurable features should be built into the work environment. Put on your favorite music when writing, for instance, or settle in to read with your favorite drink or snack.

The final set of self-leadership strategies fosters self-confidence through positive thinking. Think in terms of opportunities rather than limitations. Eliminate critical and destructive self-talk, and challenge unrealistic beliefs and assumptions. In the case of a term paper, damaging self-statements like "I can't complete this project" can be changed to "There's no reason I can't finish if I set my goals and follow my timeline." Irrational beliefs like "I must get an A on this paper or I'm a failure" can be reframed as "I'm going to give this paper my best effort, but I can't expect to excel in every situation." Use mental rehearsal as a preparation tool.

Former president Ronald Reagan provided one of the best examples of opportunity thinking when he was wounded in an assassination attempt. He tried to relieve the tension of the nation rather than focusing on his own condition. Reagan told his wife: "Honey, I forgot to duck." He pleaded with his doctors: "Please say you're Republicans." To the medical staff, he quipped: "Send me to L.A. where I can see the air I'm breathing." (Another example of an opportunity thinker can be found in box 5.8.)

> Our life is what our thoughts make it.
>
> —Marcus Aurelius

Box 5.8   Opportunity Thinking in Action
The Blind Traveler[35]

I wish to pass through, not vanquish. Do not vanquish me.

—James Holman

When it comes to opportunity thinking, few people can match James Holman (1786–1857). Holman had a promising career as an officer in the British navy, but rheumatism and blindness ended his military service when he was in his twenties. He faced a grim future. Rheumatism causes painful swelling of the joints, and the blind in Holman's time were generally seen as helpless invalids. Some who lost their sight were forced to beg while others were warehoused in asylums. Young blind men in particular were stigmatized because blindness was a marker of the latter stages of venereal disease. The affliction was seen as a sign of God's punishment.

Holman soon began to overcome physical barriers as well as social stigmas. Adopting a positive mind-set toward his new circumstances, he learned how to navigate using a walking stick to gather information through touch and sound. He also learned to write using a primitive device for writing in the dark. The retired lieutenant refused to go into seclusion or to hide his infirmity by wrapping his eyes when on the street. Instead, he strode around in public, eyes uncovered, dressed in his naval uniform. Holman then began a series of journeys that would make him internationally famous as the Blind Traveler. Traveling alone on a small pension, he made his way first through Europe, followed by trips to Russia, Africa, South America, Sri Lanka, India, China, Australia, and elsewhere. Along the way he braved a Siberian winter, helped fight the slave trade, climbed to the crater of an active volcano, and pursued rogue elephants in Ceylon. Holman became a celebrated travel writer and was elected a member of the prestigious scientific Royal Society of London. Charles Darwin cited him as an expert on the fauna of the Indian Ocean.

By the time his travels ended, the Blind Traveler had racked up at least a quarter of a million miles, reaching every continent and coming in touch with at least 200 separate cultures. He never took a railroad and only occasionally boarded a steam ship. Instead, he explored the world on foot, in carriages and carts, on horseback (he taught himself how to ride after becoming blind), and on sailing ships. Biographer Jason Roberts sums up his achievements this way: "Alone, sightless, with no prior command of native languages and with only a wisp of funds, he had forged a path equivalent to wandering to the moon."

Holman's refusal to give in to physical or societal limitations was vividly demonstrated whenever he sailed on a Royal Navy vessel during his travels. He would start the voyage by climbing the mainmast of the ship, a highly dangerous practice (banned on some vessels) called skylarking. One miscalculation of the roll of the ship and he would have died at sea. Usually only the youngest sailors attempted this feat. Holman would clamber to the highest point ("where the sway rivaled the bucking of a horse"). There he would shout and wave before descending to the deck below. Any thought that he was a fragile invalid was immediately banished from the minds of his shipmates.

CHAPTER TAKEAWAYS

- Power is defined as *the ability to influence others*. Leadership is impossible without power since a leader must modify attitudes and behaviors. Yet influencing others does not automatically qualify as leadership; power must be used in pursuit of group goals to merit leadership classification.
- *Coercive power* is based on the ability to administer punishment or to give negative reinforcements.
- *Reward power* rests on the ability to deliver something of value to others.
- *Legitimate power* resides in the position rather than in the person. People with legitimate power have the right to prescribe our behavior within specified parameters.
- *Expert power* is based on the person, not the position. Experts are influential because they supply needed information and skills.
- *Referent power* is role model power.
- Group members prefer leaders who rely on power associated with the unique characteristics of the person (expert and referent) rather than leaders who rely on power related to their position (coercion, reward, legitimate).
- A number of language features have been identified as "powerful" or "powerless" by researchers. Powerful talk makes speakers seem knowledgeable and confident; powerless talk is tentative and submissive.
- Leaders gain more power by empowering others. There are five major reasons why leaders choose to share power: (1) distributing power increases the job satisfaction and performance of employees; (2) sharing power fosters greater cooperation among group members; (3) distributing power means collective survival—the group endures rather than fails; (4) effective leadership helps personal growth and learning; and (5) sharing power prevents power abuses.
- Components of the empowerment process include modifying the environment to eliminate situational factors that create feelings of powerlessness; building intrinsic motivation though meaning, choice, competence, and impact; and supplying information and other resources.
- In the Leading the Journey empowerment model, leaders determine vision and direction, remove obstacles, develop ownership, and stimulate self-directed action.
- "Superleaders" help followers learn to lead themselves, guiding them from dependence to independence. "Self-leaders" are followers who act on their own through self-behavior modification, finding enjoyment in the task, and building self-confidence through positive thinking.

APPLICATION EXERCISES

1. Is power the last dirty word? Discuss your answer to this statement in class or in a reflection paper.

2. Create your own cost/benefit ratios for each type of power. Do you agree that leaders should strive for expert and referent power?

3. Identify the sources of power you respond to most/least favorably. Analyze the differences.

4. Develop a strategy for overcoming your powerless talk using the techniques discussed in the chapter. Report on your progress to another person in the class.

5. Brainstorm a list of strategies for eliminating environmental factors that cause powerlessness.

6. Evaluate your intrinsic task motivation as a student using the four factors described in the chapter. Share your analysis with others in the class.

7. Interview employees (leaders and followers) in an organization to determine how empowerment is/is not used effectively. Share your results with others.

8. Write a paper describing why an empowerment effort succeeded or failed based on the components and models of empowerment presented in the chapter.

9. Identify the job/situation/or context in which you have felt most/least empowered as a follower. Compare your effectiveness in these two situations.

10. Select a major task or project facing you this term (a major speech, a professional exam, getting in shape, training for a long race) and apply the self-leadership strategies described in this chapter to completing this task. Develop specific goals and determine how you will observe and evaluate your behavior, reward yourself, modify the physical environment, and rehearse. Consider the elements of the project that might be naturally rewarding and how you can think in terms of opportunities instead of limitations. Turn in your preliminary plan. At the end of the quarter or semester, after the project has been completed, reflect on your performance. Did using these tactics produce better results? How would you rate yourself as a self-leader? Record your conclusions and submit them to your instructor.

CULTURAL CONNECTIONS: A DIFFERENT VIEW ON POWER: THE SOUTH AFRICAN CONCEPT OF UBUNTU[36]

As we have discussed in this chapter, using power effectively is critical to the success of leadership. Whether power is centralized or distributed, its use or misuse has much to do with overall leadership outcomes. This becomes more complex, however, when crossing cultural boundaries. Inhabitants of different countries have sometimes radically dissimilar viewpoints on power. In some countries, such as Israel, Denmark, and New Zealand, workers often expect that power will be shared. In countries like Malaysia, India, and the Philippines, followers are generally much more willing to be directed. One country with a very unique view on power is South Africa.

Since the collapse of the oppressive apartheid system, black empowerment has been a priority. Over three-fourths of the population in South Africa is black, yet many of these indigenous people live in poverty in rural settlements outside major cities. The South African government has been working to integrate traditional black African cultural values into mainstream society. One option for development that has gained popularity embraces the traditional African concept of ubuntu. In Zulu, ubuntu roughly translates as: "a person is a person through other persons." As such, ubuntu is based on caring for the well-being of others through a spirit of mutual support and the promotion of individual and societal well-being. Ubuntu basically views an enterprise as a community of relationships that reflect group solidarity. The ubuntu philosophy of democracy is not based simply on majority rule; rather it focuses on building consensus through shared power. The ubuntu philosophy helps to create a community built on interdependent and equal participation.

This can be seen in the nearly one million South African collectives known as stokvels. These joint undertakings—savings clubs, burial societies, and other cooperatives—offer community-based services to members and are led through a process of shared decision making based on the ubuntu philosophy. Power is distributed within South African society in ways that place the good of the collective above the needs of the individual. For the stokvels, making a profit is important, but never if it involves the exploitation of others. Although similar practices are found in many other cultures, this approach would seem quite different than the view of power held by many in Western industrialized society, which often focuses on maximizing profits whatever the costs.

SPOTLIGHT ON TECHNOLOGY: THE PERSON OF THE YEAR IS YOU

Each year since 1927 *Time* magazine has selected the individual or group of individuals who have had the biggest impact on the year's news. Known as the Person of the Year, past winners have included almost all sitting U.S. presidents, various foreign heads of state, business leaders, popes, and astronauts. In 2006, *Time* made an unusual selection, naming "You" as Person of the Year. The magazine cover featured a computer monitor with a reflective image, allowing each reader to see him- or herself. The selection was a testament to the empowering nature of technology. Through the Internet individuals are empowered as never before to shape how products and services are developed, marketed, and consumed. As Jeff Howe explains, technology allows individuals to *make, name, participate, and find*.[37]

You make it. Technology allows for new forms of expression. User-generated content, media subject matter created by end users (as opposed to traditional media producers such as professional writers, publishers, journalists, licensed broadcasters, and production companies) is widespread on the Net. From YouTube to Flickr to Bloglines, the Web allows individuals to post and share creative content in ways that were not possible in the past.

You name it. The sheer mass of information online (according to Yahoo you can search over 20 billion Web pages on some 100 million Web sites) creates problems for organizing data. Sites that enable social bookmarking and collaborative tagging can be used to classify large volumes of data. Known as a "folksonomy," these networks allow individual users to personalize data to meet their needs. Folksonomic tagging is intended to make a body of information easier to search, discover, and navigate over time. One such site is del.icio.us. This site is designed to allow users to store and share bookmarks on the Web, instead of inside their browsers. Bookmarks can be accessed from anywhere—home, work, the library, or on a friend's computer. Bookmarks can be also be shared publicly, so friends, coworkers, and other people can view them for reference, amusement, collaboration, or anything else. In this way users can find other people on del.icio.us who have interesting bookmarks and add their links to their own collection.

You work on it. In the past, most work was contracted to professionals. If you needed a caterer, a wedding photographer, or a gardener, you would consult a traditional source of information like the yellow pages to find those available in your area. Today, jobs formerly performed by professionals are outsourced to groups connected by technology in a process known as "crowdsourcing." Pharmaceutical maker Eli Lilly funded the launch of a crowdsourcing site, InnoCentive, in 2001 as a way to connect with brainpower outside the company. From the outset, InnoCentive threw open the doors to other firms eager to access the network's ad hoc experts. Companies like Boeing, DuPont, and Procter & Gamble now post their most vexing scientific problems on Inno-Centive's Web site where anyone on InnoCentive's network can take a shot at cracking them. The companies—or seekers, in InnoCentive parlance—pay solvers anywhere from $10,000 to $100,000 per solution. (They also pay Inno-Centive a fee to participate.) Jill Panetta, InnoCentive's chief scientific officer, says more than 30 percent of the problems posted on the site have been cracked, "which is 30 percent more than would have been solved using a traditional, in-house approach." The solvers are not who you might expect. Many are hobbyists working from their garages, like the chemist with experience pouring concrete who came up with a way to use machinery from the concrete industry to clean up oil spills in Alaska or the patent lawyer who devised a novel way to mix large batches of chemical compounds.[38]

You find it. Even the largest brick-and-mortar stores can't afford to stock merchandise that won't sell in volume. But Web retailers can offer an endless array of obscure products. Sites like Amazon.com, Netflix, and iTunes generate revenues from customer purchases of best-selling items as well as even larger sales volume from little known products. When inventory storage and distribution costs are low, it becomes economically viable to sell relatively unpopular products. Take movie rentals as an example—a traditional movie rental store has limited shelf space, which it pays for in the form of building overhead. To maximize its profits, it must stock only the most popular movies to ensure that no shelf space is wasted. Because Netflix stocks movies in centralized warehouses, its storage costs are far lower and its distribution costs are the same for a popular or an unpopular movie. Netflix is therefore able to build a viable business stocking a far wider range of movies than a traditional movie rental store. Netflix finds that, in aggregate, "unpopular" movies are rented more than popular movies.

LEADERSHIP ON THE BIG SCREEN: *COACH CARTER*

Starring: Samuel L. Jackson, Rob Brown, Robert Ri'chard, Rick Gonzalez, Nana Gbewonyo, Ashanti

Synopsis: Samuel Jackson stars as real-life Ken Carter, a former basketball star at Richmond High School in California who returns as coach. Coach Carter must contend not only with rebellious players but also with the low academic expectations of the school and community. Few players overcome the temptations of drugs and gangs to graduate, much less go on to college. Carter uses strict discipline to turn a losing squad into one of the best teams in the region. However, winning is not enough. In a move that draws national attention, Carter locks the team out of the gym until his players pass all their classes so that they can have a chance at college careers. His efforts (and those of his players who buy in to his vision) succeed. Several team members do go on for further education.

Chapter Links: power and leadership; coercive, reward, legitimate, expert and referent power; empowerment; self-leadership

Leadership and Influence

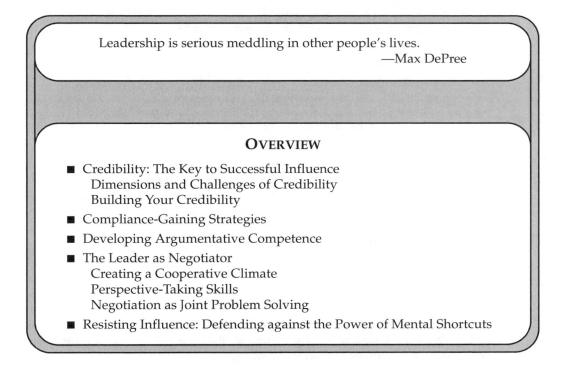

Leadership is serious meddling in other people's lives.
—Max DePree

OVERVIEW

- Credibility: The Key to Successful Influence
  Dimensions and Challenges of Credibility
  Building Your Credibility
- Compliance-Gaining Strategies
- Developing Argumentative Competence
- The Leader as Negotiator
  Creating a Cooperative Climate
  Perspective-Taking Skills
  Negotiation as Joint Problem Solving
- Resisting Influence: Defending against the Power of Mental Shortcuts

Exercising influence is the essence of leadership. Leading means influencing since leaders must shape the attitudes and behavior of others to help groups reach their goals. In the last chapter, we examined the sources and uses of power. In this chapter, we continue our discussion of influence by taking a closer look at how leaders modify the behavior of others through symbolic communication. We will focus on four sets of influence tools particularly significant to leaders: (1) credibility building behaviors, (2) compliance-gaining strategies, (3) argumentation skills, and (4) negotiation tactics. We'll conclude by examining ways to resist unethical influence attempts.

Credibility: The Key to Successful Influence

Credibility is the foundation for successful influence because the success or failure of a particular influence strategy ultimately depends on the credibility of the influencer. The results of a survey of 15,000 managers from North America, Mexico, Asia, Europe, and Australia demonstrate how important credibility is to leaders. When the managers were asked what characteristics they admired most in their leaders, the answers were forward looking, honest, inspirational, and competent. Taken together, these elements comprise what researchers label as believability or credibility.

> Above all else, people want leaders who are credible. We want to believe in our leaders. We want to have faith and confidence in them as people. We want to believe that their word can be trusted, that they have the knowledge and skill to lead, and that they are personally excited and enthusiastic about the directions in which we are headed. Credibility is the foundation of leadership.[1]

Credibility has always been central to the study of communication and leadership. The ancient Greeks studied the public speaking techniques of leaders and used the term "ethos" for what we now call credibility. For Plato, Aristotle, and others, ethos consisted of high moral standards, intelligence, and other speaker character traits.[2] An orator swayed an audience through logic (logos), emotion (pathos), and, most importantly, personal characteristics (ethos). Interest in credibility among communication scholars remains high today.[3]

The strong tie between credibility and influence is the reason why scholars have been interested in ethos through the ages. No matter what the setting, credible sources are more effective. Consider the following:

- Highly credible public speakers are more likely to convince audiences to accept their arguments. By citing credible sources, speakers build their own credibility and generate greater attitude change.[4]
- Successful counselors first earn the trust of their clients.[5]
- Salespeople are more productive if they sell themselves (build their credibility) before they sell their products.
- Editorials are more persuasive if they come from highly credible newspapers like the *New York Times* or the *Chicago Tribune*.[6]
- Trust in leadership significantly affects basketball team performance.[7]
- Juries are more swayed by credible witnesses.

> Leader credibility is the cornerstone of corporate performance and global competitiveness.
>
> —Tom Peters

Dimensions and Challenges of Credibility

Modern investigators no longer treat credibility as a set of speaker traits. Instead, they isolate factors that audiences use to evaluate the believability of speakers. The most significant elements or dimensions of credibility are *competence*, *trustworthiness*, and *dynamism*.[8]

Competence can be defined as knowledge of the topic at hand, intelligence, expertise, skill, or good judgment. The term "value-added" best describes the kind of competence that leaders need to demonstrate.[9] A leader must provide the skills that the group needs at a particular time. For example, boards of directors often look for top executives who can take their organizations in new directions. In one case, they may be looking for someone with a strong marketing or fund-raising background to increase sales or donations. In another, they may want a chief executive who knows how to cut costs or streamline operations.

Trustworthiness (Character) is another name for honesty and consistency.[10] This dimension of credibility is critical to effective leadership since the leader-follower relationship is built on trust. Managers rate honesty as the most important leader quality; the most influential public opinion leaders are also the most trustworthy. Unfortunately, the collapse of Enron, the decision of United Airlines to default on its employees' pension plan, scandals involving executive stock options, and other corporate misdeeds have undermined worker trust. Nearly half of those responding to a *USA Today* poll said that corporations can be trusted only a little, or not at all, to care for the best interests of their employees.[11] Over 40 percent of the sample believed that executives care solely about meeting their own needs.

Dynamism refers to perceptions of a source's confidence, activity, and assertiveness. Dynamic leaders communicate confidence in their visions for the future. They inspire others to work harder and to make greater sacrifices. Dynamism appears to be an integral part of what many people call charismatic leadership, a topic we discussed in detail in chapter 4.

Leaders face some special challenges when it comes to establishing and maintaining their credibility.[12] First, followers pay more attention to leaders than leaders do to followers. As a result, they are quick to note when leaders fall short. Any failure (a supervisor violating a promise, for example) is seen as evidence of the leader's poor character rather than as the product of situational factors (the supervisor may have been forced to break the commitment by top management). One negative incident can undo the goodwill built with followers over a long period of time and makes receivers more sensitive to possible future violations. Heightened scrutiny also leads to charges of inconsistency when leaders present themselves in different ways to different audiences (stockholders, customers, employees).

Second, leaders must respond to the conflicting demands of multiple constituencies. Fulfilling the expectations of one group may mean violating the expectations of another. For instance, a pledge to increase the budget of the marketing department may mean a reduction in the amount previously committed to research and development. Third, leaders often feel the pressure to treat organizational "stars" better than their peers, creating perceptions of injustice. Fourth, leaders may seek to improve performance by communicating high expectations that turn out later to be unrealistic. Fifth, following the latest management fads can lead to a gap between words and deeds because leaders start using new terminology ("empowerment," "total quality") that doesn't match reality. Finally, leaders hired solely for their technical competencies may overlook the importance of interpersonal skills like acting consistently, treating others justly, and following through on promises.

While the challenges of building leadership credibility are great, so are the rewards for doing so. Followers who believe that their leaders are trustworthy, for example, are more satisfied with their jobs as well as more committed to their organizations. These followers are more willing to help out coworkers and to treat others with respect. They are also more supportive of organizational decisions and receive higher performance evaluations.[13] (We'll take a closer look at the importance of building a trusting organizational culture in chapter 8.)

> A single lie destroys a whole reputation for integrity.
> —Baltasar Gracian

Building Your Credibility

Discovering how others assess your competence, trustworthiness, and dynamism is an excellent way to start building your credibility as a leader. Rate yourself on the credibility scales found in the first application exercise on p. 194 in this chapter. Then ask someone else to rate you and compare the responses. You will probably rank higher on one dimension of credibility than on others. In addition, your self-ratings might be either above or below the ratings you receive from your partner. Once you've targeted the dimension(s) of credibility most in need of improvement, you can start to change your behaviors in order to generate more favorable impressions. In chapter 1, we called this process impression management. The following sets of behaviors are particularly effective in managing perceptions of credibility. These tactics boost your credibility by increasing your perceived similarity with observers and linking you to groups that have reputations for competence and integrity.[14]

Self-presentation behaviors. Use statements that reveal that you are "human" with similar emotions, limitations, and experiences as your audience. Distance yourself from untrustworthy groups by pointing out how dissimilar you are to them. For example: you are *not* a manager who follows the latest management fads or you are *not* like other salespeople who will lie to sell their products. Introduce your qualifications (job title, experience, research) to address the issue at hand. Identify your credentials at or near the beginning of messages to have the greatest impact.[15] However, your message can change attitudes and behavior even if you don't have impressive qualifications. According to the "sleeper effect," the source is forgotten as time passes, but the message is remembered and judged on its own merits. If the ideas you introduce are well-crafted and supported (see the discussion of argumentation to follow), they may be adopted later.[16]

Language. Avoid technical, jargon-laced language that will distance you from your audience and may give the impression that you are hiding behind the terminology because you don't really understand the topic. Use common, clear, and understandable terms.

Physical appearance and other nonverbal behaviors. Dress appropriately for your profession; choose a style similar to that of your audience; reject clothing or accessories that might match negative stereotypes. For instance, avoid darkly tinted glasses or sunglasses. The stereotype holds that untrustworthy people wear dark eyeglasses. Since the endomorphic (round) body type is perceptually linked with low self-confidence and low competence, wear neutral colors rather than bright colors if weight is a problem. Bright colors draw attention to body size while neutral colors do not. In addition:[17]

- Make sustained eye contact when communicating with others. Avoid shifting your eyes, looking away, keeping your eyes downcast, or excessive blinking.

- Use gestures to add emphasis to the points that you make. Try to appear spontaneous and unrehearsed; let your gestures convey the depth or intensity of your emotions. Hand wringing, finger tapping, tugging at clothing, and tentative movements undermine credibility.

- Maintain a relaxed, open posture when talking with others. Lean forward and smile when answering a question in order to establish rapport. Change your posture frequently and forcefully to communicate responsiveness. Try to avoid those behaviors that make you look timid or non-assertive—holding your body rigid, keeping arms and hands crossed and close to the body, and so on.

- Pay attention to your voice. Strive to sound confident by using a conversational speaking style and vary your rate, pitch, and volume. Sounding nasal, tense, or flat can make you appear significantly less credible. In addition, frequent pauses, speaking too rapidly, repeating words, and stuttering have a negative impact on credibility.

Modifying behaviors to make the desired impression on others is the first step to building your credibility. However, our credibility as leaders also depends on the quality of the relationships we maintain with followers. Ellen Whitener and her colleagues identify five sets of behaviors that foster perceptions of trustworthiness in manager-employee relationships.[18] These include: (1) *Behavioral consistency.* Acting consistently over time and in a variety of situations makes it easier for followers to predict your behavior and to take risks. (2) *Behavioral integrity.* Match what you say and do, particularly by telling the truth and keeping promises. (3) *Sharing and delegation of control.* Inviting participation in decision making enables employees to protect their interests, reduces the likelihood that you will take advantage of the situation, and signals trust and respect for their worth and standing in the organization. (4) *Communication.* Provide accurate information, supply explanations for decisions, and reveal your openness through sharing your thoughts and feelings. (5) *Demonstration of concern.* Reflect your concern for followers by focusing on their needs and interests, protecting their rights, and refusing to take advantage of them (i.e., keep confidences, give credit to others).

James Kouzes and Barry Posner emphasize that perceptions of all three dimensions of credibility build over time. They outline the following credibility building practices that are effective in the long term.[19]

Discovering yourself. Identify your values in order to lay the foundation for consistent behavior. As we noted in chapter 4, values represent what we consider to be important. They also serve as principles or standards by which we evaluate our actions and the actions of others. Writing your personal credo or leadership philosophy is a way to clarify what you believe. To develop your credo, imagine that you'll be going on a six-month sabbatical to a location where you cannot be reached by phone, letter, fax, or e-mail. Write a short memo before you go in which you identify the values and beliefs you think should guide the decision making and actions of colleagues when you're gone. (Turn to application exercise 2 on pp. 194–195 for a complete description of this project.)

Increasing skills and confidence. A well-defined leadership philosophy is not sufficient in and of itself. You must also possess the necessary skills or competencies to put your beliefs into action and have the confidence to do so. Skill and confidence levels can be built by taking classes or training seminars, reading, mastering current tasks and adding new ones, following effective role models, and seeking support from others.

Appreciating constituents. Credible leaders have a deep understanding of the values, needs, and beliefs of constituents. In particular, they appreciate the perspectives of an increasingly diverse workplace (see chapter 10 for a discussion of leading diversity). To cultivate an in-depth understanding of followers, listen (visit the sales force, hold feedback sessions, call customers), be willing to learn from others, solicit feedback from superiors and subordinates, encourage dissent or controversy about ideas, and put your trust in others at the same time you live up to the trust they put in you.

Affirming shared values. Kouzes and Posner refer to shared values as the "common language with which we can collaborate." Speaking this common language increases job satisfaction, promotes unity, encourages loyalty, enables individuals to make decisions on their own, and increases productivity. We've already seen how important it is for a leader to have a clear set of personal values. However, you must not unilaterally impose your values on others. Instead, work together with followers through discussion groups and other forums to develop shared values statements. Additional ways to encourage shared beliefs and actions include advocating cooperation; assigning projects that require individuals to work together to achieve success; and developing hiring procedures, orientation programs, and other organizational structures that highlight organizational values.

Developing capacity. Like leaders, followers need to develop skills and self-confidence to put their beliefs into action. You can help constituents increase their capacity by (1) providing educational opportunities, (2) giving followers the latitude and authority to make significant decisions, and (3) helping followers believe in their own abilities (for a discussion of empowerment strategies, turn to chapter 5). The most credible leaders create a climate where risk taking is encouraged, and they promote an atmosphere of sharing information.

Serving a purpose. Serving a purpose refers to creating a sense of direction for the group. Leaders can communicate direction by:

- *going first.* Demonstrate commitment by taking the initial step, like being the first to volunteer to work overtime to get a product out on schedule.

- *staying in touch.* Maintain daily, personal contact with constituents.

- *making meaning on a daily basis.* Send consistent messages about attitudes and values through how you respond to routine events like interruptions, stress, meetings, and complaints.

- *teaching during moments of learning.* In the life of any group there are key moments called critical incidents that test the credibility of leaders and teach important lessons. To pass these tests, you must act on your principles, often at a significant cost. For instance, if as a shift manager you say that quality comes first, then you must let line workers reject products that are substandard even if such rejections lower production numbers and threaten your bonus.

- *storytelling.* Stories are vivid reminders of what the group or organization thinks is important.

- *handling failure and the loss of credibility.* Every leader, no matter how conscientious or successful, will fail on occasion. The effects of such failures do not have to be permanent, however. Restoring your credibility involves the six "As" of leadership accountability: accept responsibility, admit mistakes, apologize, take immediate remedial action, make amends or reparation (you should share in any penalty for the mistake), and pay close attention to the reactions of followers. (More information on trust repair can be found in chapter 8.)

- *establishing systems.* Rewards, team meetings, performance reviews, presentations, and other organizational practices should be designed to help you create a sense of institutional purpose.

> Example is not the main thing in influencing others. It is the only thing.
>
> —Albert Schweitzer

Sustaining hope. Leaders play a critical role in boosting the spirits of followers in a world marked by rapid change. As employees at Compaq Computer, Sharper Image, and Intel have discovered, organizations are vulnerable to new competitors and technologies, mergers, government deregulation, and other changes. If you want to keep hope alive in an uncertain economic and social climate, you must demonstrate optimism, inspiration, and supportiveness. Optimistic leaders believe that the future offers many opportunities for success and take the necessary steps to see that they achieve their goals. They treat failures as temporary setbacks that are out of their control (see chapter 4). When things go wrong, optimists don't blame themselves or followers. Instead, they take steps to reduce the likelihood of failure in the future. Inspirational leaders share in the suffering of followers. Their salaries and benefits are frozen along with those of other employees when company earnings drop, for example. Supportive leaders show genuine concern for others by listening to their problems, offering words of encouragement, and helping out when needed.

Compliance-Gaining Strategies

Compliance-gaining strategies are the verbal tactics that leaders and others use to get their way in face-to-face encounters. These strategies are based on the types of power we described in chapter 5. Attempts to get others to do what we want are a frequent occurrence in everyday life. Requesting notes from a classmate, convincing a friend to take a cab rather than driving home drunk from a party, enlisting volunteers for a fund drive, and persuading a neighbor to keep her dog chained up are all examples of interpersonal compliance-gaining situations.

John Hunter, Franklin Boster, and others suggest that persuaders in interpersonal settings select and reject compliance-gaining strategies based on the impact they have on the emotional state of both the compliance seeker and the target of the request.[20] Compliance gainers prefer "friendly persuasion"—messages that put both parties in a positive frame of mind.[21] Tactics that produce a positive emotional climate are:

- *Supporting evidence.* Giving reasons why the target of the request should comply (arguments, evidence, appeals to rules, fairness, tradition, etc.)

- *Other benefit.* Emphasizing how the target of the request will benefit by complying with the request ("You'll feel good about yourself if you help in the cleanup project on Saturday.")

- *Exchange.* Offering to trade or exchange things of value like favors, money, and services

- *Referent influence.* Appealing to how much the target and actor (persuader) have in common ("We both need to pass this course, so why don't we study together.")

Strategies likely to generate negative feelings include deceit, coercion, and making the target feel guilty, sad, or selfish for not going along.

In chapter 5 we developed a cost/benefit ratio for each of the five types of power. The same approach can be used to determine the best compliance-gaining strategy for an interpersonal situation. Conduct an emotional cost/benefit analysis when choosing a compliance-gaining strategy. Whenever possible, select the strategy that is most likely to generate positive feelings for both you and the target of your request.

Organizational compliance seekers face a number of constraints not present in the interpersonal context. First, they have less freedom to decide whether or not to engage in persuasion. Middle managers and supervisors must influence others if they are to perform their roles. Second, the statuses of both the compliance seeker and the target of the request in an organization are clearly defined. Third, organizational influence agents aren't free to pursue their personal goals only; they must direct most of their efforts at achieving organizational objectives like increasing productivity, reducing tardiness, and improving service. Fourth, the rules and culture of the organization may favor some influence methods while discouraging others.

Since 1980 researchers have tried to determine how, given the constraints described above, managers influence others at work. David Kipnis, Stuart Schmidt, and their colleagues found that managers are most likely to use reason and the support of coworkers when approaching superiors.[22] Making direct demands or appealing to a higher authority are the least popular strategies. When influencing subordinates, managers also rely heavily on reason, but they are much more likely to be direct and forceful (insisting, setting timelines, etc.). The relative power of the compliance seeker and the target of the request often determines the strategy selected. Kipnis and Schmidt speculate that there is an "Iron Law of Power" that dictates that the greater the difference in power between the influencer and the target of the request, the greater the probability that directive strategies will be used. Large power differences tempt managers to use coercive tactics with subordinates even when positive strategies could be more appropriate.

Kipnis and Schmidt also found that managers have different influence profiles. Shotgun managers, generally those with the least experience, make indiscriminate use of all types of influence strategies to achieve their goals. Tactician managers rely heavily on reason but revert to other tactics when needed. They usually have the most expert power in the organization and are the most satisfied and successful. Bystander managers make fewer compliance-gaining attempts and exercise less organizational influence. Based on their findings, the researchers argue that successful organizational leaders (those who fit the tactician profile) take a careful, rational, and flexible approach to influencing superiors and subordinates. Rather than employ any tactic that comes to mind, they carefully consider which strategy to use. Effective leaders prefer reason (which, like the use of supportive evidence in the interpersonal context, helps to promote a positive emotional climate), but they shift tactics when appropriate.

While Kipnis and Schmidt were the first scholars to take an in-depth look at compliance gaining in organizations, Gary Yukl of the State University of New York at Albany has directed what is perhaps the most extensive research program. Yukl and his associates identified the following common managerial influence tactics.[23]

- *Rational persuasion.* Use of logical arguments and factual evidence to demonstrate that a request or proposal will attain organizational objectives

- *Apprising.* Explaining how compliance will benefit the target and his/her career

- *Inspirational appeals.* Generating enthusiasm by appealing to values and ideals; arousing emotions
- *Consultation.* Seeking suggestions for improvement; asking for input for planning an activity, strategy, or change
- *Collaboration.* Providing resources and assistance if the target complies
- *Ingratiation.* Use of flattery and praise before or during a request; expressing confidence in the target's ability to fulfill a difficult request
- *Personal appeals.* Appealing to feelings of loyalty and friendship when asking for something
- *Exchange.* Trading favors; promising to reciprocate later or to share the benefits when the task is completed
- *Coalition tactics.* Soliciting the aid of others or using the support of coworkers to convince the target to go along
- *Legitimating tactics.* Claiming the right or authority to make a request; aligning the request with organizational policies, rules, traditions, etc.
- *Pressure.* Demanding, threatening, checking up; persistent reminders

In evaluating the effectiveness of individual managerial influence tactics, Yukl concludes that any given strategy is more likely to be successful if: (1) the target perceives the influence attempt as socially acceptable; (2) the influencer has the position and personal power to use the tactic; (3) the strategy makes the request seem more desirable to the target; (4) the tactic is used skillfully; and (5) the request is legitimate and doesn't violate the needs and values of the recipient.[24] Rational persuasion, consultation, collaboration, and inspirational appeals are most likely to generate commitment to the task, whether the target is a superior, peer, or subordinate. Ingratiation, exchange, and apprising are moderately effective with subordinates and peers but not with superiors. Personal appeals secure compliance in friendly relationships. A coalition can encourage support for a major organizational change but may be seen as ganging up on a target when used to convince someone to carry out an assignment or to improve her or his performance. Pressure and legitimating tactics gain compliance at the expense of long-term commitment.

Combinations of tactics also vary in effectiveness. "Soft tactics" (rational persuasion, apprising, consultation, ingratiation, inspirational appeals) work better when combined than when used alone. Combining a soft tactic with supporting evidence generally increases the chances of success. However, there is no similar cumulative impact for hard tactics. Using several hard tactics in a compliance-gaining attempt is no more effective than using just one. Further, mixing incompatible strategies (i.e., pressuring someone while asking him or her to do a favor based on loyalty or friendship) can derail a request.

Yukl reminds us that we can't take effective influence for granted. Subjects in his studies report many examples of when they originated or received "inept influence attempts."[25] Managers may combine incompatible tactics, make clumsy attempts at being helpful or friendly, fail to recruit allies, try to gain compliance for an improper or unethical request, and so forth. One common mistake is using hard tactics when softer ones would have been more successful.

> The humblest individual exerts some influence, either for good or evil, upon others.
>
> —Henry Ward Beecher

Developing Argumentative Competence

When two or more people take different sides on a controversial issue like stem cell research or how to fund local schools, they generally try to establish the superiority of their positions through argument. To be successful, arguers must build a strong case for their positions while simultaneously refuting the arguments of those who take other positions. The introduction of controversy and dialogue sets argumentation apart from compliance-gaining strategies, which also rely on reason and evidence. Compliance gainers may provide evidence even when there is no significant disagreement, and compliance-gaining messages often take only a few seconds to deliver. Argumentation always involves controversy and extended discussion.

Argumentation is important to leaders at every level. In small groups, argumentative individuals are more likely to emerge as leaders, and groups that argue about ideas generate higher quality solutions.[26] In organizations, supervisors must defend their own ideas and argue on behalf of subordinates.[27] In the public arena, political leaders, public relations specialists, or social activists engage in argument to support new government regulations, promote industry interests, or defend the rights of disadvantaged groups. (Complete the argumentativeness scale in box 6.1 to determine how likely you are to engage in arguments.)

While argumentation is an essential leadership activity, many of us view arguments with suspicion. Although you have probably had enjoyable arguments that stimulated your thinking, chances are you've also been in unpleasant arguments that resulted in hurt feelings and broken relationships. The key to understanding the mix of good and bad experiences we've had while arguing lies in distinguishing between argumentativeness and verbal aggression.[28] Argumentativeness involves presenting and defending positions on issues. Verbal aggressiveness is hostile communication aimed at attacking the self-concepts of others instead of (or in addition to) their positions on the issues.

Aggressive tactics include:

- *Character attacks*
- *Background attacks*
- *Insults*
- *Teasing*
- *Ridicule*
- *Profanity*
- *Threats*
- *Competence attacks*
- *Physical appearance attacks*
- *Nonverbal indicators that express hostility* (looks of disgust, clenched fists, rolling eyes, demeaning tone of voice

If our arguments have been unpleasant, it is probably because one or both parties engaged in verbal aggression. Verbally aggressive communication is

Box 6.1   Self-Assessment

Argumentativeness Scale[29]

Instructions: This questionnaire contains statements about arguing controversial issues. Indicate how often each statement is true for you personally by placing the appropriate number in the blank to the left of the statement. If the statement is almost never true for you, place a "1" in the blank. If the statement is rarely true for you, place a "2" in the blank. If the statement is occasionally true for you, place a "3" in the blank. If the statement is often true for you, place a "4" in the blank. If the statement is almost always true for you, place a "5" in the blank.

_____   1. While in an argument, I worry that the person with whom I am arguing will form a negative impression of me.

_____   2. Arguing over controversial issues improves my intelligence.

_____   3. I enjoy avoiding arguments.

_____   4. I am energetic and enthusiastic when I argue.

_____   5. Once I finish an argument I promise myself that I will not get into another.

_____   6. Arguing with a person creates more problems for me than it solves.

_____   7. I have a pleasant, good feeling when I win a point in an argument.

_____   8. When I finish arguing with someone I feel nervous and upset.

_____   9. I enjoy a good argument over a controversial issue.

_____ 10. I get an unpleasant feeling when I realize I am about to get into an argument.

_____ 11. I enjoy defending my point of view on an issue.

_____ 12. I am happy when I keep an argument from happening.

_____ 13. I do not like to miss the opportunity to argue a controversial issue.

_____ 14. I prefer being with people who rarely disagree with me.

_____ 15. I consider an argument an exciting intellectual challenge.

_____ 16. I find myself unable to think of effective points during an argument.

_____ 17. I feel refreshed and satisfied after an argument on a controversial issue.

_____ 18. I have the ability to do well in an argument.

_____ 19. I try to avoid getting into arguments.

_____ 20. I feel excitement when I expect that a conversation I am in is leading to an argument.

Argumentativeness Scoring:

1. Add your scores on items: 2, 4, 7, 9, 11, 13, 15, 17, 18, 20.

2. Add 60 to the sum obtained in step 1.

3. Add your scores on items: 1, 3, 5, 6, 8, 10, 12, 14, 16, 19.

4. To compute your argumentativeness score, subtract the total obtained in step 3 from the total obtained in step 2.

Interpretation:

73–100 = High in Argumentativeness

56–72 = Moderate in Argumentativeness

20–55 = Low in Argumentativeness

destructive. Such behavior has been linked to spousal abuse and family violence, for example, and reduces student learning and instructor credibility. In contrast, argumentativeness produces a variety of positive outcomes. Organizational followers prefer to work for supervisors who are argumentative but not aggressive, and such leaders have higher salaries and career satisfaction. Organizational leaders favor followers who have similar traits, giving argumentative (but not aggressive) subordinates higher performance reviews.[30]

Recognizing the difference between argument and aggression is the first step to building our argumentative competence.[31] We may need to jettison our negative images of the term argument and recognize its positive features. We must avoid the aggressive behaviors listed above and sharpen our argumentation skills instead. Dominic Infante outlines five skills that, collectively, constitute argumentative competence: stating the controversy in propositional form; inventing arguments; presenting and defending your position; attacking other positions; and managing interpersonal relations.[32]

Stating the controversy in propositional form. Productive arguments begin with a clear understanding of the argumentative situation. Stating the problem in the form of a proposition or proposal is the best way to clarify what the conflict is about. Propositions of fact deal with what happened in the past ("The college grew in the 1990s largely due to its president's leadership."), the present ("Enrollment is down due to higher tuition."), or future ("Unless the college cuts its rate of tuition increase, it will be in financial trouble within five years."). Propositions of value deal with issues of rightness or wrongness: "It's unethical to lay off employees when profits are rising"; "Everyone ought to do their part on the group project." Propositions of policy are concerned with what course of action should be taken, such as how to reduce the number of homeless people in a city or how to market a new financial service. By framing an argument in the form of a proposal, we identify the sides that people are likely to take on the issue, clarify where we stand, and determine who has the burden of proof. Those who favor a proposition must demonstrate that the status quo ought to be changed.

Inventing arguments. Careful examination of the proposition is the key to developing a case either for or against the proposal. The set of questions in box 6.2 can help us analyze controversies systematically. To illustrate how this system works, we'll use the example of a student government faced with the following proposition: "Student activity fees should be increased to help pay for a new fitness center on campus." Proponents of this idea might argue that long waiting lists for racquetball courts, weight rooms, gyms, and physical education classes are signs that current facilities are too small. Overcrowding means that students can't exercise when they want and can't get the classes they need for graduation (specific harm). The problem appears widespread because of the large number of students who express frustration with the current situation.

In answering questions related to blame and possible solutions, proponents might conclude that the problem of overcrowding stems from the fact that student enrollment has outgrown current facilities. A change is in order because current facilities are inadequate (sub-issues b and c). More efficient scheduling and sharing community facilities might help relieve some of the pressure, but the best solution appears to be to build a new, larger building on

Box 6.2

Inventional System[33]

Major Issues and Sub-Issues:

1. Problem
   a. What are the signs of a problem?
   b. What is the specific harm?
   c. How widespread is the harm?

2. Blame
   a. What causes the problem?
   b. Is the present system at fault?
   c. Should the present system be changed?

3. Solution
   a. What are the possible solutions?
   b. Which solution best solves the problem?

4. Consequences
   a. What good outcomes will result from the solution?
   b. What bad outcomes will result from the solution?

campus. Since the college does not currently have enough money to build the center, student activity fees must be raised to pay for the project.

Possible positive outcomes or consequences of using fees for the building include more health and human performance classes, an expanded intramural program, additional recreational opportunities, and a higher level of fitness on campus. These positive benefits, proponents might suggest, should outweigh the negative consequence—having to pay higher fees.

Those who oppose the idea of using student fees to pay for a new fitness center could use the same set of questions to generate arguments for opposing the project (the problem does not affect that many students, other solutions can be found, the hardship caused by the additional fees would outweigh any benefits, etc.).

Presenting and defending your position. Most arguments involve four parts—claim, evidence, reasons, and summary. Begin by stating what you want others to accept—the conclusion or claim of your argument. Provide evidence in the form of statistics, examples, or testimonials from others and supply reasons or logic for taking your position. Common patterns of logic include: (1) inductive (generalizing from one or a few cases to many), (2) deductive (moving from a larger category to a smaller one), (3) causal (one event causes another), and (4) analogical (argument based on similarities). All four types of reasoning could be used in the fitness center argument. If you supported this idea, you could argue that the frustration experienced by some students is typical of the student body at large (inductive), that most colleges have developed new fitness facilities in the past 10 years (deductive), that building a new fitness center will improve student retention (causal), or that billing students for a new fitness center worked well for a similar college in the next town (analogical). End your presentation with a summary that shows what you've established. Be prepared to supplement your position with further evidence and reason once it comes under attack.

Attacking other positions. This argumentative skill is based on identifying weaknesses in the evidence and reasoning of the other party. Questions to ask when attacking evidence include: Is the evidence recent enough? Was enough evidence presented, and was it from reliable sources? Is the evidence consistent with known facts? Can it be interpreted in other ways, and is it relevant to the claim of the argument? Look for these common fallacies or errors when evaluating reasoning.[34]

- *False analogy.* The differences in the two items being compared outweigh their similarities.

- *Hasty generalization.* Drawing conclusions based on a sample that is (a) too small or (b) isn't typical of the group as a whole.

- *False cause.* Assuming that one event caused another just because it happened first, or using only one cause to explain a complex problem like illegal immigration or international terrorism.

- *Slippery slope.* Assuming that an event (outlawing the use of torture on suspected terrorists) is the first in a series of steps that will inevitably lead to a bad outcome (more terrorist attacks). No proof is offered for the claim that the subsequent events will actually take place.

- *Begging the question (Circular Reasoning).* Using the premise of the argument to support the claim instead of bringing in outside evidence. (For example: "Tom Cruise is popular because he is a movie star.")

- *Non-sequitur ("It Does Not Follow").* The evidence doesn't support the arguer's claim.

- *Misdirection.* Diverting attention from the central argument to an irrelevant argument. This includes attacking the opponent instead of his/her position, appealing to popular opinion or tradition, and destroying a weak or false version of an opponent's case (a "straw" or "strawperson" argument).

- *Equivocation.* Exploiting the fact that a word has more than one meaning to generate a false conclusion. Television ads for indoor air filters, steak knives, and juicers often promise to include an extra "free" item if we call now. "Free" for the consumer means without cost. However, in this case, the cost of the additional item is already built into the original price and the buyer ends up paying for both products.

- *Amphiboly.* Using grammatical structure to mislead or confuse. For example: "Our product is new and improved." There is no basis of comparison offered in this claim. Is the current product better than previous versions or better than other brands?

- *Emotive language.* Selecting words that generate positive ("innovative," "captivating," "luxurious") or negative ("outdated," "dull," "cheap") emotional images and associations that undermine the ability to judge proof and reasoning.

Managing interpersonal relations. There are a number of tactics that can be used to keep an argument from deteriorating into verbal aggression. When others are not as skilled in argument as you, don't humiliate them by showing off your argumentative skills. Save your best efforts for those times when you are matched with someone of equal ability. Reaffirm the sense of competence of other participants through appropriate complements ("Though I don't agree, I can see that you've studied this issue thoroughly."). Emphasize what you have in common and show that you're interested in their views. Let your opponents finish what they're saying instead of interrupting, and deliver your messages in a calm voice at a deliberate pace. If opponents become verbally aggressive, you can point out the differences between argument and verbal aggression, ask them to focus on the point of controversy, or appeal to them to act in a rational manner. You may need to leave if these tactics fail. As a general rule of thumb, never respond to verbal aggression with aggressive tactics of your own.

The Leader as Negotiator

Like argumentation, negotiation comes into play when leaders must influence those who actively disagree with them. However, while the goal of argumentation is to establish the relative superiority of one position over another, the goal of negotiation is to reach a conclusion that is satisfying to both sides. Negotiation consists of back-and-forth communication aimed at reaching a joint decision when people are in disagreement. A mix of compatible and incompatible interests marks all negotiation situations. Negotiators must have some common goal or they wouldn't negotiate. On the other hand, at least one issue must divide them or they wouldn't need to negotiate to reach an agreement. Consider the relationship between members of the production and marketing departments. Although both share a common interest in seeing company sales increase, marketing wants fast product turnaround to capture a new market; production wants to minimize costs while maintaining quality. These departments must resolve their differences through negotiation in order to be successful. Similar disagreements can be found in small groups. Everyone working in your class project group probably wants a high grade. However, some group members may prefer to spend their time relaxing or studying for other classes instead of meeting with the group or gathering research. The amount of work each member does for the group then becomes a matter for negotiation.

> The very essence of all power to influence lies in getting the other person to participate.
> —Harry A. Overstreet

The significance of negotiation to leading becomes particularly apparent when a leader introduces change. Take the case of a law originating in the House of Representatives. The author of the legislation may have to negotiate for cosponsors and then negotiate passage through one or more committees and the House. Once the bill passes, any differences in the House version of the bill must be reconciled with the Senate's version in another committee. Changes must be ratified by both bodies before the bill goes to the president, who may or may not sign the legislation. A presidential veto may mean further negotiations as the House and Senate try to enact the bill without a presidential signature. To complicate matters, this whole process takes place under the scrutiny of special interest groups, the media, and the public—all of whom may try to negotiate their own changes to the bill.

Creating a Cooperative Climate

Our discussion of compliance gaining and argumentation emphasized the activities of the persuader. The outcome of the negotiation process depends on the *joint* efforts of the parties involved. As we indicated earlier, negotiators have compatible and incompatible goals. Since they have both similar and different interests, the two parties simultaneously possess the incentive to cooperate and to compete. Participants must foster cooperation and reduce competition if they are to reach a mutually satisfying solution. According to conflict expert Morton Deutsch, there are sharp differences between cooperative and competitive negotiation climates:[35]

Cooperation	Competition
Open and honest communication	Very little communication; messages often negative and misleading
An emphasis on similarities	An emphasis on differences
Trusting, friendly attitudes	Suspicion, hostility
Mutual problem solving	One party wins over the other
Reduction of conflicting interests	Escalation of conflict and negative emotions

Those who want others to cooperate act in a cooperative manner. Conversely, those who compete meet resistance. Both cooperation and competition get "locked in" to a negotiation relationship at an early stage and persist throughout the negotiation process.[36] One way to foster cooperation is by using the Tit for Tat strategy. The three rules of Tit for Tat are (1) be nice, (2) respond to provocation, and (3) be forgiving. Begin the negotiation by offering to cooperate. If the other negotiator tries to take advantage of you, respond in kind. When he or she switches to a cooperative approach, begin to cooperate again.[37] Promises and concessions are two ways to signal that you are willing to cooperate. Offer to share important information, for example, or back away from one of your initial demands. If the other party responds in kind, make further concessions. However, if the other party does not match your concession, he or she may be looking to compete rather than to cooperate. In this case, follow the rules of the Tit for Tat strategy and make no further concessions until the other negotiator becomes more conciliatory.

To prevent being taken advantage of, it helps to know some of the common destructive tactics used by competitive negotiators. Some common deceptive tactics that promote competition rather than collaboration include:[38]

- *Good cop/bad cop.* This is a variation of interrogation techniques portrayed on *Law & Order* and other police shows. The good cop is friendly and cooperative, while the other is tough and demanding. The temptation is to offer more information and concessions than you should to the "good" negotiator. A variation of this approach is the good cop asking for concessions that he or she can offer to his or her unreasonable partner.
- *Bad-faith negotiation.* The other party states that he or she is willing to collaborate but is really just stalling for time or looking for more information to use against you later. The negotiator may also try to reopen discussion on earlier points of agreement in hopes of getting greater concessions. You may yield based on the belief that you have come too far to back out now.
- *Lack of authority.* Your counterpart claims that a third party who doesn't participate in the discussion must approve agreements. This technique is common at auto dealerships where salespeople turn to the sales manager for approval. The third party often overrules or changes the agreement, bringing pressure to bear to complete the negotiation.
- *Inaccurate data.* Information supplied by the other negotiator may be inaccurate, deceptive, or incomplete, putting you at a serious disadvantage.
- *Many for one.* This tactic rests on the norm of reciprocity (to be discussed in more detail later in the chapter). The other party makes small concessions early in the negotiations only to ask for large, important concessions from you near the end of the talks.
- *Information overload.* The other negotiator tries to overload you by providing a flood of data. This mass of information may be intimidating (there is too much to read and understand); can be used to stall talks or manipulate them; and may hide errors and distortions.

To cope with these strategies, be firm but reasonable. Identify the tactic being used and warn the other party that such deceptive strategies may undermine any hope of reaching an agreement. State that you'll keep talking as long as he or she appears to be genuinely interested in reaching a mutually satisfying solution.

Perspective-Taking Skills

Understanding the other negotiator's perspective is a valuable leadership skill. A negotiator with high perspective-taking ability anticipates the goals and expectations of the other party. He/she can encourage concessions that lead to agreement. Perspective taking reduces the defensiveness of the other negotiator and makes him/her more conciliatory. The result is faster, more effective negotiations.[39] However, trying to see the other person's point of view in a negotiation is difficult for these reasons:

- strong emotions, such as anger, may be aroused;
- both parties may be highly committed to their positions;
- negotiators may have significantly different values, beliefs, and experiences; and

- interactants may be unequal in power, which increases uncertainty about how the other person will respond.

Perspective taking begins before any actual negotiation. Start by gathering information about the issues and individuals involved in the future negotiation. For example, if you want to negotiate for more funding for your organization from the student government, find out the amount of money available, past grants to your group and other campus organizations, the interests of those serving on the funding committee, and other relevant facts.

It is also important to identify the negotiating style of the other party. Interpersonally oriented negotiators are sensitive to relational aspects of the negotiation. They want to get to know the other negotiator before they do business. (See box 6.3 for one example of highly interpersonal-oriented negotiators in action.) In contrast, high task negotiators do not want coffee, doughnuts, or small talk; they want to attack the issues right away. Cooperative negotiators have an interest in others, while competitive bargainers only seek benefits for themselves. Knowing where the other party falls on these orientations can help you target your approach more effectively. A high task/competitive negotiator will want to focus solely on task issues and may try to intimidate you at first. A cooperative/high interpersonal/high task bargainer will expect you to be enthusiastic and highly involved.[40]

Box 6.3

Interpersonally Oriented Negotiation in Action[41]

I had a client in West Virginia who bought from me for several years. He had a family business that he'd started in a small town with his grandfather, and it had now grown to be the major employer in the town. We had developed quite a close relationship. Every few months, I would make a trip up from North Carolina to see him, knowing after a while that he would need to place an order with me as long as I spaced our visits out every few months. When we got together, at first we would talk about everything but business, catching up with each other. I would ask him about his life, the business, his family, the town, etc., and he would ask me about my work and the company and life in the big city in North Carolina where I lived and worked. Once we'd caught up with each other, we would get down to some business, and this was often after lunch. Each and every time, it would take a few hours of this and that, but I'd always leave with an order, and it was always a pleasant break, at least for me, from my usual hectic pace.

One day I phoned in preparation for my next trip to see if he would be in, and he told me that he'd like me to meet a friend of his the next time I was up there to visit him. His friend, he said, was interested in some of the things my company was selling, and he thought I should meet him. Of course I was delighted, and we arranged a convenient day for the three of us to meet.

When I arrived at my client's office, his friend, Carl, was already there. We were very casually introduced, and my client began explaining Carl's work, and how he thought what my company sold could be useful to him. Carl then took over and spoke a little about what he did, and I thought for a moment that we were going to go straight into business talk. However, in just a few moments, the conversation between the three of us quickly turned back to discussions of life in town, North Carolina, our respective families, and personal interests. It turned out that Carl liked to hunt, and he and my client began regaling me with stories of their hunting adventures. I'd

(continued)

hunted a little and shared my stories with them. One thing led to another and soon we were talking about vacations, the economy, baseball—you name it.

Occasionally, we would make a brief journey back to the business at hand, but it always seemed to be in conjunction with the small talk, like how the tools we manufactured were or were not as precise as the mechanisms on the guns we used for hunting, things like that. I realized that quite a lot of information about our mutual work, my company, their needs, and their work, was being exchanged in all this, even though business was never directly addressed. I remember the first few meetings my client and I had had with each other many years ago—how we learned about each other this way then, too. I was struck with how quaint it felt now, how different it was from the way I usually had to sell, and yet how much I enjoyed working like this!

Well, our discussions went on this way through the rest of the morning, weaving some business back and forth through the larger context of informal chitchat about each other and our lives. Just before lunch, my client leaned back and began what seemed to be a kind of informal summary of who I was and what I did, and how what I did seemed to be just the thing that Carl and his company could use. Carl agreed, and my client asked him almost on my behalf, how much he wanted to order, and Carl thought for a moment and gave me the biggest order I ever got from West Virginia. "Now that that's done," my client said, "how about some lunch?" We all went to the same place we always go to when I'm in West Virginia, talking about life and things and some business. By mid-afternoon I said I had to be heading home. We all agreed to stay in touch. We've been in touch ever since, and now I've got two clients to visit whenever I'm in West Virginia.

Once you've gathered as much information as you can, role play the negotiation by taking the part of the other negotiator. This should give you a greater understanding of that person's vantage point. For instance, if you are a manager preparing for labor negotiations, act out the role of the union negotiator. Do symbolic role playing if you can't physically role play. Imagine how the other party thinks and feels in the situation. As a manager in contract negotiations, consider the relationship between the union negotiator and the union membership. This person may have to make unreasonable demands at first in order to satisfy union members.

Active listening skills are critical once the negotiation begins. Ask for clarification when needed and paraphrase the speaker's comments. By making an effort to listen actively to the other negotiator, you demonstrate that you want to understand his or her point of view. This makes conciliation more likely. (A comprehensive list of productive negotiation behaviors is found in the research highlight in box 6.4.)

Box 6.4   Research Highlight

Effective Negotiation Skills[42]

Researchers in a variety of fields, including communication, management, economics, law, psychology, sociology, political science, and psychology, study negotiation. Those who want to become better negotiators must draw on insights from many different disciplines. Michael Roloff, Linda Putnam, and Lefki Anastasiou analyzed the results of studies from across academic fields to develop a comprehensive list of negotiation skills. They examined projects that focused on (a) professional negotiators or (b) successful negotiation outcomes.

Planning emerged as a critical negotiation skill based on Roloff, Putnam, and Anastasiou's analysis of the behavior of experts. Professionals who negotiate as part of their jobs are well informed on the issues and are therefore better able to question the position of the other party and to stay away from personal attacks. They are more flexible because they have considered a larger range of options. Once discussions begin, professionals exercise self-control, actively seek additional information, and keep the process from being competitive.

The researchers found that, when it comes to generating successful outcomes, the most effective negotiation behaviors vary depending on whether parties take a win-lose (distributive) or problem-solving (integrative) orientation toward negotiation. Successful distributive negotiators who seek to maximize their personal outcomes are tough bargainers who may mislead their opponents. However, the distributive approach has many limitations, including unethical behavior, increased resistance, and potential deadlock. Those who want to avoid the pitfalls of hard bargaining should engage in the following behaviors instead. Roloff, Putnam, and Anastasiou report that these skills consistently produce high-quality solutions that benefit both parties:

1. **Set specific and reasonably high goals**. Failure to specify objectives encourages participants to take shortcuts (split the difference) instead of working toward a creative solution. Negotiators who set challenging goals are motivated to analyze the situation in more detail and to come up with a win-win outcome. However, setting unrealistically high goals makes it harder to reach integrative solutions. Discouraged participants may give up.

2. **Lower goals reluctantly.** Successful negotiators resist the temptation to back off their objectives once talks begin. They recognize that giving in leads to a compromise instead of a mutually beneficial outcome. They practice flexible rigidity, holding on to their goals but identifying many ways these objectives can be reached.

3. **Share information about priorities and make trade-offs among issues of differing importance**. Effective negotiators build momentum by logrolling. In this technique (visualize a log rolling down a hill, gathering speed as it travels), participants build momentum by trading concessions on low priority items to get agreement on more significant issues. Successful logrolling depends on acquiring accurate information about the priorities of the other party.

4. **Be aware of and control cognitive biases**. Thinking errors can undermine negotiation. The first important bias is the mistaken assumption that the priorities of negotiators are identical. This false assumption prevents logrolling. The second error is the faulty belief that all of the positions and priorities of the negotiators are incompatible when they are not. This fallacy encourages the parties to compromise instead of reaching integrative agreements.

5. **Be selectively contentious**. Integrative negotiators function as problem solvers, analyzing the issues and engaging in cooperative behaviors. However, being contentious signals that negotiators are committed to their goals and may lead to a better understanding of the positions of the other parties. The best negotiators take care to reduce the potential damage that can come from contention. They are specific about their concerns and use threats sparingly—to keep the negotiations moving and to avoid repeating issues. Their challenges are focused on solutions, not on the personality of the other party or on that individual's interests and goals. They also try not to take unsupportive comments from others personally, recognizing that these remarks may be mistakes or may be the product of poor preparation.

6. **Signal concern about the opponent's needs and interests**. Effective negotiators signal flexibility by communicating concern about the other party. They express commitment to generating joint benefits, use "we" instead of "I" language, and create rapport through accommodating nonverbal communication (mirroring the other person's posture, matching gestures, using appropriate facial expressions).

Negotiation as Joint Problem Solving

As we've seen, effective negotiators create a cooperative atmosphere and take the perspective of others. The most productive approaches to negotiation incorporate these two elements by viewing negotiation as a problem-solving process rather than as a competitive tug of war. In contrast to the win-lose approach, problem-solving negotiation fosters cooperation and focuses on generating solutions that will meet the interests of both sides. Perhaps the best known example of the problem-solving style of negotiation is the principled negotiation model developed by Roger Fisher, William Ury, and associates of the Harvard Negotiation Project.[43] Following the four steps of principled negotiation will help you reach a solution that is satisfactory to both you and the other party. After you've read the description of the four steps, apply them to the case study in box 6.5.

(1) *Separate the people from the problem.* Avoid defining the situation as a test of wills. Focus instead on working side by side on a common goal—resolving the issues at hand. Build trust to defuse strong emotions and to keep conflict from escalating. Colonial activist John Woolman is an excellent example of a negotiator who was able to tackle tough issues without attacking the people with whom he disagreed.[44] Woolman, a prominent Quaker cloth merchant in Philadelphia, spent 30 years negotiating the end of slavery in Pennsylvania. Woolman assumed that there was good in everyone, including slave owners. He believed that slaveholders, rather than being evil, were "entangled" in a corrupt system. They had been socialized to believe that blacks were lazy and didn't want to oppose the practice of slavery for fear of alienating their parents and the rest of the community. Woolman was friendly and cheerful when he confronted slave owners and encouraged consensus building and experimental learning. As a group, Woolman and local farmers designed an experiment that freed a few slaves to sharecrop. The productivity of the sharecroppers was higher than that of the slaves, proving that blacks could be just as industrious as whites. Woolman's "friendly disentangling" strategy paid off. By 1770 Quakers were forbidden to own slaves, and by 1800 Pennsylvania became the only state south of New England to make slavery illegal.

(2) *Focus on interests, not positions.* A negotiating position is the negotiator's public stance (i.e., "I want $60,000 a year in salary from the company."). An interest, on the other hand, is the reason why the negotiator takes that position ("I need to earn $60,000 so that I can save for a down payment on a house."). Focusing on positions can blind you and the other negotiator to the fact that there may be more than one way to meet the underlying need or interest. The company in the example above might pay less in salary and yet meet the employee's need for housing by offering a low-cost home loan. The Camp David peace treaty between Egypt and Israel demonstrates how making a distinction between interests and positions can generate productive settlements. When the two nations first sat down to negotiate with the help of President Jimmy Carter in 1978, they argued over the return of the Sinai Peninsula, which had been seized by Israel from Egypt during the Six-Day War in 1967. Egypt took the position that all occupied lands should be returned, while Israel took the position that only some of the Sinai should be returned to Egyptian control.

As a result, the talks stalled. However, once the negotiators realized that Israel's real interest was national security and Egypt's interest lay in regaining sovereignty over her land, an agreement was reached. Israel gave back the occupied territory in return for pledges that Egypt would not use the Sinai for military purposes.[45] Despite recent unrest in the region, the two nations remain at peace.

(3) *Invent options for mutual gain.* Spend time brainstorming solutions that can meet the needs of both negotiators. Obviously, this is impossible unless you first separate the people from the problem and focus on interests rather than on negotiating positions. Fisher and Ury offer the following example of a creative solution, which met the interests of both parties.

> Consider the story of two men quarreling in a library. One wants the window open and the other wants it closed. They bicker back and forth about how much to leave it open: a crack, halfway, three quarters of the way. No solution satisfies them both. Enter the librarian. She asks one why he wants the window open: "To get some fresh air." She asks the other why he wants it closed: "To avoid the draft." After thinking a minute, she opens wide a window in the next room, bringing in fresh air without a draft.[46]

(4) *Insist on objective criteria.* Find a set of criteria on which you both can agree when determining the terms of the settlement. This reduces the possibility that one party will force the other into accepting an unsatisfactory solution. In most cases, negotiators will be comfortable with an agreement that corresponds to widely accepted norms. Such standards can range from used car price books to legal precedents for insurance settlements to industry standards for wages.

Box 6.5   Case Study

Negotiating Homes for Students

Higgins College is a private, residential four-year liberal arts school located in a small rural community in the Northeast. Over the past three years it has experienced a surge in enrollment, growing from 1,400 to 1,900 students. Unable to build student housing fast enough to meet demand, the college has purchased houses in the adjoining neighborhood as a temporary solution to its housing crisis. Unfortunately, resentment toward the college grows with each additional house it buys. Neighbors complain that student tenants are noisy and that the college lets the condition of its properties deteriorate. Some individuals who sold their homes to the school believe that they were paid less than full market value.

Imagine that you are the special assistant to the president at Higgins, newly hired with special responsibility for property acquisition. You must negotiate the purchase of two additional homes to help house this fall's incoming freshman class, the largest in the college's history. Higgins' president, a forceful personality largely credited with the college's rapid growth, has made it clear that this is to be your top priority. You've also received several e-mail messages from the student housing director, who says she needs to know if you can complete the deal in three weeks so she can finish housing assignments. The two most desirable properties are located next to each other right across the street from the college's science building. Other options are located much farther away from campus in a more expensive area. Fearful of being "ripped off," the owners of the homes near the science building have hired a real estate agent to represent them in this transac-

(continued)

tion. When you call the realtor to set up a meeting, you learn that members of the neighborhood association have urged the homeowners to sell to private individuals, not to the college. You have three days to get ready for the first negotiation session.

Discussion Questions

1. What steps will you take to build a cooperative climate?
2. Describe the perspectives of all the parties, including yourself.
3. What are the interests of both sides and how can they be met?
4. What solutions could meet the needs of both parties?
5. What objective criteria could be used to determine the terms of the settlement?
6. What alternatives does each side have to reaching a settlement? How will this influence the likely outcome of the negotiation?

Resisting Influence: Defending against the Power of Mental Shortcuts

Up to this point in the chapter we've focused on how leaders exercise influence to carry out their roles. Yet, leaders must resist influence as well as exert it. Succumbing to dishonest or poorly reasoned persuasive appeals can be costly to leaders and to their groups and organizations. Among the possible negative consequences are paying too much for goods and services, giving to unworthy causes, and engaging in illegal activities.

Arizona State University social psychologist Robert Cialdini believes that mental shortcuts leave leaders and others vulnerable to unethical influence.[47] In the modern age it is impossible to carefully evaluate every piece of information that comes our way through cable television, cell phones, Blackberries, the Internet, and other channels. Faced with a flood of data, we often make decisions based on a single piece of information that we believe accurately represents the total situation—we use shortcuts to save time.[48] Automatic responses produce poor choices if advertisers and others manipulate information to their advantage. Cialdini believes in the adage "forewarned is forearmed." If you are aware of the following tactics, you are more likely to analyze persuasive attempts critically and to avoid negative consequences.[49]

Reciprocation (give and take). The rule of reciprocity (that people are obligated to return favors) appears to be a universal guideline, which encourages individuals of every culture to cooperate with one another. People can offer assistance to others with the confidence that they will be repaid in the future, thus creating mutually advantageous relationships where none existed before. Solicitors and advertisers take advantage of this basic standard of human behavior. The March of Dimes, the Audubon Society, and other charities send out free address labels and calendars in hopes that recipients will return the favor by making donations. Other examples of this strategy (known as "foot-in-the-door") are the product representatives who line supermarket aisles on weekends handing out samples of cheese, sausage, pizza, and other foods. Shoppers often respond by buying the items, partly out of a sense of obligation.

One sobering example of the effectiveness of the foot-in-the-door strategy came during the Korean War. People were shocked by the fact that many captured U.S. soldiers readily informed on one another and offered other help to the enemy. This collaboration was not forced through torture or harsh treatment; it was the product of a series of small commitments. First, the captors convinced their prisoners to agree to such statements as "the United States is not perfect." Interrogators then asked these same men to make a list of problems in the United States and to sign their names. These lists were shown to other prisoners, and the prisoners wrote essays expanding on the nation's weaknesses. Later the names and essays were broadcast to other POW camps and U.S. soldiers still fighting in South Korea. Now the prisoners were publicly identified as collaborators. Knowing that they had written their statements without strong coercion, the captives began to live up to the "collaborator" label, giving further aid to their jailers.

The reciprocal concessions strategy (referred to as the "door-in-the-face" technique) is an interesting variation on the theme of give and take. In this strategy, persuaders make an extreme request and then back off, asking for less. Making a smaller request is viewed as a concession and, as a result, targets are more likely to comply with the second attempt. Also, the follow-up request appears more reasonable in contrast to the original one. Cialdini and his colleagues first tested this procedure by asking strangers to make a two-year commitment as youth volunteers. The researchers then followed up their initial request by asking these same individuals to take children to the zoo for two hours. To create a comparison group, they approached a separate group of strangers with only the second request. Those who had first been asked to make the long-term commitment were more likely to agree to go to the zoo.[50]

The reciprocity rule can result in unwanted debts and trigger unequal exchanges. Concerns about the dangers of reciprocity are behind attempts to restrict gifts from lobbyists. Accepting meals, golf outings, and overseas junkets can put legislators in debt to special interest groups.

Cialdini outlines three strategies for resisting the power of reciprocity. One, turn down initial favors. Some political candidates refuse large contributions, for instance, and universities return contributions from controversial donors. Two, do not feel obligated to return favors that are tricks, not genuine favors. Three, turn the tables on unethical influencers by exploiting the exploiters. Take the free gift (a cracker, a free weekend visit at a time-share resort, a road atlas) and walk away without giving anything in return.

Commitment and consistency. This shortcut is based on the desire to appear consistent with previous choices and actions. Consistency prevents feelings of dissonance while reducing the need to think carefully about an issue after making a choice. Commitment goes hand in hand with the drive for consistency. Once we've made a commitment, no matter how small, we want to remain consistent with that decision or action.

Voluntary, public decisions increase the commitment of people who made the choice. They can't attribute their behavior to outside pressures. Consider the popularity of college hazing rituals, for example. Sorority and fraternity pledges (of their own free will) publicly commit themselves to a particular Greek affiliation. When they are subsequently subjected to strenuous (and perhaps dangerous) initiation ceremonies, they become even more committed. Despite the efforts of many college administrators, the new inductees continue the tradition and insist that future pledges go through similar initiation rites. Voicing concern about the initiation hazing could be interpreted as inconsistent with the previous commitment to the sorority or fraternity. Having endured an unpleasant experience, there is a desire to embrace the commitment even more strongly.

Persuaders use a variety of strategies to invoke the power of commitment. *Lowballing* (popular with auto dealers) is securing an initial commitment to an attractive option (low price) and then raising the cost (revoking the deal, adding on options and high cost financing). *Labeling* consists of giving someone a label that is consistent with what the persuader wants this person to do. For example: calling someone an "above average citizen" to encourage him or her to vote in local elections. *Tapping into existing commitments* means offering ideas and products that tie into pre-existing ideas and behaviors. This tactic is frequently used to sell product warranties. The buyer is encouraged to extend the warranty to support his or her decision to purchase a new computer, sound system, or automobile.

Your best defense against the pull of commitment and consistency is listening to internal signals. Being trapped into complying with an undesirable request produces a tight, queasy stomach and generates negative emotions. Respond to these feelings by drawing the attention of the persuader to the tactic being used and to the faulty logic of being consistent for consistency's sake. Also, ask yourself: "If I could go back in time, would I make the same choice again?" If you wouldn't make the same decision twice, then don't make it in the first place.

> Moderation in temper is always a virtue, but moderation in principle is always a vice.
>
> —Thomas Paine

Social proof (validation). Social proof refers to deciding how to act based on what others are doing. Television producers use laugh tracks, for example, to convince viewers that situation comedies are funny. Campaign managers hope to pick up additional support by trumpeting the fact that their candidates are leading in the polls. Publishers tout their books as best sellers. Social proof exerts the most influence in ambiguous situations when observers don't know how to interpret information. Take the case of someone lying on a busy city sidewalk. This individual could be drunk, asleep, or sick. A drunk or sleepy person can be ignored; an individual with a medical emergency needs help. To determine how to respond, pedestrians look around and see how others react. If other passers-by stop to help, they are more likely to offer assistance as well. The influence exerted by social proof can be deadly. Members of Heaven's Gate (the Hale-Bopp cult) committed mass suicide in response to social pressure from other members of their group.

Social proof has less impact when you recognize that influencers are making false claims and/or creating false impressions. For instance, producers of infomercials pay actors to participate in "spontaneous" demonstrations designed to convince us that juicers and other products are effective and easy to use. Supporters of the president pack the gallery during the State of the Union address and applaud at every opportunity, hoping to make the chief executive look more popular. In addition to being on the look out for misleading influence attempts, you can also increase your resistance to this shortcut by periodically testing the crowd's reactions against established facts as well as against your past experiences and personal judgments.

Liking. As targets of influence, we are more swayed by people we like. Avon, Amway, and other marketers take advantage of this fact by having their representatives sell directly to friends and neighbors. This strategy has been so successful that the Tupperware corporation has abandoned its retail locations and largely moved from the U.S. market to cultures in Latin America, Asia, and Europe where friends and family exert a stronger influence over behavior. (A Tupperware party begins somewhere in the world every 2.7 seconds, according to the company.) Liking is based on a variety of factors, including: (1) physical attractiveness (attractive people are more likely to get elected, hired, and paid more money); (2) similarity (in appearance, attitude, nonverbal behavior, ethnic background); (3) compliments (flattery, praise); (4) familiarity and frequent cooperative contact; and (5) association with positive events and people (the Olympics, winning sport teams, celebrities).

Preventing liking is almost impossible. The key, according to Cialdini, is to determine if you like someone too much given the circumstances and to separate the merits of the proposal from the person. Ask yourself, for example: "Am I ignoring a lower bid just because I like another contractor better?" "Do I support an applicant for a job opening only because he/she shares the same ethnic background as me?" "Do I find it hard to say 'no' to a request when I've received compliments first?" If you say "yes" to any of these questions, you need to reconsider your choices.

Authority. Receivers frequently overlook the content of the message and respond instead based on status cues like titles, clothes, nice jewelry, and fine automobiles. The higher the perceived status of the persuader, the more likely it is that targets will comply. In one investigation, for example, hospital nurses were telephoned by a "doctor" (really an experimenter) they had never met who told them to administer a large amount of an unauthorized drug to a patient. Despite the fact that prescribing medications over the phone was expressly forbidden by hospital policy and the drug was not cleared for use, 95 percent of the nurses went straight to the patient's room to administer the dosage, only to be stopped by the researchers.[51]

Expertise is another element of authority. Experts are more effective when they deal with complex issues, speak against what appears to be their self-interests, and point out the weaknesses of their case before the other side has the chance to.

The best way to undermine the influence of authority is to engage in critical thinking. Probe the merits of the argument instead of relying on status cues. Consider whether the person is truly an expert on the topic at hand. Consider too whether this person will likely be truthful in this situation. Be on guard against those who will benefit personally if you go along with their recommendations.

Scarcity. Scarcity appeals are a staple of advertising. Television offers are good only if viewers call now, supermarket ads run for one week only, the most popular holiday toys always seem to be in short supply, and some furniture outlets always seem to be going out of business. Retailers recognize that items appear more valuable when they appear to be less available. Two principles underlie this mental shortcut. The first is the belief (often supported by experience) that items in short supply are better than common ones. The second is that people react against any attempt to limit their freedoms, particularly when something is newly scarce or when competition develops. Notice how fast lines form at service stations at the first hint that supplies of gas will be running low, for example, and how shoppers fight over limited supplies of the "hot" Christmas gift. Attempts to restrict information can have a similar effect. Censoring information makes it more desirable and believable. Further, influence targets are more persuaded by the thought of losing something than by the thought of gaining an advantage. Physicians in one study persuaded more smokers to quit when they described the number of years of life the subjects would lose if they kept up the habit. This was more effective than telling smokers how many years of life they would gain if they stopped.

Scarcity generates physical arousal (i.e., increased blood pressure and adrenaline), making a rational response difficult. The best way to defend against physiological arousal is to calm the nervous system. Take a break in the negotiations or refuse to commit to a major decision until thinking about it overnight. Realize, too, that limited availability doesn't make an object any better. If you want the car, property, or service for its function to you or your organization, its ultimate usefulness should determine how much you pay for it, not its scarcity. Forgetting this principle has been costly to the owners of sports teams. Bidding against other owners for players encourages these leaders to pay too much for free agents. Often they lose sight of the fact that, despite the scarcity of good talent, no player is worth the cost if his or her signing means the franchise will lose money.

Chapter Takeaways

- Credibility, which is built on perceptions of our competence, trustworthiness, and dynamism, is the key to any successful influence attempt.

- Enhance your credibility through self-presentation behaviors that establish commonalities with your audience and distance yourself from untrustworthy groups. Avoid jargon and modify your nonverbal behaviors (appearance, voice, posture, eye contact). Build quality relationships with followers through discovering yourself, increasing your skills and confidence, appreciating constituents, affirming shared values, developing capacity, serving a purpose, and sustaining hope.

- Compliance-gaining strategies are the verbal tactics used to influence others in face-to-face encounters. In the interpersonal context, use "friendly persuasion"—positive strategies that put you and the other party in a positive frame of mind. As a leader in the organizational context, take a rational yet flexible approach. Offer reasons for compliance but switch tactics when appropriate.

- Avoid hard tactics like applying pressure or appealing to authority, whenever possible. These strategies may gain compliance but often at the expense of long-term commitment. Whenever possible, use a combination of soft tactics (consulting with others, pointing out benefits, putting the other person in a good mood, arousing enthusiasm), which often work better together than alone. However, be careful not to mix incompatible strategies like applying pressure while trying to put the other person in a good mood.

- Argumentation involves controversy and extended discussion over issues. Never confuse argument with verbal aggression, which attacks the self-worth of others. Argumentation produces a wide array of positive outcomes; verbal aggression is destructive.

- In order to sway others to your point of view, you will need to avoid aggression and to develop argumentative competence. Argumentative competence consists of stating the controversy in propositional form, inventing arguments, presenting and defending your position, attacking other positions, and managing interpersonal relations.

- Negotiation is back-and-forth communication aimed at reaching a joint decision when people are in disagreement. The most effective negotiations generate solutions that benefit both parties. To reach integrative (win-win) agreements, you'll need to build a cooperative atmosphere, take the perspective of the other person, and view the discussion as a problem-solving process.

- Joint problem-solving negotiation involves separating the people from the problem, identifying the interests of each party, brainstorming options for mutual gain, and basing the settlement on objective criteria.

- As a leader, you'll need to resist influence as well as exert it. Mental shortcuts can lead to poor choices. Be prepared to resist manipulative influence tactics that appeal to: the principle of reciprocation (give and take), the desire for consistency, social proof/validation (looking to others), liking, authority, and the principle of scarcity.

APPLICATION EXERCISES

1. Evaluate Your Credibility

   Rate your credibility on form 1 below. You may want to evaluate yourself based on your image in a particular situation. For example: how competent, trustworthy, and dynamic do you appear in class or at your job? Next, have someone else rate you on form 2, while you evaluate that person. After you have finished your evaluations, discuss your reactions to this exercise. Were you surprised at how your partner rated you? Pleased? Displeased? Why did you rate yourself as you did? Would others rate you the same way?

Form 1: Self-Analysis[52]

Competence

Experienced	__	__	__	__	__	__	__	Inexperienced
Informed	__	__	__	__	__	__	__	Uninformed
Skilled	__	__	__	__	__	__	__	Unskilled
Expert	__	__	__	__	__	__	__	Inexpert
Trained	__	__	__	__	__	__	__	Untrained

Trustworthiness

Kind	__	__	__	__	__	__	__	Cruel
Friendly	__	__	__	__	__	__	__	Unfriendly
Honest	__	__	__	__	__	__	__	Dishonest
Sympathetic	__	__	__	__	__	__	__	Unsympathetic

Dynamism

Assertive	__	__	__	__	__	__	__	Hesitant
Forceful	__	__	__	__	__	__	__	Meek
Bold	__	__	__	__	__	__	__	Timid
Active	__	__	__	__	__	__	__	Passive

Form 2: Partner Rating

Competence

Experienced	__	__	__	__	__	__	__	Inexperienced
Informed	__	__	__	__	__	__	__	Uninformed
Skilled	__	__	__	__	__	__	__	Unskilled
Expert	__	__	__	__	__	__	__	Inexpert
Trained	__	__	__	__	__	__	__	Untrained

Trustworthiness

Kind	__	__	__	__	__	__	__	Cruel
Friendly	__	__	__	__	__	__	__	Unfriendly
Honest	__	__	__	__	__	__	__	Dishonest
Sympathetic	__	__	__	__	__	__	__	Unsympathetic

Dynamism

Assertive	__	__	__	__	__	__	__	Hesitant
Forceful	__	__	__	__	__	__	__	Meek
Bold	__	__	__	__	__	__	__	Timid
Active	__	__	__	__	__	__	__	Passive

2. Credo Memo

To help you develop your leadership philosophy, complete the following exercise developed by James Kouzes and Barry Posner.

Imagine that your organization has afforded you the chance to take a six-month sabbatical, all expenses paid. You will not be permitted to communicate to anyone at your office or plant while you are away. Not by letter, phone, fax, e-mail, or other means. But before you depart, those with whom you work need to know the principles that you believe should guide their decisions and actions in your absence. They need to know the values and beliefs that you think should steer the organization while you're away. After all, you'll want to be able to fit back in on your return.

You are not to write a long report, however. Just a one-page "Credo Memo." Get a single sheet of paper and write that memo.

It usually takes about five to ten minutes to write a Credo Memo. We do not pretend that this exercise is a substitute for more in-depth self discovery, but it does provide a useful starting point for articulating your guiding principles. To deepen the clarification process, identify the values you listed in your memo (usually they appear as key words or phrases) and put them in order of priority. Or rank them from low to high. Or place them on a continuum. Forcing yourself to express preferences enables you to see the relative potency of each value.[53]

3. In a research paper, evaluate the credibility of a well-known leader. Rate this individual on each of the three dimensions of credibility. Support your evaluation with examples, experts, and other evidence. Draw conclusions about why this person succeeded or failed in establishing and maintaining his or her credibility. Identify insights that you can apply to building your credibility as a leader.

4. In a group, identify the costs and benefits of each of the 11 types of organizational influence tactics described on pp. 173–174. Based on your analysis, which tactics generate the most positive feelings? What guidelines would you offer for using each tactic? Which seems to be most effective in most situations? Report your findings to the rest of the class.

5. Analyze your effectiveness as a compliance gainer both in an interpersonal and in an organizational setting. Describe a recent situation in which you were the persuader in an interpersonal encounter and as an organizational leader or follower. Which strategy or combination of strategies did you use in each situation? Did they differ? Why did you choose those tactics? How successful were your efforts? Were you more effective in one context than the other? What would you do differently next time?

6. Think of a time when you had an enjoyable argument with someone over a controversial issue, one that stimulated your thoughts and interest. Briefly describe that argument. Now think of a time when you had an unpleasant argument that resulted in hurt feelings and may have damaged the relationship. Briefly describe that situation. Was the first discussion an example of genuine argument and the second a case of verbal aggression? Why or why not?

7. Participate in a debate in class. Your instructor will give you the topic and ground rules. Use the inventional system presented in box 6.2 to construct your argument. When the debate is complete, evaluate your performance using the guidelines presented in the chapter.

8. Tape a political talk show and then evaluate the evidence and reasoning of the host and callers. Identify examples of faulty evidence and reasoning and share your tape and analysis in class.

9. Prepare for a negotiation using material presented in the chapter. Outline specific steps for putting these strategies and skills into action.

10. Analyze an infomercial to identify its unethical, poorly reasoned persuasive appeals. As an alternative, identify similar appeals found in all the commercials that appear during a one-hour television broadcast.

CULTURAL CONNECTIONS: COMPLIANCE GAINING IN CHINA[54]

Managers in the United States generally take a straightforward approach to exercising influence. Assertive and individualistic, they like to deal directly with others when making requests or resolving disputes. They rely heavily on rational arguments and exchanging benefits and favors. American managers only turn to others for assistance when the direct approach fails.

Chinese managers are more concerned with maintaining relationships *(guan-xi)* and saving face by keeping the respect of others and showing respect *(mian-zi)*. As a consequence, they are more likely to use indirect forms of influence like turning to a third party for help. Enlisting others to make a difficult request supports *guan-xi*, and keeps the influence agent from losing face. In addition, the involvement of another individual demonstrates that the proposal is legitimate. Often the third party is someone of higher status, which reflects Chinese respect for authority and power differences. Gift giving also plays an important role in Chinese compliance gaining. Gifts are routinely exchanged to strengthen workplace relationships and when seeking favors. In the United States, coupling a gift with a request is often seen as a bribe.

Not all American and Chinese managers follow the pattern described above. Factors in addition to national culture, such as personal traits and organizational rules and procedures, also help determine the selection of compliance-gaining tactics. While Chinese leaders may not rely as heavily on rational persuasion as do their American counterparts, they do think that offering reasons and evidence is an effective strategy. Managers from both nations frown on the use of pressure tactics like demanding and threatening.

SPOTLIGHT ON TECHNOLOGY: VIRAL MARKETING[55]

The term *viral marketing* refers to marketing techniques that use social networks to increase brand awareness. Like a pathological or computer virus, the marketing message is spread from person to person by word of mouth or, most commonly, through mediated contexts such as e-mail, video clips, interactive Flash games, images, or text messages. Examples of viral marketing are common on the Web. Any time you learn about a Web site by word of mouth, through a blog entry, via a link on another Web site, or even in this book, you are experiencing viral marketing.

Two of the more successful viral campaigns were launched by Hotmail and Burger King. When Hotmail was initiated as a free e-mail service, there were very few users. To boost traffic, a footer was attached to the bottom of each outgoing e-mail. The message read: To get your FREE e-mail account go to www.hotmail.com. As a result, every message sent on Hotmail was a viral advertisement encouraging others to sign up for the service. Within just a year-and-a-half after the launch of the free service, there were more than 8 million Hotmail subscribers—a penetration rate that led to the acquisition of the company by Microsoft. Burger King's viral marketing campaign consisted of a Web site featuring a person in a chicken costume. Dubbed the Subservient Chicken, the actor performed a wide range of actions based on user input. With more than 300 commands, the Subservient Chicken responded to requests ranging from "lay an egg" to "do a cartwheel." Designed by the advertising agency of Crispin Porter + Bogusky, the link to the Web site was initially only given to 15 people. Once the details of the site become known, Burger King reported some 20 million hits on the site.

LEADERSHIP ON THE BIG SCREEN: *RULES OF ENGAGEMENT*

Starring: Tommy Lee Jones, Samuel L. Jackson, Ben Kingsley, Guy Pearce, Anne Archer

Rating: R for graphic war violence and language

Synopsis: Samuel L. Jackson is Marine Colonel Terry Childers, who stands accused of ordering his men to open fire on unarmed civilians during a rescue mission in Yemen. Facing a court martial for breaking the Marines' rules of engagement, Childers turns to his friend, recently retired military lawyer Hays Hodges (Tommy Lee Jones), for help. The pair face an uphill battle. Hays is a mediocre lawyer at best, and government officials sabotage their defense by destroying evidence and committing perjury. Hays still manages to cast doubt on the prosecution's case, however. In so doing, he repays the debt he owes Childers for saving his life during the Vietnam War.

Chapter Links: credibility, verbal aggression, argumentative competence, evidence, reasoning, reciprocity

CHAPTER

seven

Leadership in Groups and Teams

The well-run group is not a battlefield of egos.

—Lao Tzu

OVERVIEW

- Fundamentals of Group Interaction
  Viewing Groups from a Communication Perspective
  Group Evolution
- Emergent Leadership
  How *Not* to Emerge as a Leader
  Useful Strategies
  Idiosyncratic Credits
  Appointed vs. Emergent Leaders
- Leadership in Meetings
- Group Decision Making
  Functions and Formats
  Avoiding the Pitfalls
- Team Leadership
  When Is a Group a Team?
  Developing Team-Building Skills
  Self-Directed Work Teams
  Leading Virtual Teams

Small groups play a major role in all of our lives. Every week we are members of planning committees, dorm councils, social clubs, condominium associations, and countless other groups. Often our most enjoyable memories are of group experiences like playing on a winning softball team or developing a new product on a task force. Yet, at the same time, some of our greatest frustrations arise out of group interaction. Many classroom project groups, for example, get low grades because group members dislike one another. In other instances, members fail to show up for meetings, leaving one person to do most of the work on the project at the last minute.

The purpose of this chapter is to improve your chances of having a productive group experience by building your understanding of group and team leadership. There are no formulas to guarantee that you will become a group leader or that your group will be successful. However, learning about how group leadership works can increase the likelihood that both will happen. We'll start by looking at some fundamentals of group behavior and then talk about emergent leadership, leading meetings, decision making, and team leadership.

Fundamentals of Group Interaction

As you read this book you may be learning a number of new terms, or you may be discovering new meanings for familiar terms. The symbols we master during our academic training focus our attention on some parts of the world and away from others. Kenneth Burke calls this focusing influence of language the "terministic screen."[1] Phillip Tompkins describes the following case of terministic screens in action:

> For example, suppose we assemble an economist, a psychologist, and a sociologist in the college cafeteria and ask each to give explanations of food choices made by a customer. Suppose further that the customer we observe happens to select custard rather than either cake or pie. The economist might explain that, because custard is less "labor intensive" and therefore cheaper than the other desserts, it was the only dessert the customer could afford. The psychologist might explain the choice by means of the customer's history; for instance, he or she might say that the customer's "past reinforcement schedule" provides the answer. The sociologist might explain the choice by pointing to the "ethno-social background" of the customer and showing how different classes of people favor different desserts. . . . Thus, the terministic screen of vocabulary causes each to focus on elements and interpretations of the situation to the exclusion of others.[2]

Viewing Groups from a Communication Perspective

The terministic screens of academic languages operate when scholars from different disciplines study groups. Psychologists, for example, are often interested in the "personalities" of group members and focus on how these characteristics shape group behaviors and outcomes. Sociologists pay attention to other factors like the "social status" of group members. Communication scholars are most interested in the communication that occurs within groups, which they label as "interaction." They argue that group success or failure often rests most heavily on what group members say and do when the group is together rather than on what group members bring with them to the discussion.

Supreme Court decisions are good examples of how group outcomes can't necessarily be predicted by knowing the characteristics of members. Presidents often try to influence Supreme Court decisions by appointing justices who favor either a conservative or liberal point of view. They are frequently surprised when their appointees violate their expectations after deliberating with other justices. In your own experience, there probably have been times when you went into a group meeting with your mind made up only to change your opinion as a result of the discussion. From a communication perspective, then, any definition of a group must take into account that communication is the essential characteristic of a group. A survey of small group communication texts reveals that the following elements define small groups.[3]

A common purpose or goal. A group is more than a collection of individuals. Several people waiting for a table at a restaurant would not constitute a group. Group members have something that they want to accomplish together, whether it is to overcome drug dependency, to decide on a new site for a manufacturing plant, or to study for an exam. As an outgrowth of this common goal and participation in the group, a sense of belonging or identity emerges. For example, a number of strangers enrolled in an evening class that met weekly; seven months later class members felt such a strong sense of group identity that they bought shirts with the name of the class imprinted on the back.

> Cooperation can be set up, perhaps, more easily than competition.
> —B. F. Skinner

Interdependence. The success of any one member of the group depends on everyone doing his or her part. When student group members fail to do their fair share of the work, the grade of even the brightest individual goes down. Interdependence is reflected in the roles that members play in the group. One person may gather materials for the meeting; another may take notes; a third may keep the group focused on the task.

Mutual influence. Not only do group members depend on each other, they influence each other through giving ideas, challenging opinions, listening, agreeing, and so on.

Ongoing communication. In order for a group to exist, members must engage in regular communication. For example, although employees working on an assembly line share the common goal of producing a product, they do not constitute a group unless they interact with one another.[4] Group members in the same location engage in face-to-face communication. Workers at different sites are linked through e-mail, online meetings, videoconferences, faxes, and telephone calls. (We'll have more to say about dispersed or virtual teams later in the chapter.)

Specific size. Groups range in size from 3 to 20 people. The addition of a third person makes a group more complex than a dyad. Group members must manage many relationships, not just one. They develop coalitions as well as sets of rules or norms to regulate group behavior. The group is also more stable than a dyad. While a dyad dissolves when one member leaves, the group (if large enough) can continue if it loses a member or two. Twenty is generally considered the maximum size for a group because group members lose the ability to communicate face-to-face when the group grows beyond this number.

John Cragan and David Wright summarize the five elements described above in their definition of a small group: "a few people engaged in communication interaction over time, usually in face-to-face settings, who have common goals and norms and have developed a communication pattern for meeting their goals in an interdependent manner."[5]

Group Evolution

Groups change and mature over time. A number of models that describe the evolution of groups, particularly the development of decision-making groups, have been offered. One early model was developed by Thomas Scheidel and Laura Crowell.[6] These two researchers suggested that group decisions are not made through a linear, step-by-step process. Instead, an idea is introduced, discussed, and then dropped. Later that same idea is reintroduced and developed further. After several such starts and stops, agreement is reached and the decision emerges. This process is called the spiral model because the discussion spirals in greater and greater loops as the discussion continues.

B. Aubrey Fisher relied heavily on the spiral model when developing his influential theory of group decision making.[7] As they listened to groups communicate, Fisher and his coworkers noted what each group member said (labeled a speech act) and how the next person responded. This pairing of speech acts is called an interact. A group interact might look something like this:

Carmen: I think we ought to get away from the office for a day and do some planning for next year.

Tim: I don't think we can cover everything in one day.

By looking at series of interacts, Fisher discovered four phases in group decision making.

1. *Orientation phase.* Participants are uncertain and tentative when groups first get together. They are not sure how to tackle the group's task or what kind of behavior will be accepted in the group. Individuals may be asking themselves such questions as, "What kinds of jokes can I tell?" or "What happens when I disagree with the rest of the group?" In this initial stage, statements about what the group should do are ambiguous, and members try hard not to offend others.

2. *Conflict phase.* In the second phase, members are no longer tentative and ambiguous. Instead, they express strong opinions about decision proposals and provide evidence to support their positions. Members who support the same ideas band together. Interacts frequently reflect disagreement in this stage. A statement of support for an idea will often be followed by a negative opinion.

3. *Emergence phase.* At this point the group begins to rally around one solution or decision. Coalitions formed during the second phase disband while dissent and social conflict die out.

4. *Reinforcement phase.* Consensus develops during the final stage. Interacts are positive in nature, reflecting support for other group members and for the solution that emerged in phase three. Tension is gone, and the group commits itself to implementing the decision.

Not everyone is convinced that groups develop through a single series of phases. For example, Marshall Scott Poole argues that groups go through multiple stages of development.[8] Poole suggests that at any given time a group may be at one point in its social development and at another in its task development. One group might start by proposing solutions and stop later to socialize, while another group might build relationships before tackling the task. Important moments of change in a group's development are called *breakpoints*. These breakpoints can involve naturally occurring topic changes, moments of delay, or, most seriously, disruptions caused by conflict or failure. Consensus about who the leader is will result in fewer delays and disruptions in the group's decision-making process.

Though scholars may describe the process in different ways, the concept of group evolution has important implications. First, timing is critical. It's not just what you say, it's when you say it. A good proposal made too early in the discussion, for instance, may not be accepted. Second, since groups take time to develop successfully, any attempt to rush a group's development is likely to meet with failure. Third, effective groups are characterized by a high degree of cohesion and commitment. Consensus both speeds the development of groups and is the product of effective group interaction. Finally, the evolution of groups suggests that group leadership also develops in stages or as a process.

Emergent Leadership

Ernest Bormann and others at the University of Minnesota studied emergent or "natural" leadership in small groups.[9] The researchers found that the group selects its leader by the *method of residues*. Instead of choosing a leader immediately, the group eliminates leader contenders until only one person is left. This procedure is similar to what happens in the presidential primary system. Many candidates begin the race for their party's presidential nomination; gradually the field shrinks as challengers lose primaries, run out of money, get caught in ethics violations, and so forth. Eventually, only one candidate remains. This same principle of selection by elimination operates in the small group. Although all members enter the group as potential leaders, contenders are disqualified until only one leader emerges.

According to Bormann and others, the elimination of potential leaders occurs in two phases. In the first phase, those deemed unsuitable for leadership are quickly removed from contention. Unsuitable candidates may be too quiet or they may be too rigid and aggressive. Many would-be leaders stumble because they appear to be unintelligent and uninformed. Once these cuts have been made, the group then enters the second phase. At this point, about half the group is still actively contending for leadership. Social relations are often tense during this stage. Communication behaviors that lead to elimination in phase two include dominating other group members and talking too much.

Such factors as social standing outside the group may be used to eliminate other aspiring leaders.

Four major patterns of leader emergence were found in the Minnesota studies. In the first pattern, the ultimate winner recruits an ally or "lieutenant" who helps him/her win out over another strong contender. In the second pattern, each of the remaining contenders has a lieutenant and, as a result, the leadership struggle is prolonged, or no strong leader emerges. In the third pattern, a crisis determines leader emergence. The successful leader is the person who helps the group handle such traumatic events as unruly members or the loss of important materials. In the fourth pattern, no one emerges as a clear leader. The result is a high level of frustration. Bormann says that people find such groups to be "punishing."[10]

The Minnesota researchers seem to rule out the possibility that more than one person can act as a group leader or that leadership tasks can be shared among group members. While the emergence of a single leader may be the norm for most groups, there are times when two or more individuals share the functions of leadership, as described in chapter 3.

How *Not* to Emerge as a Leader

Since natural leaders emerge through the process of elimination, it can be useful to identify those behaviors that virtually guarantee you won't become the group's leader. B. Aubrey Fisher and Donald Ellis offered the following "rules" for those who want to secure a low-status position in the group.[11]

Rule 1: Be absent from as many group meetings as possible. Don't explain why you didn't attend.

Rule 2: Contribute very little to the interaction.

Rule 3: Volunteer to be the secretary or the record keeper of your group's discussion. This is an important role, but a recorder or secretary rarely ends up as the group's leader.

Rule 4: Indicate that you are willing to do what you are told. While disinterest guarantees avoiding leadership responsibilities, subservience is not perceived as a leadership quality.

Rule 5: Come on [too] strong early in the group discussions. Be extreme; appear unwilling to compromise.

Rule 6: Try to assume the role of joker. Make sure your jokes are off the topic and never let on that you are serious about anything.

Rule 7: Demonstrate your knowledge of everything, including your extensive vocabulary of big words and technical jargon. Be a know-it-all and use words that others in the group won't understand.

Rule 8: Demonstrate a contempt for leadership. Express your dislike for all kinds of leaders and the idea of leadership itself.

Avoiding the behaviors identified by Fisher and Ellis works in the reverse and increases the possibility of eventually emerging as the leader of a group.

Useful Strategies

Identifying negative behaviors that eliminate leader contenders is easier than isolating positive behaviors that are essential to leadership emergence. However, the following communication strategies can boost your chances of emerging as a group leader:

Participate early and often. The link between participation and leadership is the most consistent finding in small group leadership research.[12] Participation demonstrates both your motivation to lead and your commitment to the group. Impressions about who would and would not make a suitable leader begin to take shape almost immediately after a group is formed.[13] Begin contributing in the group's first session.

Focus on communication quality as well as quantity. Frequent participation earns you consideration as a leader. However, communicating the wrong messages (rigidity, contempt, irrelevance) can keep you from moving into the leadership position. Communication behaviors that are positively correlated with emergent leadership include: setting goals, giving directions, managing tension and conflict, and summarizing.[14] Not only is quality communication essential to becoming a leader, but effective leadership communication helps the group as a whole. Groups are most likely to make good decisions when their most influential members facilitate discussion by asking questions, challenging poor assumptions, clarifying ideas, and keeping the group on track.[15] (We'll have more to say about group decision making later in the chapter.)

Demonstrate your competence. Not surprisingly, the success of would-be leaders depends heavily on their ability to convince others that they can successfully help the group complete the job at hand. Doing your homework in preparation for a project, for example, gives your leadership bid a major boost. Along with competence, you will also need to demonstrate your character and dynamism. Group members want to know that the leader candidate has the best interests of the group in mind and is not manipulating the group for personal gain. Being enthusiastic and confident makes other members more receptive to your suggestions and ideas. As we noted in chapter 6, nonverbal communication plays an important role in building perceptions of all three dimensions of credibility. One study of the nonverbal behaviors of emergent small group leaders found that they gestured frequently, established good eye contact, and expressed agreement through nodding and facial expressions.[16]

Help build a cohesive unit. You must also demonstrate that you want to cooperate with others if you want to become a group leader. Successful leader candidates pitch in to help, work to build the status of others, and don't claim all the credit for decisions.

> The path to greatness is along with others.
> —Baltasar Gracian

Idiosyncratic Credits

Another useful tool for understanding group leadership is Edwin Hollander's concept of idiosyncratic credits. The process of accumulating idiosyncratic credits is similar to starting an account at a bank. Members generate positive impressions in the group that are then deposited in their accounts.[17] Those with the highest idiosyncratic balances emerge as leaders. Credits are accumulated two ways. The first and most important way to build credits is by contributing to the completion of the group's task. The second is by conforming to group expectations. These expectations involve (1) general group norms (not being rude or overly emotional, for example) and (2) role expectations for a leader (such as representing the group well in front of other groups). Idiosyncratic credits are lost through incompetence and norm violations.

Leaders, because they have accumulated a large number of idiosyncratic credits, have greater freedom to deviate from group norms than do other group members. The right to deviate is granted only after leadership has been achieved, however. To demonstrate the important relationship between timing and the acceptance of deviance, one group of researchers planted confederates in groups who would either support or violate group norms such as speaking in turn and majority rule. Confederates who deviated early in the group process had more trouble convincing others to accept their opinions than those who deviated later in the session.[18] Although group leaders have more freedom to disobey rules, they should be very careful not to violate expectations associated with the leader role. A group leader may get away with being late to meetings or interrupting; she or he probably will not be able to act unfairly or selfishly regardless of the number of idiosyncratic credits earned.[19]

Appointed vs. Emergent Leaders

By this time you may wonder if anyone has paid any attention to groups who have appointed rather than emergent leaders. In many cases, a leader is assigned to a group before it meets for the first time. As you might have discovered from personal experience, groups are often successful in spite of, not because of, their official leaders. Many appointed leaders fail to function as leaders; in addition, an incompetent leader slows group progress because members must spend time and energy developing alternative leadership. Groups spend less time on leadership issues if the appointed leader earns the leader label by doing an effective job.[20]

Researchers comparing the impact of assigning or choosing leaders have discovered that followers expect more from natural leaders than appointed leaders. Since they have more invested in leaders that they have selected for themselves, members have higher expectations and tolerate less failure. Yet, at the same time, group members give natural leaders more room to operate. Emergent leaders have greater freedom to make decisions on behalf of the group.[21] One of the most common assignments for appointed group leaders is to plan and to preside over meetings, the subject of the next section.

Leadership in Meetings

For many people, the thought of attending a meeting conjures up images of long, boring sessions spent doodling on a notepad while endless amounts of useless information are presented. The reason for this negative impression of meetings is simple: most meetings are poorly planned and ineptly led. That's unfortunate because U.S. workers spend lots of time in meetings. As many as 11 million meetings take place each day, and some managers spend up to 80 percent of their time in group sessions.[22] Effective meeting leaders plan and prepare before a meeting to be certain that the content is both informative and useful. Adopting the following guidelines can help to ensure that your meetings are successful.

Determine if a meeting is necessary before calling people together. The first step before calling a meeting is to determine if you are justified in taking people away from other activities. Bert Auger, a supervisor with the 3M corporation for over 30 years, provides a checklist outlining when you should and should not call a meeting.[23]

When to Call a Meeting

- Organizational goals need clarification.
- Information that may stimulate questions or discussion needs to be shared.
- Group consensus is required regarding a decision.
- A problem needs to be discovered, analyzed, or solved.
- An idea, program, or decision needs to be sold to others.
- Conflict needs to be resolved.
- It is important that a number of different people have a similar understanding of the same idea, program, or decision.
- Immediate reactions are needed to assess a proposed problem or action.
- An idea, program, or decision is stalled.

*When **Not** to Call a Meeting*

- Other communication networks, such as telephone, fax, e-mail, letter, or memo will transmit the message as effectively.
- There is not sufficient time for adequate preparation by participants or the meeting leader.
- One or more of the key participants are not available.
- Issues are personal or sensitive and could be handled more effectively by talking with each person individually.

Have a clear agenda. A leader should outline the items he or she wishes to address before a meeting begins. Dividing a meeting into thirds is an effective way to structure an agenda. Devote the first third of the meeting, the warm-up phase, to announcements and items that are easy to decide. Tackle the most difficult issues during the middle third of the agenda, when the group is at peak functioning. During the final third of the session, "cool down" by addressing items that are up for discussion but not decision.[24] A copy of this agenda should be circulated in advance of the meeting. Participants should be encouraged to add items to the agenda (within reason) that they feel are important. The agenda should be constructed with time constraints in mind. Additions that greatly increase the number of topics to be discussed should be tabled or scheduled for a separate meeting. Remember, it is the leader's responsibility to decide how much meeting time is available and to keep the meeting on schedule. As with writing a report or delivering a presentation, a meeting leader should always have a clear purpose and a plan for achieving his or her goals. Always ask: "Why are we having this meeting?"

Lay the groundwork. According to John Tropman of the University of Michigan's Meeting Master Research Project, meeting experts or masters put a great deal of effort into preparing for group sessions. In addition to marshalling the information that participants will need, meeting masters hold a series of "rehearsals" prior to the session. The goal of these rehearsals is to sharpen the performance of participants and to prevent surprises:

> The whole purpose of rehearsal is to bring to the front of consciousness skills, perspectives, and ideas that participants have and to allow them to freshen their own minds or explore their own minds with respect to these elements. What the meeting masters were anxious to avoid was any sense of trapping or capturing participants unaware in a meeting. . . . [Masters recognize] that many of us do not know how we are going to feel about something until we have had a chance to chew on it a bit. The informal setting allowed this to happen without a great deal of personal peril. Thus, it becomes a very important vehicle for moving ahead.[25]

Meeting masters meet one on one with group members to test out ideas and to gather feedback. In particular, they touch base with members who will be impacted by the group's decisions. Meeting masters also get together with subgroups preparing for a presentation or discussion and make sure subcommittees are carrying out their tasks. In some cases they hold a full dress rehearsal, a premeeting gathering with everyone present that highlights the key elements of the upcoming agenda.

Maintain focus on the agenda throughout the meeting. Unless leaders maintain sharp focus, meetings have a tendency to drift away from the intended agenda. When the meeting digresses significantly, the leader needs to redirect the group. Comments like, "I think we're getting away from the real issue here. Sam, what do you think about . . ." steer the discussion back to the original agenda. A meeting leader must engage in communication behaviors that help stimulate and maintain group interest and attention. Effective meeting leaders use language that is precise yet understandable. They speak loudly and clearly (not in a mumble), and they avoid distracting gestures or movements.

Listen to others. Effective meeting leaders are active, attentive listeners. Listening involves more than merely hearing what others say; it involves incorporating the meaning of messages. University of Minnesota professor Ralph Nichols pioneered the research on effective listening. Nichols suggests several strategies for improving listening skills.[26]

- *Focus on the content of the message, not the speaker's delivery.* Information is contained in the symbols the speaker uses. Although certain habits or mannerisms such as pacing, pushing up eyeglasses repeatedly, or the excessive use of powerless forms of language (see chapter 5) can be distracting, the content of the message should be the most important focal point. Effective listeners focus on the information that is important and useful while ignoring distracting elements of delivery.

- *Listen for ideas, not just facts.* Good listeners focus on the big picture. Effective listeners don't just collect facts; they listen for concepts. If you miss some of the facts but understand the main idea, it is easy to conduct research to fill in the missing details. On the other hand, a listener who tries to memorize all the facts may miss the larger and more important issues being addressed. It's always much more difficult to fill in the big picture later.

- *Don't let yourself get distracted.* Avoid distractions by any means possible. If you are distracted by a talkative group member, get up and move. If you are hungry, bring a snack with you to the meeting. Don't let external or internal distractions get in the way of your listening. One of the most common distractions experienced in meetings is complex or technical information. Many listeners simply tune out when information becomes difficult to comprehend; whereas effective listeners concentrate even harder. A good listener works to avoid all forms of distraction that interfere with effective listening.

- *Be open-minded.* Most of us respond instantly when someone says something with which we disagree. We may not blurt out our rebuttal immediately, but we almost always begin thinking of our response. The problem with this habit is that it interferes with our ability to listen intently to the other person's point of view. Effective listeners are open-minded and don't overreact to divergent points of view.

- *Use thought speed to your advantage.* Various researchers have suggested that we think from 4 to 20 times as fast as we speak.[27] This capability sometimes causes us to lose concentration while listening—everyone daydreams! Effective listeners use the ability to think more rapidly to their advantage. They use internal thought processes to anticipate the next point, to summarize or paraphrase information that has already been presented, or to focus on nonverbal behaviors such as facial and body movements that illustrate key ideas.

> We have been given two ears and but a single mouth in order that we may hear more and talk less.
>
> —Zeno of Citium

Involve all participants. Effective meeting leaders encourage the involvement of all participants. Meetings are designed as a forum for the exchange of information and ideas. Remember, a leader calls a meeting because he or she is eager to receive immediate information. Don't stifle participants. Always encourage an atmosphere in which discussion flourishes. When making particularly important decisions, you may want to poll each person individually to make sure the group hears from every member.

Keep a record. A written record serves as the group's memory. The minutes of a meeting generally include: (1) when and where the session took place, (2) the names of those attending, and (3) a summary of the main points of the discussion (not what each person said) and important decisions. Action plans focus on implementation by recording *what* the group decided, *who* will carry out the action or decision, and *when* the task will be completed. For example:

What	Who	When
Key Actions/Decisions	Person(s) Responsible	Target Date
Set a timeline for spending cuts	Juan/Pam	June 1
Decided to have movie night	Alisha	March 23

Evaluate your performance. Stopping periodically to talk about the effectiveness of your group's meetings is a good way to improve your collective performance over time. Be sure to include everyone when evaluating the agenda as well as the behavior of the chair and other participants.[28] Professor Tropman offers the Keep, Stop, Start (KSS) technique as one simple strategy to evaluate the success of your meetings. At the end of every session, pass out a sheet with the following questions: (1) What in this meeting went well and should be KEPT?; (2) What in this meeting did not go so well and should be STOPPED?; and (3) What did not happen at this meeting that should be STARTED?[29]

> A manager's ability to turn meetings into a thinking environment is probably an organization's greatest asset.
>
> —Nancy Kline

Group Decision Making

Decision making and problem solving, as we noted earlier, are important reasons for calling group members together for a meeting. Groups are often charged with making choices because they have access to more information than do individuals. Members bring a variety of perspectives to the problem and challenge errors in thinking that might go unrecognized by a lone decision maker. Groups don't always make effective decisions, of course. But they are more likely to succeed when leaders and other members carry out important problem-solving functions, while avoiding the pitfalls that contribute to faulty solutions.

> The art of management is the art of making meaningful generalizations out of inadequate facts.
>
> —Stanley Teele

Functions and Formats

Group experts Dennis Gouran and Randy Hirokawa believe that high-quality solutions emerge from group deliberations when participants use communication to complete four tasks or functions: problem analysis, goal setting, identification of alternatives, and evaluation of possible solutions.[30] We'll use the example of a group made up of homeless shelter staff members to demonstrate the role that each of these functions plays in the decision-making process. The shelter team is meeting to discuss a year-long decline in the number of individuals and families seeking temporary housing at their facility.

(1) *Analysis of the problem.* Clearly identifying the nature and extent of the dilemma is critical to resolving it. Analysis includes recognizing that there is a problem, determining its size and scope, isolating causes, figuring out who is impacted by the problem, and so on. Analysis is a critical first step because initial decisions shape the rest of the group's deliberations. Our shelter team might decide that last year's decline in demand was a random occurrence, not a trend. If this is the case, then the situation doesn't need to be addressed for now. Even if the group determines that housing fewer residents poses a problem that must be solved, members could identify a variety of causes, each of which calls for a different solution. For example, low visibility in the community means more publicity is needed. If run-down facilities are discouraging potential clients, then the shelter house needs to be upgraded.

(2) *Goal setting.* Outlining goals and objectives clarifies what the group wants to accomplish in addressing the problem. To succeed, members must formulate clear objectives and set goals that, if achieved, will produce a reasonable solution. Identifying criteria or standards for evaluating solutions is also part of goal setting. The group from the homeless shelter may agree that it wants to come up with a plan to rebuild numbers over the course of the next year, without a significant increase in the budget.

(3) *Identification of alternatives.* The greater the number of potential solutions, the better the chances of coming up with a workable plan. Shelter staff members could consider a variety of options to draw more clients, including advertising their services, building better relations with social service agencies and religious groups, renovation of facilities, and more staff training designed to improve service to residents.

(4) *Evaluation of solutions.* In this function, decision makers evaluate the merits and demerits of each possible solution using the criteria developed earlier. Advertising would probably attract more people to the homeless shelter, for instance, but would be expensive. Renovation of the facilities would also be too costly. On the other hand, establishing better relations with social service agencies and religious congregations who refer clients would likely increase occupancy rates without the high costs that are associated with advertising and remodeling.

Using a decision-making format is one way to encourage a group to carry out the functions described above. Following a set of predetermined steps increases the likelihood that members will carefully define the problem and develop criteria instead of rushing to potential solutions. There is no consensus as to which format is best, but evidence suggests that groups following a structure are generally more effective than those who don't.[31]

The oldest and most widely used decision-making format is the Standard Agenda. Originally developed by educator John Dewey to describe the process that individuals follow when making choices, the Standard Agenda consists of the following steps:[32]

1. *Identify the problem.* Formulate the problem in the form of a question. A question of fact addresses whether or not something is true ("Is the defendant guilty?"). A question of value asks for a judgment involving right or wrong, good or bad ("Is it fair to allow only upperclassmen to live off campus?"). A question of policy asks what course of action should be followed ("Should taxes be raised to maintain public services?"). Questions of policy are the most common problems faced by groups. (See our earlier discussion of propositions of fact, value, and policy in chapter 6.)

2. *Analyze the problem.* Determine the cause(s), scope, and impact of the problem (number of people affected, costs to the organization or town, etc.).

3. *Develop criteria.* Criteria should in place before entering the solution phase since these standards play a critical role in sorting through proposals.

4. *Generate possible solutions.* Strive for quantity. Produce a variety of alternatives without passing judgment.

5. *Evaluate and select a solution.* In this stage, apply the criteria generated earlier to eliminate options and to identify the best choice. The final solution may combine elements of several proposals.

6. *Implement the solution.* This seems like an obvious step but all too often groups make a decision only to fail to follow through on their choice. Before disbanding, determine who will take action (see our earlier discussion of action plans), if future meetings are needed, and so forth.

An alternative to the Standard Agenda is the Single Question Format. This procedure incorporates the communicative functions of effective group decision making by asking participants to formulate, analyze, and then solve the problem through a series of questions. A description of this procedure is found in box 7.1

Avoiding the Pitfalls

Using a format is the first step to effective problem solving; avoiding common decision-making pitfalls is the second. Groups make significant mistakes at every stage of the decision-making process. Members fail to recognize that there is a problem or come up with the wrong cause(s), for example. They set unclear or inappropriate goals that fail to adequately address the situation and misjudge the negative and positive consequences of alternative solutions. Faulty information and/or the faulty use of information also derail group deliberations. Problem solvers often ignore important details or rely on inaccurate information. Even if their information is sound, they may misinterpret or misapply the data.[33]

In light of the logical pitfalls of group decision making, Gouran and Hirokawa argue that counteractive influence—statements that highlight problems in reasoning and get the group back on track—are particularly important to group success. Leaders and followers exercising counteractive influence draw attention to faulty problem definitions, information, assumptions, and inferences. They challenge the group when it deviates from its mutually agreed upon procedures and aren't afraid to take issue with high-status members who are leading the rest of the participants astray.[34]

Poor logic isn't the only cause of faulty decision making. The relationships between members, referred to as the social or emotional dimension of the group, can also lead to poor choices.[35] Members who don't trust each other aren't likely to share important information, for instance, or to work hard on a

---

Box 7.1

The Single Question Format[36]

1. Identify the Problem
What is the *single question* to which the group needs to find an answer to accomplish its purpose for meeting?

2. Create a Collaborative Setting
  a. Agree on principles for discussion.
   What principles should we agree on in order to maintain a reasonable and collaborative approach throughout the process?
   Examples: We will:
   1. Invite and understand all points of view.
   2. Remain fact-based in our judgments.
   3. Be tough on the issues, not on each other.
   4. Put aside any personal agenda.

  b. Surface any assumptions and biases.
   What assumptions and biases are associated with the single question identified in step 1, and how might they influence the discussion?
   Examples:
   1. We tend to assume we know our customers' needs.
   2. We believe we have efficient processes.
   3. We think our level of customer service is acceptable.
   4. We assume our past approach should be our future strategy.

3. Identify and Analyze the Issues (Subquestions)
Before responding to the single question in step 1, what *issues,* or *subquestions, must be answered* in order to fully understand the complexities of the overall problem?
  • Limit opinions by focusing on the facts.
  • If facts are unavailable, agree on the *most reasonable* response to each subquestion.

4. Identify Possible Solutions
Based on an analysis of the issues, what are the two or three most reasonable solutions to the problem? Record the advantages/disadvantages of each.

	Advantages	Disadvantages
Solution 1		
Solution 2		
Solution 3		

5. Resolve the Single Question
Among the possible solutions, which one is *most desirable?*

project. On the other hand, too much emphasis on strong relationships (which puts cohesion above performance) can also be detrimental.

Social psychologist Irving Janis developed the label *groupthink* to characterize groups that put unanimous agreement above all other considerations.[37] Groups that suffer from this syndrome fail to: consider all the alternatives, reexamine a course of action when it doesn't seem to be working, gather additional information, weigh the risks of their choices, work out contingency plans, or discuss important ethical issues. Janis noted faulty thinking in groups of ordinary citizens but is best known for his analysis of major U.S. policy disasters like the failure to anticipate the attack on Pearl Harbor, the Bay of Pigs invasion of Cuba, the invasion of North Korea, and the escalation of the Vietnam War. In each case, some of the smartest political and military leaders in U.S. history made poor choices.

Janis identified the following as symptoms or signs of groupthink:

Signs of Overconfidence

1. *Illusion of invulnerability.* Members are overly optimistic and prone to take extraordinary risks.

2. *Belief in the inherent morality of the group.* Participants ignore the ethical consequences of their actions and decisions.

Signs of Closedmindedness

3. *Collective rationalization.* Group members invent rationalizations to protect themselves from feedback that would challenge their assumptions.

4. *Stereotypes of outside groups.* Participants believe that members of other groups are evil, weak, or stupid; they underestimate the capabilities of others.

Signs of Group Pressure

5. *Pressure on dissenters.* Members coerce dissenting members to go along with the prevailing opinion in the group.

6. *Self-censorship.* Individuals keep their doubts about group decisions to themselves.

7. *Illusion of unanimity.* Group members mistakenly assume that the absence of conflicting opinions means that the entire group agrees on a course of action.

8. *Self-appointed mindguards.* Group members take it upon themselves to protect the leader from dissenting opinions that might disrupt the group's consensus.

A number of factors contribute to the emergence of groupthink, including failing to follow a decision-making procedure, group isolation, time pressures, homogenous members (same background and values), external threats, and low individual and group esteem caused by previous failures. However, leadership may be the most important influence contributing to groupthink.[38] Directive leaders who push for a particular solution cut off discussion and reduce the number of alternatives considered by the group.

Fortunately, leaders can prevent groupthink as well as promote it.[39] As a leader, don't express your preference for a particular solution; urge members to participate in the deliberations and to look at a variety of alternatives. Encourage every group member to be a critical evaluator and assign individual participants the role of "devil's advocate" to argue against prevailing opinion. Follow a set of decision-making guidelines like those outlined earlier. Divide regularly into subgroups and then come back to negotiate differences. Invite outside experts or colleagues to the group's meetings to challenge the group's ideas. Keep in regular contact with other groups in the organization. Role-play the reactions of rival organizations and groups to reduce the effects of stereotyping and rationalization. Visualize successful collective performance and eliminate negative talk and thought ("we can't succeed"; "the task is too difficult") within the group. Help members challenge the assumption that whatever they do is right and discuss the moral implications of choices.

After the decision has been made, give members one last chance to express any remaining doubts about the solution. The ancient Persians provide one example of how to revisit decisions. They made every major decision twice— once when sober and again when under the influence of wine!

In addition to poor logic and unhealthy relationships, the anxieties of individual members can undermine group problem solving. George Washington University management professor Jerry Harvey argues that it is often individual fears, not conformity pressures, that get groups in trouble.[40] He notes that we always have a choice about how to act in a group and must take responsibility for our behavior. Harvey introduces the concept of mismanaged agreement as an alternative to groupthink.

Mismanaged agreement refers to the tendency of group members to publicly support decisions that they oppose in private. As a result, groups continue to fund software installations that no one believes will ever become operational, for example, or engage in business practices that everyone in the group knows are illegal.[41] Professor Harvey calls mismanaged agreement the Abilene Paradox based on an experience his family had many years ago. He, his wife, and his in-laws decided to drive 100 miles from Coleman to Abilene, Texas, in 100-degree-plus heat in a car without air conditioning. They made this trip to eat bad cafeteria food that "could serve as a first-rate prop in an antacid commercial." After arriving home, the family discovered that nobody had wanted to make the trip in the first place. Harvey believes that many groups and organizations also embark on needless excursions. They act in direct contradiction to their true desires and thereby undermine their goals.

Groups caught in the Abilene Paradox display several symptoms. Participants agree in private about the definition of the problem and the right course of action. However, they fail to accurately communicate their thoughts and feelings to others, which misleads their fellow members into thinking that a consensus exists. Members express support for the nonexistent consensus and make decisions that run contrary to their own beliefs. These decisions have negative consequences for the group and organization. The level of anger, frustration, and dissatisfaction skyrockets as a result. Members point the finger of blame at other groups, other members, and their leaders. If the cycle is not interrupted, it will repeat itself, resulting in even greater destruction.

The causes of the Abilene Paradox are rooted in fear. Individuals know what ought to be done but are too anxious to follow through (action anxiety). They would rather endure the negative consequences of going along (economic costs, moral failure, career damage) than speak up. Members have negative fantasies about what will happen if they do act on what they believe ("I'll be criticized for not being a 'team player.'" "I'll get a lower quarterly evaluation."). They also fear separation. Group members dread being cut off or separated from their colleagues. This drives them to accede to what they think is the collective will of the group even when they have serious reservations about the decision.

Diagnosis and confrontation are the keys to breaking out of the Paradox.[42] You can use the self-assessment in box 7.2 to determine if your group is suffering from mismanaged agreement. If you are on an unproductive "trip," take the initiative to challenge the group's direction. Call a meeting where you state your true opinion and invite feedback, discussion, and debate. Reward those who confront the group instead of, as is too often the case, "shooting the messenger." Create an organizational climate where group members feel free to

---

Box 7.2   Self-Assessment
Mismanaged Agreement Diagnostic Survey[43]

Instructions: For each of the following statements, please indicate whether it is or is not characteristic of your group or organization. The more responses you identify as "characteristic," the more likely it is your group is on its way to its own "Abilene."

1. There is conflict in the group [organization].

2. Group [organizational] members feel frustrated, impotent, and unhappy when trying to deal with conflict. Many are looking for ways to escape. They may avoid meetings at which the conflict is discussed, they may be looking for new jobs, or they may spend as much time away from the office as possible by taking unneeded trips or sick leave.

3. Group [organizational] members place much of the blame for the dilemma on the boss or other groups. In "backroom" conversations among friends, the boss is termed incompetent, ineffective, "out of touch," or a candidate for early retirement. Nothing is said to his/her face, or at best, only oblique references are made concerning the group's or organization's problems. If the boss isn't blamed, some other group, division, or unit is seen as the culprit: "We would do fine if it were not for the damn fools in Division X."

4. Small subgroups of trusted friends and associates meet informally over coffee, lunch, and so on, to discuss group/organizational problems. There is a lot of agreement among the members of these subgroups regarding the cause of the troubles and the solutions that would be effective in solving them. Such conversations are frequently punctuated with statements beginning with "We should do . . ."

5. In meetings where those same people meet with members of other subgroups to discuss the problem, they "soften" their positions, state them in ambiguous language, or even reverse them to suit the apparent positions taken by others.

6. After such meetings, members complain to trusted associates that they really didn't say what they want to say, but they also provide a list of convincing reasons why the comments, suggestions, and reactions they wanted to make would have been impossible. Trusted associates commiserate and say that the same was true for them.

7. Attempts to solve the problem do not seem to work. In fact, such attempts seem to add to the problem or make it worse.

8. Individuals seem to get along better, be happier, and operate more effectively outside the group [organization] than they do within it.

express their opinions; where changing one's mind is seen as a sign of strength, not weakness; and where reaching shared goals is more important than pleasing the boss.

> Nothing is impossible to those who act after wise counsel and careful thought.
>
> —Tiruvalluvar

Team Leadership

We noted earlier that two of the distinguishing features of groups are commonality of purpose and interdependence. Members of every small group rely on each other as they work toward their objectives. Yet, some groups are more focused than others. Members of these groups are much more dependent on one another. Compare, for example, a task force designing a software product due on the market in six months to a board of directors that oversees a business. The task force has a narrow goal that cannot be achieved unless members coordinate their activities on a daily basis. The board can reach its broad objective by meeting a few times a year and by assigning ongoing tasks to individual members.

> When a team outgrows individual performance and learns team confidence, excellence becomes a reality.
>
> —Joe Paterno

When Is a Group a Team?

In recognition of the fact that groups such as task forces and boards of directors function in different ways, some observers argue that we ought to differentiate between groups and teams. They suggest that while every team is a group, not every group is a team. The two leading proponents of this position are Jon Katzenbach and Douglas Smith. See the following page for the contrasts they draw between working groups and teams.[44]

Working Group	Team
Individual work products	Collective work products
Individual accountability	Individual and group accountability
Group's purpose is the same as the broader organizational mission	Specific team purpose
Measures performance indirectly by how it influences others (e.g., financial performance of the business)	Measures its effectiveness directly by assessing collective work products
Runs meetings and active problem-solving meetings	Encourages open-ended discussion
Discusses, decides, and delegates	Discusses, decides, and does real work together
Strong, clearly focused leader	Shared leadership roles

Katzenbach and Smith believe that the key difference between a working group and a team lies in what each produces. In a working group, members meet to share information, discuss ongoing projects, and make decisions. They don't produce anything collectively and are judged largely on their individual efforts. In a team, on the other hand, members work together to produce a joint product, such as an assigned class paper, a science experiment, or a marketing strategy. While the working group shares the overall mission of the organization and measures its effectiveness by how well the whole organization does, the team has a unique purpose and clearly defined performance goals ("cut working defects on the assembly line by 25 percent"; "recommend a new site for the plant by August"). Leaders of formal working groups often control the agenda and make most of the decisions and assignments. Team leaders share decision-making responsibilities, let team members take the initiative in their areas of expertise, and are active participants in the work.

Common types of teams include (1) teams that recommend things (choosing a new computer system; planning a reorganization), (2) teams that make or do things (sell or service products, for example), and (3) teams that run things (managing the development of a product line). There are many potential advantages to taking a team approach.

- Teams are more flexible than departments or organizations.
- Teams are more productive and fun than working groups.
- Teams help the organization adapt to change.
- Teams encourage individual learning and foster new behaviors.
- Teams build trust and confidence between members.
- Teams focus attention on the group agenda rather than on individual agendas.

Despite their many advantages, teams aren't the answer in every situation. Top-level executives are one category of employees who generally function in working groups because their goals overlap those of the entire organization, their rewards are based on individual efforts, and their performance is mea-

sured indirectly through the success of their units.[45] The director of a government agency, for instance, will likely take a group approach to running her
organization, asking department heads to meet regularly to coordinate their
activities. However, when she wants to make a major change in the structure or
operations of the agency, a team approach will probably produce better results.
The crucial decision for a leader, then, is to determine whether a group
approach or a team approach is best. If performance levels can be met through
individual activities, then stick with working groups. Make the shift from
groups to teams only when the potential payoff outweighs the costs (effort, disruption, expense, etc.) of making the change.

Katzenbach and Smith use the team performance curve diagrammed in
figure 7.1 to describe how an existing working group becomes a team. The first
stage in the curve—the pseudo-team—reflects a decline in performance. When
a group decides to become a team, but hasn't yet set performance standards,
individual performance declines without any corresponding increase in group
performance. Or, to put it another way: "In pseudo-teams, the sum of the
whole is less than the potential of the individual parts."[46] The second stage of
the curve reflects a sharp increase in performance as the group makes a strong
effort to improve its output, even though members have yet to establish collective accountability. Performance increases still further when the group becomes
a real team, which Katzenbach and Smith define as "a small number of people
with complementary skills who *are equally committed to a common purpose, goals,
and working approach for which they hold themselves mutually accountable.*"[47] The
peak of the performance curve comes when the group evolves into a high-per-

Figure 7.1   The Team Performance Curve[48]

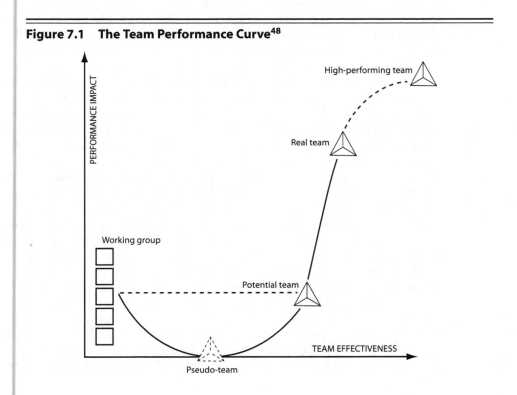

formance team made up of members who are very committed to each other's growth and success.

Developing Team-Building Skills

Successful leaders use team-building skills to help groups move up the performance curve. Carl Larson and Frank LaFasto spent nearly three years studying more than 75 diverse teams.[49] Larson and LaFasto interviewed key members of these teams, including the leader of the Boeing 747 project, a person who served on several presidential cabinets, members of cardiac surgery teams, the founder of the U.S. Space Command, a member of a Mount Everest climbing expedition, and several players from the 1966 Notre Dame championship football team. From their groundbreaking work, Larson and LaFasto identified eight strategies that they believe are essential to effective team performance.

Establish clear and inspiring team goals. Effective teams are clearly focused on goals that maximize team outcomes. Further, these goals inspire the team to perform at peak levels. The team leader is primarily responsible for defining and articulating goals and for motivating followers. Team failure can be caused by a lack of clarity in the identification of a team agenda, the loss of focus from the agenda, or from distractions associated with individual demands at the expense of the group.

Maintain a results-oriented team structure. Within effective teams, each member clearly understands his or her role in the overall successful functioning of the group. Further, team members are accountable for their behavior in all situations. Every member of a successful team knows what is expected and takes responsibility for making sure tasks are done correctly. Members of a surgical team, for example, all play an important role in the overall success of an operation. The anesthesiologist monitors the patient's breathing, the nurse prepares the instruments, and the surgeon performs the procedure. Each member of the team must perform his or her task in concert with others in order to achieve a successful outcome. Communication within results-oriented teams is open and honest. Effective team leaders communicate in a highly democratic manner. (You may want to refer back to chapter 2 to reacquaint yourself with the qualities of the democratic leadership communication style.) Information is easily accessible, and questions and comments are always welcomed from all members of the group. Successful team leaders also provide frequent evaluation and feedback to members. Identifying strengths and weaknesses of group members is necessary in order to reward excellence and to suggest strategies for improving deficiencies. Finally, results-oriented teams base their decisions on sound factual data. Although "gut" feelings and hunches may produce positive results on occasion, successful decision making is based on objective criteria.

Assemble competent team members. Effective teams are comprised of competent team members. Both technical and interpersonal competencies are essential to team success. Technical competence refers to the knowledge, skills, and abilities relevant to the team's goals. Interpersonal competence relates to the ability of team members to communicate feelings and needs, to resolve conflict, and to think critically. Google has a reputation as one of the most innovative organizations in the computer industry. One reason for the company's success is that Google hires only the most highly regarded talent. In 2004, Google placed a billboard advertisement in the heart of Silicon Valley along congested Highway 101. The white ad with black lettering posed a complex mathematical question.

The billboard read: "{first 10-digit prime found in consecutive digits *e*}.com." The answer, 7427466391.com, would lead a puzzle-sleuth to a Web page with yet another equation to solve, with still no sign the game was hosted by Google. Mastering that equation would lead someone to a page on Google Labs, the company's research and development department, which read: "One thing we learned while building Google is that it's easier to find what you're looking for if it comes looking for you. What we're looking for are the best engineers in the world. And here you are."[50]

Strive for unified commitment. The members of successful teams are wholly committed. Leaders seeking this type of unified commitment must work to create a team identity. Team identity is enhanced when team members are involved in decision making, policy implementation, and analysis. Indeed, involvement begets commitment. The president's cabinet and staff are examples of unified teams with a collective identity. Members of these groups feel such a strong sense of duty that they are literally on call to handle any crisis that may arise.

Provide a collaborative climate. Cooperation and teamwork are essential to allow teams to function smoothly. Teams that work well together perform most effectively. Trust is the key ingredient in teamwork. An open, honest environment in which team members trust and respect one another promotes collaboration. In such an atmosphere, team members feel free to express dissenting opinions, thus avoiding groupthink.

Encourage standards of excellence. Successful teams have high expectations regarding outcomes. These standards of excellence define acceptable performance. High standards mean hard work, and top performing teams spend a great deal of time preparing and practicing. They are ready for virtually any contingency. The cockpit crew of United Airlines Flight 232 performed an almost impossible task in July 1989 during a crash landing at Sioux City, Iowa. Although over 100 passengers died, aviation experts lauded the crew for maneuvering the plane under the most extreme emergency—a complete failure of the hydraulic system. Fortunately for the surviving 185 passengers, the crew believed that they could do the impossible. Standards of excellence are found everywhere within successful teams. Individual team members expect excellence from themselves and others. Perhaps most importantly, the leaders of highly effective teams demand that a standard of excellence be upheld. They will accept nothing less from themselves or the team. (Turn to Leadership on the Big Screen at the end of the chapter for an example of one team that wouldn't accept failure.)

Furnish external support and recognition. External support in the form of material or social rewards is important to the success of teams. These rewards alone do not guarantee success, but the absence of any form of external recognition or support appears to be detrimental to a team's overall effectiveness. According to Larson and LaFasto, recognition and support are most critical when the team is performing either extremely well or extremely poorly.

Apply principled leadership. The leaders of effective teams employ transformational leadership techniques. As discussed in chapter 4, the transformational leader is creative, interactive, visionary, empowering, and passionate. Larson and LaFasto found that three qualities seemed most important to effective team leadership: (1) establishing a vision; (2) creating change; and (3) unleashing talent. Effective team leaders have a clear vision for the team. The specific actions required to achieve this vision are clearly presented to team members. Further, this vision represents an inspiring and desirable goal for the group. Effective leaders also create change. Change is essential to improving and progressing. Effective team leaders encourage team members to seek out new and better ways to perform tasks and solve problems. Successful team leaders are not completely satisfied with the present level of achievement; they are always looking to the next challenge. Finally, effective team leaders empower their followers by unleashing the talent of all members of the team.

> The most effective leaders, as reported by our sample, were those who subjugated the needs of their ego in favor of the team's goals. They allowed team members to take part in shaping the destiny of the team's effort. They allowed them to decide, to make choices, to act, to do something meaningful. The result of this approach was the creation of the "multiplier effect." It created a contagion among team members to unlock their own leadership abilities.[51]

> It is not the individual but the team that is the instrument of sustained and enduring success in management.
> —Anthony Jay

LaFasto and Larson extended their exploration of successful teams with *When Teams Work Best*.[52] In this book, the authors report the results of data collected from 6,000 team members over a 14-year period. They conclude that five dynamics—*the team member, team relationships, team problem solving, team leadership,* and *the organizational environment*—are fundamental to team success.

The team member. Successful teams are most often a collection of effective individuals. Six factors differentiate effective from ineffective team members. (1) Experience—they know the task, are technically competent, and have a clear sense of vision. (2) Problem-solving ability—they proactively assist the team in resolving critical problems. (3) Openness—they address issues in a straightforward manner and promote an open exchange of ideas within the team. (4) Supportiveness—they provide encouragement and demonstrate a willingness to help others succeed. (5) Action orientation—they are willing to take action and prod others on the team to take initiative as well. (6) Personal style—they display behavior that is energetic, optimistic, engaging, fun-loving, and confident.

Team relationships. Although the individual qualities of each team member form the basic building blocks of team success, how well the team works together is critical in determining overall team effectiveness. LaFasto and Larson suggest the most significant barrier in building effective team relationships is the inability to give and receive feedback. To improve feedback ability and to strengthen existing interpersonal relationships, they recommend following the seven steps in The Connect Model. The first letter of each of the steps form the acronym CONNECT.

Step 1: Commit to the relationship. Let the other person know that you are interested in strengthening your relationship with him/her. Tell the other person why you believe it is worth having a conversation and reinforce your willingness to work to improve the relationship.

Step 2: Optimize safety. After you commit to the relationship, help the other person feel safe by letting him/her know you will try your hardest not to make him/her feel defensive. This means you will commit to making every effort to understand and appreciate the other person's point of view and try to suspend judgment.

Step 3: Narrow to one issue. After creating a safe environment for discussion, the next step is to identify a single issue to be addressed. The issue might be the scheduling of breaks, statements that have been made in team meetings, the level of trust in the relationship, or your roles on an upcoming project.

Step 4: Neutralize defensiveness. Before the conversation begins, think about the types of words, statements, or behaviors that might cause a defensive reaction in the other person. Avoid these provoking actions. While engaging in discussion, ask the other person to let you know if he/she is feeling defensive at any point. Use this feedback to work to diffuse defensive reactions.

Step 5: Explain and echo. Explain what you observe, how it makes you feel, and the long-term consequences. For example:

> What I observe, Sally, is that you have a tendency to interrupt me in group meetings. In the budget meeting the other day, for instance, I had an idea that I tried to bring up a couple of times, and each time you interrupted me, and I had to wait. Eventually, the idea came out, but maybe we could have gotten to it sooner if I had been given a chance. It makes me feel less valued, like my ideas don't have a lot of merit. It makes me feel frustrated because I can't seem to get my ideas on the table. And I am starting to feel resentful. The consequences are, if we don't change this, I don't think I'm going to want to be in meetings with you in the future.[53]

After providing the explanation, ask the other person to echo (paraphrase) your concerns. Allow the other person to state his or her concerns and echo back your understanding of those issues.

Step 6: Change one behavior each. Based on the discussions in steps one through five, initiate a conversation about a change that both of you could make to improve the situation. Agree on one behavior each person will initiate or terminate.

Step 7: Track it. Monitor progress on the agreement by selecting some specific follow-up times to give one another feedback on the effectiveness of the agreements reached in step six.

Team problem solving. A major part of any team's work consists of solving problems to advance the team toward its goals. The team members in LaFasto and Larson's research suggest that three key factors are critical to effective team problem solving—the degree to which team members are focused and clear about what they are trying to accomplish; the creation of a team climate that emphasizes a relaxed, comfortable, and accepting atmosphere; and open and honest communication. Team problem solving is further enhanced by the use of a systematic strategy like the Standard Agenda and Single Question Format approaches presented earlier in this chapter.

Team leadership. Successful team leaders share six consistent leadership competencies. (1) Focus on the goal—establish a common goal for the team and continue to reinforce that goal to keep the team on track. (2) Ensure a collaborative climate—promote a safe environment where team members can openly discuss issues. (3) Build confidence—work to strengthen the self-confidence of team members by building and maintaining trust and offering meaningful levels of responsibility. (4) Demonstrate sufficient technical know-how—be technically competent in matters relating to team tasks and goals. (5) Set priorities—keep the team focused on a manageable set of priorities. (6) Manage performance—offer clear performance expectations, recognize and reward superior performance, and provide developmental feedback to team members.

The organizational environment. The organizational environment is the psychological atmosphere that permeates the broader organization within which a team operates. Like the concept of organizational culture we will discuss in chapter 8, the environment can enhance or inhibit the achievement of successful outcomes. A productive work environment depends on the effectiveness of three organizational dimensions: management practices that set direction, align effort, and deliver results; structure and processes that ensure the best decisions are made as quickly as possible by competent people; and systems that provide relevant information and drive behavior toward desired results.

Self-Directed Work Teams

One type of team seen with increasing frequency in organizations is the self-directed work team (SDWT)—an intact, interdependent group of approximately six to ten highly trained employees who are responsible for managing themselves and their work.[54] SDWTs are generally responsible for a complete product or process. Unlike traditional group or team structures, where an organizational segment may be divided by functional specialties (for example, accounting or marketing), SDWTs are usually responsible for the delivery of an entire service or product. In this way, SDWTs operate like small businesses within a larger organization.

Several characteristics typically distinguish SDWTs from other types of teams:

- SDWTs consist of multiskilled, cross-trained employees who are responsible for an entire job.
- Quality and process control are an ongoing, key SDWT responsibility.
- SDWTs are empowered to share a wide variety of management and leadership functions, including: scheduling, budgeting, purchasing, inventory control, and, in many cases, hiring and firing.
- Leadership is shared by the SDWT, rather than assigned to a supervisor. (If there is a designated team leader, he or she plays the role of facilitator, supporting the group as a coach, rather than acting as a boss.)

- SDWTs meet regularly to diagnose and to solve their own problems.
- Customer satisfaction and overall business needs are the primary focus of SDWTs. Information generally reserved for management is passed on to the team so members can make informed decisions.
- SDWTs engage in ongoing training as a means for enhancing team skills.[55]

> As we look ahead into the next century, leaders will be those who empower others.
>
> —Bill Gates

In practice, SDWTs can be classified by their degree of empowerment. Figure 7.2 illustrates responsibilities delegated to a team at four levels of empowerment. The first level on the continuum describes the responsibilities generally assigned to a newly formed team. These team duties include such tasks as running meetings ("housekeeping"), cross-training, and scheduling. As the team matures and the level of empowerment increases, members may take responsibility for continuous improvement of their processes, monitoring external customer relationships, recruiting and selecting new members, and

Figure 7.2   Team Empowerment Continuum[56]

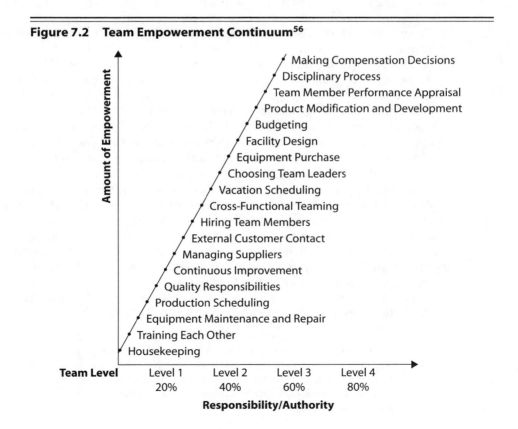

making decisions about capital expenditures and budgeting. At level four, the mature self-directed team assumes the responsibilities related to performance appraisal, discipline, and even compensation. At this level, the team controls about 80 percent of their total work responsibilities. The remaining responsibilities, mostly administrative and strategic in nature (e.g., establishing administrative policies, long-range planning), are generally performed by leaders outside the team.[57]

Although the SDWT approach has only recently begun to receive widespread attention, SDWTs have been successfully used in organizations for many years. In 1951, management professor Eric Trist and his student Kenneth Bamforth trained British coal miners to work in SDWTs.[58] The miners were taught to assist one another with key tasks and to trade jobs when workloads became unbalanced or tedious. Further, each work team was permitted to set its own rate of production and was responsible for handling its own conflicts. The output of these self-directed teams was compared with that of groups in the same organization using traditional hierarchical management. Trist and Bamforth discovered clear indications of higher productivity and job satisfaction among workers in the self-directed teams. The miners in SDWTs outperformed their hierarchically managed counterparts by approximately 34 percent, or 1.8 tons of coal per shift.

Application of self-direction didn't begin in the United States until the early 1960s. The earliest SDWT experiment was undertaken by Procter & Gamble. The results of this experiment with self-direction were so successful that the company declared them trade secrets, with all the restrictions and security precautions associated with product development.[59] In 1990, 26 percent of all organizations in the United States had employees working in SDWTs.[60] By 1999, nearly half of all Fortune 1000 organizations had integrated SDWTs into their operations.[61] Over the past decade a wide variety of large (Boeing, Bristol-Myers Squibb, Corning, General Electric, Hewlett-Packard, IBM, and Xerox) and small (Ampex, Johnsonville Foods, Lake Superior Paper, and Sterling Winthrop Limited) companies have had success with SDWTs.[62] These numbers will likely continue to increase as more organizations become aware of the dramatic results of self-directed work teams (see the chart in box 7.3).

Making the transition from a traditional organizational structure to a SDWT environment can be difficult. The transition is, perhaps, most difficult for managers who must make the switch from playing the role of supervisor to playing the role of facilitator. The key differences between the traditional manager and the SDWT facilitator are outlined in box 7.4. As a facilitator, emphasis is placed on developing the leadership skills of team members while, at the same time, serving as an advocate for the team by enabling team members to free themselves from internal and external obstacles to group effectiveness.[63] Making this change can be difficult, as Kenneth Labich notes:

> Managers are often directly on the firing line when a company begins experimenting with a new management method. They are asked to learn entirely new ways of behaving, and their worth to the company can suddenly depend on their willingness to do something adults generally hate to do: change. The pressures can be intense, leading at times to a professional identity crisis.[64]

Box 7.3   Research Highlight
The Effectiveness of Self-Directed Work Teams

An increasing number of organizations have implemented the self-directed work team approach. Research suggests self-directed team members are more innovative, able to share information, involved, and task-skilled than those in more traditional organizational structures.[65] These outcomes appear to relate directly to increased productivity and satisfaction. Consider the following examples:

Organization	Results
AT&T Credit Corporation	Teams process 800 lease applications per day versus 400 per day before SDWTs.[66]
Carrier	Reduced unit turnaround time from two weeks to two days.[67]
Corning	Decrease in defect rate from 1,800 parts per million to 9 parts per million.[68]
Federal Express	Reduced service errors (incorrect bills and lost packages) by 13 percent in one year.[69]
General Mills	Productivity 40 percent higher than traditional factory.[70]
Hewlett-Packard	Cut financial transaction processing costs by 27 percent, realizing a savings of nearly $14 million.[71]
Honeywell	Output increased 280 percent.[72]
Miller Brewing Company	Reduced labor hours needed to produce a barrel of beer by 30 percent.[73]
Shenandoah Life Insurance	Case handling time reduced from 27 days to 2 days, resulting in $200,000 savings per year.[74]
Xerox	Teams are 30 percent more productive than traditionally managed counterparts.[75]

Box 7.4
The Self-Directed Work Team Facilitator as Leader[76]

Typical behaviors of the traditional manager and the self-directed work team (SDWT) facilitator.

The Traditional Manager	The SDWT Facilitator
Supervise	Empower
Direct	Develop
Focus on tasks	Focus on people
Make decisions for others	Assist with decision making
Set policies and procedures	Remove barriers for team
Tell people what to do	Listen to team members
Control people	Trust people
Meet with staff when necessary	Be visible and available
Punish mistakes	Reward risk taking
Manage change	Embrace change
Focus on the bottom line	Focus on the customer and the employee
Set limits	Believe there are no limits

Management consultant Kimball Fisher suggests four primary reasons why it is difficult for managers to make the transition to SDWT facilitation.[77] (See the case study in box 7.5 for an example of how difficult this transition can be.)

1. *Perceived loss of power and status.* Equality is emphasized in the SDWT environment. As a result, managerial titles and perks (such as preferred parking and office space) are generally relinquished. Although these symbols of power do little to engender respect among subordinates, they are often perceived by managers themselves as important indicators of organizational status. The egalitarian approach to leadership in SDWTs is problematic for some. In one organization using SDWTs, prospective employees are asked if they can work in an environment where there are no promotions (there are pay raises, but there are no increasing levels in which job titles change). The answer for many is, "No."

2. *The role of team facilitator may feel ambiguous.* Acting as a facilitator is an unfamiliar role for many managers. To be successful, supervisors at all levels need to have a clear understanding of the team facilitator role and how the role differs from traditional management.

3. *Job security concerns may frustrate supervisory change.* The phrase "self-directed" leads many managers to fear that supervisors are unnecessary. Although some companies have used the transition to SDWTs as an excuse for downsizing, the most successful transitions have capitalized on managerial experience by using former managers as team leaders and facilitators, trainers, consultants, and, in some cases, team members.

4. *Facilitators may be victims of a management "double standard."* Even if a manager successfully adapts to the role of facilitator, she may be caught in a double bind. The facilitator's superiors may still be using traditional management practices in dealing with her. For instance, the team may be responsible for its own performance appraisals and salary reviews based on team goals, while the facilitator is likely to be evaluated by her superiors using traditional appraisal standards that are based on individual, rather than team, performance. This "double standard" makes it difficult to play the role of team facilitator successfully.

While making the transition from a supervisor to facilitator role may be challenging, organizational leaders can smooth the way by screening out those who are unwilling to share power; by providing training that carefully outlines the responsibilities of facilitators; by ensuring job security during the transition period; and by adopting appraisal standards that evaluate team achieve-

Box 7.5   Case Study
Learning to Let Go: The Role of the Self-Directed Work Team Facilitator

Martin Kelly spent four years working as a sales representative in the marketing department at Aircom Industries. He traveled around the globe meeting with customers considering the purchase of various airplane components. Although Martin enjoyed this job, he decided he needed to gain additional experience to advance his career. The vice president of marketing and several of Martin's colleagues suggested he should seek an opportunity that would enable him to develop his skills as a manager. Martin applied for several positions in other Aircom departments. After two interviews he was offered a position in financial services.

The vice president of financial services, Judy Morton, was impressed with Martin's energy and eagerness. Though Martin had no previous experience managing others, Judy hired him as a manager in her department of 50 employees. Judy was certain that Martin would be a good choice to help her implement a new organizational structure—self-directed work teams (SDWTs). Martin was introduced to the staff at a luncheon. His enthusiasm was a breath of fresh air in a department that had experienced little turnover in the past decade. Shortly after he joined the department, Judy and Martin announced that employees would be reorganized into eight SDWTs. Martin would be the facilitator for four of the teams and another manager in the department, Anna Garcia, would be facilitator for the remaining teams.

Judy, Martin, and Anna consulted with other managers in Aircom who had successfully implemented SDWTs. They kicked off the project with a five-day training session that provided instruction regarding the use of SDWTs and the role of the SDWT facilitator. After the training, most people in the department were eagerly anticipating the change in their work environment.

It was quickly apparent that Anna was better prepared to serve as a facilitator than Martin. Anna encouraged her teams to make their own decisions; when approached with an idea or suggestion, she told team members to "give it a try." Martin, on the other hand, was much more controlling. When one of his teams approached him with the suggestion that a particular order management form was redundant and should be eliminated, he accused the team of trying to "get out of work" and called those who presented the idea "immature" and "irresponsible." Within a matter of months Anna's teams were developing process improvements, setting their own work schedules, managing daily work flow, and implementing training plans. Martin's teams were still closely supervised. Each day Martin would send several e-mails to his teams outlining what he considered to be the most urgent tasks to be completed. Since Martin was new in the department, his priorities were not always on target, and customers' needs were sometimes not met. Many on Martin's teams were dissatisfied, and morale was steadily declining.

Nearly a year after the introduction of SDWTs in financial services, Anna's teams had improved their productivity by nearly 15 percent. Those on Martin's teams were operating at levels 10 percent below where they were prior to the introduction of SDWTs. The problem became critical when three team members working for Martin transferred to other departments. In their exit interviews with Judy, the team members complained they were treated with a lack of respect. They added that they felt as if there was *less* autonomy working with Martin than there had been *before* the introduction of SDWTs. The productivity numbers and the information gained in the exit interviews convinced Judy it was time to discuss the situation with Martin.

Discussion Questions

1. What are the characteristics of an effective SDWT facilitator? How do these behaviors differ from those of a traditional manager?

2. Do you think anyone can learn to be an effective SDWT facilitator? Why? Why not? Are there any factors that Judy should have considered before hiring Martin?

3. Research suggests the effective use of SDWTs generally results in increased productivity and satisfaction. Why do you think this occurs? What made Anna's teams more successful than Martin's?

4. If you were Judy, what would you say to Martin?

5. What should be done to improve the morale on Martin's teams? How would you advise Martin to reestablish his credibility in the financial services department?

ments. The time, money, and effort leaders invest in the transition process will likely be rewarded with significant increases in productivity, quality, efficiency, and profits.

Leading Virtual Teams

Technological advances enable teams to function across space and time. No longer do members have to meet face-to-face. Now individuals working in different geographic locations and at different times of the day coordinate their efforts through *virtual teams*. Virtual teams use e-mail, videoconferencing, online bulletin boards, groupware, project management software, and other electronic means to carry out their work.[78] Large organizations like IBM, Sun Microsystems, Intel, NCR, Microsoft, Price Waterhouse Coopers, Eastman Kodak, and Hewlett-Packard rely on virtual teams to carry out marketing, consulting, project engineering, customer service, and other functions. Sabre, which processes 40 percent of the world's travel reservations, uses virtual teams in the United States and Canada to sell and maintain reservation systems. The company credits these teams for dramatic increases in market share and customer satisfaction.[79] Virtual teams are becoming more popular as organizations expand their international operations. Businesses and nonprofits want to draw on a wide variety of expertise from around the world without the expense of relocating employees or flying them to a central location. In addition, virtual global teams can respond more rapidly to changing international conditions than conventional teams, reducing product development times and costs.[80]

Some experts argue that leading a virtual team is more challenging than leading a traditional team.[81] Virtual teams add a layer of complexity. Leaders must carry out all the functions we described earlier in the chapter—making effective decisions, building a collaborative climate, encouraging unified commitment, and so forth. At the same time, they also have to cope with the problems created by space, time, and cultural differences as well as computer-mediated communication channels. Members often feel isolated and find it hard to stay committed to other team members they might never meet in person. Some in the group may have to get up early or stay up late to meet with those in other time zones. In virtual global teams, members have to manage cultural differences. Because electronic communication is not as "rich" (it doesn't carry as much information) as face-to-face communication, miscommunication is more likely. E-mail recipients have to decode messages without the benefit of verbal and nonverbal cues like tone of voice, facial expressions, and posture.

Research into virtual team leadership is still in its infancy. However, investigators suggest that effective leaders meet the added challenges of virtual teams through the following strategies.[82] You can draw on these tactics if you find yourself in charge of a dispersed team.

1. *Task-oriented team building.* In traditional groups, cohesion comes in large part from the informal interaction between group members, like gathering after work or impromptu discussions in the hallway. In virtual teams, team collaboration is more dependent on task performance—consistently carrying through on promises and assignments, responding quickly to requests, and so on. Effec-

tive virtual team leaders don't ignore the social dimension of group work. They may devote a good portion of initial e-mails and meetings to informal interaction about hobbies, work background, and family, for instance. However, the social component of team building complements the task dimension.

Team members generally come to the group with the expectation that other members are qualified based on their expertise and organizational roles. Perceptions of trustworthiness of other members form within "the first few keystrokes."[83] Brusque comments, ambiguous messages, and other credibility reducing behaviors undermine trust. Leaders can help build a trusting climate by rallying the group around a common project or task and expressing their commitment and enthusiasm. (We'll have more to say about trust building in the next chapter.)

How leaders and members respond to messages is particularly important to fostering collaboration in the virtual environment. Timely e-mail responses signal involvement, attraction, and attachment. Often the responder can provide information to help clarify the original message. Delayed responses frustrate communicators, can be interpreted as a signal of disinterest or dislike, and deprive senders of vital information needed to interpret earlier communication. The leaders of successful virtual teams encourage team members to respond quickly to messages. Predictability, like promptness, also plays a significant role in building cohesion. Group members don't always need to communicate often but they should do so in a consistent fashion (such as at the same time every week). They ought to notify others if they are going to be gone and can't participate in an upcoming discussion.

2. *A proactive approach to creating and maintaining structure.* While structure is necessary for on-site teams, it takes on added importance in virtual teaming. Dispersed teams need clear guidelines and structure to help overcome the barriers of distance, diverse backgrounds, and competing demands on their time. Effective leaders are proactive, outlining the group's purpose and member roles before the team is formed. They provide detailed instructions in writing, describe workflow, and outline operating rules (e.g., members should respond to all e-mails within 24 hours). They also set forth clear performance standards. Sabre Inc., for example, uses a balanced scorecard to evaluate its virtual teams. Teams are judged on growth of market share, profitability for each travel booking, process improvements (cycle time, installation time), and customer satisfaction. Once the group is underway, successful leaders make a continuous effort to maintain and improve structure. They continuously monitor group interaction as well as individual and collective performance, providing ongoing feedback to members on how well they are fulfilling their roles and meeting objectives.

3. *Mastery of communication technology and channels.* Since virtual groups are linked through computer-mediated communication, skillful use of technology is critical. Members must have access to the right technology and know how to use it. Leaders of productive teams ensure that followers have the necessary equipment and software and provide training. Yet, equipping and training are just the beginning. Effective leadership involves matching message content with the proper technology or format. To succeed, virtual team leaders must accurately determine which form of communication—e-mail, videoconferencing, online meetings—should be used in which situation. E-mails sent at differ-

ent times (*asynchronous* messages) work well for routine communication. However, as the need for information and coordination increases, real-time forums (*synchronous* communication) are required. These include online chats, regularly scheduled online meetings, and phone calls. Managing conflicts, reinforcing group cohesion, and dealing with the most complex project issues requires even richer channels—videoconferencing and, whenever possible, face-to-face meetings. (Read the Cultural Connections at the end of the chapter to see how culture should influence the selection of communication formats.)

CHAPTER TAKEAWAYS

- From a communication viewpoint, a small group has five essential elements: (1) a common purpose or goal, (2) interdependence, (3) mutual influence, (4) ongoing communication, and (5) a size of 3 to 20 members.

- Groups evolve over time. Both group decisions and group leaders emerge as the group changes and matures. Emergent group leaders (leaders who aren't appointed by someone outside the group) are selected through a process of elimination called the *method of residues*. Leader contenders are eliminated until only one remains.

- To emerge as a leader, avoid actions that eliminate you from contention like being silent, constantly joking around, or trying to impress others with your knowledge. Instead, participate frequently in the group discussion, make constructive contributions, demonstrate your competence, and help build a cohesive unit.

- Establish your leadership credentials or idiosyncratic credits by demonstrating that you can help the group complete its task and that you will conform to group norms.

- Followers expect more from emergent than from appointed leaders. On the other hand, they are willing to give emergent leaders more freedom to act on behalf of the group.

- To provide effective leadership in meetings: (1) determine if a meeting is necessary before calling people together; (2) have a clear agenda; (3) maintain focus on the agenda throughout the meeting; (4) listen to others; (5) involve all participants; (6) keep a record; and (7) evaluate the group's performance.

- Groups charged with making decisions are more likely to succeed when they use communication to fulfill key problem-solving functions—analysis of the problem, goal setting, identification of alternatives, and evaluation of solutions—through the use of such formats as the Standard Agenda and Single Question Format.

- Avoid logical pitfalls that undermine group decision making through counteractive influence. Highlight problems in reasoning and get the group back on track.

- Combat groupthink, which is the tendency to put cohesion above performance, by soliciting input rather than pushing for your own choices. Encourage diverse opinions and constructive group thought patterns.

- Be alert to the danger of mismanaged agreement, the tendency for members to support in public what they oppose in private. Mismanaged agreement (the Abilene Paradox) causes groups to make choices that undermine their goals. To break the Paradox, publicly challenge the direction of the group and encourage others to do likewise.

- A working group shares the overall mission of the organization and measures its effectiveness by how well the organization as a whole performs. Group members meet to share information and ideas, but they are judged on their individual efforts. In contrast, a team has a unique purpose and clearly defined performance standards. Members work together to produce a joint product, and the team is accountable for achieving its objectives.

- Successful leaders use team-building skills to help working groups move up the performance curve. Eight characteristics essential to effective team performance include: clear and inspiring team goals; results-oriented team structure (clear roles and responsibilities, an effective communication network, frequent feedback, objective criteria); competent team members; unified commitment; a collaborative climate; standards of excellence; external support and recognition; and principled (transformational) leadership.

- Key team dynamics include skilled members, effective problem solving, giving and receiving feedback, competent leadership, and a supportive organizational environment.

- Self-directed work teams (SDWTs) are empowered to operate like small businesses within a larger organization. Leaders can help managers who must switch from a supervisory to a facilitator role deal with perceived loss of power and status, feelings of ambiguity, job security concerns, and outdated appraisal standards by screening out unsuitable candidates, by providing training, by ensuring job protection, and by developing team-oriented evaluation guidelines.

- Virtual teams consist of members who work at different locations (often around the globe) and at different times who coordinate their efforts though e-mail, online meetings, videoconferencing, and other forms of electronic communication. To meet the challenges posed by spatial, time, and cultural differences, virtual team leaders need to: (1) engage in task-oriented team building; (2) take a proactive approach to providing and maintaining team structure; and (3) master communication technology and channels.

APPLICATION EXERCISES

1. Brainstorm a list of possible group norms. Which norms do leaders always have to follow? Which can they violate?

2. Discuss the pattern of leadership emergence in a group to which you belong. First, describe the communication patterns that eliminated members from leadership contention. Next, describe the communica-

tion behaviors of the leader (if one emerged) that contributed to that person's success. Evaluate your own performance. Why did you succeed in your attempt to become the leader or why did you fail? Finally, choose the leadership pattern that describes your group from the four identified in the Minnesota studies. Write up your findings.

3. Add to the list of reasons why you should or should not hold a meeting. What happens if you have a meeting when there isn't a valid reason for doing so?

4. Develop an agenda for an upcoming meeting using the guidelines provided in the chapter.

5. Form a group and use the Standard Agenda or Single Question Format to solve one of the following problems.

   • Due to a budget shortfall, one of your college or university's sports teams must be cut. The president of the school will act on the recommendation of your student panel. Decide which sport will be eliminated.

   • A wealthy donor has given $5 million to your institution "to be spent by students for the benefit of students." As members of student government, come up with recommendations for spending this gift.

   • Your college/university task force has been charged with developing a plan for improving relationships with the surrounding community. Outline a strategy for achieving this goal.

6. Determine if your group or organization is suffering from mismanaged agreement by completing the self-assessment instrument in box 7.2. If your group is caught in the Abilene Paradox, develop a plan for confronting the problem.

7. Analyze the performance of a team using the eight characteristics of effective teams presented in the chapter. Which elements are present? Which are missing? What can the team do to become more productive?

8. Describe a high performing team of which you have been a member. What made this team so successful? Why do you think other teams you were on were less successful?

9. Interview someone who has been a member of a self-directed work team or virtual team. Report your findings in class.

10. Write a research paper on virtual team leadership. What do you identify as the behaviors of effective virtual team leaders and members?

CULTURAL CONNECTIONS: DEVELOPING A GLOBAL TEAM CHARTER

There are many challenges in working as a member of a global team. Language and cultural barriers can lead to misunderstanding; geographic distances may contribute to feelings of isolation; and technical problems have the potential to derail communication. For these and other challenges, it is vitally important that global teams have a clear sense of direction and purpose. Michael Marquardt and Lisa Horvath suggest one way a global team can stay on track is to develop a Global Team Charter. [84] The essential elements of the charter include:

Goals. The charter should list *both* task and process goals in clear, specific, and measurable terms.

Expectations. Five to six expectations for performance should be identified. These expectations might address issues such as attendance, timeliness, conduct, communication norms, and deadline expectations, among other issues.

Policies and procedures. The boundaries for team behavior help to clarify when team members have met team expectations for performance. Examples of global team policies and procedures might include: a team member who fails to participate in the weekly status meeting without first notifying the team leader will be given a verbal warning; or team rewards will be based on overall team performance, not accomplishments at a single site.

Timeline and project plan. The charter divides the project into tasks with an appropriate timeline and completion dates. Tasks are assigned to specific team members and/or subgroups with regularly scheduled checkpoints noted.

Roles. Both task *and* process roles are clearly assigned.

Although this level of clarity is helpful for any team, Marquardt and Horvath argue that a Global Team Charter is crucial for the success of a geographically and culturally dispersed team. Sustaining team identity is very difficult in a global and predominately electronic environment—unless team members have a shared identity and objectives.[85]

SPOTLIGHT ON TECHNOLOGY:
VIRTUAL TEAMS: EAST/WEST DIFFERENCES IN E-MAIL USE[86]

Electronic mail has emerged as the communication channel of choice for corporations in the United States. Managers increasingly rely on e-mail messages instead of faxes, letters, phone calls, or even face-to-face discussions. E-mail is not as popular in East Asia, however. In Japan, for example, corporate leaders prefer faxes. They may find it easier to write Japanese characters on paper than to write them in e-mails. Yet even in Korea, which has an alphabet similar to English, business leaders do not use e-mail as often as do leaders in the United States.

Respect for elders, both in the workplace as well as in the family, may explain why employees in Japan, Korea, and China are more reluctant to use e-mail. Workers need to show deference to those senior in rank or age through special language and codes of conduct. They can't do so effectively through e-mail, which has a limited range of cues for interpreting messages. Sending e-mail could be seen as being rude (too easy or casual), thereby communicating disrespect. The results of a study of one virtual marketing team at a South Korean electronics manufacturer suggest that this is indeed the case. Team members used e-mail frequently for communicating with peers. However, e-mail messages between team members and the team leader were generally one sided. When the leader sent out extensive orders, followers responded with very short messages indicating that they would comply.

East/West differences in e-mail use mean that virtual team leaders need to pay careful attention to cultural factors when choosing communication channels. How they communicate with followers (and encourage followers to communicate with each other) should be based in part on the cultural background of team members.

LEADERSHIP ON THE BIG SCREEN: *APOLLO 13*

Starring: Tom Hanks, Ed Harris, Bill Saxton, Gary Sinise, Kevin Bacon, Kathleen Quinlan

Rating: PG for language and intensity

Synopsis: Based on the crisis that made the phrases "Houston, we have a problem" and "Failure is not an option" famous. The *Apollo 13* moon mission is aborted after an explosion on the ship. Getting the crew safely back to earth requires the extraordinary efforts of both the space crew led by Jim Lovell (played by Hanks) and the team at Houston mission control led by Gene Kranz (played by Harris). The two groups work together to cope with depleted oxygen and energy supplies, cold, dangerous levels of carbon dioxide, and damage to the capsule's heat shield. At one point, team members on earth figure out how to help the crew fit a square filter into a round hole on the ship using only items (socks, booklet cover, duct tape) available to the astronauts.

Chapter Links: group decision making, counteractive influence, team leadership, team building

Leadership in Organizations

> Good leaders make people feel they're at the heart of things,
> not at the periphery.
>
> —Fred Kofman

OVERVIEW

- Symbolic Leadership in the Organization
  - Communicating and Organizing
  - Elements of Organizational Culture
  - The Nature of Symbolic Leadership
  - Shaping Culture
  - Creating a Learning, Trusting Culture
- The Power of Expectations: The Pygmalion Effect
  - The Communication of Expectations
  - The Galatea Effect
  - Putting Pygmalion to Work

Leaders and organizations: it's hard to talk for very long about either topic without mentioning the other. Although this chapter is devoted to a discussion of leadership in organizations, we've already talked at length about organizational leadership in this book. For example, most of the leadership theories presented in chapters 3 and 4 were developed by organizational scholars. Interest in organizational leadership is not surprising when you consider that leaders are extremely important to the health of organizations and that we spend a good deal of our time in organizations. Amitai Etzioni sums up the importance of organizations this way:

> We are born in organizations, educated by organizations, and most of us spend much of our lives working for organizations. We spend much of our leisure time paying, playing, and praying in organizations. Most of us will die in an organization and when the time comes for burial, the largest organization of all—the state—must grant official permission.[1]

In the pages that follow we will focus, first of all, on the nature of organizations and symbolic leadership. Then we'll explore the ways that leader expectations can either increase or decrease follower performance.

Symbolic Leadership in the Organization

Organizational experts have traditionally taken a "container approach" to organizational life. When the organization is seen as a container, communication becomes only one of many variables that determine the health of the organization.[2] Textbooks written from this perspective talk about how leaders design organizational structures, manage information, oversee tasks and relationships, use technology, and so forth. The container approach understates the role of communication in organizing.

Communicating and Organizing

Earlier we noted that humans have the ability to create reality through their use of symbols, and this is readily apparent in the organizational context. Organizations are formed through the process of communication. As organizational members meet and interact, they develop a shared meaning for events. Communication is not contained within the organization. Instead, communication *is* the organization.

In recent years communication scholars and others have borrowed the idea of culture from the field of anthropology to describe how organizations create shared meanings.[3] From a cultural perspective, the organization resembles a tribe. Over time, the tribe develops its own language, hierarchy, ceremonies, customs, and beliefs. Because each organizational tribe shares different experiences and meanings, each develops its own unique way of seeing the world or culture. Anyone who joins a new company, governmental agency, or nonprofit group quickly recognizes unique differences in perspectives.

New employees often undergo culture shock as they move into an organization with a different language, authority structure, and attitude toward work and people. Even long-term members can feel out of place if they change positions within the same organization. Each department or branch office may represent a distinct subculture. Salespeople, for example, generally talk and dress differently than engineers employed by the same firm.[4]

Elements of Organizational Culture

Dividing organizational culture into three levels—assumptions, values, and symbols—provides important insights into how culture operates. Members of every organization share a set of assumptions that serve as the foundation for the group's culture. Assumptions are unstated beliefs about: human relationships (are relationships between organizational members hierarchical, group oriented, or individualistic?); human nature (are humans basically good or evil or neither?); truth (is it revealed by authority figures or discovered on one's own through testing?); the environment (should we master the environment, be subjugated to it, or live in harmony with it?); and universalism/particularism (should all organizational members be treated the same, or should some individuals receive preferential treatment?).[5] How an organization answers these questions will determine the way it treats employees and outsiders, whether or not members will respond favorably to directives from management, what sorts of products a company manufactures, and so on.

Values make up the next level of organizational culture. Frequently (but not always) recognized and acknowledged by members, values reflect what the organization feels it "ought" to do. They serve as the yardstick for judging behavior. One way to identify important values is by examining credos, vision and mission statements, and advertising slogans. Words like "concern," "quality," and "corporate responsibility" articulate the official goals and standards of the organization. At times, however, the official or espoused values conflict with what people actually do, as in the case of an organization that touts its commitment to the environment but engages in illegal dumping.

Symbols and symbolic creations called artifacts make up the top level of an organization's culture. By analyzing these visible elements, used in everyday interaction, we gain insights into an organization's assumptions and values.[6] Common organizational symbols and artifacts include:

language	buildings
stories and myths	products
rites and rituals	technology
written materials	heroes
metaphors	logos
dress and physical appearance	office decor

While there are far too many symbols to examine each in detail, experts pay particularly close attention to the first three symbols when they analyze organizational culture. We will review them briefly.

A good way to determine how an organization views itself and the world is by listening carefully to the *language* that organizational members use. Word choices reflect and reinforce working relationships and values. The selection of the word "we" is revealing. It reflects a willingness to share power and credit and to work with others (see chapter 5). The choice of terms to describe followers also provides important insights into organizational life. For example, using the term "associates" rather than "employees" suggests that all organizational participants are important members of the team. Workers at Disney theme parks are called "cast members" to emphasize that they have significant roles to play in the overall performance for visitors who are, in turn, called "guests."

Language is a powerful motivator that focuses attention on some aspects of experience and directs it away from others. Those who speak of innovation or quality workmanship ("BMW—The Ultimate Driving Machine") are generally more likely to provide creative and well-crafted products. In addition, a common language binds group members together. To demonstrate this fact, brainstorm a list of terms that you use frequently at school and on the job. Many verbal symbols like "student union" or "pull an all-nighter" that you take for granted as a student might not be familiar to those at your workplace. On the other hand, some of the terms you use at work might be new to other students.

Organizational *stories* carry multiple messages. They reflect important values, inspire, describe what members should do, and provide a means to vent emotions. In many cases, organizational members are more likely to believe the stories they hear from coworkers than the statistics they hear from management.[7] For example, workers at Intel tell the story of a manager who was fired after receiving an average performance evaluation. She was dismissed because "there are no average employees at Intel." This story makes it clear that the company has high expectations of its members. (Turn back to chapter 1 for more information on types of stories and storytelling.)

> The key to effective leadership in corporations is reading and responding to cultural cues.
>
> —Terrence Deal

Rituals, rites, and *routines* involve repeated patterns of behavior: saying "hello" in the morning to everyone on the floor; an annual staff retreat; or disciplinary procedures. Harrison Trice and Janice Beyer identify some common organizational rites:[8]

- *Rites of passage.* These events mark important changes in roles and statuses. When joining the army, for instance, the new recruit is stripped of his or her civilian identity and converted into a soldier with a new haircut, uniform, and prescribed ways of speaking and walking.

- *Rites of degradation.* Some rituals are used to lower the status of organizational members, such as when a coach or top executive is fired. These events are characterized by degradation talk aimed at discrediting the poor performer. Critics may claim, for example, that the coach couldn't get along with the players or that the executive was overly demanding.

- *Rites of enhancement.* Unlike rites of degradation, rites of enhancement raise the standing of organizational members. Giving medals to athletes, listing faculty publications in the college newsletter, and publicly distributing sales bonuses are examples of such rituals. Recall the example of Mary Kay Cosmetics in chapter 1. The Mary Kay Cosmetic Company is one organization that makes effective use of enhancement rituals. At Mary Kay seminars, high performers are rewarded with jewelry, fur stoles, and pink Cadillacs in front of cheering audiences. The pink Cadillac is a clear symbol of high status for the Mary Kay sales force, since this is the type of car that Mary Kay herself drove.

- *Rites of renewal.* These rituals strengthen the current system. Many widely used management techniques like management by objectives and organizational development are rites of renewal because they serve the status quo. Such programs direct attention toward employee evaluation, goal setting, long-range planning, and other areas that need improvement.

- *Rites of conflict reduction.* Organizations routinely use collective bargaining, task forces, and committees to resolve conflicts. Even though committees may not make important changes, their formation may reduce tension, since they signal that an organization is trying to be responsive.

- *Rites of integration.* Rites of integration tie subgroups to the large system. Annual stockholder meetings, professional gatherings, and office picnics all integrate people into larger organizations.

- *Rites of creation.* These rites celebrate and encourage change, helping organizations remain flexible in turbulent environments marked by rapid shifts in markets and technology. Some groups rotate individuals in and out of the role of devil's advocate to challenge the status quo, for example. One company went so far as to appoint a "vice-president for revolutions." Every four years he made dramatic changes in the organization's structure and personnel in order to introduce new perspectives.

- *Rites of transition.* Meetings, speeches, and other strategies can help organizational members accept changes that they didn't plan, as in the case of an unexpected merger. Addressing what the group has lost (past values, symbols, heroes) can ease the transition to a new culture.

- *Rites of parting.* When organizations die, parting ceremonies are common. Members meet to reminisce and to say goodbye, often over meals. These events help participants understand and accept the loss and provide them with emotional support.

The Nature of Symbolic Leadership

Viewing organizations as the product of symbol using suggests that organizational leaders play an important role in the creation of organizational meaning or culture. In particular, the organizational leader is actively involved in "symbolic leadership" by using symbols to determine meaning and the direction of the organization. Leaders can't always control what happens in organizations, but they can exert significant influence over how events are understood. Helping followers interpret events like mergers, market shifts, and new programs is an important task of organizational leadership. Organizational experts Gail Fairhurst and Robert Sarr use the term "framing" to describe how leaders encourage constituents to adopt one particular interpretation or frame instead of alternative explanations.[9] To translate a new corporate vision into action, for example, lower-level leaders must: (1) help followers understand the new concepts associated with the vision, (2) show followers how the new vision is relevant to their jobs, (3) demonstrate enthusiasm for the vision, (4) relate new ideas with established programs and practices, and (5) help stakeholders see the next steps in implementing the vision.

> Those who give voice and form to our search for meaning, and who help us make our world purposeful, are leaders we cherish, and to whom we return gift for gift.
>
> —Margaret Wheatley

Another important task of symbolic leadership is directing people's attention to future goals. At any given time, an organization can veer in many different directions. Even a successful company must: decide on new products and services, react to new government regulations, and maintain or change production methods. Rosabeth Moss Kanter calls these choices "action possibilities."[10] A successful leader uses his or her vision (created with the input of constituents) to guide the organization down one particular path—in Kanter's words, to one particular action possibility that meets both individual and collective needs. In doing so, a leader provides direction for an organization and, at the same time, may strengthen employee identification with the company. Complete the self-assessment in box 8.1 to determine how strongly you identify with a particular organization.

Symbolic leaders concern themselves with much more than organizational charts, information management systems, and all the other traditional subjects of management training. They pay close attention to the assumptions, values, and symbols that create and reflect organizational culture. Organizational psychologist Edgar Schein highlights the significant role that leaders play in the creation of organizational culture:

> Neither culture or leadership, when one examines each closely, can really be understood by itself. In fact, one could argue that the only thing of real importance that leaders do is to create and manage culture and that the unique talent of leaders is their ability to understand and work with culture.[11]

Schein notes that the responsibilities of symbolic leaders shift as the organization matures. The founder/owner, in addition to determining the group's purpose, imparting values, and recruiting followers, provides stability and reduces the anxiety people feel when an organization is just starting out.[12] A new organization often struggles with meeting its payroll, developing a market niche, and managing growth. The seeds of future problems are often sown during the organization's initial stage of development. For example, the founder/leader might emphasize teamwork but continue to make all major decisions. Other founders do not perform as effectively as leaders once the organization has been firmly established. Founders/leaders often lay the groundwork for future change by promoting people who will share some, but not all, of their values. Once the organization reaches mid-life and maturity, leaders (frequently someone other than the founder) become change agents who intervene

Box 8.1   Self-Assessment

Organizational Identification Questionnaire[13]

Think of an organization you currently work for or have worked for in the past. For each item below, select the answer that best represents your attitude toward or belief about the organization.

7 = agree very strongly   3 = disagree
6 = agree strongly   2 = disagree strongly
5 = agree   1 = disagree very strongly
4 = neither agree nor disagree

1. _____ I would probably continue working for _____ even if I didn't need the money.

2. _____ In general, the people employed by _____ are working toward the same goals.

3. _____ I am very proud to be an employee of _____.

4. _____ _____'s image in the community represents me as well.

5. _____ I often describe myself to others by saying, "I work for _____." or "I am from _____."

6. _____ I try to make on-the-job decisions by considering the consequences of my actions for _____.

7. _____ We at _____ are different from others in our field.

8. _____ I am glad I chose to work for _____ rather than another company.

9. _____ I talk up _____ to my friends as a great company to work for.

10. _____ In general, I view _____'s problems as my own.

11. _____ I am willing to put in a great deal of effort beyond that normally expected in order to help _____ be successful.

12. _____ I become irritated when I hear others outside _____ criticize the company.

13. _____ I have warm feelings toward _____ as a place to work.

14. _____ I would be quite willing to spend the rest of my career with _____.

15. _____ I feel that _____ cares about me.

16. _____ The record of _____ is an example of what dedicated people can achieve.

17. _____ I have a lot in common with others employed by _____.

18. _____ I find it difficult to agree with _____'s policies on important matters relating to me.

19. _____ My association with _____ is only a small part of who I am.

20. _____ I like to tell others about projects that _____ is working on.

21. _____ I find that my values and the values of _____ are very similar.

22. _____ I feel very little loyalty to _____.

23. _____ I would describe _____ as a large "family" in which most members feel a sense of belonging.

24. _____ I find it easy to identify with _____.

25. _____ I really care about the fate of _____.

(continued)

Scoring:

1. Reverse your scores on items 18, 19, and 22 so that 7 becomes 1; 6 becomes 2; 5 becomes 3; 3 becomes 5; 2 becomes 6; and 1 becomes 7 (4s remain unchanged).

2. Tally your reversed scores on these items.

3. Compute your scores on the remaining items.

4. Add your scores from steps 2 and 3 to come up with your grand total.

If your total score is **137 or above** you have a strong identification with the organization you evaluated; if your total score is **113 to 136** you have moderate identification; if your total score is **112 or below** you have a weak identification.

Discussion Questions

1. Do you think the results you obtained on this questionnaire were accurate? Why? Why not?

2. Do you believe there is a link between organizational identification and organizational culture? If so, what is the connection?

3. How can organizational identification be strengthened?

4. How well do you identify with your college or university? How does this impact your performance as a student?

to challenge cultural assumptions, reinforce key values, or create new symbols. (For one example of a company that is intent on capitalizing on its core values, see box 8.2).

Shaping Culture

Your effectiveness as a symbolic leader will depend in large part on how well you put your "stamp" on an organization's culture or subcultures either

Box 8.2

Imprinting and Maintaining Cultural Values at Starbucks

Over the past decade Starbucks has been one of the world's fastest growing retail chains. The specialty coffee retailer, which began in Seattle with a single store in 1971, now has some 15,000 outlets in 42 countries employing more than 147,000 people.[14] The company's rapid expansion helped create the gourmet coffee craze and introduced lattes, cappuccinos, mochas, and other European coffee drinks to the United States.

Starbucks CEO Howard Schultz is the driving force behind the firm. Schultz joined the company in 1982 as a salesman. A visit to Italy convinced him that the coffee bar culture, an important part of Italian social life, could be re-created in the United States. The company's founders and a number of outside investors were skeptical, but by 1987 Schultz had raised enough money to buy the firm. In 1992 the company began selling shares to the public. Starbucks stock value soared more than 2,200 percent in the 1990s, surpassing Wall Street giants such as General Electric, Microsoft, and IBM in total return.[15] Schultz stepped down as CEO in 2000 but took over the top position again in 2008 after a period in which Starbucks stock value declined and competitors, such as McDonald's, began to erode market share.

Schultz attributes the company's early success to a variety of factors—financial supporters, a solid business plan, dedicated employees, a talented management team, risk taking, and sophisticated operating systems. However, he gives most of the credit to the corporation's values. From the moment he took over, Schultz was very conscious of the fact that one of the major tasks of an entrepreneur is imparting or "imprinting" values.

> Whatever your culture, your values, your guiding principles, you have to take steps to inculcate them in the organization early in its life so that they can guide every decision, every hire, every strategic objective you set. Whether you are the CEO or a lower-level employee, the single most important thing you do at work each day is communicate your values to others, especially new hires. Establishing the right tone at the inception of an enterprise, whatever its size, is vital to its long-term success.[16]

The following are the values that Schultz tried to imprint at Starbucks when the firm consisted of a handful of stores in the Northwest:

- a passion for quality coffee products and educating consumers
- outstanding customer service that creates a bond with consumers
- creation of a comfortable atmosphere for casual social interaction
- recognition that employees (referred to as "partners") are the company's greatest asset
- concern for local communities and the environment
- continuous innovation

Ironically, rapid global growth (the chain has a goal of operating 40,000 outlets) has threatened the very value system that fueled the company's expansion. The greater the number of employees and stores around the globe, the harder it is for Schultz to communicate his passion for coffee and his values to employees. Critics have accused Starbucks of becoming just another "soulless" large chain that takes advantage of small coffee farmers. Some communities have resisted the opening of Starbucks outlets, fearing that the retailer will drive out local businesses.[17]

Schultz has always believed the key to success is for Starbucks to "stay small" as the company gets bigger. To encourage employee identification with the corporation and its values, Starbucks pays higher-than-average wages, offers stock options, provides health insurance for part-time workers, recognizes outstanding partners, and holds quarterly open forums. The company has responded to criticisms by supporting local charity programs, contributing to the CARE international relief agency, offering Fair Trade coffee (shade-grown beans that guarantee a living wage to growers), and placing more of its stores in middle- and lower-class neighborhoods.

Some observers are skeptical that Starbucks will be able to maintain its values as it continues to expand. Recent concerns about the quality of customer service and the limited knowledge level of some employees are worrisome for the company. Yet, Schultz is committed to a strategy that holds fast to core values while fostering flexibility and innovation:

> No matter how many avenues Starbucks pursues, and no matter how much we grow, our fundamental core values and purpose won't change. I want Starbucks to be admired not only for *what* we have achieved but for *how* we achieved it. I believe we can defy conventional wisdom by maintaining our passion, style, entrepreneurial drive, and personal connection even as we become a global company.[18]

Discussion Questions

1. Do you think Starbucks is maintaining its values as it continues to expand? Why or why not?

2. What additional strategies could the company use to "stay small" as it grows big?

3. Would you want to work for Starbucks? Do you or would you shop at its stores? Why?

4. If you were to found a corporation or nonprofit organization, what values would you try to imprint on its culture?

5. What challenges do you think Starbucks faces as it becomes increasingly global in its focus?

as a founder or as a change agent. Perhaps you want to introduce more productive values and practices or encourage innovation as part of your vision or agenda. Cultural change, while necessary, is far from easy. Some organizational consultants sell programs that promise to modify organizational culture in a quick and orderly fashion. Such claims, which treat culture as yet another element housed in the organizational container, are misleading.

> Nothing is inevitable until it happens.
>
> —A. J. P. Taylor

Change is difficult because cultures are organized around deeply rooted assumptions and values that affect every aspect of organizational life. Current symbols and goals provide organizational and individual stability, so any innovation can be threatening. However, knowing how culture is embedded and transmitted can help you guide the cultural creation and change process. According to Edgar Schein, there are six primary and six secondary mechanisms you can use to establish and maintain culture. Primary mechanisms create the organization's "climate" and are the most important tools for shaping culture. Secondary mechanisms serve a supporting role, reinforcing messages sent through the primary mechanisms.[19]

Primary Mechanisms

1. *Attention.* Systematically and persistently emphasize those values that undergird your organization's philosophy or plan. If your vision emphasizes customer service, for example, then you need to focus the organization's attention on service activities. Your claim that service should be the company's first priority will not be taken seriously unless you as a leader perform service, honor good service, and penalize those who fail to respond to customer needs. In this way, others are encouraged to act as you do, to share your meaning that good service is important, and to believe service activities are critical. Some, like Ren McPherson of the Dana Corporation, argue that paying attention is the key activity of leader/managers. In McPherson's words: "When you assume the title of manager, you give up doing honest work for a living. You don't make it, you don't sell it, you don't service it. What's left? Attention is all there is."[20] Focused attention takes on even more importance when undertaking major transformation efforts (see box 8.3).

2. *Reactions to critical incidents.* The way you respond to stressful events sends important messages about underlying organizational assumptions. Compare the way that organizations handle financial crises, for example. Some use layoffs as an efficient way to balance the books. Others, who put cooperation ahead of efficiency, cut costs by asking everyone to work fewer hours. (See chapter 13 for more information on how to prepare for crisis situations.)

3. *Resource allocation.* How an organization spends its money is a key indicator of where it is headed. Looking at projected expenses reveals

Box 8.3   Research Highlight

Leading Transformation[21]

Introducing significant change is one of the toughest challenges facing organizational leaders. Harvard business professor John Kotter studied 100 companies in the United States and abroad who launched a variety of change initiatives under such labels as "restructuring," "downsizing," and "total quality management (TQM)." He found that only a handful of these firms succeeded at transforming the way they do business. The rest were only partially successful or total failures.

Why do so few transformation efforts succeed? Kotter identifies eight common errors, any one of which can slow a change effort.

Error 1: Not establishing enough sense of urgency. Creating motivation for change is critical. Without a sense of urgency, organizational members don't have any reason to take on the extra work and psychological discomfort associated with change. Top executives often underestimate how hard it is to get people to abandon their current behaviors, or they start the transformation process without the buy-in of their management teams. In Kotter's sample, successful reform movements were sparked by such factors as poor financial results, changing markets, and customer complaints. Three-quarters or more of the managers in the transformed companies supported the change efforts.

Error 2: Not creating a powerful guiding coalition. A top executive can spearhead transformation, but he or she must soon be joined by other powerful leaders (senior managers, union leaders, board members, key customers). This coalition typically operates outside the normal chain of command because, by definition, reform threatens the status quo. Companies fail in their change efforts when they don't assemble enough influential leaders who can work as a team, or assign the responsibility for the change effort to one department instead of including members from many different units.

Error 3: Lacking a vision. One of the change coalition's most important tasks is coming up with a clear, achievable vision that is easily communicated to internal and external constituencies. All too often, lists, plans, and programs replace a compelling picture of the end result. The change initiative then disintegrates into a series of fragmented projects that confuse and alienate employees.

Error 4: Undercommunicating the vision by a factor of ten. A single meeting, speech, or memo will not encourage the kind of sacrifice needed for transformation. Instead, the vision needs to be constantly communicated in every kind of forum and through every channel (e-mail, newsletters, annual reports, department meetings, company celebrations, advertising). Leaders also need to model the desired new behaviors (i.e., commitment to quality, cost cutting, team building)—backing their rhetoric with action.

Error 5: Not removing obstacles to the new vision. The organization's current structure, compensation guidelines, and performance appraisal systems can all undermine renewal. For instance, the current pay and evaluation structure may reflect past, not current, values. The greatest danger to transformation, though, comes from those who actively resist change. They must be won over to the change effort or be removed from the organization.

Error 6: Not systematically planning and creating short-term wins. Major change efforts take years to complete. Members lose their sense of urgency when leaders focus solely on the end results of the change program. Setting intermediate goals marks the progress of the group and provides opportunities to reward gains through money, public recognition, promotions, and other means.

Error 7: Declaring victory too soon. Initial victories, while important for sustaining momentum, don't signal the end of the change battle. In fact, confusing short-term wins with long-term transformation puts change supporters at ease and emboldens resisters, bringing change to a halt. Major transformations take 5–10 years to complete.

Error 8: Not anchoring changes in the corporation's culture. Changes may seem solidly in place, but they can be undone unless they become part of the group's deeply held norms and values. Drawing attention to how the new systems and behaviors have improved collective performance is one way to anchor changes; making sure the next generation of leaders champions the reforms is another.

whether a company will invest in new product lines, for example. Further, the process of budgeting reveals a great deal about organizational values and assumptions. The greater the organization's faith in the competence of its employees, for instance, the more likely it is to involve people from all levels of the organization in setting financial targets. Because budgeting sends such strong cultural signals, think carefully about what you want to communicate when deciding how to create the departmental or organizational spending plan.

4. *Role modeling.* Effective leaders work to develop others who share their vision. Become a coach and teacher to followers, particularly to those who are directly underneath you on the organizational ladder. You can also instill organizational philosophy through formal training programs. Hewlett-Packard estimates that one-third of its initial training session is devoted to discussing the "Hewlett-Packard Way." Employee evaluation is partially based on how well workers adhere to the HP philosophy.

5. *Rewards.* Rewards and punishments go hand in hand with the mechanism of attention described earlier. If service is your goal, then honor those who provide good service (through expanded job responsibilities, pay raises, etc.) and discipline those who don't.

6. *Selection.* Since organizations tend to perpetuate existing values and assumptions by hiring people who fit into the current system, reform the culture by recruiting members who share your new perspective rather than the old one. Promote those who support your vision; if necessary, help those who won't or can't change find employment at another organization.

Secondary Mechanisms

1. *Structure.* Organizational design and structure affect how leaders divide up such things as product lines, markets, and work responsibilities. Some structures emphasize the interdependence of organizational units, for example, while others encourage each department or branch to operate as independently as possible. With this in mind, determine what your current structure says about your underlying premises and make changes when appropriate.

2. *Systems and procedures.* Quarterly reports, monthly meetings, work routines, and other recurring tasks occupy much of our time in organizations. You can use these organizational routines to reinforce the message that you care about certain activities. For example, requiring a weekly sales report is a reminder that you are concerned about marketing results.

3. *Rites and rituals.* To encourage change, nonessential rituals (those with little meaning for participants) can be dropped, essential rituals can be adapted to new purposes, and new rituals can be created. For instance, the annual Christmas party that has been a source of discomfort can become an annual banquet at which the organization promotes cooperation and teamwork. Harrison Trice and Janice Beyer suggest that rites of passage and enhancement are the best ways to encourage change.[22] Develop new ways to help organizational members pass from one status

to the next and publicly celebrate the accomplishments of those who meet the new standards.

4. *Physical space.* The physical layout of your organization's facilities can transmit your values, but only if you pay close attention to the messages you send through these elements. Restaurants are good examples of how physical settings can communicate important themes. The harsh lights, stainless steel counters, bright colors, and uncomfortable seats of fast-food restaurants invite customers in for a cheap, pleasant, and quick meal. The muted lighting, plush carpeting, and linen tablecloths at fancy restaurants encourage customers to linger over expensive dinners complete with drinks and dessert. Determine what type of message you want to send through your use of physical space (collegiality, stability, familiarity) and design accordingly.

5. *Stories.* Consider creating new stories and changing old ones. If you are faced with a negative story that is already part of the organizational culture (perhaps a tale of how management is insensitive to worker needs), work to change the behaviors that made the story believable.

6. *Formal statements.* Most of what an organization believes never makes it into a formal statement. Nonetheless, as we noted earlier, credos and mission statements do reflect important values. Writing such statements can help you and your constituents clarify your thinking. If members understand the philosophy of the organization and have a statement of its goals, they can quickly make decisions about what actions will help their company or nonprofit group. (Remember the example in chapter 1 of the Procter & Gamble employee who bought all the mislabeled Jif peanut butter jars he found at his local store.)

> We must be the change we wish to see in the world.
> —Mahatma Gandhi

Creating a Learning, Trusting Culture

The cultures of successful organizations take a variety of forms based on group history and membership, the environment, goals, values, and other factors. However, effective organizations generally share two cultural distinctives in common: a commitment to learning and a trusting organizational climate. In this section we'll outline ways you can promote organizational learning and build trust.

Leading the Learning Organization

Organizations, like individuals, must learn in order to survive and prosper. They must continually master new technologies, respond to changing market conditions and competitors, develop new products and services, react to rising energy costs, and so on.[23] Groups that fail to learn (or learn too slowly) are doomed to failure. As evidence of this fact, consider that one-third of the Fortune 500 industrials disappeared between 1970–1983, and that the largest industrial companies live less than half as long as the average person.[24]

Effective leaders build learning organizations that are skilled at generating and acquiring knowledge and then using that information to modify behavior.[25] They model learning by reading, attending workshops, visiting customers, touring factories, and so on. Learning leaders also function as teachers who challenge the assumptions of the group, ask probing questions (see box 8.4), and allow others to experiment and fail.[26] Further, they ensure that their organizations make effective use of three types of learning: intelligence, experience, and experimentation.[27]

Box 8.4   Research Highlight

The Power of Questions[28]

Asking effective questions is a critical skill for leaders. In his book, *Leading with Questions*, professor and consultant Michael Marquardt builds a case for exercising leadership through questioning. To discover how successful leaders use inquiries, Marquardt interviewed 22 leaders from around the world who are known for their questioning abilities. His sample included top-level executives at Dupont, Novartis, and ConocoPhillips Petroleum, as well as academic leaders and nonprofit officials drawn from Brazil, Finland, North America, Malaysia, Korea, Mauritius, and Switzerland,

Professor Marquardt found that asking questions instead of providing answers creates a "questioning culture." In a questioning culture, members challenge assumptions, encourage inquiries, and find creative ways to solve problems. Both groups and individuals benefit as a result. Questions promote organizational learning; improve collective problem solving and decision making; produce greater adaptability; energize followers; encourage teamwork; and foster innovation. Individuals working in a questioning climate experience greater self-awareness, self-confidence, openness, and personal flexibility. They become better listeners; are more comfortable expressing and managing conflict; develop keener insight into organizational dynamics and relationships; and demonstrate stronger commitment to learning and personal development.

Unfortunately, leaders are often quick to provide answers instead of asking questions, based in part on their belief that followers are looking to them for solutions. When leaders do ask questions, they may put others on the defensive. Examples of judgmental questions include: "Why are you behind schedule?" and "What's the problem with this project?" According to Marquardt, leaders must admit when they don't have the answers and ask questions that encourage followers to come up with their own solutions. For example: "How do you feel about the project thus far?"; "What have you accomplished so far that you are most pleased with?"; "What key things need to happen to achieve your objective?"

Moving from judgmental questions to productive ones takes a shift in mind-set as well as behavior. Leaders need to begin with a commitment to learn rather than to judge. They should frame questions in a nonthreatening manner to express curiosity and to open dialogue. They can set the stage for inquiries by spelling out what they desire from the conversation ("I hope to get a better idea of why costs are up." "I want to understand your feelings about the reorganization plan."). The questioning leader should allow the other person enough time to reflect and to respond and show genuine interest in the reply. Finally, it is critical to follow up on information and concerns. As one nonprofit executive in Marquardt's sample noted: "The power of questions can only be realized through learning, follow up, and change. The leader who asks questions and doesn't pay attention to the answers quickly loses credibility."

Intelligence consists of the collection and interpretation of information gathered from sources outside and inside the organization. **Search intelligence** involves scanning and analyzing data that already exist or are readily available through public sources like newspapers, patent filings, information databases, and Internet Web sites. Searching can reveal cultural or industry trends or market growth, for instance. (We'll have more to say about identifying important trends or issues in the next chapter.) **Inquiry intelligence** must be used when existing information is incomplete or unavailable. For example, a university may want to discover why MBA students chose its program over others in the area. Administrators might use interviews, questionnaires, and/or focus groups to gather this information, asking closed-end questions like "How many MBA programs did you investigate before choosing this one?" or posing open-ended queries like "Why did you enroll in our program?" **Observation intelligence** is appropriate when respondents have trouble communicating their real needs or feelings. Most employees can describe their formal job duties, for instance. However, by observing their behavior, you might discover that they spend much of their time on responsibilities not spelled out in their job descriptions. (Turn to box 8.5 to see how one organization makes effective use of intelligence.)

Experience learning is based on doing—entering a new overseas market, acquiring a competitor, surviving a crisis, solving an ethical dilemma. Learning organizations analyze their successes and, often more importantly, their failures. The IBM 360 computer series provides one model of learning through defeat. One of the company's most successful product lines, the 360 series, was built on the failure of the earlier Stretch computer. Learning leaders develop case studies based on organizational experiences, or they draw side-by-side comparisons between average and superior products. Boeing used the comparison approach to make sure that problems with the 737 and 747 airplanes weren't repeated. These models were contrasted to the 707 and 727 rollouts, which were highly successful. You can also conduct reviews to determine why individuals (engineers, leaders), groups (project development teams), and entire organizations are effective.

Experimentation comes into play when organizations enter unfamiliar territory. Through experiments, learners introduce changes, observe, and then draw conclusions. They may test different explanations or interpretations to account for why sales are down or customer complaints are up, for example. Exploration is a form of experimentation that introduces prototype products (clothing lines, soft drinks, software) and processes (automated assembly lines) and then refines them based on feedback. Demonstration projects test significant changes in one location before they are rolled out to the rest of the organization. GE took this approach when it created an entirely new manufacturing plant to produce an advanced refrigerator compressor. At the facility, engineers developed a new manufacturing process and modified existing machines to meet more rigorous specifications. Employees received extensive training in order to master additional responsibilities and to succeed in newly created work teams. Many of the lessons learned at the plant were then adopted by managers and workers in other divisions of the company.[29]

The leaders of learning organizations effectively manage the knowledge gained through intelligence, experience, and experimentation.[30] They realize

Box 8.5   Case Study

Learning from Customers at L.L. Bean[31]

Outdoor clothing and equipment manufacturer L.L. Bean goes to unusual lengths to learn from those who purchase its products. This connection with its customer base goes back to the firm's founder, who came up with the idea of combining rubber soles with leather uppers to create comfortable hunting boots. Bean had to give full refunds for 90 of the first 100 pairs of boots he sold in 1912 but soon came up with a more durable model based on feedback from buyers. He continued to stand behind his products as his mail order business grew, testing the gear he sold and often responding to complaint letters himself.

Today L.L. Bean Inc. does nearly $1.5 billion in sales annually. The company has retained the customer focus of its founder. Of particular note are the firm's strategies for soliciting input when developing and testing products. Bean has an extensive database of product testers who are selected after they submit essays, profiles, and product evaluations. These testers are divided into three categories. *Lead users* are those, like mountaineering and fishing guides, who depend on products for their livelihood and personal safety. They often modify clothing and equipment to better meet their needs. *Demanding users* are just as enthusiastic about outdoor activities as lead users but don't make their living from these pursuits. *Happy customers* like the products but only use them once in awhile. For example: a family that hikes, camps, or backpacks once or twice a year.

Testers generally receive samples from Bean and from one competitor to use for three months. They may be asked to assess particular product attributes like the ease of putting up a tent or the comfort of a sweater. Users provide feedback when the product is first received (to record first impressions right out of the box); at the midpoint (to identify opportunities and problems); and at the end of the trial (for a comprehensive review and evaluation). Company leaders use a number of creative strategies to structure the midpoint evaluations, including bringing groups of testers together for conversations while participating in outdoor activities. Suppliers and manufacturers are sometimes invited along. When revamping the Cresta Hiker boot, testers trekked near Mt. Washington in New Hampshire, sharing their notes and observations as they periodically switched pairs of shoes from Bean and competitors, waded through streams to test waterproofing, and wore mismatched pairs to test for comfort. Modifications were made and submitted to the testers. Sales of the revamped boot, which had been declining, jumped 85 percent.

L.L. Bean developed a process called "concept engineering" that is specifically tailored for radical redesigns and for creating entirely new products. The concept engineering process begins when a cross-functional team meets to determine its agenda (e.g., develop a new fly rod or outdoor "sleeping system"). The team then generates 5–6 broad questions to draw out as many details and impressions as possible from evaluators. A hunting boot team asked: "Describe what went through your mind when you purchased your last pair of boots. Describe the experience." "If you could build your own custom hunting boots, what would they look like?" Interviewees are chosen from the tester database along with a few noncustomers. Interviews take place at the homes or workplaces of the testers with one company official asking questions while another records the answers word for word. Major themes and images are developed and recorded on Post-it notes. When the team reconvenes, members spend three days combining and eliminating Post-it notes to come to a common understanding of customer concerns and to agree on the most important product requirements. Needs are rank ordered and confirmed through a questionnaire sent to 1,000 users. Brainstorming then produces solutions that are matched to customer requirements. Finally, prototypes are created and sent to testers for feedback. Concept engineering was used to develop the company's popular "Burrito Bag." This sleeping bag is made up of multiple layers of fleece that can be wrapped and unwrapped to regulate the temperature of the sleeper.

Discussion Questions

1. What are the advantages and disadvantages of L.L. Bean's approach to learning from customers?
2. Could L.L. Bean's learning strategies be applied to products and services in other industries? Why or why not?
3. Can you think of other organizations that go to unusual lengths to keep in touch with the wants and needs of their customer base? What strategies do they use?
4. Select a product you use. Would you qualify as a lead user, a demanding user, or a happy customer? What feedback would you like to give to the manufacturer?
5. How can leaders encourage their organizations to develop a stronger connection to customers/users/clients?
6. What lessons about organizational learning did you take from this case?

that information has little value unless it is shared or disseminated. In fact, failing to share knowledge can be expensive. A department at AT&T, for example, spent $79,449 to collect information that was already available to the public in a Bell Lab technical document priced at $13.[32] To encourage knowledge sharing rather than knowledge hoarding, knowledge management experts William Ives, Ben Torrey, and Cindy Gordon argue that you will need to address all of the following elements.[33]

- *Business context.* Link knowledge sharing to shared goals and the success of the organization. The greatest dissemination of knowledge occurs when employees are highly committed to the mission and values of the group, are informed of the organization's strategy, and understand the challenges and opportunities posed by the organizational environment.

- *Organizational structure and roles.* Create a competent staff of knowledge management professionals (IT staff, corporate librarians, chief knowledge officers) who can assist employees. Within business units, identify and encourage those who sponsor and reward knowledge-sharing activities, serve as experts in content areas, integrate new information into daily operations, and train employees.

- *Organizational processes.* Knowledge sharing should become part of the average job description. Specify how new knowledge is to be contributed and captured. Examples of knowledge-sharing processes include open forums, team debriefings, recording best practices, and knowledge fairs.

- *Organizational climate.* Knowledge sharing should become an organizational priority. Emphasize this behavior in orientation and training sessions, reward it, promote open communication between individuals and units, and include questions on knowledge sharing in project reviews.

- *Physical environment.* Create quiet spaces where employees can reflect and record their insights as well as attractive spots (kitchens, cafes, lobbies) where they can meet to share ideas. Install network connections to allow interaction with those located off-site.

- *Direction.* Guide the knowledge-sharing process. Create guidelines and processes; focus on action steps; provide structured questions for analysis and reflection.

- *Measurement.* Assess individual and group knowledge sharing behavior by measuring contributions (participation in online discussions, submissions to databases) and through cost-benefit analyses (reduced product development time, improved efficiency). Texas Instruments estimates that it retained $1.5 billion in business by improving its delivery times through knowledge management; Dow Chemical saved over $40 million in patent maintenance fees.

- *Means.* Facilitate knowledge sharing through technologies like e-mail, the Internet, groupware, and videoconferencing.

- *Ability.* Help followers develop information-sharing skills (networking, relationship building) and tools for capturing knowledge (logs, computer programs). Support their attempts to reflect on and to record their learning as they perform on the job.

- *Motivation.* Emphasize the intrinsic rewards of sharing data—saving time and money, completing a project, interacting with others, pride in being recognized as an expert. External rewards should not undermine team efforts or pit individuals against each other. Pay particular attention to the interpersonal dimension of information sharing by creating learning communities made up of groups of employees with similar tasks and interests. Demonstrate respect for the ideas of every follower.

> Power comes from transmitting information to make it productive, not hiding it.
>
> —Peter Drucker

Building a Trusting Climate

Trust, like learning, is essential to organizational success. Organizations with trusting climates are generally more productive, innovative, competitive, profitable, and effective.[34] Trust boosts collective performance by (1) fostering teamwork, cooperation, and risk taking; (2) increasing the flow and quality of information; and (3) improving problem solving. Those who work in a trusting environment are more productive because they have higher job satisfaction, enjoy better relationships, stay focused on their tasks, feel committed to the group, sacrifice for the greater organizational good, and are willing to go beyond their job descriptions to help out fellow employees.

Organizational trust is defined as the collective level of positive expectations that members have about others and the group as a whole. These optimistic expectancies are based on the belief that coworkers, work units, and the entire organization will honor their commitments. As we noted in chapter 4, trusting cultures are marked by high expectations of collective: (a) competence (the effectiveness of coworkers, leaders, and the entire organization); (b) openness and honesty; (c) concern for employees; (d) reliability (consistent and dependable behavior); and (e) identification—connection to the organization's culture, management, and fellow workers.[35]

Unfortunately, trust is fragile.[36] One untrustworthy act can quickly undermine a pattern of credible behavior. Former American Airlines CEO Don Carty found this out when he asked employees to take significant pay and benefit cuts during an economic downturn. Workers rebelled when word leaked out that the CEO and other senior executives were receiving large bonuses at the same time they were asking others to scale back. Carty apologized and resigned.[37]

To preserve trust, we need to remove those factors that destroy it and act in a trustworthy manner (see chapter 6). Listed below are some common "trust busters" to eliminate.[38]

inconsistent messages and behavior	dishonesty
unjust rewards	"us" versus "them" mentality
incompetence and low standards	restricted social interaction
inconsistent rules and procedures	negative moods (anger, frustration)
secrecy	finger pointing; blaming
concentration of power	micromanaging
hierarchy	failure to delegate
monitoring and surveillance	high turnover
unclear priorities and vision	unmet expectations and promises
organizational underperformance	

> Trust has rightly moved from a bit player to center stage in contemporary organizational theory and research.
> —Roderick Kramer

It isn't always possible to preserve trust. For example, you may promise extra vacation time only to be overruled by your supervisor, or employees may be bitter about the organization's pay structure. When trust has been significantly damaged, you will need to engage in trust repair. Following these four steps can help rebuild trust after it has been breached.[39]

Step 1. *Determine what happened.* The causes may not be as obvious as you think. Ask yourself:

- How fast did trust break down? If the deterioration was gradual, study the process to try to prevent similar failures in the future. However, don't expect to recover quickly from any breach of trust, slow or rapid.

- When did the violation of trust become known to you and to the larger organization? A significant gap between when the problem was recognized and when it was addressed will intensify feelings of betrayal.

- Was there a single cause? Responding to an isolated event is easier than dealing with a series of events, but don't ignore the possibility that several factors—poor performance, inconsistent standards, unfair rewards—could be at work.

- Was the loss of trust reciprocal? If both parties feel betrayed, then it is likely that neither side will respond objectively. Avoid retaliation and start a conflict resolution process if needed.

Step 2. *Determine the depth and breadth of the loss of trust.* Adjust your response to each affected group. In the case of layoffs, for example, some locations and departments will feel the impact more than others. More effort will need to be expended to restore the trust of these groups.

Step 3. *Own up to the loss (don't ignore or downplay it).* Acknowledge that trust has been broken as soon as possible. Promise to address the problem even if you don't have action steps in mind yet. Set a time when you will return with more specifics about how the issue will be addressed.

Step 4. *Identify what you must accomplish in order to rebuild trust.* Rebuilding trust may require providing more information, reconciling competing departments, or reducing pay inequities. List the changes that need to occur to reach these objectives. You may need to hold monthly informational meetings, merge work units, or form a compensation task force. Be careful not to overlook the details. Determine the extent of your involvement in the changes, for example; decide who else will be engaged in the process; and set a timeline for implementation.

> Whatever matters to human beings, trust is the atmosphere in which it thrives.
>
> —Sissela Bok

The Power of Expectations: The Pygmalion Effect

What a leader expects is often what a leader gets. This makes the communication of expectations one of a leader's most powerful tools. Our tendency to live up to the expectations placed on us is called the Pygmalion effect. Prince Pygmalion (a figure in Greek mythology) created a statue of a beautiful woman whom he named Galatea. After the figure was complete, he fell in love with his creation. The goddess Venus took pity on the poor prince and brought Galatea to life. The Pygmalion effect has been studied in a number of settings. Consider the following examples of the power of expectations in action.

- Patients often improve when they receive placebos because they believe they will get better.

- Nursing home residents are less depressed and go to hospitals less often when nurses and aides are told that they will progress more quickly.[40]

- Clients labeled as "motivated" by their therapists are less likely to drop out of alcohol treatment programs than those described as "unmotivated."[41]

- The expectations of teachers can influence the test and IQ scores of students. The most widely publicized investigation of the Pygmalion effect in education was conducted by Robert Rosenthal and Lenore Jacobson, who randomly assigned students in a San Francisco area elementary school to a group labeled as intellectual "bloomers." These investigators told teachers to expect dramatic intellectual growth from these students during the school year. The "bloomers" made greater gains on intelligence tests and reading scores than the other children.[42]

- Military personnel perform up to the expectations of their superiors. At an Israeli army training base, for example, instructors were told that trainees had high, regular, or unknown command potential. The high-potential soldiers (who really had no more potential than the other trainees and who were not told that they were superior) outperformed the members of the other groups, were more satisfied with the training course, and were more motivated to go on for further training.[43] In an investigation conducted in the U.S. Navy, the performance of problem sailors improved significantly after they were assigned to mentors and given a special training seminar designed to promote personal growth.[44]

Patterns created through expectations tend to persist. One long-term study of 500 students revealed that their standardized math test scores in the twelfth grade were influenced, in part, by the expectations that teachers had of their mathematical abilities in the sixth grade.[45] David Berlew and Douglas Hall examined the careers of two groups of AT&T managers and found that new managers performed best if they worked for supervisors who had high but realistic expectations.[46] These new employees internalized positive attitudes and standards and were entrusted with greater responsibilities. Six years later, they were still highly productive. On the other hand, managers who worked for bosses who expected too much or too little performed poorly throughout the test period. These workers either failed to develop high standards or didn't get recognition for the work that they did complete. As a result, they may have decided to perform at minimal levels. Berlew and Hall conclude that the first 12–18 months are critical to the career success of any new employee. Patterns set during this initial period often continue throughout a worker's tenure at a company.

There can be little doubt that leader expectations exert a long-lasting influence on performance. Yet, it would be a mistake to conclude that the Pygmalion effect has a dramatic impact on all followers. Disadvantaged groups (those stereotyped as low achievers) tend to benefit most from positive expectations, as do those who lack a clear sense of their abilities or find themselves in a novel situation (new hires, for example). Men seem to be more influenced by the expectancies of their managers than do women.[47]

Two characteristics of leaders moderate the impact of their expectations. The first is their level of self-esteem. Even when placed with subordinates with superior abilities, some leaders fail to communicate positive expectations because they lack confidence in their own abilities. One study of sales managers at a Metropolitan Life Insurance agency demonstrates the important relationship between leader self-confidence and the Pygmalion effect. Sales agents were randomly divided into high, average, and poor performance groups. Sales of the high performer unit dramatically increased, while sales of the weakest unit declined and members dropped out. Significantly, the performance of the "average" group went up because the leader of this group refused to accept the fact that he or his sales force were any less capable than the supposedly outstanding sales unit. The superior manager's confidence in his or her ability to develop and stimulate high levels of performance results in the belief that expectations will be met. Doubts about one's ability lead to lowered expectations and less confident interactions.[48]

A second characteristic of leaders that moderates the influence of the Pygmalion effect is the level of expectations. As we saw in the case of the AT&T managers, expectations must be high but also realistic. Setting standards too low does not challenge the abilities of followers, since there is little satisfaction to be gained by fulfilling minimal expectations. Yet, setting expectations too high guarantees failure and may start a negative self-fulfilling prophecy. Having failed once, the organization member expects to fail again. Goal-setting theorists argue that high performance comes from setting specific, challenging objectives, not vague, easy ones. (Being told to "try your best" is not very motivating, for instance.) Employees must be adequately trained for their tasks and then rewarded when they reach their targets.[49]

> We are not only our brother's keeper; in countless large and small ways, we are our brother's maker.
>
> —Bonaro Overstreet

To summarize, followers often perform up to expectations, whether in the nursing home, the classroom, the military, or the corporation. Leaders must have confidence in their own abilities and set realistic goals for followers in order for the positive Pygmalion effect to operate. However, the confidence that leaders have in themselves and their followers will have no impact on group behavior unless group members know that this confidence exists. Leaders must clearly communicate their expectations to followers. With this in mind, we turn now to a description of how expectations are communicated.

The Communication of Expectations

Telling others that they have ability, offering them compliments, and saying that you expect great things from them communicates high expectations. Subordinates also get the message that leaders have high or low expectations of them even when expectancies are not explicitly stated. Expectations are communicated through four important channels.[50]

1. *Climate.* Climate refers to the type of social and emotional atmosphere leaders create for followers. When dealing with people whom they like, leaders act in a supportive, accepting, friendly, and encouraging manner. Nonverbal cues play a major role in creating climates. Communication experts John Baird and Gretchen Wieting recommend that organizational managers use nonverbal behaviors that emphasize concern, respect, equality, and warmth—while avoiding behaviors that communicate coolness, disinterest, superiority, and disrespect.[51] (See box 8.6 for a summary of nonverbal cues that communicate positive expectations.)

Box 8.6

Nonverbal Cues that Communicate Positive Expectations[52]

Nonverbal Category	Positive Behaviors
Time	Don't keep employees waiting, give adequate time, make frequent contacts.
Setting	Meet in pleasant, attractive surroundings and avoid using furniture as a barrier.
Physical Proximity	Sitting or standing close to an employee promotes warmth and decreases status differences.
Gestures	Make frequent use of open palm gestures.
Head Movements	Use head nods, but do not indicate suspicion by cocking the head or tilting it backward while the other person is speaking.
Facial Expression	Smile frequently.
Eye	Make frequent, direct eye contact.
Voice	Combine pitch, volume, quality, and rate to communicate warmth. Avoid sounding bored or disinterested.

2. *Input.* In an organizational setting, positive expectations are also communicated through the number and type of assignments and projects given employees. Those expected to perform well are given more responsibility, which creates a positive performance spiral. As employees receive more tasks and complete them successfully, they gain self-confidence and the confidence of superiors. These star performers are then given additional responsibilities and are likely to meet the new challenges as well.

3. *Output.* Those expected to reach high standards are given more opportunities to speak, to offer their opinions, or to disagree. Superiors pay more attention to these employees when they speak and offer more assistance to them when they need to come up with solutions. This is similar to what happens in the classroom when teachers call on "high achievers" more than "low achievers," wait less time for low achievers to answer questions, and provide fewer clues and follow-up questions to low achievers.[53]

4. *Feedback.* Supervisors give more frequent positive feedback when they have high expectations of employees, praising them more often for success and criticizing them less often for failure. In addition, managers provide these subordinates with more detailed feedback about their performance. However, superiors are more likely to praise minimal performance when it comes from those labeled as poor performers. This reinforces the perception that supervisors expect less from these followers.

The Galatea Effect

Our focus so far has been on the ways that leaders communicate their expectations to followers. Once communicated, these prophecies can have a significant impact on subordinate performance. The same effects can be generated by expectations that followers place on themselves, however. Earlier we noted the example of Israeli army trainees who performed up to instructor expectations. In a follow-up experiment, a psychologist told a random group of military recruits that they had high potential to succeed in a course. These trainees did as well as those who had been identified as high achievers to their instructors. In this case, the trainees became their own "prophets."[54] The power of self-expectancies has been called the Galatea effect in honor of Galatea, the statue who came to life in the story of Pygmalion.

Figure 8.1 depicts the relationship between supervisor and self-expectations. In the positive Pygmalion effect, the chain starts with the manager's expectations (circle A), which causes him/her to allocate (arrow 1) more effective leadership behavior (circle B). These leadership behaviors then positively influence (arrow 2) the expectations that followers have of themselves, particularly their sense of self-efficacy or personal power (circle C). This increases motivation (arrow 3), leading to more effort (circle D), greater performance (arrow 4), and higher achievement (circle E). Subordinate performance then completes the chain because employee behavior raises or lowers the manager's expectations for future assignments (arrow 5). High expectations may also help the manager structure the subordinate's job to facilitate performance by eliminating obstacles, shielding him/her from outside interference (arrow 7). This leads to higher achievement without necessarily impacting follower motivation. Circles A and B and arrows 1 and 2 are eliminated in the Galatea effect. Subordinates perform better if they set high standards for themselves (circles C, D, and E). When they reach their goals, they expect to achieve even more in the future (arrow 6).

Figure 8.1   A Model of the Self-Fulfilling Prophecy at Work[55]

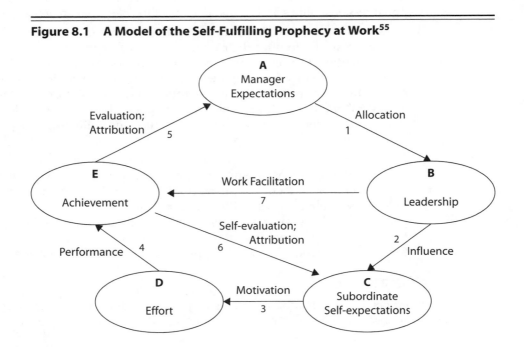

> We usually see only the things we are looking for—so much that we sometimes see them where they are not.
>
> —Eric Hoffer

Putting Pygmalion to Work

Since expectations can have a powerful influence on performance, we need to know how to put the power of Pygmalion to work. As leaders, we often aren't conscious of the expectations we have for others, or we don't realize how we communicate these expectations. We may assume that we treat all followers alike. Nevertheless, we've already noted that there are significant differences in how managers, teachers, and others treat high and low performers. Take inventory of how you communicate expectations using the four channels we discussed earlier: climate, input, output, and feedback. Analyze your nonverbal communication: do you engage in the behaviors described in box 8.6? Examine how assignments are distributed, how frequently some employees are given the opportunity to offer their opinions, whom you help most often, and the type of feedback you provide. Finally, identify the steps that you can take to communicate high expectations to your subordinates; try to put these behaviors into action.

In addition to taking steps as an individual leader to "harness" the power of Pygmalion, there are strategies that your organization can use to institute a positive expectation/performance cycle.[56] Eliminate organizational labels ("low performers," "fast trackers") that reflect low expectancies or suggest that only a few individuals are capable of outstanding performance. All supervisors should learn about the power of expectations and develop confidence in their ability to foster improvement in *all* of their subordinates. Because the patterns of high expectations/high success and low expectations/low success are established early in organizational careers, try to ensure that new employees work under effective managers. Often new subordinates are exposed to the worst leadership the organization has to offer—inexperienced supervisors or those who are trapped in low-level management positions because of poor past performance. Try instead to place new workers with the best leaders in the organization—those with high self-confidence who set challenging, yet realistic, goals. The positive patterns new subordinates establish under the guidance of these managers will pay off for both the individual and the organization for years to come. Consider moving established low performers to new situations where they can break the influence of old, negative self-fulfilling prophecies.

We can also put the power of Pygmalion to work as followers. Dov Eden argues that as subordinates we can protect ourselves from the force of negative leadership expectations by being aware of how such expectancies operate. We can also encourage supervisors to have high expectations of us by meeting and exceeding standards. In essence, this approach uses the Galatea effect to create positive expectations in leaders. Eden summarizes subordinate use of expectations this way:

Subordinates could be taught how to behave in a manner that would evoke more effective leadership from their supervisors. This would be harnessing Pygmalion in reverse, subordinates "treating" their supervisors in such a way that they mold their supervisory behavior in accordance with subordinate desires. Similarly, awareness of interpersonal expectancy effects might help immunize certain subordinates against the debilitating effects of poor leadership from supervisors who harbor low expectations toward them.[57]

CHAPTER TAKEAWAYS

- Organizations are the product of communication. As organizational members communicate, they develop shared meanings that form the organization's unique way of seeing the world—an organization's culture.

- Cultures are made up of underlying assumptions, values, symbols, and symbolic creations called artifacts. The organization is the product of symbol using, and organizational leaders are symbolic leaders who use symbols to interpret events and to help determine the direction of the group.

- You can embed and transmit culture by primary and secondary mechanisms. Primary mechanisms are the most important elements for shaping culture: what you pay attention to; how you react to critical incidents; the way you spend budgeted monies; how you role model; the criteria you select for allocation of rewards; and the criteria you use for selection. Secondary mechanisms reinforce primary messages: how you mold the organizational structure; how you utilize organizational systems and procedures; your use of rites and rituals; how you design physical space to reinforce key values; the stories you tell about important events and people; and the way you communicate organizational philosophy.

- Effective leaders build cultures that are committed to learning. Learning organizations are skilled at generating and acquiring knowledge and then using that information to modify their behavior. You will need to function as a learner/teacher who promotes information gathering through intelligence (collection of data), collective experience, and experimentation. Then make sure that this knowledge is widely shared or disseminated.

- Trust is critical to the success of any organization. Organizational trust is the collective level of positive expectations that coworkers, work units, and organizations will honor their commitments. Trusting organizational cultures are marked by high expectations of collective competence, openness and honesty, concern for employees, reliability, and identification with the organization.

- When trust is broken, you will need to (1) determine what happened, (2) determine the depth and breadth of the loss of trust, (3) own up to the loss (don't ignore or downplay it), and (4) identify what you must accomplish in order to rebuild trust.

- Expectations shape motivation and performance. The Pygmalion Effect refers to our tendency to live up to the expectations of others. Generally, the higher the expectancy, the higher the performance. Leaders communicate expectations through climate (social and emotional atmosphere), input (the number and type of assignments they give to employees), output (the number of opportunities that followers have to voice opinions), and feedback (the frequency of praise or criticism).

- To create a high expectations/high performance cycle, build a warm climate, delegate important responsibilities, solicit ideas, and provide frequent positive feedback.

- Self-expectations (called the Galatea effect) also influence performance. Protect yourself from the power of negative leadership expectations by setting high standards for yourself.

APPLICATION EXERCISES

1. For a major research paper, conduct your own organizational culture analysis. Be sure to identify the following:
   - the role of the founder and current leadership
   - assumptions
   - values
   - important symbols, such as myths and stories, rituals, and language
   - important artifacts, such as buildings, products, and technology
   - efforts at change

2. In a group, identify important rites at your college or university and categorize them using the framework presented on pp. 240–241. What messages do these rituals send? How could they be modified to encourage cultural change?

3. Develop your own definition of "symbolic leadership." Provide examples of symbolic leadership in action.

4. Framing Scenario
   Imagine that you work for the public relations office of Lake Okiboji University (L.O.U.). Your college is merging with a smaller school that was just about to close its doors for good. Your frame is that the merger will help both schools. The student body at L.O.U. will grow (increasing tuition revenue), and the merger will create an attractive new branch campus. Students at the smaller college (who would have been forced to transfer) can now finish their degrees without leaving town. The presence of a stronger university will also benefit the community as a whole. In addition to offering classes and cultural and athletic events, L.O.U. will become the area's largest employer when the merger is complete. Not everyone agrees with your perspective, however. You've heard the following comments from students, faculty, donors, and others in the community:
   - L.O.U. is getting too big and impersonal.
   - The leaders of L.O.U. are "empire builders."
   - The needs of students have been ignored in the rush to merge.
   - L.O.U. is more interested in collecting more tuition and acquiring property than in meeting the needs of the community.

Generate some possible responses to these competing frames and then pair off with a classmate. Take turns playing the role of the public relations professional and a stakeholder who is critical of the merger. When you're done, evaluate how well each of you constructed and communicated the university's frame to the hostile stakeholder.

5. Develop a case study based on a learning organization. Describe how that organization learns and shares knowledge. Generate a list of best practices that other organizations could adopt.

6. Distribute the Organizational Identification Questionnaire (p. 243) to several other members of your organization. How do their responses compare to yours? Does your organization demonstrate higher or lower than average levels of identification? Report your findings to classmates and/or organizational leaders.

7. Identify a situation in your organization that calls for trust repair. Outline a strategy for restoring trust based on the process described in the chapter. Write up your findings.

8. Form a small group and brainstorm ways that teachers, managers, and others communicate both low and high expectations. Report your findings during class discussion.

9. Develop a strategy for communicating high expectations to someone you lead but do not like. Analyze what expectations you have for that person now and how you communicate these expectancies. Identify steps that you can take to create a positive Pygmalion Effect. Is it possible to modify your expectations? To mask your negative feelings? Write up your conclusions.

10. Develop a strategy for creating positive expectations in those who lead you.

CULTURAL CONNECTIONS: MCDONALD'S SERVES UP A GLOBAL APPROACH TO ORGANIZATIONAL CULTURE[58]

One multinational company that has been very adept at honoring local customs is McDonald's. While the signature McDonald's sandwich, the Big Mac, is served in much the same way around the globe, McDonald's also serves regional items such as kosher hamburgers in Israel, vegetable McNuggets in India, sandwiches on rye bread in Finland, teriyaki beef in Japan, and the Kiwi Burger in New Zealand—a local favorite featuring a fried egg and beetroot. Unlike many other large global corporations, McDonald's restaurants are mostly locally owned—affording restaurant franchisees an intimate understanding of regional culture. In Muslim countries McDonald's offers prayer rooms, while in Greece it significantly alters its menu during Lent. In Asia, students often sit in McDonald's for hours—turning the restaurants into youth clubs—a practice that would not be tolerated in the United States but is encouraged by local owners in places like Hong Kong, Seoul, and Beijing. This adaptation to local customs by a globally branded company has been dubbed "glocalization."

Of course, much of the McDonald's experience is standardized around the globe—from the golden arches to the core menu items—making dining at McDonald's much the same from Atlanta to Nairobi to Warsaw. Entrepreneurs from all over the world are taught McDonald's product and service-quality principles at one of four Hamburger Universities. Yet, these local owners are given wide latitude to adapt the McDonald's concept to their native cultures. The results have been positive. McDonald's sales in the United States have been on the increase lately after declines in previous years. The company is doing well in other parts of the world as well. Sales increased by nearly 6 percent in Europe in 2006, the best annual results in nearly 15 years. France, of all places, is outpacing performance in most markets around the world. McDonald's has been successful in winning over French consumers, with restaurants featuring barstools made from bicycle seats and wood-and-stone interiors reminiscent of a chalet. Further, French customers spend an average of $9 per visit compared to only $4 in the United States, even though a Big Mac costs roughly the same in Paris and New York. In Germany, supermodel Heidi Klum is a spokesperson for the company. The emphasis in this campaign is on the restaurant chain's commitment to fitness and health.

McDonald's financial future will depend on its continuing ability to connect with global customers. The company serves 50 million people every day in about 30,000 restaurants in 119 countries. To continue to increase sales volume, McDonald's will need to continue to suit the tastes of customers around the world by acknowledging local cuisine and culture.

SPOTLIGHT ON TECHNOLOGY:
THE INSTANT MESSAGING REVOLUTION

Instant messaging (IM) is quickly replacing e-mail as the communication tool of choice in organizations around the globe. IM is not just a social networking medium for teenagers; it is a serious tool for sharing business information. According to one estimate 90 percent of companies are using some form of IM. As Nancy Flynn explains, there are several advantages to IM.[59]

Instant communication. IM allows for instantaneous communication among employees, vendors, and customers. Further, IM enables workers to determine the availability of others in real-time from any location. This eliminates unnecessary phone tag and e-mail responses.

Enhanced customer service. An increasing number of businesses are using IM to communicate with customers. Alaska Airlines allows customers to IM to get quick information about flights. Land's End allows online shoppers to use IM to contact customer service. The company found that those who use the IM service are 70 percent more likely to make a purchase than those who call the Land's End 800 telephone number with questions.

Improved multitasking. Employees can IM while engaged in other activities. This reduces the need for subsequent interactions. According to one study, IM reduced phone usage by 72 percent; voice mail by 69 percent; e-mail by 85 percent; and face-to-face meetings by 50 percent.

Cost savings. With IM multiple people can be involved in conversations at the same time from any location. Since IBM introduced IM it has realized a savings of $4 million a month in reduced costs for travel. Further, telephone costs have also declined at IBM by some 4 percent.

Although IM can have some disadvantages (too much time spent on IM, messages not read or attended to, for example), it appears that this form of communication will have an increasing presence within the workplace.

LEADERSHIP ON THE BIG SCREEN:
ENRON: THE SMARTEST GUYS IN THE ROOM

Starring: Peter Coyote (narrator), Bethany McLean, Peter Elkind, Amanda Martin, Ken Lay, Jeff Skilling, Sherron Watkins

Rating: R for language and brief nudity

Synopsis: This documentary, based on the book by *Fortune* reporters Bethany McLean and Peter Elkind, chronicles one of the most famous business scandals in U.S. history. Once the nation's seventh largest corporation, Enron collapsed due to massive accounting fraud. The producers interview McLean and Elkind along with a number of Enron employees and outside observers. Video and audio from corporate meetings and the company's trading desks provide a chilling look at a culture driven by greed and arrogance.

Chapter Links: elements of organizational culture, cultural transmission, trust busters

Public Leadership

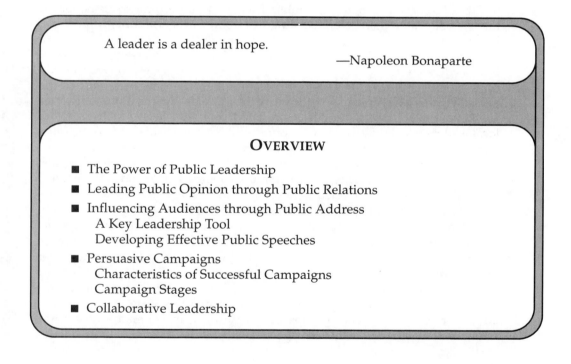

A leader is a dealer in hope.

—Napoleon Bonaparte

OVERVIEW

- The Power of Public Leadership
- Leading Public Opinion through Public Relations
- Influencing Audiences through Public Address
  A Key Leadership Tool
  Developing Effective Public Speeches
- Persuasive Campaigns
  Characteristics of Successful Campaigns
  Campaign Stages
- Collaborative Leadership

The Power of Public Leadership

Public leadership is one of the most visible and dynamic forms of social influence. Religious and political authorities, educators, social activists, and other public leaders attempt to modify the attitudes and behaviors of mass audiences. The influence of public leaders on the course of history is a matter of conjecture. Some scholars adopt the viewpoint of Thomas Carlyle, suggesting that history is essentially the story of "heroic" leaders.[1] Others agree with Herbert Spencer that no single leader is capable of changing the evolutionary development of history.[2]

Conventional wisdom supports Carlyle's notion that powerful leaders shape history. Many public leaders have had a profound effect on human affairs. Robert Tucker, a Princeton University political scientist, argues that the atrocities committed under the leadership of Adolph Hitler in Nazi Germany and Joseph Stalin in the then Soviet Union were directly attributable to the "paranoid" personalities of those two ignoble public leaders.[3]

It is important to note that public leadership is not limited to nationally known political, religious, or social figures. John Gardner, former secretary of Health, Education, and Welfare in the Lyndon Johnson administration and the founder of Common Cause, used the term "dispersed leadership" to describe how leaders are found at all levels, including social agencies, universities, the professions, businesses, and minority communities.[4] Gardner believed that dispersed leadership is essential to the health of complex organizations and societies. Lower-level leaders can deal more effectively with local problems. When local leaders take initiative, they encourage higher-level leaders to do the same. At times the efforts of lower-level leaders trigger events that change society as a whole. For example, Lech Walesa (an electrician) and Vaclav Havel (a writer) mobilized public sentiment against communist regimes in Poland and the Czech Republic and were later elected as the democratic leaders of those two nations.

Every public leader, from the president of the United States down to the president of a local chamber of commerce, must influence the attitudes and behaviors of groups within a social system. This process of influence is called opinion leadership. Since public leaders deal with large audiences, they often use different tactics than leaders in other contexts. In an interpersonal encounter, a leader can target a persuasive message to the special needs of one follower using face-to-face communication. In a public setting, a leader must address messages to what groups of people have in common—health and financial worries, political beliefs, age, ethnic heritage—through both mediated and interpersonal channels.[5] Effective public leaders shape public opinion through public relations activities, public speaking, and persuasive campaigns.

Leading Public Opinion through Public Relations

Communication professionals use the term public relations to describe how groups and organizations influence important audiences (publics) through a cluster of coordinated activities. Sparked by the growth of the mass media and the rising importance of public opinion, the practice of public relations has become a multibillion-dollar industry. Common public relations tasks include:[6]

- working with media representatives
- researching public attitudes
- disseminating financial information
- lobbying government agencies
- publicizing company events
- creating internal communication programs aimed at organizational members
- supporting marketing programs
- maintaining positive relationships with community groups
- responding to activists
- advising top management
- dealing with customer concerns
- fund raising
- planning promotional events
- writing and delivering speeches and presentations
- organizing persuasive campaigns

The mix of activities that leaders use to influence public opinion will vary depending on the needs of the group. The leader of a private charity may concentrate on fund-raising and attracting donors. The leader of a publicly held corporation will likely devote attention to marketing and, by law, must provide information about the company's financial condition to important news sources.

Whatever their differences, the best public relations programs have a number of elements in common, according to a major research project commissioned by the International Association of Business Communicators (IABC). Researchers James Grunig, Larissa Grunig, and David Dozier surveyed public relations directors, CEOs, and employees at 300 organizations in the United States, Canada, and Great Britain.[7] They report that excellent public relations efforts—those that increase organizational effectiveness and benefit society as a whole—share the following characteristics.

1. *Empowered.* To be excellent, public relations functions must be valued and promoted by top management. The IABC researchers found that the most effective efforts are housed in a single department that functions separately from marketing. Top organizational leaders see public relations as a "critical management function." Public relations officials serve on the senior management team, often reporting directly to the CEO.

2. *A strategic management role.* The leaders of excellent public relations departments are managers, not technicians. Their success depends more on their ability to set policy, solve problems, and administer budgets than on writing, media production, event planning, and other technical skills. These leaders play a significant role in determining organizational strategy. They shape the organization's direction, in part, through **issues**

management. Issues management is the ongoing process of (a) monitoring the environment for societal developments that pose threats or opportunities to the organization, and then (b) responding in a way that reduces the threats and builds on the opportunities.[8] Thanks to issues managers, Bank of America changed its lending policies two years before Congress required banks to reveal whether or not they were engaged in "redlining"—refusing to loan money in minority neighborhoods. Bank of America reports that its proactive response reduced the cost of compliance and spared it from criticism from cities and public interest groups.[9] Other organizations have not been as successful at issues management. R. J. Reynolds came under fire from health organizations and legislators for encouraging children to smoke through its Joe Camel ads.[10] Many school districts were slow to respond to rising concerns about childhood obesity. They are now under governmental and parental pressure to remove fast food, unhealthy snacks, and soft drinks from school grounds. (To read about a variety of organizational responses to electronic waste, turn to the case study in box 9.1.)

Issues management begins with scanning the environment—reading a wide variety of publications, monitoring news outlets, surfing the Web, tracking legislation—to identify potential issues, which are defined as differences of opinion or concerns that could impact the organization. PR managers monitor the issues to determine their trajectory (some issues disappear, others get national attention) and to determine if they are a concern to key organizational publics. The most pressing and important issues get top priority, and leaders outline a potential plan of action. Initiating a persuasive campaign is one option. (We'll have more to say about persuasive campaigns later in the chapter.) Instead of launching a campaign, an organization may need to take steps to repair its reputation. It may apologize to the public, change policies, fire unethical employees, support community projects, etc. (See chapter 13 for more information on image restoration.)

Box 9.1   Case Study

E-Waste: A Tale of Three Companies

Every year 20–50 million tons of mobile phones, televisions, iPods, Blackberries, and other electronic equipment end up in landfills around the world. The U.S. Environmental Protection Agency estimates that Americans replace 65 million personal computers and 130 million cell phones in a year. Only 10%–15% of this material is recycled. E-waste is highly toxic, containing heavy metals like arsenic, barium, mercury, and chromium that leach into groundwater or are released into the air when burned. Discarded computers are a particularly hazardous form of e-waste. Old computer monitors can contain four to eight pounds of lead. Circuit boards contain cadmium and lead. Computer cables are sprayed with toxic fire retardant chemicals.[11]

E-waste has emerged as a significant global issue. Activist groups note that many electronic products targeted for recycling in the West end up in workshops in China, Africa, and India. There they are dismantled by workers without protective gear who allow toxic materials to enter the soil and air. The European Union has set limits on the number of toxic materials in new electronic products. Japan and South Korea require manufacturers to fund and manage recycling programs for their products. In the United States, California made it illegal to throw away most used electronic equipment. Maine, Washington, and Maryland have passed laws requiring electronics makers to take back their products, and other states are considering similar legislation.

Hewlett-Packard (HP) was the first major U.S. computer manufacturer to take significant steps to tackle the problem of e-waste. For over 20 years, the firm has invested in recycling equipment that has lowered production costs. HP joined with environmentalists to persuade lawmakers to pass the "take back" laws in Washington and Maine over the opposition of IBM and several television manufacturers. The company's vice president for corporate, social, and environmental responsibility summarizes the advantages of this proactive approach: "A lot of companies haven't stepped up to the plate. . . . If we do this right, it becomes an advantage to us."[12] Hewlett-Packard estimates that, in one year alone, it recycled over 140 million tons of its products, collecting approximately 2.5 million units to be refurbished for sale or donation. HP accepts computers from any manufacturer, though the owner has to pay for shipping. It also started a battery recycling effort and reduced levels of heavy metals in its newer products.

Compared to HP, Dell is a relative newcomer to the e-waste recycling movement. However, the computer maker has quickly taken a leadership role. Dell too will recycle any PC regardless of the manufacturer. Representatives will come to a home or place of business to pick up the old computer. It is also phasing out toxic chemicals in the manufacturing process. Dell has gone a step further than Hewlett-Packard by addressing the problem of greenhouse emissions. Consumers can give a donation ($2 for a laptop, $6 for a desktop computer) that goes to planting trees in managed forests. These trees will help absorb the carbon dioxide released by the electricity that powers their computer systems. Dell founder and CEO Michael Dell challenged the computer industry to follow his company's lead, stating: "It's the right thing to do for our customers. It's the right thing to do for our earth."[13]

Apple lags behind HP and Dell when it comes to e-waste. The company would seem a natural for take-back programs given its progressive image, loyal customer base, and retail network. Instead, the firm recycles relatively few of its products and fought against the take back legislation in Maine. When shareholders complained about the firm's stance at the company's annual meeting, CEO Steven Jobs answered with a profanity. Greenpeace gives Apple low ratings for its e-waste efforts because the company hasn't eliminated polyvinyl chloride (PVC) from its products and doesn't have a timeline for doing so. The firm refuses to list the regulated substances that are found in its products.

Apple officials defend their e-waste record by noting that the company has cut lead use and that many of its products are small and light, reducing the volume of waste. They believe that recycling is not just the responsibility of the manufacturer. Chief Operating Officer Timothy Cook argues: "Recycling is a responsibility of the person who makes the product, the people who use the product, the people who sell the product, and the government." Environmental critics don't agree. They point out that Nokia also makes small devices but has a much better recycling record. They promise to push company leaders to improve their e-waste performance. Said one activist: "They are laggards in a number of ways on the issue of e-waste. It's come to the point where we need to have the company confronted."[14]

Discussion Questions

1. Who is responsible for the problem of e-waste?

2. What potential threats and opportunities does e-waste pose to Hewlett-Packard, Dell, and Apple?

3. How well has each company responded to these threats and opportunities?

4. What advice would you give to the leaders of Apple Computer on how to deal with the e-waste issue?

5. Can you think of other emerging issues that might have a significant impact on computer makers? How should they respond in order to shape public opinion?

3. *Two-way communication, symmetrical relationships.* In the popular imagination, public relations is viewed as a form of one-way communication. PR specialists, according to this view, craft messages and develop strategies designed to benefit the group or organization by shaping public attitudes. Little thought is given to the desires and needs of external audiences. As a result, the organization often gets its way at the expense of employees, neighbors, local governments, small businesses, unions, and other groups. The IABC researchers discovered, however, that outstanding public relations programs engage in two-way, not one-way, communication. Leaders of these programs still craft and deliver messages designed to shape public opinion, but they make an active effort to identify and to respond to the needs of important publics. They conduct ongoing research (using focus groups, surveys, community meetings, and other means) to determine the attitudes and behaviors of audiences. Just as important, they are willing to adjust their goals to develop collaborative or symmetrical relationships with outside groups. Consider the siting of a new county prison, for instance. An asymmetrical approach would be to identify a site, announce the location, and then ask county public relations personnel to develop a strategy to win over opponents. A symmetrical approach would be to solicit public input before making a final decision and then tailor the plan to meet local concerns. Officials might, for example, select an alternative site or change the building design.

4. *Ethical.* Engaging in two-way communication and building symmetrical relationships encourages ethical behavior. Excellent practitioners disclose accurate information to publics whom they treat as partners. As noted above, they listen and respond to the concerns of outsiders. These experts engage in dialogue, which seeks mutual benefit, rather than in monologue, which serves the interests of the organization at the expense of outsiders. The community as a whole benefits from the ethical, symmetrical relationships. Grunig, Grunig, and Dozier report that excellent public relations departments often become ethics counselors to management. They serve as advocates of social responsibility, which is doing business in a way that benefits society as well as the organization.

5. *Supportive structure.* Excellent public relations programs are nurtured by, and reflect, a supportive organizational structure. Supportive structure is organic: decentralized, less formal, less stratified into organizational layers, and more complex. Such structure facilitates participation by empowering employees, delegating responsibility, and soliciting input and feedback. Employees and managers engage in two-way communication and develop symmetrical relationships based on openness and trust. Women and minorities have more opportunities for advancement, and workers report a high degree of job satisfaction.

Of all the elements that go into a public relations program, public speaking and persuasive campaigns deserve special attention because they play such a critical role in shaping and responding to public opinion. In the next two sections of the chapter, we'll take a closer look at the relationship between public address and public leadership and outline ways to use persuasive campaigns to full advantage.

Influencing Audiences through Public Address

A Key Leadership Tool

Public speaking is a significant tool for all types of public leaders—from student body officers to environmental activists to religious figures. As a matter of fact, it is hard to think of effective leaders who don't have at least some public speaking ability.[15] (See box 9.2 for examples of the wide variety of leaders who used public address to influence U.S. society during the past century.)

As an exercise in discovering the essential role of public address in public life and public leadership, clip out all the news stories about public speakers from an edition of your newspaper (see application exercise 4 on p. 293). Included below are stories that appeared in just one issue of a metropolitan daily.[16]

- Speakers gathered on the steps of the state capital to express their support for more school funding.
- Union leaders briefed members on allegations against a former union treasurer and answered questions.
- County officials held public hearings to hear comments on improving a local park.
- President George W. Bush praised George Washington in a speech delivered on the grounds of Washington's Mount Vernon estate.
- A Republican presidential candidate criticized former Secretary of Defense Donald Rumsfeld's handling of the Iraq War.
- A rescued mountain climber described his ordeal in front of television cameras and print reporters.
- The governor of a neighboring state announced her support of a new professional basketball arena.

Box 9.2   Research Highlight

Words That Shaped a Century

Words don't merely record historical events, they make history. That's the thesis of a book edited by former New Jersey Senator Robert Torricelli and Andrew Carroll, founder of the Legacy Project (a national organization dedicated to preserving historically significant correspondence and documents). *In Our Own Words* is a collection of speeches that demonstrates the power of public address in U.S. society. Citizens from all walks of life can have an impact through public communication, according to Torricelli and Carroll.

From some more distant perspective the century might appear to be punctuated solely with the grandiloquence of Roosevelt, Kennedy, or Reagan. But the most lasting impression we hope to leave with this collection is that the power of words is not reserved for the powerful. The use of language to effect change or communi-

(continued)

cate ideas is limited only by imagination, not birthright.... The sound track of democracy, as it is recorded here, emanates from well beyond the Oval Office or the gilded halls of Congress. Indeed, it is all around us.[17]

The 150 speeches found in the book include messages delivered in traditional settings (policy speeches, commencement addresses, eulogies) and in other contexts (testimony before Congress, courtroom summations, radio broadcasts). The speakers come from a variety of ethnic and cultural backgrounds and include famous politicians, a drug addict, an AIDS victim, ministers, actors, judges, lawyers, poets, coaches, military officers, civil rights activists (and their opponents), and others. Here are some of the speakers and speeches that appear in the collection. This sample makes it clear that public speaking is a significant tool for all kinds of leaders, whatever their position in society.

1900–1909	Social worker Jane Addams pays tribute to George Washington on the anniversary of his birthday.
	Civil rights activist W. E. B. Du Bois issues a call to arms to fellow African Americans.
1910–1919	A union organizer uses a memorial service for seamstresses killed in an industrial fire to criticize society's apathy toward workers.
	Suffragette Carrie Chapman Catt urges Congress to extend voting rights to women.
1920–1929	Preacher Billy Sunday condemns alcohol as "God's worst enemy."
	Helen Keller endorses communism and the Russian Revolution when addressing a crowd of socialists.
1930–1939	Radio broadcaster Herb Morrison reports live on the crash of the *Hindenburg* dirigible.
	Baseball star Lou Gehrig, suffering from a fatal illness, thanks his fans and declares himself the "luckiest man on the face of the earth."
1940–1949	General George S. Patton extols the virtues of war to his troops.
	U.S. Attorney General Robert Jackson demands guilty verdicts for Nazi war criminals at the Nuremberg trials.
1950–1959	Architect Frank Lloyd Wright encourages his students to create buildings that benefit humankind.
	Environmentalist Rachel Carson reflects on the beauty of the Earth and its impact on the human spirit while addressing a women's group.
1960–1969	George Wallace, in his inaugural address as governor of Alabama, declares that his state will practice segregation forever.
	Robert F. Kennedy calms an angry black crowd after telling them that Martin Luther King, Jr., had just been assassinated.
1970–1979	An inmate reads prisoner demands during a hostage crisis at Attica Prison in New York.
	A soldier describes to army investigators the atrocities committed at the Vietnamese town of My Lai.
1980–1989	Sixteen-year-old AIDS victim Ryan White describes to a presidential commission the hatred directed at him because of his illness.
	President Ronald Reagan honors the memory of the astronauts killed in the *Challenger* explosion.
1990–1999	Supreme Court nominee Clarence Thomas denies charges of sexual harassment during confirmation hearings.
	Singer Barbra Streisand defends the role of the arts in society to an audience of Harvard students.

- The U.S. Secretary of State read a statement describing slow progress in Israeli-Palestinian peace talks

- The owner of a pro football team announced the hiring of a new coach.

- Anglican church leaders meeting in Africa debated the issues of gay bishops and same-sex couples

> Of all the talents bestowed upon men [women], none is so precious as the gift of oratory. . . . Abandoned by his [her] party, betrayed by his [her] friends, stripped of his [her] offices, whoever can command this power is still formidable.
>
> —Winston Churchill

Developing Effective Public Speeches

Because public address is such an important skill for leaders, we need to understand the key elements that go into effective public messages. Regardless of where you speak—whether in the classroom, at a political rally, or in a business meeting—you will discover that the delivery of an effective public speech enhances audience perceptions of your personal power and leadership potential. The effectiveness of a public speech depends on six primary elements: prespeech planning, organization, language, rehearsal, delivery, and responding to questions.

Prespeech Planning

Planning is essential in the development of successful public messages. The following factors should be considered before delivering a public presentation. In particular, think carefully about possible modes of delivery and audience analysis.

The principal modes of delivery are *impromptu, extemporaneous,* and *manuscript.* Impromptu speeches are delivered "off the cuff," with little advance preparation. Situations that might require an impromptu presentation include responding to an unexpected disaster or crisis or participating in a meeting. One of President George W. Bush's most memorable speeches was an impromptu message delivered to rescue workers through a bullhorn at Ground Zero in New York City. When speaking in the impromptu mode, try to maintain a clear focus or theme. Always avoid long, rambling impromptu messages.

Speaking from a prepared outline or set of notes is known as extemporaneous speech. This is the most common mode of public address. Extemporaneous speech gives you an opportunity to develop a clear presentational purpose or goal and adequate reasoning and support. The extemporaneous speech also offers you freedom in the construction of the message. Since your notes consist of an outline or a few key phrases, you have greater flexibility.

Working from a manuscript—a written transcript of the speech—allows for the greatest control of subject matter. Many political leaders use the manuscript mode of delivery. Manuscripts are most effective when the content of the message must be very precise, such as when the president announces the details of a treaty or when law enforcement officials reveal the results of an investigation. Because the manuscript mode does not allow a speaker to be spontaneous, it is advisable to use a teleprompter or similar mechanical device in order to maintain eye contact with the audience.

Regardless of the delivery style chosen, it is essential that you have an understanding of the attitudes and expertise of your listeners. Although audience size may vary from a small group to a worldwide conference, an understanding of the needs, aspirations, experiences, and intellectual abilities of listeners helps to create a more effective message. For example, a political candidate addressing a group of union employees will be more effective if he or she is aware of the issues that have the greatest impact on union members. A well-prepared speaker will seek information about the audience from a variety of sources. The speaker might research the previous positions of audience members; observe the group's current actions; or question, interview, or survey selected audience members as a means of uncovering information. In addition, he or she will have a clear grasp of the demands of the speaking situation (see box 9.3).

Organization

The logic and structure of the ideas presented within a public speech are critical. Successful presentations are organized around a central theme with supporting points. Developing a thesis, arranging ideas, linking primary points, and crafting a beginning and ending are the four most important factors in organizing a public speech.

The purpose or objective of a speech is known as the thesis. In general terms, the thesis identifies your goals—to inform, persuade, or entertain. More specifically, the thesis outlines exactly what you hope to achieve in your presentation. A thesis statement is prepared in the initial stages of speech organization and usually consists of one declarative sentence. The thesis statement itself should be as specific as possible in identifying the feelings, knowledge, or understanding you wish to convey to your audience. For example, "My speech is on John F. Kennedy," is ineffective. This thesis provides no explanation regarding the specific purpose of the speech. A better thesis would be, "John F. Kennedy was one of the most effective public communicators of the twentieth century." This thesis statement provides a detailed description of the argument you wish to make.

> Many leaders, in all fields, are too quick to patronize their public, assuming that people are selfish, dull, or uninterested in global or universal questions. Quite the contrary, the public is eager to hear, eager to engage, and eager to act when called to contribute to just causes that are larger than themselves.
>
> —Terry Pearce

After the thesis has been developed, arrange the main points you have selected to support your thesis. The number of main points should be kept to a minimum, and each main point should be supported with statistics, examples, illustrations, anecdotes, or other forms of evidence. Main points can be arranged (1) in chronological order (from the earliest to the most recent event), (2) in spatial order (by some physical or geographical relationship), (3) in order of size or impact (from largest to smallest or vice versa), (4) in a problem-solution format (a problem definition followed by a resolution), or (5) in a cause-effect

---

Box 9.3

Leading Through Special Occasion Speeches[18]

Leaders are often called on to speak at special occasions like funerals, dedications, conventions, award ceremonies, and banquets, either as invited guests or as representatives of the group. On these occasions, speakers must pay particular attention to the requirements of the situation. Leaders who violate audience expectations for the setting, such as the CEO who delivers an off-color toast at an employee's wedding reception or the politician who delivers a campaign speech at a graduation ceremony, do significant damage to their credibility. They also diminish the occasion as well as those gathered to celebrate it. You can avoid the same fate by following the guidelines outlined below.

Type	Purpose	Techniques
Speech of Introduction	To prepare the audience for the speech to follow To build the speaker's credibility To make the speaker feel welcome	Be brief Be accurate Don't exaggerate by overstating the speaker's qualifications
Speech of Presentation	To present a gift, award, or honor	Adapt remarks to the audience Create a sense of anticipation Explain the background of the award Acknowledge the achievements of the recipient
Acceptance Speech	To accept or respond to an award	Express gratitude Acknowledge others Focus on the values represented in the award
Commemorative Speeches (eulogies, dedications, testimonials)	To pay tribute	Provide information about the subject of the tribute
After-Dinner Speeches	To entertain and celebrate	Arouse and heighten appreciation for the person, group, institution, or idea Be positive and light hearted Communicate a central theme or idea Use humor (but cautiously)
Speech of Inspiration	To arouse the audience to pursue common goals or values	Incorporate vivid descriptions and imagery Be enthusiastic Review shared experiences Focus on shared values

arrangement (based on a causal connection between two elements or events). When no other logical pattern seems appropriate, a topical arrangement may work best. Topical arrangement involves creating an organizational pattern that fits the ideas presented. For example, a persuasive speech describing the benefits of a particular university would be difficult to organize chronologically, spatially, in relation to size, or in a problem-solution or cause-effect format. Developing a series of arguments strung together in a topical pattern would be more effective. Topics could include tuition and housing costs, location, and the quality of the faculty. (Other organizational patterns may be more appropriate in other cultures—see the Cultural Connections section at the end of the chapter.)

Statements that link ideas together are known as transitions. Be careful to include transitions in your presentation so that audience members can follow your message. Phrases such as, "Now that we have discussed the affordable housing at State University, let's focus on the desirability of the surrounding area," help to shift an audience's attention from one main point to the next.

> A bad beginning makes a bad ending.
>
> —Euripedes

Once you've planned the body of your speech, then it is time to consider how you will introduce and conclude your presentation. An effective introduction serves four purposes.[19] First, it captures the attention of audience members and identifies the topic. Many speakers launch into their speeches by announcing their subject. For example: "Today I'm going to talk about empowerment" or "Hi, I'm Karen and I will explain the reorganization plan." While such statements leave no doubt as to the subject of the presentation, they do little to pique the interest of audience members. To create an effective introduction, begin with a memorable quotation or startling statistic, refer to a current event, tell a story, use an audiovisual aid, or ask a question. Give your audience a reason to listen. This can be done by establishing how the topic relates to the everyday lives of listeners as well as to their needs and motivations. An activist promoting stricter industry pollution standards will be more successful if she can establish that pollution poses a danger to local residents and lowers property values. Next, establish your credibility on this particular topic by describing your experience, research, and/or interest in the subject. Finally, preview the main points of the speech, generally in the form of a short statement that summarizes your thesis and transitions into the body. For example: "Today I will describe the personal and organizational benefits of empowering your employees."

A memorable conclusion leaves audience members with a positive impression of you and your topic and provides a sense of closure. Summarize your major points or thesis when informing an audience; ask for agreement and action when persuading. Make sure that the audience knows you are done by tying back to your introduction, posing a challenge or question, or using a quotation.

> Always leave them wanting more.
>
> —Helen Hayes

Language

The effective use of language is the key to producing memorable and moving public speeches. We remember Martin Luther King, Jr.'s "I Have a Dream" speech as one of the greatest of the twentieth century primarily because of the way King used words to create dramatic images. King spoke of coming to cash in on the promise of equal rights at the "bank of justice" and urged followers to refuse to drink from "the cup of bitterness and hatred." At one point he declared his hope that his children would "one day live in a nation where they will not be judged by the color of their skin, but by the content of their character." Successful speakers follow the example set by King by using language that is clear, vivid, and appropriate.

The best rule of thumb in a presentation is to use clear, specific, understandable language. Technical and complicated words should be used sparingly, particularly when dealing with mass audiences. Further, avoid the use of jargon and euphemisms. Government officials often try to create pleasant descriptions for unpleasant events, referring to missiles as "peace-keepers," taxes as "revenue enhancements," and death as "exceeding survivability."[20] This type of "doublespeak" confuses and distracts audience members. The more you complicate your message by using technical or convoluted language, the more likely it is that your message will be misunderstood.

Clear language does not have to be dull. Public speeches should be descriptive and distinctive. The use of affect and imagery enliven public address. Affective language sparks emotion, while imagery creates visual connections for the audience. Franklin Roosevelt's Declaration of War following the Pearl Harbor attack of 1941 began as follows:

> Yesterday, December 7, 1941—a date which will live in infamy—the United States was suddenly and deliberately attacked by naval and air forces of the Empire of Japan.

Roosevelt's words expressed the shock of a nation. To this day, many people look at the calendar on December 7 and are transported back to the attack. The mark of effective public speakers is their ability to create vivid, stirring representations for audiences. While a picture may paint a thousand words, it is equally true that a gifted speaker can fashion a word into a thousand pictures. (See box 9.4 for other examples of vivid language.)

Avoid using language that might offend members of the audience. The use of profane, obscene, or inappropriate language can irreparably damage a speaker's image. In 2002, Mississippi Senator Trent Lott offended many and lost his position as majority leader of the Senate when he claimed that the United States might have been better off if the racist segregation policies outlined in the 1948 presidential campaign of Strom Thurmond had been adopted.

Box 9.4

Vivid Speech Samples[21]

We're an army going out to set other men free. . . . Here you can be *something*. Here's a place to build a home. It isn't the land—there's always more land. It's the idea that we all have value, you and me, we're worth something more than the dirt. . . . What we're fighting for, in the end, is each other.

Joshua Lawrence Chamberlain, 2nd Maine regiment,
prior to the Battle of the Little Round Top at Gettysburg

At the stroke of the midnight hour, when the world sleeps, India will awake to life and freedom. A moment comes, which comes but rarely in history, when we step out from the old to the new, when an age ends, and when the soul of a nation, long suppressed, finds utterance. It is fitting that at this solemn moment we take the pledge of dedication to the service of India and her people and to the still larger cause of humanity.

Jawaharlal Nehru, speaking at the
granting of Indian independence following World War II

Now if this blind pursuit of licentious trade continues, political instability will return big time. The rise of fascism, brutal nationalism, and the ethnic racism we see on continent after continent are not an accident.
Demagogues *prey* on insecurity and fear; they breed in the darkness of poverty and desolation. If we do not build an economic growth that helps sustain communities, cultures, and families, the consequences will be severe. Even if our politics somehow survives, our globe will not.

Body Shop President Anita Roddick, advocating that the
International Chamber of Commerce become more socially responsible

Today I am an inquisitor, and hyperbole would not be fictional and would not overstate the solemnness that I feel right now. My faith in the Constitution is whole, it is complete, it is total. And I am not going to sit here and be an idle spectator to the diminution, the subversion, the destruction of the Constitution.

Representative Barbara Jordan,
testifying at an impeachment hearing for President Richard Nixon

A typical bank—including my bank—was once monolithic, homogeneous, self-contained and self-absorbed. For many years, conventional wisdom held that a bank's commitment ended where the sidewalk began. But now we've changed. We are in the streets. We are "out there," active, engaged and involved, building bridges to the many communities that make up society today, chipping away at the old, stereotypical view of banks.

Bank of Montreal CEO Matthew Barrett,
outlining the future of banking and his company's vision

Indifference elicits no response. Indifference is not a response. Indifference is not a beginning; it is an end. And, therefore, indifference is always the friend of the enemy, for it benefits the aggressor—never his victim, whose pain is magnified when he or she feels forgotten. The political prisoner in his cell, the hungry children, the homeless refugees—not to respond to their plight, not to relieve their solitude by offering them a spark of hope is to exile them from human memory. And in denying their humanity, we betray our own.

Concentration camp survivor Elie Wiesel,
speaking on behalf of oppressed peoples of the world

Some types of humor lower a speaker's credibility. One type of humor that can be detrimental involves making oneself or others the brunt of a joke. Disparagement focusing on personal shortcomings (such as height, weight, complexion, or social skills) does not enhance a speaker's image. Speakers who belittle themselves are rated as less competent, less expert, and less likable, while speakers who belittle others are rated as having lower character.[22] Other research suggests that a speaker's use of milder forms of disparaging humor aimed at one's occupation or profession are not as harmful.[23] Most evidence suggests that public speakers should generally avoid using disparaging humor.

Rehearsal

Practicing gives you the opportunity to simulate a public presentation. This experience helps you refine content and increase your confidence level. Just as a dress rehearsal makes a marriage ceremony or theater production less confusing and stressful, a speech rehearsal helps polish a public presentation.

The most important thing to remember when rehearsing a speech is that you must practice out loud. We think more rapidly than we speak. As a result, internal thought and external speech operate differently. Thought is characterized by condensed grammar and syntax, which makes the structure of internal thought incomplete. Our thoughts are composed of fleeting images and words. External speech, on the other hand, is grammatically and syntactically complete. Speech consists of fully constructed messages that follow a distinctive organizational pattern. Since presentations are delivered in external speech, the external form of communication must be used during rehearsal. Rehearsing only in internal thought (just thinking about what you will say without saying it out loud) may contribute to the same feelings of anxiety that are associated with inadequate speech preparation.[24]

Delivery

Delivery refers to the physical aspects of speechmaking. A speaker's delivery should not be awkward or distracting. The delivery of a message is most effective when it appears natural. Physical appearance, gestures, movement, eye contact, and voice quality all directly affect the delivery of public messages.

Public speakers should be appropriately groomed and clothed. Audience expectations regarding hygiene and dress vary from one situation to another. For example, it is usually acceptable to deliver a classroom presentation dressed in jeans and a t-shirt, but this casual attire would not be acceptable for a speech to a group of civic leaders. In general, it is best to tailor your appearance to the situation, region, or culture in which you will be speaking. Your audience analysis should help you decide what will be acceptable.

Gestures occur naturally in conversation, and that tendency should be followed in public address. When did you last worry about gesturing while conversing casually with your best friend? Unfortunately, many speakers are uncomfortable about body language during their presentations. Instead of allowing the natural tendency to gesture to operate, they plan where to insert gestures in the speech. As a result, their movements are awkward and distracting. Pay attention to your natural pattern of gestures. When rehearsing, include natural gestures in your presentation. You'll then be more relaxed and natural when you make your appearance in front of an audience.

Movement can be used to heighten interest in a speech. Movement that minimizes physical distance between speaker and audience also creates a sense of psychological closeness that communication scholars call "immediacy." Audiences are more receptive to speakers who signal warmth, liking, and friendliness through movement and other nonverbal behaviors. You can assess how well you communicate a sense of immediacy as a public speaker by completing the self-assessment exercise in box 9.5.

In Western culture, looking others in the eyes is a sign of respect and honesty. Effective public speakers maintain eye contact with audience members. Staring at your notes or letting your eyes dart around leads to the perception that you are not trustworthy. Use your notes sparingly. Maintain focus for a few seconds on individuals seated in one section of the audience, and then sustain eye contact with another section. Avoid monotonous or strident tones. An expressive voice conveys emotion and interest without being harsh. Most unpleasant vocal patterns can be improved with training and practice.

Responding to Questions

The delivery of a speech is often followed by a question and answer session. Responding to questions can be stressful; speakers must "think on their feet." The advantage of taking questions is that it provides immediate feedback about how the audience reacted to the presentation and gives the speaker an opportunity to clarify misunderstandings. Effective responses can help a leader establish a stronger bond with the audience and build commitment to her or his message.[25]

Try to anticipate possible questions when preparing a speech and learn to distinguish between types of questions. Some questions are really statements of support that elaborate on points you made in your speech. They're easy to handle—just agree when the response is appropriate to what you've said. Other questions ask for additional information and clarification and should be acknowledged and answered as directly as possible. The most difficult queries are disputes or challenges offered in the form of a question. In these cases, listen to the questioner's words, tone of voice, and body language to determine her/his true intent. The question "When will we get our next raise?" might really be a criticism of the fact that employees in some departments got pay increases while members of other departments did not. Try to address both the stated question and the questioner's intention, acknowledging the feelings behind the dispute or challenge. Find commonalities between the challenger's position and yours if possible; differentiate your position when appropriate. In response to the question about raises, a corporate executive might answer:

> Linda, you've asked about upcoming raises, but I also sense that you have some frustration about unequal pay. Let me speak to both your question and other concerns you might have. It's true that union employees recently received pay increases even though we instituted a hiring and wage freeze in January. We were legally obligated to pay those increases to union employees under the previous contract. However, like many of you, I don't think that's fair. Now that the freeze has been lifted, the next round of raises is scheduled for July 1. At that time, we will give top priority to increasing the salaries of nonunion staff.

Box 9.5   Self-Assessment

Nonverbal Immediacy Scale[26]

Instructions

Originally developed to assess the nonverbal immediacy of teachers, this scale has been revised to reveal nonverbal immediacy in all types of public presentations. For each item, indicate how likely you would be to engage in the nonverbal behaviors while speaking before a large group. Use the following scale:

5-extremely likely   4-likely   3-maybe/unsure   2-unlikely   1-extremely unlikely

_____   1.   I would sit behind a table or desk while speaking.

_____   2.   I would use a lot of purposeful gestures while talking to the group.

_____   3.   I would use a monotone/dull voice when speaking.

_____   4.   I would look directly at my audience while presenting.

_____   5.   I would smile at the group while talking.

_____   6.   My entire body would feel tense and rigid while giving my speech.

_____   7.   I would approach or stand beside individual audience members.

_____   8.   I would move around the room while speaking.

_____   9.   I would avoid looking at individual audience members during my speech.

_____ 10.   I would look at my notes frequently during my presentation.

_____ 11.   I would stand behind a podium or desk while giving my speech.

_____ 12.   I would have a very relaxed body position while talking to the group.

_____ 13.   I would smile at individual members in the audience.

_____ 14.   I would use a variety of vocal expressions while talking.

_____ 15.   I would engage in a lot of nervous gestures or body movements, such as shuffling my note cards or switching my weight from one foot to the next.

Calculating Your Score

Step 1: Total your responses to items 1, 3, 6, 9, 10, 11, and 15 _____.

Step 2: Total your responses to items 2, 4, 5, 7, 8, 12, 13, and 14 _____.

Complete the following formula:

42 minus total from step 1 =   _____

Plus total from step 2 =   _____

YOUR TOTAL SCORE   _____

Interpreting Your Score

Your score should fall between 15 and 75. The average or midpoint is around 45. If your score totals 50 or higher, you are high in nonverbal immediacy and are likely to be seen as approachable and likable. If your score falls below 40, you might want to learn and practice the specific immediacy behaviors reflected in the items listed in step 2. Nonimmediate speakers are perceived as cold and distant and are more likely to bore their audiences.

Persuasive Campaigns

As we've seen, public speaking is an important tool for public leaders. However, much like a single television advertisement or a single newspaper editorial, a single speech does not always change the attitudes or behaviors of large numbers of people. For this reason, public leaders frequently put together persuasive campaigns in order to influence public opinion.

Characteristics of Successful Campaigns

Persuasion expert Herbert Simons defines campaigns as "organized, sustained attempts at influencing groups of people . . . through a series of messages."[27] Campaigns use both the mass media and interpersonal communication networks to achieve their goals. There are six types of persuasive campaigns: (1) product/commercial (selling goods and services), (2) public relations (building public awareness, providing information, educating the public, modifying behavior), (3) political (electing candidates to office), (4) issue (changing or implementing government or corporate policy), (5) image (building positive images for individuals or organizations), and (6) social movements (proposing or opposing change in societal norms and/or values).[28]

Not all campaigns are successful. The failure of many heavily promoted Hollywood movies, Web sites, and political candidates demonstrates how even well-planned and well-financed commercial campaigns can go astray. Other types of campaigns often suffer a similar fate. For example, the popular DARE (Drug Abuse Resistance Education) program for elementary school children has had no measurable long-term effect on drug usage. Teens who participated in campaign activities when they were younger are just as likely to take illegal substances as those who didn't go through the program.[29]

While many campaigns fail, others meet their objectives. One of the longest running and most successful campaigns is the Smokey Bear fire prevention program. Since the campaign began in 1942, the number of acres lost to wildfires has dropped from 30 million to 5 million a year. One survey found that 98 percent of the population knows who Smokey is and Smokey Bear headquarters has its own zip code to handle the volume of cards and letters requesting fire prevention kits.[30] Another successful campaign encourages the use of designated drivers. The number of drinkers who choose designated drivers has risen dramatically since the program began in 1988. The belief that drivers should not drink has now become a widely accepted norm in society.[31]

Why do some campaigns have a significant impact on public attitudes and behavior while others have little influence at all? In order to answer this question, Everett Rogers and Douglas Storey surveyed 40 years of campaign research.[32] Rogers and Storey identified the following as eight characteristics of successful campaigns. Subsequent research has confirmed their conclusions.[33]

Pretest messages and identify market segments. Organizers of effective campaigns rely on research to help them shape their messages. Doing market research prior to a campaign reveals what audiences currently believe, if receivers understand campaign advertisements and themes, and which messages are best suited to particular segments of the market. Soul City, a nonprofit health organization in South Africa, is one group that uses research to identify issues and audiences. The group's leaders conduct focus groups, interviews, and pretesting to identify important national health concerns (HIV prevention, alcohol abuse, domestic violence) and public attitudes about these issues. The mix of campaign media activities and materials is then adapted to target audiences. Television reaches urban populations while radio programs are directed at rural listeners. Education packets for youths consist of a comic book and set of workbooks. Education packets for adults include a health booklet, audiotapes, and Soul City posters.[34]

Expose a large segment of the audience to clear campaign messages. Message exposure is a prerequisite for campaign success. Audiences must be aware of campaign messages before they can act on the information contained in those messages. Similarly, in most cases it is important that messages be clear. The "Life Takes Visa" advertising campaign, for example, may fall short on this standard. It's not obvious exactly what the tagline of its commercials—"but no matter what it takes, life takes Visa"—means. Even the company's explanation of its campaign message could stand some clarification. According to a company spokesperson: "We want consumers to take away that Visa can really help you do everything to let you live life the way you want. That ranges from everything you need to do, want to do, and some of the things you never thought possible."[35]

Use the most accessible media for target groups. Successful campaigns utilize those media that are most accessible to audiences. In some countries few people have access to either television or newspapers. In these situations, campaign organizers must rely on radio and other media. The timing of messages is also critical. Effective campaigns reach audiences when they are most receptive. For example, when the Olympic Games are in session (and public interest in the Olympics is at its peak), corporations use media spots to trumpet the fact that their products are endorsed by the U.S. Olympic Committee.

Use the media to raise awareness. The media are most effective when they are used to provide important information, stimulate interpersonal conversations, and recruit additional people to participate in the campaign. Media messages raise awareness and get people talking about the merits of politicians, products, organizations, and causes. In addition, many people volunteer for food drives, fund-raisers, clean-up campaigns, and other projects after hearing about them through advertisements or news stories.

Rely on interpersonal communication, particularly communication between people of similar social backgrounds, to lead to and reinforce behavior change. Interpersonal communication networks play a particularly important role in persuasive campaigns designed to change people's behaviors. Behavioral change is more likely when the desired behaviors are modeled by others. Rogers and Storey note, "While the mass media may be effective in disseminating information, interpersonal channels are more influential in motivating people to act on that information."[36] The national crime prevention campaign that urges listeners and viewers to "Take a bite out of crime" is one example of how media and interpersonal channels can complement each other. Although many people learn about crime prevention behaviors through the campaign's media spots, listeners often put these behaviors into action only after they become involved in neighborhood watch groups. The groups reinforce the message and demonstrate that crime prevention activities are socially acceptable.

Certain individuals—called opinion leaders—play a major role in convincing others to adopt new products, techniques, or ideas. Enlisting the participation of these individuals greatly increases a campaign's chances for success. Opinion leaders share four characteristics: (1) they have greater exposure to the media, outside change agents, and other key external communication sources; (2) they participate in a variety of social networks and rapidly spread new ideas to others; (3) they generally have a higher socioeconomic status than opinion followers; and (4) they are more innovative when the norms of the social system favor change.[37] (See box 9.6 for more information on how a few individuals can bring about major social changes.)

Use high credibility sources. Successful campaigns use highly credible representatives. (Refer to chapter 6 for more information on the dimensions of

---

Box 9.6   Research Highlight

Starting Positive Epidemics[38]

New Yorker staff writer Malcolm Gladwell believes that products, behaviors, and ideas are contagious and spread like viruses. In his book *The Tipping Point,* he argues that social trends ranging from clothing styles to crime rates are transmitted in the same way as the flu or AIDS. The "tipping point" refers to the critical moment when a social epidemic becomes highly contagious, bringing rapid change. For example, 1998 marked a tipping point for cellular phones in the United States. By that year mobile phones had become cheap and easy to use. The number of cellular users then exploded. Gladwell offers three rules of social epidemics.

The first is the "law of the few," which describes the types of people who play a key role in spreading trends. *Connectors* know lots of people from a variety of social groups and spread information about ideas through their social networks. *Mavens* are eager to share information to help others; they are experts on topics like supermarket prices, movies, and cars. *Salespeople* actively persuade those who are reluctant to buy a new product or adopt a new behavior.

The second rule is "the stickiness factor." For information to have an impact, it must "stick" or be retained. The producers of *Sesame Street* (who were out to create a literacy epidemic among 3–5 year-olds) used this principle to make their show memorable to children. They made sure that human actors always appeared on screen with Muppet characters after they discovered that young viewers tuned out when the adults were shown on their own.

The third law is the power of context. Environment plays a critical role in shaping human activity, and small modifications in the setting can bring about significant behavioral changes. For instance, the rapid drop in the New York City crime rate between 1992 and 1997 is attributed in large part to crackdowns on such minor offenses as graffiti tagging and cheating on subway fares.

The fact that a few people introducing small changes can produce major effects is good news for leaders who want to start positive epidemics like lowering teen pregnancy or school drop-out rates. Gladwell introduces San Diego nurse Georgia Sadler as one example of someone who is making a significant difference through a series of small steps. Sadler wanted to increase awareness of breast cancer and diabetes in her African American community. When she didn't make much progress contacting church groups, she took her message to local beauty salons. Sadler trained stylists in how to present breast cancer information through stories and kept supplying new anecdotes for them to share. Information was written in large print on laminated sheets so stylists could refer to it when needed. Follow-up evaluation revealed that women who went to the salons were having more mammograms and diabetes testing.

credibility.) For instance, many people criticized the Nestlé company for taking advantage of the credibility of medical personnel by using women dressed as nurses to promote the use of infant formula in third world countries. Infant formula is extremely expensive in developing areas and is unsafe when mixed with dirty water. Audiences keep the motives of sources in mind when evaluating their credibility. An actor who promotes AIDS prevention as a public service is generally seen as more credible than an actor paid to promote a product.

Direct messages at the individual needs of the audience. Audiences are most influenced by messages aimed directly at personal needs. Effective political campaigns emphasize how the candidate will help the voter by lowering taxes, providing more jobs, building better roads, lowering crime, and so on. Campaigns for popular products link the purchase of the item with a specific need felt by the audience (e.g., smoke detectors for safety, cosmetics to enhance physical appearance, frozen dinners for convenience).

Emphasize positive rewards rather than prevention. Many campaigns (such as the one urging us to wear our seat belts) try to help audiences avoid future, unwanted events. These campaigns often fall short of their goals because the consequences of noncompliance are uncertain. In the case of safety belts, many of us drive without them because we believe that we will never be in a serious auto accident. Effective campaigns emphasize the immediate positive rewards that come from adopting a value, belief, or behavior. Campaign planners may use our fear of suffering a heart attack to encourage us to start a regular exercise program. However, we are more likely to adopt a regular exercise routine if campaign messages emphasize weight loss, stress reduction, and other *immediate* benefits.

Campaign Stages

Even with an understanding of the factors that contribute to successful campaigns, organizing a campaign can seem like an overwhelming task. Successful campaigns involve research, the careful construction of messages, and effective use of both the media and interpersonal networks. To make the campaign process more manageable, Gary Woodward and Robert Denton suggest that you follow the six steps described in box 9.7.[39]

Situation analysis is the foundation for the rest of the campaign. In this first stage, begin by identifying key audience characteristics. These include: (1) demographic variables (age, education, occupation), (2) geographic variables (urban versus suburban, West versus Midwest), and (3) psychographic variables (lifestyle, interests, activities, and opinions). If your campaign is product oriented, then size up the competition and determine attitudes toward your product. Your research can be both informal and formal. Informal research is the process of gathering information from libraries, personal contacts, industry publications, and other sources. Formal research is based on the statistical analysis of data collected through surveys and interviews.

Once the preliminary research is complete, goals should be set in stage 2. *Objectives* can center on increased awareness, attitude change, or changes in behavior. Many campaigns fail because they are too ambitious. When you seek significant behavioral change, set more modest goals. For example, you might

---

Box 9.7

Campaign Implementation Overview[40]

Stage	Components
1. Situation analysis	target audience product/issue/idea competition or opponent
2. Objectives	mission goals outcomes
3. Strategies	messages media presentation activities
4. Budget	labor material media talent production
5. Implementation	timing follow-up
6. Evaluation	what people say what people think what people do

---

be able to convince a large percentage of your audience that recycling reduces our dependence on landfills. Yet, only a portion of those who believe in recycling will actually participate in recycling programs.

The third stage of the campaign is concerned with *strategies* to get things done. Structure messages to appeal to market segments, determine how you will use the media to reach audiences, and plan presentational activities like press conferences, rallies, and conventions. (See box 9.8 for a list of communication channels or vehicles commonly used in persuasive campaigns.)

In the fourth stage, prepare a *budget*. Financial resources will frequently determine the scope of your campaign. Labor, material, media, talent, and production costs must all be taken into consideration.

Implementation is the fifth stage. The campaign goes into action during this phase. Monitor your progress and determine the timing of messages through ongoing research. Poll voters to test attitudes; check and recheck reactions. By periodically gathering data, you will know if your campaign is on target or if you should modify your campaign messages and strategies.

The *evaluation* stage completes the ongoing campaign and lays the groundwork for future projects. In order to determine if you reached the campaign objectives you set earlier, you will need to survey target audiences, measure sales, and determine if favorable attitudes translate into desired action. What you learn from the successes and failures of one persuasive campaign can serve as the foundation for the next.

Box 9.8

Campaign Communication Channels[41]

Issues advertising	Placed and commissioned articles
Sponsored books, editorials	Employee communication
Negotiation	Internal and external newsletters
Executive comments	Speakers bureaus
Public affairs programming	Annual financial or special topic reports
Press releases, media relations	Videos mailed to key audiences and on request
Personal contact with opinion leaders by key staff and management personnel	Op-eds placed on editorial pages
Video and satellite presentations to internal and external audiences	Talk show appearances
	Electronic mail and bulletin boards
Congressional testimony, public hearings	Billboards
Mailings to constituencies	Special issue documents
Bill stuffers	Scholarly papers (commissioned)
Conference paper presentations	Citizens advisory committees
Trials	Lobbying
Open houses, issue workshops	Web sites
Education information relevant to activist, government, or industry issues that can be distributed through schools	Legislative position papers
	Collaborative decision making
	Joint research efforts

Collaborative Leadership

In a pluralistic society such as ours, encouraging groups to cooperate on behalf of the common good is often a public leader's greatest challenge.[42] Attempts to restore salmon and steelhead runs in the Pacific Northwest are a case in point. Billions of dollars have been spent to bolster these fish populations, but their numbers continue to decline due to dams, overgrazing, urban pollution, logging, irrigation, fishing, and other factors. Reversing this trend will take the cooperative efforts of biologists, government agencies, power companies, ranchers, barge owners, water districts, tribes, city councils, environmental activists, governors, and congressional representatives. Unless these groups look beyond their individual interests and work together, many species (which used to return to the region's rivers by the millions) will become extinct.

Fortunately, collaborative efforts can succeed if led effectively. Collaborative leaders focus on the process of decision making rather than on any particular outcome.[43] They believe that diverse groups will generate reasonable solutions if interested parties work together in constructive ways. These leaders have little formal power but function as "first among equals" who encourage their peers to take ownership in the collaborative process. They convene

the discussions, help the group reach agreement, and work with other participants to implement the solution.

David Chrislip and Carl Larson conducted a comprehensive investigation
of successful collaborative public leadership efforts in Phoenix, Denver, Balti-
more, and other cities. Each produced concrete, tangible results and was hailed
as a success by those involved. The collaborative efforts brought together
diverse members of communities with varied (and often contradictory) needs
and interests to tackle problems such as homelessness, decaying city infrastructure, poor school performance, and racism. Based on their observations, Chrislip and Larson identified 10 factors necessary for successful collaboration.[44]

- *Good timing and a clear need.* Stakeholders must be ready to act in
  response to a clear need. Whether the issue is roads in need of repair or
  programs for pregnant teens, collaborative leadership will not be successful until people in a community feel it is time to address a problem.

- *Strong stakeholder groups.* The ability to voice public opinion accurately is
  an important ingredient in successful collaboration. Strong stakeholder
  groups can represent their constituents effectively. Successful collaborative leadership depends on strong stakeholder groups who are able to
  voice public opinion accurately. When a group such as the chamber of
  commerce speaks and acts credibly for its members, collaborative leadership is more likely to succeed.

- *Broad-based involvement.* Collaborative efforts are most successful when
  participants from different segments of the community are involved.
  Successful collaborative initiatives often involve people from government, business, education, and other key community groups. (To test
  your ability to identify important stakeholder groups, respond to the
  case study in box 9.9.)

- *Credible and open process.* At the beginning of almost any broad-based collaborative process, there is suspicion and cynicism. Participants in successful
  collaborative efforts work to create an atmosphere of trust and openness.
  This is accomplished by actions such as treating all stakeholder groups
  fairly and consistently, establishing ground rules for engaging in civilized
  disagreement, and working to depoliticize the decision-making process.[45]

- *Participation of high level, visible community leaders.* The support of leaders
  such as mayors, city council members, CEOs of local organizations, and
  school administrators gives visibility to collaborative goals. Although
  these leaders need not always be directly involved in every step of the
  process, their commitment to the collaborative venture is critical.

- *Formal support.* Support from established authorities such as government
  agencies, city councils, and school boards is critical to the success of community-based collaborative decision making. For example, the former
  mayor of Phoenix, Paul Johnson, assigned each member of the Phoenix
  city council the task of implementing a recommendation made by a citizen task force. The task force had no power to put its recommendations
  into action, and Johnson realized that support from the formal power
  structure was a mandatory ingredient.

- *Ability to overcome mistrust and skepticism.* Many participants begin the collaborative process with little hope that substantive progress can be made. They worry that certain stakeholders will behave poorly or that the collaborative effort will be derailed. Successful collaborative groups overcome their mistrust and skepticism, particularly in the early stages of their deliberations.

- *Strong leadership of the process.* As we noted earlier, successful collaborative efforts are characterized by strong leadership of the process. This leadership is exhibited in many ways: keeping stakeholders at the table through periods of frustration and skepticism, helping stakeholders negotiate difficult points, and enforcing group ground rules. Process leaders are excellent listeners who address problems head-on while, at the same time, expressing respect and appreciation for all group members.[46]

- *Celebration of ongoing achievement.* Whether it involves reaching an interim goal, overcoming a difficult obstacle, attracting new resources, or

---

Box 9.9   Case Study

Building the Bypass: Identifying the Stakeholders

For nearly 25 years, residents of Bloomburg have talked about the need for a bypass to carry traffic around their small city. Currently a major highway, which connects the state's major population center to the coast, runs through downtown. On week days the road is clogged with semis, logging trucks, and commuters. On summer weekends, traffic backs up for miles as vacationers head for the beach. Local residents find it difficult to get from one side of town to the next, frustrated travelers blame the city for their lengthy delays, and downtown businesses are fleeing to the neighboring community. City officials and the local chamber of commerce want to launch a downtown revitalization effort but there is little chance of success unless the highway is relocated.

Tom Hirokawa was recently hired as Bloomburg's first full-time planning director. One of his major responsibilities is to start work on the bypass project. He knows that a number of earlier bypass efforts failed. Local farmers and orchard growers viewed the bypass as a threat to their livelihoods, and highway funds weren't available. Hirokawa realizes that the farmers and growers still object to the bypass, but he has been told by local legislators and the area's congressional representative that the state and federal government will now pay for the project. According to plans drawn up earlier, the proposed route would not only cut across farmland and orchards but would also border a federally protected wetland. A small manufacturing facility and several homes would have to be relocated to accommodate the new road.

Tom knows that the critical first step in the project is identifying all the important stakeholder groups. Groups left out of the deliberations could later undermine the collaborative process. He also realizes that it is important to identify the interests and perspectives of stakeholders before he gathers them together to meet for the first time.

Discussion Questions

1. Who are the important stakeholder groups for the bypass project?

2. What are the needs and interests of each group?

3. Are there any groups that Tom shouldn't invite to participate in the discussions? Why?

4. Which groups have conflicting interests? How should Tom respond to these conflicts?

5. Based on your analysis of the stakeholder groups, how difficult is it going to be to reach consensus? Do you think the bypass will ever be built?

bridging a gap with a reluctant stakeholder, highly effective collaborative groups acknowledge their successes. From the use of pizza parties to
formal award ceremonies, small signs of progress are celebrated.

- *Shift to broader concerns.* As collaborative efforts progress, successful
  groups focus less on narrow issues and more on the broader interests of
  the community.

Chrislip and Larson emphasize that collaborative leadership both produces tangible results and also creates effective problem-solving mechanisms
for the future. The process of collaboration changes the way organizations and
communities function. Thus, collaborative leadership is effective in dealing
with current problems and in setting the stage for addressing future issues. It
helps create an energized constituency primed to address the problems of an
organization or community.

Chapter Takeaways

- Public leaders influence the attitudes and behaviors of large audiences at
  all levels of society through the use of public relations activities, public
  address, and persuasive campaigns.

- Excellent public relations programs share the following characteristics:
  (1) empowered (valued and promoted by top management); (2) a strategic management role that helps shape organizational policy and direction; (3) two-way communication and symmetrical relationships that
  identify and respond to the needs of publics while fostering collaboration with outside groups; (4) ethical behavior that discloses accurate
  information, engages in dialogue, and advocates social responsibility;
  and (5) supportive structure that encourages participation and fosters
  the advancement of women and minorities.

- Your speech will be effective if it is based on careful prespeech planning
  (deciding on a mode of delivery, audience analysis); clear organization
  (developing a thesis statement, arranging and linking ideas, crafting a
  memorable introduction and conclusion); clear, vivid, and appropriate
  language; extensive rehearsal; delivery that appears natural and creates a
  sense of immediacy; and skillful anticipation and response to questions
  after the presentation is over.

- A persuasive campaign consists of a series of messages aimed at changing the beliefs and behaviors of others. To create a campaign with significant impact, pretest messages and identify market segments; expose a
  large portion of the audience to campaign messages; use the media most
  accessible to target groups; rely on the media to raise awareness; utilize
  interpersonal communication to bring about behavior change; employ
  high credibility sources; direct messages at individual needs; and
  emphasize positive rewards rather than prevention.

- There are six steps or stages to any type of persuasive campaign: (1) situation analysis, which identifies key audience characteristics and possible
  competitors; (2) objectives, which center on increased awareness, atti-

tude change, or changed behavior; (3) strategies, which identify types of messages and communication activities; (4) budget, which determines the resources available to pay for labor, material, media, talent, and production costs; (5) implementation, which puts the campaign into action and evaluates progress; and (6) evaluation, which gathers feedback and measures outcomes.

- Collaborative leaders focus on the decision-making process instead of promoting a particular solution. They have little formal power but get discussions started, help the group reach agreement, and work with other participants to implement the solution.

- Ten necessary conditions for successful collaborative public ventures include: (1) good timing and a clear need; (2) strong stakeholder groups; (3) broad-based involvement; (4) a credible and open process; (5) committed, high-level, visible community leaders; (6) formal support; (7) an ability to overcome mistrust and skepticism; (8) strong leadership of the process; (9) celebration of ongoing achievement; and (10) shift to broader concerns.

APPLICATION EXERCISES

1. Consider the impact of public leaders on history. Do you agree with Carlyle's perspective that history is shaped by powerful leaders or with Spencer's claim that history develops according to patterns that cannot be altered by a single individual? Think of some examples that support your position.

2. As a research project, examine the public relations efforts of a large organization. Does the program meet the standards of excellence outlined in the chapter?

3. In a small group, identify emerging issues that will likely have an impact on your college or another organization of your choice. How should the organization respond in order to lead public opinion?

4. Locate all the articles related to public speaking from one newspaper. Classify the news stories as local, regional, national, or international. What conclusions can you draw about the relationship between public address and public leadership based on your sample?

5. Practice your ability to deliver impromptu speeches. You instructor will provide you with a list of topics and set time limits.

6. Use the techniques discussed in the chapter to prepare a speech. Concentrate on prespeech preparation, organization, language, rehearsal, and delivery. After the speech, evaluate your performance and record ways that you can make your future presentations more effective.

7. Evaluate a speech delivered by someone else based on concepts presented in the chapter. Write up your analysis.

8. In a research paper, describe the public speaking techniques of a well-known leader (e.g., Abraham Lincoln, Winston Churchill, Margaret Thatcher, Martin Luther King, Jr., or Eleanor Roosevelt). What made

this individual an effective speaker? What can we learn about public address from this person?

9. Analyze a recent persuasive campaign based on the characteristics of successful campaigns presented in the chapter. Based on these elements, why did the campaign succeed or fail? Write up your findings.

10. Analyze the effectiveness of a collaborative public venture using Chrislip and Larson's 10 characteristics of successful collaborative groups. Report your findings in a class presentation.

CULTURAL CONNECTIONS: PUBLIC SPEAKING IN KENYA[47]

Culture has a significant impact on public speaking patterns. The qualities that characterize an effective speaker in the United States and Canada often do not translate to other cultures. Consider the contrast between public address in Kenya, East Africa, and in the United States, for example. Ann Neville Miller, a professor at Daystar University in Nairobi, discovered that Americans and Kenyans view the prospect of speaking very differently. While a majority of Americans say they fear speaking in public, Kenyans expect to give speeches as part of everyday life.

> For most Kenyans public speaking is an unavoidable responsibility. Life events both major and minor are marked by ceremonies which occasion multiple public speeches. The normal procedure at wedding receptions, for example, is to include not only a speech by the best man and the parents of both bride and groom, but also addresses by the grandparents, various uncles and aunts, representatives of the bridal party's respective workplaces, and any of a host of other individuals and groups. Even the woman selected to cut the cake expects to give a brief word of advice before performing her duty.

North Americans give lots of persuasive and informative speeches that are supported by expert testimony and statistics. Kenyans, for the reasons described above, deliver more special occasion speeches that are supported with personal stories, parables that leave the audience to infer the main point, and proverbs. They may break out into song and encourage audience participation by leading chants or by having listeners fill in the end of sentences. East African speakers establish their credibility by virtue of their status (wealth, social standing, age, education, tribal affiliation) instead of through their expertise, as is the case in North America. Linear organizational patterns, like those outlined earlier in the chapter, are less common in African speeches. Instead, presenters often use a circular pattern that resembles a bicycle wheel. The main point serves as the hub. Personal stories, proverbs, and parables radiate out like spokes to the rim and then return to the hub or thesis.

SPOTLIGHT ON TECHNOLOGY:
POLITICAL CAMPAIGNING MOVES INTO CYBERSPACE

A growing number of political candidates are using social networking sites (such as YouTube, MySpace, and Facebook), blogs, campaign Web sites, and even text messaging for everything from recruiting volunteers and spreading the word about their campaigns to posting unflattering and embarrassing information about their opponents. A search on YouTube one year prior to the 2008 general election yielded over 15,000 clips related to Hillary Clinton. Some, like a *Sopranos* spoof intended to introduce the campaign theme song (Celine Dion's *You and I*), were posted by the Clinton campaign. Others, like a video from a Clinton rally in Denver in which a campaign worker confronted someone carrying a placard for another candidate, were posted by opponents. YouTube (which attracts 20 million visitors a month) provides unique access to campaign videos, events, and debate footage. It also provides an international platform for embarrassment. When Montana's Republican Senator Conrad Burns fell asleep during a farm bill hearing, a worker for the opposing campaign caught the nap on tape. It was immediately posted on YouTube. Now campaigns are sending staff members to tape opposing candidates at events in the hopes that they will make a mistake worth posting. The fact that these sites are free and can reach millions of people, especially younger voters, has made them especially attractive to political candidates who have previously had to spend hundreds of thousands of dollars on 30-second television ads. Further, such exposure can reach voters who do not watch candidate debates or traditional television news programming.[48]

The challenge in managing a campaign in cyberspace is that it is difficult for candidates to control the information that is posted. On open-source sites, such as Wikipedia, both supporters and opponents have the ability to make changes to candidate profiles. Even on authorized pages, online "friends" can post negative or offensive messages. The trend toward the use of cyberspace in politics is not just a uniquely American phenomenon. The Labour party in the U.K. began posting its Party Conference on the Internet in the 1990s, allowing for online interaction among politicians and constituents. Similarly, political parties in Sweden, Italy, and the Netherlands have a very active Web presence. Former Swedish Prime Minister Carl Bildt even went so far as to personally answer e-mails sent to him by citizens.[49] Exactly how cyberspace will be used in political campaigns in the future remains to be seen, but it is clear that the trend toward using such forms of delivery to reach voters will continue to increase.

LEADERSHIP ON THE BIG SCREEN: *GOOD NIGHT, AND GOOD LUCK*

Starring: David Strathairn, George Clooney, Robert Downey, Jr., Patricia Clarkson, Jeff Daniels

Rating: PG for language and themes

Synopsis: David Strathairn plays CBS television's Edward R. Murrow, the most influential electronic journalist of his day, during the McCarthy era of the 1950s. Senator Joseph McCarthy fanned anti-communist hysteria by falsely accusing those appearing before his committee of being communist sympathizers. In this highly charged political atmosphere, even CBS news staffers have to prove their loyalty to the country. Despite the dangers, Murrow and producer Fred Friendly (Clooney) broadcast a series of reports critical of McCarthy's methods. This effort helps turn the tide of public opinion against the senator. Fellow politicians and President Eisenhower join the effort to discredit McCarthy. "Good night, and good luck" was Murrow's signature sign-off phrase. Filmed in black and white.

Chapter Links: the power of public opinion, opinion leadership, public speaking, media effects

Leadership and Diversity

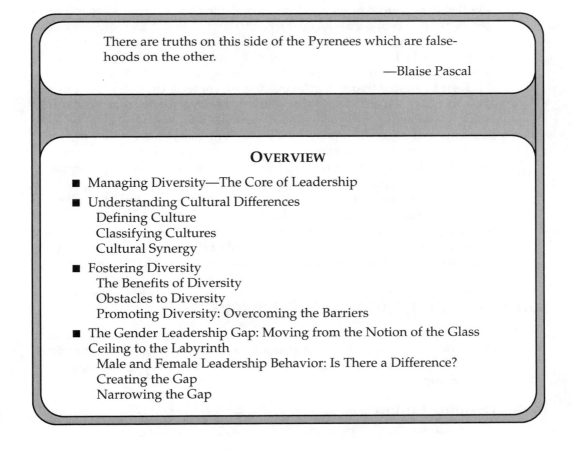

There are truths on this side of the Pyrenees which are false-hoods on the other.

—Blaise Pascal

OVERVIEW

- Managing Diversity—The Core of Leadership
- Understanding Cultural Differences
    Defining Culture
    Classifying Cultures
    Cultural Synergy
- Fostering Diversity
    The Benefits of Diversity
    Obstacles to Diversity
    Promoting Diversity: Overcoming the Barriers
- The Gender Leadership Gap: Moving from the Notion of the Glass Ceiling to the Labyrinth
    Male and Female Leadership Behavior: Is There a Difference?
    Creating the Gap
    Narrowing the Gap

Managing Diversity—The Core of Leadership

Cultural diversity is a growing force both at home and abroad. In the United States, minorities generated two-thirds of the nation's population growth between the 1990 and 2000 censuses, a trend that is expected to continue. By the year 2015, 35 percent of those in the United States between the ages of 16 and 64 are expected to be nonwhite. Similarly, most of the growth in the workforces of other industrialized nations is coming from immigrants or groups currently underrepresented in the workplace. Along with these demographic trends, four main forces—known as the four Ts—have brought the world into a global age: *technology, travel, trade,* and *television.* Members of different cultures have more frequent contact and exposure to one another through: the Internet, satellite hookups, and fiber optic lines; increased international travel with millions of people visiting other nations each year; multinational organizations and open markets; and rapidly expanding broadcasting bandwidth. Nestlé, for example, has 97 percent of its employees working outside its headquarters in Switzerland, and Philips has 82 percent of its workforce located in countries outside the Netherlands. Many U.S. companies, such as Ford and IBM, have more than 50 percent of their staff outside the United States, and AT&T, General Electric, PepsiCo, and General Motors have between one-third and one-fifth of their employees working beyond U.S. borders.[1]

Taylor Cox concludes that managing diversity is the "core" of modern organizational leadership.[2] To Cox and others, diversity management means taking advantage of the benefits of a diverse labor force while coping with the problems that arise when people from different backgrounds work together.[3] The goal is to enable all employees, regardless of ethnicity, gender, age, or physical ability, to achieve their full potential and to contribute to organizational goals and performance. While most experts focus their attention on the organizational work setting, diversity management is essential to leaders in group and public contexts as well. In this chapter we will explore the topic of leadership and diversity by identifying important cultural differences, by examining the impact of culture on leadership behavior, by outlining ways to overcome diversity barriers, and by discussing the gender leadership gap.

Understanding Cultural Differences

In chapter 8 we defined an organization's culture as a unique way of seeing the world, based on particular assumptions, values, rituals, stories, practices, artifacts, and physical settings. These same elements make up the cultures of larger groups.

Defining Culture

Everett Rogers and Thomas Steinfatt define culture as "the total way of life of a people, composed of their learned and shared behavior patterns, values, norms, and material objects."[4] Because cultures are human (symbolic) creations, they take many different forms. Cultural teachings result in very different assumptions, expectations, and rules for interaction. If we are not aware of these cultural differences, we can ascribe meanings to behaviors that are inaccurate and divisive.

Communication patterns are the verbal and nonverbal codes used to convey meanings in face-to-face encounters; these patterns vary from culture to culture. One important ingredient is language. Languages help people organize their perceptions and shape their worldviews. The grammar of Spanish, for instance, reflects a number of levels of respect that reinforces status distinctions. English reinforces individualism by being the only language that capitalizes the pronoun "I" in writing.

Nonverbal codes help individuals interpret the meaning of gestures, posture, facial expressions, time, touch, and space. Again, culture teaches the meanings of nonverbal behaviors. A simple action like sticking out the tongue can be interpreted many different ways. Tongue protrusion can signal everything from polite deference (Tibet), to embarrassment (south China), negation (Marquesa Islands), and contempt (United States).[5]

Patterns of relationships are strongly influenced by the culture in which one was raised. A son or daughter in the United States has much more freedom than his or her counterpart in South Korea. In Korean families, the oldest male relative has the right to determine where children go to school, what careers they pursue, and whom they marry.

Formal organizations structure the activities of significant numbers of people. Important institutions include governments (which sponsor schools to teach cultural knowledge and values), social and professional organizations, work organizations, and religions. Religious faiths organize people differently. In Christianity or Judaism, adherents attach themselves to a particular church or synagogue, which sponsors a program of worship activities. Followers of Hinduism, on the other hand, worship whenever they want at the most convenient temple. Religions hold conflicting views about the meaning of existence, salvation, sin, and other questions.

Cultures create or borrow inventions necessary to maintain or enhance day-to-day functions. *Artifacts* is the term frequently used to describe the tools used by a culture. The personal computer is one technological creation that has greatly impacted U.S. culture. PCs have increased office productivity, encouraged more people to work at home, shortened the production time of books and other written materials, increased the flow of information, linked users from around the world, and introduced new terms like "Google," "hackers," "computer virus," "YouTube," and "e-commerce" into the national vocabulary.

The *collective wisdom* of a culture is shaped by historical events such as immigration, invasions, wars, economic crises, legal decisions, legislative acts, and the decisions of prior leaders. For example, the rise of communism in Vietnam was spurred by the oppression of French colonialism. In the United States, the Social Security system and other entitlement programs are a legacy of the Great Depression.

A culture's external *environment*, including climate, geographical features, and natural resources, influences a wide variety of cultural elements, such as interaction patterns and population density. People from warm climates (the Middle East or the Mediterranean, for example) are more involved with each other, maintain closer distances, and engage in more touch than individuals from cold-weather climates like Scandinavia and Great Britain. In the United States, most major cities are located near lakes and rivers because they provide drinking water, serve as sources of hydroelectric power, and act as transportation corridors. The most sparsely populated regions of the country (portions of the Dakotas, Nebraska, Nevada, Oregon, Kansas, and Texas) generally receive very little rainfall.

Classifying Cultures

Researchers group cultures according to common characteristics. These commonalities help leaders recognize and respond to the needs of diverse groups.

Five cautions should be kept in mind when studying cultural categories. First, cultures change over time, so older groupings may not be as accurate as newer ones. Second, scholars disagree about how to categorize some nations and have not studied some regions (such as Africa and the Middle East) as thoroughly as others. Third, not every member of a cultural group will respond the same way. Statements about cultural patterns are generalizations that don't account for the behavior of every individual on every occasion. Americans are generally regarded as highly individualistic, but some groups in the United States (religious orders, communes) are much more collectively oriented. Fourth, political and cultural boundaries are not always identical, as in the case of the Basque people, who live in both Spain and France. Fifth, Westerners have developed most of the cultural category systems and may have overlooked values that are important to non-Western societies. (See box 10.1 for an Eastern approach to leadership currently attracting considerable interest in North America.)

There are a number of cultural classification systems; Edward Hall and Geert Hofstede developed two of the most notable.

Box 10.1   Research Highlight
Taoism: Leadership Insights from Nature[6]

Scholars in the United States and Europe developed nearly all of the theories presented in this and other Western leadership texts. However, there is one non-Western approach to leadership that is becoming increasingly popular in the United States. Advocates of Taoism (pronounced Daoism) claim that leaders who follow its principles achieve better results with less stress.[7]

The original Taoists were a group of philosophers who offered advice to the rulers of warring city-states in China during the years 600–300 BC. Taoist teachers hoped to restore peace and order by encouraging leaders to follow natural principles. The *Tao Te Ching* is Taoism's most important text. Over the centuries this book has been translated more often than any other book except the Bible. Many believe that a royal librarian named Lao-Tzu was the author, but most experts conclude that this short volume (approximately 5,000 words long) is a collection of the teachings of several sages.[8]

Taoists emphasize simplicity and integrity in life and in leadership based on their understanding of nature. Ideal leaders resemble uncarved blocks of stone or wood. They reject wealth, status, and cleverness. Instead, they accept what comes—success or failure, life or death—and do not intrude in the lives of followers. Such leaders demonstrate integrity or character *(te)* that comes from living in harmony with natural processes. They are in tune with how the universe works because they are as innocent and honest as children. The power of a childlike character can be seen in the life of Mahatma Gandhi. Gandhi dressed simply, owned almost nothing, and did not seek political office. Yet, he was one of the twentieth century's most influential leaders.

Central to the Taoist approach to leadership is the notion of *wu wei*, or positive inaction. Nature can't be rushed but takes its own course. The wise leader, then, knows when to intervene and when to step back. According to the *Tao Te Ching*:

> He [she] who takes action fails.
> He [she] who grasps things loses them.
> For this reason the sage takes no action and therefore does not fail.
> He [she] grasps nothing and therefore he [she] does not lose anything.[9]

The martial art called t'ai chi is based on the principle of *wu wei*. Practitioners of this art never attack; instead they wear their enemies out by yielding, deflecting the force of their opponents' attacks back to them. In the same way, wise leaders seldom take aggressive action to get their way. Instead, they are sensitive to the natural order of things (circumstances, the needs and interests of followers, stages of group development) and work with events instead of against them. They use less energy but get more done.

Along with advocating positive inaction, Taoism also encourages leaders to be weak rather than strong. To the Taoists (and to many other Chinese), the universe is made up of two forces: the yin (negative, dark, cool, female, shadows) and the yang (positive, brightness, warmth, male, sun). While our culture highlights the yang or masculine side of leadership, the Taoists draw more attention to the yin. They urge leaders to be valleys (which reflect the yin) instead of prominent peaks (which reflect the yang). The *Tao Te Ching* describes the action of water to illustrate that weakness overcomes strength:

> There is nothing softer and weaker than water,
> And yet there is nothing better for attacking hard and strong things.
> For this reason there is no substitute for it.
> All the world knows that the weak overcomes the strong and the soft overcomes the hard.[10]

Just as water cuts the hardest rock over time, the weak often overcome the powerful in human society. For example, authoritarian governments in Soviet Russia, Argentina, and the Philippines were overthrown through the efforts of ordinary citizens. Leaders who use "soft" tactics (listening, empowering, collaborating) rather than "hard" ones (threats and force) are more likely to overcome resistance to change in the long term.

Flexibility is an important attribute of weakness. Weak things are more likely to survive because they can adapt. Pliability is a sign of life; stiffness signals death. Like young grass and saplings, successful leaders bend rather than break, adjusting their strategies to meet changing conditions. The *Tao* sums up the advantages of flexibility and adaptability this way:
> When a man is born, he is tender and weak.
> At death, he is stiff and hard.
> All things, the grass as well as trees, are tender and supple while alive.
> When dead, they are withered and dried.
> Therefore the stiff and the hard are companions of death.
> The tender and the weak are companions of life.
> Therefore if the army is strong, it will not win.
> If a tree is stiff, it will break.
> The strong and the great are inferior, while the tender and the weak are superior.[11]

> To lead the people, walk behind them.
>
> —Lao Tzu

High- and Low-Context Cultures

Hall, an anthropologist and nonverbal communication expert, categorizes cultures as high or low context based on the way people in the culture communicate.[12] In high-context cultures such as Japan, China, and South Korea, most of the information about the meaning of a message is contained in the context or setting. Group members assume that they share common meanings and prefer indirect or covert messages that rely heavily on nonverbal codes. In low-context cultures such as Germany and Great Britain, much more meaning is embedded in the words that make up the verbal message, and speakers are more direct. Other differences between high- and low-context cultures center on group membership, interpersonal relationships, and orientations toward time. A summary of the differences between high- and low-context cultures is found in box 10.2.

Leaders can run into serious difficulties when dealing with followers who prefer a different communication style. Take the case of the German manager who deals with conflict by confronting his Japanese employees directly. The supervisor's low-context culture encourages him to be honest and straightforward. However, his followers, who have been raised in a high-context society, would rather ignore tensions or deal with them indirectly through hints and nonverbal cues like making less eye contact.

Keep off the grass.

—Lawn sign in the United States

Since we have a broad road, why should we open small paths?

—Lawn sign in China

Box 10.2

Characteristics of High- and Low-Context Cultures[13]

High-Context Cultures	Low-Context Cultures
Covert and implicit	Overt and explicit
Messages internalized	Messages plainly coded
Much nonverbal coding	Details verbalized
Reactions reserved	Reactions on the surface
Distinct in-groups and out-groups	Flexible in-groups and out-groups
Strong interpersonal bonds	Fragile interpersonal bonds
Commitment high	Commitment low
Time open and flexible	Time highly organized

Programmed Values Patterns

Geert Hofstede of the Netherlands conducted a massive study of cultural patterns. In order to determine important values that are "programmed" into members of various cultures, Hofstede surveyed 116,000 IBM employees in 72 countries. He then validated his findings by correlating his results with data collected by other investigators in many of the same nations.[14] In his original research, Hofstede found four values dimensions that characterize cultures. With Michael Harris Bond, he later identified a fifth category that has its roots in Eastern culture.[15] These dimensions and some of their implications for leader/follower relations are described below.[16]

Power distance.   The first value dimension identified by Hofstede looks at the importance of power differences in a culture. "All societies are unequal," Hofstede states, "but some are more unequal than others."[17] In high power-distance cultures, inequality is considered to be a natural part of the world. Superiors are a special class of people who deserve special privileges. However, at the same time, they are obligated to take care of their less fortunate subordinates. High-status individuals try to look as powerful as possible and exert influence through coercive and referent power bases. In contrast, low power-distance cultures are uncomfortable with differences in wealth, status, power, and privilege; they promote equal rights. Members of these groups emphasize interdependence and rely on reward, legitimate, and expert power. Superiors are similar to subordinates and may try to appear less powerful than they actually are. Citizens of the Philippines, Mexico, Venezuela, India, and Singapore ranked among the highest in power distance; residents of New Zealand, Denmark, Israel, Austria, and Sweden the lowest. Power distance has a number of implications for leadership.

- The larger the power distance between leaders and followers, the greater the fear of disagreeing with a superior and the closer the supervision of follower activities.

- Followers in high power-distance countries expect managers to give direction and feel uncomfortable when asked to participate in decision making.

- Coercive, authoritarian leadership is more common in high power-distance countries; democratic leadership is more often the norm in low power-distance cultures.

- Organizations operating in low power-distance countries are less centralized and distribute rewards more equally.

Individualism-collectivism.   The second of Hofstede's value dimensions distinguishes cultures by their beliefs about individuals and groups. Individualistic cultures emphasize that the needs and goals of the individual and his or her immediate family are most important. Decisions are based on what benefits the person rather than the group. Collectivist cultures emphasize group identity. Individuals do not function as independent agents; rather, they define themselves and make decisions on the basis of their connection to an extended family, tribe, clan, or organization. The United States ranked as the most individualistic culture in Hofstede's sample, followed by Australia, Great Britain, Canada, and the Netherlands. Among the most collectivistic cultures were

Colombia, Mexico, Pakistan, Taiwan, and South Korea. The following are implications for leadership along the individualism-collectivism continuum.

- Followers in individualistic societies generally respond well to material rewards that honor individual effort (commissions, bonuses for winning sales contests). Followers in collectivistic cultures don't feel comfortable with individual recognition and prefer team rewards instead.

- Members of collectivist societies expect mutual loyalty between organizational leaders and followers and feel betrayed when companies furlough or fire employees.

- To be accepted, new ideas in collectivist countries must come from the group as a whole rather than from any individual.

- Decision making is identified with a single leader in individualistic societies. Leaders in collectivist groups rely more heavily on group norms and social values to manage the behavior of followers.

- The ideal leader for individualists is someone who provides autonomy and opportunities for personal growth. The ideal leader for collectivists takes an active role in nurturing followers and fostering the growth of the group as a whole.

- Followers with a collectivist orientation prefer indirect criticism, while followers with individualistic values expect to be confronted directly about poor performance and conflicts.

Masculinity-femininity. The third value dimension looks at roles assigned to the sexes. In masculine cultures, men are thought to be assertive, decisive, competitive, ambitious, and dominant. They are concerned with material success and "respect whatever is big, strong, and fast." Women are encouraged to serve; responsibilities include nurturing interpersonal relationships and caring for the family and weaker members of society. In feminine cultures, sex roles overlap. Neither sex is expected to be competitive, ambitious, or caring at all times. These cultures stress intuition, interdependence, and concern; there is respect for the small, weak, and slow. Japan, Austria, Venezuela, and Italy were the most masculine cultures surveyed, while Sweden, Norway, the Netherlands, and Denmark were the most feminine. The masculinity-femininity implications for leadership include the following.

- Females in masculine cultures have a harder time emerging as leaders and are more likely to be segregated into a few specialized occupations.

- Decision makers in feminine cultures put a greater emphasis on intuition and consensus.

- Leaders and constituents in masculine cultures put a higher priority on work (they "live to work"); leaders and constituents in feminine cultures put more emphasis on the quality of life (they "work to live").

- Leaders in feminine societies are more likely to demonstrate an interpersonally-oriented leadership style.

- Members of masculine cultures are more motivated by achievement, recognition, and challenge.

> If a [hu]man can be gracious and courteous to strangers, it shows he[she] is a citizen of the world.
>
> —Francis Bacon

Uncertainty avoidance.   The fourth dimension measures (1) the extent to which people feel uncomfortable in unstructured or unpredictable situations, and (2) the lengths to which they will go to avoid ambiguity by following strict codes of behavior or by believing in absolute truths. Members of high uncertainty-avoidance cultures view uncertainty as a threat, are less tolerant, face high stress, seek security, believe in written rules and regulations, and readily accept directives from experts and those in authority. Individuals in low uncertainty-avoidance cultures accept uncertainty as a fact of life, are more contemplative, experience less stress, take more risks, are less concerned about rules, are more likely to trust their own judgments or common sense rather than experts, and believe that authorities serve the citizens. Citizens of Greece, Portugal, Belgium, and Japan reported some of the highest uncertainty-avoidance ratings; residents of Jamaica, Denmark, Sweden, and Ireland among the lowest. Uncertainty-avoidance has several implications for leadership.

- High uncertainty-avoidance cultures give more weight to age and seniority when selecting leaders.
- Managers in low uncertainty-avoidance societies emphasize interpersonal relations and are more willing to take risks. Managers in high uncertainty-avoidance countries seem unapproachable and are more likely to try to control the activities of followers.
- Organizational constituents in high uncertainty-avoidance cultures prefer clear instructions, are more willing to follow orders, disapprove of competition between employees, and are more loyal than their low uncertainty-avoidance counterparts.

Long-term–short-term orientation.   The fifth value dimension is concerned with how citizens view the past, present, and future. Cultures with a long-term orientation (LTO) encourage norms and behaviors that lead to future rewards. Members of these societies sacrifice immediate gratification (leisure time, luxuries, entertainment) for long-term benefits. They put a high value on persistence and perseverance, spend sparingly, and save a lot. Status relationships (teacher-student, manager-worker, parent-child) are clearly defined and honored. Feelings of shame come from violating social contracts and commitments. Cultures with a short-term orientation (STO) focus on the past and the present, respecting tradition and expecting quick results. Members of these groups put much less importance on persistence, spend freely, and have lower savings rates. China, Hong Kong, Taiwan, Japan, and South Korea ranked highest on long-term orientation; Pakistan, Nigeria, the Philippines, Canada, and Zimbabwe ranked lowest. Long-term or short-term orientations have the following implications for leadership.

- Leaders in LTO cultures can expect greater sacrifice from followers on behalf of long-term goals. Leaders in STO societies are under greater pressure to demonstrate immediate progress.

- Feelings of shame can be powerful motivational tools to encourage follower compliance in LTO nations.

- Short-term orientation, with its emphasis on spending instead of saving, interferes with economic development in emerging countries, making the task of national leaders and aid agencies more difficult.

The GLOBE Studies

Recently a cultural classification system related specifically to leadership has been developed. The GLOBE studies, short for Global Leadership and Organizational Behavior Effectiveness, were initiated in 1991 by Robert House. Working with over 160 colleagues around the world, House and his research team have published two volumes with nearly 2,000 pages of material focusing on the relationship between culture and leadership.[18] The GLOBE research is based on analysis of the responses of 17,300 managers in more than 950 organizations across 62 cultures. The GLOBE studies produced a cultural classification system consisting of nine dimensions. Some of these dimensions overlap with previous research, while others add new elements. The dimensions are as follows:[19]

Uncertainty avoidance is the extent to which members of an organization or a society strive to avoid uncertainty by relying on established social norms, rituals, and bureaucratic practices. People in high uncertainty-avoidance cultures actively seek to decrease the probability of unpredictable future events that could adversely affect the operation of organizations or society. In the GLOBE research, those in Switzerland, Singapore, Germany, and Austria scored high on this dimension. Citizens of Russia, Hungary, Guatemala, Bolivia, and Venezuela were low in uncertainty avoidance. Individuals in those countries more easily tolerate unstructured and unpredictable situations.

Power distance is the degree to which members of an organization or society expect and agree that power should be concentrated at higher levels of an organization or government. Those in Morocco, Nigeria, El Salvador, Zimbabwe, Argentina, and Thailand had high levels of power distance behavior. Individuals in these countries do not expect equality and are more willing to accept a leader's authority based solely on position. GLOBE subjects in Denmark, South Africa, the Netherlands, Bolivia, Albania, and Israel were low on this dimension and, as a result, more likely to challenge status and authority.

Collectivism I—Institutional collectivism is the degree to which organizational and societal practices encourage and reward collective distribution of resources and collective action.

Collectivism II—In-group collectivism is the degree to which individuals express pride, loyalty, and cohesiveness in their organizations or families. Citizens of Greece, Hungary, Germany, Argentina, Italy, Switzerland, and the United States scored low on the two collectivism dimensions, indicating a greater focus on individual needs and goals. Those in Sweden, South Korea, Japan, Singapore, New Zealand, China, and the Philippines were high on these dimensions, indicating a greater tendency to be concerned for the welfare of others and the needs of the larger familial, organizational, and societal groups.

Gender egalitarianism is the degree to which organizations and societies minimize gender role differences while promoting gender equality. Those in Hungary, Russia, Poland, Slovenia, Denmark, Namibia, Kazakhstan, and Sweden scored high on this dimension, suggesting countries where differences in the educational levels, leadership opportunities, and distribution of authority is relatively equal between men and women. GLOBE subjects in South Korea, Kuwait, Egypt, Morocco, Turkey, India, Switzerland, and China were low on gender egalitarianism, suggesting cultures where men have higher social status and women hold fewer positions of authority.

Assertiveness is the degree to which individuals in organizations or societies are assertive, confrontational, and aggressive in social relationships. The most assertive individuals in the GLOBE studies were found in Albania, Nigeria, Hungary, Germany, Hong Kong, Austria, El Salvador, South Africa, Greece, and the United States. Those in Sweden, New Zealand, Switzerland, Japan, Kuwait, Thailand, Portugal, Russia, and India were the least assertive, valuing modest and tender behavior over assertive and competitive stances.

Future orientation is the degree to which individuals in organizations or societies engage in future-oriented behaviors such as planning, investing in the future, and delaying individual or collective gratification. Future-oriented citizens were found in Singapore, Switzerland, South Africa, the Netherlands, Malaysia, Austria, and Denmark. Individuals in these countries have a propensity to save for the future and demonstrate a longer time horizon for decision making. Those in Russia, Argentina, Poland, Hungary, Guatemala, Italy, Morocco, Kuwait, and Colombia were low on this dimension, placing more emphasis on short-term outcomes and instant gratification.

Performance orientation is the degree to which an organization or society encourages and rewards group members for performance improvement and excellence. High performance-orientation scores were noted among GLOBE subjects in Switzerland, Singapore, Hong Kong, New Zealand, Canada, and the United States. Citizens in these societies value training and development opportunities and strive to take initiative to improve performance. Those in Greece, Venezuela, Russia, Hungary, Qatar, Italy, Portugal, and Argentina had low performance orientation scores. In these countries, individuals focus more on family background and group membership, as opposed to performance, as a means for achieving success.

Humane orientation is the degree to which individuals in organizations or societies encourage and reward individuals for being fair, altruistic, friendly, generous, caring, and kind to others. Those in Zambia, the Philippines, Ireland, Malaysia, Thailand, Egypt, India, Canada, and Denmark were high on this dimension, reflecting a focus on sympathy and support for the weak. Citizens of Germany, Spain, Greece, Hungary, France, Singapore, Switzerland, Poland, Italy, and Brazil were low on humane orientation, reflecting more importance given to power, material possessions, and self-interest.

Since the GLOBE studies were specifically concerned with the impact of culture on leadership, the researchers were interested in identifying the specific leader characteristics and actions that were considered to be effective in different cultures. To this end, the GLOBE researchers identified six global leadership behaviors and the cultural contexts in which these behaviors are most positively viewed.[20]

Charismatic/Value-based leadership. This broadly defined leadership dimension reflects the ability to inspire and motivate and expects high performance from others based on shared core values. This type of leadership involves being visionary, inspirational, self-sacrificing, trustworthy, decisive, and performance oriented. Such leadership is viewed most positively in Finland, Sweden, the Netherlands, Australia, the United Kingdom, Ireland, the United States, Argentina, Colombia, Mexico, Greece, China, Hong Kong, Singapore, and India.

Team-oriented leadership. This leadership dimension emphasizes team building and a common purpose among team members; it includes characteristics such as being collaborative, integrative, diplomatic, and administratively competent. This type of leadership is viewed most positively in Finland, Sweden, the Netherlands, Portugal, Spain, Argentina, Colombia, Mexico, Greece, Turkey, China, Hong Kong, Singapore, and India.

Participative leadership. This leadership dimension reflects the degree to which leaders involve others in decision making and implementation and thus includes being participative and nonauthoritarian. This type of leadership is viewed most positively in Austria, Germany, Switzerland, the United States, France, and Argentina.

Humane-oriented leadership. This leadership dimension reflects supportive, considerate, compassionate, and generous behavior; it also includes modesty and sensitivity to the needs of others. This type of leadership is viewed most positively in New Zealand and China.

Autonomous leadership. This leadership dimension refers to independent and individualistic leadership. This type of leadership is viewed most positively in Russia.

Self-protective leadership. This leadership dimension reflects behavior that ensures the safety and security of the leader and the group. This includes leadership that is leader-focused, status conscious, face saving, and procedural. This type of leadership is viewed most positively in Argentina, Mexico, Turkey, and Hong Kong.

Understanding cultural differences lays the groundwork for leading groups in a variety of cultures as well as for leading groups made up of diverse members. The successful leader recognizes and responds to cultural differences; the leader who fails to appreciate cultural influences is doomed to frustration and failure. Consider, for example, the interaction described in box 10.3.

> A [hu]man's feet must be planted in his[her] country, but his[her] eyes should survey the world.
>
> —George Santayana

Cultural Synergy

Cultural synergy is the ultimate goal of recognizing and responding to cultural variations. Synergy refers to the production of an end product that is greater than the sum of its parts. In cultural synergy, decision makers draw on the diversity of the group to produce a new, better-than-expected solution.

Box 10.3

When Cultural Values Clash: American Leader/Greek Follower[21]

Bob is a U.S. manager from a low power-distance/low uncertainty-avoidance culture. His Greek subordinate, Ari, ranks high on both these dimensions.

Verbal Conversation	Attribution
Bob: How long will it take you to finish this report?	Bob: I asked him to participate.
	Ari: His behavior makes no sense. He is the boss. Why doesn't he *tell* me?
Ari: I do not know. How long should it take?	Bob: He refuses to take responsibility.
	Ari: I asked him for an order.
Bob: You are in the best position to analyze time requirements.	Bob: I press him to take responsibility for his own actions.
	Ari: What nonsense! I better give him an answer.
Ari: 10 days.	Bob: He lacks the ability to estimate time; this time estimate is totally inadequate.
Bob: Take 15. Is it agreed you will do it in 15 days?	Bob: I offer a contract.
	Ari: These are my orders—15 days.

In fact, the report needed 30 days of regular work. So Ari worked day and night, but at the end of the fifteenth day, he still needed one more day's work.

Verbal Conversation	Attribution
Bob: Where is the report?	Bob: I am making sure he fulfills his contract.
	Ari: He is asking for the report.
Ari: It will be ready tomorrow.	
Bob: But we had agreed it would be ready today.	Bob: I must teach him to fulfill a contract.
	Ari: The stupid, incompetent boss! Not only did he give me wrong orders, but he does not even appreciate that I did a 30-day job in 16 days.
Ari hands in his resignation.	Bob is surprised.
	Ari: I can't work for such a man.

According to cross-cultural management expert Nancy Adler, culturally synergistic problem solving is a four-step process.[22]

The first step is identifying the dilemma or conflict facing the dyad or group. Due to differing cultural perspectives, some communicators may not realize that there is a problem. In the U.S. manager/Greek employee interaction described in box 10.3, Bob didn't think that asking for input would cause difficulties. After all, involving employees in decision making is what a "good" leader would do in the United States. Bob can't begin the synergistic process until he recognizes that soliciting participation is problematic for his follower. Further, he needs to identify the conflict without making negative value judgments about Ari's response. Ari will need to approach Bob in the same nonjudgmental fashion.

In step two, communicators try to determine why members of other cultures think and act as they do. The underlying assumption is that all people act rationally from their culture's point of view. Communicators identify both similarities and differences in cultural perspectives and recognize that cultural values can cluster together in different ways. For instance, some collectivist societies are low in power distance. Others, such as Malaysia, are characterized by "vertical collectivism"—a combination of collectivism and high power distance.[23] Constituents in all collectivist cultures expect to work in groups, but vertical collectivists try to ensure that group decisions are acceptable to people in authority.[24]

Step three begins by asking the question: "What can people from one culture contribute to people from another culture?" Problem solvers then generate alternatives and come up with a creative answer that incorporates the cultural assumptions of all group members but also transcends them.

Consider the dilemma faced by American and Japanese sales representatives of a U.S.-based freight company that promised customers specific flight arrival times.[25] American customers would accept delays with adequate explanation, but Japanese customers would not. As a result, company officials in Japan refused to promise delivery times until they were certain they would be kept, thus saving face. American customers wanted specific delivery times and began to lose faith in the freight business. The firm needed to come up with a "promising" system that was appropriate for both cultures. It had to be definite for the Americans and close enough to actual arrival times to satisfy the Japanese. The sales representatives from both countries came up with a creative, synergistic solution. They began to promise delivery within a time range rather than at specific times. For example: "late Wednesday morning" instead of "at 11:30 AM." The Americans were able to keep making promises and the Japanese were able to save face by never promising something they couldn't deliver.

Effective implementation of a solution in step four also requires synergistic thinking based on cultural awareness. Synergistic implementation of a sales reward system at a multinational corporation, for example, would give managers in host countries plenty of leeway in distributing awards appropriate for the specific cultural settings.[26] As we noted earlier, stakeholders in individualistic societies expect to be compensated for their personal efforts, but a greater share of the rewards will go to the group in collectivistic cultures. One oil company took the collectivist orientation of its employees into account when it rewarded a group of workers by building a well in their African village. The new water system helped the community and, at the same time, raised the status of the employees.

> Luck is when opportunity meets preparation.
> —Denzel Washington

Fostering Diversity

So far we've highlighted the importance of responding to cultural differences. We've seen that leaders improve their effectiveness if they recognize and incorporate differences into their problem solving. However, the best leaders go beyond simply responding to cultural differences; they actively promote diversity in the groups they lead. In this section of the chapter we provide a rationale for fostering diversity, discuss some of the obstacles that keep members of minority groups from reaching their full potential, and suggest ways to promote diversity in the organizational context.

The Benefits of Diversity

Perhaps the best reason for encouraging diversity is that it is the right thing to do. Fostering diversity reduces inequities and gives everyone a chance to make a meaningful contribution. While ethical considerations alone should be sufficient motivation for promoting diversity, there are also a number of practical benefits that come from making maximum use of the members of various constituencies. Taken together, these make the "business case" for promoting organizational diversity.[27]

- *Cost savings.* Absenteeism and turnover rates in organizations are often higher for women and ethnic minorities than they are for white males. Finding temporary substitutes and permanent replacements is expensive. Addressing diversity concerns lowers the number of absences and resignations and reduces the likelihood of sexual harassment and racial discrimination lawsuits.

- *Resource acquisition and utilization.* Organizations with reputations for managing diversity will attract the best personnel out of a shrinking labor pool. They will also help talented minority employees break out of low-level positions.

- *Keeping and gaining market share.* Diverse organizations are in the best position to take advantage of markets both at home and abroad. Such organizations understand the needs of a variety of target audiences and have minority representatives who can appeal to members of many different cultural groups. The Avon company illustrates how diversity can boost the bottom line. The corporation gave African American and Hispanic managers authority over unprofitable inner-city markets. These territories are now among the company's most productive.

- *Better decision making.* Earlier we argued that cultural differences can be the basis for higher quality solutions. Forming heterogeneous groups is one way to stimulate cultural synergy. Members of diverse groups are also less likely to succumb to groupthink (see chapter 7). Having a variety of opinions forces group members to pay more attention to all aspects of an issue, consider more viewpoints, and use a wider variety of problem-solving strategies.[28]

- *Greater innovation.* Nurturing a variety of cultural perspectives makes an organization more open to ideas. Innovative organizations employ more women and minorities and work harder at eliminating racism and sexism.[29]

Organizations experience more of the benefits of diversity when their senior leaders strive for the cultural synergy we described earlier. These executives adopt a *learning-and-effectiveness* approach that recognizes cultural differences as valuable organizational assets.[30] Drawing on the insights of diverse members can dramatically improve how organizations carry out their tasks—helping them to think in new ways about markets, products, goals, and organizational structures. This synergistic approach stands in sharp contrast to the diversity paradigms adopted by the leaders of most organizations. Executives in some groups view diversity initiatives solely as a way to provide equal opportunity; they strive to treat everyone the same way and try to ignore cultural differences rather than building on them. Executives in other groups value minorities solely as marketing agents who can sell to their ethnic groups. Diversity in these two situations has little impact on the way that these organizations conduct their core businesses.

Obstacles to Diversity

While the benefits of fostering diversity are substantial, so too are the barriers that prevent leaders and followers from reaching cultural synergy. Diversity barriers can be found at every level of society—personal, group, and institutional. Barriers found at the individual level include prejudice, discrimination, stereotyping, and perceptual bias.[31] The term prejudice refers to negative attitudes toward people from other backgrounds. Surveys reveal that whites, for example, typically believe that minorities are less intelligent, do not work as hard, and are less patriotic.[32] These negative attitudes produce discriminatory behavior, which likely accounts for the fact that minorities receive fewer organ transplants, are underrepresented in the media, serve on fewer corporate boards, earn less money than whites, and so on. Stereotyping is the process of classifying group members according to their perceived similarities, either good or bad. According to widely held stereotypes in U.S. culture, disabled workers are seen as less productive, and Asian Americans are seen as excelling at technical but not managerial skills. As a consequence of these stereotypes, organizations are reluctant to hire disabled people and hire Asian Americans primarily for technical positions. Perceptual biases reinforce the power of stereotypes. Individuals generally attribute their failings to external factors and their successes to internal factors. The opposite is true when it comes to evaluating the behavior of members of marginalized groups. When we fail, outside forces (other people, chance, bad weather) are to blame. When members of low status groups fail, internal forces (laziness, poor character, low intelligence) are to blame. Our success is based on our skills and motivation. When minorities perform well, we attribute their success to help from others rather than to their individual abilities and efforts.

> What is repugnant to every human being is to be reckoned as a member of a class and not an individual person.
> —Dorothy Sayers

On a group level, ethnocentrism—the attitude (conscious or unconscious) that regards one's own culture as the measure by which all others should be judged—is a significant barrier to incorporating diversity. Ethnocentrism is less hostile than prejudice, but it still leads to preferential treatment for insiders. Most of us would rather socialize with people from similar backgrounds (complete the self-assessment in box 10.4 to determine if this is true for you) and prefer to recruit, promote, and reward those who share our values. Intergroup conflicts also serve as diversity obstacles. Religious, social, political, and economic differences generate tensions that tear groups and societies apart.

At the institutional level, large power differences between cultural groups reduce the motivation of minority group members and make it more difficult for them to be perceived as leaders. Many organizations (often without meaning to do so) engage in practices that keep minority groups from fully participating. Here are some of the practices that serve as organizational barriers to diversity. You may be able to identify others (see application exercise 5 on p. 331).[33]

Practice	Impact
50-hour-plus workweeks with weekend and evening meetings	Increases stress for working mothers who have more responsibility for children and home chores.
Self-promotion (selling oneself) and self-evaluations	Uncomfortable for people from cultures that value modesty (i.e., Japanese, Chinese).
Informal networks	Women, the disabled, and others may be excluded from "old boy networks" that are important sources of information and contacts for promotion.
Inaccessible facilities	Despite passage of the American Disabilities Act some schools, businesses, and houses of worship remain inaccessible to disabled workers.

Promoting Diversity: Overcoming the Barriers

Strategies for promoting diversity must address the obstacles described above. Modifying our attitudes is an excellent place to start. We can greatly reduce the power of stereotypes, prejudice, biased perceptions, and ethnocentrism if we engage in *mindful* communication. Mindfulness refers to focused attention, which stands in sharp contrast to the *mindlessness* that characterizes our typical interactions. Most of the time, we operate mechanically without giving much conscious thought to our behaviors and to the behaviors of the other person. This mind-set, which relies on the scripts we've learned through experience, characterizes such routine encounters as chatting with a fellow student before class or discussing the latest movie with friends. Mindlessness can be dangerous when interacting with individuals of diverse backgrounds, however. Scripted responses make us susceptible to prejudice, stereotypes, and per-

Box 10.4   Self-Assessment

Diversity Profile[34]

Complete each sentence by placing a check in the appropriate box(es).

	African American	Asian American	Caucasian	Hispanic	Native American	Other
I am						
Most of the students in this class are						
Most of my friends on campus are						
Most of my professors are						
Most of the people with whom I work at my most recent job are (were)						
My boss is (was)						
My high school was predominantly						
My neighbors when I was growing up were						
My dentist is						
My doctor is						
People who live in my home are						
People who regularly visit my home are						
The music I listen to is generally performed by artists who are						
My favorite actor or actress is						
My favorite author is						
My personal hero is						

Discussion Questions

1. Are you involved primarily with members of only one ethnic group?

2. Identify any patterns in your diversity profile (e.g., school, work, home, social) that divide along ethnic boundaries. Do these patterns contribute to prejudice or ethnocentrism?

3. How could you expand your involvement with members of ethnic groups underrepresented in your diversity profile?

4. What advantages or disadvantages could you envision from interacting regularly with members of diverse ethnic groups?

5. Does a diverse membership make an organization more or less effective?

ceptual biases. If we do not engage in mindful communication, we are less likely to challenge the assumption that our culture is best or work to create cultural synergy.

A mindful state consists of three intrapersonal processes.[35] The first is the creation of new categories. Breaking old categories increases sensitivity to differences. We are then able to make finer distinctions within broad categories based on age, disabilities, race, gender, sexual orientation, and other factors. For instance, we recognize that not all older people find it difficult to learn new skills. In a mindful state, we are less likely to stereotype individuals or to act in a prejudiced manner. The second intrapersonal process is welcoming new information. In a mindless state, we are closed off to new data, which blinds us to potential cultural differences and prevents us from adjusting our behavior to meet the demands of the situation. In a mindful state, we monitor our actions and the actions of others. Heightened awareness enables us to modify our responses and to reach better conclusions. The third component of mindfulness is openness to different points of view. Recognizing that there are different perspectives on events and behaviors reduces the likelihood of cultural misunderstandings and opens the way for solutions that combine the insights of a variety of cultures.

Dignity, integrity, and inclusion are also important tools for overcoming personal and group barriers to diversity.[36] We need to recognize the dignity of others by respecting their views, even when we disagree. We need to retain our integrity by confronting others who demonstrate prejudice (e.g., use a racial slur, discriminate against a person of color). We need to include, not exclude, those of different backgrounds, applying the same rules of fairness to them as we apply to members of our group. Acting with dignity, integrity, and inclusion encourages followers to do the same, creating a more ethical and accepting group climate.

Organization-wide strategies for promoting diversity address accountability, training, recruitment, development, and work-life flexibility.[37] (Complete the self-assessment in box 10.5 to determine your perceptions of the current diversity climate of your work organization.)

Accountability starts with the top leaders in an organization. Unless they are committed to holding lower-level leaders accountable for fostering diversity, any diversity effort will fail. Top executives need to define the vision for change, outlining what diversity success looks like. They need to set a personal example by presenting and attending diversity training sessions, collecting feedback on diversity issues, dealing quickly and forcefully with sexual harassment complaints and so on. Diversity efforts need to be integrated into organizational strategy by demonstrating how diversity serves the mission of the group. In universities, diversity improves the quality of teaching and learning. In business, as we noted earlier, diversity increases profitability. Responsibility for diversity is neither limited to CEOs and vice presidents nor relegated to the human resources department. Every manager must develop nontraditional leaders as a routine part of her or his job description.

Training and education are essential for all forms of organizational change, including diversity initiatives. Such training can cover a number of topics, such as the value of diversity, cultural differences, stereotypes and prejudice, and developing skills for working effectively with multicultural team members. An

Box 10.5 Self-Assessment

The Diversity Perceptions Scale[38]

Respond to each item by circling the appropriate number. 1 = strongly disagree, 6 = strongly agree.

1. I feel that I have been treated differently here because of my race, gender, sexual orientation, religion or age.

   1   2   3   4   5   6

2. Managers here have a track record of hiring and promoting employees objectively, regardless of their race, gender, sexual orientation, religion, or age.

   1   2   3   4   5   6

3. Managers here give feedback and evaluate employees fairly, regardless of employees' race, gender, sexual orientation, religion, age, or social background.

   1   2   3   4   5   6

4. Managers here make layoff decisions fairly, regardless of factors such as employees' race, gender, age, or social background.

   1   2   3   4   5   6

5. Managers interpret human resource policies (such as sick leave) fairly for all employees.

   1   2   3   4   5   6

6. Managers give assignments based on the skills and abilities of employees.

   1   2   3   4   5   6

7. Management here encourages the formation of employee network support groups.

   1   2   3   4   5   6

8. There is a mentoring program in use here that identifies and prepares all minority and female employees for promotion.

   1   2   3   4   5   6

9. The "old boys network" is alive and well here.

   1   2   3   4   5   6

10. The company spends enough money and time on diversity awareness and related training.

    1   2   3   4   5   6

11. Knowing more about the cultural norms of diverse groups would help me be more effective in my job.

    1   2   3   4   5   6

12. I think that diverse viewpoints add value.

    1   2   3   4   5   6

13. I believe diversity is a strategic business issue.

    1   2   3   4   5   6

14. I feel at ease with people from backgrounds different from my own.

    1   2   3   4   5   6

15. I am afraid to disagree with members of other groups for fear of being called prejudiced.

    1   2   3   4   5   6

16. Diversity issues keep some work teams here from performing to their maximum effectiveness.

    1   2   3   4   5   6

Scoring

This scale measures two dimensions—the organizational and the personal—which each contain two factors as follows:

I. Organizational dimension

  a. Organizational fairness factor (items 1–6)

  b. Organizational inclusion factor (items 7–10)

II. Personal dimension

  c. Personal diversity value factor (items 11–13)

  d. Personal comfort with diversity (items 14–16)

Reverse scores on items 1, 9, 15, and 16 (1 = 6, 2 = 5, 3 = 4, 4 = 3, 5 = 2, 6 = 1). Then add up your responses to all 16 items (maximum score 96). The higher your total score, the more positive your view of the diversity climate. Similarly, the higher your score or each of the item subsets described above, the more positive your perceptions are on that factor.

important element of any effective training program is instruction about the organization's specific diversity policies. The best training programs are customized to the needs of the organization, allow sufficient time for discussion, and are led by skilled facilitators who can deal with controversial topics and conflict.

Recruitment of nontraditional members remains a problem for many organizations. Lower salaries can make it difficult for governments, educational institutions, and charities to compete with business for qualified candidates. Many organizations have little contact with minority populations. Effective strategies for recruiting more diverse members include:

- develop relationships with schools with a high percentage of minority students
- create internship and work-study programs for students of color and women
- recruit key managers from the outside
- publicize diversity efforts to interest potential employees
- provide incentives for nontraditional candidates
- use diverse recruiting teams

Development has been overlooked in many diversity efforts. Too many leaders have mistakenly assumed that nontraditional workers would automatically work their way up the organizational hierarchy. Managed development opportunities produce better results. Development strategies include annual meetings with supervisors to create individual development plans; programs designed to help nontraditional managers move up the organizational ladder by providing challenging job assignments, education, assessment, and feedback; and pairing diverse managers with mentors (see chapter 12) who act as coaches and sponsors. Some organizations also encourage the formation of affinity groups like Deaf and Hard of Hearing at Microsoft or Filipinos at Microsoft. These groups connect members to one another, providing greater access to information and social support. In some cases, these employee networks meet with top management and lobby for changes to organizational policy. Organizational leaders can take steps to ensure that minorities aren't excluded from advancement by (1) ensuring that jobs are posted so that members of all groups can apply for them, and by (2) requiring that women and minorities be included on all promotion and succession lists. (See the research highlight in box 10.6 for more suggestions on how to develop minority leaders.)

Work-life flexibility benefits make it easier for women and minorities to juggle job and family responsibilities and eliminate many of the practices identified earlier that serve as organizational barriers to diversity. Such benefits include flexible scheduling (choosing arrival and departure times, compressing the work week to four days); job sharing; moving to part-time status when family demands are high (such as when raising young children or helping ill parents); working from home; and longer parental leaves.

> Leadership has a harder job to do than just choose sides. It must bring sides together.
>
> —Jesse Jackson

Box 10.6   Research Highlight
Breaking Through to the Executive Ranks[39]

Harvard professors David Thomas and John Gabarro compared the careers of African American, Asian, and Hispanic executives with minorities who had plateaued in their careers. Their goal was to identify the organizational and personal factors that promote the development of minority leaders. The investigators conducted an in-depth study of three demographically diverse organizations (a law firm, bank, and consulting firm), and collected data at nine additional companies and nonprofits that were more homogeneous. Thomas and Gabarro offer the following seven "lessons" (divided into three categories) for executives interested in developing and promoting minorities to upper management and executive posts.

Creating an Enabling Organizational Context

- *Lesson 1: Become personally involved in diversity initiatives.* Executives must champion the diversity process, mentor and sponsor minority managers, outline the way that diversity initiatives relate to the organizational mission and strategy, and so forth.

- *Lesson 2: Build partnerships to ensure long-term success of diversity efforts.* Top leaders must remain involved, rather than shifting the responsibility to a diversity office or human relations department. If diversity initiatives become compartmentalized, they are quickly jettisoned when costs must be cut. Partnerships should include members of minority groups who are most directly impacted by diversity initiatives and need to help implement them.

- *Lesson 3: Understand that diversity initiatives will both maintain and change corporate culture.* Diversity efforts imply change, meaning that top leaders and others act as change agents. However, successful initiatives are tied to an organization's unchanging core values.

Ensuring Opportunity

- *Lesson 4: Monitor the distribution of and pathways to opportunity.* Promotion models that quickly label people as "executive material" work to the disadvantage of both minorities and talented whites who are not identified as potential high achievers. Understand the norms or rules that determine rewards as well as the pathways that lead to top-level positions.

- *Lesson 5: Spotlight the threshold between upper-middle management and executive level positions.* Determine which positions lead to executive appointments and make sure that qualified minorities are placed in these threshold jobs. In many cases, a technical position doesn't develop the skills necessary to function effectively as a vice president, a position that requires many emotional as well as cognitive competencies.

Ensuring the Development Takes Place

- *Lesson 6: Facilitate the formation of developmental relationships.* Finding a mentor early in a career is particularly important to people of color (we'll have more to say about developmental relationships in chapter 12.)[40] Make sure that minorities are given assignments that pair them with people who are skilled at developing others.

- *Lesson 7: Directly address attitudes that create low expectations for minority performance.* White managers should not accept substandard work as the price of diversity efforts. High expectations lead to high performance that benefits minorities and organizations alike.

Thomas and Gabarro, based on their analysis of the career paths of high performers, also offer seven lessons for aspiring minority leaders.

- *Lesson 1: Choose work and an organization that suit your personality.* Hating the job or the company will cause you to leave too soon, before you can take advantage of the opportunities the position has to offer. Minorities, in particular, pay a high price for making poor career choices because biased observers interpret premature job changes as evidence of low ability. According to Thomas and Gabarro, most of the minority candidates for CEO positions have spent the majority of their careers at one firm.

- *Lesson 2: Choose high quality experiences over fast advancement.* Quality experiences build credibility and confidence. Early in a career they are superior to so-called "fast track" experiences for which you are unprepared.

- *Lesson 3: Build a network of developmental relationships.* Find those who can help your career, whether they be sponsors, mentors, or peers.

- *Lesson 4: The organization matters.* Avoid companies that have a poor track record of minority advancement. Chances are, one individual is not going to have much impact on the entire organizational system. Be on guard against organizations that set low expectations for minorities or that have failed to align their diversity strategies with their cultures and values. Minorities in these organizations rarely get promoted to the executive suite. Expect, too, to play a role in promoting corporate diversity efforts.

- *Lesson 5: Take charge of your own career.* People of color cannot count on the system working on their behalf. As a result, they must set personal goals, seek to learn, solicit feedback, and so forth. Remember that commitment to high performance is important whatever the position.

- *Lesson 6: Race matters, but it alone does not determine your fate.* Minority executives are comfortable with who they are and talk freely about racial issues. They have integrated their racial identities with their professional roles. As a result, these executives solve race-related problems the same way they handle other dilemmas. Race may play a role in a conflict with a boss, for example, but other factors like personality and communication styles also come into play. An effective minority manager is able to talk to a superior about all the issues that may be interfering with effective communication.

- *Lesson 7: Make sure it is worth the price.* Success comes at a price—long hours, time away from children, moves. Determine if you are willing to endure these costs while, at the same time, meeting your personal needs and maintaining important personal relationships.

The Gender Leadership Gap: Moving from the Notion of the Glass Ceiling to the Labyrinth

Over the past century, the number of women occupying leadership positions has risen dramatically. In 1900, women held only 4 out of 100 managerial positions. By the beginning of the new millennium, nearly half of all managerial and professional positions in the workforce in the United States were held by females. Few women, however, have moved into the highest level of government or business positions. They hold 71 seats in the House of Representatives (including Nancy Pelosi, who in 2007 became the first woman to hold the top leadership position in the House of Representatives) and 16 seats in the Senate. These 86 legislators represent 16 percent of the total seats in the U.S. Congress. While encouraging, this figure still places the United States well below other countries such as Sweden (47 percent), Spain (31 percent), and Switzerland (25 percent) in terms of the number of women with seats in the national governing body. In the workforce, males in the same occupations earn more than their female counterparts, and males dominate occupations with higher pay scales. In 2007, only 15 percent of board members of Fortune 500 companies were women and only 12 of the Fortune 500 companies had a female CEO.[41] Many have called this barrier to top-level leadership roles *the glass ceiling*.[42] The argument is that while women are represented more proportionately at lower levels of leadership there is a barrier to women's advancement to higher-level leadership positions. This barrier is viewed as being almost impossible to shatter. Recently Alice Eagly and Linda Carli proposed a new metaphor—*the labyrinth*. As they explain:

> With continuing change, the obstacles that women face have become more surmountable, at least by some women some of the time. Paths to the top exist, and some women find them. The successful routes can be difficult to discover, however, and therefore we label these circuitous paths a labyrinth.[43]

We agree with Eagly and Carli that the glass ceiling metaphor of the past is outdated and that the notion of the labyrinth is a more accurate depiction of the challenges that women face. The existence of the gender leadership gap, and the labyrinth it creates for women, raises three significant questions: (1) Are there differences in how males and females lead? (2) What factors hinder the emergence of women as leaders? (3) Can the gender leadership gap be narrowed? To answer these questions, we'll begin by taking a look at what researchers have discovered about female and male leadership behavior.

Male and Female Leadership Behavior: Is There a Difference?

There has been much debate about whether differences between male and female leadership behaviors are genuine or merely a matter of perception. Judy Rosener, for instance, argues that female leaders are more likely to use an interactive style of leadership that encourages participation, shares power and information, and enhances the self-worth of others.[44] (See the case study in box 10.7 for an example of how one woman's approach to leadership has proven successful.)

Box 10.7   Case Study

Applying Feminist Ideals at The Body Shop[45]

In March 1976, Anita Roddick opened a small cosmetics shop in Brighton, England. Despite a threatened lawsuit from two neighboring funeral parlors unhappy with her choice of store name, Roddick dubbed her venture The Body Shop. The initial product line consisted of 15 natural-based skin and hair care products packaged in reusable bottles with handwritten labels. These products were inspired by Roddick's previous travels where she observed how women in other cultures, without access to expensive cosmetics, cared for their bodies naturally. On the shop's first day, Roddick took in $225.

Within seven months a second Body Shop was opened in Chichester, England. By 1984, The Body Shop went public on the London Stock Exchange with a value of over $12 million. In 2006, the company was sold to the French cosmetics giant L'Oreal, and in 2007 company founder Anita Roddick died. Despite this, the company's culture and values thrive. Its sales volume continues to grow with 2,265 stores in 56 countries generating sales of over $1 billion.

The key to The Body Shop's success is twofold—a powerful social conscience and a commitment to feminist ideals. All products sold at The Body Shop use natural-based and biodegradable ingredients; packaging is kept to a minimum; recyclable materials are used whenever possible; and customers are encouraged to bring bottles back to be refilled when making subsequent purchases. All this is in response to Roddick's claims that her rivals in the cosmetics industry produce mostly "packaging and garbage."

The Body Shop's model of commerce-with-a-conscience also extends to important social issues. The Body Shop strictly forbids the testing of any of its products on animals. Further, through window displays, pamphlets, posters, and messages on shopping bags, each Body Shop retail outlet highlights issues ranging from AIDS awareness to preservation of rain forests.

Conventional business practices used by others in the cosmetics industry are generally ignored at The Body Shop. Products are not hyped. The word "beauty" is not used in conjunction with any Body Shop product. Packaging is plain and practical, and there has never been one cent spent on product-based advertising. When the first franchise opened in the United States in 1988, the *Wall Street Journal* quoted a Harvard Business School professor as saying that a major advertising campaign would have to be launched for The Body Shop to succeed in the United States. In response, Roddick stated she would "never hire anybody from Harvard Business School."

Roddick's greatest disdain, however, was reserved for the cosmetics industry itself. She believed that women are "enslaved by the images of beauty and glamour" portrayed by her competitors. She explained:

> It is immoral to trade on fear. It is immoral to constantly make women feel dissatisfied with their bodies. It is immoral to deceive a customer by making miracle claims for a product. It is immoral to use a photograph of a glowing sixteen-year-old to sell a cream aimed at preventing wrinkles in a forty-year-old.[46]

The Body Shop is also guided by feminist philosophy. Honesty, caring, intuition, and a concern for women are core company values. In 1990, The Body Shop opened a day care center at its corporate headquarters. The facility took nearly two years to build and cost over $1 million. The Body Shop pays a subsidy for employees using the center, and the facility has been made available to those who work elsewhere in the community but are unable to afford reliable, high quality day care. Further, employee training, whether related to work or merely of a personal interest, is paid for by the company. As Roddick explained, "Most businesses today are concerned with maximizing profits for the few. We try to create a humanized workplace that is joyful to be in, creative, and encourages brilliance."[47]

(continued)

Also grounded in feminist ideology is The Body Shop's approach to retailing. The objective of employees is not only to sell merchandise but also to educate customers. "The idea that everyone should walk out of our shops having bought something is anathema to me," Roddick insisted. "We prefer to give staff information about the products, anecdotes about the history and derivation of the ingredients, and funny stories about how they came [to be] on The Body Shop shelves. We want to spark conversations with our customers, not brow-beat them to buy."[48] This manner of customer interaction (which emphasizes conversation over control, coercion, and hierarchy) represents a practical application of feminist principles.

Commitment to The Body Shop values is the cornerstone of the organization. Before a potential franchisee is offered a Body Shop outlet, she or he must work in an existing store so that the store's staff can evaluate how well the prospect fits into The Body Shop culture. Then the potential franchisee must go through extensive interviews at corporate headquarters with top executives before being invited to join The Body Shop family.

Some detractors argue that The Body Shop is "off-beat" and "loony." To those critics Roddick explained: "The big mistake they make is to equate our feminine values with weakness and inefficiency. We know how to run a business. We do it differently, but we do it well."[49]

Discussion Questions

1. Do you think The Body Shop would be more or less successful if it were led in a more "traditional" manner?

2. What was the impact of Roddick's social conscience and commitment to feminist ideals on employees? Customers? Competitors?

3. Do you agree with Roddick when she suggested the "feminine values" of The Body Shop are often misinterpreted?

4. Can you identify other organizations that demonstrate a commitment to feminist ideals? Would you like to work for such a company?

5. Are there any types of organizations that could not be effectively led using feminist ideals?

Other researchers argue that differences in male/female leadership are a matter of perception. These investigators note that most of the data supporting differing leadership patterns among males and females come from laboratory studies. Such controlled environments are more likely to yield results supporting stereotypical views of gender behavior because the research models are often biased.[50] These studies assume that men, being masculine, will be higher in task-oriented behavior and women, being feminine, will demonstrate greater interpersonally oriented behavior. In actual leadership situations, such differences are not generally evident.

For example, in studies of cadet leaders at the Air Force Academy, cadets rated female leaders less favorably before they saw the women in action. After serving with the women leaders over a period of time, the cadets gave female and male leaders equal evaluations.[51] Related findings have been reported in large-scale investigations. In a survey of nearly 3,000 employees from Fortune 500 companies, respondents gave men and women managers similar ratings on such criteria as fairness, keeping workers informed, and providing recognition and support.[52]

Alice Eagly uses the concept of gender spillover to explain why there are usually only slight differences in female/male leadership patterning in organizational settings.[53] She argues that variation in the behavior of men and women is greatest in contexts where there are few constraints, such as when friends interact informally. In these settings, gender role expectations are more likely to "spill over" and influence behavior. In contrast, when there are clear guidelines about how to act, there is less room for variation and less gender role spillover. In managerial positions there are relatively fewer gender differences because both males and females receive similar training, carry out the same job responsibilities, and work toward similar goals.

Creating the Gap

The gender leadership gap is the product of the obstacles to diversity identified earlier in this chapter. One way to visualize the development of the gender leadership gap is to think of women and men competing against each other on a track. Both are running in a 440-yard race. However, women run the 440 hurdles while men run the 440 dash. With each hurdle, more women fall behind, and the gap between male and female leadership aspirants widens. These hurdles have eliminated most of the female competitors by the time both contenders reach the finish line.

A study of female executives conducted by the Center for Creative Leadership illustrates the difficulties shared by women who had reached significant leadership positions within organizations.[54] The researchers discovered that all 76 of the successful female executives relied on the assistance of a senior mentor while making their climb to the top of the corporation. Mentors offered wide-ranging advice from assistance with key projects to support for promotions. (See chapter 12 for further discussion of mentoring.) Although mentors are valuable to both men and women, the investigators discovered that it was absolutely necessary for a woman to have a mentor to reach the highest levels of organizational leadership.

The study also found that successful female executives reported a willingness to take career risks and a desire for success that exceeded that of their male colleagues. These female executives, in many instances, felt a need to sacrifice family and relationships as the price for success. To overcome the hurdles to leadership success, women needed influential mentors and a commitment to exceed the standards usually set for males striving to reach the same top leadership positions.

Of all the barriers to diversity, stereotyping has the greatest negative impact on female leaders. Gender stereotypes are based on cultural definitions of what it means to be male or female. Sex is biologically based, but gender orientation—the way we think about acting female and male—is the product of symbolic communication. Julia Wood summarizes the relationship between sex, gender, and culture this way:

> There is nothing a person does to acquire her or his sex. It is a classification based on genetic factors and one that is enduring. Gender, however, is neither innate nor necessarily stable. It is acquired through interaction in a social world, and it changes over time. One way to understand gender is to think of it as what we learn about sex. We are born male or female—a classification based on biology—but we learn to be masculine and feminine. Gen-

der is a social construction that varies across cultures, over time within a given culture, and in relation to the other gender.[55]

In the United States (which ranks toward the masculine end of Hofstede's masculine-feminine typology), masculine characteristics are equated with strength, aggression, ambition, independence, stoicism, and rationality. Feminine characteristics are associated with sensitivity to the needs of others, concern for family and relationships, emotionality, and nurturing. Gender expectations are communicated to us from the moment we're born. Girl babies are dressed in pink, boy babies in blue. Parents engage in more rough-and-tumble play with their infant sons than with their infant daughters. Boys are encouraged to engage in adventurous activities and to avoid tears while girls are encouraged to be careful, to share, and to look pretty.

These expectations shape the roles we play in society. Despite a recent shift to greater role flexibility, women remain the primary caregivers (in a dual career family, for instance, the mother is the parent who generally leaves work to pick up a sick child). Men are still considered the primary breadwinners and are most likely to build their identities around their careers.

Unfortunately, cultural expectations work against women who aspire to leadership. Not only are women and men viewed in different ways, but those characteristics defined as masculine are given higher status. As a culture, we put more value on decisiveness, assertiveness, competition, and other characteristics traditionally associated with males.[56] Compounding the problem of gender bias is the notion that the prototypical leader is masculine.

The damaging impact of gender typing can be seen at every step in leadership development. Many women never seriously consider becoming leaders because the process of socialization has taught them that leadership is the province of males or that some professions are open to men but not to women. Negative stereotypes and discrimination lower the self-confidence of some females, making them reluctant to take risks and to strive for leadership positions.[57] Because our culture highlights the nurturing role of women, most females enter service professions (teaching, nursing) or work in departments (such as human resources) that support the larger organization.[58] Female-dominated careers like clerical support, day care, and library science have less status than comparable male-dominated fields.

Women who do enter departments or professions that are overwhelmingly male face difficulties common to all who act as token representatives of their social groups.[59] Female tokens often find themselves treated as mothers or daughters. They may turn against other women as a result of the perceived need to adopt the attitudes of the dominant male culture. There is also a more narrow range of acceptable behavior for female leaders. Women who act "too aggressive," for example, risk being criticized for behaving in an unfeminine manner.[60]

In her book *Beyond the Double Bind*, Kathleen Jamieson explores a number of the traps and restrictions women confront. She describes a double bind as a rhetorical concept "that posits two and only two alternatives, one or both penalizing the person being offered them. . . . The strategy defines something 'fundamental' to women as incompatible with something the woman seeks— be it education, the ballot, or access to the workplace."[61] Thus, for example, it is often assumed that women cannot be both female and competent.

Other examples of double binds are plentiful. Historically, women were forbidden to speak, yet are now criticized for not producing great oratory. In the mid-twentieth century (and continuing in moderated form), the trap was that women could choose either parenting or intellectual/economic pursuits. Discussions of similarities and/or differences between men and women use men as the standard, skewing the discussion from the start or, at a minimum, assuming that a "gain" for one "side" is a "loss" for the other. Jamieson points out that the double bind is "durable, but not indestructible."[62] She urges us to examine the binds as rhetorical forms to understand them, to manipulate them, and then to dismantle them.

> The test of whether or not you can hold a job should not be the arrangement of your chromosomes.
>
> —Bella Abzug

Narrowing the Gap

The best practices for fostering diversity outlined earlier in this chapter address many of the barriers generated by negative gender stereotypes. Aggressive recruitment, greater accountability for developing female leaders, formation of advocacy groups, mentorship, and executive development programs can help bridge the gender leadership gap. At the individual level, Alice Eagly and Linda Carli suggest two key principles that are critical in allowing women to ease their route through the labyrinth—thus narrowing the gap.[63] First, women must *blend agency with communion*. As Eagly and Carli explain, most people believe that leaders should be agentic—tough, decisive, and action oriented. Similarly, women are often viewed as being more communal—warm, friendly, and caring. These two perceptions create a conflict for female leaders. Nice, friendly female leaders may be criticized for not being assertive and decisive enough while strong, action-oriented female leaders may seem too harsh. For women, establishing both agency and communion can be challenging. To succeed in these dual demands, a woman must first establish an exceptional level of competence. This competence can be demonstrated, for example, by mastering job-relevant knowledge or being exceptionally well prepared for meetings. As Eagly and Carli suggest, although it isn't fair, women often need to be exceptionally good to be credited with the abilities of less-competent men. Once competence is established, a woman can finesse the agency/communion conflict by combining assertive task behavior with kindness, niceness, and helpfulness. Secondly, Eagly and Carli suggest that it is critical for women to *build social capital*. Those who create social capital through good relationships with colleagues, both within and outside their organization, are more likely to rise to positions of authority. This social capital can be earned through a variety of means, including developing informal relationships, participating in social networks, and establishing a mentor/protégé relationship.

Linguist Deborah Tannen believes female communication patterns are keeping women from getting the credit they deserve in organizational settings. Tannen begins by suggesting that communication styles are developed through childhood interactions with same-sex peer groups in which girls foster cooperation and boys promote competition. Female children are encouraged to play indoors in small groups or best-friend pairs and to build a sense of closeness and equality with their playmates. They are discouraged from boasting and giving orders, announcing their achievements, or expressing their preferences. Instead, girls are socialized to express their feelings and desires as helpful suggestions. Boys, on the other hand, are encouraged to play outdoors in large, hierarchically structured groups. They create and follow strict rules for competition where there are clearly defined winners and losers. Boys achieve status and maintain a degree of independence by giving orders, boasting, telling jokes and stories, and challenging the assertions of other boys in the group.[64]

The result of this early childhood training, according to Tannen, is a set of conversational patterns or rituals that contribute both to confusion on the job and to the gender leadership gap. Some of the more important differences in communication practice are listed below.[65]

- *Apologies.* Women often say "I'm sorry" to express understanding rather than to apologize for doing something wrong. Sharing the blame fosters equal positions for both parties. Men are reluctant to apologize because they perceive admitting mistakes as a subordinate act. Problems arise in conversations when women apologize to create equal status. Women expect a response like "It's partially my fault, too." Instead, they generally receive a response from men such as "I accept your apology." This pattern of interaction places women in an inferior position.

- *Softening criticism.* To foster cooperation, women soften their criticism by injecting positive comments ("I really like the first section of the article, but the second section needs some more work"), while men are more likely to address only the critiques ("The second section of this article is poorly done").

- *Saying thanks.* Politeness enhances feelings of goodwill and closeness. Women frequently say thanks as a way to signal the end of a conversation. Men, on the other hand, believe that expressions of gratitude place them in a subordinate position and will not respond in kind. This lack of an "appropriate" response may be perceived by women as rude and can create confusion and conflict.

- *Ritual fighting.* Males are socialized to express their preferences through open challenge and criticism; women are socialized to offer helpful suggestions in a spirit of camaraderie. Females are discouraged from ritual fighting and find open challenges and criticisms alien to the sense of cooperation they strive to foster.

- *Giving compliments.* Striving for equality, women are more willing to risk lessening their position of control by recognizing others' strengths and complimenting them on those strengths. Men associate giving compliments with low status and are less likely to respond in kind. These perceptions create one-up and one-down positions that place women at a disadvantage in male-dominated workplaces.

- *Complaining*. Females are trained to nurture and support. Listening and sharing problems and feelings foster an environment where rapport is highlighted. Males perceive complaints and problems as something that must be fixed by those in charge. Women who share problems and feelings may be perceived by men as difficult.

- *Humor*. Early childhood socialization of male humor involves teasing and hostility while female humor in childhood focuses on self-deprecation. Men are apt to take women's self-deprecation literally and fail to understand that it is actually understatement. When men accept this form of humor at face value, women are placed in an adverse position.

- *Boasting*. Females are discouraged from publicly acclaiming their efforts; they are encouraged to focus on the welfare of the group. Males, on the other hand, are encouraged to trumpet their accomplishments in order to achieve higher individual recognition and status. Organizational standards that encourage personal acclaim place women at a disadvantage.

- *Downplaying authority*. In order to create feelings of equality, women are less likely than men to remind subordinates of their lower status or to behave in an authoritarian manner.

Tannen is careful to note that there is no one best conversational style and that not all men and women fit the descriptions she provides. Gender socialization is only one of many cultural influences on conversational styles. Ethnic background, regional differences, family influences, and personality variables also determine how we interact. However, Tannen suggests that the gender gap may be largely a "wall of words." Ritual apologies, thank yous and compliments, frequent complaints, soft criticism, self-deprecating humor, the preference for modesty, and downplaying authority are often perceived as lower-status behaviors—making women and their ideas invisible. As a consequence, women are less likely to be rewarded or considered for advancement.

Kathleen Kelley Reardon supports the belief that differing communication styles are keeping women from advancing to the top levels of many organizations.[66] She notes that men are more comfortable with self-promotion, verbal sparring, and the language of team sports. The contrasting male/female communication styles have created a number of dysfunctional communication patterns (DCPs) that belittle women and reinforce male bias. Common DCPs include (1) excluding women from the decision-making process; (2) dismissing their contributions by interrupting, talking over, or ignoring ideas expressed; (3) retaliation based on male fear of female competence; and (4) patronizing responses such as treating female participation as unimportant or as an afterthought. Reardon encourages women managers (who often opt for silence) to confront these patterns head on. They should draw attention to the fact that they've been excluded from important meetings, claim credit for good proposals, challenge retaliatory statements, refuse to honor patronizing comments, and so on (see the case study in box 10.8).

Critics suggest that focusing on gender communication differences is counterproductive. Highlighting differences reinforces sexual stereotypes. Male communication is frequently seen as the norm, and female communication is viewed as deviant. This, skeptics argue, negates the unique and valuable contributions of women.[67] Further, there are many more similarities than differences in male and female communication patterns. While popular culture has embraced the notion that men and women are from different planets (Mars and Venus), in reality it may be more appropriate to suggest "men are from South Dakota and women are from North Dakota."[68] South Dakotans and North Dakotans may believe that they are significantly different, but to the rest of the world the residents of the two states look and act very much alike. There are

---

Box 10.8   Case Study

Downsizing at Simtek[69]

Karen Jacobs-McKinney is the manager of a group of 10 sales representatives at Simtek, a large computer components manufacturer. The company was founded by President and CEO John Simmons and has grown from a small, privately held start-up company to a publicly held corporation.

Simtek has been known for fair treatment of its nonunion employees and for employee relations policies that are above average. Pay and benefits are in the top fourth of the industry. The only major criticism leveled at Simtek was a charge that the company was not committed to its stated pro-diversity policy. Of its 400 employees, women and minorities represent less than 2 percent.

Jacobs-McKinney was the first woman of color hired by Simtek and is the only female manager in the company. She has been employed for five years and has worked very hard to be recognized as a fair and capable manager in a white, male-dominated organization. Karen has just been faced with an extremely difficult task. Her immediate supervisor has told her that Simtek is reengineering and her unit will have to downsize by two or three people. There will be a moderate severance package. Karen has to decide who will be released. She has both flexibility and responsibility for selecting among employees who have roughly equal work histories, skills, and potential.

The employees in Ms. Jacobs-McKinney's unit consist of seven white males, one white female, one African American male, and one Asian American female. When she compares the work performance of the 10, she finds that all have performed equally well. All have similar knowledge of the products, and their sales levels are also very similar. The white female, the African American male, and the Asian American female have all been hired in the past two years in an effort to increase diversity within the organization. The white males have all been employed there at least five years. If Karen relies on seniority to determine who should be laid off, then the department will lose all of the diversity that the company has tried increase in the past two years. However, she also knows that if she decides to keep any of the new employees, then most likely she will be involved with the company in a reverse discrimination suit. White males have threatened legal action, complaining that Simtek now hires almost exclusively women and minorities.

The personnel manager has just called Karen requesting the names of the employees who will be terminated. She has one week to decide what to do.

Discussion Questions

1. What will be the likely impact if the three minority employees are terminated?

2. What will be the likely impact if more senior employees are terminated?

3. What criteria should Karen use in making her decision?

4. Who should Karen terminate? Why?

5. Can you think of other leaders and organizations who have faced similar decisions? How did they respond? What happened as a result of their choices?

differences in how the sexes communicate due to cultural and biological factors, but these variations are frequently exaggerated. A more productive approach highlights the potential of women's communication to increase leadership effectiveness. Many of the behaviors Tannen identifies—softening criticism, being polite, recognizing achievement, and downplaying status differences—are qualities of exceptional leadership. As Carole Spitzack and Kathryn Carter explain, we should "begin to question the qualities proposed for leadership and conduct investigations which do not begin by assuming that female behaviors impede group progress. Female leadership may, in fact, promote cohesiveness, openness, trust, and commitment."[70]

> The new leader is a facilitator, not an order giver.
> —John Naisbitt

Leaders perceived as transformational, whether male or female, exhibit gender balance—displaying characteristics traditionally regarded as masculine and feminine.[71] Transformational leaders are emotional and nurturing as well as independent and ambitious—cooperative as well as competitive. The most effective leaders narrow the gender gap by combining the talents traditionally thought of as masculine and feminine to create a well-balanced leadership style.

CHAPTER TAKEAWAYS

- To be an effective organizational leader in an increasingly global society, you will need to manage diversity. Managing diversity means taking advantage of a diverse labor force while coping with the problems that arise when people of different backgrounds work together. The goal of diversity management is to help all employees reach their full potential.

- Culture refers to the total way of life of a group of people. Key cultural elements include communication patterns, formal organizations, artifacts, collective wisdom, and external environment.

- As human (symbolic) creations, cultures vary widely. However, recognizing cultural commonalities can help you respond to the needs of diverse groups.

- In high-context cultures, members prefer indirect or covert messages and determine meaning based largely on the context or setting. In low-context cultures, members communicate through overt messages and embed much more information in the language used to construct the message.

- Hofstede identified five values dimensions to analyze cultures: power distance (how societies deal with inequities); individualism-collectivism (the relative emphasis on the individual or the group); masculinity-femininity (the definition and differentiation of sex roles); uncertainty avoidance (the extent to which people feel uncomfortable in unstructured situations); and long-term–short-term orientation (the extent to which societies sacrifice immediate gratification).

- The GLOBE studies produced a cultural classification system consisting of nine dimensions: (1) uncertainty avoidance, (2) power distance, (3) collectivism I—institutional collectivism, (4) collectivism II—in-group collectivism, (5) gender egalitarianism, (6) assertiveness, (7) future orientation, (8) performance orientation, and (9) humane orientation.

- Successful leaders recognize and respond to cultural differences, adapting their behaviors to meet cultural expectations. They also strive for cultural synergy. In cultural synergy, decision makers draw on the diversity of the group and cultural awareness to produce and implement a better than expected solution.

- The benefits of fostering diversity include cost savings, improved resource acquisition and utilization, greater market share, better decision making, and higher creativity.

- Obstacles to diversity operate at the personal, group, and institutional levels. Individuals engage in prejudice, discrimination, stereotyping, and perceptual bias. Group members often suffer from ethnocentrism and experience conflicts based on cultural differences. Institutions sponsor practices that limit the progress of women and minorities.

- Organization-wide strategies that promote diversity include: (1) making existing leaders accountable for diversity progress; (2) offering diversity training and education; (3) recruiting more diverse members; (4) helping nontraditional employees develop leadership skills and move up the organizational ladder; and (5) providing work-life flexibility benefits that make it easier for women and minorities to juggle job and family responsibilities.

- While women are represented more proportionately at lower levels of leadership, there is a barrier to women's advancement to high-level leadership positions. This barrier has been described as the glass ceiling and, more recently, as the labyrinth.

- There has been much debate about whether differences between male and female leadership behaviors are genuine or merely a matter of perception.

- Two key principles are critical in allowing women to ease their route through the labyrinth. First, women must blend agency with communion. Secondly, it is critical for women to build social capital.

- Deborah Tannen believes female communication patterns are keeping women from getting the credit they deserve in organizational settings. A set of conversational patterns or rituals contribute both to confusion on the job and to the gender leadership gap. Some of the more important differences in communication practice are: apologies, softening criticism, saying thanks, ritual fighting, giving compliments, complaining, humor, boasting, and downplaying authority.

APPLICATION EXERCISES

1. In a research paper, compare and contrast the cultural classification systems described in the chapter with others not mentioned in the

text. What common themes and differences do you note? What generalizations can you draw? How do your conclusions relate to leaders and followers?

2. Review the GLOBE research. Take a particular culture (or set of cultures) you are familiar with and analyze how effectively you believe the GLOBE research captures the nuances of this culture(s). Share your reactions in class.

3. Which of the Taoist leadership principles described in box 10.1 is most helpful to you? Least helpful? What other metaphors or images from nature might provide useful insights into leadership? How do Taoist leadership principles compare to those found in other philosophical/religious traditions like Christianity, Judaism, Islam, or Buddhism? Discuss your thoughts in a group or write up your conclusions.

4. As a small group, develop a culturally synergistic solution for the conflict involving Bob and Ari in box 10.3.

5. Create your own list of organizational practices that serve as barriers to diversity either on your own or in a small group. Share your findings with the rest of the class.

6. Share your scores from the Diversity Perceptions Scale in box 10.5 with a partner or in a small group. What do your responses reveal about your perceptions of your organization's fairness and inclusiveness? The value you put on diversity and your comfort with diversity issues? How do your answers compare with those of your partner or other members of the group?

7. Analyze the current diversity efforts of your college or work organization. What is the composition of the membership? The surrounding area? What steps have been taken to promote diversity? How effective have they been? Write up your findings.

8. Divide into debate teams and argue for or against each of the assertions listed below. Your instructor will determine the debate format.

    • There is too much emphasis on the differences in the ways that men and women communicate.

    • Gender stereotypes will change significantly in the next 10 years.

    • Prejudice and discrimination are a natural part of the human condition.

9. Interview a successful female leader. Share your findings with the rest of the class.

10. Discuss whether you believe the challenges women face in obtaining top-level leadership roles are best described by the metaphor of the glass ceiling or the labyrinth.

CULTURAL CONNECTIONS:
THE NOT SO UNIVERSAL LANGUAGE OF SPORTS[72]

American business executives are in love with sports jargon. They lace their speech with terms from baseball, football, basketball, and other sports.

Here are some of the sports phrases used by U.S. corporate leaders and what they mean in the business setting:

- *Step up to the plate.* Baseball: take your turn at bat, often in an important situation. Business: confront a problem, make a critical decision.

- *Ducks on the pond.* Baseball: runners on base. Business: a situation where the organization has a good chance at succeeding.

- *Curve.* Baseball: A pitch that breaks before it gets to the plate. Business: anything that happens that is unexpected.

- *All the bases covered.* Baseball: all fielders in the right position to get an out. Business: being prepared for every contingency.

- *Red zone selling.* Football: being inside the opponent's 20-yard line. Business: stakes get higher as the sale is about to close.

- *Hail Mary pass.* Football: desperate, last-second pass with little chance of being completed. Business: a desperate attempt to turn a situation around with little chance of success.

- *Calling an audible.* Football: quarterback changing the play at the line of scrimmage. Business: changing an agenda or plan at the last minute.

- *Jump ball scenario.* Basketball: throwing the ball up between two players to determine possession. Business: neither side has an advantage.

- *Slam dunk.* Basketball: scoring by putting the ball in from above the rim. Business: a can't miss opportunity.

- *Under par.* Golf: scoring better than average. Business: exceeding the target.

While such jargon may make sense to many American executives, it confuses their counterparts from other cultures (India, Europe, Great Britain) where these sports are not played. On the other hand, sports terminology from other nations can puzzle U.S. residents. Latin Americans may talk about "parar la pelota" (or "stop the ball") from soccer, which refers to pausing and taking stock before the next move. The use of sports metaphors leads to misunderstanding and may slow down the communication process. (One British executive reports that he spent 45 minutes trying to explain cricket terms like "sticky wicket" and "hitting a six" to his American audience without success.) Further, leaders in some nations, like the Czech Republic, apparently don't use sports jargon in business.

U.S. leaders and their colleagues from other nations should limit the use of sports terminology. Such jargon should only be used with audiences who share the same sports (baseball is popular in Japan and the United States, for instance) and when sports language is considered appropriate for the business context.

SPOTLIGHT ON TECHNOLOGY: MEN AND WOMEN AND THE INTERNET

In 2005, the Pew Research Center—a nonpartisan Washington DC based organization that conducts surveys on different aspects of technology, media, and Internet usage—released a report detailing how men and women in the United States use the Internet.[73] The report concluded that men continue to pursue Internet activities more than women, and that men are still on the leading edge in seeking the most recent technological advances. At the same time, the survey results suggest that women are catching up in overall Internet usage and are structuring their online experiences to include a greater emphasis on creating connections with people. Some highlights from the report show how men's and women's use of the Internet differs.

- The percentage of women using the Internet still lags slightly behind the percentage of men. Women under 30 are online more than their male peers, but older women trail considerably behind older men.

- Men are slightly more intense Internet users than women. Men log on more often and spend more time online. In most categories of Internet activity, more men than women are participants, but women are catching up.

- More than men, women are keen online communicators. Women are more likely than men to use e-mail to write to friends and family about a variety of topics: sharing news, planning events, forwarding jokes and funny stories. Women are more likely to feel satisfied with the role e-mail plays in their lives, especially when it comes to nurturing their relationships. And women include a wider range of topics and activities in their personal e-mails. Men use e-mail more than women to communicate with various kinds of organizations.

- More men than women perform online transactions. Men and women are equally likely to use the Internet to buy products and take part in online banking, but men are more likely to use the Internet to pay bills, participate in auctions, trade stocks and bonds, and pay for digital content.

- Men are more avid consumers of online information and men look for information on a wider variety of topics and issues than women do.

- Men are more interested than women in technology, and they are also more tech savvy.

Overall, the Pew data suggest that men and women are more similar than different in their online lives, starting with their common appreciation of the Internet's strongest suit: efficiency. Both men and women appreciate online transactions that simplify their lives by saving time on such mundane tasks as buying tickets or paying bills. Men and women also value the Internet for its access to information. Men reach farther and wider for topics, from getting financial information to political news, while women are more likely to dig deeper into areas where they have the greatest interest, including health and religion.

LEADERSHIP ON THE BIG SCREEN: *WHALE RIDER*

Starring: Keisha Castle-Hughes, Rawiri Paratene, Vicky Haughton, Cliff Curtis
Rating: PG-13 for language and a drug reference
Synopsis: Keisha Castle-Hughes stars as 12-year-old Pai who lives in a small Maori village in New Zealand. Pai's twin brother, who died at birth, was to take the mantle of tribal leadership, restoring the fortunes of the village according to ancient legend. Her grandfather Karo (Paratene), the group's

patriarch, believes that only males can lead and excludes Pai from his leadership training school for boys. She refuses to be deterred, however, and becomes the whale rider described in tribal myth. Pai demonstrates that Maori customs can be renewed when both sexes share leadership responsibilities.

Chapter Links: cultural differences and leadership patterns, male/female leadership, gender stereotypes, discrimination

Ethical Leadership and Followership

Most people wish to be good, but not all of the time.

—George Orwell

The Importance of Ethics

As we have suggested throughout this book, effective leadership is the product of the creation and delivery of inspiring and compelling messages. Humans, unlike other species, are capable of shaping reality through the manipulation of symbols. We do not passively react but rather *act* to change the world around us.

The power of human communication means that the question of ethics, in the words of Gerald Miller, is "inextricably bound up with every instance of human communication."[1] Ethics refer to standards of moral conduct, to judgments about whether human behavior is right or wrong.[2] The investigation of ethics is critical when focusing on leadership. A leader communicates a plan of action to his or her followers. The ethical implications of a leader's plans must be considered, since the exercise of unethical leadership can have devastating results. If you consider, for example, the negative impact of leaders such as Adolph Hitler and Joseph Stalin, you begin to see how important the relationship between leadership and ethics is.

Whether a leader is guiding a problem-solving group, a small business, a multimillion-dollar organization, or a national government, he or she exerts significant influence. Leaders must weigh the impact they have on their followers as well as on others external to the group, organization, or society.

Educational writer and consultant Parker Palmer introduces a powerful metaphor to highlight the importance of leadership ethics and to dramatize the difference between moral and immoral leadership. According to Palmer, the distinction between ethical and unethical leaders is as sharp as the contrast between light and darkness, between heaven and hell.

A leader is a person who has an unusual degree of power to create the conditions under which other people must live and move and have their being, conditions that can be either as illuminating as heaven or as shadowy as hell. A leader must take special responsibility for what's going on inside his or her own self, inside his or her consciousness, lest the act of leadership create more harm than good.[3]

The Ethical Challenges of Leadership: Casting Light or Shadow

Functioning as a leader means taking on a unique set of ethical challenges in addition to a set of tasks and expectations. These dilemmas involve issues of information, responsibility, power, privilege, loyalty, and responsibility. How leaders respond to these ethical challenges will determine if they cast more light than shadow.[4]

The Challenge of Information Management

Leaders typically have more access to information than do followers. They participate in decision-making groups, receive financial data, keep personnel files, network with managers from other units, and so on. Being "in the know" raises a number of complicated ethical dilemmas. One such dilemma is decid-ing whether or not to tell the truth. Sissela Bok, in her book *Lying: Moral Choice in Public and Private Life*, defines lies as messages designed to make others believe what we ourselves don't believe.[5] We have all probably told a lie (even if it was merely "little" or "white"). Leaders also practice deception, either to further their own interests or to promote the interests of the group. Prominent pastor Ted Haggard denied that he engaged in sexual encounters with a male prostitute, only to confess later. Officers at a number of high-tech firms secretly changed the dates of stock options to benefit their executives and then covered up their activities. Members of the Bush administration and intelligence com-munity are accused of overstating the danger posed by Saddam Hussein in order to justify the invasion of Iraq.

Most ethical experts agree that lying is wrong because it (a) damages the character of the liar by supplanting such virtues as honesty and consistency; and (b) damages organizational performance by destroying trust, lowering employee job satisfaction, driving out ethical workers, undermining the group's reputation, and corrupting the flow of information required for mak-ing decisions and coordinating activities.[6] However, there appear to be justified exceptions to the adage that states that honesty is the best policy. We admire informants who infiltrate terrorist cells or criminal gangs. Reporters who go underground to uncover fraud and corruption win journalism awards.

Determining whether or not to tell or conceal the truth is not the only dilemma surrounding access to data. Leaders also must choose when to release information and to whom and whether or not to reveal that they possess important knowledge. Law enforcement officials wrestle with both these issues when solving major crimes. Citizens have a right to know what their officials are doing, and tips from the public are instrumental in bringing many offend-ers to justice. However, releasing too much information too soon can jeopardize cases by alerting perpetrators to hide incriminating evidence. Revealing details about the crime to the media disperses knowledge previously known only to the perpetrator—and investigators lose one of their tools for assessing guilt.

How leaders get information can be a concern too. For example, civil liber-tarians oppose antiterrorism measures like eavesdropping on conversations between suspected terrorists and their lawyers and opening the mail of U.S. cit-izens. Google retains records of all searches to better target advertisements and routinely responds to requests for information from the federal government (you can read more about Google and the ethics of censorship in Spotlight on Technology at the end of this chapter). Some employers secretly monitor worker behavior through hidden video cameras and recording systems as well as through spyware that records computer keystrokes.

When it comes to the challenge of information management, leaders cast more shadow than light when they:

- lie, particularly for selfish ends;
- use information solely for personal benefit;
- deny having knowledge that is in their possession;
- gather data in a way that violates privacy rights;
- withhold information that followers legitimately need;

- share information with the wrong people;
- put followers in moral binds by insisting that they withhold information that others have a right to know.

The Challenge of Responsibility

Followers are largely responsible for their own actions, but leaders are held accountable for the actions of others. They must answer for the performance of the entire group, whether an academic department, a business, a nonprofit, a government agency, or a sports franchise. This challenge is particularly important given the fact that leaders set the ethical tone for an entire organization. The commitment of senior-level executives determines whether or not a corporation takes its moral responsibilities seriously. Nearly all of the nation's largest firms have taken steps to address ethical problems (e.g., adopting codes of ethics, appointing ethics officers, setting up complaint systems). However, in many cases these programs have little impact on day-to-day operations. CEOs rarely talk about ethics with employees or their ethics officers; workers rarely refer to the policies or call the complaint lines, and so on.[7] This helps account for the moral meltdowns of such companies as WorldCom, Tyco, Adelphia, Xerox, Fannie Mae, and AIG Insurance. Only when top leaders personally commit themselves to moral responsibility do ethical considerations take precedence over profit and efficiency; ethical performance becomes part of evaluation and promotion decisions.

While few would disagree with the fact that leaders are responsible for the actions of followers, determining the extent of a leader's responsibility is far from easy. For example: Can we hold the editor of a school newspaper responsible for the racist comments of a guest writer? Are university administrators liable for what faculty say off campus? Should clothing manufacturers be held accountable for working conditions in overseas factories run by subcontractors? Do these employers "owe" their followers safe working conditions, humane supervision, and a living wage? Can we blame professional football coaches when their players commit crimes during the off-season? Should military officers receive the same or harsher penalties when their subordinates are punished for following their orders?

Answers to these questions can vary depending on the particular situation. Nonetheless, there are some general expectations of leaders. Responsible leaders:

- acknowledge and try to correct ethical problems;
- admit that they have duties to followers;
- take responsibility for the consequences of their orders and actions;
- take reasonable steps to prevent crimes and other abuses by followers;
- hold themselves to the same standards as their followers.

The Challenge of Power

A leader must decide when to employ power, what types of power to use, and how much power she or he wishes to exert over followers. These decisions have moral implications. Is it ethical, for instance, to use power to pursue personal objectives as well as organizational goals? Is it ethical to dominate followers and demand action, or should power be distributed? Is it ethical for a leader to demand compliance when a follower has a moral objection to the leader's request? The U.S. government, for instance, allows those with a moral objection to war to register as conscientious objectors. Those who register for military service in this category are not assigned to combat units but serve in noncombative environments, such as hospitals. What if an employee finds a particular task morally objectionable or physically dangerous? Can a leader ethically insist that a follower perform the task? Some medical practitioners, for instance, refuse to participate in the performance of certain medical procedures such as abortions, sterilization, or euthanasia. Should these practitioners be punished for their views? Of course, followers who choose not to perform certain tasks must live with the consequences of their convictions: a demotion, a narrowing of responsibility, or reassignment to another unit. Under what conditions should a leader respect a follower's right to determine his or her own behavior?

How leaders respond to ethical questions surrounding the use of power will go a long way to determining if they cast light or shadow over the lives of followers. As we noted in chapter 5, power can exert a corrupting influence over those who possess it—the greater the power, the greater the potential for abuse. Impulsive, self-centered individuals more often seize powerful positions.[8] They then wield their influence to further their own interests (like accumulating more power or wealth) at the expense of the group. Powerful leaders frequently protect their status by attacking those they view as threats and justify their lofty positions by assuming that powerless people aren't as qualified or valuable to the organization as they are. They are tempted to use subordinates as means to achieve their ends and employ coercion to get their way.[9] Without checks and balances, those in power are free to project their inner demons on larger and larger groups. For example, Richard Scrushy, former HealthSouth CEO, would hold what his subordinates called "Monday-morning beatings." At these weekly meetings he would ask employees to account for their decisions and actions. He would often respond to explanations with the comment: "That was the stupidest thing I ever heard." He would also place calls to facility administrators at 1 AM from corporate parking lots to say he had found litter. The administrators had to come over immediately to clean up.[10] On a global scale, history's most infamous leaders—Nero, Mao, Pol Pot, Idi Amin, Saddam Hussein—used their absolute power to imprison, torture, and murder millions.

> Lust for power is the most flagrant of all passions.
>
> —Cornelius Tacitus

The Challenge of Privilege

Positions of leadership are associated with social and material rewards. Leaders may reap social benefits such as status, privilege, and respect, as well as material benefits such as high salaries and stock options. Most would agree that leaders deserve additional privileges because they have a broader range of responsibilities than followers, but just how far should these benefits extend? Is it ethical for a leader to take advantage of his or her position to achieve personal power or prestige? Should a leader's concern always be for the good of the collective? In Kenya, one of the most corrupt and poorest nations in the world, political leaders have traditionally taken advantage of their positions to enrich themselves at the expense of the general population. Government officials seize public property and use international loans and relief funds to purchase villas and luxury cars. The current government is attacking corruption, but bribery is common and scandals continue. At the same time, much of the population lives on $1 a day or less.[11]

Kenyan leaders are clearly abusing the benefits that come with their positions. However, such abuses are not limited to developing countries. Corporate executives in the United States often live like royalty; they are the highest paid in the world and enjoy such perks as chauffeur driven limousines, private jets, and executive dining rooms. Between 1993 and 2005, the average pay for chief executives of large U.S. companies quadrupled to $10.5 million (including salary, bonus, stocks, and stock option grants).[12] The paycheck of the average American barely kept pace with inflation during the same period. Soaring compensation packages might be justified if there was a consistent correlation between CEO pay and performance. There isn't.[13] To make matters worse, some failed executives have been richly rewarded. Fired Pfizer CEO Henry McKinnell received $83 million in pension benefits even though Pfizer stock declined nearly 37 percent during his tenure. Home Depot's Bob Nardelli walked away with a $210 million severance package despite the fact that the company's share price remained flat during his six years on the job.[14]

When it comes to executive excess, few can match former Tyco CEO Dennis Kowslowski. Kowslowski looted money from his company to buy art for his apartment (which cost $16.8 million to buy and $3 million to renovate) and then tried to avoid paying New York state income taxes on his purchases. He also threw a lavish $2.1 million birthday party for his wife and collected such accessories as a $6,300 sewing basket, a $6,000 shower curtain, a $2,200 metal wastebasket, $2,900 coat hangers, and a $445 pin cushion.[15]

The Challenge of Loyalty

Leaders have to balance a variety of loyalties or duties when making decisions. Officers of a publicly held corporation, for example, must weigh their obligations to stockholders, employees, suppliers, other businesses, local communities, the societies where the company does business, and the environment. These loyalties often conflict with one another. For example, converting salespeople, insurance adjusters, and other workers to independent contractors reduces company expenditures for payroll taxes and benefits packages. While this decision benefits stockholders, it comes at the expense of workers. Employees may earn less under the new system while paying more in social security taxes and funding their own health and retirement plans. (See box 11.1 for another case involving conflicting corporate loyalties.)

Admirable leaders put the needs of others above selfish concerns. Executives at Tom's of Maine (a consumer products company) and Patagonia (see

Box 11.1   Case Study

A Corporate Hero Leaves Town[16]

The Oreck Company, maker of vacuums, carpet cleaners, and air purifiers, was one of the corporate heroes of Hurricane Katrina. Ten days after the storm in August 2005, the firm reopened its assembly plant in Long Beach, Mississippi, less than a mile from the Gulf of Mexico. The building suffered $4 million in damage and $4 million in inventory was lost. Oreck officials bought trailers and apartments to house workers, supplied them with food, gasoline, and medical supplies, and installed electric generators in the plant. The company, which is owned by private investors and the Oreck family, was widely praised for its generosity and commitment to the local community.

In December 2006, 16 months after Hurricane Katrina, Oreck CEO Tom Oreck announced that the company would close its Long Beach plant and shift manufacturing to a new facility in Cookesville, Tennessee. The Cookesville plant was originally scheduled to be an alternative manufacturing location outside the hurricane zone but the firm decided instead to move its operations there. CEO Oreck explained that the decision to move was based on soaring commercial insurance rates (up over 270 percent in the Gulf Coast region), a dearth of skilled workers due to the local housing shortage, and rising labor costs caused by a surge of high-paying jobs in federal recovery and construction programs. Oreck expressed his appreciation to the 500 local employees who helped keep the Long Beach plant open and pledged to help them find new jobs before closing the facility. Workers interviewed by the press were optimistic that they could find employment in the booming job market.

Government and economic development officials blasted Oreck for its decision. They argued that business conditions would gradually improve. (Oreck was the first major employer to move out of the region, though others might follow. The firm's headquarters remain in New Orleans.) Some suspected that the company planned to move all along, in part because some of its tax breaks were set to expire. To them, the company, which had received a $3 million loan at 2.5 percent interest, tax exemptions, cheap land, a $416,000 grant, and free road access, wanted to move on before having to pay its fair share for doing business. Long Beach mayor William Skellie complained: "I think it would have been easier on everybody if they had stayed closed rather than put everyone through this and use them up while they got their deal done. It's a bigger punch in the nose."[17] Others criticized the timing of the announcement (made near the Christmas holiday) and a report that CEO Oreck called the Mississippi workforce "unproductive" (a quote that he denies). Mississippi Senator Trent Lott urged taxpayers and government officials to keep the Oreck example in mind the next time a company asks for tax incentives and to scrutinize loan applicants carefully.

Discussion Questions

1. Who are the stakeholders in this case? Who deserves the most loyalty from company leadership?

2. What might be the long-term consequences of this decision for the Oreck corporation and its owners? For other companies doing business on the Gulf Coast? For area residents? For the region?

3. Was Oreck justified in closing its Long Beach plant? Why or why not?

4. Would it have been better for the company to close the plant immediately after the hurricane rather than to reopen only to close later?

5. How would you rate Oreck as a corporate citizen?

6. What feedback would you give the company leader about the timing and announcement of this decision?

chapter 2) draw praise for giving to deserving causes, supporting local communities, and protecting the environment. In contrast, trial attorneys were criticized for keeping their suspicions about the safety of Firestone tires to themselves in order to increase their chances of winning lawsuits against the company. Their silence delayed the recall of the defective tires and may have resulted in additional injuries and deaths.[18]

Broken loyalties can also cast shadows. Employees at Enron felt betrayed by the firm's president, Kenneth Lay. He assured workers that the company was prospering even as he sold large quantities of his own stock. When the value of Enron stock evaporated, the retirement savings of many workers disappeared along with their jobs. On the other hand, well-placed loyalty can make a powerful moral statement. This happened in the case of Pee-Wee Reese, the Brooklyn Dodger who publicly demonstrated loyalty to Jackie Robinson, the first black player in the major leagues. In one particularly vivid display of support, Reese put his arm around Robinson's shoulders in front of a extremely hostile crowd in Cincinnati.[19]

The Challenge of Consistency

Leaders deal with a variety of followers, relationships, and situations, making it difficult to behave consistently. In fact, the situational and relational approaches discussed in chapter 3 are based on the premise that a leader's behavior will vary depending on such factors as the readiness levels of followers, the nature of the task, and whether subordinates are members of the in-group or out-group. Nonetheless, acting inconsistently raises significant ethical dilemmas. Those in a leader's in-group probably have no problem with the leader's favoritism; those in the out-group probably resent the preferential treatment. Deciding when to bend the rules and for whom is also problematic. A strict policy about being on time for work, for instance, may have to be relaxed during bad weather. Some coaches let their star players skip practices to rest up for big games. Resident assistants are tempted to overlook infractions of the rules committed by friends who live on their dormitory floors.

> Wrong is wrong, no matter who does it or says it.
>
> —Malcolm X

Some degree of inconsistency appears inevitable, but leaders cast shadows when they appear to act arbitrarily and unfairly. Leaders should try to be equitable with followers, making exceptions only after careful thought. In addition, they need to be evenhanded in their dealings with those outside the organization. Concerns about favoritism are at the heart of attempts to reform campaign financing and lobbying. "Buying" access to political officials means that those who make large campaign contributions and pay for meals and trips for law makers generally receive better treatment in the form of favorable legislation. The rest of us end up bearing a larger portion of the total tax burden and pay more for goods and services because of laws that protect everyone from farmers to automobile manufacturers to prescription drug companies.[20]

Meeting the unique ethical challenges of leadership is difficult, and we may disagree on what courses of action are appropriate. However, because moral judgments are critical to the practice of leadership, we have a responsibility to make reasoned, ethical decisions and to act on those choices. We can better fulfill this responsibility if we understand the components of ethical behavior and study some widely accepted ethical perspectives for guidance.

Components of Ethical Behavior

James Rest and his colleagues at the Center for the Study of Ethical Development at the University of Minnesota believe that ethical behavior is the product of four intrapersonal and interpersonal communication processes. Ethical failure occurs when one of these processes malfunctions. By taking a closer look at each of these components, we can improve our performance and help our followers do the same.[21]

Component 1: Moral sensitivity (recognition). Moral sensitivity is identifying the existence of ethical problems. We can't solve a moral problem unless we first recognize that one exists. This component involves acknowledging that our behavior impacts others, identifying possible courses of action, and determining the consequences of each possible strategy. Empathy and perspective taking skills are essential if we are to predict the possible consequences of our actions and to evaluate the effectiveness of various options. We need to imagine how others might feel or react. However, we can be victimized by moral tunnel vision when our mental scripts don't include ethical considerations. When buying clothes, for example, we may focus solely on getting a good deal, ignoring the fact that our purchase might help keep a sweatshop operating in the third world. (The research highlight in box 11.2 provides an in-depth look at how one group of leaders ignored the moral implications of their choices with tragic consequences.) Moral muteness is also problem. All too often leaders are reluctant to use ethical terminology when describing situations, perhaps because they want to avoid conflict or believe that their silence will make them appear in control.[22]

You can increase your moral sensitivity if you: (a) engage in active listening to learn about the possible ethical consequences of your choices; (b) challenge your schemas to make sure that you're not overlooking important moral considerations; and (c) use ethical terms like *right, wrong, values, fairness,* and *immoral* when describing problems and solutions.

Component 2: Moral judgment. Moral judgment is deciding which course of action identified in the first component is the right one to follow. Decision makers determine what is the right or wrong thing to do in this particular situation. Moral judgment is the most studied component of Rest's model. Researchers have conducted over a thousand studies of moral judgment using an instrument called the Defining Issues Test. Respondents read moral dilemmas (Should a model escaped prisoner be reported to the police? Should a doctor help a dying patient take her own life?) and then rank a series of items that reveal what they take into consideration when making ethical choices. According to Rest, the highest form of ethical reasoning is based on broad principles like justice, cooperation, and respect for others.[23]

Box 11.2   Research Highlight
Anatomy of an Ethical Failure[24]

The Bridgestone/Firestone/Ford scandal, which involved accidents of Ford Explorers equipped with Wilderness ATV tires, was not the first time that the Ford Motor Company was accused of ignoring serious safety problems. In the late 1970s, the automaker faced a serious crisis based on its refusal to recall and repair gas tanks on Pinto subcompacts manufactured between 1970–1976. Gas tanks on these models were located behind the rear axle. In low-speed, rear-end collisions, bolts from the differential housing (the large gear that transfers power from the drive shaft to the rear axle) could puncture the tank, causing a leak. At the same time, the filler pipe that carries gas to the tank often tore loose, causing additional leaks. Any spark would then ignite the gas, and the car would be engulfed in flames.

Despite the fact that fixing the problem would cost only $11 per vehicle, the company failed to act, based in part on the belief that all small cars were inherently unsafe and that "safety wouldn't sell." The company also conducted a cost-benefit analysis and determined that the costs in human life (at $200,000 per fatality and $67,000 per injury) were substantially less than the costs to repair the problem on 12.5 million vehicles. In 1978, the National Highway and Transportation Administration declared the Pinto defective, and Ford reluctantly issued a recall. That same year, the company lost a major lawsuit brought by a burn victim and was indicted by a grand jury for criminal negligence in the deaths of three teens who died in a rear-end crash in Indiana (Ford was acquitted in the subsequent trial). This marked the first time that a major firm had faced criminal, not civil, charges for manufacturing faulty products. Ford stopped producing the Pinto in 1980.

Business professor Dennis Gioia was Ford's Recall Coordinator between 1973 and 1975. This put him in the research role of a participant-observer. Gioia initiated a discussion about recalling the Pinto but voted with the rest of the safety committee in recommending against any further action. Most of the criticism of Ford came after Gioia left the automaker, when the gas tank problem had been clearly identified, and Ford stonewalled its critics. Yet Professor Gioia wonders why he didn't define the defective tanks as an ethical problem rather than as a business decision. Somehow his high moral standards (which included trying to make Ford more socially responsive) did not translate into action.

Gioia offers a number of explanations for his failure to act, including company pressure and personal moral weakness. In the end, however, he lays the blame on his moral insensitivity. He concludes that his typical way of processing information, or *script*, blinded him to the ethical dimension of the problem. Scripts, like other mental shortcuts, enable decision makers to process data rapidly and to make quick choices. At the first signs of trouble with the Pinto, Gioia was dealing with as many as 100 possible recalls. His script (shared by others at Ford) defined problems based on their size and costs. To attract the attention of the safety group, there had to be lots of reports about a particular defect. The decision about how to respond to the faulty part was based on balancing the costs against the potential benefits. In the case of the Pinto, only a few exploded, so the problem didn't seem as pressing as defects in other models, which occurred much more frequently. Further, the expense of fixing the gas tank didn't appear to be justified. Sadly, ethical considerations were not part of the standard script. Gioia and his colleagues didn't question the morality of putting a dollar value on human life and allowing customers to die in order to save money.

Gioia argues that organizations should strive to integrate ethics into the scripts of organizational members. Codes of ethics and written policies will not be enough. Instead, ethical responsibilities should be included in job descriptions, and ethics ought to be an important theme in training and mentoring. Experienced employees may have to revise their scripts through training and experiences that explicitly focus on ethical issues. Unless ethics becomes part of the cognitive structure that decision makers use every day, they are likely to remain insensitive to the existence of moral problems. According to Gioia:

Most models of ethical decision making in organizations implicitly assume that people recognize and think about a moral or ethical dilemma when they are confronted with one. I call this seemingly fundamental assumption into question. The unexplored ethical issue for me is the arguably prevalent case where organizational representatives are not aware that they are dealing with a problem that might have ethical overtones. If the case involves a familiar class of problems or issues, it is likely to be handled via existing cognitive structure or scripts—*scripts that typically include no ethical component in their cognitive content.*[25]

Results from the Defining Issues Test indicate that we can increase our ethical competence. There is a strong link between higher education and reasoned decision making.[26] People in college and graduate school demonstrate the greatest gains in moral development. However, insecurities, greed, and ego can subvert the reasoning process, contributing to the downfall of such prominent leaders as Martha Stewart and former House majority leader Tom DeLay.

To improve your moral judgment, maximize the ethical benefits of your college education by taking courses on ethics and by participating in internships that raise real-life ethical dilemmas. Base your decisions on widely accepted ethical principles (see the discussion of ethical perspectives to follow). Be alert to the possibility of faulty reasoning—consult with others to check your perceptions against reality and stay close to people who will tell you the truth and hold you accountable.

Component 3: Moral motivation. Moral motivation refers to following through on choices. The desire to do the right thing generally comes into conflict with other values like security, wealth, and social acceptance. Ethical behavior results if moral values take precedence over other considerations. Leaders and followers are more likely to follow through when they are rewarded for doing so. Lockheed Martin, for example, encourages ethical behavior by evaluating ethical performance as part of the review process and by giving out an annual ethics award to senior-level managers. On the other side of the coin, employees are encouraged to inflate sales figures, lie to investors, produce shoddy products, and take kickbacks from suppliers when guilty parties prosper. In the early 1990s, mechanics and service center advisors at Sears Roebuck car centers sold needless parts and repairs to customers because they earned commissions for reaching sales quotas.

Emotions, like rewards, also influence ethical motivation. In general, positive feelings like happiness, joy, and optimism encourage individuals to follow through while negative emotions, like anger, frustration, stress, and depression, lower motivation and encourage aggression and other antisocial behaviors instead.[27]

You can increase your moral motivation and that of your followers by creating an ethically rewarding environment and managing your emotions. Catch people doing good. That is, reward moral behavior that might otherwise go unappreciated, such as providing outstanding customer service or eliminating wasteful spending. Don't focus solely on the bottom line but develop other measures of performance, such as community involvement and support of corporate mission and values. Evaluate based on processes as well as on results.

Provide incentives for those who reach their goals in an ethical manner and punish those who don't. (See box 11.3 for more information on how to create an ethical environment.) Monitor your emotions and regulate them to bring them in line with your goals. Note your destructive feelings and shift into a more positive frame of mind.

Component 4: Moral character (implementation). Moral character is the implementation stage of the model. Opposition, fatigue, distractions, and other factors are formidable barriers to ethical action. Overcoming these obstacles takes persistence. Those with a strong will are more likely to persist as well as those with an internal locus of control. Internally oriented people (internals) are convinced that they have control over their lives and can determine what

---

Box 11.3

Creating an Ethical Environment: Defensive and Proactive Strategies[28]

Ethical leaders increase the motivation to behave morally by shaping the group or organizational context through defensive and proactive strategies. Defensive tactics are designed to prevent unethical, destructive behaviors, including incivility (rude or discourteous actions like ignoring a coworker or stealing someone else's work), aggression aimed at hurting others or the organization, sexual harassment, and discrimination. Proactive tactics intentionally promote a positive moral atmosphere or climate.

Defensive Tactics
Create zero-tolerance policies for antisocial behaviors
Personally adhere to policies; model compliance
Confront offenders at the first sign of trouble
Punish those who break the rules
Address the root causes of destructive behaviors: oppressive supervision, injustice, stress, unpleasant working conditions, extreme competitiveness
Set up reporting systems (e.g., ethics hotlines) for ethical violations and create disciplinary procedures
Design performance evaluation systems that detect unethical behavior

Proactive Tactics
Create codes of ethics
Appoint ethics officers
Establish clear lines of accountability
Honor ethical heroes
Model moral behavior
Continually communicate the organization's core values and core purpose
Incorporate values into every organizational decision
Equip constituents to make their own moral decisions; empower them to do so
Build ethical criteria and standards into performance reviews
Reward ethical behavior (e.g., honesty, fair treatment of vendors, courtesy, excellent service)
Evaluate based on processes (how goals are reached) as well as on outcomes
Support, don't punish, whistle-blowers
Select employees based on their character and values
Integrate discussion of ethics and values into socialization processes (employment interviews, orientation, training)
Provide ongoing ethics training
Periodically audit the ethical culture of the organization

happens to them. Externally oriented people (externals) believe that what happens in life is generally outside their control and is the product of such forces as fate or luck. Internals are more likely to take personal responsibility for their actions and therefore try to do what is right. Externals are more likely to give in to situational pressures and to give up rather than to carry on.[29]

Successful implementation requires competence as well as persistence. Consider the high-tech manager who believes it is wrong to release the latest software update before it has been tested thoroughly. To delay the release, she'll need to marshal her evidence, enlist the help of her fellow managers, engage in constructive argument with her supervisors, negotiate with other departments, and so on.

You can boost the probability that you'll take moral action by (a) assessing your personal history (How well do you manage obstacles? What can you do to improve your track record?); (b) believing that you can make a difference; (c) mastering the context (organizational policies, informal networks, key decision makers) so that you can respond effectively when needed; and (d) building your communication competence so that can put your choice into action.

Ethical Perspectives

Over the centuries philosophers and other scholars have developed a variety of theories or approaches that can be applied to ethical issues. These perspectives impact all four of the components of ethical behavior described above. They can raise our ethical awareness, guide our decision making, help us prioritize our values, and strengthen our moral character. In this section of the chapter we'll look at five ethical approaches that are particularly relevant to leadership.

Kant's Categorical Imperative

German philosopher Immanuel Kant (1724–1804) argued that individuals ought to do what is morally right, no matter what the consequences. The term *categorical* means *without exception*.[30] This approach to moral reasoning is the best known example of deontological ethics. Proponents of deontological ethics believe that we ought to base our choices on our duty (*deon* is the Greek word for duty) to follow universal truths that we discover through our intuition or reason. Kant's standard can be applied by asking a simple question: Would we want everyone to make the same decision we did? If the answer is "yes," the choice is ethical. If the answer is "no," the decision is wrong. Based on this reasoning, behaviors like treating employees fairly and keeping commitments are always right. Such behaviors as cheating, lying, and abusive behavior are always wrong. For instance, if we're tempted to make up statistics to boost donations to the nonprofit group we lead, we need to ask ourselves what would happen if every charity lied in order to raise funds. A climate of suspicion and hostility might be created that would bankrupt many worthy organizations. Our duty, then, is to present accurate information—even if misleading statistics might convince people to give more to our particular cause.

Kant also advocated respect for people, which has become one of the most influential ideas in Western moral philosophy.[31] According to Kant: "Act so that you treat humanity, whether in your own person or that of another, always as an end and never as a means only." We need followers to help us reach our objectives as leaders. However, we should never treat subordinates merely as tools. Our duty is to respect the right of followers to choose for themselves. Based on this principle, it is unethical to subject them to dangerous chemicals in the workplace or to gather personal information about them without their knowledge or consent. Coercing or threatening followers is wrong because it violates their freedom of choice. Similarly, denying assistance to them is immoral because refusing help limits their options.

Utilitarianism

In sharp contrast to Kant, British philosophers Jeremy Bentham (1748–1832) and John Stuart Mill (1806–1873) argued that ethical choices should be based on their consequences rather than on individual duty. The best decisions are those that (1) generate the most benefits as compared to their disadvantages, and (2) benefit the largest number of people. The end result is that utilitarianism attempts to do the greatest good for the greatest number of people.[32]

Leaders commonly weigh outcomes when making decisions. Franklin Roosevelt, for instance, lied to Congress and U.S. citizens in order to help Great Britain in World War II. He began to send ships and materials to the embattled nation before he received congressional approval, judging that saving England justified his deceit. Harry Truman decided to drop the atomic bomb on Japan after determining that the benefits of shortening the war in the Pacific outweighed the costs of destroying Hiroshima and Nagasaki and ushering in the nuclear age.

Identifying and evaluating possible consequences can be difficult. Take the debate over ethanol fuel, for instance. Proponents of ethanol, which is a corn product used to fuel cars, argue that increasing production will reduce dependence on foreign oil and reduce pollution. Opponents point out that producing ethanol uses more energy than ethanol generates. Further, growing corn for this purpose drives up the cost of other products like beef and reduces the harvest of other crops for human consumption, contributing to world hunger. Putting more acreage into production can reduce wildlife habitats and increase agricultural runoff, which pollutes rivers and streams.

Based on the difficulty of determining potential costs and benefits in situations like the one described above, utilitarian decision makers sometimes reach different conclusions when faced with the same dilemma. Some historians, for example, criticize Truman for his decision to drop the atomic bomb. They argue that the war would have ended soon without the use of nuclear weapons and that no military objective justifies such widespread destruction.

Virtue Ethics

As we've seen, there are significant differences between the categorical and utilitarian perspectives. However, both theories involve the application of universal rules or principles to specific situations. Dissatisfaction with rule-based approaches to ethical decision making is growing. Some ethicists complain that these guidelines are applied to extreme situations, not the types of choices we typically make.[33] Few of us will be faced with the extraordinary scenarios (stealing to save a life or lying to the secret police to protect a fugitive) that are frequently used to illustrate principled decision making. Our dilemmas are generally less dramatic. For instance: Should I lie to protect someone's feelings? Tell my employer about another job offer? Confront a coworker about a sexist joke? Ethical decision makers also deal with time pressures and uncertainty. In crisis situations they don't have time to carefully weigh consequences or to determine which abstract principle to apply.[34]

Recognizing the limitations of the utilitarian and categorical approaches, some scholars are turning back to one of the oldest ethical traditions—virtue ethics. Virtue ethicists highlight the role of the person or actor in ethical decision making. They argue that individuals with high moral character are more likely to make wise ethical choices. Virtue theorists seek: (1) to develop a description of the ideal person, (2) to identify the virtues that make up the character of this ethical prototype, and (3) to outline how individuals can acquire the required virtues.[35] Let's take a closer look at each of these objectives as they apply to leadership.

Definitions of *the ideal leader* will differ to some degree depending on the context. We may value kindness and consideration in a religious figure but want toughness in a military leader. Nevertheless, descriptions of the ideal leader show a high degree of consistency, no matter what the setting. The most admired leadership characteristics (honesty, forward looking, inspiring, competent) that emerged in the study of 15,000 managers described in chapter 6 bear a striking resemblance to the things we look for in political leaders. We want elected officials who act with integrity, exercise good judgment, restrain their impulses, respect others, rally followers, persist in the face of strong opposition, and so forth.[36] Former President Clinton's affair with Monica Lewinsky demonstrated poor character. He took advantage of the power of his position, acted recklessly, and lied to cover up his unethical behavior. (See the self-assessment in box 11.4 for one tool designed specifically to measure the honesty and consistency of those in leadership roles.)

The *virtues of the ethical leader* are "deep-rooted dispositions, habits, skills, or traits of character that incline persons to perceive, feel, and act in ethically right and sensitive ways."[37] Aristotle provided one of the first comprehensive lists of virtues in Western culture. He described the ideal citizen/ leader as someone who possesses characteristics such as courage, moderation, justice, generosity, hospitality, a mild temper, truthfulness, and proper judgment. Most, if not all, of these virtues appear on the lists of contemporary ethicists and leadership scholars. Other common virtues include love, empathy, compassion, and strength.[38]

> Love is the virtue of the heart. Sincerity the virtue of the mind.
> Courage the virtue of the spirit. Decision the virtue of the will.
> —Frank Lloyd Wright

Box 11.4   Self-Assessment

Perceived Leader Integrity Scale (PLIS)[39]

The following items concern your immediate supervisor—the person who has the most control over your daily work activities. Use the following numbers to indicate how well each item describes your immediate supervisor.

1 = Not at all; 2 = Somewhat; 3 = Very much; 4 = Exactly

The higher the total score on the scale (31 is the lowest possible score, 124 the highest), the lower the perception of integrity of the person being rated. You can also use this instrument to assess the image others have of your character. You might distribute the survey to a group of followers and ask for anonymous responses or estimate how you think others would rate you on each item.

_____ 1. Would use my mistakes to attack me personally

_____ 2. Always gets even

_____ 3. Gives special favors to certain "pet" employees, but not to me

_____ 4. Would lie to me

_____ 5. Would risk me to protect himself/herself in work matters

_____ 6. Deliberately fuels conflict among employees

_____ 7. Is evil

_____ 8. Would use my performance appraisal to criticize me as a person

_____ 9. Has it in for me

_____ 10. Would allow me to be blamed for his/her mistake

_____ 11. Would falsify records if it would help his/her work situation

_____ 12. Lacks high morals

_____ 13. Makes fun of my mistakes instead of coaching me as to how to do my job better

_____ 14. Would deliberately exaggerate my mistakes to make me look bad when describing my performance to his/her superiors

_____ 15. Is vindictive

_____ 16. Would blame me for his/her own mistake

_____ 17. Avoids coaching me because (s)he wants me to fail

_____ 18. Would treat me better if I belonged to a different ethnic group

_____ 19. Would deliberately distort what I say

_____ 20. Deliberately makes employees angry at each other

_____ 21. Is a hypocrite

_____ 22. Would limit my training opportunities to prevent me from advancing

_____ 23. Would blackmail an employee if (s)he thought (s)he could get away with it

_____ 24. Enjoys turning down my requests

_____ 25. Would make trouble for me if I got on his/her bad side

_____ 26. Would take credit for my ideas

_____ 27. Would steal from the organization

_____ 28. Would risk me to get back at someone else

_____ 29. Would engage in sabotage against the organization

_____ 30. Would fire people just because (s)he doesn't like them if (s)he could get away with it

_____ 31. Would do things that violate organizational policy and then expect his/her subordinates to cover for him/her

Exemplars or role models play a critical role in the ***development of high moral character***. Virtues are more "caught than taught" in that they are acquired through observation and imitation. We learn what it means to be just, generous, and honest by seeing these qualities modeled in the lives of exemplary leaders. Exemplary leaders can be people we work for; political, religious, or military leaders; historical figures (see the case study in box 11.5); and even fictional characters. Any story about leaders, whether it is an item in the morning newspaper, a segment on CNN, a novel, a play, a biography, or a movie, can provide insights into ethical (and unethical) leader behavior. Communities encourage the formation of moral character by telling and retelling stories that illustrate and reinforce ethical values.[40]

One group of scholars and leadership practitioners believes that authenticity is the most important virtue for leaders.[41] Authentic leaders demonstrate self-awareness and act in ways that are consistent with that self-understanding. They "own" their thoughts, emotions, beliefs, wants, and needs. They express what they really think and believe and, at the same time, their behavior reflects their "true" selves. Proponents of authenticity argue that this virtue can dramatically improve organizations. Authentic leaders help constituents find meaning in work, foster optimism, build trust and commitment levels, and promote an ethical climate.

Four factors distinguish authentic leaders.[42]

1. *Heightened levels of self-awareness*. Authentic leaders know and trust their thoughts and feelings and are more aware of and committed to their values. There is little gap between what they are (the actual self) and what they would like to be (the ideal self). Such heightened self-awareness enhances personal esteem and positive emotions. Authentic leaders regulate their behaviors according to internal, not external, standards. They focus on reaching goals they set for themselves. Authentic individuals may get totally immersed in their work, for example, and are driven by feelings of accomplishment, curiosity, and learning.

2. *Balanced processing*. Authentic leaders have positive self-esteem as well as a more accurate understanding of the extent and limits of their skills and knowledge. While they can't completely avoid perceptual biases, they are less defensive about their weaknesses and take steps to improve.

3. *Authentic behavior*. Authentic leaders give priority to their values and needs rather than to conforming to the group. They resist group and organizational pressure to act in a way that is inconsistent with their principles. They don't need continual affirmation from others. However, they are always sensitive to the demands of the situation.

4. *Relational transparency*. Authentic leaders value relational truthfulness and openness. They place trust in others and freely exchange information with followers. They engage in honest but appropriate self-disclosure and encourage followers to do the same.

Reflecting on your life story is one way to become more authentic. Interpret your past experiences and put them together into a coherent whole, focusing on key moments of development (see chapter 12). In particular, think about experiences and feedback that revealed previously unrecognized strengths that

Box 11.5   Case Study
Moral Exemplars during the Holocaust[43]

If, as the virtue ethicists claim, we learn how to be virtuous by observing others, then it is important to identify examples of moral leadership. Leaders such as Mother Teresa, Archbishop Desmond Tutu, or Mahatma Gandhi fit neatly into the category of exemplary leader. Others, however, seem to blur the line between virtue and vice.

Lawrence Blum points to Oskar Schindler as someone who defies easy moral classification. The story of his life is familiar to those who have read the book *Schindler's List* by Thomas Keneally or have seen the film by the same name. Schindler was a German industrialist who hoped to get rich off the Nazi war machine during World War II. He went to Poland during the German occupation to set up an enamelware factory. He later used his position as factory manager to save the lives of 1,100 Jews who faced death through slave labor and extermination camps. In the process he was arrested several times and lost his entire fortune. None of his business ventures succeeded after the war, and he had to depend on the generosity of those he had rescued in Poland.

There are several features of Schindler's character that contribute to what Blum calls his "moral ambiguity." Schindler loved fast cars, fine clothes, and alcohol. He had two mistresses in Poland and made little effort to hide this fact. An accomplished liar, he enjoyed misleading the Nazis. Part of his motivation for rescuing his workers may have been his addiction to adventure and risk. At times he seemed too impressed with himself as a "savior" of Jews.

Blum argues that Schindler should still be considered a moral hero despite his weaknesses and ethical complexities. He brought about a great good (or prevented a great evil). While his motives were mixed, there can be no doubt that he found Nazi policies abhorrent and felt compassion for his workers. He carried out his rescue efforts at great personal cost, and his concern for others appeared to have been stronger than his need for power.

While labeling Schindler a hero, Blum concedes that there are better models of behavior. He calls these individuals "moral paragons" or "saints." Such leaders live exemplary lives, demonstrating the virtues of integrity, moderation, and good judgment that appear to be missing in Oskar Schindler. They are motivated by high ideals that call forth their best efforts no matter what the situation. In contrast, moral heroes like Schindler seem to emerge only during times of crisis.

Blum points to Andre and Magda Trocme as prototypical moral saints. Andre was a pastor in the small town of Le Chambon in occupied France during World War II. He and his wife Magda convinced their congregation to shelter Jews, provided Jewish fugitives with food and shelter, and arranged for many to escape. Like Schindler, their efforts brought about a great good. However, unlike Schindler, they only engaged in deception because they had to and were motivated by a lifelong devotion to nonviolence. Schindler seemed to lose his purpose in life after the war and faded into moral obscurity. Andre Trocme continued to work on the behalf of nonviolence, becoming the European Secretary of the Fellowship of Reconciliation. Throughout his life Andre Trocme was able to accept (not condemn) others and, at the same time, bring out the moral best in them.[44]

Discussion Questions

1. What should the criteria be for determining if someone is an exemplary moral leader?

2. Based on your criteria, is Oskar Schindler such a leader?

3. Why does a crisis bring out the ethical best in some leaders like Schindler and the worst in others? What accounts for the difference?

4. Do you agree with Blum's distinction between moral heroes (Schindler) and moral saints (Andre and Magda Trocme)? Why or why not?

5. What can we learn from Schindler's example, whether or not you consider him an exemplary moral leader? What can we learn from the Trocmes?

give you the confidence to take on new experiences. Reflect on why your role models are important to you and study the narratives of other leaders to gain new insights. Finally, attempt to live out your story. Behaving consistently now builds your potential to act authentically in the future.[45]

Altruism

Altruism makes concern for others the ultimate ethical standard. Proponents of altruistic behavior argue that we ought to help others regardless of whether we get any benefit from doing so. Altruism appears to be a universal value promoted in cultures around the world. For example, the major world religions, those that have lasted and expanded over the centuries, emphasize love for all humanity. Well-known religious altruists include Tibet's Dalai Lama, South African bishop Desmond Tutu, Gandhi, social activist Dorothy Day, Martin Luther King, hospice advocate Dame Cicely Sanders, and former UN Secretary Dag Hammarskjold.[46] Not only is altruistic behavior an ideal, it appears to be common in everyday life. Social scientists from such fields as psychology, economics, sociology, and political science report that altruism is an integral part of human nature.[47] We comfort our friends and family members, send money to tsunami victims, rebuild homes after Hurricane Katrina, push strangers' cars out of snowbanks, provide free dental and medical care, volunteer for mountain rescue teams, and so on. Altruistic behavior not only benefits the recipients but also pays dividends for society as a whole. Such actions build bonds between people and nurture the cooperation and trust necessary to take collective action (e.g., form a political party, operate a business, educate students). In sum, society functions more effectively when people act on behalf of others. (Turn to box 11.6 for examples of altruistic behaviors that can boost organizational productivity.)

> Doing good is one of the wonderful mysteries of the human universe.
>
> —Jeffrey Kottler

As you can see, altruism is a significant ethical consideration for all citizens. However, concern for others may be more important for leaders than for followers. By definition, leaders serve group goals, not their selfish interests (see chapter 1). A number of effective leadership practices described in this text—team building, listening, transformational leadership, empowerment, mentoring—have an altruistic component. Many of the qualities of virtuous leaders described earlier, like generosity, hospitality, empathy, and compassion, reflect a focus on others rather than a self-focus. Management professors Rabindra Kanungo and Manuel Mendonca argue that "organizational leaders are only effective when they are motivated by a concern for others."[48] They contrast the motives of self- and other-motivated leaders. Self-focused leaders pursue their own agenda at the cost of the organization. They seek personal achievement, want to control followers, and make heavy use of legitimate, reward, and coercive power bases. In the process they destroy loyalty and trust and put their organizations at risk. Other-focused leaders pursue institutional goals. They seek collective achievements, empower followers, and rely on referent and expert power bases. Altruistic leaders foster collaboration and their self-sacrifice demonstrates commitment to the group and its mission. When followers emulate the example of altruistic leaders, higher performance often results.

> To reveal someone's beauty is to reveal their value by giving them time, attention, and tenderness.
>
> —Jean Vanier

Box 11.6

Organizational Altruistic Behaviors[49]

Directed to Benefit Individuals
Consideration of others' needs
Technical assistance on the job
Job orientation in new jobs
Buddy system of induction for new employees
Training to acquire new skills
Empowerment practices including mentoring and modeling for others to gain competence

Directed to Benefit Groups
Team building
Participative group decision making
Protecting people from sexual harassment
Minority promotion and advancement programs
Counseling programs
Educational support programs
Interdepartmental cooperation

Directed to Benefit the Organization
Organizational commitment and loyalty
Work dedication
Equitable compensation programs
Whistle-blowing to maintain organizational integrity
Protecting and conserving organizational resources
Presenting a positive image of the organization to outsiders
Sharing of organizational wealth through profit-sharing programs

Directed to Benefit Society
Contributions to social welfare and community needs in the areas of health, education, the arts, and culture
Lobbying for public interest legislation
Affirmative action programs for minorities
Training and employment for handicapped and hard-core unemployed
Environmental pollution control
Economic sanctions against oppressive social control
Assuring product safety and customer satisfaction

Leaders as Servants

This ethical perspective specifically addresses the behavior of leaders. Contemporary interest in leaders as servants was sparked by Robert Greenleaf. He coined the term "servant leader" in 1970 to describe a leadership model that puts the concerns of followers first. Greenleaf later founded a center to promote servant leadership. His ideas have been adopted by businesses (Southwest Airlines, Synovus Financial Corporation, The Container Store, AFLAC), nonprofit organizations, and community and service-learning programs.[50] Servant leaders put the needs of followers before their own needs. Because they continually ask themselves what would be best for their constituents, servant leaders are less tempted to take advantage of followers, act inconsistently, or accumulate money and power for themselves. Five principles serve as the foundation for servant leadership.

The first principle is a concern for people—an extension of the ethical principle of altruism. Servant leaders believe that healthy societies and organizations care for their members. They use such terms as *love*, *civility*, and *community* to characterize working relationships. Servant leaders argue that the measure of a leader's success lies in what happens in the lives of followers—not in what the leader has accomplished. Greenleaf suggests that we gauge a leader's effectiveness by asking the following questions: "Do those served grow as persons? Do they, while being served, become healthier, wise, freer, more autonomous, more likely themselves to become servants?"[51]

The second principle of servant leadership is stewardship. Servant leaders hold their positions and organizations in trust for others. They act on behalf of followers who have entrusted them with leadership responsibilities; they act on behalf of society by making sure that their organizations serve the common good. Stewards are accountable for results but reach their goals by serving others, not by controlling or coercing them.[52]

> The highest of distinctions is service to others.
>
> —George VI

The third principle of servant leadership is equity or justice. Servant leaders make a concerted effort to create a level playing field by distributing resources fairly. For example, as we noted in chapter 1, at Costco the CEO, Jim Sinegal, earns a salary of $350,000 a year—a figure that has held steady over the past six years.[53] This is a sharp contrast to the typical CEO salaries noted earlier in this chapter. The principle of equity extends to the distribution of power. Servant leaders view followers as partners. They practice empowerment by giving followers the space to develop and exercise their talents, by delegating authority for important tasks, and by sharing information. Former Herman Miller Chairman of the Board Max DePree urges organizational leaders to engage in "lavish" communications, sharing information about every aspect of the operation. "Information is power," says DePree, "but it is pointless power if hoarded. Power must be shared for an organization or a relationship to work."[54] When DePree was CEO of Herman Miller, top executives reported monthly to employees on company profits and productivity.

> One thing I know: The only ones among you who will be truly happy are those who have sought and found how to serve.
> —Albert Schweitzer

The fourth principle of servant leadership is indebtedness. For those who view leadership as a form of service, leaders have certain responsibilities to their followers. According to DePree, followers can expect the following rights from their leaders.[55]

- *Right to be needed.* Followers have the right to use their gifts and be connected in a meaningful way to the mission of the organization.
- *Right to be involved.* Everyone has a right to participate and to have input. In addition, leaders must respond to suggestions and work with followers to meet the needs of customers.
- *Right to a covenantal relationship.* Contractual relationships are based on legal agreements that define pay, working conditions, vacations, etc. Covenantal relationships are based on a commitment to common goals and values; such relationships meet deeper needs and help provide meaning to work.
- *Right to understand.* Followers have a right to know and understand the following elements: organizational mission, personal career paths, the competition, the working environment, terms of employment.
- *Right to affect one's own destiny.* Followers should always be involved in their performance evaluations and in promotion and transfer decisions that impact their careers.
- *Right to be accountable.* Accountability includes contributing to the achievement of group goals and sharing ownership in group problems and risks. Contributions should be evaluated according to clear, acceptable criteria.
- *Right to appeal.* Everyone should have the right to appeal decisions that might threaten one or more of the rights described earlier.
- *Right to make a commitment.* In order to make a commitment, followers must know that they can do their best and not be held back by leaders, particularly leaders who act in an irrational manner.

The fifth principle of servant leadership is self-understanding. Like the virtue ethicists, proponents of servant leadership believe that ethical choices should be based on character rather than on codes of conduct. Servant leaders analyze their motives, seek out opportunities for personal growth, and regularly take time to examine their attitudes and values. They create a positive ethical climate for followers by striving to be trusting, insightful, open to new ideas, strong, and courageous.[56]

Following servant leadership principles can have a significant impact on how organizational leaders think and act. For a summary of the differences between traditional bosses and those who seek to serve, see box 11.7.

Box 11.7

Traditional Bosses vs. Servant Leaders: A New Kind of Leadership[57]

Traditional Boss	Servant as Leader
Motivated by personal drive to achieve.	Motivated by desire to serve others.
Highly competitive; independent mind-set; seeks to receive personal credit for achievement.	Highly collaborative and interdependent; gives credit to others generously.
Understands internal politics and uses them to win personally.	Sensitive to what motivates others and empowers all to win with shared goals and vision.
Focuses on fast action. Complains about long meetings and about others being too slow.	Focuses on gaining understanding, input, and buy-in from all parties.
Relies on facts, logic, or proof.	Uses intuition and foresight to balance facts, logic, or proof.
Controls information in order to maintain power.	Shares big-picture information generously.
Spends more time telling and giving orders. Sees too much listening or coaching as inefficient.	Listens deeply and respectfully to others— especially to those who disagree.
Feels that personal value comes from individual mentoring.	Feels that personal value comes from one's own talents and working collaboratively with others.
Sees network of supporters as power base and titles as a signal to others.	Develops trust across a network of constituencies; breaks down hierarchy.
Eager to speak first; feels his/her ideas are more important; often dominates or intimidates opponents.	Most likely to listen first; values others' input.
Uses personal power and intimidation to leverage what he/she wants.	Uses personal trust and respect to build bridges and do what's best for the "whole."
Accountability is more often about who is to blame.	Accountability is about making it safe to learn from mistakes.
Uses humor to control others.	Uses humor to lift others up and make it safe to learn from mistakes.

Meeting the Ethical Challenges of Followership

So far we have focused our attention on the ethical responsibilities of leaders. However, followers also make moral choices. Followers are charged with doing the work and implementing the decisions of leaders. They also have less status and power. Their special ethical challenges center around:[58]

Obligation. Followers are obligated to their leaders and their organizations, which provide them with paychecks, health insurance, friendships, training, meaningful work, and other benefits. Yet, they must decide how far those obligations extend. Followers should meet minimal responsibilities by showing up to work on time, faithfully carrying out job duties, and respecting company property. However, some organizations ask too much of their members, as in the case of technology firms that require their employees to work 70–80 hours a week or religious cults that demand total obedience. The challenge for followers lies in determining whether they are meeting their ethical obligations or giving too little or too much.

Obedience. Obeying orders and directives (even unpopular ones) is routine for followers. The challenge comes when they have to decide when to disobey. Obedience is essential if organizations are to function smoothly. Yet, time and time again, followers blindly follow authority with devastating consequences, as in the case of the mass genocide in Nazi Germany and more recently in Rwanda and Darfur. As business and government consultant Ira Chaleff notes, being a follower does not justify unethical behavior. He points to the Nuremberg trials held after World War II as proof that we must take ownership of our actions as followers. Convened to try Nazi war criminals, the international tribunal rejected the argument that German officials should be exempt from punishment because they were "following orders."

> The bottom line of followership is that we are responsible for our decision to continue or not to continue following a leader . . . we have the choice of supporting an anathema to our values or not. This is the Nuremberg trials principle. The fact that we are following orders absolves us from nothing.[59]

Cynicism. Cynicism is a common trait of many followers, and it is easy to see why. Followers enjoy less information, power, and privilege than leaders. They get left out of important decisions. At times, the actions of their superiors seem to defy logic. Far too many hard working, loyal employees have lost their jobs and pension plans at places like Enron, Arthur Andersen, United, and Delta. Nonetheless, cynicism acts like acid, lowering personal commitment and effort, destroying trust, and cutting off communication. The challenge is to maintain a level of healthy skepticism (which prevents exploitation) while avoiding unhealthy cynicism, which poisons the organizational atmosphere while eroding performance.

Dissent. Followers can't change policies, procedures, salary schedules, working conditions, and other factors themselves so they have to express their disagreement to those who can. To begin, they have to decide when to speak up and when to keep their objections to themselves. Followers who raise too many issues earn the "whiner" label. On the flip side, silence can be immoral, as in the case of the accountant who discovers that her company is lying to investors. Followers who decide to protest face the additional challenge of determining how to dissent, whom to contact with their concerns, how to respond to rejection, and when to go outside the organization with complaints.

Bad news. Delivering bad news is risky. Followers who tell their leaders what they don't want to hear can incur their wrath and retribution. The risk is greatest when the bearer of bad news is at fault. Not surprisingly, subordinates routinely keep negative information to themselves, even feedback about leader behaviors that could be keeping the group from achieving its goals.[60] Organizations suffer when followers cover up or hide bad news or try to blame others.

Serious deficiencies, like financial or product quality problems, may remain undetected and uncorrected. Members focus on defending themselves instead of on resolving issues. Leaders remain blind to their ineffective habits.

Understanding the components of moral action and major ethical perspectives can help us meet the moral demands of followership just as they can help us master the ethical challenges of leadership. However, to close out this chapter we'll look at two approaches—servant followership and courageous followership—that are specifically designed to help us act ethically in a follower role.

Servant Followership

Servant followership is the flip side of servant leadership. According to Robert Kelley, servant followership is more important than servant leadership because most people spend most of their time in follower roles and followers contribute more to organizational success.[61] Kelley defines a servant-follower as someone who wants to remain in a follower role rather than to seek a leadership position. This reduces the likelihood of destructive competition and conflict and keeps the focus on organizational goals.

Servant-followers demonstrate the exemplary behaviors described in chapter 2. They take initiative and think for themselves. In particular, they know how to "disagree agreeably" about policies and procedures by employing seven strategies. One, servant-followers are proactive, assuming that their leaders want the best outcomes. They provide leaders with the information they need to change course. Two, they gather their facts and try to educate their superiors. Three, servant-followers seek wise counsel from trusted advisors who understand the organization and its leadership. Four, they play by the rules, signaling that they want to be part of the community by using the system. Five, they speak the language of the organization, tying their arguments to the group's values and vision. Six, servant-followers prepare themselves to go to top leaders if lower-level managers ignore their concerns. Seven, they either enlist others to stand with them or make contingency plans (saving plans, other job offers) if they must stand alone.

Max DePree argues that servant-followers have responsibilities to their leaders just as servant leaders have responsibilities to their followers. Followers owe the following to their leaders and institutions:[62]

- understand the institution and its goals, customers, limitations, etc.
- take responsibility for reaching personal goals
- be loyal to the idea behind the organization even when not in agreement with all of the organization's goals and procedures
- resist fear of the new and unknown
- understand the value of others as members of the group and their contributions
- make a personal commitment to be open to change
- build constructive relationships
- ask a great many questions of leaders, including what they believe, how they have prepared themselves for leadership, and whether they can help followers reach their potential

Courageous Followership

Ira Chaleff believes that courage is the most important virtue for followers. He defines courage as accepting a higher level of risk.[63] It is risky, for instance, for a student to confront a professor about an unfair grading policy, for a vice president to oppose the pet project of the CEO, or for a congressional chief of staff to challenge the position of a member of the House or Senate. Exhibiting courage is easier if followers recognize that their ultimate allegiance is to the purpose and values of the organization, not to the leader. Chaleff outlines five dimensions of courageous followership.

The Courage to Assume Responsibility

Followers must be accountable both for themselves and for the organization as a whole. Taking responsibility utilizes many of the strategies outlined in our discussion of self-leadership in chapter 5. Courageous followers take stock of their skills and attitudes, seek feedback and personal growth, maintain a healthy private life, and care deeply about the organization's goals. They take initiative to change organizational culture by challenging rules and mind-sets and by improving processes.

The Courage to Serve

Courageous followers support their leaders through hard, often unglamorous, work. This labor takes a variety of forms, including:

- helping leaders conserve their energies for their most significant tasks
- organizing the flow of information from and to the leader
- controlling access to the leader
- defending the leader from unjust criticism
- relaying a leader's messages in an accurate, effective manner
- acting in the leader's name when appropriate
- shaping a leader's public image
- helping the creative leader focus on the most useful ideas generated
- presenting options during decision making
- encouraging the leader to develop a variety of relationships
- preparing for crises
- helping the leader and the group cope if the leader becomes ill
- mediating conflicts between leaders
- promoting performance reviews for leaders

The Courage to Challenge

Inappropriate behavior damages the relationship between leaders and followers and threatens the purpose of the organization. Leaders may break the law; scream at or use demeaning language with employees; display an arrogant attitude; engage in sexual harassment; abuse drugs and alcohol; and misuse funds. Courageous followers need to confront leaders acting in a destructive manner. In some situations, just asking questions about the wisdom of a policy decision is sufficient to bring about change. In more extreme cases, followers may need to disobey unethical orders. (For examples of leader/followers who took the initiative to influence their bosses, see box 11.8.)

Chaleff offers a number of suggestions for those who must stand up to their leaders. First, recognize that leaders are particularly prone to self-delusion because they have strong egos and their strategies have been successful in the past. The very traits that elevated them to positions of responsibility—decisiveness, independence, and attention to detail—may now be weaknesses in light of current organizational realities (see our discussion of organizational leadership in chapter 8). Next, confront destructive behavior when it first occurs—before it becomes a habit that undermines the organization and the leader. Defuse defensiveness by prefacing comments with statements of support and respect. Finally, aim negative feedback at a behavior or policy, not at

---

Box 11.8   Research Highlight
Courage in Action: Leading Up[64]

University of Pennsylvania leadership scholar Michael Useem uses the phrase "leading up" to describe leader/followers who take the initiative to influence their bosses as well as their subordinates. These individuals move beyond their assigned responsibilities, taking charge when they see a need and persuading their superiors to support their efforts. According to Useem, as organizations decentralize authority, modern managers must increasingly lead up as well as down. However, he cautions that while some organizations want followers to speak up, many do not. Leading up in these situations takes courage.

To come forward when an organization or superior does not encourage it can be both tremendously rewarding and extremely risky. If the upward leadership works, we can help transform incipient disaster into shining triumph. If handled poorly, such upward courage may prove little more than reckless abandon—a career-shortening or even career-ending move. Either way, though, we will have embraced a responsibility whose absence we deplore in others.[65]

In his book *Leading Up*, Useem describes a number of contemporary and historical leaders who either succeeded or failed in their attempts to influence their superiors. He then draws implications from their experiences. Some of his examples of leading up (or failing to lead up) include:

- Charles Schwab president David Pottruck. Through careful planning and reasoning, he convinced the firm's founder to move his brokerage onto the Internet.

- Civil War generals Joseph Johnson, George McClellan, and Robert E. Lee. Johnson and McClellan were replaced because they failed to keep their superiors—Jefferson Davis and Abraham Lincoln—informed. Lee, on the other hand, succeeded in keeping his post because he regularly communicated with Davis and treated him with respect.

- United Nations peacekeeper Romero Dallaire. Dallaire tried to convince his superiors to intervene in the 1994 genocide in Rwanda but failed because he didn't effectively communicate the gravity of the situation. Even without the permission of the UN secretary general, he could have taken additional steps to curb the bloodshed.

- CEOs Robert Ayling of British Airways, Eckerd Pfeiffer of Compaq computer, and Thomas Wynan of CBS. All three lost their jobs when they forgot that they worked for their boards of directors and kept their superiors in the dark about profits and business strategies.

- Old Testament patriarchs Abraham, Moses, and Samuel. These prophets were able to intercede with God, persuading the Supreme Being to modify His decrees to better serve His chosen people.

the person. Be specific about what the problem behavior is, its negative consequences, and the potential long-term impact if it continues.

The Courage to Participate in Transformation

Negative behavior, when unchecked, often results in a leader's destruction. Yet overcoming ingrained habits and communication patterns is a long, difficult process. Leaders may deny the need to change, or they may attempt to justify their behavior. They may claim that whatever they do for themselves (embezzling, enriching themselves at the expense of stockholders, etc.) ultimately benefits the organization. To succeed in modifying their behavior patterns, leaders must admit they have a problem and acknowledge that they should change. They need to take personal responsibility and visualize the outcomes of the transformation—better health, more productive employees, higher self-esteem, restored relationships. Followers can aid in the process of transformation by: drawing attention to what needs to be changed; providing honest feedback; suggesting resources; creating a supportive environment; modeling openness to change and empathy; and providing positive reinforcement for positive new behaviors.

The Courage to Leave

When leaders are unwilling to change, courageous followers may take principled action by resigning from the organization. Departure is justified when the leader's behaviors clash with the leader's self-proclaimed values or the values of the group, or when the leader degrades or endangers others. Sometimes leaving is not enough. In the event of serious ethical violations, the misbehavior of the leader must be brought to the attention of the public by going to the authorities or the press. Such a response would be justified when police commanders order the torture of suspects, corporate executives ask employees to ignore serious safety problems, or the founders of activist groups call for acts that endanger the lives of citizens. Those who decide to leave can reduce the risks by setting contingency funds aside, by having written references on file should the need to change jobs arise, by developing good relations with the media in case they need to go public, and by building support groups.

> The brave carve out their own fortune.
>
> —Cervantes

CHAPTER TAKEAWAYS

- Standards of moral judgment are critical to the practice of leadership because unethical leaders can do significant damage to groups, organizations, and societies.
- When you take on the role of leader, you take on ethical challenges in addition to a set of tasks and expectations. The moral demands of the leadership role include: (1) issues related to truthfulness and the release and collection of information; (2) the extent of responsibility for the

actions of followers; (3) use of power; (4) accumulation of social and material rewards; (5) conflicting and broken loyalties; and (6) inconsistent treatment of subordinates and outsiders. How you respond to these challenges will determine if you cast light or shadow over the lives of your followers.

- Four processes or components lead to ethical behavior: moral sensitivity, moral judgment, moral motivation, and moral action.

- Moral sensitivity (recognition) is the identification of the existence of moral problems. This component involves acknowledging that our behavior impacts others, identifying possible courses of action, and determining the consequences of each possible strategy. You can build your moral sensitivity through: listening to others and working on perspective-taking skills; including moral considerations in decision-making processes; and using moral terminology when discussing problems.

- Moral judgment is deciding which course of action is best. The highest form of ethical reasoning employs widely held moral standards. You can improve your moral judgment by focusing on ethics during your college education, basing your choices on ethical principles, and being alert to the possibility of faulty reasoning.

- Moral motivation refers to following through on ethical choices, which requires putting moral values ahead of competing values. Rewards and positive emotions increase the likelihood of ethical follow through. Boost the moral motivation of your organization by creating an ethically rewarding environment. Boost your personal moral motivation by regulating your emotions and setting aside destructive feelings for more constructive ones.

- Moral character (implementation) is the action stage of the ethical behavior model. Opposition, fatigue, distractions, and other obstacles must be overcome through persistence. Competence—knowing whom to influence and how—is also essential to successful implementation. You are more likely to put your decisions into action if you assess your personal history, believe that you can make a difference, master the context, and build your communication competence.

- Kant's categorical imperative argues that leaders ought to do what is morally right no matter what the consequences (without exception). Such behaviors as exaggeration, lying, stealing, and murder are always wrong because we wouldn't want others to engage in them. Respect for people is an important corollary to Kant's imperative. Never treat followers as a means to an end. They have a right to choose for themselves.

- The premise of utilitarianism is that ethical choices should be based on their consequences. The best decisions are those that generate the most advantages as compared to disadvantages and that benefit the greatest number of people.

- Virtue ethics highlights the role of the person making ethical choices. Leaders with high moral character (who display virtues such as courage, integrity, justice, wisdom, and generosity) are more likely to behave in an ethical manner. Authenticity is a particularly important character trait for leaders. Authentic leaders demonstrate self-awareness and act in ways that are consistent with their self-understanding.

• Altruism makes concern for others the ultimate standard. Altruistic behavior is critical for leaders who must pursue group goals rather than selfish interests. Many effective leadership practices have an altruistic component. To be an effective leader, you will need to promote collective achievements while empowering followers and engaging in self-sacrificing behavior.

• Servant leaders put the needs of followers before their own needs. Five principles serve as the foundation of servant leadership: (1) concern for people; (2) stewardship (holding your position and organization in trust for followers and society); (3) equity or justice created by distributing rewards fairly and treating your followers as partners; (4) indebtedness—the recognition that leaders and followers "owe" each other certain responsibilities; and (5) self-understanding based on character.

• The ethical challenges of followership involve obligation, obedience, cynicism, dissent, and communicating bad news.

• Servant-followers want to remain followers rather than compete for leadership positions. In so doing, they reduce destructive conflict and build trust. They are highly engaged, independent thinkers who know how to "disagree agreeably" with their leaders.

• Courage (accepting a higher level of risk) is critical for those in the follower position. As a follower you must: take responsibility for yourself and the organization; serve your leaders through hard work; challenge leaders when they engage in destructive behaviors; help leaders overcome destructive patterns and habits; and leave when a leader's behaviors clash with important values or when the leader degrades or endangers others.

APPLICATION EXERCISES

1. Look for examples of unethical leadership behavior in the media and classify them according to the six ethical challenges. Which challenge(s) did the leader fail to meet? What shadows did she/he cast? Do you note any patterns? Are there additional ethical dilemmas unique to leadership beyond those discussed in the chapter?

2. Think of an ethical dilemma you have faced and analyze your response based on Rest's four-component model. Why did you identify this problem as an ethical issue? What considerations played a part in your decision about what to do? What values impacted your motivation to implement your choice? Did you follow through on your decision and take the action you had determined to be appropriate? Why or why not? Write up your analysis in a 4–5 page paper.

3. Form a small group and analyze the Oreck case on p. 341 using each of the major ethical perspectives described in the chapter. Record your conclusions. Did you reach different solutions based on the perspective you used? Do some perspectives apply better than others? What is

your overall conclusion after using all the theories? Did employing a variety of perspectives improve your final solution?

4. What is the most important virtue for leaders? Defend your choice.

5. Use the chart of defensive and proactive strategies for creating an ethical environment in box 11.3 to evaluate your organization. Does your organization have a positive moral climate? Why or why not?

6. Select a segment from the television show *60 Minutes* and analyze it from a virtue ethics perspective. Choose a story that raises ethical issues about leadership or followership (an employee who blows the whistle on an unethical organization, a world leader who demonstrates courage). What virtues do the subjects in the story exhibit or fail to exhibit? How would you evaluate their ethical character? What ethical lessons can we learn about leadership and followership from this story? Write up your analysis.

7. Do you agree with the list of universal values on p. 366? Are there any values that you would add to the list? Subtract? Should the search for ethical common ground be abandoned? Why or why not? Present your conclusions to other class members.

8. Conduct a class debate concerning whether or not leaders should act as "servants" to their followers. As an alternative, debate whether altruism is part of human nature.

9. Interview someone you would consider to be a servant-follower to determine how this individual manages the moral demands of followership. Write up your findings.

10. Practice confronting leaders by role playing the following scenarios in class:

   • You have been at your new job for six months and really enjoy it. However, you are becoming increasingly uncomfortable with the way that your supervisor touches you. At first he gave you brief pats on the shoulder and back. Now his hand lingers for 2–3 seconds. You are concerned that he will become even more intimate, so you set up an appointment to talk about his behavior.

   • Your supervisor at the ad agency is a "hard charger" who has dramatically increased billings for new clients. Unfortunately, this highly competent and confident leader demeans employees who don't meet her high standards. In the most recent incident, she screamed obscenities at an account executive during a staff meeting. You decide to confront her in private.

   • You admire your supervisor who is kind and generous with all employees. However, she can't seem to stay focused on important tasks. As a result, you get stuck with a lot of last minute details that aren't in your job description. You worry that your supervisor and your department will suffer if she doesn't start finishing projects on time and paying attention to the overall direction of your group. Your weekly appointment with your supervisor is about to begin.

- You are assistant director at a nonprofit organization that serves the developmentally disabled. The director founded the agency 25 years ago. He recently suffered a series of strokes and cannot carry out many of his responsibilities, including raising money and setting the budget. He refuses to step down or even to take a temporary leave. You decide to discuss his future with him.

CULTURAL CONNECTIONS:
IDENTIFYING A GLOBAL CODE OF ETHICS[66]

Is there such a thing as a global code of ethics—a set of values that all cultures can agree on? According to Rushworth Kidder of the Global Ethics Foundation, the answer to this question is a resounding "yes." He argues that there are common ethical standards that cross political, social, and cultural boundaries. Further, identifying these shared values is more important than ever before due to "worldshrink" and "technobulge." The world is becoming increasingly interdependent due to rapid transportation, the mass media, and international commerce. While the world is shrinking, technology is expanding. Technological progress generates new ethical dilemmas with far-reaching consequences. Development of the atomic bomb raised the specter of global holocaust for the first time in human history. Genetic mapping and weather control raise additional ethical issues for contemporary leaders and ethicists. Kidder believes that finding moral common ground is the way to ensure global survival. Adhering to shared values can bind the international community together and enable diverse cultures to solve world problems jointly.

To identify universal values, Kidder interviewed two dozen "ethical thought leaders" from around the world. These men and women included officials from the United Nations, leaders from the United States and New Zealand, former heads of state from Costa Rica and Lebanon, a Buddhist monk and a Catholic priest, and writers from Sweden, Australia, and England. Each of the interviews began with this question: "If you could create a global code of ethics, what would be on it?" Once the data was collected, Kidder and his colleagues looked for common threads in the tapes and transcripts. What they found were eight core values:

- love (compassion that transcends cultural and political differences)
- truthfulness (honesty, keeping promises, not keeping secrets)
- fairness (even-handedness, fair play, a concern for justice and equality)
- freedom (right to express ideas and to act on individual conscience)
- unity (putting emphasis on community, solidarity, cooperation)
- tolerance (respect for the dignity, rights, and ideas of others)
- responsibility (for oneself, others, future generations)
- respect for life (not killing)

The researchers don't claim to have isolated *the* global code of ethics, but they believe that their findings prove that world leaders can find an ethical common ground. The fact that the list contains few surprises is proof that these values are widely shared. According to Kidder:

This eight-point set of values bears striking resemblance to lists of values derived by participants in numerous ethics seminars conducted recently around the United States by the staff at the Institute for Global Ethics. This is not, in other words, an off-the-wall, unique, bizarre list. It may even strike us as familiar, ordinary, and unsurprising. That's a comforting fact. Codes of ethics, to be practicable, need to have behind them broad consensus. The originality of the list matters less than its consistency and universality.[67]

SPOTLIGHT ON TECHNOLOGY

The Internet has changed the way that humans access information. For many, one of the first actions taken to get the latest news or stock quotes, check the weather forecast, or conduct research is to search the World Wide Web. Among the most poplar methods for accessing such data is the search engine Google. Indeed, the Google search engine is so widely used that the company name has morphed into a verb (to google), which means to search for information on the Internet. Many assume that access to information is the same around the globe. This is not the case. In 2006 Google set up a site in China (Google.cn) that was heavily censored by the Chinese government. In exchange for agreeing to censor sensitive Web sites on topics such as independence for Taiwan and the 1989 Tiananmen Square massacre, Google was granted wider access to the burgeoning Chinese market and its more than 100 million Internet search users.

The decision to allow the Chinese government to dictate the content of Web searches on Google.cn was a difficult one for company officials. The company motto is "don't be evil," and senior Google leaders were concerned about their alliance with the Chinese government. When Google censors results in China, it posts notifications alerting users that some content has been removed to comply with local laws. The company provides similar alerts in Germany and France when, to conform to national laws, it censors results to remove references to Nazi Web sites. Even the U.S. version of Google is censored to limit access to sites containing child pornography. Limitations such as these, which deny access to hateful, menacing, and morally questionable Web sites, have not created concern. However, the Chinese censorship limitations that deny Google users in China access to basic information have been controversial. Sergey Brin, one of the cofounders of Google, admitted in 2007 that, "on a business level the decision to censor [in China] was a net negative."[68] As Internet access expands into other global markets and as governments continue to debate how much information should be available via the World Wide Web, ethical issues will continue to arise as to how much access should be granted to those who search on the Internet.

LEADERSHIP ON THE BIG SCREEN:
THE LORD OF THE RINGS: THE RETURN OF THE KING

Starring: Elijah Wood, Ian McKellen, Liv Tyler, Viggo Mortensen, Cate Blanchett

Rating: PG 13 for violence and frightening special effects

Synopsis: Final installment of the film series based on J. R. R. Tolkien's popular *Lord of the Rings* fantasy trilogy. Winner of 11 Academy Awards, including best picture. The forces of good (humans, dwarves, elves) fight the forces of evil (orcs, trolls, dark spirits) who serve Lord Sauron. Sauron needs a powerful ring, carried by Hobbit Frodo Baggins, in order to complete his conquest of Middle Earth. As the final battle rages, Frodo (played by Wood) continues his quest to destroy the ring in the fires of Mount Doom where it was created. It takes the heroic efforts of Frodo, as well as his friends and their allies, to save Middle Earth and to restore the rightful king to his throne. Good triumphs because leaders and followers demonstrate such qualities as courage, loyalty, self-sacrifice, love, friendship, hope, and persistence.

Chapter Links: moral motivation and action, moral duty, virtue ethics, servant leadership, courageous followership

twelve

Leader and Leadership Development

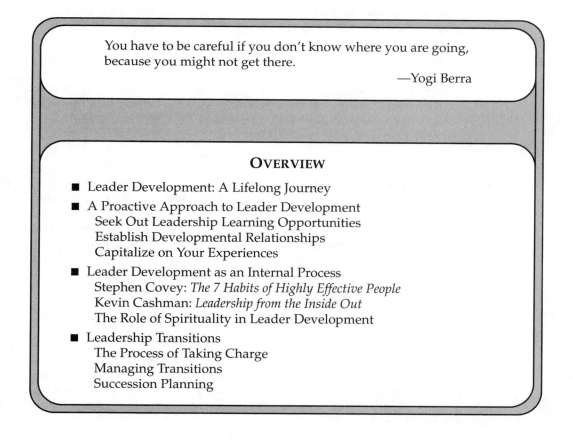

You have to be careful if you don't know where you are going, because you might not get there.

—Yogi Berra

OVERVIEW

- Leader Development: A Lifelong Journey
- A Proactive Approach to Leader Development
  Seek Out Leadership Learning Opportunities
  Establish Developmental Relationships
  Capitalize on Your Experiences
- Leader Development as an Internal Process
  Stephen Covey: *The 7 Habits of Highly Effective People*
  Kevin Cashman: *Leadership from the Inside Out*
  The Role of Spirituality in Leader Development
- Leadership Transitions
  The Process of Taking Charge
  Managing Transitions
  Succession Planning

Leader Development: A Lifelong Journey

Every year growing numbers of adult learners over the age of 25 return to college classrooms to complete their undergraduate and graduate degrees and to upgrade their job skills. Approximately one-quarter of students enrolled at U.S. colleges and universities are age 30 or older.[1] Adult learners (you may be one of them) believe in lifelong learning. We do, too. Developing leadership communication skills is an ongoing process or journey, not a single event. Like other journeys, leader development unfolds step by step. How far we go and how much we get out of the trip depends on us. We need to prepare for the journey and be open to new experiences. The moment we think we have "arrived" as leaders, our progress stops.

Ellen Van Velsor and Cynthia McCauley of the Center for Creative Leadership define the goal of the leader development journey as "the expansion of a person's capacity to be effective in leadership roles and processes."[2] Two elements are central to this definition:

1. Leadership can be learned. Individuals can expand their leadership capacities at any age. People do learn, grow, and change.

2. Leader development helps to make a person effective in a variety of formal and informal leadership roles. While developing leader abilities improves leadership effectiveness among those who serve in formal leadership roles such as supervisors, managers, and project leaders, it can be equally as important in developing competencies for those who play informal leadership roles in their campus, community, workplace, or religious organization.

Van Velsor and her colleagues make a distinction between *leader development* and *leadership development*.[3] Leader development promotes personal growth, helping individuals develop their abilities to manage themselves, to work effectively with others, and to ensure that the work gets done. Leadership development promotes organizational growth, helping the group as a whole develop the leaders it needs to carry out such tasks as securing the commitment of members and setting direction. In keeping with this distinction, we have titled this chapter "Leader and Leadership Development." Our primary focus will be on how you can continue your development as a leader. However, we'll also look at how organizations promote their collective leadership capacity.

A Proactive Approach to Leader Development

Satisfying journeys don't generally happen by accident. If you want to become an effective leader, you will need to be proactive, taking responsibility for your development. This proactive approach includes an ongoing commitment to leadership learning, building developmental relationships, and taking advantage of developmental experiences.

Seek Out Leadership Learning Opportunities

There is no shortage of opportunities to learn about leadership. As a matter of fact, it would be hard to avoid hearing about leaders. We track their successes and failures in the newspaper, read about them in history books, and follow them at school and on the job. Some of the strategies and behaviors we witness are excellent models for our own attempts to lead. Unfortunately, we sometimes learn very little from the examples of other leaders because we merely observe them without understanding the reasons behind their successes and failures.

One way to become a more perceptive student of leadership is to keep current with leadership research. The explosion of leadership knowledge in recent years demonstrates why it is so important to view leadership learning as an ongoing process. A search on Amazon.com in 2008 yielded over 8,200 books related to leadership communication, while the word leadership produced over 220,000 results!

> Leadership and learning are indispensable to one another.
> —John F. Kennedy

According to one estimate, there are approximately 1,000 leader development programs offered at institutions of higher education in the United States, ranging from small liberal arts colleges to major state schools and Ivy League universities.[4] In addition, leadership topics are integrated into the curriculum in many courses. Over three-quarters of the communication departments we surveyed include material on leadership in at least one course.[5] A rapidly increasing number of colleges and universities are offering minors, majors, and even graduate degrees in leadership studies.

Within work organizations, formal training programs are widely used to improve leadership effectiveness. Corporations around the globe have recognized that leadership skills can be developed. Companies like Motorola, Southwest Airlines, Hewlett-Packard, Xerox, American Express, and PepsiCo, among others, spend millions of dollars each year on training. Much of this training is devoted to improving leadership effectiveness. Over $6 billion is spent each year on programs specifically devoted to developing corporate leaders.[6]

Jay Conger and Beth Benjamin surveyed a dozen organizations that offer innovative in-house training programs and identified three approaches to leadership development.[7] Chances are you'll participate in one or more of the following types of programs during your career.

1. *Individual preparation.* Historically, training programs have focused on developing the individual leader in the belief that improving a leader's effectiveness will improve the organization as a whole. *Conceptual awareness* workshops develop cognitive understanding. Trainers use case studies, lecture, and discussion to present leadership models or to introduce participants to the differences between leadership and management. *Feedback sessions* provide information to participants about leadership behaviors. Armed with this knowledge, they can address their weaknesses and build on their strengths. Feedback comes from trainers who observe in-class exercises, from fellow trainees, and from self-assessment instruments like those found in each chapter of this text.

Skills-based training helps leaders master such skills as public speaking, listening, and conflict management through modeling and hands-on practice. *Personal growth* programs put leaders into challenging situations that encourage reflection about working relationships and personal priorities while building confidence. Completing a ropes course, white-water rafting, rappelling, and other strenuous activities are designed to get trainees thinking about teamwork, risk taking, creativity, and goal setting in hopes that they will take these insights back to their workplaces and homes.

2. *Socializing company vision and values.* Transmitting a group's culture, as we saw in chapter 8, is one of the most important responsibilities of organizational leaders. In recognition of this fact, Federal Express, Intel, Nordstrom, and the U.S. Army use leadership training as a socialization tool. Their training programs highlight corporate vision and values, encourage commitment to organizational priorities, develop a shared interpretation of the group's culture, and provide a forum for dialogue between new and established leaders.

3. *Strategic leadership initiatives.* In this approach, participants learn how to lead change while working toward actual corporate objectives. Strategic programs involve leaders at every level of the organization, and concepts and knowledge covered in training sessions relate directly to the problem at hand. Often teams are assigned to conduct research and then report their findings and recommendations in presentations to management. At General Electric, for example, learning groups carry out consulting projects for business units. Teams have assessed the overall strategy of the European plastics division and helped the locomotive division identify markets for leasing engines.[8]

The action learning focus of the strategic initiatives approach has become the centerpiece of many corporate leadership programs.[9] Action learning benefits both the individual and the organization. Adults learn best when they immediately apply concepts to the problems they face at work, while companies see visible results from these initiatives. Effective action learning programs involve: (1) careful selection of projects—significant ones that build the skills of individuals; (2) clearly defined objectives and results; (3) periodic opportunities for individuals and groups to discuss and reflect on what they are learning about the project and their personal strengths and weaknesses; (4) sponsorship, participation, and review by top management; and (5) expert facilitation and coaching, generally by outside consultants. Unfortunately, many action learning formats fail to live up to their potential. Too often they require just one learning experience, not repeated experiences that reinforce learning. Little opportunity is provided for reflection, and participants don't get to implement their recommendations.[10]

Establish Developmental Relationships

Establishing connections with those who can help you achieve your goals will greatly increase your chances of emerging as a leader in an organizational context. Some of these supportive relationships can be established with peers.[11]

Information peers are casual acquaintances who provide useful information. *Collegial peers* help with career strategies and provide job-related feedback as well as friendship. *Special peers* act like best friends—giving confirmation, emotional support, and personal feedback. However, the most beneficial relationships will pair you with senior leaders. An established leader can help you by serving as an example that you can emulate from a distance or by taking an active role in your development through acting as your mentor.[12]

The term "mentor" originated from the character Mentor who was the friend of the ancient Greek king Ulysses in Homer's *Odyssey.* He watched the king's son while Ulysses was away, acting as a personal and professional counselor and guide. Modern mentors perform many of the functions of the original. Mentoring expert Kathleen Kram divides mentor functions into two types: career and psychosocial.[13] Career functions are aspects of the relationship that help protégés in their career advancement. Psychosocial functions build the sense of competence and self-worth of both mentors and protégés.

It is important to note that individuals can serve in a mentor role even if they carry out only one set of functions. Some men, for example, find it hard to provide emotional support to protégés but are eager to offer career advice.[14] The shifting needs of protégés will also have an impact on the functions that mentors perform. An inexperienced protégé may need more reassurance; a long-time protégé may want more advice about how to achieve career goals.[15] With this in mind, here is a brief description of the specific functions that fall into each category.

Career Functions

- *Sponsorship.* Mentors fight for their protégés by standing up for them in meetings, putting their names in for promotions, and so forth. Protégés also gain power and more chances for advancement through their association with powerful mentors.

- *Coaching.* Mentors help protégés learn the ins and outs of the organization, including how decisions are made, what the key values are, and who holds power. Mentors have been totally immersed in the corporate culture and can help acclimate the protégé. In addition, they make specific suggestions about how to get the work done, give advice about how to achieve career goals, and supply valuable feedback about job performance.

- *Protection.* Mentors shield their protégés when things aren't going well. They take the blame for slow progress on projects, talk to senior officials when their mentees aren't ready to do so, and step in when their junior partners aren't up to the task.

- *Challenging assignments.* As we noted in our discussion of the Pygmalion Effect in chapter 8, the type of assignments that a new manager receives can determine whether that person becomes a low or a high performer. Low expectations communicated through unchallenging or overly demanding assignments can generate a negative performance cycle. Effective mentors set challenging yet realistic goals and work with protégés to help them achieve their objectives. Protégés learn key skills and develop a sense of accomplishment as they master challenges.

Psychosocial Functions

- *Role modeling.* Mentors are role models who demonstrate leadership skills. During their apprenticeships, protégés learn how to manage conflict, build teams, gather information, and make ethical choices by observing the behavior of their senior colleagues.

- *Acceptance-and-confirmation.* Positive regard develops in a healthy mentor/mentee relationship. Each side enjoys the feeling of respect and encouragement that comes from interacting with the other party. When a protégé feels accepted and affirmed, she or he is more willing to take risks and to explore new behaviors.

- *Counseling.* Mentors often become sounding boards for their protégés, helping them work through conflicts that detract from work performance. Three issues are particularly important for those just starting out in a career: (1) how to develop job competence and satisfaction, (2) how to relate to the organization without compromising values and individuality, and (3) how to balance work and family responsibilities.

- *Friendship.* In many successful mentor/protégé partnerships, the parties become friends who develop a mutual liking for one another and engage in informal interaction. The emergence of this function signals that the protégé has become more of a peer than a subordinate. Even when the original relationship ends because of a promotion, job transfer, or some other factor, the friendship often remains.

> Make yourself necessary to someone.
> —Ralph Waldo Emerson

Based on what mentors can do for their protégés, it's not surprising that those who have organizational sponsors are generally more successful. They typically earn higher salaries, get promoted more often, enjoy greater recognition, and experience higher job satisfaction.[16] These advantages carry over into the university setting. Instructors who receive mentoring help have higher rank and pay, are more likely to be tenured, and feel more committed to their institutions.[17] Undergraduates who receive individual attention from a faculty member generally do better in school.[18]

Protégés aren't the only ones to profit from the establishment of mentor/protégé partnerships. The organization as a whole benefits because those who have been successfully mentored are more productive and more committed to the institution. Mentors benefit from the help they get with tasks as well as from the affirmation, confirmation, and friendship provided by protégés. They enjoy passing on their values and insights and seeing their protégés develop.

While there are a great many advantages to mentoring, there are potential difficulties as well. Linda Phillips-Jones identified the common problems and possible solutions described below after interviewing mentors and protégés at companies around the United States.[19]

Problem	Solution
Mentor/protégé makes excessive demands on the time and energy of the other person.	Decide in advance how much time you can commit and set limits. Continually monitor time and energy commitments. If one party or the other appears undercommitted, terminate the relationship.
Inappropriate choice of mentor or protégé; i.e., someone who can't help you reach your goals or an individual who might endanger your position in the organization.	Don't rush into a binding relationship; choose carefully. Be willing to break off the arrangement if necessary.
Unrealistic expectations for mentors or protégés; i.e., giving too much responsibility to a protégé too soon.	Check to see if you're expecting perfection from the other person. List the other party's strengths and weaknesses and lower expectations when necessary. Monitor verbal and non-verbal messages for signs of tension.
Expectations of protégé failure.	Don't mentor if you have serious doubts about the other individual.
Protégé's feelings of inferiority.	Instead of judging yourself by a mentor's accomplishments, set personal goals and determine how well you've reached those objectives.
Unfair manipulation by a mentor or protégé.	Double-check to make sure you really are being treated unfairly. Ask yourself if you have contributed to the problem by hiding your needs or volunteering for extra work. Discuss the issues and break off the relationship if they can't be resolved.
Jealousy from mentors or protégés about the success of the other party.	Try to figure out why you feel jealous or what you're doing that might generate these emotions. Talk about these feelings with your partner.
Jealousy from others.	If the envious individuals are important to you, work together with your partner to determine what might be provoking jealous responses. Make sure the relationship really hasn't become a threat to spouses, business partners, coworkers, and others.
Overdependence on mentors or protégés.	Expect the most dependence at the beginning of the relationship and greater independence as the relationship matures. Maintain a network of other relationships and become more self-reliant (learn to judge your own work, for example).
Unwanted romance and sexual involvement.	Take steps to reduce contact (only meet at work, for instance) and back away to analyze romantic feelings if they develop. Communicate about these feelings and end the relationship if necessary.

Ernst & Young, Pulte Homes, and a number of other organizations sponsor mentorship programs to promote the benefits of mentoring while, at the same time, they try to reduce the risks associated with the mentor/protégé relationship. Well-designed programs generally include the following elements:[20]

- criteria and process for selecting both protégés and mentors
- tools for diagnosing the needs of protégés
- strategies for matching protégés with mentors
- formal, negotiated agreements between mentors and protégés
- a coordinator who trains participants, maintains the program, and monitors the mentor/protégé pairs
- periodic evaluation to make necessary adjustments and to determine outcomes for the protégés, mentors, and organization

Joining an organization that has a mentoring program will simplify your search for a mentor. However, most organizations do not have systematic mentoring efforts. In these cases, you'll need to identify the person or persons who might aid in your leadership development. This takes more effort on your part, but research suggests that informal mentor/protégé relationships are generally more productive than those established through formal mentoring programs. Unofficial partnerships last longer and are more supportive than those where protégés are assigned to mentors.[21] Linda Phillips-Jones recommends the following steps when searching for a mentor.[22]

1. *Identify what (not whom) you need.* Before you zero in on people who can help, think first about the kind of help you need. Do you need to sharpen your public speaking or management skills? Polish your writing? Learn how to close sales deals? Developing a list of needs will help you know what kind of assistance to ask for, and some of the items on the list might be satisfied through reading, training sessions, and other resources.

2. *Evaluate yourself as a prospective protégé.* Consider how prepared you are to be mentored. Not everyone is ready for such a relationship. If you're holding back, try to determine why. It may be that you find it hard to ask for help.

3. *Identify mentor candidates.* Go back to the list you generated in step one and think of individuals who can provide the help you seek. Some important questions to consider are: Who are the most influential people I know? Who can help me or would like some help? Where are they in their careers? Have they mentored before and with what results? What's their current job situation?

4. *Prepare for the obstacles.* Before you approach anyone, do the same kind of preparation you would do for a job interview. Find out about this person's job responsibilities and special interests and talk to others who know this candidate. Anticipate possible questions and concerns.

5. *Approach possible mentors.* Indirect tactics for contacting a mentor candidate include asking for help from a mutual acquaintance and letting him or her see you in action on committees and in other settings. The direct approach is to set up an appointment and spell out exactly what you desire from that individual.

In recent years, more and more leaders are turning to *formal coaches* to supplement or even to substitute for mentor relationships.[23] Mentors and peers can act as informal coaches, but formal coaches are outside experts hired to work one on one with leaders. Typically, a coaching program has three phases. In the preprogram phase, the coach meets with the coachee to determine his/her level of readiness and to design a development plan. A coachee might want help in leading a corporate turnaround, learning to delegate more effectively, or becoming more accessible to followers. The plan will include details on the length of the coaching relationship; how the pair will interact (online, in person) and how often; the release of information; and assessment tools. During the program implementation stage, the coach and coachee establish their relationship, collect and review data on the coachee's performance, and then construct and implement a personal learning agenda with goals, action steps, and measurable outcomes. In the postprogram phase, the participants review and evaluate the coachee's performance and the coach's input.

Capitalize on Your Experiences

Any setting where you can master your communication skills (whether at home, at work, or at school) is preparation for leadership. The most useful experiences, though, are those that put you in the leader role. Since leadership experience is so vital, seek out chances to act as a leader. Volunteer to coordinate a campus or community activity, be a crew manager, teach a skill to a group, or offer to serve in any capacity to further your leadership skills. What you learn from your successes—and perhaps more importantly, from your failures—is preparation for future leadership assignments.

> Experience is not what happens to a man [woman]. It is what a man [woman] does with what happens to him [her].
>
> Aldous Huxley

Certain kinds of experiences are extremely helpful in developing leadership abilities. Patricia Ohlott, a research associate at the Center for Creative Leadership, calls these types of experiences developmental job assignments.[24] The key characteristic in all developmental job assignments is challenge. These ventures involve risk and require people to leave their comfort zones. Ohlott identifies five broad types of developmental job opportunities.

- *Job transitions.* Moving from one position to another puts people in new situations where job responsibilities are often unfamiliar. Transitions require people to alter their routines and to find new ways to frame and to solve problems. The greater the change in job function, the more opportunity for leadership development.

- *Creating change.* Job experiences that require a person to create change challenge individuals to find new ways to face ambiguous circumstances. A leader may be asked to develop a new product or process, reorganize a work unit, or develop a strategy for dealing with a crisis.

Such situations provide fertile experiences for leaders to develop and enrich leadership skills.

- *High levels of responsibility.* Leadership assignments with high levels of responsibility provide potent learning opportunities. These jobs generally involve complex, strategic issues that have a significant impact on an organization. Although these assignments may be stressful, they offer an opportunity for greater visibility and can be a great boon to a leader's self-confidence.

- *Managing boundaries.* Most leaders are accustomed to managing downward. When they have to work with peers, clients, or others with whom they do not have direct authority, they must learn to work collaboratively. Leaders in these assignments need to develop skills in relationship building, problem solving, negotiation, and conflict resolution.

- *Dealing with diversity.* As noted in chapter 10, leaders must learn to work with and to manage those who have significantly different experiences, backgrounds, values, and needs. This requires them to understand diverse perspectives and to manage differences. (See box 12.1 for examples of each of the developmental job assignments.)

Another type of developmental experience is **hardship.** Hardships differ from the other developmental opportunities because people encounter them with little or no warning. Popular author and speaker John Maxwell argues that the difference between average and exceptional leaders lies in their response to adversity and failure.[25] Typical leaders "fail backward" by blaming others, repeating their errors, setting unrealistically high expectations, internalizing their disappointments, and quitting. Successful leaders "fail forward" by taking responsibility for their errors and learning from them, maintaining a positive attitude, taking on new risks, and persevering. To learn from adversity, Maxwell suggests that you ask yourself the following questions every time you encounter failures or mistakes.

What caused the failure: the situation, someone else, or myself? You must identify what went wrong before you can put it right. Don't confuse failure with being a failure. Instead, view what happened as a learning experience and start by locating the source of the problem.

Was this truly a failure, or did I just fall short? Some "failures" are really attempts to meet unrealistic expectations (generally those we put on ourselves). Falling short of an unrealistic goal is not a failure.

What successes are contained in the failure? Failures often contain the keys to future success. For example, Kellogg's Corn Flakes is the result of accidentally leaving boiled corn in a baking pan overnight, and Ivory soap floats because excess air was pumped into a batch when the mixer was left on too long.[26]

What can I learn from what happened? Failure can teach us more than success. When we succeed, we generally use the same approach again. When we fail, we look for different, better ways to proceed.

Am I grateful for the experience? Gratitude can be the key to a teachable mindset. If nothing else, falling short teaches us how to live with disappointments.

How can I turn this into a success? Mistakes teach us how to avoid future miscues and (as we saw above) can lead to important discoveries. Bernie Marcus provides one example of the principle of turning failure into success. After being fired from the Handy Dan hardware chain, Marcus and a partner opened their own home improvement store called The Home Depot. The Home Depot now generates approximately $80 billion in sales annually.

Box 12.1

Developmental Challenges and Examples of Assignments Where They May Be Found[27]

Development Component	Examples of Assignments
Job transitions	Being the inexperienced member of a project team Taking a temporary assignment in another function Moving to a general management job Managing a group or discipline you know little about Moving from a line job to a corporate staff role Making a lateral move to another department
Creating change	Launching a new product, project, or system Serving on a reengineering team Facilitating the development of a new vision or mission statement Dealing with a business crisis Handling a workforce reduction Hiring new staff Breaking ground on a new operation Reorganizing a unit Resolving subordinate performance problems Supervising the liquidation of products or equipment
High levels of responsibility	Managing a corporate assignment with tight deadlines Representing the organization to the media or influential outsiders Managing across geographic locations Assuming additional responsibilities following a downsizing Taking on a colleague's responsibilities during his or her absence
Managing boundaries	Presenting a proposal to top management Performing a corporate staff job Serving on a cross-functional team Managing an internal project such as a company event or office renovation Working on a project with a community or social organization
Dealing with diversity	Negotiating with a union Managing a vendor relationship Taking an assignment in another country Managing a workgroup made up of people with racial, ethnic, or religious backgrounds different from your own Managing a group of employees from a different generation who seem to be motivated in different ways than you are Training in your organization's diversity program Leading an organizational effort to revise policies about harassment; or the development of the skills of people of different genders, races, sexual orientations, and so on Managing a group that consists largely of expatriates

Who can help me with this issue? Learning from adversity is easier with the help of mentors, families, peers, and others. The best advice comes from those who have successfully dealt with their own failures.

Where do I go from here? You can't claim to have learned from an experience unless it leads to a change in behavior.

Research suggests that there are five primary types of hardship events.[28]

- *Business mistakes and failures.* These take the form of lost advertising clients, disgruntled employees, failed mergers, discontinued product lines, bankruptcies, and other organizational mishaps. They offer excellent opportunities for failing forward, teaching important lessons about how to manage others, coping with adversity, and the need for humility.

- *Career setbacks.* An individual's career can be derailed in a number of ways: not getting a promotion, being stuck in a dead-end job, or being demoted or fired. Such career setbacks should be viewed as a wake-up call. They offer the opportunity to see how others perceive you and your contributions. For those who are willing to learn, career setbacks can provide valuable information that can enhance readiness for future leadership endeavors. (See the case study in box 12.2.)

- *Personal trauma.* In many instances a personal trauma such as an illness, death in the family, divorce, or difficulties with children can provide a powerful jolt to a leader. These traumas may prompt a leader to soften his or her behavior, focus more attention on a work-life balance, or learn the value of perseverance.

- *Problem employees.* Dealing with difficult employees offers an opportunity for leader development. Whether it is the employee who behaves in a fraudulent or unethical manner, has a poor work ethic, or is just difficult to get along with, problem employees teach a leader how to deal directly with problem situations.

- *Downsizing.* Being downsized is a hardship that offers a leader a chance to reflect on her or his current situation and to make choices for the future. Although many victimized by downsizing feel a powerful sense of anger, distrust, and loss, those who use the time to take stock and to consider anew what's important in life and their career can ultimately improve their effectiveness.

Box 12.2   Case Study

Profile in Hardship: Abraham Lincoln[29]

The leaders we admire the most are often the ones who have endured the greatest hardships. William Wilberforce, for example, fought for 46 years to eliminate slavery in Great Britain. Nelson Mandela, Alexander Solzhenitsyn, and Vaclav Havel served prison sentences. Mother Teresa lived in poverty in order to serve the poor. Franklin Roosevelt had to conquer the ravages of polio.

When it comes to rising above hardship, few can match the record of Abraham Lincoln. Lincoln was a small-town lawyer from Illinois who lost two bids for the Senate before his election to the presidency in 1860. He received only 40 percent of the popular vote in a field of four candidates. Assassination threats forced him to sneak into Washington DC to take his oath of office. He then presided over a war that cost the lives of one out of every five male citizens between the ages of 15 and 40. Some members of Lincoln's extended family fought for the South, and during his first term his beloved son Willie died from illness.

Instead of breaking under the strain, Lincoln grew in stature. He gained confidence and became more committed to the cause of maintaining the Union. The Emancipation Proclamation is one example of how Lincoln matured as a moral and political leader. He bypassed congressional opposition to freeing blacks by issuing the proclamation as a military order. Later, members of the House and Senate followed his example and passed the Thirteenth Amendment, the measure that permanently outlawed slavery in the United States. Few leaders can match Lincoln's generous spirit. He invited his political rivals William Seward, Salmon Chase, and Edward Bates to serve on his cabinet. He specifically instructed Ulysses S. Grant to offer lenient surrender terms to the Confederate army. On the very day he was shot, Lincoln urged his cabinet to welcome Robert E. Lee and other Confederate leaders back into the Union fold.

What was the secret of Lincoln's grace under pressure? No one can say for sure, but three factors seem particularly important. (1) Lincoln tried to understand the meaning underlying the tragic events around him. He was convinced that there was a moral pattern in history and that the suffering of the nation was its punishment for slavery. (2) Lincoln was committed to the cause of continuing the "American experiment" in democracy. He believed that the United States was a model for other nations. (3) Lincoln found a spiritual anchor, placing his confidence in God and seeing himself as an imperfect servant of God's will. Never a member of any particular religious group, he nonetheless devoted himself to prayer and to the study of scripture and has been described as the nation's most spiritual president. Lincoln's search for meaning, belief in the American cause, and spiritual understanding are reflected in his second inaugural address. This message, which is etched on his memorial, is considered by some to be the finest political statement of the 1800s. Lincoln concludes his address with these words:

> Fondly do we hope, fervently do we pray, that this mighty scourge of war may speedily pass away. Yet, if God wills that it continue until all the wealth piled by the bondsman's two hundred and fifty years of unrequited toil shall be sunk, and until every drop of blood drawn with the lash shall be paid by another drawn with the sword, as was said three thousand years ago, so still it must be said "the judgements of the Lord are true and righteous altogether."
>
> With malice toward none, with charity for all, with firmness in the right as God gives us to see the right, let us strive on to finish the work we are in, to bind up the nation's wounds, to care for him who shall have borne the battle and for his widow and his orphan, to do all which may achieve and cherish a just and lasting peace among ourselves and with all nations.

Discussion Questions

1. Can you think of other leaders, famous or not, who endured significant hardship?

2. What role has hardship played in your development as a leader?

3. Why do some people mature when faced with hardship, while others become bitter and disillusioned?

4. What can we learn from Lincoln's struggle with adversity?

5. Why don't contemporary political leaders follow Lincoln's example and reach out to their opponents?

6. How does Lincoln demonstrate the principle of failing forward?

> Never, never, never, never give up.
>
> —Winston Churchill

As you can see, some developmental experiences are planned while others are not. Further, such experiences can take place both on and off the job. University of Nebraska professor Bruce Avolio argues that nearly every important event (moving to a new city, battling cancer) or person (parent, sibling, a favorite teacher or coach) in our "life stream" shapes our development as leaders. He notes that both the former president of Poland, Lech Walesa, and the former president of South Africa, Nelson Mandela, boxed when they were young. Skilled boxers know when to punch and when to cover up. This experience, in turn, shaped their leadership behavior: "Both of these men [Walesa and Mandela] stood toe to toe with awesome regimes that had all of the institutional power, and yet they took the punches and survived."[30]

The experiences of our life stream create a life model that contains our views of the world and our perspective on how we should lead others (see our discussion of schemas in chapter 2). In other words, how we lead can't be separated from who we are. That means we need to reflect on all the meaningful people and events in our lives to determine how they have impacted our development and to draw useful insights to improve our performance. You can begin to identify these significant relationships and circumstances by completing the self-assessment in box 12.3, which asks you to draw a map of your personal leader journey.

Box 12.3   Self-Assessment

Leader Journey Map

Step 1

Create a map of your journey as a leader to this point in your life. Draw your leadership path or road. Put in important twists and turns as well as highs and lows. Mark important events or experiences that have shaped who you are and how you think and act as a leader. Identify important people who played a role along the way. Then share your map with a partner or small group. Describing your drawing will deepen your self-understanding and provide others with important insights into your leader behavior.

Step 2

Extend your map 5–10 years out into the future. Identify the learning opportunities, experiences, and relationships you want to have to become a more effective leader. Describe your map and the action steps you will take to reach your goals.

In sum, when it comes to our growth as leaders, we need to capitalize on our developmental experiences whenever and wherever they arise—structured or unstructured, at work or at home, painful or pleasurable. We need to reflect on them and discover what they can teach us. Rather than being trapped by our experiences, we can build on the past to anticipate and to shape future events. The research highlight in box 12.4 provides more information on how effective leaders grow even when faced with the most challenging of circumstances.

Box 12.4   Research Highlight

Crucible Experiences[31]

Warren Bennis and Robert Thomas surveyed over 40 leaders in the private and public sectors who were born before 1925 ("geezers") or after 1970 ("geeks"). They discovered that these individuals from very different eras had one characteristic in common. Both geezers and geeks had passed through intense, sometimes traumatic, experiences that had profoundly changed them and helped them develop their distinctive leadership abilities. Bennis and Thomas call these experiences "crucibles" because such experiences serve as places of testing and refinement. Leaders in their sample were forced to question their values, assumptions, and judgment, but they came out of their crucibles stronger and more self-confident, with a greater sense of purpose.

Crucible experiences come in many different forms. Suffering cultural, sexual, racial, or ethnic prejudice served as a crucible moment for some interviewees. Being the subject of gender bias, anti-Semitism, or racist remarks helped many get a clearer sense of their identities, including their strengths. Others had to endure illness or violence or imprisonment. Not all crucible experiences are negative. For example, meeting the high expectations of a supervisor or mentor can bring about significant change. Judge Nathaniel R. Jones of the U.S. Court of Appeals for the Sixth Circuit attributes his success to his mentor, J. Maynard Dickerson, the first black city prosecutor in the United States. Dickerson invited Jones to join his conversations with civil rights activists and demanded that he communicate clearly.

Bennis and Thomas believe that successful leaders are able to cope with, and grow from, these intense and often negative experiences because they have four skills. First, they find meaning in the experience and then employ that new understanding. Sidney Harman, the chief executive of Harman International (then Harman Kardon), used a strike at a manufacturing plant to develop a participative approach to management that empowered workers. Second, effective leaders speak with a unique and moving voice. In the midst of trouble, they can get others to listen and respond. Jack Coleman, former president of Haverford College in Pennsylvania, was able to defuse a confrontation in the 1960s between protesting students who wanted to take down the American flag and burn it and angry football players who wanted to keep it flying. He convinced the protestors to take the flag down and wash it instead. Third, notable leaders demonstrate a strong sense of values and integrity that sustains them through the crucible event and rallies others. Fourth, and most importantly, they demonstrate "adaptive capacity." Adaptive capacity is the ability to emerge from adversity stronger than before. Those with adaptive capacity understand the context so they can connect with their constituents and put the situation into perspective. They are also hardy and resilient, able to emerge from terrible circumstances with their hope intact.

> It is the combination of hardiness and ability to grasp context that, above all, allows a person to not only survive an ordeal, but to learn from it, and to emerge stronger, more engaged, and more committed than ever. These attributes allow leaders to grow from their crucibles, instead of being destroyed by them—to find opportunity where others might find only despair. This is the stuff of true leadership.[32]

> What good is experience if you do not reflect?
> —Frederick the Great

Leader Development as an Internal Process

The fact that how we lead (our doing) can't be separated from who we are (our being) means that we need to pay close attention to the inner dimension of leader development. In this section we'll examine leader development as a process that occurs *within* an individual. First, we'll review two acclaimed models that are based on the premise that a great deal of a leader's development happens internally. We will then probe the possible link between spirituality and leader development.

Stephen Covey: *The 7 Habits of Highly Effective People*

This may be the most popular leadership development program in the United States. The seven habits, developed by business consultant Stephen Covey, are described in the best-selling book by the same name. Thousands of businesses, nonprofit groups, and government agencies have participated in workshops offered by the Covey Leadership Center. Covey argues that a leader's effectiveness is based on such character principles as fairness, integrity, honesty, service, excellence, and growth. (Refer to chapter 11 for more information on virtue or character ethics.) He defines a habit as a combination of *knowledge* (what to do and why to do it), *skill* (how to do it), and *motivation* (wanting to do it).[33] Leadership development is an "inside-out" process that starts within the leader and then moves outward to impact others.

Habit 1. Be proactive. Proactive leaders realize that they can choose how they respond to events. For example, when insulted or unfairly criticized, they decide to remain calm instead of getting angry. Proactive individuals also take the initiative by opting to attack problems instead of accepting defeat. Their language reflects their willingness to accept rather than to avoid responsibility. A proactive leader makes such statements as "let's examine our options" and "I can create a strategic plan." A reactive leader makes such comments as "the organization won't go along with that idea," "I'm too old to change," and "that's just who I am."

> No one can hurt you without your consent.
> —Eleanor Roosevelt

Habit 2. Begin with the end in mind. Effective leaders always keep their ultimate goals in mind. Creating personal and organizational mission statements is one way to identify end results. Covey urges leaders to center their lives on inner principles rather than on external factors like family, money, friends, or work.

Habit 3. Put first things first. This principle is based on the notion that a leader's time should be organized around priorities. Too many leaders spend their time coping with emergencies and neglect long-range planning and relationships. They mistakenly believe that urgent items are always important. Effective leaders carve out time for significant activities by identifying their most important roles, selecting their goals, creating schedules that enable them to reach their objectives, and modifying these plans when necessary. They also know how to delegate tasks and have the courage to say "no" to requests that don't fit their priorities.

Habit 4. Think win/win. Those with win/win perspectives take a mutual gains approach to communication, believing that the best solution benefits both parties. The win/win habit is based on: character (integrity, maturity, and a willingness to share); trusting relationships committed to mutual benefit; performance or partnership agreements that spell out conditions and responsibilities; organizational systems that fairly distribute rewards; and principled negotiation that guarantees that the solution is generated by both parties and not imposed by one side or the other. (For an in-depth look at principled negotiation, turn to chapter 6.)

Habit 5. Seek first to understand, then to be understood. Effective leaders put aside their personal concerns to engage in empathetic listening. They seek to understand instead of evaluating, advising, or interpreting. Empathetic listening is an excellent way to build a trusting relationship. Covey uses the metaphor of the emotional bank account to illustrate how trust develops. Principled leaders make deposits in the emotional bank account by showing kindness and courtesy, keeping commitments, paying attention to small details, and seeking to understand. These strong relational reserves help prevent misunderstandings and increase the likelihood that leaders and followers will quickly resolve any problems that do arise.

Habit 6. Synergize. As we noted in our discussion of cultural differences in chapter 10, synergy creates a solution that is greater than the sum of its parts. Synergistic, creative solutions can only come out of trusting relationships (those with high emotional bank accounts) where participants value their differences.

Habit 7. Sharpen the saw. Sharpening the saw refers to continual renewal of the physical, social/emotional, spiritual, and mental dimensions of the self. Healthy leaders care for their bodies, nurture their inner values through study and/or meditation, encourage their mental development through reading and writing, and generate positive self-esteem through meaningful relationships with others.

Kevin Cashman: *Leadership from the Inside Out*

Kevin Cashman argues that too many leadership development books focus on the external act of leadership.[34] He believes that leadership comes from within and is an expression of who we are as people. Leadership is not something that one does; it comes from somewhere inside. Cashman defines leadership as "authentic self-expression that creates value."[35] This form of leadership can be found at all levels in organizations and can be exhibited by anyone.

> A life without purpose is an early death.
>
> —Johann Wolfgang von Goethe

To develop self-leadership skills, Cashman identifies seven pathways that allow a person to lead from the inside out. (See figure 12.1.) These pathways are not stages of development arranged in a sequential or hierarchical order. Rather, they are viewed holistically as integrated pieces of a collective framework.

Pathway One: Personal Mastery. The ongoing commitment to exploring who you are is the key to personal mastery. This understanding allows a person to lead through authentic self-expression. Learning what is important to you will impact how you lead. Cashman suggests exploring such questions as:

- What do I believe about myself?
- What do I believe about other people?
- What do I believe about life?
- What do I believe about leadership?

Questions such as these bring your beliefs to the forefront and help to guide your leadership efforts.

Pathway Two: Purpose Mastery. Learning how you make a difference is key to the second pathway. Purpose mastery focuses on understanding and using your gifts and talents to add value to those around you. This pathway encourages a leader to explore his or her purpose in life by identifying activities that are energizing and exciting. Cashman suggests that a leader's journey involves seeking ways to move from doing what you "have to do" to doing what you "want to do."

Pathway Three: Change Mastery. Letting go of old patterns and taking a fresh approach allows a leader to enhance his or her creativity. This pathway

Figure 12.1   Seven Pathways to Mastery[36]

emphasizes the need to be adaptable and willing to change. Being open to change allows a leader to be open to the possibilities presented by each situation, whether it is the opportunity to start your own business, go back to school, or simply try a new restaurant. Change challenges current reality and allows a leader to see a new reality.

Pathway Four: Interpersonal Mastery. This pathway focuses on the development of interpersonal competencies. Many leaders are not skilled in building relationships with others. A study of 6,403 middle and upper managers conducted by the Foundation for Future Leadership found that managers receive their highest evaluations for their intellect and technical expertise and their lowest marks for their interpersonal skills.[37] To develop interpersonal mastery, seek feedback from others and use that information to improve personal relationships.

Pathway Five: Being Mastery. Being is at the core of an individual. Being mastery involves using periods of peace and silence to understand one's innermost depths of character and being. Quiet moments, a favorite piece of music, a walk in the country, or inspirational reading can serve as a catalyst for exploring one's being.

Pathway Six: Balance Mastery. Taking time for self, family, and friends is critical to maintaining balance in life. Without balance, a leader can become irritable, uninspired, unfocused, and nervous. Achieving balance may be among the most difficult of the pathways to mastery to achieve. Interviews with 53 CEOs and presidents of corporations indicated that 92 percent felt balance mastery was the biggest challenge for them in their professional lives.[38]

> The number one reason leaders are so unsuccessful is their inability to lead themselves.
>
> —Truett Cathy

Pathway Seven: Action Mastery. Action mastery involves leading as a whole person. In this pathway, a leader gets in touch with his or her authentic self and expresses it to others. During the 1996 presidential campaign, Bob Dole appeared as a somewhat tough and ill-at-ease candidate. After he lost the election, many people were surprised to see the calm and funny person who surfaced. As Dole told David Letterman when he appeared as a guest on his show, "After 18 months I can be myself again."[39] It would have been interesting to note the electorate's perception of Dole if he had acted as himself throughout the campaign.

The Role of Spirituality in Leader Development

The topic of spirituality, once relegated to the margins of organizational and leadership studies, has entered the academic mainstream. More and more researchers are studying the impact of spiritual beliefs and practices on organizational and leadership performance, examining the relationship between spirituality and job satisfaction, turnover, decision making, employee commitment, productivity, and other variables. Their findings are reported in a variety of journals (*Journal of Organizational Change Management, Journal of Managerial Psychology, Leadership Quarterly*) and books (*Handbook of Workplace Spirituality and Organizational Performance, Spiritual Intelligence at Work, Religion in the Workplace*). So far investigators have discovered that spirituality fosters organizational learning and creativity, improves morale, generates higher productivity, encourages collaboration, and enhances commitment to the organizational mission, core values, and ethical standards.[40] Spirituality in the workplace has also attracted popular attention. Some organizations sponsor groups for spiritual seekers, and those interested in the subject can attend a variety of business and spirituality conferences and seminars. Tom's of Maine, TD Industries, Toro, and Medtronic are a few of the companies that put spiritual values at the center of their organizational cultures.

Connectedness is key to understanding the nature of spirituality in organizations. Workplace spirituality is about integration and connection, not separation and differentiation. According to one widely cited definition, for example, workplace spirituality is "a framework of organizational values evidenced in the culture that promotes employees' experience of transcendence through the work process, facilitating their sense of being connected to others in a way that provides feelings of completeness and joy."[41] Ian Mitroff and Elizabeth Denton describe organizational spirituality as "the basic feeling of being connected with one's complete self, others, and the entire universe."[42] Feeling connected with self means getting in touch with our inner longings and emotions while reintegrating thoughts and feelings. Feeling connected with others is lived out through concern for coworkers, respect, teamwork, and community involvement. Feeling connected to "the entire universe" describes developing relationships with larger forces like nature, a higher power, or God. Many scholars distinguish between religion and spirituality. While the two overlap, they are not identical. Religion involves belief systems and institutions (temples, meetings, churches) that nurture and structure spiritual experiences, but spiritual encounters can occur outside formal religious settings.

A number of leaders report that spirituality has played a critical role in their development, helping them to make and follow through on their moral choices, develop virtues and character, identify their values and purpose, reach out to others, and benefit from (rather than being overwhelmed by) challenging job assignments and hardships. Spiritual leadership expert Laura Reave reviewed over 150 studies and found a correlation between spiritual values and leader effectiveness.[43] Spiritual values play an important role in both leader and follower motivation. Leaders and followers alike want to serve worthy purposes, to view work as a calling that serves the needs of others and a higher power. Promoting spiritual values reduces stress, absenteeism, and turnover while improving morale and profitability. Spiritual values also promote leader integrity and humility. As we saw in our discussion of credibility in chapter 6, organizational trust in chapter 8, and character in chapter 11, these qualities are essential to personal and collective success.

Reave also found that the following common spiritual practices also promote leader effectiveness.

1. *Treating others fairly.* Fairness is an outcome of viewing others with respect, an important tenet in most belief systems and spiritual paths.

Employees put a high priority on fairness at work. They are more likely to trust leaders who treat them fairly and to go beyond their job descriptions to help coworkers.

2. *Expressing caring and concern.* Spirituality often takes the form of supportive behavior. Those working for caring leaders are more satisfied and build better relationships with their supervisors. As we noted in our review of LMX theory in chapter 3, fulfilling relationships lead to increased productivity. Caring and concern for the community also pays off. Employees of organizations known for corporate philanthropy rate their work environments as excellent and ethical, get a higher sense of achievement from their work, and take more pride in the company. Examples of socially responsible organizations include Starbucks, The Body Shop, Whole Foods Markets, and Ben and Jerry's.

3. *Listening responsively.* Listening and responding to the needs of others is another practice endorsed by many spiritual traditions. Good listeners are more likely to emerge as group leaders, and organizational leaders who demonstrate better listening skills are rated as more effective. Successful leaders also respond to what they hear. Eastman Kodak provides one example of responsive listening in action. Kodak executives publish replies to employee letters and meet regularly for discussions with workers. This listening process has been credited with doubling quality and productivity while reducing costs by 24 percent.

4. *Appreciating the contributions of others.* Most of the world's faiths view people as creations of God (or some other powerful force) who are worthy of praise. Praise for God's creation, in turn, expresses gratitude to God. In the workplace, recognizing and praising employee contributions generates goodwill toward the organization, creates a sense of community, and fosters continuing commitment and contribution.

5. *Engaging in reflective practice.* Spiritual practice doesn't end with demonstrating fairness, caring, and appreciation to others. It also has a self-reflective component. Meditation, prayer, journaling, and spiritual reading deepen spirituality and also pay practical dividends.[44] Leaders who engage in such practices improve their mental and physical health by reducing stress levels, becoming more productive, and developing stronger relationships with others. They are better equipped to rebound from crises and to discover the deeper meaning in the defining moments of their lives. Self-reflective leaders also have more control over their emotions and exercise more self-discipline.

Evidence that spiritual values and practices can improve leader effectiveness provides a link between spiritual development and leader development. As we develop spiritually, we can expand our capacity to function as leaders. Kazimierz Gozdz and Robert Frager offer the following model of spiritual development that measures both personal and organizational spiritual growth.[45] You can use this model to track your spiritual progress as well as the spiritual progress of your organization.

Stage I. Unprincipled. Unprincipled individuals are egocentric and narcissistic (focused on personal pleasure). They are unwilling to give up their needs for anyone or anything else. At this stage, people want to have their own way and seek to dominate and control others. At the same time, they refuse to admit that their actions are problematic. Such individuals break or bend the rules when they can and only obey out of fear of punishment. Stage I organizations "are dysfunctional for society and for the planet."[46] They are greedy and pursue selfish interests. To them, the world is a battleground. In the fight for survival, anything goes—cheating, lying, overcharging, polluting the environment. These dysfunctional institutions are frequently run by tyrannical bosses.

Stage II. Conventional. People in this stage have a good deal of self-doubt, so they turn to rules and organizational structure for comfort instead of relying on their own judgment. These individuals are often subservient to those above them and abusive to those below them. They rarely question the system and are more interested in getting on with the job. The Stage II institution (a family business, for example) promotes obedience to the system and the rules. The group is conservative, relying on strategies that have worked in the past. Hard work is more important than taking initiative. Leaders in these organizations are often autocratic and patriarchal, managing through detailed procedures and regulations as well as through threats of punishment.

Stage III. Self-Actualizing. Individuals in the third stage are committed to personal growth and demonstrate a high degree of self-awareness. They can articulate their values and are inner-directed. Stage III people are more willing to challenge assumptions and regulations than their Stage I and Stage II counterparts. However, they often experience burn out because they work long and hard to reach their goals. Egocentric, they may also lose sight of organizational and societal goals and interests as they compete with others. Organizations in this stage put a premium on growth and innovation. Like sports teams, they encourage teamwork while at the same time they strive to beat other "teams." Stage III groups are good at strategic planning and responding to change. They reward both individual initiative as well as teamwork. Bill Gates is an example of a Stage III leader. His organization—Microsoft—also functions at this third stage.

Stage IV. Integral. At this final stage, individuals move beyond their egos and demonstrate deeper levels of spirituality. They have experienced powerful feelings of connection to others and larger ("transcendent") forces outside themselves. These moments have made them more humble and compassionate, shifting them from self-concern to a willingness to surrender to greater, higher causes. People in this stage of development feel an integration between their inner and outer selves. They are committed to questioning and challenging assumptions and realize that the world is always changing. As a result, they value change, growth, and flexibility. Stage IV institutions are learning organizations (see chapter 8). They anticipate change and respond quickly and effectively to threats and opportunities. Their structures are fluid, based more on functional and project groups than on hierarchy and authority. Such organizations make decisions based on what is good for society, the world, and the environment. These groups actively seek feedback and set aside competition for collaboration that produces win/win solutions. Leaders of Stage IV organizations have a clear vision that they articulate in an inspiring manner. Such leaders are servants (see chapter 11) who build others up rather than using them. As a result, followers also move to higher stages of spiritual development.

Leadership Transitions

Leadership transitions are critical to both personal and organizational success. Not only do we need to acquire the knowledge and skills necessary to carry out new leadership roles, we also need to help ensure that the group as a whole chooses the right successors when positions open up. Any transition is risky. Estimates are that 40 percent of newly promoted managers and two-thirds of senior leaders appointed from outside the organization have to be replaced within 18 months.[47] A number of prominent CEOs like Jill Barad of Mattel, Douglas Ivester of Coca-Cola, Carly Fiorina of Hewlett-Packard, Robert Nardelli of Home Depot, and Robert Ayling of British Airways have been forced out after only a few years on the job. In this final section of the chapter, we will outline how successors master their new roles, describe ways to smooth the transition from one leader to another, and identify the characteristics of effective succession planning programs.

> Nothing is permanent but change.
>
> —Heracleitus

The Process of Taking Charge

John Gabarro uses the term "taking charge" to describe how newly appointed managers become leaders.[48] Gabarro (who developed the process model of succession to leadership found in figure 12.2) notes that new managers rely heavily on legitimate power, which is based on organizational position. If they want to become leaders, they must extend their influence by developing other power bases. Appointees take charge by developing an understanding of the leadership situation, gaining acceptance as leaders, and having an impact on organizational performance. To achieve these outcomes, they engage in three types of work or processes: *cognitive* (learning about the organization and its culture, acquiring technical knowledge, diagnosing problems, understanding issues); *organizational* (developing a set of shared expectations with followers, working out conflicts, and building a cohesive management team); and *interpersonal* (developing good working relationships with superiors, subordinates, and peers).

The cognitive, organizational, and interpersonal work that results in a leader taking charge is accomplished over time. Through interviews with successful and unsuccessful new leaders and their subordinates, Gabarro discovered that taking charge involves five stages.[49]

- *Taking hold.* Taking hold is a period of intense activity lasting from three to six months. Newly appointed managers have a great deal of information to absorb. As they learn, they evaluate the situation and take corrective action to solve pressing short-term problems.

- *Immersion.* This stage (lasting four to eleven months) is less hectic than the first. Instead of making changes, new managers immerse themselves in day-to-day operations and develop a deeper understanding of the organization. In-depth understanding often produces a new plan for improving performance.

- *Reshaping.* During the reshaping phase (three to six months), new leaders implement the concepts they developed during the immersion period, making changes in the organization's structure, processes, and personnel.

- *Consolidation.* In the consolidation phase (three to nine months), leaders follow through on the changes made during the reshaping stage. They identify and deal with remaining implementation problems, correct any unanticipated difficulties produced by changes made during the reshaping period, and implement changes they could not make earlier.

- *Refinement.* Refinement signals the end of the taking-charge process. By this time, successors are no longer viewed as new, and their major changes are

Figure 12.2   A Process Model of Succession to Leadership[50]

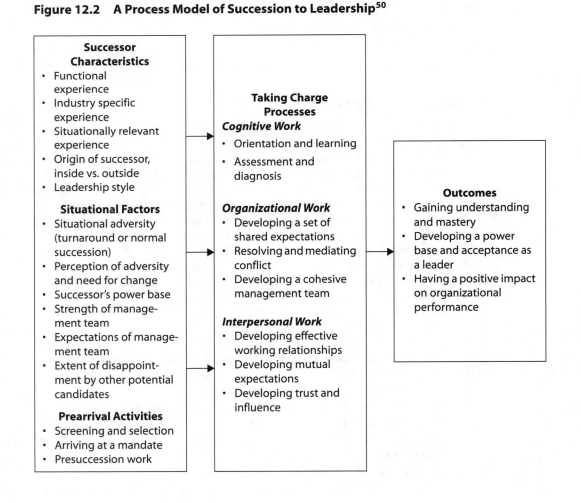

in place. They continue to learn and to make changes, but they have much less new information to master. Any adjustments they make are minor.

There are a number of variables (summarized in the left column in figure 12.2) that either facilitate or complicate the task of taking charge.[51] Some of these variables have to do with the characteristics of the successor. Those brought in from outside the organization generally make more changes and have more to learn. A close match between the successor's previous experience and the demands of the new position make for a smoother transition, but conflicts will likely develop if the successor's leadership communication style is inconsistent with her or his predecessor's. Other variables are situational in nature. Those faced with significant performance problems must make greater changes. A perceived need for change; a strong power base built on competence, position, and other factors; and a strong, supportive management team make taking charge easier. Disgruntled employees who were turned down for the leader's position make the successor's job harder. The final cluster of variables involves the selection process itself and how the organization prepares for the arrival of the new leader. The successor who clearly understands the expectations of the organization and is given a mandate for change has the greatest chance of success. The new leader's superior can defuse the hostility of disappointed candidates by telling them why they weren't chosen for the position.

Managing Transitions

The process model of leadership succession highlights the fact that taking charge is a complex, difficult, and demanding task. However, Gabarro makes these suggestions to help manage transitions either as a successor or as someone overseeing the succession process.

- *Recognize that taking charge takes time.* It takes over two years to master a new leadership role. Be patient; don't expect instant miracles of yourself or others. Discourage short-term assignments because they don't give new leaders a chance to immerse themselves in the situation and to reshape the department or organization.

- *Develop effective working relationships immediately.* Building strong working relationships with key subordinates and the boss is essential during the taking-hold period. Gabarro found that failure to build effective relationships was "the most prominent characteristic that distinguished between successful and failed succession."[52] To build productive relationships, negotiate specific differences with subordinates and keep superiors informed of changes. Instead of tackling problems on your own (acting as a "Lone Ranger"), seek out the opinions of others and develop a cohesive working group with a common vision.

- *Assess and act on prior experience.* Realistically assess your skills as well as the skills and experience of those you choose for leadership positions. Then develop strategies that reflect these assessments. Build on your strengths as you acquaint yourself with less familiar elements of the job. If you have strong organizational skills but lack technical expertise, for instance, you may want to restructure the department before you tackle problems that require technical solutions. When supervising others, identify the potential problems successors will face and provide the support they will need to overcome these challenges (additional training, key subordinates, etc.). The smoothest transitions, as we noted earlier, are usually made by individuals who have performed similar tasks (accounting, engineering, teaching) in another organization or in another position.

- *Clarify expectations.* Learn exactly what is expected of you and make the "going-in mandate" of a successor as clear as possible. For example, are you to increase market share? Reduce costs? Reorganize? Will the successor you choose have the power to lay employees off? Increase the budget? Develop new systems? After the succession has been made, you or the new appointee should meet with constituents to identify important issues and concerns.

Succession Planning

A growing number of large organizations are developing succession-planning programs that take a systematic approach to identifying and developing future leaders. Anticipating leadership transitions makes sense for several reasons. As we saw earlier, the importance of leadership changeover and the high failure rate of new leaders suggests that succession planning should not be left to chance. The need for future leaders is likely to increase as baby boomers reach retirement at the same time that there are fewer younger workers to replace them. Corporate layoffs may also contribute to a leader shortfall by reducing the number of middle management positions that have traditionally served as training grounds for executives. Further, a systematic approach to leadership transitions reduces the likelihood of a mismatch between the person and the position as well as the tendency for job incumbents (who are often white males) to choose successors who resemble themselves (other white males). (Complete the self-assessment in box 12.5 to determine if your organization has a systematic process for leadership succession.)

Experts report that effective succession-planning programs share the following characteristics:[53]

- *Participation and support of top management.* When top leaders are involved, others are more likely to devote time and effort to succession concerns.

- *Include all leadership levels.* Succession planning is important for low-level management positions as well as for executive ones.

- *Organizational needs assessment.* Organizations must decide on the direction in which they are headed before they know what types of skills their future leaders must develop.

- *Competency focused.* Focusing on competencies means equipping people to take a variety of positions, not just the next one up the organizational ladder.

- *Accountability.* Accountability comes from appointing one person to oversee the succession program as well as from evaluating current leaders on how well they are preparing potential replacements.

Box 12.5   Self-Assessment

Succession Planning Survey[54]

Complete the following survey to determine the status of your work group or organization's succession-planning process. "No" responses indicate potential weaknesses. Outline steps that your work group or organization can take to address these problem areas.

Question	Yes	No	Your Comments
A. Is there a systematic means to identify possible replacement needs stemming from retirement or other predictable losses of people?			
B. Is there a systematic approach to performance appraisal so as to clarify each individual's current performance?			
C. Is there a systematic approach to identifying individuals who have the potential to advance one or more levels beyond their current positions?			
D. Is there a systematic approach by which to accelerate the development of individuals who have the potential to advance one or more levels beyond their current positions?			
E. Does a means by which to keep track of possible replacements by key positions exist?			

- *Development.* Future leaders must be developed. Development tools include job rotation, training programs, and mentoring. While organizations provide development opportunities, every employee is ultimately responsible for acquiring the competencies he or she needs to move into new leadership positions. Key developmental passages in large organizations—in increasing order of complexity and responsibility—include: (1) from managing self to managing others (acting as a frontline supervisor); (2) from managing others to managing managers (overseeing first-level supervisors); (3) from managing other managers to managing a particular function (e.g., operating a plant, supervising production); (4) from functional manager to managing an entire business or division of the company; (5) from business manager to managing several corporate businesses (serving as a group manager); and (6) from group manager to managing the entire enterprise.[55]

CHAPTER TAKEAWAYS

- Leader development promotes individual growth, helping a person expand his/her capacity to be effective in a variety of formal and informal leadership roles.
- Leadership development promotes organizational growth, helping the group as a whole develop the leaders it needs to be successful.

- Leader development is a lifelong journey. To become an effective leader, you will need to be proactive, seeking out leadership learning opportunities, building developmental relationships, and capitalizing on your experiences.

- Leadership learning can be achieved through reading, attending college or university courses, and training. Three common types of training programs include: (1) individual preparation, (2) socializing company vision and values, and (3) strategic leadership initiatives.

- Establishing connections with those who can help you achieve your goals will greatly increase your chances of emerging as a leader in an organizational context. The most beneficial relationships are with mentors. Mentors act as sponsors; provide coaching; protect protégés; give challenging assignments; serve as role models; supply acceptance and confirmation; function as counselors or sounding boards; and become friends.

- To locate a mentor when formal mentoring programs are not available, determine what (not whom) you need. After this vital first step, evaluate yourself as a prospective protégé, identify mentor candidates, prepare for the obstacles that might arise, and approach potential mentors.

- Formal coaches can be used to supplement or even to substitute for mentor relationships. Coaches help coachees design, implement, and evaluate personal development plans.

- Leadership experiences enable us to expand our leadership skills. The richest experiences occur in developmental job assignments. These experiences fall into five categories: job transitions, creating change, taking on a high level of responsibility, managing boundaries, and dealing with diversity. Another type of developmental experience is hardship. Successful leaders "fail forward" by learning from adversity. The most common hardships are business mistakes and failures; career setbacks; personal trauma; problem employees; and downsizing.

- Unstructured experiences also contribute to your development as a leader. Reflect on and learn from all the important events and relationships in your life stream.

- Two models view leadership development as an internal process. Stephen Covey prescribes seven habits for effective leadership: (1) be proactive; (2) begin with an end in mind; (3) put first things first; (4) think win/win; (5) seek first to understand, then to be understood; (6) synergize; and (7) sharpen the saw. Kevin Cashman's *Leadership from the Inside Out* offers a holistic approach consisting of seven pathways to leadership: (1) personal mastery; (2) purpose mastery; (3) change mastery; (4) interpersonal mastery; (5) being mastery; (6) balance mastery; and (7) action mastery.

- Spiritual development can be tied to leader development. Common spiritual practices that promote leadership effectiveness include treating others fairly, expressing caring and concern, listening responsively, appreciating the contributions of others, and engaging in reflective practice (meditation, prayer, journaling, spiritual reading). There are four stages of personal and organizational spiritual development: Stage I. Unprincipled (egocentric, self-centered); Stage II. Conventional (bound by rules and structure); Stage III. Self-Actualizing (committed to individual and collective growth, inner-directed); and Stage IV. Integral (deeply spiritual, connected, other-focused).

- Taking charge as a new leader means developing an understanding of the leadership context, gaining acceptance as a leader, and having an impact on organizational performance. The five stages of the taking-charge process are: taking hold, immersion, reshaping, consolidation, and refinement. Succession-planning programs systematically identify and develop future leaders.

APPLICATION EXERCISES

1. Talk with someone who is employed in a company that offers leadership training to its workers. Compare your experiences in this course to the training received in the organization. Share your findings in class.

2. Read a book on leadership. Give a presentation to your classmates outlining the major concepts in the book and your evaluation of the strengths and weaknesses of the book you selected.

3. Look at the course catalog at your school and see how many different leadership courses are offered. Compare the results with other schools by viewing their course catalogs online.

4. Profile a famous leader and identify hardships she/he has suffered. Discuss these examples in class, and try to determine if these experiences were valuable in the leader's development.

5. Pair off with someone and discuss mentor relationships. Have you served as a mentor or protégé? Been a part of a formal mentoring program? How would you evaluate this experience? If you haven't been in this type of relationship, follow the steps outlined in the chapter to identify someone who could serve in this capacity and how you might ask him/her to be your mentor. Describe peer relationships that have been most helpful to you at work or at school.

6. Read either *The 7 Habits of Highly Effective People* by Stephen Covey or *Leadership from the Inside Out* by Kevin Cashman. Attempt to use either of these models to develop your internal approach to leadership. Report your experiences to your classmates.

7. Write a research paper on spirituality and leadership. What do you conclude about the relationship between spiritual development and leader development?

8. Attend a leadership-training seminar and measure its effectiveness based on material covered in this text and in class. Write up your findings.

9. Develop a taking-charge case study based on the experiences of a new leader. What challenges did this leader face? How did he/she accomplish the three tasks of taking charge? Did she/he pass through the

four stages described in the chapter? How successful was the leadership transition? Write up your findings.

10. Evaluate your organization's succession-planning process. Share your findings with the organization's leadership team.

CULTURAL CONNECTIONS: LEADERSHIP DEVELOPMENT[56]

All too often corporate trainers and consultants assume that training programs developed for U.S. audiences will automatically work in other countries. Trainers believe that challenge and practical experience promote development and that leaders should periodically measure their progress and get feedback from others. They are disappointed when participants from other nations refuse to enter into discussions, demand a rationale for every activity, or resist giving and receiving feedback. According to Center for Creative Leadership senior associate Michael Hoppe, U.S. trainers operate under a unique set of cultural assumptions. As we've seen in this chapter, leader development programs in the United States generally focus on the advancement of the individual and are based on the conviction that everyone can develop leadership capacities.

How well training strategies developed in the United States transfer to another country will depend on the overlap between U.S. values and beliefs and those of the host nation. Consider how different European nations promote their "fast-tack" managers, for example. In Sweden, many managers don't want to be singled out as having high potential because promotions damage relationships with coworkers and mean less time with family. Germans equate leader development with technical expertise and use an apprentice system. Careers in France are highly structured, and only a favored few are selected for leader development programs.

Hoppe uses the 360-degree feedback instrument to highlight some of the difficulties in transferring training techniques from the United States to other cultural settings. A 360-degree survey asks many different people (direct reports, peers, supervisors, customers) to rate an individual leader. This instrument is highly popular in the United States, where managers believe in data-driven, "objective" performance measures and giving direct feedback (positive or negative). It is not so successful in a variety of other cultures. For instance, managers from Japan, Mexico, South Korea, and Taiwan welcome positive but not negative feedback. While the individual may control how the results of the instrument are used in U.S. society, such data may be considered organizational property in collectivist societies like China and Japan. Leaders in hierarchical cultures like France and Saudi Arabia may believe that they have a right to the results of 360-degree evaluations conducted on their subordinates.

Because leader development draws on deeply rooted cultural values and beliefs, Hoppe declares that "there are no shortcuts" when it comes to transferring training models and practices from any one nation to another. Successful cross-cultural leader development trainers look for cultural similarities and differences. When given an overseas assignment, they learn as much as they can about the host culture, consult cultural insiders when designing programs, and make their content, activities, and assessment methods appropriate for the intended audience.

SPOTLIGHT ON TECHNOLOGY: E-LEADER DEVELOPMENT

The spread of information technology is changing the context for leadership. Many leaders will spend more time leading virtual teams than face-to-face groups. Information that once was closely held by top management is now available to employees, customers, suppliers, and even competitors through e-mail and the Internet. In the brave new world of computer communication, those at lower levels of the organization will be equipped with the knowledge they need to manage their own tasks. Collective or shared leadership will be more common, and individuals will rapidly alternate between their leader and follower roles.

Leader development expert Bruce Avolio argues that our effectiveness as leaders will depend on our ability to adapt to the realities of the information age, to become "e-leaders."[57] He identifies five technological "points of impact" that you should keep in mind as part of your personal development plan.

1. Is the spirit of your leadership consistent with the spirit of the information technology available to your followers? There could be conflict if you are directive and the technology fosters collaboration.

2. As more people know what you know, how can you make sure that they share their knowledge with others in order to improve performance?

3. How prepared are you to move from being a content leader to a process leader? Increasingly you will need to facilitate the work of experts in areas where you lack expertise.

4. What strategy will you use to balance face-to-face interactions with distance interactions that occur via technology? You will have to determine which type of communication should occur online or in person and avoid overusing technology.

5. What learning plan do you have in place to help coach yourself and others on how to best use information technology to improve one another's work and quality of life?

LEADERSHIP ON THE BIG SCREEN: *MILLION DOLLAR BABY*

Starring: Clint Eastwood, Hillary Swank, Morgan Freeman

Rating: PG-13 for violence, disturbing images, language

Synopsis: Clint Eastwood (who also directed and produced the film) plays Frankie Dunn, an aging boxing trainer and manager haunted by his professional and personal failures. When waitress Maggie McDonald (Swank) shows up to work out at his gym, he refuses to coach her, declaring: "I don't train girls." Her determination soon wins him over, however. Within a year and a half Maggie is competing for the title. Then tragedy strikes. Dunn must then decide if he should honor his protégé's final wishes. Morgan Freeman—the movie's narrator—plays Scrap, the gym caretaker and former fighter who acts as an informal coach to the aspiring boxer. The film took Oscars for best director and best film, best actress (Swank), and best supporting actor (Freeman).

Chapter Links: developmental relationships, developmental experiences, dealing with hardship and failure, the inner dimension of leadership

Leadership in Crisis

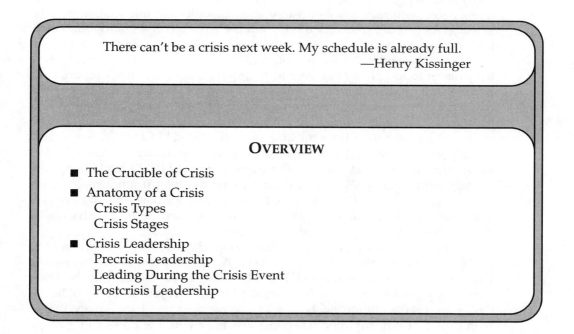

There can't be a crisis next week. My schedule is already full.
—Henry Kissinger

OVERVIEW

- The Crucible of Crisis
- Anatomy of a Crisis
  Crisis Types
  Crisis Stages
- Crisis Leadership
  Precrisis Leadership
  Leading During the Crisis Event
  Postcrisis Leadership

The Crucible of Crisis

We live in an age of crisis. Stories of hurricanes, corporate and political scandals, terrorist attacks, epidemics, tsunamis, school shootings, earthquakes, and other crises headline the news. Evidence suggests that some types of crises are happening with greater frequency. Significant industrial accidents (those with 50 or more deaths) are more common, and deliberate attacks (bombings, kidnappings, cyber attacks, sabotage) have risen sharply over the past decade.[1] At the same time, global warming disrupts weather patterns, increasing the number and strength of hurricanes.

The proliferation of crises means that leaders must act as crisis managers. They have to be alert to dangers, prepare their groups and organizations for trouble, and respond quickly and effectively when a crisis breaks out. Crisis management may be the most demanding task of leadership. In the crucible of a crisis, the organization is threatened and comes under media and public scrutiny. Jobs and property are lost, and lives may be at stake. Events move at lightning speed, requiring quick decisions even though vital information may be missing. As a result, crises often bring out the worst in organizations and their leaders.[2] Hurricane Katrina, for example, is rapidly becoming a textbook case of how *not* to handle a crisis. A House congressional committee investigating the disaster found plenty of blame to go around. The committee's report, entitled "A Failure of Initiative," faulted state and local officials for delaying a mandatory evacuation, stranding thousands of New Orleanians who didn't have cars. Incomplete evacuation led to "deaths, thousands of dangerous rescues, and horrible conditions for those who remained."[3] Committee members (largely Republicans) blamed Homeland Security Secretary Michael Chertoff for appointing an unqualified disaster manager to head the Federal Emergency Management Agency (FEMA) and for waiting too long to implement emergency response plans. They also noted that the White House should have gotten involved sooner. In sum, the government's response to Katrina was a "litany of mistakes, misjudgments, lapses, and absurdities."

Fortunately, some organizations respond quickly and forcefully when a crisis strikes and emerge stronger than ever. A case in point is the Johnson & Johnson company, the makers of Tylenol. When six people died in the 1980s after taking extra-strength Tylenol capsules laced with cyanide, the firm, led by CEO James Burke, immediately recalled the capsules and later replaced them with caplets. Company officials cooperated fully with the press and government authorities. Public confidence in Johnson & Johnson was restored, and Tylenol sales are higher now than they were before the tampering incident.

The goal of this chapter is to help you and your organization manage crises rather than falling victim to them. In the first section of the chapter, we'll dissect crises in order to understand them better. In the second section of the chapter, we will examine the communication strategies essential to successful crisis leadership.

Anatomy of a Crisis

"Know your enemy" is the first step to effective crisis leadership. We can't prepare for or manage crises until we have a better understanding of what they are and how they unfold. Crises can be categorized by type and by stages of development.

Crisis Types

A crisis is any major unpredictable event that has the potential to damage an organization and, in extreme cases, to threaten its survival.[4] There is no one universally accepted list of all potential crises. However, a number of investigators divide crises into types. Researchers at the Center for Crisis Management at the University of Southern California, for example, report that crises generally fall into the following categories:[5]

- *Economic:* labor strikes and unrest; major decline in stock price, market price, and earnings; market crash
- *Informational:* loss of proprietary and confidential information; false information; computer tampering
- *Physical:* loss of key equipment, plants, supplies, and facilities; equipment breakdowns
- *Human resources:* loss of key executives and personnel; workplace violence
- *Reputational:* slander, gossip, rumors, damage to corporate reputation
- *Psychopathic acts:* product tampering; kidnapping and hostage taking; terrorism
- *Natural disasters:* earthquakes, fires, floods, mudslides, typhoons, tsunamis

This classification system and others like it can help leaders better prepare for emergency situations. Different types of crises call for different responses. Recovering from flood damage to corporate headquarters calls for one set of tactics; coping with a case of product tampering requires another. Classifying crises can also help leaders determine where their organizations are most vulnerable. A high school must be on guard against student violence, for example, while a software manufacturer must contend with computer hackers. In addition, no organization can prepare for every potential crisis. Crisis managers can, nonetheless, develop a plan that can be used for incidents that occur within each category.

Crisis Stages

While crises differ, they all appear to follow a similar pattern of development. Each passes through the same three stages: precrisis, crisis event, and postcrisis.[6]

Stage 1: Precrisis

Organizations spend most of their time between crises. During these periods of normalcy, leaders typically assume that the risks of a crisis occurring are low. Further, they believe that their organizations are adequately prepared for any potential contingency. The longer the period between crises, the more confident leaders become. They may cut back crisis training programs as well as funding for backup operational sites and other crisis containment measures. Sadly, such overconfidence makes disaster more likely. Officials at NASA, for example, became overconfident about the safety of shuttle missions between the *Challenger* and *Columbia* disasters. Safety concerns were a priority after the *Challenger* crash. Seventeen years later, other goals, like keeping the shuttle program on schedule, took precedence. Top managers dismissed concerns that the *Columbia* had been damaged during its launch. However, a small hole opened by a debris strike shortly after liftoff allowed superheated gas to enter the craft when it returned to earth. *Columbia* disintegrated, taking the lives of seven astronauts.[7]

As a leader, you'll need to fight the tendency to become complacent. Even during periods of relative calm, there are likely to be indications that another crisis is brewing. Crisis expert Steven Fink uses the term "prodomes" (taken from the Greek term meaning "running before") to describe the warning signs that something is seriously amiss.[8] Catholic cardinals and bishops knew that priests were sexually abusing children decades before victims began suing for damages. Computer simulations demonstrated that the levees in New Orleans wouldn't withstand the force of a hurricane as strong as Katrina.

In addition to battling complacency, leaders must also overcome: (1) *human biases* (errors in decision making and judgment); (2) *institutional failures* (organizational breakdowns in processing information); and (3) *special-interest groups* (resistance from groups that look out for the interests of their own members). Box 13.1 summarizes the ways in which these barriers can undermine crisis readiness.

Max Bazerman and Michael Watkins use the term "predictable surprises" to describe situations where organizations have all the information they need to predict what will happen but fail to take action due to the decision barriers listed above.[9] The attacks of 9/11 are a case in point. Between 1987 and 2000, the General Accounting Office (GAO) and two presidential commissions issued reports warning of weaknesses in the airline industry's security systems and outlining steps for improvement. Further, government officials were aware of the growing hatred of Islamic extremists and that knives had been used in previous highjackings. Nevertheless, little was done to enhance security on the ground or in the air due to pressure from the airline industry (security is expensive) and inaction at the Federal Aviation Administration (FAA).

> One of the extraordinary things about human events is that the unthinkable becomes thinkable.
> —Salman Rushdie

Stage 2: Crisis Event

This stage begins with a "trigger event" that initiates the crisis and ends when the crisis is resolved. Harm is done to people, property, and the environment. Organizational members experience strong emotions like surprise, fear, and anger. They are confused about how to respond and worried about what will happen to the organization and themselves. The crisis erupts into public consciousness.

Box 13.1

Barriers to Crisis Prevention[10]

Human Biases

- positive illusions that falsely convince decision makers that a problem doesn't exist or isn't severe enough to require action
- interpreting events in an egocentric manner that favors the leader and the organization while blaming outsiders
- discounting the future by ignoring possible long-term costs; refusing to invest resources now to prevent future crises
- maintaining the dysfunctional status quo by refusing to inflict any harm (such as higher social security taxes) that would address a mounting problem (the danger that the social security system will become insolvent)
- failure to recognize problems because they aren't vivid (they are not personally experienced as direct threats)

Institutional Failures

- failure to collect adequate data due to (a) ignoring certain problems and discounting evidence, (b) the presence of conflicting information, and (c) information overload
- information is not integrated into the organization as a whole because departments operate independently and managers maintain secrecy
- members lack incentive to take action because they are rewarded for acting selfishly or believe that everyone agrees with a course of action
- leaders fail to learn from experience or to disseminate lessons learned because information is not recorded or shared or because key organizational members are lost

Special-Interest Groups

- impose social burdens (higher taxes, water pollution, high drug prices) in order to benefit themselves
- blame complex problems on individuals rather than on systems that are at fault
- oppose reform efforts

During the crisis event, the focus shifts to damage control. The group implements its crisis management plans, communicates to internal and external publics, responds to outside pressures, and tries to resume normal operations. Containing the problem (controlling the oil spill, rescuing villagers stranded by an earthquake) is an important component of this stage.

Stage 3: Postcrisis

The postcrisis stage begins when the immediate danger is past and the organization has been able to resume its normal operations. This is a period of evaluation, analysis, and restoration. Crisis-savvy leaders try to learn from their experiences. They make sure that the organization evaluates its response in order to determine the extent of the damage and to determine how well contingency plans worked. They record the results of the analysis to help ensure that the crisis lessons become part of the organization's memory and institute needed changes. Effective crisis managers also help their organizations recover from the trauma and move forward.

Crisis Leadership

The three-stage model of crisis development provides a useful framework for crisis leadership. Each crisis stage makes unique demands on leaders. Successful leaders must recognize and meet these challenges by shifting communication strategies as the crisis develops.

Precrisis Leadership

During the precrisis stage, the leader's primary responsibility is to move the organization from crisis prone to crisis ready.[11] The crisis ready organization is alert to warning signs, identifies potential trouble spots, develops a crisis management plan, and creates a reservoir of credibility and good will. You can determine your organization's crisis readiness by completing the self-assessment in box 13.2.

Recognize Danger Signs

Leaders can prevent many crises by being alert to prodomes, the warning signs that something is amiss. To pick up on these signals, they must encourage their organizations to scan the environment continually. Environmental scanning looks both outward and inward. In external scanning, the organization surveys the news media, trade journals, public opinion polls, online publications, Web sites, and other sources to identify potential dangers. For instance, reports of avian (bird) flu not only moved health officials to mobilize but also alerted other organizational leaders that an outbreak could increase absentee rates and lower productivity.

Warning signs often come from those who have an ongoing relationship with the organization, like customers, donors, and suppliers. Indicators of trouble include product returns, public criticism, complaints, and protests. Failure to respond to these signals can spell trouble, as Procter & Gamble (P&G) discovered in the "devil case." P&G initially dismissed phone inquiries that the company was connected to the Church of Satan. By not taking these calls seriously, the company soon found itself fielding 15,000 devil-related calls every month in the early 1980s, and rumors about its satanic connections still linger.[12]

Internal scanning looks for organizational deficiencies that could lead to crisis situations. These might include signs of overconfidence, inadequate safety procedures, decaying equipment, and overloaded transportation systems.[13] Unfortunately, obtaining accurate information about internal conditions is difficult. Warnings threaten the group's sense of well-being and whistle-blowers are often punished. Lower-level employees distort information by sending only positive messages to their superiors and by downplaying risks. As a consequence, leaders may be surprised by organizational crises while their employees are not. The flow of negative information generally increases if leaders create a trusting atmosphere, being particularly careful not to punish those who bring bad news.

> Prediction is very difficult, especially about the future.
> —Niels Bohr

Box 13.2   Self-Assessment

Crisis Preparedness Scale[14]

To determine how ready your organization is to deal with a crisis, answer yes or no to the following questions.

Statement	Yes	No
1. Our organization has the necessary abilities to assess the potential numbers and types of injuries (to people, animals, the environment) associated with any crisis.		
2. Our organization has the capabilities required to treat whatever injuries might result.		
3. Our organization's values system or culture gives priority to treating injuries promptly.		
4. Our organization gives priority to covering up or denying a crisis.		
5. Legal considerations do not override ethical and human concerns.		
6. Our organization has a trained crisis management team (CMT) that can assemble quickly and make effective decisions.		
7. Our organization has the capabilities to investigate and determine		
a. the precise type or nature of whatever crisis could occur.		
b. the early warning signals that precede each type of crisis.		
c. whether such signals were blocked or ignored.		
d. the exact, human, organizational, and technical causes of a crisis.		
8. Our organization has properly designed, constantly maintained, and regularly tested damage containment systems in place.		
9. Our organization has backup manufacturing equipment and computers so that it can resume operations as quickly as possible.		
10. Our organization has recovery mechanisms to restore full site and organizational operations.		
11. Our organization has recovery mechanisms to restore the surrounding community and environment.		
12. Our organization has the capabilities to communicate effectively, notify the proper authorities, respond to the media, and reassure a wide array of stakeholders.		

If you answered no to two or more of these statements it is likely that your organization will have a crisis and that it will have difficulty handling it properly.

Look for Trouble

Looking for trouble means revealing weaknesses that could prove harmful or fatal to the organization. One trouble-shooting tactic is to brainstorm a list of possible crises. Here, for example, are some potential crises that might strike your college or university (see application exercise 1 on p. 423).

- asbestos contamination
- murder
- dramatic decrease in enrollment
- earthquake
- explosion in the science lab
- faculty member or administrator accused of illegal or immoral conduct
- food poisoning in the cafeteria
- financial problems
- fire
- flood
- lawsuits against the university
- staff or faculty strike
- student protests
- students arrested for serious crimes
- controversial speaker or art exhibit
- students hurt or killed while participating in school-sponsored activities

Crisis management experts Ian Mitroff and Murat Alpasian offer four additional techniques that can be used along with brainstorming to help leaders highlight organizational vulnerabilities.[15]

Wheel of crises. Build a wheel complete with a spinner. List all the types of crises that a company or nonprofit can face. Take turns spinning the wheel. When the spinner stops, brainstorm all of the kinds of possible crises that might occur in that category. In a variation of this technique, combine two crises. This will drive home the point of the magnitude for potential disaster. In 1997, for example, the Red River flood combined with fire to destroy most of Grand Forks, North Dakota's downtown area. New Orleans was devastated by both high winds and high water during Hurricane Katrina.

Internal assassins. Ask members of your organization to play the role of villains and to imagine ways to destroy products and processes. Have these teams of assassins think of ways to disrupt the manufacturing process, embezzle money, hide accounting losses, steal personal data and so on. Then develop strategies for foiling such attacks.

Mixed metaphors. Look to other industries to determine if the dangers they face pose a threat to your type of organization. One large electronics manufacturer imagined itself as part of the food industry. Leaders at this company thought about how "bugs" and "microbes" might "infect" their products. They went so far as to hire an infectious disease specialist to help prevent such infections. Based on this analysis, executives determined that disgruntled employees could introduce pathogens (computer viruses or faulty parts, for example) into company products. They decided to quarantine suspect shipments until the items were inoculated (repaired).

Spy games. Hire journalists, private investigators, consumer experts, lawyers, and others to expose weaknesses. These impartial outsiders can visit plant facilities to determine security breaches, write investigative stories, or produce simulated videos attacking the organization, employees, or products.

> A degree of paranoia helps protect organizations.
> —Yiannis Gabriel

Create a Crisis Management Plan (CMP)

Once potential crises have been identified, develop an action plan to cope with each type of emergency. Every crisis management plan (CMP) should contain the following elements.[16]

1. *Cover page*. This cover sheet should identify the document, and, in many cases, state that it is confidential and not to be shown to those outside the organization. Be sure to include dates when the plan was written and revised to help readers determine how current the document is.

2. *Introduction*. The introduction generally should be written by the organization's top executive in order to highlight the importance of the CMP.

3. *Acknowledgements*. This removable page is signed by employees and put on file with the human resources department. It serves as an official record that employees have read and understood the plan.

4. *Rehearsal dates*. Record when the plan has been practiced. Responses to the most likely and most damaging crises should be practiced at least once a year. Hospitals, for example, hold disaster drills on a regular basis, complete with volunteers who play the role of patients.

5. *Crisis management team (CMT)*. Identify who is in charge during the incident and how this person can be reached. Describe when the CMP should be activated and by whom. The composition of the crisis management team will vary depending on the exact nature of the crisis. However, the typical team for a large organization will consist of the following members:[17]

   - Attorney to review messages, reduce legal risk, outline legal requirements

   - Public relations director or coordinator to manage internal and external communication strategies and media relations

   - Operational managers to coordinate recovery

   - Controller or another financial manager with knowledge of financial assets and insurance coverage

   - Institutional technology manager to help keep communication channels open and to maintain databases

- Regulatory expert to coordinate with government agencies and represent the interests of the public
- The CEO or a representative from his/her office

6. *Crisis management directory.* List the names of team members, their organizational roles, and areas of expertise. Also include outsiders, like emergency personnel, insurance agents, key suppliers, and consultants, who should be contacted during an emergency. The contact sheet should make it easy to identify and reach members of the crisis management team.

7. *Crisis risk assessment.* This section incorporates the analysis done during the precrisis stage. Identify possible crises and evaluate risk based on probability (likelihood of occurring) and impact (potential damage). In addition to helping an organization prepare for crises, the risk assessment demonstrates that your group has engaged in due diligence to try to prevent these crises.

8. *Incident report.* Keep detailed records of your organization's activities during the crisis. Record when the incident started and where, what happened during the crisis, and who was contacted during the emergency. This documentation will help the group evaluate its crisis management efforts and to respond to lawsuits and government investigations.

9. *Proprietary information.* Some information should not be revealed during a crisis without the express consent of the CEO and legal counsel. This might include, for instance, certain manufacturing processes and product ingredients. Also, never release the names of victims before notifying their families.

10. *CMP strategy worksheet.* This element of the plan emphasizes that every message sent during a crisis needs to serve a clear purpose and documents crisis actions. Crisis managers should record the specific audiences they address as well as their goals and include copies of the messages they send. Communicators may need to be reminded to avoid technical jargon and to define organizational terms in a way that outsiders can understand.

11. *Secondary contact sheet.* On this contact sheet, identify other groups that should be notified during the crisis, either because they have important information or because they will be affected by the emergency. Identify the type of stakeholder and important contact information. Specify who should get in touch with each stakeholder and document who made the contact and when.

12. *Stakeholder contact worksheet.* Some stakeholders will contact the organization directly for information. The media, in particular, will demand a prompt response. Outline procedures for responding to calls from the press as well as from families, employees, and community leaders. Determine how to route these calls and who should speak on behalf of the organization. Document responses, including who contacted the organization and when, the communication channel used to make the contact, the nature of the inquiry, the response, and any required follow up.

13. *Business resumption plan.* Getting back to regular operations as soon as possible is an important organizational goal. The plan should spell out how your organization will respond when communications systems and facilities are damaged, data is lost, and so on.

14. *Crisis control center.* Designate a place where crisis team members can gather and coordinate their efforts. Some larger organizations have developed permanent crisis command centers for use during emergencies.

15. *Postcrisis evaluation.* Develop an evaluation form to help the group learn from the crisis. Determine how well the CMP functioned, including its activation, contacts, message strategy, stakeholder relations, and business resumption measures.

Establish Credibility

Organizations with a reputation for integrity and competence in environmental concerns are better equipped to weather a crisis (for more information on the dimensions of credibility, see chapter 6). They create goodwill that encourages government officials and the public to treat them more leniently when they come under attack or make mistakes. The importance of establishing credibility can be seen in public responses to airline disasters. Delta recovered rapidly from the 1985 crash of a jet during a thunderstorm in part because it had an excellent service record at that time as well as a "family image." Two years later Northwest Airlines stock declined after a DC-9 crashed on takeoff. Prior to the crash, Northwest was embroiled in labor disputes and led the industry in customer complaints. The company's out-of-control image carried over into its recovery efforts. Observers criticized Northwest for not taking charge and for ignoring the needs of victims' families. Some relatives filed lawsuits less than a week after the crash.[18]

Work hard to build and maintain credibility by producing quality products, providing excellent customer service, keeping promises and commitments, and acting in a socially responsible manner. Treat employees well, support community programs, be a responsible steward of the environment, and so on. Stay close to stakeholders (see chapter 9) by engaging in regular two-way communication.

Leading during the Crisis Event

Leaders take charge of the organization's response when crises break out. They initiate action, serve as spokespeople, engage in vigilant decision making, and connect to core values.

Initiate Action and Coordinate Activities

The leader's first responsibility is to recognize that a crisis has occurred. In many cases, such as industrial accidents or natural disasters, this determination is easy to make. Some crises are subtler, however. Intel failed to recognize that it faced a crisis in 1994 when it learned that its processor chip made mistakes when doing advanced calculations. The company decided to replace the chip only after the problem had been posted on the Internet and customers were angered.[19] Be prepared to convince your organization that the event is very important (poses a great risk), is an immediate threat, and can't be solved through ordinary measures and procedures. Put the crisis management plan into action and mobilize the crisis management team. Focus on containing the threats to people, property, and the environment.

Crises intensify the need for coordination. Resources and group members often have to be redeployed. For example, transportation personnel normally assigned to routine road maintenance operate snowplows and sanding trucks during blizzards. New systems and safeguards may also have to be put into place. Johnson & Johnson developed new tamper resistant packaging for Tylenol, for instance, and the Catholic Church adopted new guidelines for dealing with priests suspected of sexual abuse. In addition, leaders and their representatives have to contact and then coordinate with local government officials, emergency personnel, and the media.

Act as a Spokesperson

In case of an emergency, one person should take primary responsibility to speak on behalf of the entire organization in order to eliminate conflicting messages and to prevent the spread of misinformation. Generally the chief operating officer should fill this role, receiving assistance from others when needed. This leader's performance in front of the media will have a significant impact on public perceptions, for better or for worse. Successful spokespeople communicate in a clear, succinct, and forthright manner under pressure and handle hostile questions without getting angry or flustered. Taping and evaluating mock interviews and press conferences is one way to prepare for this role (see application exercise 7).

Those directly affected by the crisis have special information needs.[20] In addition to learning what happened, they also have to know how to protect themselves. Neighbors downwind of a chemical leak will need to be told how to evacuate; those in the path of a tornado will need to take shelter; potential victims of a virus will need to receive vaccinations. Communicating to these groups should be the top priority of the spokesperson and crisis management team.

Because leaders are the faces and voices of the organization, they need to respond quickly and forcefully when crisis breaks out. News of a disaster gets out fast and creates a demand for information. If your organization doesn't fill the information void, other groups (the media, critics) will, often supply misinformation. A rapid response ensures that the public gets accurate data and signals that the organization is taking control of the situation. Slow moving organizations appear inept and incompetent. They allow others to define the crisis situation. (See box 13.3 for an example of an organization that failed to move quickly enough in the face of a crisis.)

Leaders should appear before the media immediately even if they don't have the complete story. Spokespeople should never say "no comment," however. This statement is often taken as an admission of guilt. Instead, if you don't have information, admit that fact and promise to provide the data when it becomes available. Getting to the scene of the crisis is important as well. Rudolph Giuliani was praised for getting to Ground Zero within hours of the terrorist attacks. President George W. Bush was criticized for staying on vacation at his Texas ranch after Katrina struck the Gulf Coast.

Plan to cooperate with the media in order to encourage more accurate and favorable coverage. Make sure the spokesperson is available to the press at all

Box 13.3   Case Study
Information Insecurity at the Veterans Administration[21]

Computerization of records has created a new type of crisis: large-scale data theft. The largest loss of government records occurred when an external hard drive containing the names, birth dates, and Social Security numbers of 26 million veterans was stolen from the Maryland home of a Department of Veterans Affairs (VA) analyst. The VA collects this data in order to carry out its mission of providing health care, disability payments, home loans, and even burial plots to service people. It is against VA policy to take data files from the office, but the analyst had done so for years in order to work on a project.

Immediately after the hard drive and computer were stolen, the employee reported the theft to police and to his superiors at the VA. However, it took VA officials another 12 days to report the loss to VA Secretary Jim Nicholson. (The FBI wasn't asked to investigate until two weeks after the burglary.) Secretary Nicholson, in turn, did not notify veterans and the public until another week had passed, approximately three weeks after the theft took place. Department security officials and local police initially believed that only someone with a statistical software package could access the data but later reported that the information was readily available. When the two thieves who stole the computer and files in a burglary spree were apprehended, the FBI determined that they had not opened the files.

Observers blasted the VA for both its lax attitude toward information security and its slow response to the crisis. Said one veteran: "If we had done something like that in the military, we'd be punished by courts-martial. We protect America, and do they protect our personal information? No. It's galling."[22] The agency's inspector general criticized VA officials for demonstrating "little sense of urgency or responsibility" during the crisis. They apparently made little attempt at first to determine the extent of the data loss. VA Secretary Nicholson acknowledged that the agency's response was unacceptable. He then fired the analyst and forced out several supervisors who had been slow to report the theft. Nicholson did not explain why he waited several days to announce that the data was missing, however.

Secretary Nicholson vowed to make the VA a "goal standard and recognized leader in security of personal information" going forward. If so, then he and his department have a long way to go. Veterans Affairs earned an "F" on the annual computer security report card that measures compliance with the Federal Information Security Management Act. The VA's former chief information security officer reports that he was unable to implement significant security improvements in his three years on the job and that he only spoke to Nicholson once during his tenure, at a social event. The agency has yet to act on earlier recommendations made by its inspector general that background checks be performed on VA and contract workers; that off-duty workers be denied access to sensitive information; and that all employees receive annual security awareness training.

Discussion Questions

1. Why do you think it took so long for VA officials to respond to this crisis?

2. What immediate steps should have been taken?

3. Can you think of other examples of massive data theft? How did leaders respond in these cases?

4. How would you rate data security procedures at your college or university? Do you see any potential weaknesses that could produce a crisis?

5. How can leaders at the Veterans Administration and other organizations prevent future data security breaches?

6. What advice would you give VA officials to regain the trust of veterans and to restore the organization's public image? To the leaders of other organizations who have also experienced a similar crisis?

times. Compile press kits that describe the organization and its officers. Set up a crisis center with additional phone lines, copiers, and fax machines. Conduct press conferences well before newspaper and television deadlines.

When it comes to a crisis, honesty is the best policy. If your organization is at fault, take responsibility. Don't try to hide damaging information (chances are it will be discovered anyway), and correct your mistakes when necessary. At the beginning of the Tylenol tampering crisis, the Johnson & Johnson company stated that cyanide was not present in the manufacturing process. When the company later discovered that small amounts of the chemical were used, it admitted the error. Demonstrate genuine concern by acting as quickly as possible to repair the damage and by communicating your compassion for victims. Don't appear aloof and detached, as NASA did when it proclaimed that there was "an apparent malfunction" in the *Challenger* spacecraft as millions watched replays of the explosion on television. NASA spokespeople performed much better when the shuttle *Columbia* burned up. Officials expressed shock and sadness immediately after the tragedy.

Engage in Vigilant Decision Making

The stress of a crisis puts incredible demands on organizational leaders. Lives may have been lost, property damaged, or products recalled from shelves. Mental and physical fatigue sets in. Under such conditions, both individual leaders and groups of decision makers are tempted to make quick decisions. They need to be vigilant instead.[23] Vigilant decision makers examine a wide variety of options and weigh the costs and benefits of each alternative. They seek out new information and reevaluate their choices in the face of what they discover. (See the research highlight in box 13.4 for more information on how to remain vigilant in extreme crisis situations.)

Be sure to carry out the decision-making functions described in chapter 7—analyze the problem, set goals, and then identify and evaluate alternatives—whether working alone or with others. Be alert to possible decision-making biases that can intensify the crisis. When deciding in a group, be particularly attuned to symptoms of groupthink (which are more likely to appear when groups are under pressure) and the tendency to escalate commitment.

Box 13.4   Research Highlight
Wilderness Survival and Crisis Decision Making[24]

Research into wilderness survival provides important insights into how crisis decision makers should manage extreme stress. Outdoor writer and enthusiast Laurence Gonzales estimates that only 10–20 percent of those faced with a wilderness emergency (getting lost, being caught in an avalanche, crash landing on a mountain, capsizing on a boat) can think clearly enough to survive. More often than not, the physically strong lie down and perish while the weak push on and are rescued. To answer the question of who lives and who dies in these situations, the author examined historical records, interviewed survivors, studied brain physiology, met with experts, and attended survival camps.

Gonzales concludes that the key to survival lies in vigilance and in managing emotions. Survivors are highly sensitive to the environment and changing conditions. They also master their feelings in order to think rationally. In particular, they manage fear, which paralyzes at least 75 percent of those in a catastrophe. Victims of fear either freeze or wander around in a daze. That fact helps explain why a number of office workers in the World Trade Center attacks stayed near their desks rather than heading for the emergency exits.

Gonzales offers the following tips to those faced with danger, whether in the woods or in an office building or on the plant floor:

1. *Perceive, believe (look, see, believe).* Pay close attention to details from the moment the crisis starts. Immediately acknowledge and accept the reality of the situation. Don't blame the circumstances but focus on what you can do to address the situation.

2. *Stay calm (use fear to focus, use humor).* Make fear an ally; use it to sharpen your focus. Be on guard against emotional distractions. Keep a sense of humor. (Survivors are often able to make light of themselves and their circumstances.)

3. *Think/analyze/plan (get organized; set up small, manageable tasks).* Survivors quickly get organized, set up routines, and impose discipline. If you take such actions, you're likely to emerge as the group leader. Push aside the inner voice that declares that the situation is hopeless and follow the rational one that expects success.

4. *Take correct, decisive action (be bold and cautious while carrying out tasks).* Convert thought into action. Take necessary risks to help yourself and others. Break down major tasks into manageable steps. Deal with what is in your power to address; live moment to moment.

5. *Celebrate success (take joy in completing tasks).* Take joy in even the tiniest of successes. This joy increases motivation, prevents a feeling of hopelessness, and provides momentary relief from stress.

6. *Count your blessings (be grateful—you're alive).* Become a rescuer who focuses on the needs of others.

7. *Play (sing, play mind games, recite poetry, count anything, do mathematical problems in your head).* The more exposure you have had to art, poetry, mathematics, and literature, the more resources you'll have to draw on in an emergency. These resources are critical in calming emotions.

8. *See the beauty.* Survivors often report feelings of awe and wonder that come from being in tune with the natural world. Such appreciation can help reduce stress, enable you to take in new information, and motivate you to go on.

9. *Believe that you will succeed (develop a deep conviction that you'll live).* Fix your attention on making it through the emergency. Admonish yourself to be careful and do your best; believe that you will prevail if you do so.

10. *Surrender (let go of your fear of dying; "put away the pain").* Don't let the fear of death, pain, or failure stop you. Mountain climber Joe Simpson modeled this principle. He was abandoned by his climbing partner and left for dead on a peak in the Andes. Instead of giving up, for three days he crawled and hopped down the mountain on a severely broken leg until he reached safety.[25]

11. *Do whatever is necessary (be determined; have the will and the skill).* Have an accurate grasp of your abilities; don't under- or overestimate them. Be realistic about the situation; get what you need; do what you have to do.

12. *Never give up (let nothing break your spirit).* "There is always one more thing you can do." Don't get frustrated or discouraged by setbacks but recognize that the environment (natural, business, political) is constantly in flux. Start over again and keep your mind occupied with the resources described in step 7. Look for the opportunity in adversity. If you do, you may be like many other survivors who learn from, and are even grateful for, their survival experiences once they've reached safety.

> I take it we are all in complete agreement on the decision here. . . .
> Then I propose we postpone further discussion of this matter
> until our next meeting to give ourselves time to develop dis-
> agreement and perhaps gain some understanding of what the
> decision is all about.
>
> —Alfred P. Sloan

Connect with Vision and Values

One of a leader's major responsibilities during a crisis is to remind followers of the group's purpose and values, reinforcing their use as a set of operating
principles. Guided by a clear mission and a set of operating principles, organizational members can respond quickly and effectively in emergency situations.
Followers empowered to make decisions generally act decisively during a crisis.[26] If they are part of an organization with a commitment to people and society, their actions will likely be marked by integrity and compassion. During the
Tylenol tampering crisis, for instance, employees of Johnson & Johnson were
guided by the company's credo, which states that the firm is responsible to
local communities as well as to the world community.

Postcrisis Leadership

During the postcrisis phase, the leader spearheads the organization's
recovery. He or she helps the group restore its image, learn from the crisis experience, and experience healing.

Rebuild the Organization's Image

An organization can make it through the crisis stage but ultimately be
doomed if it cannot restore its image. Customers may boycott the company's
products; lawmakers may call for stricter regulation; voters may desert the
party; donors quit giving; and so on. Pan Am Airways went out of business in
part because the company was seen as callous and uncaring after Flight 103
was blown up over Scotland. Victims' families, the media, and the public
blamed Pan Am for inadequate security and ignoring a bomb threat.[27] World-
Com imploded after an accounting scandal. PTL (Praise the Lord) Ministries,
once a highly successful and visible religious organization, collapsed after
accusations of securities fraud and wasteful spending.

Because public image is so critical, leaders must help the group repair its
reputation when the immediate crisis is past. Communication professor William Benoit offers one widely used typology of image restoration strategies that
can be used in crisis situations.[28]

Denial. Organizational leaders try to avoid blame by (a) denying they were
responsible, or (b) shifting the responsibility to someone else. PepsiCo is one
organization that successfully used denial to avoid blame. The public accepted
its claim that it was not responsible for syringes in cans of its diet cola. On the
other hand, Bridgestone/Firestone and Ford unsuccessfully tried to shift blame
to each other during a tire crisis. Ford Explorers equipped with Firestone ATX
tires were involved in hundreds of crashes and deaths. Bridgestone/Firestone

blamed rollover problems on the design of the Ford Explorer; Ford faulted the tire manufacturer.[29]

Evading responsibility. Those who can't deny that they contributed to a crisis can try instead to lessen their responsibility for what happened. First, leaders may claim that they were provoked into action (provocation). The Bush administration, for example, argued that its controversial invasion of Iraq was justified because Saddam Hussein refused to stop his weapons program. Second, officials may claim that they can't be held accountable because of lack of information or factors like strikes or market forces beyond their control (defeasibility). Third, leaders may offer excuses (freak weather conditions, time pressures, lack of resources) to lower accountability. Fourth, leaders may evade responsibility by claiming good intentions. Actors may admit to a wrongdoing but claim that they were acting out of honorable intentions (they were trying to prevent a larger problem, help others, etc.).

Reducing offensiveness. There are several variations of this strategy, which is designed to reduce the audience's negative feelings toward the act and/or actor. *Bolstering* is attempting to boost the audience's positive affect for the leader and organization. Listeners may still be angry about what happened but these feelings may be offset in part by reminding them of the organization's past service to the community, excellent products, contributions to the local economy, and so on. *Minimization* reduces the damage caused by the crisis by convincing publics that what happened wasn't as bad as it seemed. There weren't as many injuries as first feared, for example, or that the damage caused by an oil spill will soon dissipate. *Differentiation* distinguishes the act in question from other similar but more damaging actions. A company might point out, for instance, that a misstatement of earnings does not equate to widespread accounting fraud. *Transcendence* places a harmful act in a broader context to justify behavior. For instance, a police officer accused of shooting an unarmed suspect may claim that all traffic stops are potentially dangerous and that the suspect appeared to be holding a gun. *Attacking the accusers* turns the tables by reducing the credibility of the critics. Such attacks can deflect attention away from the speaker and reduce damage to his/her image. Former House majority leader Tom DeLay used this approach with limited effect, publicly condemning the Texas prosecutor who accused him of campaign finance violations (he still had to resign his post and stand trial). *Compensation* attempts to reduce the damage of an action by offering payments to those, for example, who were hospitalized after eating tainted food or lost their loved ones in a plant explosion.

Corrective action. In corrective action, organizational leaders pledge to correct the problem by restoring conditions to what they were before the crisis or by taking steps to make sure that the problem doesn't reoccur. Often this strategy is combined with an apology, but an organization can take corrective action without admitting guilt. Corrective action differs from compensation. While compensation is designed to counterbalance the damage, corrective action promises to rectify the situation. The Schwan Food Company took swift corrective action after a number of customers came down with salmonella poisoning after eating the firm's signature ice cream products. The problem arose when pasteurized ice cream mix was transported from a supplier to the firm's

Marshall, Minnesota, plant in a truck that had previously carried raw eggs. In response, the company built its own plant to pasteurize the ice cream mix and dedicated a fleet of tanker trucks specifically to transport the product.[30]

Mortification. Mortification consists of admitting responsibility and asking for forgiveness. If the apology is seen as sincere, stakeholders often pardon the organization. AT&T used this strategy following a breakdown in New York City long-distance phone service in 1991. After initially trying to shift the blame to low-level workers, company leaders admitted responsibility for the disruption.[31]

Benoit applies his typology to a number of significant crises, such as the Exxon *Valdez* oil spill, the Bhopal tragedy, the Sears auto repair scandal, and court battles over the safety of Dow Corning breast implants. Based on his analysis, he offers several suggestions for leaders engaged in image restoration. First, if you and your organization are at fault, acknowledge that fact right away. Credibility can be severely damaged if an organization initially denies responsibility but then is forced to accept blame later. Second, denial, if backed by solid evidence, can restore a tarnished reputation. Third, shifting blame generally is only effective when attention shifts away from the organization and onto a plausible scapegoat or when there does appear to be factors beyond the organization's control. (Exxon was unable to shift blame to the captain of the *Valdez* oil tanker, for example.) Fourth, outline plans to correct the immediate effects of the crisis and to prevent a recurrence in the future. Fifth, minimizing the damage can backfire if the organization is seen as trying to trivialize a significant problem. Sixth, a combination of image restoration strategies (mortification and corrective action, bolstering and defeasibility) often works better than one tactic alone. Seventh, employing several groups to reinforce the message (top management, customers, employees, suppliers) is generally more effective than one group speaking on its own. Eighth, the more important or salient a disaster is to an audience, the harder it will be to restore the image of the organization linked to the crisis. Ninth, the power of image restoration is limited. If your group has made serious mistakes, it can expect to suffer serious consequences.

Learn from the Experience

Image restoration must be coupled with learning or the crisis is likely to repeat itself. That's why detailed record keeping and evaluation are built into the crisis management plan. Three forms of organizational learning should take place in the postcrisis phase.[32] In *retrospective sensemaking,* organizational members look back to identify what they previously overlooked and to highlight faulty assumptions that contributed to the emergency. Such self-reflection can lead to greater understanding and improve crisis planning and response. The *Columbia* Accident Investigation Board, for instance, put much of the blame for the disaster on the organization's culture, which, as we've seen, became overconfident about safety and prevented communication between the agency departments and levels. Faulty assumptions led engineers to believe that all materials covering the spacecraft were equally durable when they were not.

Reconsidering structure addresses the structural problems. Crisis disrupts the current organizational structure and provides opportunity for change. In many cases, changes in leadership, practices, and processes are required in order for the group to regain its legitimacy. One major organizational restructuring took place after the events of 9/11 when the Department of Homeland Security (DHS) was created. The DHS combined the Coast Guard, FEMA, the Transportation Safety Agency, and other departments into one unit.

Since crises are so public, organizations can often learn from the examples of others. *Vicarious learning* consists of observing models of crisis management or mismanagement and then applying the insights learned. Take the case of Hurricane Katrina. We can learn from the mistakes of local, state, and national officials to prepare for the next major natural disaster. (Read about some of the positive lessons that can be learned from the events of 9/11 in box 13.5.)

> Adversity is the first path to truth.
>
> —Lord Byron

The ultimate goal of crisis learning is to rebuild the organization so that it rarely fails even though it may face lots of unexpected events. According to University of Michigan business professors Karl Weick and Kathleen Sutcliffe, high reliability organizations (HROs) have mindful cultures.[33] They are very sensitive to even the weakest signs that trouble is brewing and respond forcefully. Weick and Sutcliffe use the nuclear aircraft carrier as the prototypical HRO. A carrier's deck has been called "the most dangerous four and one-half acres in the world." This small space is filled with jet aircraft (armed with lethal weapons) that are constantly launching and landing. It is covered with a slippery mix of seawater and oil. There are few safe places to stand, and vocal communication is difficult. Those who run the ship's operations are generally 19- and 20-year-olds who may never have seen a jet close up or who have never been on a large, ocean-going vessel. (For another example of a high reliability naval organization, see Leadership on the Big Screen at the end of the chapter.)

Despite the dangers, mishaps on aircraft carriers are rare. Weick and Sutcliffe argue that adopting the practices of this high-reliability organization can help other complex groups (health care facilities, railroads, nuclear power plants) reduce their odds of crisis.

Carrier captains build a high reliability culture that is *preoccupied with (mindful of) failure*. Every landing is filmed and graded, and near misses require detailed debriefings. Any deviation is seen as a potential sign of a larger, more significant problem. Crewmembers of every rank routinely walk the deck to spot any object (a bolt, a wrench) that could get sucked into a fighter engine and cause a crash. Carrier crews are *reluctant to simplify*, taking nothing for granted. Every plane is inspected several times, and responsibilities are clearly communicated through uniform color, hand signals, and voice signals. The entire ship is *concerned with operations*. Officers engage in continuous communication during flight operations. The captain who is in charge of the ship and the commander of the Air Wing (who directs the aircraft) are positioned to observe every step of the operation. Crews are *committed to resilience*. They know the importance of routines but can improvise in the face of surprises. For example, the first captain of the nuclear carrier *Carl Vinson* drove the ship at 10 knots in reverse during an intense storm. This reduced wind speeds across the

Box 13.5   Research Highlight
The Crisis Communication Lessons of 9/11[34]

The terrorist attacks on September 11, 2001, marked one of the most significant crises in the history of American business. Companies located in and near the World Trade Center lost employees, offices, records, and communication systems. Other corporations were unable to fill orders, airlines were grounded, stock trading was suspended, and business activity declined dramatically. Even companies not directly or indirectly impacted by the crisis had to respond to employees traumatized by these events.

Paul Argenti, a professor of management and corporate communication at Dartmouth College, interviewed managers and executives after 9/11 to identify guideposts for future leaders who find themselves in crisis situations. He discovered that internal communications take priority in extreme circumstances. Employee morale and confidence must be restored before an organization can take any constructive action (serving customers, covering news stories, resuming flights, managing investments). Professor Argenti identifies five crisis communication lessons from 9/11.

Lesson 1: Get on the Scene. During the crisis, the most effective leaders maintained a high profile. New York City Mayor Rudolph Giuliani arrived at the World Trade Center (WTC) within minutes of the first attack, held several press conferences near Ground Zero, and attended many funerals and memorial services for victims. Top officials at Verizon visited thousands of employees near the WTC. At *The New York Times*, the president, CEO, and publisher formed a crisis management team that walked through the building every day to answer questions and to thank employees. According to Argenti, followers needed to hear the voices of their leaders:

> Written statements have their place, but oral statements and the sound of an empathic human voice communicate sincerity. And if the voice belongs to a company leader, the listener has reason to think that the full weight of the company stands behind whatever promises and assurances are being made.

Lesson 2: Choose Your Channels Carefully. The terrorist attacks disrupted normal channels of communication. Morgan Stanley, for example, lost the voice mail system that served 3,700 employees in the Two World Trade Center and Five World Trade Center buildings. Leaders had to become creative about how they communicated with followers. Workers at Morgan Stanley confirmed that they were safe by calling one of the toll-free lines at the firm's Discover Card call center. This number was broadcast by the television networks and placed on the ticker display on the Times Square building. American Airlines president Don Carty updated his labor force through the SABRE machines that print itineraries and tickets as well as through e-mail and the Internet.

Lesson 3: Stay Focused on the Business. Concentrating on work provides an outlet to employees, provides a sense of normalcy, builds pride in the company, and creates bonds with suppliers and customers. The Dell Corporation, headquartered in Texas, wasn't a target of the attacks. Yet its customers were. Dell employees (who had records of what customers had lost) worked overtime to ship replacement products. At the same time, corporate communications officials provided regular updates on the crisis to personnel.

Lesson 4: Have a Plan in Place. Crisis plans need to be backed by alternate work sites. The New York Board of Trade established two backup sites after the truck bombing at the WTC in 1993. These contingency locations enabled the organization to quickly resume trading in 2001. While operations can be scattered among several sites, decision making and communication should be centralized. American Airlines operated out of a specially designed crisis command center. Messages at Oppenheimer Funds came directly from the corporate affairs director and CEO. Many respondents told Argenti that having experienced communications professionals on hand was essential to coping with the crisis. These professionals didn't panic and could be used in a variety of jobs.

Lesson 5: Improvise, but from a Strong Foundation. When a crisis strikes, managers and employees have to think on their feet. However, they are more likely to make the right choices if they are prepared. Preparation extends beyond training to include instilling corporate values. One of the key values in the Starbucks mission statement is, "Contribute positively to our communities and our environment." Driven by this precept, managers at several undamaged stores near Ground Zero kept their locations open even though all other stores around the country were ordered shut. Starbucks employees provided coffee and pastries to medical personnel and rescue workers and also pulled pedestrians to safety.

Like many other tragedies, the trauma of 9/11 brought people closer together. Many of the executives interviewed by Professor Argenti reported that their companies sustained a sense of community by keeping the communication lines open long after the immediate danger had past.

deck to allow planes to land safely. Finally, team members *defer to expertise.* A lower-level officer may override a superior if he or she has more knowledge about, for example, how to land an aircraft with mechanical problems.

Promote Healing

Taking corrective action is an important step to healing. Addressing vulnerabilities (reinforcing flood levees, tighter security measures) reduces stress and promotes recovery. In addition to correcting problems, carefully shape the memories of what happened. Honor heroes, like the firefighters who died while rescuing the victims of 9/11 or students and professors who barricaded classroom doors during the shootings at Virginia Tech. Remember the bravery and sacrifice of those touched by the tragedy. Observe the anniversary of the crisis. In some cases, plaques, trees, and other memorials are appropriate.

The goal of healing is renewal, although many organizations never reach this state. Renewed organizations focus on the future, on how they can explore new opportunities. They put aside blame to tell stories about support and rebuilding. Former FEMA Director James Lee Witt argues that, when it comes to natural disasters at least, crisis can be turned into triumph:

> I'm taken by the fact that I meet people all the time who start their stories about surviving a crisis with words along the lines of "I think the storm was a blessing." Their tales usually turn to the ways that the disaster forced them to work with people they didn't know beforehand, or to find out how they or their neighbors could be heroes, or to realign the priorities in their life, or to make their town a safer place. A crisis gives your people a chance to demonstrate leadership that can be valuable not just in a crisis. It allows you to solidify relationships with suppliers, clients, or partners. It forces you to see the weaknesses in the way you do business and turn them into strengths.[35]

CHAPTER TAKEAWAYS

- A crisis is any major unpredictable event that threatens an organization. Common types of crises include economic, informational, physical, human resources, reputational, psychopathic acts, and natural disasters.
- Regardless of type, crises pass through the same series of stages. The pre-crisis stage is a period of normalcy when the group should be alert to

warning signs (prodomes) that signal that a crisis is developing. The crisis event stage begins when trouble breaks out and ends when the immediate danger is over. The postcrisis phase of evaluation and analysis starts when the immediate danger is past and the organization has resumed normal operations.

- Each stage of the crisis process requires different communication skills and strategies. Your duty as a leader in the precrisis stage is to move the organization from crisis prone to crisis ready. Crisis readiness requires (a) recognizing danger signs through scanning the external and internal environments; (b) identifying trouble spots or vulnerabilities; (c) developing a crisis management plan (including a crisis management team); and (d) building organizational credibility.

- During the crisis event, you will need to initiate action by convincing the organization that a crisis exists, by implementing the crisis management plan, and by mobilizing the crisis management team. Coordinate such activities as redeploying resources and group members, instituting new systems and safeguards, containing the damage, and working with outside agencies. Act as a spokesperson during the crisis, appearing before the media and providing information to protect victims. Effective spokespeople respond quickly and forcefully by getting to the scene of the crisis whenever possible, cooperating with media outlets, and expressing honesty and compassion.

- In the midst of the emergency, engage in vigilant decision making. Resist the temptation to reach decisions quickly and seek out new information instead, reevaluating your choices based on what you discover. In addition, connect with the organization's ethical foundation, encouraging followers to use shared vision and values as operating principles during the crisis.

- After the immediate threat is past, help your organization restore its reputation, learn from the experience, and promote healing. Commonly used image restoration strategies include: (1) denial (denying or shifting responsibility); (2) evading responsibility (lessening the degree of responsibility for what happened); (3) reducing offensiveness (minimizing the audience's negative feelings toward the act and actor); (4) corrective action to repair the damage and to prevent a reoccurrence of the problem; and (5) mortification (admitting guilt and apologizing). When at fault, acknowledge that fact right away and outline plans for correcting the immediate problem and for preventing a recurrence in the future.

- Learning is facilitated by thorough record keeping during the crises event and takes place through retrospective sensemaking (reflecting on past events), organizational restructuring and through observing the examples of other organizations. The ultimate goal of crisis learning is to create a high reliability organization. High reliability organizations are mindful of failure, taking nothing for granted while improvising in the face of surprises.

- Corrective action promotes healing, as does shaping the memories of events, focusing on the future, and recognizing that triumph can come out of tragedy.

APPLICATION EXERCISES

1. In a group, create your own list of possible crises that could strike your college or university. Place these potential crises in the categories outlined in the chapter.

2. Choose one crisis from your list in exercise 1 and develop a response plan.

3. Use one of the trouble-shooting tactics in the chapter to prepare your organization for a crisis.

4. Share your response to the self-assessment in box 13.2 with a partner. What does your score reveal about the crisis preparedness of your organization? What steps should it take to better prepare for potential crisis events?

5. Describe a time when you and/or your organization were in a crisis situation. Identify what you learned from the experience.

6. Create a crisis case study. Describe the type and development of the crisis and how it was managed. Evaluate the effectiveness of the leader and organization. Determine the long-term effects of the crisis event and the organization's learning, healing, and renewal. Identify a set of lessons you can draw from this event.

7. Role-play a crisis press conference. Choose 6–8 class members to be the crisis team and assign a specific organizational role (CEO, public relations director, chief engineer) to each. The rest of the class will be the reporters. Separate the groups to prepare for the news conference. Begin with a statement from the crisis management team, followed by questions from the reporters. Make sure that the entire CMT participates. Film the proceedings and debrief, evaluating the performance of both sides.

8. Evaluate your survival ability based on the research highlight in box 13.4. Write up your conclusions.

9. As a class, brainstorm a list of the ways that groups and organizations can promote healing after a crisis.

10. What crisis leadership lessons do you take away from the attack on the World Trade Center in 2001? How do these compare to those outlined in box 13.5?

CULTURAL CONNECTIONS: CAUGHT IN THE CROSSFIRE[36]

Multinational corporations face crises when they get caught in the crossfire of religious and political disputes. Angry Muslims, for example, retaliated against Dutch businesses after unflattering cartoons featuring the Prophet Mohammed appeared in newspapers in the Netherlands. Some U.S. residents urged a boycott of French products after the government of France refused to support the Iraqi invasion.

Italian companies found themselves under attack in the late 1990s. The Italian government refused to extradite Kurdish rebel Abdullah Öcalan to Turkey. The rebel leader was scheduled to stand trial for crimes committed during the conflict between the majority Turks and minority Kurds. Thousands of Turks took to the streets to protest against Italy and Italian businesses such as Fiat, Ferrari, and Perelli. They burned Italian flags and silk ties, threatened to attack stores, and shunned Italian and Italian-sounding products.

Many Italian companies tried to convince the public through newspaper ads that Turkish subsidiaries, run by Turks, should not be blamed for the actions of the Italian government. Most Turks were unwilling to accept this rational argument, which assumed that they would think like Italian corporate executives. Clothing manufacturer Benetton-Turkey decided to take a different approach. The company's corporate response team took out ads that sided emotionally with the Turkish people. These print ads proclaimed: "First and foremost, we are Turks too! Our first allegiance and loyalty is to Turkey! We feel the same way that you do towards the Italians!"

Benetton-Turkey backed up its public statements by altering the company's famous logo "The United Colors of Benetton." This logo stands for the unification of people in the midst of their diversity. However, with the support of store managers, the firm removed the colors from the corporate symbol. It placed black wreaths in its storefronts and dressed mannequins in black to signal a state of mourning. During the crisis, top executives eliminated store quotas to reduce the economic pressure caused by the boycotts. These efforts paid off. The company survived the crisis with a minimum of financial damage. Grateful Turkish citizens taped Post-it notes and poems expressing support to Benetton store windows.

Benetton-Turkey's example demonstrates the importance of thinking outside the typical "corporate box" when dealing with crises, particularly those involving cultural differences. The company's appeal to national emotions turned Benetton-Turkey from a victim to a hero.

SPOTLIGHT ON TECHNOLOGY: DEALING WITH CRISIS AT COLLEGES AND UNIVERSITIES[37]

An ever-growing number of physical disasters, such as Hurricane Katrina and the Northridge earthquake, and human crises, like the Duke lacrosse scandal, the Virginia Tech and Northern Illinois shootings, and the privacy data leak affecting 300,000 people at Ohio University, have led many colleges and universities to be more aware of the potential for a crisis on campus. One of the major challenges in such crises is the question of how to communicate to large numbers of students, parents, faculty, staff, and community members in a short period of time. There are a wide variety of technologies available to communicate in a crisis. Each communication tool has a number of characteristics that should be taken into consideration.

Landline telephone. Traditional landlines still account for the bulk of communication at most institutions. Widespread events such as flooding, chemical release, or a serious epidemic may result in a lapse in the maintenance necessary for reliable performance. Further, power failure, equipment failure, and damage to cables can render landlines unusable. Landlines are also limited to those in close proximity to their telephone receiver.

Cell phones. Cell phones have been widely adopted, particularly among students. In a crisis they can be invaluable tools, but as with fixed networks, mobile networks are subject to overload from a massive increase in demand and outages from significant infrastructure damage. Further, cell phones must be switched on to receive a call.

Text messaging. Text messaging allows mobile and computer devices to send and retrieve simple messages up to 160 characters in length. Longer messages can be joined together, but this is not normally recommended in crisis situations where brevity and clarity are important. Text messages are less resource intensive than mobile voice calls, so networks can better cope with increased demand. Unfortunately, evidence of delivery does not confirm that the message has been read, or perhaps more importantly, understood.

E-mail. E-mail is suitable for long and detailed messages and can be sent to large groups relatively quickly. There are no delivery guarantees and obtaining return information is less effective when dealing with a large number of respondents. E-mail systems generally require Internet access or access to fixed communications networks, and these are vulnerable to disruption in times of crisis.

Internet (Web, IM, podcasting, Web cams, etc.). The flexibility of the Internet provides a wide variety of communication media (including instant messaging, podcasting, Web cams, application sharing, and others). As long as users are familiar with them, they can all be used with great effectiveness—provided that access to the Internet is available with a reasonable degree of speed. The Web is a very efficient means of broadcasting messages, and the simple addition of a news update on a college or university Web site can be read by large numbers of people quickly and efficiently.

LEADERSHIP ON THE BIG SCREEN:
MASTER AND COMMANDER: THE FAR SIDE OF THE WORLD

Starring: Russell Crowe, Paul Bettany, Billy Boyd, James D'Arcy, Lee Ingleby
Rating: PG-13 for violence
Synopsis: Russell Crowe stars as "Lucky" Jack Aubrey, captain of the British ship HMS *Surprise* during the Napoleonic wars. Aubrey leads his crew of nearly 200 men into battle against a much larger, faster, better-armed, and better-fortified French frigate off the coast of South America. The captain must help his crew cope with a series of emergencies, including surprise attacks, a sudden storm, an accidental shooting, a suicide, and the threat of mutiny. He leads them to victory through a mixture of vigilance, discipline, preparation, flexibility, and creativity. Based on a series of naval novels by Patrick O'Brian.

Chapter Links: crisis readiness, crisis response, vigilant decision making, crisis learning and recovery, building a high reliability organization

Endnotes

Chapter 1

[1] For more information on the history of leadership study, see: Bass, B. M. (Ed.). (1990). *Bass and Stogdill's handbook of leadership* (3rd ed., ch. 1). New York: Free Press.

[2] See, for example: Meindl, J. R., Ehrlich, S. B., & Dukerich, J. M. (1985). The romance of leadership. *Administrative Science Quarterly, 30,* 78–102; Meindl, J. R. (1995). The romance of leadership as a follower-centric theory: A social constructionist approach. *Leadership Quarterly, 6,* 329–341; Kiechel, W. (1988, November 21). The case against leaders. *Fortune,* 217–218.

[3] Bass, ch. 1.

[4] Staw, B. M., & Sutton, R. (1993). Macro organizational psychology. In J. K. Murnighan (Ed.), *Social psychology in organizations: Advances in theory and research* (pp. 350–384). Englewood Cliffs, NJ: Prentice-Hall; Meindl.

[5] Fairhurst, G. T., & Sarr, R. A. (1996). *The art of framing.* San Francisco: Jossey-Bass.

[6] Adapted from Tichy, N. M. (1997). *The leadership engine.* New York: HarperBusiness, pp. 215–216. Copyright © 1997 by Noel M. Tichy. Reprinted by permission of HarperCollins Publishers.

[7] An IMAX film crew was on Mt. Everest during the 1996 disaster and recorded the rescue efforts. The video and DVD of *Everest* (Miramax Films, 1998) are available for purchase or rental. Krakauer, J. (1997). *Into thin air.* New York: Villard.

[8] Dance, F. E. X. (1982). A speech theory of human communication. In F. E. X. Dance (Ed.), *Human communication theory* (pp. 120–146). New York: Harper & Row, p. 126.

[9] White, L. A. (1949). *The science of culture.* New York: Farrar, Strauss and Cudahy, p. 25.

[10] Information concerning differences among human and animal communication systems is extensive. The following sources serve as a good starting point for reading in this area: Adler, J. J. (1967). *The difference of man and the difference it makes.* New York: Holt, Rinehart and Winston; Pearce, W. B. (1989). *Communication and the human condition.* Carbondale: Southern Illinois University Press; Sebeok, T. A., & Rosenthal, R. (Eds.). (1981). *The clever Hans phenomenon: Communication with horses, whales, apes, and people* (Annals of the New York Academy of Sciences, Vol. 364). New York: New York Academy of Sciences; Sebeok, T. A., & Umiker-Sebeok, J. (1979). *Speaking of apes: A critical anthology of two-way communication with man.* New York: Plenum; Terrace, H. S., Pettito, L. A., Sanders, R. J., & Bever, T. G. (1979). Can an ape create a sentence? *Science, 206,* 891–902; Walker, S. (1983). *Animal thought.* London: Routledge & Kegan Paul.

[11] Barnlund, D. C. (1962). Toward a meaning-centered philosophy of communication. *Journal of Communication, 12,* 197–211.

[12] Burns, J. M. (1978). *Leadership.* New York: Harper & Row, p. 2.

[13] Rost, J. C. (1991). *Leadership for the twenty-first century.* New York: Praeger.

[14] Bogardus, E. S. (1934). *Leaders and leadership*. New York: Appleton-Century.

[15] Bingham, W. V. (1927). Leadership. In H. C. Metcalf, *The psychological foundations of management*. New York: Shaw.

[16] Hersey, P. (1984). *The situational leader*. Escondido, CA: Center for Leadership Studies, p. 14.

[17] Bass, B. M. (1960). *Leadership, psychology, and organizational behavior*. New York: Harper & Row, p. 90.

[18] Alvesson, M. (2002). *Understanding organizational culture*. Thousand Oaks, CA: Sage, p. 105.

[19] Hemphill, J. K. (1949). The leader and his group. *Journal of Educational Research, 28*, 225–229.

[20] Stogdill, R. M. (1950). Leadership, membership and organization. *Psychological Bulletin, 47*, p. 4.

[21] Rost, J. C. (1993). Leadership in the new millennium. *The Journal of Leadership Studies*, 91–110, p. 99; Rost, *Leadership for the twenty-first century*.

[22] See, for example: Block, P. (1993). *Stewardship*. San Francisco: Berrett-Koehler; Greenleaf, R. K. (1977). *Servant leadership*. New York: Paulist Press.

[23] Northouse, P. (2007). *Leadership: Theory and practice* (4th ed.). Thousand Oaks, CA: Sage, p. 3.

[24] Yukl, G. (2006). *Leadership in organizations* (6th ed.). Upper Saddle River, NJ: Prentice-Hall, p. 8.

[25] Nahavandi, A. (2006). *The art and science of leadership* (4th ed.). Upper Saddle River, NJ: Prentice-Hall, p. 4.

[26] Manning, G., & Curtis, K. (1988). *Leadership: Nine keys to success*. Cincinnati: South-Western.

[27] Witherspoon, P. D. (1997). *Communicating leadership: An organizational perspective*. Boston: Allyn & Bacon, p. 19.

[28] Kouzes, J. M., & Posner, B. Z. (1987). *The leadership challenge: How to get extraordinary things done in organizations*. San Francisco: Jossey-Bass, pp. 31–32.

[29] Bennis, W., & Nanus, B. (1985). *Leaders: The strategies for taking charge*. New York: Harper & Row, p. 21.

[30] Bennis, W. (1976). *The unconscious conspiracy: Why leaders can't lead*. New York: AMACOM, p. 154.

[31] Kotter, J. P. (1990). *A force for change: How leadership differs from management*. New York: Free Press p. 6. Reprinted with the permission of The Free Press, a Division of Simon & Schuster Adult Publishing Group, from *A force for change: How leadership differs from management* by John P. Kotter. Copyright © 1990 by John P. Kotter, Inc. All rights reserved.

[32] Lieber, R. B. (1998, January 12). Why employees love these companies. *Fortune*, pp. 72–74.

[33] Peters, T. (1994). *The pursuit of wow!* New York: Vintage Books, p. 165.

[34] Freiberg, K., & Freiberg, J. (1996). *Nuts! Southwest Airlines crazy recipe for business and personal success*. New York: Broadway Books, p. 288.

[35] Freiberg & Freiberg, p. 148.

[36] Labich, K. (1994, May 2). Is Herb Kelleher America's best CEO? *Fortune*, 46–50.

[37] Herskovitz, J. (2002, June 8–9). Job candidates queue up. *New Zealand Herald*, p. C7.

[38] Wow, are they that good? (2002, August 5). *Business Week*, 14.

[39] Peters, T. (1992). *Liberation management*. New York: Ballantine, p. 656.

[40] Kotter, pp. 56, 65–67.

[41] Kotter, pp. 6–7.

[42] Kotter, J. P. (1999). *On what leaders really do*. Boston: Harvard Business School Press.

[43] Gardner, J. W. (1986). The tasks of leadership *(Leadership Paper No. 2)*. Washington, DC: Independent Sector, p. 7.

[44] Peters, T., & Austin, N. (1985). *A passion for excellence: The leadership difference*. New York: Random House, p. 328.

[45] Kellerman, B. (2004). *Bad leadership*. Boston: Harvard University Press; Lipman-Blumen, J. (2005). *The allure of toxic leaders*. New York: Oxford University Press.

[46] This notion of making a distinction between leaders and power wielders comes from Burns.

[47] Kellerman, B. (1999). Hitler's ghost: A manifesto. In B. Kellerman & L. Matusak (Eds.), *Cutting edge leadership 2000* (pp. 65–68). College Park, MD: Burns Academy of Leadership.

[48] Definitions and examples from Kellerman, *Bad leadership*.

[49] Adapted from Lipman-Blumen, pp. 19–22. Used by permission.

[50] Pearce, C. L., & Conger, J. A. (2003). All those years ago: The historical underpinnings of shared leadership. In C. L. Pearce & J. A. Conger (Eds.), *Shared leadership: Reframing the hows and whys of leadership* (pp. 1–16). Thousand Oaks, CA: Sage; Pearce, C. L. (2004). The future of leadership: Combining vertical and shared leadership to transform knowledge work. *Academy of Management Review, 18*, 47–57; O'Toole, J., Galbraith, J., Lawler, E. E. (2002). When two (or more) heads are better than one: The promise and pitfalls of shared leadership. *California Management Review, 44*, 65–83.

[51] Hollander, E. P. (1992, April). The essential interdependence of leadership and followership. *Current Directions in Psychological Science*, 71–75.

52 Litzinger, W., & Schaefer, T. (1982, September–October). Leadership through followership. *Business Horizons,* 78–81.

53 Heenan, D. A., & Bennis, W. (1999). *Co-leaders: The power of great partnerships.* New York: John Wiley & Sons, p. 6.

54 Heenan & Bennis, p. 6.

55 Kelley, R. (1992). *The power of followership: How to create leaders people want to follow and followers who lead themselves.* New York: Doubleday/Currency, p. 41.

56 Summaries of the development of the Willingness to Communicate construct can be found in: McCroskey, J. C., & Richmond, V. P. (1998). Willingness to communicate. In J. C. McCroskey, J. A. Daly, M. M. Martin, & M. J. Beatty (Eds.), *Communication and personality: Trait perspectives* (pp. 119–131). Cresswell, NJ: Hampton Press; Richmond, V. P., & Roach, K. D. (1992). Willingness to communicate and employee success in U.S. organizations. *Journal of Applied Communication Research, 20,* 95–115; McCroskey, J. C., & Richmond, V. P. (1991). Willingness to communicate: A cognitive view. In M. Booth-Butterfield (Ed.), *Personality and interpersonal communication* (pp. 129–156). Newbury Park, CA: Sage.

57 McCroskey, J. C., & Richmond, V. P. (1990). Willingness to communicate: Differing cultural perspectives. *Southern Communication Journal, 56,* 72–77.

58 McCroskey, J. C., & Richmond, V. P. (1996). *Fundamentals of human communication: An interpersonal perspective.* Long Grove, IL: Waveland Press, pp. 53–54. Used by permission.

59 Johnson, C., Dixon, B., Hackman, M. Z., & Vinson, L. (1995). Willingness to communicate, the need for cognition and innovativeness: New Zealand students and professionals. In J. E. Aitken & L. J. Shedletsky (Eds.), *Intrapersonal communication processes* (pp. 376–381). Plymouth, MI: Midnight Oil and the Speech Communication Association; Hackman, M. Z., & Johnson, C. (1994). *A cross-cultural investigation of innovativeness, willingness to communicate and need for cognition.* Paper presented at the Speech Communication Association convention, New Orleans, LA.

60 Harvey, M. (2006). Leadership and the human condition. In G. R. Goethals & G. L. J. Sorenson (Eds.), *The quest for a general theory of leadership* (pp. 39–45). Northampton, MA: Edward Elgar, p. 42.

61 Denning, S. (2005). *The leader's guide to storytelling.* San Francisco: Jossey-Bass.

62 Mirvis, P. (1996, March). Can you teach your people to think smarter? *Across the Board,* 26–27.

63 Definitions and examples from Denning.

64 Freiberg & Freiberg, p. 290.

65 Information and quotes from: Clark, E. (2004). *Around the corporate campfire: How great leaders use stories to inspire success.* Sevierville, TN: Insight. Goldberg, A. B., & Ritter, B. (2006, August 2). Costco CEO finds pro-worker means profitability. *ABC News* online; Greenhouse, S. (2005, July 17). How Costco became the anti-Wal-Mart. *New York Times* online edition; Harris, C. (2007, December 9). Costco sticks to concept. *The Gazette,* p. B4; *The Costco Connection* (2006, October).

66 For an overview of the development of the field of emotional intelligence, see Mayer, J. D. (2001). A field guide to emotional intelligence. In J. Ciarrochi, J. P. Forgas, & J. D. Mayer (Eds.), *Emotional intelligence in everyday life: A scientific inquiry* (pp. 3–24). Philadelphia: Psychology Press.

67 Goleman, D. (1995). *Emotional intelligence: Why it can matter more than IQ.* New York: Bantam Books.

68 Goleman, D. (1998). *Working with emotional intelligence.* New York: Bantam Books; Cherniss, C., & Goleman, D. (Eds.). (2001). *The emotionally intelligent workplace: How to select for, measure, and improve emotional intelligence in individuals, groups and organizations.* San Francisco: Jossey-Bass.

69 Goleman, D., Boyatzis, R., & McKee, A. (2002). *Primal leadership: Realizing the power of emotional intelligence.* Boston: Harvard Business School Press.

70 Cherniss, C. (2000). Social and emotional competence in the workplace. In R. Bar-On & J. D. A. Parker (Eds.), *The handbook of emotional intelligence: Theory, development, assessment, and application at home, school, and in the workplace.* San Francisco: Jossey-Bass; Goleman, *Working with emotional intelligence;* Cooper, R. K., & Sawat, A. (1996). *Executive EQ: Emotional intelligence in leadership and organizations.* New York: Grosset/Putnam; Weisinger, H. (1998). *Emotional intelligence at work: The untapped edge for success.* San Francisco: Jossey-Bass.

71 Johnson, C. (2002). Evaluating the impact of emotional intelligence on leadership performance: Resonance or dissonance? *Selected Proceedings of the 2002 International Leadership Association convention* [online]. Available from http://www.academy.umd.edu/ILA.

72 Salovey, P., Bedell, B. T., Detweiler, J. B., & Mayer, J. D. (2000). Current directions in emotional intelligence research. In M. Lewis & J. M. Haviland-Lewis (Eds.), *Handbook of emotions* (2nd ed., pp. 504–520). New York: Guilford Press.

73 Goffman, E. (1959). *The presentation of self in everyday life*. Garden City, NY: Doubleday; Brissett, D., & Edgley, C. (Eds.), The dramaturgical perspective. In D. Brissett & C. Edgley (Eds.), *Life as theater: A dramaturgical sourcebook* (2nd ed., pp. 1–46). New York: Aldine de Gruyter; Gardner, W. L., & Martinko, M. J. (1988). Impression management in organizations. *Journal of Management, 14*, 321–338.

74 Gardner, W. L. (1992). Lessons in organizational dramaturgy: The art of impression management. *Organizational Dynamics, 21*, 33–46; Gardner, W. L., & Cleavenger, D. (1998). The impression management strategies associated with transformational leadership at the world-class level: A psychological assessment. *Management Communication Quarterly, 12*, 3–41; Gardner, W. L., & Avolio, B. J. (1998). The charismatic relationship: A dramaturgical perspective. *Academy of Management Review, 23*, 32–58; Sosi, J. J., Avolio, B. J., & Jung, D. I. (2002). Beneath the mask: Examining the relationship of self-presentation attributes and impression management to charismatic leadership. *Leadership Quarterly, 13*, 217–242.

75 Keegan, J. (1987). *The mask of command*. New York: Viking Penguin.

76 Keegan, p. 11.

77 Keegan, p. 318.

78 Gardner & Avolio.

79 Rosenfeld, P., Giacalone, R. A., & Riordan, C. A. (1995*). Impression management in organizations: theory, measurement, practice*. New York: Routledge, p. 133.

80 Planalp, S. (1999). *Communicating emotion: Social, moral, and cultural processes*. Cambridge, UK: Cambridge University Press.

81 Planalp, p. 200.

82 Emirates cancels orders for 20 Airbus jets (2006, October 30), MSNBC.com; FedEx cancels Airbus aircraft order (2006, November 7), MSNBC.com.

83 Matlack, C. (2006, October 23). Wayward Airbus. *Business Week*, 46–48.

Chapter 2

1 Adapted from Capezio, P., & Morehouse, D. (1997). *Secrets of breakthrough leadership*. Franklin Lakes, NJ: Career Press; Manning, G., & Curtis, K. (1988). *Leadership: Nine keys to success*. Cincinnati: South-Western; DuBrin, A. J. (1995). *Leadership*. Boston: Houghton Mifflin.

2 Lewin, K., Lippitt, R., & White, R. K. (1939). Patterns of aggressive behavior in experimentally created "social climates." *Journal of Social Psychology, 10*, 271–299.

3 See, for example: Bass, B. M. (1990). *Bass & Stogdill's handbook of leadership* (3rd ed., ch. 25). New York: Free Press.

4 Wasden, M., & Guzley, R. (2004, November). *Guided freedom leadership: Competent and capable individuals in the 21st century*. Paper presented at the International Leadership Association Conference, Washington, DC.

5 Kriegel, R. J., & Patler, L. (1991). *If it ain't broke . . . break it!* New York: Warner Books; Looney, D. S. (1989, September 4). A most unusual man. *Sports Illustrated*, pp. 118–124; Ortmayer, R. (personal communication, May 13, 1999).

6 Lewin et al.

7 White, R., & Lippitt, R. (1968). Leader behavior and member reaction in three "social climates." In D. Cartwright & A. Zander (Eds.), *Group dynamics* (pp. 318–335). New York: Harper & Row.

8 Shaw, M. E. (1955). A comparison of two types of leadership in various communication nets. *Journal of Abnormal and Social Psychology, 50*, 127–134; Hise, R. T. (1968, Fall). The effect of close supervision on productivity of simulated managerial decision-making groups. *Business Studies, North Texas University*, pp. 96–104.

9 Cammalleri, J. A., Hendrick, H. W., Pittmen, W. C., Jr., Blout, H. D., & Prather, D. C. (1973). Effects of different leadership styles on group accuracy. *Journal of Applied Psychology, 57*, 32–37.

10 Vroom, V. H., & Mann, F. C. (1960). Leader authorization and employee attitudes. *Personnel Psychology, 13*, 125–140.

11 Rudin, S. A. (1964). Leadership as psychophysiological activation of group members: A case experimental study. *Psychological Reports, 15*, 577–578.

12 Day, R. C., & Hamblin, R. L. (1964). Some effects of close and punitive styles of supervision. *American Journal of Sociology, 69*, 499–510.

[13] Ley, R. (1966). Labor turnover as a function of worker differences, work environment, and authoritarianism of foremen. *Journal of Applied Psychology, 50,* 497–500.

[14] Argyle, M., Gardner, G., & Ciofi, F. (1958). Supervisory methods related to productivity, absenteeism, and labor turnover. *Human Relations, 11,* 23–40.

[15] Mohr, L. B. (1971). Organizational technology and organizational structure. *Administrative Science Quarterly, 16,* 444–459; Bass, B. M., Burger, P. C., Doktor, R., & Barrett, G. V. (1979). *Assessment of managers: An international comparison.* New York: Free Press.

[16] Hespe, G., & Wall, T. (1976). The demand for participation among employees. *Human Relations, 29,* 411–428.

[17] Ziller, R. C. (1954). Four techniques of group decision making under uncertainty. *American Psychologist, 9,* 498.

[18] Farris, G. F. (1972). The effect of individual roles on performance in innovative groups. *R & D Management, 3,* 23–28.

[19] Meyer, H. H. (1968). Achievement motivation and industrial climates. In R. Tagiuri & G. H. Litwin (Eds.), Organizational technology and organizational structure. *Administrative Science Quarterly, 16,* 444–459.

[20] Farris.

[21] Aspegren, R. E. (1963). A study of leadership behavior and its effects on morale and attitudes in selected elementary schools. *Dissertation Abstracts, 23,* 3708.

[22] Baumgartel, H. (1957). Leadership style as a variable in research administration. *Administrative Science Quarterly, 2,* 344–360.

[23] Muringham, J. K., & Leung, T. K. (1976). The effects of leadership involvement and the importance of the task on subordinates' performance. *Organizational Behavior and Human Performance, 17,* 299–310.

[24] Weschler, I. R., Kahane, M., & Tannenbaum, R. (1952). Job satisfaction, productivity, and morale: A case study. *Occupational Psychology, 26,* 1–14; Meltzer, L. (1956). Scientific productivity in organizational settings. *Journal of Social Issues, 12,* 32–40.

[25] Information in this case comes from: Chouinard, Y. (2005). *Let my people go surfing.* New York: Penguin Press; *Patagonia case study.* (1999). Greenleaf.

[26] Chouinard, p. 178.

[27] Chouinard, p. 181.

[28] Zemke, R., Raines, C., & Filipczak, B. (2000). *Generations at work.* New York: AMACOM.

[29] Stech, E. L. (1983). *Leadership communication.* Chicago: Nelson-Hall, ch. 4.

[30] See: Katz, D., Maccoby, N., Gurin, G., & Floor, L. (1951). *Productivity, supervision, and morale among railroad workers.* Ann Arbor: University of Michigan, Institute for Social Research; Katz, D., Maccoby, N., & Morse, N. (1950). *Productivity, supervision, and morale in an office situation.* Ann Arbor: University of Michigan, Institute for Social Research.

[31] Although the one-dimensional view of leadership communication has been criticized as being overly simplistic, some one-dimensional models are still routinely discussed in leadership courses. For an example of a commonly cited one-dimensional model see: Tannenbaum, R., & Schmidt, W. H. (1958). How to choose a leadership pattern. *Harvard Business Review, 36,* 95–101.

[32] Kahn, R. L. (1956). The prediction of productivity. *Journal of Social Issues, 12,* 41–49.

[33] Stogdill, R. M., & Coons, A. E. (1957). *Leader behavior: Its description and measurement.* Columbus: Ohio State University, Bureau of Business Research.

[34] Stogdill, R. M. (1965). *Managers, employees, organizations.* Columbus: Ohio State University, Bureau of Business Research.

[35] McGregor, D. (1960). *The human side of enterprise.* New York: McGraw-Hill.

[36] Blake, R. R., & McCanse, A. A. (1991). *Leadership dilemmas—grid solutions.* Houston: Gulf; Blake, R. R., & Mouton, J. S. (1985). *The managerial grid III: The key to leadership excellence.* Houston: Gulf.

[37] The Leadership Grid Figure for *Leadership Dilemmas—Grid Solutions* by Robert R. Blake and Anne Adams McCanse (formerly the Managerial Grid Figure by Robert R. Blake and Jane S. Mouton). Austin: Grid International, p. 29. © 1991 by Grid International. Reproduced by permission.

[38] See: Blake & McCanse; Blake, R. R., Mouton, J. S., Barnes, L. B., & Greiner, L. E. (1964). Breakthrough in organization development. *Harvard Business Review, 42,* 133–155.

[39] Kelley, R. (1992). *The power of followership: How to create leaders that people want to follow and followers who lead themselves.* New York: Doubleday/Currency; Kelley, R. (1988, November–December). In praise of followers. *Harvard Business Review, 66,* 142–148.

40 From *The power of followership* (pp. 89–97) by Robert E. Kelley, copyright © 1992 by Consultants to Executives and Organizations, Ltd. Used by permission of Doubleday, a division of Random House, Inc.

41 DePree, M. (1992). *Leadership jazz*. New York: Currency/Doubleday, pp. 197–217.

42 Pittman, T. S., Rosenbach, W. E., & Potter, E. H. III. (1998). Followers as partners: Taking the initiative for action. In W. E. Rosenbach & R. L. Taylor (Eds.), *Contemporary issues in leadership* (pp. 107–120). Boulder, CO: Westview Press.

43 Material from this section drawn from: Brown, D. J., Scott, K. A., & Lewis, H. (2004). Information processing and leadership. In J. Antonakis, A. T. Cianciolo, & R. J. Sternberg (Eds.), *The nature of leadership* (pp. 125–147). Thousand Oaks, CA: Sage.

44 Brown et al., p. 126.

45 See, for example: Vygotsky, L. (1986). *Thought and language* (Trans. A. Kozulin). Cambridge, MA: MIT Press; Vygotsky, L. (1978). *Mind in society*. M. Cole, V. John-Steiner, S. Scribner, & E. Souberman (Eds.). Cambridge, MA: Harvard University Press; Luria, A. R. (1982). *Language and cognition*. J. V. Wertsch (Ed.). New York: John Wiley & Sons; Johnson, J. R. (1984). The role of inner speech in human communication. *Communication Education, 33,* 211–222.

46 Connelly, M. S., Gilbert, J. A., Zaccaro, S. J., Threlfall, K. V., Marks, M. A., & Mumford, M. D. (2000). Exploring the relationship of leadership skills and knowledge to leader performance. *Leadership Quarterly, 11,* 65–86.

47 Lord, R. G., & Maher, K. J. (1991). *Leadership and information processing: Linking perceptions and performance*. Boston: Unwin Hyman.

48 Lord & Maher.

49 Lord, R. G., & Brown, D. J. (2004). *Leadership processes and follower self-identity*. Mahwah, NJ: Lawrence Erlbaum; Lord, R. G., Brown, D. J., & Freiberg, S. J. (1999). Understanding the dynamics of leadership: The role of follower self-concepts in the leader/follower relationship. *Organizational Behavior and Human Decision Processes, 78,* 167–203; Shamir, B., House, R. J., & Arthur, M. B. (1993). The motivational effects of charismatic leadership: A self-concept based theory. *Organization Science, 4,* 577–594; van Knippenberg, D., van Knippenberg, B., De Cremer, D., & Hogg, M. A. (2004). Leadership, self, and identity: A review and research agenda. *Leadership Quarterly, 15,* 825–856.

50 Derr, C. B., Roussillon, S., & Bournois, F. (2002). Conclusion. In C. B. Derr, S. Roussillon, & F. Bournois (Eds.), *Cross-cultural approaches to leadership development* (pp. 289–303). Westport, CT: Quorum Books, pp. 290–292.

51 Kakabadse, A., Myers, A., McMahon, T., & Spony, G. (1995). Top management styles in Europe: Implications for business and cross-national teams. *European Business Journal, 7,* 17–27.

52 Hoefling, T. (2003). *Working virtually*. Sterling, VA: Stylus.

53 Fisher, K., & Fisher, M. D. (2001). *The distance manager*. New York: McGraw-Hill.

54 Fisher & Fisher, p. 21.

55 Fisher & Fisher, p. 33.

56 Williams, V. (2002). *Virtual leadership*. Edison, NJ: Shadowbrook.

Chapter 3

1 Stogdill, R. M. (1948). Personal factors associated with leadership: A survey of the literature. *Journal of Psychology, 25,* 35–71.

2 Stogdill, p. 64.

3 Stogdill, R. M. (1974). *Handbook of leadership*. New York: The Free Press.

4 Stogdill, *Handbook*, p. 72.

5 Kenny, D. A., & Zaccaro, S. J. (1983). An estimate of variance due to traits in leadership. *Journal of Applied Psychology, 68,* 678–685 (a reanalysis of Barnlund's consistency of emergent leadership in groups with changing tasks and members published in *Speech Monographs* in 1962); Lord, R. G., De Vader, C. L., & Alliger, G. M. (1986). A meta-analysis of the relation between personality traits and leadership perceptions: An application of validity generalization procedures. *Journal of Applied Psychology, 71,* 402–410 (a reanalysis of Mann's review of the relationships between personality and performance in small groups published in *Psychological Bulletin* in 1959).

6 Foti, R. J., Fraser, S. L., & Lord, R. G. (1982). Effects of leadership labels and prototypes on perceptions of political leaders. *Journal of Applied Psychology, 67,* 326–333.

7 Boyatzis, R. E. (1982). *The competent manager*. New York: John Wiley; Fiedler, F. E., & Garcia, J. E. (1987). *New approaches to effective leadership: Cognitive resources and organizational performance*. New

York: John Wiley; Howard, A., & Bray, D. W. (1988). *Managerial lives in transition: Advancing age and changing times.* New York: Guilford Press; Kirkpatrick, S. A., & Locke, E. A. (1991). Leadership: Do traits matter? *The Executive, 5,* 48–60; Lombardo, M. M., & McCauley, C. D. (1988). *The dynamics of management derailment.* Technical Report No. 34. Greensboro, NC: Center for Creative Leadership; McCall, N. W., Jr., & Lombardo, M. M. (1983). *Off the track: Why and how successful executives get derailed.* Technical Report No. 21. Greensboro, NC: Center for Creative Leadership; Zaccaro, S. J., Kemp, C., & Bader, P. (2004). Leader traits and attributes. In J. Antonakis, A. T. Cianciolo, & R. J. Sternberg (Eds.), *The nature of leadership* (pp. 101–124). Thousand Oaks, CA: Sage.

[8] See, for example: Gardner, H. (1983). *Frames of mind.* New York: Basic Books; Johnson, C. E., & Hackman, M. Z. (1995). *Creative communication: Principles and applications.* Long Grove, IL: Waveland Press, chapters 2 and 4.

[9] Goldberg, L. R. (1990). An alternative "description of personality": The big-five factor structure. *Journal of Personality and Social Psychology, 59,* 1216–1229; McCrae, R. R., & Costa, P. T. (1987). Validation of the five-factor model of personality across instruments and observers. *Journal of Personality and Social Psychology, 52,* 81–90.

[10] Judge, T. A., Bono, J. E., Ilies, R., & Gerhardt, M. W. (2002). Personality and leadership: A qualitative and quantitative review. *Journal of Applied Psychology, 87,* 765–780.

[11] Howard, P. S., & Howard, J. M. (2001). *The owner's manual for personality at work.* Atlanta: Bard Press.

[12] Case based on material from Gerber, R. (2002). *Leadership the Eleanor Roosevelt way: Timeless strategies from the first lady of courage.* New York: Prentice-Hall.

[13] Gerber, p. 169.

[14] Gerber, p. 7.

[15] Gerber, pp. 4–5.

[16] See, for example: Burns, T., & Stalker, G. M. (1961). *The management of innovation.* Chicago: Quadrangle Books; Lawrence, P. R., & Lorsch, J. W. (1967). *Organization and environment.* Cambridge, MA: Harvard University Press; Woodward, J. (1965). *Industrial organization: Theory and practice.* Oxford: Oxford University Press.

[17] Mayo, A. J., & Nohira, N. (2005). *In their time: The greatest business leaders of the twentieth century.* Boston: Harvard Business School Press.

[18] See, for example: Fiedler, F. E. (1967). *A theory of leadership effectiveness.* New York: McGraw-Hill; Fiedler, F. E. (1972). Personality, motivational systems, and the behavior of high and low LPC persons. *Human Relations, 25,* 391–412; Fiedler, F. E. (1978). The contingency model and the dynamics of the leadership process. In L. Berkowitz (Ed.), *Advances in experimental social psychology* (pp. 60–112). New York: Academic Press.

[19] Fiedler, F. E., Chemers, M. M., & Mahar, L. (1976). *Improving leadership effectiveness: The leader match concept.* New York: John Wiley. Used by permission.

[20] See, for example: Ashour, A. S. (1973). The contingency model of leadership effectiveness: An evaluation. *Organizational Behavior and Human Performance, 9,* 339–355; Kerr, S., & Harlan, A. (1973). Predicting the effects of leadership training and experience from the contingency model: Some remaining problems. *Journal of Applied Psychology, 57,* 114–117; Schriesheim, C. A., & Kerr, S. (1977). Theories and measures of leadership: A critical appraisal. In J. G. Hunt & L. L. Larson (Eds.), *Leadership: The cutting edge* (pp. 9–45). Carbondale: Southern Illinois University Press.

[21] See, for example: House, R. J. (1971). A path-goal theory of leader effectiveness. *Administrative Science Quarterly, 16,* 321–338; House, R. J., & Mitchell, T. R. (1974). Path-goal theory of leadership. *Journal of Contemporary Business, 3,* 81–97.

[22] Fiedler, *A theory of leadership effectiveness.* Used by permission.

[23] Hersey, P., Blanchard, K. H., & Johnson, D. (2008). *Management of organizational behavior: Leading human resources* (9th ed.). Upper Saddle River, NJ: Prentice-Hall.

[24] Center for Leadership Studies, © copyright 2006. Reprinted with permission of the Center for Leadership Studies, Inc. Escondido, CA 92025. All rights reserved.

[25] Barnard, C. I. (1938). *The functions of the executive.* Cambridge, MA: Harvard University Press.

[26] Benne, K. D., & Sheats, P. (1948). Functional roles of group members. *Journal of Social Issues, 4,* 41–49.

[27] Krech, D., & Crutchfield, R. (1948). *Theory and problems of social psychology.* New York: McGraw-Hill.

[28] Bowers, D. G., & Seashore, S. E. (1966). Predicting organizational effectiveness with a four-factory theory of leadership. *Administrative Science Quarterly, 2,* 238–263.

[29] Cartwright, D., & Zander, A. (1968). Leadership and performance of group functions: Introduction. In D. Cartwright & A. Zander (Eds.), *Group dynamics* (pp. 301–317). New York: Harper & Row.

[30] See, for example: Graen, G. (1976). Role-making processes within complex organizations. In M. D. Dunnette (Ed.), *Handbook of industrial organizational psychology* (pp. 1201–1246). Chicago:

Rand-McNally; Graen, G. B., & Cashman, J. F. (1975). A role-making model of leadership in formal organizations: A developmental approach. In J. G. Hunt & L. L. Larson (Eds.), *Leadership frontiers* (pp. 143–165). Kent, OH: Kent State University Press; Dansereau, F., Graen, G. B., & Haga, W. (1975). A vertical dyad linkage approach to leadership in formal organizations. *Organizational Behavior and Human Performance, 13,* 46–78; Graen, G. B., & Scandura, T. (1987). Toward a psychology of dyadic organizing. *Research in Organizational Behavior, 9,* 175–208; Duchon, D., Green, S. G., & Taber, T. D. (1988). Vertical dyad linkage: A longitudinal assessment of antecedents, measures, and consequences. *Journal of Applied Psychology, 71,* 56–60.

31 Uhl-Bien, M. (2003). Relationship development as a key ingredient for leadership development. In S. E. Murphy & R. E. Riggo (Eds.), *The future of leadership development* (pp. 129–147). Mahwah, NJ: Lawrence Erlbaum.

32 Gerstner, C. R., & Day, D. V. (1997). Meta-analytic review of leader-member exchange theory: Correlates and construct issues. *Journal of Applied Psychology, 82,* 827–844; Mueller, B. H., & Lee, J. (2002). Leader-member exchange and organizational communication satisfaction in multiple contexts. *Journal of Business Communication, 39,* 220–244.

33 Adapted from Graen, G., & Uhl-Bien, M. (1998). Relationship-based approach to leadership: Development of leader-member exchange (LMX) theory of leadership over 25 years: Applying a multi-level multi-domain perspective. In F. Dansereau & F. J. Yammarino (Eds.), *Leadership: The multiple-level approaches* (Vol. 24, p. 123). New York: Elsevier. With permission from Elsevier.

34 Graen & Uhl-Bien, pp. 103–158.

35 Schriesheim, C. A., Castro, S. L., & Cogliser, C. C. (1999). Leader-member exchange (LMX) research: A comprehensive review of theory, measurement, and data-analytic practices. *Leadership Quarterly, 10,* 63–113; Northouse, P. (2007). *Leadership: Theory and practice* (4th ed., chapter 8). Thousand Oaks, CA: Sage; Greguras, G. J., & Ford, J. M. (2006). An examination of the multidimensonality of supervisor and subordinate perceptions of leader-member exchange. *Journal of Occupational and Organizational Psychology, 79,* 433–465.

36 Hofstede, G. (2001). *Culture's consequences: Comparing values, behaviors, institutions, and organizations across nations* (2nd ed.). Thousand Oaks, CA: Sage; Hofstede, G. (1993). Cultural constraints in management theories. *Academy of Management Executive, 7,* 81–94; Hofstede, G. (1980). Motivation, leadership and organization: Do American theories apply abroad? *Organizational Dynamics, 9,* 42–63.

37 Haire, M., Ghiselli, E. E., & Porter, L. W. (1966). *Managerial thinking: An international study.* New York: John Wiley.

38 AIIM & Kahn Consulting. (2005). *Electronic communication policies and procedures: A 2005 industry study.* Silver Spring, MD: Author.

39 Connaughton, S. L., & Ruben, B. D. (2005). Millennium leadership inc.: A case study of computer and Internet-based communication in a simulated organization. In K. St. Amant & P. Zemliansky (Eds.), *Internet-based workplace communications* (pp. 40–67). Hershey, PA: Information Science.

40 Kruger, J., Epley, N., Parker, J., & Ng, Z. (2005). Egocentrism over e-mail: Can we communicate as well as we think? *Journal of Personality and Social Psychology, 89,* 925–936.

41 Brady, D. (2006, December 4). *!#?@ the e-mail: Can we talk? *Business Week,* 109.

42 Adapted from Fisher, K., & Fisher, M. D. (2001). *The distance manager.* New York: McGraw-Hill, ch. 18.

Chapter 4

1 Burns, J. M. (1978). *Leadership.* New York: Harper & Row.

2 Maslow, A. H. (1970). *Motivation and personality.* New York: Harper & Row.

3 See for example: Bass, B. M. (1985). *Leadership and performance beyond expectations.* New York: The Free Press.

4 Bass, B. M. (1990). *Bass & Stogdill's handbook of leadership* (3rd ed., p. 53). New York: The Free Press.

5 Burns, p. 4.

6 Bass, *Leadership*; Bass, B. M., & Avolio, B. J. (1994). *Improving organizational effectiveness through transformational leadership.* Thousand Oaks, CA: Sage.

7 Bass, *Leadership*, p. 17.

8 Bass, *Leadership*; Bass, B. M. (1990). From transactional to transformational leadership: Learning to share the vision. *Organizational Dynamics, 18,* 19–31; Bass & Avolio.

9 Zorn, T. E. (1991). Construct system development, transformational leadership and leadership messages. *Southern Communication Journal, 56*, 178–193.

10 Avolio, B. J., & Yammarino, F. J. (Eds.). (2002). *Transformational and charismatic leadership: The road ahead*. Boston: JAI.

11 Peters, T. J., & Waterman, R. H., Jr. (1982). *In search of excellence*. New York: Harper & Row.

12 Peters, T. J., & Austin, N. K. (1985). *A passion for excellence: The leadership difference*. New York: Warner Books.

13 Peters, T. (1992). *Liberation management*. New York: Ballantine.

14 Bennis, W. G., & Nanus, B. (1997). *Leaders: The strategies for taking charge* (2nd ed.). New York: Harper & Row.

15 Kouzes, J. M., & Posner, B. Z. (1995). *The leadership challenge: How to get extraordinary things done in organizations*. San Francisco: Jossey-Bass.

16 Neff, T. J., & Citrin, J. M. (1999). *Lessons from the top*. New York: Doubleday; Avolio, B. J., & Bass, B. M. (2002). *Developing potential across a full range of leadership: Cases on transactional and transformational leadership*. Mahwah, NJ: Lawrence Erlbaum.

17 Snyder, N. H., & Graves, M. (1994). Leadership and vision. *Business Horizons, 37*, 1–7.

18 Kriegel, R. J., & Patler, L. (1991). *If it ain't broke . . . break it!* New York: Warner Books.

19 Parnes, S. J. (1975). "Aha!" In I. A. Taylor & J. W. Getzels (Eds.), *Perspectives on creativity* (pp. 224–248). Chicago: Aldine.

20 Mednick, S. A. (1962). The associative basis of the creative process. *Psychological Review, 69*, 221.

21 Wallas, G. (1926). *The art of thought*. New York: Harcourt.

22 von Oech, R. (1986). *A kick in the seat of the pants*. New York: Harper & Row, pp. 30, 32.

23 Orsag Madigan, C., & Elwood, A. (1983). *Brainstorms and thunderbolts*. New York: Macmillan.

24 Johnson, C. E., & Hackman, M. Z. (1995). *Creative communication: Principles and applications*. Long Grove, IL: Waveland Press, ch. 2.

25 Adams, J. L. (1986). *Conceptual blockbusting* (3rd ed.). Reading, MA: Addison-Wesley.

26 Sanders, D. A., & Sanders, J. A. (1984). *Teaching creativity through metaphor*. New York: Longman, p. 19.

27 Getzels, J. W. (1975). Problem-finding and the inventiveness of solutions. *Journal of Creative Behavior, 9*, 12–18; Getzels, J. W. (1973, November 21). Problem finding: The 343rd Convocation Address, the University of Chicago. *The University of Chicago Record, 9*, 281–283; Mackworth, N. H. (1965). Originality. *American Psychologist, 20*, 51–66.

28 Kriegel, R., & Brandt, D. (1996). *Sacred cows make the best burgers: Paradigm-busting strategies for developing change-ready people and organizations*. New York: Warner Books.

29 Peters & Waterman, p. 223.

30 Garvin, D. A. (1993, July–August). Building a learning organization. *Harvard Business Review, 86*.

31 Martin, F. (2002, April). So you failed . . . so what? *Unlimited*, p. 48.

32 Bennis, W. G., & Nanus, B. (1985). *Leaders: The strategies for taking charge*. New York: Harper & Row.

33 Conceiao, P., Hamill, D., & Pinheiro, P. (2002). Innovative science and technology commercialization strategies at 3M: A case study. *Journal of Engineering and Technology Management, 19*, 25–38; Dubashi, J. (1992, February 18). 3M: New talent and products outweigh the costs. *Financial World, 19*; Hindo, B. (2007, June 11). At 3M, a struggle between efficiency and creativity. *Business Week*, 8–14; Katauskas, T. (1990, November). Follow-through: 3M's formula for success. *Research and Development*, 46–52; Lehr, L. W. (1988). Encouraging innovation and entrepreneurship in diversified corporations. In R. L. Kuhn (Ed.), *Handbook for creative and innovative managers* (pp. 211–229). New York: McGraw-Hill; Mitchell, R. (1989, April 10). Masters of innovation: How 3M keeps its new products coming. *Business Week*, 58–63; Mitchell, R. (1989, Innovation Issue). Mining the work force for ideas. *Business Week*, 121; Mitsch, R. A. (1992, September–October). R&D at 3M: Continuing to play a big role. *Research Technology Management*, 22–26; Zand, D. E. (1997). *The leadership triad: Knowledge, trust, and power*. New York: Oxford University Press.

34 Peters & Austin, ch. 2.

35 Neff & Citrin.

36 Neff & Citrin, pp. 39–40.

37 Pasternack, B. A., & O'Toole, J. (2002, second quarter). Yellow light leadership: How the world's best companies manage uncertainty. *Strategy + Business*, 74–83.

38 Holzman, D. (1993, August). When workers run the show. *Working Woman*, 38–41, 72–74; Managing the journey (1990, November). *Inc.*, 45–54; Peters, *Liberation management*, 238–243; Pomeroy, A. (2004, July). Great places, inspired employees. *HR Magazine*; Stayer, R. (1990, November–December). How I learned to let my workers lead. *Harvard Business Review*, 66–83.

[39] Guarrero, C. A. (1998, October). The leadership challenge. *Security Management*, 27–29.

[40] Masters, C. (2007, September 10). How Boeing got going. *Time*, 1–6.

[41] Gumbel, P. (2007, July 16). BMW drives Germany. *Time*, 1–6

[42] Bennis & Nanus.

[43] Nanus, B. (1992). *Visionary leadership*. San Francisco: Jossey-Bass.

[44] Collins, J. C., & Porras, J. I. (1994). *Built to last*. New York: Harper Business.

[45] Kotter, J. P. (1990). *A force for change: How leadership differs from management*. New York: Free Press, p. 36.

[46] The vision thing. (1991, November 9). *The Economist*, 89.

[47] The vision statements listed come from the following sources: Abrahams, J. (1995). *The mission statement book*. Berkeley, CA: Ten Speed Press; Collins, J. C., & Porras, J. I. (1996, September–October). Building your company's vision. *Harvard Business Review*, 65–77; Disney Institute. (2001). *Be our guest*. New York: Disney Enterprises; Hughes, R. L., & Beatty, K. C. (2005). *Becoming a strategic leader*. San Francisco: Jossey-Bass; Zaccaro, S. J., & Banks, D. J. (2001). Leadership, vision, and organizational effectiveness. In S. J. Zaccaro & R. K. Klimoski (Eds.), *The nature of organizational leadership* (pp. 181–218). San Francisco: Jossey-Bass.

[48] Rokeach, M. (1973). *The nature of human values*. New York: Free Press. Reprinted with the permission of The Free Press, a Division of Simon & Schuster Adult Publishing Group, from *The nature of human values* by Milton Rokeach. Copyright © 1973 by The Free Press. Copyright © renewed 2001 by Sandra Ball-Rokeach. All rights reserved.

[49] Jones, L. B. (1996). *The path: Creating your mission statement for work and life*. New York: Hyperion, p. 71.

[50] Levin, I. M. (2000). Vision revisited. *Journal of Applied Behavioral Science, 36*, 91–107.

[51] Baum, R. J., Locke, E. A., & Kirkpatrick, S. (1998). A longitudinal study of the relations of vision and vision communication to venture growth in entrepreneurial firms. *Journal of Applied Psychology, 83*, 43–54.

[52] Capodagli, B., & Jackson, L. (1999). *The Disney way*. New York: McGraw-Hill, p. 87.

[53] Shockley-Zalabak, P., Ellis, K., & Cesaria, R. (2000). *Measuring organizational trust*. San Francisco: International Association of Business Communicators.

[54] DePree, M. (1989). *Leadership is an art*. New York: Doubleday, p. 9.

[55] Carlzon, J. (1987). *Moments of truth*. New York: Harper & Row.

[56] Neff & Citrin, p. 188.

[57] Sanders, B. (1995). *Fabled service*. San Francisco: Jossey-Bass, p. 75.

[58] Spector, R., & McCarthy, P. (1995). *The Nordstrom way*. New York: John Wiley & Sons, p. 97.

[59] Heskett, J. L., Sasser, W. E., Jr., & Hart, C. W. L. (1990). *Service breakthroughs*. New York: Free Press, pp. 13–14.

[60] Spector, R. (2001). *Lessons from the Nordstrom way*. New York: John Wiley & Sons, p. 68.

[61] Lundin, S. C., Paul, H., & Christensen, J. (2000). *Fish! A remarkable way to boost morale and improve results*. New York: Hyperion.

[62] Chang, R. (2001). *The passion plan at work*. San Francisco: Jossey-Bass, p. 5.

[63] Collins, J. (2001). *Good to great*. New York: HarperBusiness, pp. 109–110.

[64] Bass, B. M., & Riggio, R. E. (2006). *Transformational leadership* (2nd ed.). Mahwah, NJ: Lawrence Erlbaum.

[65] See, for example: Brown, M. E., & Trevino, L. K. (2003, August). *The influence of leadership styles on unethical conduct in work groups: An empirical test*. Paper presented at the meeting of the Academy of Management, Seattle, WA; Parry, K. W., & Proctor-Thompson, S. B. (2002). Perceived integrity of transformational leaders in organisational settings. *Journal of Business Ethics, 35*, 75–96; Turner, N., Barling, J., Epitropaki, O., Butcher, V., & Milner, C. (2002). Transformational leadership and moral reasoning. *Journal of Applied Psychology, 87*, 304–311.

[66] Howell, J. M., & Avolio, B. J. (1992). The ethics of charismatic leadership: Submission or liberation. *Academy of Management Executive, 6*, 43–54.

[67] Bass, *Leadership*, ch. 3. Some contemporary Christian groups also consider their leaders to be gifted by God. The term "charismatic" can also refer to a particular style of religious worship.

[68] Weber, M. (1947). *The theory of social and economic organization* (A. M. Henderson & T. Parsons, Trans.). Glencoe, IL: The Free Press, pp. 358–359.

[69] Trice, H. M., & Beyer, J. M. (1993). *The cultures of work organizations*. Englewood Cliffs, NJ: Prentice-Hall, p. 259.

[70] Bass, *Handbook*, p. 187. Bass summarizes the concerns regarding the centrality of crisis in the definition of charismatic leadership and provides an example of charisma without crisis. Bass notes that financial investment brokers often have devoted, unquestioning followers who perceive them as being charismatic even in times of financial calm.

[71] Conger, J. A., & Kanungo, R. N. (1987). Toward a behavioral theory of charismatic leadership in organizational settings. *Academy of Management Review, 12*, 637–647.

[72] House, R. J. (1977). A 1976 theory of charismatic leadership. In J. G. Hunt & L. L. Larson (Eds.), *Leadership: The cutting edge* (pp. 189–207). Carbondale: Southern Illinois University Press; Bass, *Handbook*, ch. 3.

[73] Bass, *Leadership*, p. 61.

[74] Conger & Kanungo.

[75] Richardson, R. J., & Thayer, S. K. (1993). *The charisma factor.* Englewood Cliffs, NJ: Prentice-Hall, p. 27.

[76] Geertz, C. (1977). Centers, kings, and charisma: Reflections on the symbolics of power. In J. Ben-David & T. Nichols (Eds.), *Culture and its creation: Essays in honor of Edward Shils* (pp. 150–171). Chicago: University of Chicago Press, p. 151.

[77] Dow, T. (1969). The theory of charisma. *Sociological Quarterly, 10*, 316.

[78] Huggins, N. (1987). Martin Luther King, Jr.: Charisma and leadership. *Journal of American History, 74*, 477–481.

[79] Bass, B. M. (1997). Does the transactional-transformational leadership paradigm transcend organizational and national boundaries? *American Psychologist, 52*, 130–139; Bass, B. M., & Avolio, B. J. (1993). Transformational leadership: A response to critiques. In M. M. Chemers & R. Ayman (Eds.), *Leadership theory and research: Perspectives and directions* (pp. 49–80). New York: Academic Press; Den Hartog, D. N., House, R. J., Hanges, P. J., & Ruiz-Quintanilla, S. A. (1999). Culture specific and cross-culturally generalizable implicit leadership theories: Are attributes of charismatic/transformational leadership universally endorsed? *Leadership Quarterly, 10*, 219–256.

[80] Tapscott, D., & Williams, A. D. (2006). *Wikinomics: How mass collaboration changes everything.* New York: Penguin Books.

[81] Tapscott & Williams, p. 244.

Chapter 5

[1] Kanter, R. M. (1979, July–August). Power failure in management circuits. *Harvard Business Review, 57*, 65.

[2] Pfeffer, J. (1992, Winter). Understanding power in organizations. *California Management Review*, 29–50.

[3] Gardner, J. (1990). *On leadership.* New York: Free Press, pp. 55–57.

[4] Bennis, W., & Nanus, B. (1985). *Leaders: The strategies for taking charge.* New York: Harper & Row, pp. 17–18.

[5] French, J. R. P., & Raven, B. (1959). The bases of social power. In D. Cartwright (Ed.), *Studies in social power* (pp. 150–167). Ann Arbor: University of Michigan, Institute for Social Research. Although there are a number of power typologies, this is the most widely used, generating research in such fields as management, communication, and education.

[6] Modified version of Hinken, T. R., & Schriesheim, C. A. (1989). Development and application of new scales to measure the French and Raven (1959) bases of social power. *Journal of Applied Psychology, 74*, 561–567. Permission granted by the American Psychological Association. Copyright © 1989.

[7] Katzenbach, J. R. (2003). *Why pride matters more than money: The power of the world's greatest motivational force.* New York: Crown Business.

[8] The most popular social exchange theory is that of J. W. Thibault and H. H. Kelley (*Interpersonal relations: A theory of interdependence.* New York: John Wiley, 1978). For one application of social exchange theory to groups, see: Hollander, E. (1978). *Leadership dynamics: A practical guide to effective relationships.* New York: The Free Press.

[9] Information on the costs and benefits of power types are found in the following sources: Bass, B. (1990). *Bass and Stogdill's handbook of leadership* (3rd ed., ch. 13). New York: Free Press; Hersey, P., Blanchard, K. H., & Johnson, D. (2008). *Management of organizational behavior: Leading human resources* (9th ed.). Upper Saddle River, NJ: Prentice-Hall; Yukl, G., & Falbe, C. M. (1991). Impor-

tance of different power sources in downward and lateral relations. *Journal of Applied Psychology, 76,* 416–423; Baldwin, D. A. (1971). The costs of power. *Journal of Conflict Resolution, 15,* 145–155; Yukl, G. (1998). *Leadership in organizations* (4th ed., ch. 8). Englewood Cliffs, NJ: Prentice-Hall.

[10] Giles, H., & Powesland, P. F. (1975). *Speech style and social evaluation.* London: Academic Press.

[11] O'Barr, W. (1984). Asking the right questions about language and power. In C. Kramarae, M. Schulz, & W. O'Barr (Eds.), *Language and power* (pp. 260–280). Beverly Hills, CA: Sage.

[12] Bradac, J., & Mulac, A. (1984). A molecular view of powerful and powerless speech styles: Attributional consequences of specific language features and communicator intentions. *Communication Monographs, 51,* 307–319.

[13] See, for example: Burell, N. A., & Koper, R. J. (1994). The efficacy of powerful/powerless language on persuasiveness/credibility: A meta-analytic review. In R. W. Preiss & M. Allen (Eds.), *Prospects and precautions in the use of meta-analysis* (pp. 235–255). Dubuque, IA: Brown & Benchmark; Haleta, L. L. (1996). Student perceptions of teachers' use of language: The effects of powerful and powerless language on impression formation and uncertainty. *Communication Education, 45,* 16–28; Johnson, C., Vinson, L., Hackman, M., & Hardin, T. (1989). The effects of an instructor's use of hesitation form on student ratings of quality, recommendations to hire, and lecture listening. *Journal of the International Listening Association, 3,* 32–43.

[14] Johnson, C., & Vinson, L. (1987). "Damned if you do, damned if you don't?": Status, powerful speech and evaluations of female witnesses. *Women's Studies in Communication, 10,* 37–44.

[15] Vinson, L., Johnson, C., & Hackman, M. (1992). *I like you just the way you are: Student evaluations of favorite and least favorite instructors using hesitant speech.* Paper presented at the Speech Communication Association convention, Chicago, IL; Vinson, L., & Johnson, C. (1990). The relationship between the use of hesitations and/or hedges and listening: The role of perceived importance as a mediating variable. *Journal of the International Listening Association, 4,* 116–127.

[16] Sorensen, R., & Pickett, T. (1986). A test of two teaching strategies designed to improve interview effectiveness: Rating behavior and videotaped feedback. *Communication Monographs, 35,* 13–22.

[17] Bass, *Handbook.*

[18] Kanter, R. M. (1977). *Men and women of the corporation.* New York: Basic Books, ch. 7; Fuller, B. J., Morrison, R., Jones, L., Bridger, D., & Brown, V. (1999). The effects of psychological empowerment on transformational leadership and job satisfaction. *Journal of Social Psychology, 139,* 389–391; Seibert, S. C., Silver, S. R., & Randolph, R. W. (2004). Taking empowerment to the next level: A multiple-level model of empowerment, performance, and satisfaction. *Academy of Management Journal, 47,* 332–349.

[19] Kouzes, J. M., & Posner, B. Z. (2007). *The leadership challenge: How to get extraordinary things done in organizations* (4th ed.). San Francisco: Jossey-Bass, p. 20.

[20] Bennis, W. (1976). *The unconscious conspiracy: Why leaders can't lead.* New York: AMACOM, p. 167.

[21] Bies, R., & Tripp, T. M. (1998). Two faces of the powerless: Coping with tyranny in organizations. In R. M. Kramer & M. A. Neale (Eds.), *Power and influence in organizations* (pp. 203–219). Thousand Oaks, CA: Sage. See also: Hornstein, H. A. (1996). *Brutal bosses and their prey.* New York: Riverhead Books.

[22] Fiske, S. T. (1993, June). Controlling other people: The impact of power on stereotyping. *American Psychologist,* pp. 621–628.

[23] Adams, S. (1996). *The Dilbert principle: A cubicle's eye view of bosses, meetings, management fads & other workplace afflictions.* New York: HarperBusiness; Adams, S. (1998). *The Dilbert future: Thriving on business stupidity in the 21st century.* New York: HarperBusiness; Adams, S. (1998). *The joy of work: Dilbert's guide to finding happiness at the expense of your co-workers.* New York: HarperBusiness.

[24] Adams, *The Dilbert principle,* p. 325.

[25] Thomas, K. W., & Velthouse, B. A. (1990). Cognitive elements of empowerment: An "interpretive" model of intrinsic task motivation. *Academy of Management Review, 15,* 666–681; Spreitzer, G. M. (1995). Psychological empowerment in the workplace: Dimensions, measurement, and validation. *Academy of Management Journal, 38,* 1422–1465; Spreitzer, G. M. (1996). Social structural characteristics of psychological empowerment. *Academy of Management Journal, 39,* 483–504; Spreitzer, G. M., Kizilos, M. A., & Nason, S. W. (1997). A dimensional analysis of the relationship between psychological empowerment and effectiveness, satisfaction, and strain. *Journal of Management, 23,* 679–704; Quinn, R. E., & Spreitzer, G. M. (1997). The road to empowerment: Seven questions every leader should ask. *Organizational Dynamics, 26,* 37–49.

[26] Conger, J. (1989). Leadership: The art of empowering others. *The Academy of Management EXECUTIVE, 3,* 17–24, p. 22. Used by permission.

27 Bandura, A. (1977). Self-efficacy: Toward a unifying theory of behavioral change. *Psychological Review, 84,* 191–215; Bandura, A., & Wood, R. (1989). Effect of perceived controllability and performance standards on self-regulation of complex decision making. *Journal of Personality and Social Psychology, 84,* 805–814.

28 See: Conger, J. A., & Kanungo, R. N. (1988). The empowerment process: Integrating theory and practice. *Academy of Management Review, 13,* 471–482; Conger, *Leadership,* pp. 17–24.

29 Kanter, Power failure.

30 Belasco, J. A., & Stayer, R. C. (1994). *Flight of the buffalo.* New York: Warner Books.

31 Seifter, H., & Economy, P. (2001). *Leadership ensemble: Lessons in collaborative management from the world's only conductorless orchestra.* New York: Times Books.

32 Belasco & Stayer, p. 351.

33 Charles Manz, Henry Sims, Jr., and Christopher Neck have described superleadership and self-leadership in a variety of sources. Material for this section was taken from: Sims, H. P., Jr., & Manz, C. C. (1996). *Company of heroes: Unleashing the power of self-leadership.* New York: John Wiley; Manz, C. C., & Sims, H. P., Jr. (2001). *The new superleadership: Leading others to lead themselves.* San Francisco: Berrett-Koehler; Manz, C. C., & Neck, C. P. (1999). *Mastering self-leadership: Empowering yourself for personal excellence.* Upper Saddle River, NJ: Prentice-Hall; Neck, C. P., & Houghton, J. D. (2006). Two decades of self-leadership theory and research: Past developments, present trends, and future possibilities. *Journal of Managerial Psychology, 21,* 270–295.

34 Manz & Sims, p. 69. Used by permission.

35 Roberts, J. (2006). *A sense of the world: How a blind man became history's greatest traveler.* New York: HarperCollins.

36 Hough, J., & Neuland, E. W. (2000). *Global business.* Oxford: Oxford University Press; Louw, D. J. (2001). *Ubuntu and the challenges of multiculturalism in post-apartheid South Africa.* Retrieved from: http://www.phys.uu.nl/~unitwin/ubuntu.html; Van der Merwe, W. L. (1996). Philosophy and the multi-cultural context of (post)apartheid South Africa. *Ethical Perspectives, 3,* 1–15.

37 Howe, J. (2006, December 25). Your web, your way. *Time,* pp. 60–61.

38 Howe, J. (2006, June). The rise of crowdsourcing. *Wired.* Retrieved from http://www.wired.com/wired/archive/14.06

Chapter 6

1 Kouzes, J. M., & Posner, B. Z. (2003). *Credibility: How leaders gain and lose it, why people demand it.* San Francisco: Jossey-Bass, p. 22.

2 Sattler, W. M. (1947). Conceptions of ethos in ancient rhetoric. *Speech Monographs, 14,* 55–65.

3 McCroskey, J. C., & Young, T. J. (1981). Ethos and credibility: The construct and its measurement after three decades. *Central States Speech Journal, 32,* 24.

4 Haiman, F. S. (1949). An experimental study of the effects of ethos in public speaking. *Speech Monographs, 16,* 190–202; Warren, I. D. (1969). The effects of credibility in sources of testimony and audience attitudes toward speaker and topic. *Speech Monographs, 36,* 456–458.

5 Strong, S. R., & Schmidt, L. D. (1970). Expertness and influence in counseling. *Journal of Counseling Psychology, 17,* 81–87; Strong, S. R., & Dixon, D. N. (1971). Expertness, attractiveness, and influence in counseling. *Journal of Counseling Psychology, 18,* 562–570.

6 Hovland, C. I., & Weiss, W. (1951). The influence of source credibility on communication effectiveness. *Public Opinion Quarterly, 15,* 635–650.

7 Dirks, K. T. (2000). Trust in leadership and team performance: Evidence from NCAA basketball. *Journal of Applied Psychology, 85,* 1004–1012.

8 Brembeck, W. L., & Howell, W. S. (1976). *Persuasion: A means of social influence* (2nd ed.). Englewood Cliffs, NJ: Prentice-Hall.

9 Kouzes, J. M., & Posner, B. Z. (2007). *The leadership challenge: How to get extraordinary things done in organizations* (4th ed.). San Francisco: Jossey-Bass.

10 Carl Hovland, a pioneer in credibility research, was among the first to argue that a distinction should be made between competence and trustworthiness. He pointed out that a message from a competent source will be rejected if hearers believe that this person is lying. See: Hovland, C., Janis, I., & Kelley, H. H. (1953). *Communication and persuasion.* New Haven, CT: Yale University Press.

11 Amour, S. (2002, February 5). Employees' new motto: Trust no one. *USA Today,* pp. 1A, 1B.

[12] Dirks, K. T., & Skarlicki, D. P. (2004). Trust in leaders: Existing research and emerging issues. In R. M. Kramer & K. S. Cook (Eds.), *Trust and distrust in organizations: Dilemmas and approaches* (pp. 21–40). New York: Russell Sage Foundation; Simons, T. (2000). Behavioral integrity: The perceived alignment between managers' words and deeds as a research focus. *Organization Science, 13,* 18–35.

[13] Dirks, K. T., & Ferrin, D. L. (2002). Trust in leadership: Meta-analytic findings and implications for research and practice. *Journal of Applied Psychology, 87,* 611–628.

[14] Elsbach, K. D. (2004). Managing images of trustworthiness in organizations. In R. M. Kramer & K. S. Cook (Eds.), *Trust and distrust in organizations: Dilemmas and approaches* (pp. 275–292). New York: Russell Sage Foundation.

[15] Ward, C. D., & McGinnies, E. (1974). Persuasive effects of early and late mention of credible and non-credible sources. *Journal of Psychology, 86,* 17–23; O'Keefe, D. J. (1987). The persuasive effects of delaying identification of high and low-credibility communicators: A meta-analytic review. *Central States Speech Journal, 38,* 63–72.

[16] Kelman, H. C., & Hovland, C. L. (1953). "Reinstatement" of the communicator in delayed measurement of opinion change. *Journal of Abnormal and Social Psychology, 48,* 327–335.

[17] Leathers, D. G. (1997). *Successful nonverbal communication: Principles and applications* (2nd ed.). New York: Macmillan. See also: McMahan, E. M. (1976). Nonverbal communication as a function of attribution in impression formation. *Communication Monographs, 43,* 287–294.

[18] Whitener, E. M., Brodt, S. E., Korsgaard, J. A., & Werner, J. M. (1998). Managers as initiators of trust: An exchange relationship framework for understanding managerial trustworthy behavior. *Academy of Management Review, 23,* 513–530.

[19] Kouzes & Posner, *Credibility.*

[20] Hunter, J. E., & Boster, F. J. (1987). A model of compliance-gaining message selection. *Communication Monographs, 54,* 63–84; Vinson, L. (1988, November). *An emotion-based model of compliance-gaining message selection.* Paper presented at the Speech Communication Association convention, New Orleans, LA; Grant, J. A., King, P. E., & Behnke, R. R. (1994). Compliance-gaining strategies, communication satisfaction, and willingness to comply. *Communication Reports, 7,* 99–108.

[21] Marwell, G., & Schmitt, D. (1967). Dimensions of compliance-gaining behavior: An empirical analysis. *Sociometry, 30,* 350–364. Some researchers use the terms prosocial and antisocial to distinguish between friendly and unfriendly types of compliance gaining. For more information on the differences between pro- and antisocial tactics, see: Falbo, T. (1977). Multidimensional scaling of power strategies. *Journal of Personality and Social Psychology, 35,* 537–547; Kearney, P., Plax, T. G., Sorensen, G., & Smith, V. R. (1988). Experienced and prospective teachers' selections of compliance-gaining messages for "common" student misbehaviors. *Communication Education, 37,* 150–164; Roloff, M. E., & Barnicott, E. F. (1978). The situational use of pro- and antisocial compliance-gaining strategies by high and low Machiavellians. In B. Ruben (Ed.), *Communication Yearbook 2* (pp. 193–208). New Brunswick, NJ: Transaction Books.

[22] Kipnis, D., & Schmidt, S. M. (1988). Upward-influence styles: Relationship with performance evaluations, salary, and stress. *Administrative Science Quarterly, 33,* 528–542; Kipnis, D., Schmidt, S. M., Swaffin-Smith, C., & Wilkinson, I. (1984, Winter). Patterns of managerial influence: Shotgun managers, tacticians, and bystanders. *Organizational Dynamics,* 58–67; Kipnis, D., Schmidt, S. J., & Wilkinson, I. (1980). Intraorganizational influence tactics: Explorations in getting one's way. *Journal of Applied Psychology, 65,* 440–452.

[23] Yukl, G. (2006). *Leadership in organizations* (6th ed.). Upper Saddle River, NJ: Prentice-Hall; Yukl, G., Guinan, P. J., & Sottolano, D. (1995). Influence tactics used for different objectives with subordinates, peers, and superiors. *Group & Organization Management, 20,* 272–296.

[24] Yukl.

[25] Yukl, G., Falbe, C. M., & Youn, J. (1993). Patterns of influence behaviors for managers. *Group & Organization Management, 18,* 5–28.

[26] Hill, T. A. (1976). An experimental study of the relationship between opinionated leadership and small group consensus. *Speech Monographs, 43,* 246–257; Schultz, B. (1982). Argumentativeness: Its effect in group decision making and its role in leadership perception. *Communication Quarterly, 30,* 368–375; Muscovici, S., Mugny, G., & Van Avermaet, E. (Eds.). (1985). *Perspectives on minority influence.* Cambridge, MA: Cambridge University Press.

[27] Infante, D. A., & Gorden, W. I. (1985). Superiors' argumentativeness and verbal aggressiveness as predictors of subordinates' satisfaction. *Human Communication Research, 12,* 117–125; Infante,

D. A., & Gorden, W. I. (1985). Benefits versus bias: An investigation of argumentativeness, gender, and organizational outcomes. *Communication Research Reports, 2*, 196–201; Infante, D. A., & Gorden, W. I. (1991). How employees see the boss: Test of an argumentative and affirming model of supervisors' communicative behavior. *Western Journal of Speech Communication, 55*, 294–304; Infante, D. A., & Gorden, W. I. (1989). Argumentativeness and affirming communicator style as predictors of satisfaction/dissatisfaction with subordinates. *Communication Quarterly, 31*, 81–90.

[28] Infante, D. (1988). *Arguing constructively.* Long Grove, IL: Waveland Press; Infante, D., & Rancer, A. (1996). Argumentativeness and verbal aggressiveness: A review of recent theory and research. In B. Burleson (Ed.), *Communication Yearbook 19* (pp. 319–351). Thousand Oaks, CA: Sage.

[29] Infante, D. A., & Rancer, A. S. (1982). A conceptualization and measure of argumentativeness. *Journal of Personality Assessment, 46*, 72–80. Used by permission.

[30] Hample, D. (2003). Arguing skill. In J. O. Greene & B. R. Burleson (Eds.), *Handbook of communication and social interaction skills* (pp. 439–477). Mahwah, NJ: Lawrence Erlbaum; Infante, D. A. (1995). Teaching students to understand and control verbal aggression. *Communication Education, 44*, 51–63.

[31] Rancer, A. S., & Avtgis, T. A. (2006). *Argumentative and aggressive communication: Theory, research, and application.* Thousand Oaks, CA: Sage.

[32] Infante, *Arguing constructively,* pp. 33–81.

[33] Infante, *Arguing constructively,* p. 47. Used by permission.

[34] Inch, E. S., & Warnick, B. (2002). *Critical thinking and communication: The use of reason in argument* (4th ed.). Boston: Allyn & Bacon.

[35] Deutsch, M. (1973). *The resolution of conflict.* New Haven: Yale University Press.

[36] Rubin, J. Z., & Brown, B. R. (1975). *The social psychology of bargaining and negotiation.* New York: Academic Press.

[37] An impressive demonstration of the effectiveness of the Tit for Tat strategy is found in: Axelrod, R. (1984). *The evolution of cooperation.* New York: Basic Books. Axelrod set up a tournament using a computerized version of the Prisoner's Dilemma game. The Tit for Tat strategy beat all other entries. For more information on variations of this approach, see: Pruitt, D. G., & Carnevale, P. J. (1993). *Negotiation in social conflict.* Pacific Grove, CA: Brooks/Cole, ch. 4.

[38] Isenhart, M. W., & Spangle, M. (2000). *Collaborative approaches to resolving conflict.* Thousand Oaks, CA: Sage, pp. 56–58.

[39] Neale, M. A., & Bazerman, M. H. (1983). The role of perspective-taking ability in negotiating under different forms of arbitration. *Industrial and Labor Relations, 36*, 378–388; Bazerman, M. H., & Neale, M. A. (1983). Heuristics in negotiation: Limitations to effective dispute resolution. In M. H. Bazerman & R. J. Lewecki (Eds.), *Negotiating in organizations* (pp. 51–67). Beverly Hills, CA: Sage; Kemp, K. F., & Smith, W. P. (1994). Information exchange, toughness, and integrative bargaining: The roles of explicit cues and perspective-take. *The International Journal of Conflict Management, 5*, 5–12.

[40] Tenbrusel, A. E., & Messick, D. M. (2001). Power asymmetries and the ethical atmosphere in negotiations. In J. M. Darley, D. M. Messick, & T. R. Tyler (Eds.), *Social influences on ethical behavior in organizations* (pp. 201–216). Mahwah, NJ: Lawrence Erlbaum. See also: Williams, G. R. (1993). Style and effectiveness in negotiation. In L. Hall (Ed.), *Negotiation: Strategies for mutual gain* (pp. 151–174). Newbury Park, CA: Sage.

[41] Foster, D. A. (1992). *Bargaining across borders: How to negotiate business successfully anywhere in the world.* New York: McGraw-Hill, pp. 108–109. Copyright © 1992. Reproduced with permission of The McGraw-Hill Companies.

[42] Roloff, M. E., Putnam, L. L., & Anastasiou, L. (2003). Negotiation skills. In J. O. Greene & B. R. Burleson (Eds.), *Handbook of communication and social interaction skills* (pp. 801–833). Mahwah, NJ: Lawrence Erlbaum.

[43] Fisher, R., & Ury, W. (1991). *Getting to yes* (2nd ed.). New York: Penguin Books.

[44] Nielsen, R. P. (1998). Quaker foundations for Greenleaf's servant-leadership and "friendly disentangling" method. In L. Spears (Ed.), *Insights on leadership* (pp. 126–144). New York: John Wiley & Sons.

[45] Fisher & Ury, pp. 41–42.

[46] Fisher & Ury, p. 40.

[47] Cialdini, R. B. (2001). *Influence: Science and practice* (4th ed.). Boston: Allyn & Bacon; Rhoads, K. V. L., & Cialdini, R. B. (2002). The business of influence: Principles that lead to success in commercial settings. In J. P. Dillard & M. Pfau (Eds.), *The persuasion handbook: Developments in theory and practice.* Thousand Oaks, CA: Sage. Some of the examples in this section are drawn from these sources.

48 Richard Petty and John Cacioppo's elaboration likelihood model is also based on the premise that receivers don't have the time, energy, or mental capacity to think carefully about (to elaborate on) all the persuasive messages they receive. Topics deemed important and relevant are carefully processed along the central route of persuasion. All others are processed along the peripheral route, which is heavily influenced by the mental shortcuts identified by Cialdini. See, for example: Petty, R. E., & Cacioppo, J. T. (1986). *Communication and persuasion: Central and peripheral routes to attitude change.* New York: Springer-Verlag; Petty, R., & Wegener, D. (1999). The elaboration likelihood model: Current status and controversies. In S. Chaiken & Y. Trope (Eds.), *Dual process theories in social psychology* (pp. 41–72). New York: Guilford.

49 Cialdini, R. B., Sagarin, B. J., & Rice, W. E. (2001). Training in ethical influence. In J. M. Darley, D. M. Messick, & T. R. Tyler (Eds.), *Social influences on ethical behavior in organizations* (pp. 137–153). Mahwah, NJ: Lawrence Erlbaum.

50 Cialdini, R., Vincent, J., Lewis, S., Catalan, J., Wheeler, D., & Darby, B. (1975). Reciprocal procedure for inducing compliance: The door-in-the-face technique. *Journal of Personality and Social Psychology, 31,* 206–213.

51 Hofling, C. K., Brotzman, E., Dalrymple, S., Graves, N., & Pierce, C. M. (1966). An experimental study of nurse-physician relationships. *Journal of Nervous and Mental Disease, 143,* 171–180.

52 Adapted from the credibility scales of: Berlo, D., Lemert, J., & Mertz, R. (1969). Dimensions for evaluation of the acceptability of message sources. *Public Opinion Quarterly, 33,* 563–576; McCroskey, J., & Young, T. (1981). Ethos and credibility: The construct and its measurements after two decades. *Central States Speech Journal,* 22–34.

53 Kouzes & Posner, *The leadership challenge,* p. 70.

54 Ping, P. F., & Yukl, G. (2000). Perceived effectiveness of influence tactics in the United States and China. *Leadership Quarterly, 11,* 251–266.

55 Steinberg, B., & Vranica, S. (2004, April 15). Burger King seeks some Web heat. *Wall Street Journal,* p. B3.

Chapter 7

1 Burke, K. (1968). *Language as symbolic action.* Berkeley: University of California Press.

2 Tompkins, P. K. (1982). *Communication as action: An introduction to rhetoric and communication.* Belmont, CA: Wadsworth, p. 8.

3 Books surveyed include: Cragan, J. F., & Wright, D. W. (1999). *Communication in small group: Theory, process, skills* (5th ed.). Belmont, CA: Wadsworth; Fisher, B. A., & Ellis, D. G. (1994). *Small group decision making* (4th ed.). New York: McGraw-Hill; Jensen, A. D., & Chilberg, J. G. (1991). *Small group communication.* Belmont, CA: Wadsworth; Patton, B. P., & Downs, T. M. (2003). *Decision-making group interaction: Achieving quality* (4th ed.). New York: Allyn & Bacon; Rothwell, J. D. (2004). *In mixed company: Small group communication* (4th ed.). Belmont, CA: Wadsworth; Schultz, B. G. (1996). *Communicating in the small group: Theory and practice* (2nd ed.). New York: Harper-Collins; Engleberg, I. N., & Wynn, D. R. (2003). *Working in groups: Communication principles and strategies* (3rd ed.). Boston: Houghton Mifflin.

4 Patton & Downs, p. 3.

5 Cragan & Wright, p. 9.

6 Scheidel, T. M., & Crowell, L. (1964). Idea development in small discussion groups. *Quarterly Journal of Speech, 50,* 140–145.

7 Fisher, B. A. (1970). Decision emergence: Phases in group decision making. *Speech Monographs, 37,* 53–66.

8 Poole, M. S. (1983). Decision development in small groups II: A study of multiple sequences in decision making. *Communication Monographs, 50,* 206–232; Poole, M. S. (1983). Decision development in small groups III: A multiple sequence model of group decision development. *Communication Monographs, 50,* 321–341.

9 A summary of the results of these studies can be found in Bormann, E. G. (1975). *Discussion and group methods* (2nd ed., ch. 11). New York: Harper & Row. Leader emergence findings from this research program are also reported in Mortensen, C. D. (1966). Should the discussion group have an assigned leader? *The Speech Teacher, 15,* 34–41; and Geier, J. G. (1967). A trait approach to the study of leadership. *Journal of Communication, 17,* 316–323.

[10] Bormann, p. 261.

[11] Fisher & Ellis, pp. 251–253.

[12] See, for example: Stang, D. J. (1973). Effect of interaction rate on ratings of leadership and liking. *Journal of Personality and Social Psychology, 27,* 405–408; Regula, C. R., & Julian, J. W. (1983). The impact of quality and frequency of task contributions on perceived ability. *Journal of Social Psychology, 89,* 115–122; Riecken, H. (1975). The effect of talkativeness on ability to influence group solutions of problems. In P. V. Crosbie (Ed.), *Interaction in small groups* (pp. 238–249). New York: Macmillan; Daly, J. A., McCroskey, J. C., & Richmond, V. P. (1980). Relationship between vocal activity and perception of communication in small group interaction. *Western Journal of Speech Communication, 41,* 175–187.

[13] Schultz, B. (1980). Communicative correlates of perceived leaders. *Small Group Behavior, 11,* 175–191.

[14] Schultz, B. (1979). Predicting emergent leaders: An exploratory study of the salience of communicative functions. *Small Group Behavior, 9,* 109–114; Knutson, T. J., & Holdridge, W. E. (1975). Orientation behavior, leadership and consensus: A possible functional relationship. *Speech Monographs, 42,* 107–114.

[15] Hirokawa, R., & Pace, R. (1983). A descriptive investigation of the possible communication-based reasons for effective and ineffective group decision making. *Communication Monographs, 50,* 363–379.

[16] Baird, J. E. (1977). Some nonverbal elements of leadership emergence. *Southern Speech Communication Journal, 42,* 352–361.

[17] Hollander developed the idea of idiosyncratic credits over three decades. A summary of this research is found in *Leadership Dynamics: A practical guide to effective relationships* (1978). New York: The Free Press.

[18] This study is described in Jacobs, T. O. (1970). *Leadership and exchange in formal organizations.* Alexandria, VA: Human Resources Research Organization, ch. 3.

[19] Hollander, p. 42.

[20] Poole, Decision development III.

[21] Hollander, pp. 60–64.

[22] Engleberg & Wynn, p. 3.

[23] Auger, B. Y. (1972). *How to run better business meetings.* New York: AMACOM.

[24] Tropman, J. (2003). *Making meetings work: Achieving high quality group decisions* (2nd ed.). Thousand Oaks, CA: Sage.

[25] Tropman, p. 66.

[26] Nichols, R. G. (1961). Do we know how to listen? Practical helps in a modern age. *The Speech Teacher, 10,* 120–124.

[27] See, for example: Foulke, E. (1971). The perception of time compressed speech. In D. L. Horton & J. J. Jenkins (Eds.), *The perception of language* (pp. 79–107). Columbus, OH: Charles E. Merrill; Korba, R. J. (1986). *The rate of inner speech.* Unpublished doctoral dissertation, University of Denver; Landauer, T. J. (1962). Rate of implicit speech. *Perceptual and Motor Skills, 15,* 646.

[28] Kline, T. (1999). *Remaking teams: The revolutionary research-based guide that puts theory into practice.* San Francisco: Jossey-Bass.

[29] Tropman.

[30] Gouran, D. S., Hirokawa, R. Y., Julian, K. M., & Leatham, G. B. (1993). The evolution and current status of the functional perspective on communication in decision-making and problem-solving groups. In S. Deetz (Ed.), *Communication yearbook 16* (pp. 573–600). Newbury Park, CA: Sage; Griffin, E. (2009). *A first look at communication theory* (7th ed., ch. 17). New York: McGraw-Hill.

[31] Larson, C. E. (1969). Forms of analysis and small group problem-solving. *Speech Monographs, 36,* 452–455.

[32] Dewey, J. (1910). *How we think.* Boston: D.C. Heath. There are a number of variations of Dewey's original model. The version described in this chapter is found in Rothwell, ch. 7.

[33] Hirokawa, R. Y., & Scheerhorn, D. R. (1986). Communication in faulty group decision-making. In R. Y. Hirokawa & M. S. Poole (Eds.), *Communication and group decision-making* (pp. 63–80). Beverly Hills, CA: Sage.

[34] Gouran, D. S., & Hirokawa, R. Y. (1986). Counteractive functions of communication in effective group decision-making. In *Communication and group decision-making,* pp. 81–90.

[35] Druskat, V. U., & Wolff, S. B. (2001, March). Building the emotional intelligence of groups. *Harvard Business Review,* 80–90. Robert Bales developed a coding system based on the task and social dimensions of group interaction that served as the foundation for later theories of group evolu-

tion. See: Bales, R. F. (1970). *Personality and interpersonal behavior.* New York: Holt Rinehart & Winston; Bales, R. F., & Cohen, S. P. (1979). *Symlog: A system for the multiple level observation of groups.* London: Collier.

[36] LaFasto, F., & Larson, C. (2001). *When teams work best: 6000 team members and leaders tell what it takes to excel.* Thousand Oaks, CA: Sage, p. 85, © 2001 Sage Publications, Inc. Reprinted by permission of the publisher.

[37] Janis, I. (1971, November). Groupthink: The problems of conformity. *Psychology Today, 271–279;* Janis, I. (1982). *Groupthink* (2nd ed.). Boston: Houghton Mifflin. Janis, I. (1989). *Crucial decisions: Leadership in policymaking and crisis management.* New York: The Free Press; Janis, I., & Mann, L. (1977). *Decision making.* New York: The Free Press. Groupthink has also been identified in other historical events, including the *Challenger* shuttle launch and the Iran–Contra Affair. See: Esser, J. K. (1998). Alive and well after 25 years: A review of groupthink research. *Organizational Behavior and Human Decision Processes, 73,* 116–141.

[38] Chen, Z., Lawson, R. B., Gordon, L. R., & McIntosh, B. (1996). Groupthink: Deciding with the leader and the devil. *Psychological Record, 46,* 581–590.

[39] Janis, *Groupthink;* Manz, C. C., & Peck, C. P. (1995). Teamthink: Beyond the groupthink syndrome in self-managing work teams. *Journal of Managerial Psychology, 10,* 7–15; Moorhead, G., Neck, C. P., & West, M. S. (1998). The tendency toward defective decision making within self-managing teams: The relevance of groupthink for the 21st century. *Organizational Behavior and Human Decision Processes, 73,* 327–351.

[40] Harvey, J. (1974, Summer). The Abilene Paradox: The mismanagement of agreement. *Organizational Dynamics,* pp. 63–80; Harvey, J. (1988). *The Abilene Paradox and other meditations on management.* Lexington, MA: Lexington Books.

[41] Social psychologists use the term *escalation of commitment* to describe how groups persist in failed courses of action. For more information on escalating commitment, see: Keil, M., & Montealegre, R. (2000, Spring). Cutting your losses: Extracting your organization when a big project goes awry. *Sloan Management Review, 41,* 55–68. Ross, J., & Staw, B. M. (1993). Organizational escalation and exit: Lessons from the Shoreham nuclear power plant. *Academy of Management Journal, 36,* 701–732; Staw, B. M. (2001). The escalation of commitment to a course of action. *Academy of Management Review, 6,* 577–587.

[42] Kanter, R. M. (2001). An Abilene defense: Commentary one. *Organizational Dynamics, 17,* 37–39; Carlisle, A. E. (2001). An Abilene defense: Commentary two. *Organizational Dynamics, 17,* 40–43.

[43] Harvey, *The Abilene Paradox,* pp. 31–32. Used by permission of the publisher.

[44] Katzenbach, J. R., & Smith, D. K. (1993, March–April). The discipline of teams. *Harvard Business Review,* 111–120; Katzenbach, J. R., & Smith, D. K. (1993). *The wisdom of teams.* Boston: Harvard Business School Press.

[45] Katzenbach, J. R. (1998). *Teams at the top: Unleashing the potential of both teams and individual leaders.* Boston: Harvard Business School Press.

[46] Katzenbach & Smith, *Wisdom,* p. 31.

[47] Katzenbach & Smith, *Wisdom,* p. 45.

[48] Katzenbach, J. R., & Smith, D. K. (1993). *The wisdom of teams.* Boston: Harvard Business School Press, p. 84. Used by permission.

[49] Larson, C. E., & LaFasto, F. M. J. (1989). *Teamwork: What must go right/What can go wrong.* Newbury Park, CA: Sage.

[50] Olsen, S. (2004, July 9). *Google recruits eggheads with mysterious billboard.* CNETNews.com.

[51] Larson & LaFasto, p. 128.

[52] LaFasto, F., & Larson, C. (2001). *When teams work best.* Thousand Oaks, CA: Sage.

[53] LaFasto & Larson, p. 56.

[54] Ray, D., & Bronstein, H. (1995). *Teaming up.* New York: McGraw-Hill. p. 21.

[55] See, for example: Fisher, K., Harper, B., & Harper, A. (1992). *Succeeding as a self-directed work team.* Mohegan Lake, NY: MW Corporation; Wellins, R. S., Byham, W. C., & Wilson, J. M. (1991). *Empowered teams.* San Francisco: Jossey-Bass.

[56] Wellins, Byham, & Wilson, p. 26. Permission granted by John Wiley & Sons, Inc.

[57] Wellins, Byham, & Wilson.

[58] Trist, E. L., & Bamforth, K. W. (1951). Some social and psychological consequences of the long-wall method of coal-getting. *Human Relations, 4,* 3–38.

[59] Fisher, K. (1993). *Leading self-directed work teams.* New York: McGraw-Hill, p. 5.

[60] Wellins, Byham, & Wilson, p. 9.

[61] Stewart, G. L., Manz, C. C., & Sims, H. P. (1999). *Team work and group dynamics*. New York: Wiley.

[62] Wellins, R. S., Byham, W. C., & Dixon, G. R. (1994). *Inside teams*. San Francisco: Jossey-Bass.

[63] Kayser, T. A. (1994). *Team power*. Burr Ridge, IL: Irwin, p. 36.

[64] Labich, K. (1989, May 8). Making over middle managers. *Fortune*, 58–64.

[65] Near, R., & Weckler, D. (1990, September). *Organizational and job characteristics related to self-managing teams*. Paper presented at the International Conference on Self-Managed Work Teams, Denton, TX.

[66] Hoerr, J., & Zellner, W. (1989, July 10). The payoff for teamwork. *Business Week*.

[67] Wyscoki, L. (1990, September). *Implementation of self-managed teams within a non-union manufacturing facility*. Paper presented at the International Conference on Self-Managed Work Teams, Denton, TX.

[68] Sheridan, J. H. (1990, October). America's best plants. *Industry Week*, 27–64.

[69] Dumaine, B. (1990, May 7). Who needs a boss? *Fortune*, 52–55.

[70] Dumaine.

[71] Shockley-Zalabak, P., & Burmester, S. B. (2001). *The power of networked teams*. New York: Oxford University Press.

[72] Sherwood, J. (1988). Creating work cultures with competitive advantage. *Organizational Dynamics, 16*, 4.

[73] Wellins, Byham, & Dixon.

[74] Hoerr, J., & Pollock, M. A. (1986, September 29). Management discovers the human side of automation. *Business Week, 74*–77; O'Dell, C. (1989, November). Team play, team pay: New ways of keeping score. *Across the Board*, 38–45.

[75] Hoerr & Pollock.

[76] Adapted from: Fisher, K., Harper, B., & Harper, A. (1992). *Succeeding as a self-directed work team*. Mohegan Lake, NY: MW Corporation; Wellins, Byham, & Wilson.

[77] Fisher, *Leading*, pp. 48–54.

[78] Zaccaro, S. J., Ardison, S. D., & Orvis, K. L. (2004). Leadership in virtual teams. In D. V. Day, S. M. Halpin, & S. J. Zaccaro (Eds.), *Leadership development for transforming organizations: Growing leaders for tomorrow*. Mahwah, NJ: Lawrence Erlbaum.

[79] Kirkman, B. L., Rosen, B., Gibson, C. B., Tesluk, P. E., & McPherson, S. O. (2002). Five challenges to virtual team success: Lessons from Sabre, Inc. *Academy of Management Executive, 16*, 67–79.

[80] Jarvenpaa, S. L., & Leidner, D. E. (1999). Communication and trust in global virtual teams. *Organization Science, 10*, 791–815.

[81] Kayworth, T. R., & Leidner, D. E. (2001–2002). Leadership effectiveness in global virtual teams. *Journal of Management Information Systems, 18*, 7–40.

[82] Bell, B. S. (2002). A typology of virtual teams: Implications for effective leadership. *Group & Organization Management, 27*, 14–49; Cascio, W. F. (2000). Managing a virtual workplace. *Academy of Management Executive, 14*, 81–90; Zaccaro et al.; Kayworth & Leidner; Kirkman et al.

[83] Jarvenpaa & Leidner.

[84] Marquardt, M. J., & Horvath, L. (2001). *Global teams*. Palo Alto, CA: Davies-Black.

[85] Deveraux, M., & Johansen, R. (1994). *GlobalWork: Bridging distance, culture, and time*. San Francisco: Jossey-Bass.

[86] Lee, O. (2002). Cultural differences in e-mail use of virtual teams: A critical social theory perspective. *CyberPsychology & Behavior, 5*, 227–232.

Chapter 8

[1] Etzioni, A. (1964). *Modern organizations*. Englewood Cliffs, NJ: Prentice-Hall, p. 1.

[2] Hawes, L. C. (1974). Social collectivities as communication: Perspectives on organizational behavior. *Quarterly Journal of Speech, 60*, 497–502.

[3] For an overview of the different ways that communication scholars approach the study of organizational culture, see: Eisenberg, E. M., & Riley, P. (2001). Organizational culture. In F. M. Jablin & L. L. Putnam (Eds.), *The new handbook of organizational communication: Advances in theory, research, and methods* (pp. 291–322). Thousand Oaks, CA: Sage.

[4] The number of cultures an organization has is a matter of some debate. One group of researchers argues that there is only one culture per organization. Others argue that an organization consists

of a series of cultural islands or subcultures. A third group contends that there are multiple cultures created by members as they interact. We think that there must be some common cultural elements in order for there to be an organization, but we acknowledge the presence of subcultures and that individuals shape and form culture as they coordinate their actions. For a description of the three perspectives and how each can provide useful insights into organizational behavior, see: Martin, J. (1992). *Cultures in organizations.* New York: Oxford University Press; Martin, J. (2002). *Organizational culture: Mapping the terrain.* Thousand Oaks, CA: Sage.

[5] Dyer, W. G. (1985). The cycle of cultural evolution in organizations. In R. H. Kilmann, M. J. Saxton, & R. Serpa (Eds.), *Gaining control of the corporate culture* (pp. 200–229). San Francisco: Jossey-Bass.

[6] Rafaeli, A., & Worline, M. (2000). Symbols in organizational culture. In N. M. Ashkanasy, C. P. M. Wilderom, & M. F. Peterson (Eds.), *Handbook of organizational culture and climate* (pp. 71–84). Thousand Oaks, CA: Sage.

[7] Martin, J., & Powers, M. E. (1983). Truth or corporate propaganda: The value of a good story. In L. R. Pondy, P. J. Frost, G. Morgan, & T. C. Dandridge (Eds.), *Organizational symbolism* (pp. 93–107). Greenwich, CT: JAI Press.

[8] Trice, H. M., & Beyer, J. M. (1984). Studying organizational cultures through rites and ceremonials. *Academy of Management Review, 9,* 653–669; Trice, H. M., & Beyer, J. M. (1993). *The cultures of work organizations.* Englewood Cliffs, NJ: Prentice-Hall, ch. 3.

[9] Fairhurst, G. T., & Sarr, R. A. (1996). *The art of framing: Managing the language of leadership.* San Francisco: Jossey-Bass.

[10] Kanter, R. M. (1983). *The change masters: Innovation for productivity in the American corporation.* New York: Simon and Schuster, p. 281.

[11] Schein, E. H. (1992). *Organizational culture and leadership* (2nd ed.). San Francisco: Jossey-Bass, p. 5.

[12] Schein, ch. 10; Schein, E. H. (1983). The role of the founder in creating organizational culture. *Organizational Dynamics, 12,* 13–26.

[13] Adapted from Cheney, G. (1983). On the various and changing meanings of organizational membership: A field study of organizational identification. *Communication Monographs, 50,* 342–362. Used by permission.

[14] Linn, A. (2006, October 5). Boston.com Business.

[15] Planet Starbucks. (2002, September 9). *Business Week,* 100–109.

[16] Schultz, H., & Yang, D. J. (1997). *Pour your heart into it: How Starbucks built a company one cup at a time.* New York: Hyperion, p. 81.

[17] Jones, A. (1999, July 3). Coffee shops leave a sour taste. *The London Times.* Retrieved July 4, 1999, from http://web.lexis-nexis.com/universe; Business Wire. (2002, February 26). Starbucks annual shareholder's meeting to highlight new initiatives. Retrieved April 20, 2002, from http://businesswire.com; PR Newswire. (2002, February 12). Organic consumer activists will leaflet and protest at Starbucks coffee shops. Retrieved April 20, 2002, from http://www.prnewswire.com.

[18] Schultz & Yang, p. 332

[19] Schein, *Organizational culture,* ch. 11.

[20] Peters, T., & Austin, N. (1985). *A passion for excellence: The leadership difference.* New York: Warner Books, p. 337.

[21] Kotter, J. (1999). Leading change: The eight steps to transformation. In J. A. Conger, G. M. Spreitzer, & E. E. Lawler III (Eds.), *The leader's change handbook: An essential guide to setting direction and taking action* (pp. 87–99). San Francisco: Jossey-Bass.

[22] Trice, H. M., & Beyer, J. M. (1985). Using six organizational rites to change culture. In *Gaining control of the corporate culture,* pp. 370–399. See also: Knittel, R. E. (1974). Essential and nonessential ritual in programs of planned change. *Human Organization, 33,* 394–396.

[23] Bennet, D., & Bennet, A. (2003). The rise of the knowledge organization. In C. W. Holsapple (Ed.), *Handbook on knowledge management 1: Knowledge matters* (pp. 5–20). Berlin: Springer-Verlag; Edmondson, A., & Moingeon, B. (1996). When to learn how and when to learn why: Appropriate organizational learning processes as a source of competitive advantage. In B. Moingeon & A. Edmondson (Eds.), *Organizational learning and competitive advantage* (pp. 17–37). London: Sage; Ulrich, D., Von Glinow, M. A., & Todd, J. (1993). High-impact learning: Building and diffusing learning capability. *Organizational Dynamics, 22,* 52–66.

[24] Senge, P. M. (1990, Fall). The leader's new work: Building learning organizations. *Sloan Management Review,* pp. 7–23.

[25] Garvin, D. A. (1993, July–August). Building a learning organization. *Harvard Business Review,* 78–91.

26 Senge, P. M. (1990). *The fifth discipline: The art and practice of the learning organization*. New York: Doubleday/Currency; Sadler, P. (2001). Leadership and organizational learning. In M. Dierkes, A. Berthoin Antal, J. Child, & I. Nonaka (Eds.), *Handbook of organizational learning and knowledge* (pp. 415–427). Oxford: Oxford University Press; Dubrin, A. J. (2007). *Leadership: Research findings, practice, and skills*. Boston: Houghton Mifflin, ch. 13.

27 Garvin, D. A. (2000). *Learning in action: A guide to putting the learning organization to work*. Boston: Harvard Business School Press. A number of examples of the three learning types come from Garvin's work.

28 Marquardt, M. (2005). *Leading with questions*. San Francisco: Jossey-Bass.

29 Magaziner, I. C., & Patinkin, M. (1989, March–April). Cold competition: GE wages the refrigerator war. *Harvard Business Review*, 114–124; Magaziner, I. C., & Patinkin, M. (1989). *The silent war: Inside the global business battles shaping America's future*. New York: Random House, ch. 3.

30 For purposes of this discussion, we are distinguishing between knowledge generation (learning) and knowledge management (the dissemination and storage of information). Some scholars, however, treat learning as a subset of knowledge management. See, for example: Hult, G. T. M. (2003). An integration of thoughts on knowledge management. *Decision Sciences, 34*, 189–195; Alavi, M. (2001). Review: Knowledge management and knowledge management systems: Conceptual foundations and research issues. *MIS Quarterly, 25*, 107–136; Skyrme, D. J. (2000). Developing a knowledge strategy: From management to leadership. In D. Morey, M. Maybury, & B. Thuraisingham (Eds.), *Knowledge management: Classic and contemporary works* (pp. 61–83). Cambridge, MA: MIT Press.

31 Primary source: Garvin, *Learning in action*, ch. 3. See also: Day, S. (2002, August 27). L. L. Bean tries to escape the mail-order wilderness. *The New York Times*, p. C1. Retrieved July 18, 2006, from The Newspaper Source; Entrepreneur L.L. Bean never sold out: Devotion to quality and customer service made him king of outdoor gear. (2001, October 8). *Investor's Business Daily*, p. A6. Retrieved July 18, 2006, from Newspaper Source; L. L. Bean reports 2005 net sales results: Company reports third consecutive year of strong growth. (2006, March 10). *PR Newswire*. Retrieved July 18, 2006, from Newspaper Source.

32 Skyrme.

33 Ives, W., Torrey, B., & Gordon, C. (2002). Knowledge sharing is human behavior. In *Knowledge management* (pp. 99–129). Cambridge, MA: MIT Press.

34 See, for example: Bruhn, J. G. (2001). *Trust and the health of organizations*. New York: Kluwer/Plenum; Dirks, K. T. (1999). The effects of interpersonal trust on work group performance. *Journal of Applied Psychology, 84*, 445–455; Driscoll, J. W. (1978). Trust and participation in organizational decision making as predictors of satisfaction. *Academy of Management Journal, 21*, 44–56; Gilbert, J. A., & Tang, T. L. (1998). An examination of organizational trust antecedents. *Public Personnel Management, 27*, 321–338; Kramer, R. M., & Tyler, T. R. (1996). *Trust in organizations: Frontiers of theory and research*. Thousand Oaks, CA: Sage; Mayer, R. C., & Gavin, M. B. (2005). Trust in management and performance: Who minds the shop while the employees watch the boss? *Academy of Management Journal, 48*, 874–888; McLain, D. L., & Hackman, K. (1999). Trust, risk, and decision-making in organizational change. *Public Administration Quarterly, 23*, 152–176; Shockley-Zalabak, Ellis, K., & Winograd, G. (2000). Organizational trust: What it means, why it matters. *Organization Development Journal, 18*, 35–47.

35 Shockley-Zalabak, Ellis, & Winograd. See also: Mishra, A. K. (1996). Organizational responses to crisis: The centrality of trust. In R. M. Kramer & T. R. Tyler (Eds.), *Trust in organizations: Frontiers of theory and research* (pp. 261–287). Thousand Oaks, CA: Sage.

36 Kramer, R. M. (1999). Trust and distrust in organizations: Emerging perspectives, enduring questions. *Annual Review of Psychology, 50*, 569–98; McLain & Hackman.

37 Stein, L. (2003, May 5). Flying low. *U.S. News & World Report*. Retrieved July 14, 2006, from Business Source Premier.

38 Trustbusting factors are drawn from a variety of sources, including: Bruhn; Elangovan, A. R., & Shapiro, D. L. (1998). Betrayal of trust in organizations. *Academy of Management Review, 23*, 547–566; Galford, R., & Drapeau, A. S. (2003, February). The enemies of trust. *Harvard Business Review, 81*, 88–97; McLain & Hackman; Prusak, L., & Cohen, D. (2001, June). How to invest in social capital. *Harvard Business Review*, 86–93; Simons, T. (2002, September). The high cost of lost trust. *Harvard Business Review*, 18–19; Whitener, E. M. (1997). The impact of human resource activities on employee trust. *Human Resource Management Review, 7*, 380–405; Whitener, E. M.,

Brodt, S. E., Korsgaard, M. A., & Werner, J. M. (1998). Managers as initiators of trust: An exchange relationship framework for understanding managerial trustworthy behavior. *Academy of Management Review, 23,* 513–530.

[39] Galford & Drapeau.

[40] Learman, L. A., Avorn, J., Everitt, D. E., & Rosenthal, R. (1990). Pygmalion in the nursing home: The effects of caregiver expectations on patient outcomes. *Journal of the American Geriatrics Society, 38,* 797–803

[41] Jenner, H. (1990). The Pygmalion Effect: The importance of expectancies. *Alcoholism Treatment Quarterly, 7,* 127–133.

[42] Rosenthal, R., & Jacobson, L. (1968). *Pygmalion in the classroom.* New York: Holt, Rinehart and Winston. Many other researchers have verified the findings of Rosenthal and Jackson's groundbreaking study. See, for example: Jussim, L., Madon, S., & Chatman, C. (1994). Teacher expectations and student achievement: Self-fulfilling prophecies, biases, and accuracy. In L. Heath, R. S. Tindale, J. Edwards, E. J. Posavac, F. B. Bryant, E. Henderson-King, Y. Suarez-Balcazar, & J. Myers (Eds.), *Applications of heuristics and biases to social issues* (pp. 303–334). New York: Plenum Press; Barad, E. (1993). Pygmalion—25 years after interpersonal expectations in the classroom. In P. D. Blanck (Ed.), *Interpersonal expectations: Theory, research, and applications* (pp. 125–153). Cambridge, MA: Cambridge University Press.

[43] Eden, D., & Shami, A. B. (1982). Pygmalion goes to boot camp: Expectancy, leadership, and trainee performance. *Journal of Applied Psychology, 67,* 194–199.

[44] Crawford, K. S., Thomas, E. D., & Fink, J. J. (1980). Pygmalion at sea: Improving the work effectiveness of low performers. *Journal of Applied Behavioral Science, 16,* 482–505.

[45] Smith, A. E., Jussim, L., & Eccles, J. (1999). Do self-fulfilling prophecies accumulate, dissipate, or remain stable over time? *Journal of Personality and Social Psychology, 77,* 548–565.

[46] Berlew, D., & Hall, D. (1966). The socialization of managers: Effects of expectations on performance. *Administrative Science Quarterly, 2,* 208–223.

[47] White, S. S., & Locke, E. A. (2000). Problems with the Pygmalion Effect and some proposed solutions. *Leadership Quarterly, 11,* 389–416; McNatt, D. B. (2000). Ancient Pygmalion joins contemporary management: A meta-analysis of the result. *Journal of Applied Psychology, 85,* 314–322; Madon, S., Jussim, L., & Eccles, J. (1997). In search of the powerful self-fulfilling prophecy. *Journal of Personality and Social Psychology, 72,* 791–809; Duir, T., Eden, D., & Banjo, M. L. (1995). Self-fulfilling prophecy and gender: Can women be Pygmalion and Galatea? *Journal of Applied Psychology, 80,* 253–270.

[48] Livingston, J. S. (1969). Pygmalion in management. *Harvard Business Review, 47,* 85. For another discussion of self-esteem and expectations, see: Hill, N. (1976, August). Self-esteem: The key to effective leadership. *Administrative Management,* 24–25, 51.

[49] Locke, E. A., & Latham, G. P. (1990). *A theory of goal setting & task performance.* Englewood Cliffs, NJ: Prentice-Hall.

[50] Rosenthal, R. (1993). Interpersonal expectations: Some antecedents and some consequences. In *Interpersonal expectations* (pp. 3–24).

[51] Baird, J., & Wieting, G. K. (1979, September). Nonverbal communication can be a motivational tool. *Personnel Journal,* 607–610.

[52] Baird & Wieting.

[53] Good, T., & Brophy, J. (1980). *Educational psychology: A realistic approach.* New York: Holt, Rinehart and Winston.

[54] Eden, D., & Ravid, G. (1982). Pygmalion vs. self-expectancy: Effects of instructor and self-expectancy on trainee performance. *Organizational Behavior and Human Performance, 30,* 351–364.

[55] Eden, D. (1984). Self-fulfilling prophecy as a management tool: Harnessing Pygmalion. *Academy of Management Review, 9,* 64–73. Used by permission.

[56] Eden, D. (1990). *Pygmalion in management.* Lexington, MA: Lexington Books/D. C. Heath; Eden, D. (1993). Interpersonal expectations in organizations. In *Interpersonal expectations* (pp. 154–178).

[57] Eden, Self-fulfilling prophecy.

[58] Arndt, M. (2007, February 5). McDonald's 24/7. *Business Week,* 64–72; Belasen, A. T. (2008). *The theory and practice of corporate communication.* Los Angeles: Sage; Cowan, J. (2002, November). Is McDonald's really so bad? *enRoute,* 79–84; Daniels, J. L., & Daniels, N. C. (1993). *Global vision.* New York: McGraw-Hill; Happy meal. (2007, January 27). *The Economist,* 64–65; What's this? The French love McDonald's? (2003, January 13). *Business Week,* 50.

[59] Flynn, N. (2004). *Instant messaging rules.* New York: Amacom.

Chapter 9

[1] Carlyle, T. (1907). *On heroes, hero-worship, and the heroic in history.* Boston: Houghton Mifflin. (Original work written 1840.)

[2] Spencer, H. (1884). *The study of sociology.* New York: D. A. Appleton. (First published 1873.)

[3] Tucker, R. C. (1965). The dictator and totalitarianism. *World Politics, 17,* 565–573.

[4] Gardner, J. (1990). *On leadership.* New York: The Free Press, p. xiii.

[5] For more information on the unique features of public communication, see: Hart, R., Friedrich, G., & Brooks, W. (1975). *Public communication.* New York: Harper & Row; Asante, K., & Frye, J. (1977). *Contemporary public communication.* New York: Harper & Row.

[6] Newsom, D., Van Slyke Turk, J., & Kruckeberg, D. (2004). *This is PR: The realities of public relations* (8th ed.). Belmont, CA: Wadsworth/Thompson Learning; Wilcox, D. L., Cameron, G. T., Ault, P. H., & Agee, W. K. (2003). *Public relations: Strategies and tactics* (7th ed.). New York: Longman.

[7] Grunig, L. A., Grunig, J. E., Dozier, D. M. (2002). *Excellent public relations and effective organizations: A study of communication management in three countries.* Mahwah, NJ: Lawrence Erlbaum. See also: Dozier, D. M., Grunig, L. A., & Grunig, J. E. (1995). *Manager's guide to excellence in public relations and communication management.* Mahwah, NJ: Lawrence Erlbaum; Grunig, J. E., & Grunig, L. A. (1992). Models of public relations and communication. In J. E. Grunig, D. M. Dozier, W. Ehling, L. A. Grunig, F. C. Repper, & J. White (Eds.), *Excellence in public relations and communication management* (pp. 285–325). Hillsdale, NJ: Lawrence Erlbaum.

[8] Bridges, J. A., & Nelson, R. A. (2000). Issues management: A relational approach. In J. A. Ledingham & S. D. Bruning (Eds.), *Public relations as relationship management: A relational approach to the study and practice of public relations* (pp. 95–115). Mahwah, NJ: Lawrence Erlbaum; Heath, R. L. (2002). Issues management: Its past, present and future. *Journal of Public Affairs, 2,* 209–214; Renfro, W. L. (1993). *Issues management in strategic planning.* Westport, CT: Quorum Books.

[9] Carroll, A. B., & Buchholtz, A. K. (2003). *Business & society: Ethics and stakeholder management.* Mason, OH: Thomson/South-Western.

[10] Heath, R. L. (1997). *Strategic issues management: Organizations and public policy challenges.* Thousand Oaks, CA: Sage.

[11] Sarrel, M. D. (2006, December 26). Recycling e-waste. *PC Magazine,* p. 114. Retrieved March 13, 2007, from Business Source Premier; Flynn, L. J. (2005, October 24). Poor nations are littered with old PC's report says. *The New York Times,* p. C5. Retrieved March 13, 2007, from LexisNexis; Flynn, L. J. (2006, June 29). Dell expands its computer recycling program. *The New York Times,* p. C6. Retrieved March 13, 2007, from LexisNexis; How green is your apple? (2006, August 26). *Economist,* 49. Retrieved March 13, 2007, from Business Source Premier.

[12] Woellert, L. (2006, April 10). HP wants your old PCs back. *Business Week,* 82. Retrieved March 13, 2007, from Business Source Premier.

[13] Chea, T. (2007, March 4). Tech firms go green as e-waste mounts. *Associated Press Financial Wire.* Retrieved March 13, 2007, from LexisNexis.

[14] Moran, S. (2006, May 17). Panning e-waste for gold. *The New York Times,* p. G8.

[15] Whitman, R. F., & Foster, T. J. (1994). *Speaking in public.* New York: Macmillan, ch. 1.

[16] News items were taken from the February 20, 2007, issue of *The Oregonian,* Portland, OR.

[17] Torricelli, R., & Carroll, A. (Eds.). (1999). *In our own words: Extraordinary speeches of the American century.* New York: Kodansha International, p. xxix.

[18] Lucas, S. E. (2003). *The art of public speaking* (7th ed.). Boston: McGraw-Hill.

[19] Jaffe, C. (2007). *Public speaking: Concepts and skills for a diverse society* (5th ed.). Belmont, CA: Wadsworth/Thompson; Devito, J. (2000). *The elements of public speaking* (7th ed.). New York: Longman.

[20] For more examples of this kind of deceptive communication, see: Lutz, W. (1989). *Doublespeak.* New York: Harper & Row. This highly readable and entertaining book describes how government, business, advertisers, and others use language to distort reality. Among the more comical examples: an 18-page recipe for fruitcake for army chefs that includes instructions describing how the cake should "conform to the inside contour of the can or can liner" with "no point on the top of the lid greater than ¾-inch from the side of the can where the cake did not touch the lid during baking"; and the U.S. government's description of the 1983 early morning paratroop invasion of Grenada as a "pre-dawn vertical insertion." Australian speech writer Don Watson (2003) provides a number of additional examples of distorted verbiage from his country in *Death*

Sentences: How clichés, weasel words, and management-speak are strangling public language. New York: Gotham Books.

[21] Speech samples taken from: Conger, J. A. (1991). Inspiring others: The language of leadership. *Academy of Management Executive, 5,* 30–45; Pearce, T. (2003). *Leading out loud: The authentic speaker, the credible leader.* San Francisco: Jossey-Bass; Useem, M. (1998). *The leadership moment.* New York: Times Books; Smith-Davies Publishing. (2005). *Speeches that changed the world: The stories and transcripts of the moments that made history.* London: Author.

[22] See: Hackman, M. Z. (1988). Audience reactions to the use of direct and personal disparaging humor in informative public address. *Communication Research Reports, 5,* 126–130; Hackman, M. Z. (1988). Reactions to the use of self-disparaging humor by informative public speakers. *Southern Speech Communication Journal, 53,* 175–183.

[23] Chang, M., & Gruner, C. R. (1981). Audience reaction to self-disparaging humor. *Southern Speech Communication Journal, 46,* 419–447.

[24] For a more complete discussion of the importance of internal thought and external speech in public address, see: Hackman, M. Z. (1989). The inner game of public speaking: Applying intrapersonal communication processes in the public speaking course. *Carolinas Speech Communication Annual, 5,* 41–47.

[25] Pearce.

[26] Adapted from DeFleur, M. L., Kearney, P., & Plax, T. G. (1993). *Mastering communication in contemporary America.* Mountain View, CA: Mayfield, pp. 418–419.

[27] Simons, H. W., Morreale, J., & Gronbeck, B. (2003). *Persuasion in society.* Thousand Oaks, CA: Sage, p. 211.

[28] Persuasion experts categorize campaigns in different ways. These categories are adapted from: Woodward, G. C., & Denton, R. E. (2009). *Persuasion & influence in American life* (6th ed., ch. 9). Long Grove, IL: Waveland Press. For more information on social movements, see: Stewart, C. J., Smith, C. A., & Denton, R. E. (2007). *Persuasion and social movements* (5th ed.). Long Grove, IL: Waveland Press.

[29] Lynam, D. R., & Milich, R. (1999). Project DARE: No effects at 10 year follow up. *Journal of Consulting Clinical Psychology, 67,* 590–594.

[30] Rice, R. R. (2001). Smokey Bear. In R. R. Rice & C. K. Atkin (Eds.), *Public communication campaigns* (3rd ed., pp. 276–279). Thousand Oaks, CA: Sage.

[31] Winsten, J. A., & DeJong, W. (2001). The designated driver campaign. In *Public communication campaigns* (pp. 290–294).

[32] Rogers, E. M., & Storey, J. D. (1987). Communication campaigns. In C. R. Berger & S. H. Chaffee (Eds.), *Handbook of communication science* (pp. 817–846). Newbury Park, CA: Sage. Some of the examples used in this section of the chapter also come from this article.

[33] See, for example: Atkin, C. K. (2001). Theory and principles of media health campaigns. In *Public communication campaigns* (pp. 49–68); Snyder, L. B. (2001). How effective are mediated health campaigns? In *Public communication campaigns* (pp. 181–190).

[34] Singhal, A., & Rogers, E. (1999). *Entertainment-education: A communication strategy for social change.* Mahwah, NJ: Lawrence Erlbaum, ch. 9.

[35] Raine, G. (2006, February 8). Visa putting new life in advertising theme: "It's everywhere you want to be" ends after 20 years. *San Francisco Chronicle.* Retrieved May 23, 2008, from http://www.sfgate.com/cgi-bin/article.cgi?f=/c/a/2006/02/08/BUGIIH4FD21.DTL; Simon, B. (2006, May). Visa USA. *Sales & Marketing Management.* Retrieved March 14, 2007, from Business Source Premier.

[36] Rogers & Storey, p. 837.

[37] Rogers, E. M. (1995). *Diffusion of innovations* (4th ed., ch. 8). New York: The Free Press.

[38] Gladwell, M. (2002). *The tipping point: How little things can make a big difference.* Boston: Little Brown.

[39] Woodward & Denton, ch. 9.

[40] Woodward & Denton, p. 247. Used by permission.

[41] Heath, *Strategic issues management,* p. 231. Reproduced with permission of Sage Publications, Inc.

[42] Gardner, chs. 9 & 10.

[43] Johnson, C., & Hackman, M. Z. (1998). *Public relations, collaborative leadership and community.* Paper presented at the National Communication Association convention, New York, NY.

[44] Chrislip, D. D., & Larson, C. E. (1994). *Collaborative leadership.* San Francisco: Jossey-Bass. Many of the examples in this section come from Chrislip and Larson.

[45] Acting in a trustworthy fashion is particularly important when participants are angry and hostile. To learn more about dealing with difficult constituents, see: Susskind, I., & Field, P. (1996). *Dealing with an angry public: The mutual gains approach to resolving disputes.* New York: The Free Press.

[46] Alexander, J. A., Comfort, M. E., Weiner, B. J., & Bogue, R. (2001). Leadership in collaborative community health partnerships. *Nonprofit Management & Leadership, 12*, 159–175.

[47] Miller, A. N. (2002). An exploration of Kenyan public speaking patterns with implications for the American introductory public speaking course. *Communication Education, 51*, 168–182.

[48] Political candidates ride the YouTube, MySpace wave. (2006, September, 27). *NewsHour Extra.*

[49] Noble, P. (1996, July). International cyberspacing-use of the Internet worldwide. *Campaigns & Elections.*

Chapter 10

[1] Data taken from: Branch-Brioso, L. (2001, March 13). Minorities fueled growth in last decade, census says: Hispanic population has grown by 13 million. *St. Louis Post–Dispatch*, p. A1; Hays-Thomas, R. (2004). Why now? The contemporary focus on managing diversity. In M. S. Stockdale & F. J. Crosby (Eds.), *The psychology and management of workplace diversity* (pp. 3–30). Malden, MA: Blackwell; Mor Barak, M. E. (2005). *Managing diversity: Toward a globally inclusive workplace.* Thousand Oaks, CA: Sage; Friedman, T. (2000). *The lexus and the olive tree* (Expanded Version). New York: Anchor Books; Cox, T. (1993). *Cultural diversity in organizations: Theory, research and practice.* San Francisco: Berrett-Koehler; Marquardt, M. J., & Berger, N. O. (2000). *Global leaders for the 21st century.* Albany: State University of New York Press.

[2] Cox, *Cultural diversity in organizations*, ch. 2; Cox. T. (2001). *Creating the multicultural organization: A strategy for capturing the power of diversity.* San Francisco: Jossey-Bass; Hays-Thomas.

[3] We will use the terms "managing diversity" and "diversity management" interchangeably. However, some scholars distinguish between the two phrases. See, for example: Pushkala, P., Pringle, J. K., & Konrad, A. M. (2006). Examining the contours of workplace diversity: Concepts, contexts and challenges. In A. M. Konrad, P. Prasad, & J. K. Pringle (Eds.), *Handbook of workplace diversity* (pp. 1–22). London: Sage.

[4] Rogers, E. M., & Steinfatt, T. M. (1999). *Intercultural communication.* Long Grove, IL: Waveland Press, p. 79.

[5] Larrabee, W. (1972). Paralinguistics, kinesics, and cultural anthropology. In L. Samovar & R. Porter (Eds.), *Intercultural communication: A reader* (pp. 172–180). Belmont, CA: Wadsworth.

[6] This research highlight is adapted from: Johnson, C. E. (1997, Spring). A leadership journey to the East. *Journal of Leadership Studies, 4*, 82–88.

[7] Books promoting Taoist leadership practices include: Autry, J. A., & Mitchell, S. (1998). *Real power: Business lessons from the* Tao Te Ching. New York: St. Martin's Press; Heider, J. (1985). *The Tao of leadership.* New York: Bantam Books; Dreher, D. (1995). *The Tao of personal leadership.* New York: HarperBusiness; Messing, B. (1989). *The Tao of management.* New York: Bantam Books.

[8] For additional information on the historical background of Taoism, see: Ching, J. (1993). *Chinese religions.* Maryknoll, NY: Orbis Books; Hopfe, L. M. (1991). *Religions of the world* (5th ed.). New York: Macmillan; Watts, A. (1975). *The Watercourse way.* New York: Pantheon Books; Welch, H. (1965). *Taoism: The parting of the way* (Rev. Ed.). Boston: Beacon Press.

[9] Chan, W. (1963). *The way of Lao Tzu.* Indianapolis: Bobbs-Merrill, p. 64.

[10] Chan, p. 78.

[11] Chan, p. 76.

[12] Hall, E. (1977). *Beyond culture.* Garden City, NY: Anchor.

[13] Lustig, Myron W., & Koester, J. (2006). *Intercultural competence: Interpersonal communication across cultures* (5th ed.). Boston: Allyn & Bacon. Copyright © 2006 by Pearson Education. Reprinted by permission of the publisher.

[14] Hofstede, G. (2001). *Culture's consequences: Comparing values, behaviors, institutions, and organizations across nations* (2nd ed.). Thousand Oaks, CA: Sage; Hofstede, G. (1991). *Cultures and organizations: Software of the mind.* London: McGraw-Hill; Hofstede, G. (1984). The cultural relativity of the quality of life concept. *Academy of Management Review, 9*, 389–398.

[15] Hofstede, G., & Bond, M. H. (1988). The Confucius connection: From cultural roots to economic growth. *Organizational Dynamics, 14*, 483–503; Chinese Culture Connection. (1987). Chinese val-

ues and the search for culture-free dimensions of culture. *Journal of Cross-Cultural Psychology, 18,* 143–174.

16 See, for example: Erez, M., & Earley, P. C. (1993). *Culture, self-identity, and work.* New York: Oxford University Press, ch. 8; Hofstede, *Cultures and organizations;* Hofstede, *Culture's consequences;* Offermann, L. R., & Hellmann, P. S. (1997). Culture's consequences for leadership behavior: National values in action. *Journal of Cross-Cultural Psychology, 28,* 342–351; Triandis, H. C. (1993). The contingency model in cross-cultural perspective. In M. M. Chemers & R. Ayman (Eds.), *Leadership theory and research: Perspectives and directions* (pp. 167–188). San Diego: Academic Press.

17 Hofstede, *Culture's consequences,* p. 390.

18 House, R. J., Hanges, P. J., Javidan, M., Dorfman, P. W., & Gupta, V. (2004). *Culture, leadership, and organizations: The GLOBE study of 62 societies.* Thousand Oaks, CA: Sage; Chhokar, J. S., Brodbeck, F. C., & House, R. J. (2007). *Culture and leadership across the world: The GLOBE book of in-depth studies of 25 societies.* Mahwah, NJ: Lawrence Erlbaum.

19 House et al.

20 House et al.; Chhokar et al.

21 Adapted from Harris, P. R., & Moran, R. T. (1993). *Managing cultural differences* (4th ed., p. 30). Houston, TX: Gulf Publishing.

22 Adler, N. J. (2002). *From Boston to Beijing: Managing with a world view.* Cincinnati, OH: South-Western. Adler, N. J. (1991). *International dimensions of organizational behavior* (2nd ed.). Belmont, CA: Wadsworth.

23 Singelis, T. M., Triandis, H. C., Bhawuk, D. S., & Gelfand, M. (1995). Horizontal and vertical dimensions of individualism and collectivism: A theoretical and measurement refinement. *Cross-cultural Research, 29,* 240–275.

24 Schermerhorn, R., & Bond, M. H. (1997). Cross-cultural leadership dynamics in collectivism and high power distance settings. *Leadership & Organization Development Journal, 18,* 187–193.

25 Adler, *From Boston to Beijing.*

26 Tromprenaars, F. (1994). *Riding the waves of culture: Understanding diversity in global business.* Burr Ridge, IL: Irwin.

27 Konrad, A. M. (2006). Leveraging workplace diversity in organizations. *Organization Management Journal, 3,* 164–189; Hays-Thomas, R., Kossek, E. E., Lobel, S. A., & Brown, J. (2006). Human resource strategies to manage workplace diversity: Examining "the business case." In *Handbook of workplace diversity* (pp. 53–74); Cox, T. (1991). Managing cultural diversity: Implications for organizational competitiveness. *Academy of Management Executive, 5,* 45–56.

28 For summaries of research on minority influence processes, see: Moscovici, S., Mugny, G., & Van Avermaet, E. (Eds.). (1985). *Perspectives on minority influence.* Cambridge, MA: Cambridge University Press; Maas, A., & Clark, R. D. (1984). Hidden impact of minorities: Fifteen years of minority influence research. *Psychological Bulletin, 95,* 428–450.

29 Eisenberger, R., Fasolo, P., & Davis-LaMastro, V. (1990). Perceived organizational support and employee diligence, commitment, and innovation. *Journal of Applied Psychology, 75,* 57–59.

30 Thomas, D. A., & Ely, R. J. (1996, September–October). Making differences matter: A new paradigm for managing diversity. *Harvard Business Review,* 79–90.

31 Cox, *Cultural diversity,* ch. 13; Brown, R. (1995). *Prejudice: Its social psychology.* Oxford, UK: Blackwell; Fiske S. T. (1998). Stereotyping, prejudice, and discrimination. In D. T. Gilbert, S. T. Fiske, & G. Lindzey (Eds.), *The handbook of social psychology* (Vol. 2, pp. 357–411). Boston: McGraw-Hill.

32 Smith, T. W. (1990). *Ethnic images.* National Opinion Research Center, GSS Topical Report No. 19. Chicago: University of Chicago.

33 Cox, *Cultural diversity,* ch. 13.

34 Adapted from Dickerson-Jones, T. (1993). *50 activities for managing cultural diversity.* Amherst, MA: HRD Press.

35 Langer, E. J. (1989). *Mindfulness.* Reading, MA: Addison-Wesley.

36 Gudykunst, W. B., & Kim, Y. Y. (2003). *Communicating with strangers: An approach to intercultural communication* (4th ed.). New York: McGraw-Hill. See also: Opotow, S. (1990). Moral exclusion and injustice: An introduction. *Journal of Social Issues, 46,* 1–20.

37 Material on organizational strategies for promoting diversity taken from: Cox, *Creating the multicultural organization;* Morrison, A. M. (1996). *The new leaders: Guidelines on leadership diversity in America.* San Francisco: Jossey-Bass; Konrad, Leveraging workplace diversity.

[38] Mor Barak, *Managing diversity,* pp. 296–297. Reproduced with permission of Sage Publications, Inc.

[39] Thomas, D. A., & Gabarro, J. J. (1999). *Breaking through: The making of minority executives in corporate America.* Boston: Harvard Business School Press.

[40] Thomas, D. A. (2001, April–May). Race matters: The truth about mentoring minorities. *Harvard Business Review,* 99–107.

[41] Statistics taken from: Eagly, A. H., & Carli, L. L. (2007). *Through the labyrinth: The truth about how women become leaders.* Boston: Harvard Business School Press; More women serving on boards. (2001, December 5). *Los Angeles Times,* p. C3; Catalyst. (2002, March 2). And reach for more of the pie. Retrieved from http://www.fortune.com; Sherman, E. (2001, Fall). Women in political leadership: Reflections on larger social issues. *Leadership,* 4–5; Powell, G. (1993). *Women and men in management* (2nd ed.). Newbury Park, CA: Sage.

[42] The term *glass ceiling* was first used in a special issue of the *Wall Street Journal* in 1986. The corporate woman: A special report. (1986, March 24). *Wall Street Journal,* 32-page supplement.

[43] Eagly & Carli, p. 6.

[44] Rosener, J. B. (1990, November–December). Ways women lead. *Harvard Business Review,* 119–125.

[45] Gaines, J. (1993). "You don't necessarily have to be charismatic . . .": An interview with Anita Roddick and reflections on charismatic processes in the Body Shop International. *Leadership Quarterly, 4,* 347–359; Miller, A. (1991, October 14). Reach out and prod someone. *Newsweek,* 50; Peters, T. (1992). *Liberation management.* New York: Ballantine Books; Roddick, A. (1991). *Body and soul.* New York: Crown; Wallace, C. (1990, October). Lessons in marketing—From a maverick. *Working Woman,* 81–84.

[46] Roddick, p. 15.

[47] Birchfield, D. (2002, May). Anita Roddick: In full flight. *New Zealand Management,* 41–43.

[48] Roddick, p. 25.

[49] Roddick, p. 217.

[50] Karsten, M. F. (1994). *Management and gender.* Westport, CT: Praeger.

[51] Adams, J., Rice, R., & Instone, D. (1984). Follower attitudes toward women and judgments concerning performance by female and male leaders. *Academy of Management Journal, 27,* 636–643.

[52] Shellenbarger, S. (1995, September 3). Work-force study finds loyalty is weak, divisions of race and gender are deep. *Wall Street Journal,* pp. B1, B8.

[53] See: Eagly, A. H., & Johnson, B. T. (1990). Gender and leadership style: A meta- analysis. *Psychological Bulletin, 108,* 233–256; Eagly, A. H., & Karau, S. J. (1991). Gender and the emergence of leaders: A meta-analysis. *Journal of Personality and Social Psychology, 60,* 685–710; Eagly, A. H. (1987). *Sex differences in social behavior.* Hillsdale, NJ: Lawrence Erlbaum.

[54] Morrison, A. M., White, R. P., & Van Velsor, E. (1987, August). Executive women: Substance plus style. *Psychology Today,* 18–26.

[55] Wood, J. T. (1999). *Gendered lives: Communication, gender and culture* (3rd ed., p. 22). Belmont, CA: Wadsworth.

[56] Broverman, I., Broverman, D. M., Clarkson, F. E., Rosenkranz, P. S., & Vogel, S. R. (1970). Sex-role stereotypes and clinical judgments in mental health. *Journal of Consulting and Clinical Psychology, 34,* 1–7.

[57] See: Andrews, P. (1984). Performance, self-esteem and perceptions of leadership emergence: A comparative study of men and women. *Western Journal of Speech Communication, 48,* 1–13; Instone, D., Major, B., & Bunker, B. B. (1983). Gender, self-confidence, and social influence strategies: An organizational simulation. *Journal of Personality and Social Psychology, 44,* 322–333.

[58] Epstein, C. F. (1988). *Deceptive distinctions: Sex, gender, and the social order.* New Haven: Yale University Press.

[59] Kanter, R. M. (1977). Some effects of proportions on group life: Skewed sex ratios and responses to token women. *American Journal of Sociology, 82,* 969–990.

[60] Morrison et al.

[61] Jamieson, K. H. (1995). *Beyond the double bind: Women and leadership* (pp. 13–14). New York: Oxford University Press.

[62] Jamieson, p. 20.

[63] Eagly & Carli.

[64] Tannen, D. (1990). *You just don't understand: Women and men in conversation.* New York: Ballantine.

[65] Tannen, D. (1994). *Talking from 9 to 5.* New York: William Morrow and Company.

[66] Reardon, K. K. (1995). *They just don't get it, do they?* New York: Little Brown.

[67] See, for example: Carter, K., & Spitzack, C. (1990). Transformation and empowerment in gender and communication courses. *Women's Studies in Communication, 13,* 92–110; Spitzack, C., & Carter, K. (1987). Women in communication studies: A typology for revision. *Quarterly Journal of Speech, 73,* 401–423; Aries, E. (1998). Gender differences in interaction: A reexamination. In D. J. Canary & K. Dindia (Eds.), *Sex differences and similarities in communication* (pp. 65–81). Mahwah, NJ: Lawrence Erlbaum; Weatherall, A. (1998). Re-visioning gender and language research. *Women and language, 21,* 1–9.

[68] Anderson, P. A. (1998). Researching sex differences within sex similarities: The evolutionary consequences of reproductive behavior. In *Sex differences and similarities in communication* (pp. 83–100).

[69] Adapted from: Hopkins, S. A. (1997). Case #1: Downsizing at Simtek. In W. E. Hopkins (Ed.), *Ethical dimensions of diversity* (pp. 119–121). Thousand Oaks, CA: Sage. Reproduced with permission of Sage Publications, Inc.

[70] Spitzack & Carter, p. 418.

[71] Hackman, M. Z., Furniss, A. H., Hills, M. J., & Paterson, T. J. (1992). Perceptions of gender-role characteristics and transformational leadership behaviours. *Perceptual and Motor Skills, 75,* 311–319.

[72] Jones, D. (2007, May 30). Do foreign executives balk at sports jargon? *USA Today,* pp. B1, B2.

[73] Fallows, D. (2005, December 28). *How women and men use the Internet.* Pew Internet & American Life Project. Washington, DC: Pew Foundation.

Chapter 11

[1] Miller, G. R. (1969). Contributions of communication research to the study of speech. In A. H. Monroe & D. Ehninger (Eds.), *Principles and types of speech communication* (6th brief ed., pp. 334–357). Glenview, IL: Scott Foresman, p. 355.

[2] Johannesen, R. L., Valde, K. S., & Whedbee, K. E. (2008). *Ethics in human communication* (6th ed.). Long Grove, IL: Waveland Press.

[3] Palmer, P. (1996). Leading from within. In L. C. Spears (Ed.), *Insights on leadership: Service, stewardship, spirit, and servant-leadership* (pp. 197–208). New York: John Wiley, p. 200.

[4] Material from this section is adapted from: Johnson, C. E. (2009). *Meeting the ethical challenges of leadership: Casting light or shadow* (3rd ed.). Thousand Oaks, CA: Sage.

[5] Bok, S. (1979). *Lying: Moral choice in public and private life.* New York: Vintage Books.

[6] Grover, S. L. (1997). Lying in organizations: Theory, research, and future directions. In R. A. Giacalone & J. Greenberg (Eds.), *Antisocial behavior in organizations* (pp. 68–84). Thousand Oaks, CA: Sage; Cialdini, R. B., Petrova, P. K., & Goldstein, N. J. (2004, Spring). The hidden costs of organizational dishonesty. *MIT Sloan Management Review,* pp. 67–73.

[7] Weaver, G. R., Trevino, L. K., & Cochran, P. L. (1999). Integrated and decoupled corporate social performance: Management commitments, external pressures, and corporate ethics practices. *Academy of Management Journal, 42,* 539–552; Weaver, G. R., Trevino, L. K., & Cochran, P. L. (1999). Corporate ethics practices in the mid-1990s: An empirical study of the Fortune 1000. *Journal of Business Ethics, 18,* 283–294.

[8] Keltner, D., Langner, C. A., & Allison, M. L. (2006). Power and moral leadership. In D. L. Rhode (Ed.), *Moral leadership: The theory and practice of power, judgment and policy* (pp. 177–194). San Francisco: Jossey-Bass.

[9] Fiske, S. T. (1993). Controlling other people: The impact of power on stereotyping. *American Psychologist, 48,* 621–628; Goodwin, S. A. (2003). Power and prejudice: A social-cognitive perspective on power and leadership. In D. van Knippenberg & M. A. Hogg (Eds.), *Leadership and power: Identity processes in groups and organizations* (pp. 138–152). London: Sage.

[10] Jennings, M. M. (2006). *The seven signs of ethical collapse: How to spot moral meltdowns in companies . . . before it's too late.* New York: St. Martin's Press, ch. 3.

[11] Fall in Kenyan corruption. (2004, October 20). Retrieved March 28, 2007, from http://newsbbs.co.uk; Corruption perceptions index. (2006). Retrieved March 28, 2007, from http://transparency.org.

[12] Lublin, J. S. (2006, October 12). Executive pay soars despite attempted restraints. Associated Press Financial Wire. Retrieved January 22, 2007, from LexisNexis Academic.

[13] CEO compensation not well related to companies' stock returns: Study. Canadian Press Newswire. Retrieved January 22, 2007, from LexisNexis Academic.

[14] Lublin; Grow, B., Foust, D., Thornton, E., Farzad, R., McGregor, J., Zegle, S., & Javers, E. (2007, January 15). Out at Home Depot. *Business Week*, 56–62. Retrieved January 22, 2007, from EbscoHost.

[15] Jennings, *Seven signs of ethical collapse*.

[16] Editorial board. (2006, December 26). Not only did Oreck jilt taxpayers and employees, its departure was tactless as well as heartless. *Sun Herald* (Biloxi, Mississippi). Retrieved January 22, 2007, from LexisNexis Academic; Miehl, R. (2006, December 18). Oreck closing Miss. site in wake of Katrina. *Plastic News*, pp. 1, 18. Retrieved January 22, 2007, from LexisNexis Academic; Lott, T. (2007, January 19). The Oreck challenge. *US Fed News*. Retrieved January 22, 2007, from LexisNexis Academic.

[17] Eaton, L. (2007, January 15). Vacuum maker hailed as savior quits Gulf town. *New York Times*, pp. A1, A13.

[18] Bradsher, K. (2001, June 24). Firestone tire flaw unreported for 4 years. *The Oregonian*, p. A4.

[19] Ramperstad, A. (1997). *Jackie Robinson*. New York: Knopf.

[20] Bartlett, D. L., & Steele, J. B. (2000, February 7). How the little guy gets crunched. *Time*, 38–41; Palast, G. (2003). *The best democracy money can buy* (rev. Am ed.). New York: Plume.

[21] Rest, J. R. (1986). *Moral development: Advances in research and theory*. New York: Praeger; Rest, J. R. (1994). Background: Theory and research. In J. R. Rest & D. Narvaez (Eds.), *Moral development in the professions: Psychology and applied ethics* (pp. 1–25). Hillsdale, NJ: Lawrence Erlbaum.

[22] Bird, F. B. (1996). *The muted conscience: Moral silence and the practice of ethics in business*. Westport, CT: Quorum Books.

[23] Rest, *Moral development*.

[24] Gioia, D. A. (1992). Pinto fires and personal ethics: A script analysis of missed opportunities. *Journal of Business Ethics, 11,* 379–389; Birsch, D., & Fielder, J. H. (Eds.). (1994). *The Ford Pinto case: A study in applied ethics, business, and technology*. Albany: State University of New York Press.

[25] Gioia, p. 388.

[26] Rest, J. R. (1993). Research on moral judgment in college students. In A. Garrod (Ed.), *Approaches to moral development* (pp. 201–211). New York: Teachers College Press.

[27] Eisenberg, N. (2000). Emotion, regulation, and moral development. *Annual Review of Psychology, 51,* 665–697; Guadine, A., & Thorne, L. (2001). Emotion and ethical decision-making in organizations. *Journal of Business Ethics, 31,* 175–187; Giacalone, R. A., & Greenbergh, J. (Eds.). (1997). *Antisocial behavior in organizations*. Thousand Oaks, CA: Sage.

[28] Johnson, C. E. (2007). *Ethics in the workplace: Tools and tactics for organizational transformation*. Thousand Oaks, CA: Sage.

[29] Trevino, L. K., & Weaver, G. R. (2003). *Managing ethics in business organizations: Social scientific perspectives*. Palo Alto, CA: Stanford University Press, ch. 7.

[30] Kant, I. (1964). *Ground work for the metaphysics of morals* (Trans. H. J. Ryan). New York: Harper & Row.

[31] Graham, G. (2004). *Eight theories of ethics*. London: Routledge, ch. 6.

[32] See, for example: Bentham, J. (1948). *An introduction to the principles of morals and legislation*. New York: Hafner Publishing; Gorovitz, S. (Ed.). (1971). *Utilitarianism: Text and critical essays*. Indianapolis, IN: Bobbs-Merrill.

[33] Meilander, G. (1986). Virtue in contemporary religious thought. In R. J. Nehaus (Ed.), *Virtue: Public and private* (pp. 7–30). Grand Rapids, MI: Eerdmans; Alderman, H. (1997). By virtue of a virtue. In D. Statman (Ed.), *Virtue ethics* (pp. 145–164). Washington, DC: Georgetown University Press.

[34] Johannesen et al., pp. 10–11.

[35] Solomon, R. (1988). Internal objections to virtue ethics. *Midwest Studies in Philosophy, 8,* 428–441.

[36] Johannesen, R. L. (1991). Virtue ethics, character, and political communication. In R. E. Denton (Ed.), *Ethical dimensions of political communication* (pp. 69–90). New York: Praeger.

[37] Johannesen et al., p. 10.

[38] Luke, J. S. (1994). Character and conduct in the public service. In T. C. Cooper (Ed.), *The handbook of administrative ethics* (pp. 391–412). New York: Marcel Dakker; Hart, D. K. (1994). Administration and the ethics of virtue. In *The handbook of administrative ethics* (pp. 107–123).

[39] Bartholomew, C. S., & Gustafson, S. B. (1998). Perceived Leader Integrity Scale: An instrument for assessing employee perceptions of leader integrity. *Leadership Quarterly, 9,* 127–145. Reproduced with permission of Elsevier Limited.

[40] MacIntyre, A. (1984). *After virtue: A study in moral theory* (2nd ed.). Notre Dame, IN: University of Notre Dame Press; Hauerwas, S. (1981). *A community of character*. Notre Dame, IN: University of Notre Dame Press.

[41] See, for example: Luthans, F., & Avolio, B. J. (2003). Authentic development: A positive developmental approach. In K. S. Cameron, J. E. Dutton, & R. E. Quinn (Eds.), *Positive organizational scholarship* (pp. 241–261). San Francisco: Barrett-Koehler; Terry, R. W. (1993). *Authentic leadership: Courage in action.* San Francisco: Jossey-Bass; George, B. (2003). *Authentic leadership: Rediscovering the secrets to creating lasting value.* San Francisco: Jossey-Bass.

[42] Avolio, B. J., & Gardner, W. L. (2005). Authentic leadership development: Getting to the root of positive forms of leadership. *Leadership Quarterly, 16,* 315–338; Gardner, W. L., Avolio, B. J., Luthans, F., May, D. R., & Walumbwa, F. (2005). "Can you see the real me?" A self-based model of authentic leader and follower development. *Leadership Quarterly, 16,* 343–372; Ilies, R., Morgeson, F. P., & Nahrgang, J. (2005). Authentic leadership and eudaemonic well-being: Understanding leader-follower outcomes. *Leadership Quarterly, 16,* 373–394.

[43] Blum, L. A. (1988). Moral exemplars: Reflections on Schindler, the Trocmes, and others. *Midwest Studies in Philosophy, 13,* 196–221; Keneally, T. (1982). *Schindler's list.* New York: Simon and Schuster/Touchstone.

[44] Hallie, P. (1979). *Lest innocent blood be shed: The story of the village of LeChambon and how goodness happened there.* New York: Harper & Row.

[45] Shamir, B., & Eilam, G. (2005). "What's your story?" A life-stories approach to authentic leadership development. *Leadership Quarterly, 16,* 395–417.

[46] Post, S. G. (2002). The tradition of agape. In S. G. Post, L. G. Underwood, J. P. Schloss, & W. B. Hurlbut (Eds.), *Altruism & altruistic love: Science, philosophy, & religion in dialogue* (pp. 51–64). Oxford: Oxford University Press.

[47] Piliavin, J. A., & Charng, H-W. (1990). Altruism: A review of recent theory and research. *Annual Review of Sociology, 16,* 27–65; Batson, C. D., Van Lange, P. A. M., Ahmad, N., & Lishner, D. A. (2003). Altruism and helping behavior. In M. A. Hogg & J. Cooper (Eds.), *The Sage handbook of social psychology* (pp. 279–295). London: Sage.

[48] Kanungo, R. N., & Mendonca, M. (1996). *Ethical dimensions of leadership.* Thousand Oaks, CA: Sage, p. 35.

[49] Kanungo, R. N., & Conger, J. A. (1990). The quest for altruism in organizations. In S. Srivastva & D. L. Cooperrider, and Associates (Eds.), *Appreciative management and leadership: The power of positive thought and action in organizations* (pp. 248–249). San Francisco: Jossey-Bass. Used by permission.

[50] Spears, L. (1998). Tracing the growing impact of servant-leadership. In L. Spears (Ed.), *Insights on leadership: Service, stewardship, spirit, and servant leadership* (pp. 1–15). New York: John Wiley & Sons; Ruschman, N. L. (2002). Servant-leadership and the best companies to work for in America. In L. C. Spears & M. Lawrence (Eds.), *Focus on leadership: Servant-leadership for the twenty-first century.* New York: John Wiley & Sons.

[51] Greenleaf, R. (1977). *Servant leadership.* New York: Paulist Press, pp. 13–14.

[52] Block, P. (1993). *Stewardship: Choosing service over self-interest.* San Francisco: Berrett-Koehler.

[53] Harris, C. (2007, December 9). Costco sticks to concept. *The Gazette,* p. B4.

[54] DePree, M. (1989). *Leadership is an art.* New York: Doubleday, p. 92.

[55] DePree, M. (1992). *Leadership jazz.* New York: Currency Doubleday.

[56] Fraker, A. (1996). Robert K. Greenleaf and business ethics: There is no code. In L. C. Spears (Ed.), *Reflections on leadership* (pp. 37–48). New York: John Wiley.

[57] McGee-Cooper, A., & Trammell, D. (2002). From hero-as-leader to servant-as-leader. In *Focus on leadership* (pp. 145–146).

[58] Johnson, *Ethics in the workplace.*

[59] Chaleff, I. (1995). *The courageous follower.* San Francisco: Berett-Koehler, p. 162.

[60] Roloff, M. E., & Paulson, G. D. (2001). Confronting organizational transgressions. In J. M. Darley, D. M. Messick, & T. R. Tyler (Eds.), *Social influences on ethical behavior in organizations* (pp. 53–68). Mahwah, NJ: Lawrence Erlbaum.

[61] Kelley, R. E. (1998). Followership in a leadership world. In *Insights on leadership* (pp. 170–184).

[62] DePree, *Leadership is an art.*

[63] Chaleff.

[64] Useem, M. (2001). *Leading up: How to lead your boss so you both win.* New York: Crown Business.

[65] Useem, p. 1.

[66] Kidder, R. M. (1994). *Shared values for a troubled world: Conversations with men and women of conscience.* San Francisco: Jossey-Bass; Kidder, R. M. (1994, July–August). Universal human values: Finding an ethical common ground. *The Futurist,* 8–13.

67 Kidder, *Shared values for a troubled world*, p. 312.

68 Martinson, J. (2007, January 27). China censorship damaged us, Google founders admit. *Guardian online.*

Chapter 12

1 Horn, L., Peter, K., & Rooney, K. (2002). Profile of undergraduates in U.S. postsecondary education institutions: 1999–2000. National Center for Educational Statistics. Retrieved February 8, 2008, from http://nces.ed.gov/das/epubs/2002168/profile2.asp.

2 Van Velsor, E., & McCauley, C. D. (2004). Introduction: Our view of leadership development. In C. D. McCauley & E. Van Velsor (Eds.), *The Center for Creative Leadership handbook of leadership development* (2nd ed., pp. 1–22). San Francisco: Jossey-Bass, p. 2.

3 A number of experts make a similar distinction between leader and leadership development. See, for example: Day, D. V., & Halpin, S. M. (2004). Growing leaders for tomorrow: An introduction. In D. Day, S. J. Zaccaro, & S. M. Halpin (Eds.), *Leader development for transforming organizations* (pp. 3–22). Mahwah, NJ: Lawrence Erlbaum; Day, D. V., & O'Connor, P. M. (2003). Leadership development: Understanding the process. In S. E. Murphy & R. E. Riggio (Eds.), *The future of leadership development* (pp. 11–27). Mahwah, NJ: Lawrence Erlbaum.

4 Ayman, R., Adams, S., Fisher, B., & Hartman, E. (2003). Leadership development in higher education institutions: A present and future perspective. In *The future of leadership development*, pp. 201–222; Riggio, R. E., Ciulla, J. B., & Sorenson, G. J. (2003). Leadership education at the undergraduate level: A liberal arts approach to leadership development. In *The future of leadership development*, pp. 223–236.

5 Johnson, C., & Hackman, M. (1993). The status of leadership coursework in communication. *The Michigan Association of Speech Communication Journal, 28*, 1–13. Leadership material is most often included in small group, organizational, and political communication courses.

6 Brown, P. T. (1999–2000, Winter). New directions in leadership development: A review of tends and best practices. *The Public Manager*, 37–41.

7 Conger, J. A., & Benjamin, B. (1999). *Building leaders: How successful companies develop the next generation.* San Francisco: Jossey-Bass.

8 Conger, J. A., & Toegel, G. (2003). Action learning and multirater feedback: Pathways to leadership development? In *The future of leadership development*, pp. 107–125.

9 Brown.

10 Conger & Toegel.

11 Kram, K. E., & Isabella, L. A. (1985). Mentoring alternatives: The role of peer relationships in career development. *Academy of Management Review, 28*, 110–132.

12 Crosby, F. J. (1999). The developing literature on developmental relationships. In A. J. Murrell, F. J. Crosby, & R. J. Ely (Eds.), *Mentoring dilemmas: Developmental relationships within multicultural organizations* (pp. 3–20). Mahwah, NJ: Lawrence Erlbaum. See also: Zachary, L. J. (2000). *The mentor's guide.* San Francisco: Jossey-Bass.

13 Kram, K. E. (1985). *Mentoring at work: Developmental relationships in organizational life.* Glenview, IL: Scott, Foresman and Company. See also: Hunt, D. M., & Michael, C. (1983). Mentorship: A career training and development tool. *Academy of Management Review, 8*, 475–485; Woodlands Group. (1980, November). Management development roles: Coach, sponsor, and mentor. *Personnel Journal, 9*, 18–21.

14 Crosby; Mullen, E. J. (1998). Vocational and psychosocial mentoring functions: Identifying mentors who serve both. *Human Resource Development Quarterly, 9*, 319–331.

15 Otto, M. L. (1994). Mentoring: An adult developmental perspective. In M. A. Wunsch (Ed.), *Mentoring revisited: Making an impact on individuals and institutions* (pp. 15–22). San Francisco: Jossey-Bass.

16 See, for example: Mullen; Dreyer, G. F., & Ash, R. A. (1990). A comparative study of mentoring among men and women in managerial, professional, and technological positions. *Journal of Applied Psychology, 75*, 539–546; Fagenson, E. A. (1989). The mentor advantage: Perceived career/job experiences of protégés versus non-protégés. *Journal of Organizational Behavior, 10*, 309–320.

17 Kogler Hill, S. E., Bahniuk, M. H., & Dobbs, J. (1989). The impact of mentoring and collegial support on faculty success: An analysis of support behavior information adequacy, and communication apprehension. *Communication Education, 38*, 15–33; Schrodt, P., Cawyer, C. S., & Sanders, R.

(2003). An examination of academic mentoring behaviors and new faculty members' satisfaction with socialization and tenure and promotion processes. *Communication Education, 52*, 17–29.

[18] Jacobi, M. (1991). Mentoring and undergraduate academic success: A literature review. *Review of Educational Research, 61*(4), 505–532.

[19] Phillips-Jones, L. (1983). *Mentors and protégés*. New York: Arbor House, ch. 8. See also: Kram; Myers, D. W., & Humphreys, N. J. (1985, July–August). The caveats in mentorship. *Business Horizons*, 9–14.

[20] Murray, M. (1991). *Beyond the myths and magic of mentoring*. San Francisco: Jossey-Bass; Kram, K. E., & Bragar, M. C. (1992). Development through mentoring: A strategic approach. In D. H. Montross & C. J. Shinkman (Eds.), *Career development: Theory and practice* (pp. 221–254). Springfield, IL: Charles C. Thomas.

[21] Chao, G. T., Walz, P. M., & Gardner, P. D. (1992). Formal and informal mentorships: A comparison on mentoring functions and contrast with nonmentored counterparts. *Personnel Psychology, 45*, 619–636.

[22] Phillips-Jones.

[23] Ting, S., & Hart, E. W. (2004). Formal coaching. In *The Center for Creative Leadership handbook*, pp. 116–150; Freas, A. M. (2000). Coaching executives for business results. In M. Goldsmith, L. Lyons, & A. Freas (Eds.), *Coaching for leadership: How the world's greatest coaches help leaders learn* (pp. 27–42). San Francisco: Jossey-Bass/Pfeiffer; Ting, S., & Scisco, P. (2006). *The CCL handbook of coaching: A guide for the leader coach*. San Francisco: Jossey-Bass.

[24] Ohlott, P. J. (2004). Job assignments. In *The Center for Creative Leadership handbook*, pp. 151–182. See also: McCauley, C. D. (2001). Leader training and development. In S. J. Zaccaro & R. J. Klimoski (Eds.), *The nature of organizational leadership: Understanding the performance imperatives confronting today's leaders* (pp. 347–383). San Francisco: Jossey-Bass.

[25] Maxwell, J. (2000). *Failing forward: Turning mistakes into stepping-stones for success*. Nashville: Thomas Nelson Publishers.

[26] Maxwell, p. 117.

[27] Ohlott, p. 157.

[28] Moxley, R. S., & Pulley, M. L. (2004). Hardships. In *The Center for Creative Leadership handbook*, pp. 183–203.

[29] Guinness, O. (Ed.). (1999). *Character counts: Leadership qualities in Washington, Wilberforce, Lincoln, and Solzhenitsyn*. Grand Rapids, MI: Baker Books; Goodwin, D. K. (2005). *Team of rivals: The political genius of Abraham Lincoln*. New York: Simon & Schuster.

[30] Avolio, B. J. (2005). *Leadership development in balance: Made/born*. Mahwah, NJ: Lawrence Erlbaum, p. 15

[31] Bennis, W. G., & Thomas, R. J. (2004). Crucibles of leadership. In *Harvard Business Review on developing leaders* (pp. 151–170). Boston: Harvard Business School Publishing; Bennis, W. G., & Thomas, R. J. (2002). *Geeks and geezers: How era, values and defining moments shape leaders*. Boston: Harvard Business School Press.

[32] Bennis & Thomas, p. 167

[33] Covey, S. R. (1989). *The 7 habits of highly effective people*. New York: Simon and Schuster.

[34] Cashman, K. (1998). *Leadership from the inside out*. Provo, UT: Executive Excellence Publishing.

[35] Cashman, p. 20.

[36] Cashman, p. 29. Used by permission.

[37] Cashman, p. 107.

[38] Cashman, p. 153.

[39] Cashman, p. 184.

[40] Giacalone, R. A., & Jurkiewicz, C. L. (2003). Toward a science of workplace spirituality. In R. A. Giacalone & C. L. Jurkiewicz (Eds.), *Handbook of workplace spirituality and organizational performance* (pp. 3–28). Armonk, NY: M. E. Sharpe; Duchon, D., & Plowman, D. A. (2005). Nurturing the spirit at work: Impact on work unit performance. *Leadership Quarterly, 16*, 807–833; Craigie, F. C. (1999). The spirit and work: Observations about spirituality and organizational life. *Journal of Psychology and Christianity, 18*, 45–53; Fairholm, G. W. (1996). Spiritual leadership: Fulfilling whole-self needs at work. *Leadership & Organization Development Journal, 17*, 11–17.

[41] Giacalone & Jurkiewicz, p. 13.

[42] Mitroff, I., & Denton, E. A. (1999, Summer). A study of spirituality in the workplace. *Sloan Management Review, 40*, 83–92. See also: Mitroff, I., & Denton, E. A. (1999). *A spiritual audit of corporate America: A hard look at spirituality, religion, and values in the workplace*. San Francisco: Jossey-Bass.

[43] Reave, L. (2005). Spiritual values and practices related to leadership effectiveness. *Leadership Quarterly, 16*, 655–687.

[44] For more information on self-reflective practices, see: Foster, R. J. (1998). *Celebration of discipline: The path to spiritual growth* (20th anniversary edition). San Francisco: Harper.

[45] Gozdz, K., & Frager, R. (2003). Using everyday challenges of business to transform individuals and organizations. In *Handbook of workplace spirituality and organizational performance* (pp. 475–492).

[46] Gozdz & Frager, p. 486.

[47] Gale, S. F. (2001, June). Bringing good leaders to light. *Training*, 38–42; Caudron, S. (1999, September). The looming leadership crisis. *Workforce*, 72–76; Rothwell, W. J. (2001). *Effective succession planning* (2nd ed.). New York: AMACOM.

[48] Gabarro, J. J. (1988). Executive leadership and succession: The process of taking charge. In D. C. Hambrick (Ed.), *The executive effect: Concepts and methods for studying top managers* (p. 258). Greenwich, CT: JAI Press.

[49] Gabarro, J. J. (1985, May–June). When a manager takes charge. *Harvard Business Review*, 110–123.

[50] Gabarro, Executive leadership and succession, p. 258. Used by permission.

[51] For further discussion of important variables in the succession process, see: Gordon, G. E., & Rosen, N. (1981). Critical factors in leadership succession. *Organizational Behavior and Human Performance, 27*, 227–254; House, R. J., & Singh, J. V. (1987). Organizational behavior: Some new directions for I/O psychology. In M. R. Rosenzweig & L. Porter (Eds.), *Annual Review of Psychology* (Vol. 38, pp. 669–717). Palo Alto, CA: Annual Reviews; Lord, R., & Maher, K. (1991). *Leadership and information processing*. Boston: Unwin Hyman, ch. 10; Giambatista, R. C., Rowe, W. G., & Riaz, S. (2005). Nothing succeeds like succession: A critical review of leader succession literature since 1994. *Leadership Quarterly, 16*, 963–991.

[52] Gabarro, J. J. (1987). *The dynamics of taking charge*. Boston: Harvard Business School Press, p. 131.

[53] Rothwell; Gale; Caudron.

[54] Rothwell, p. 98. Reproduced by permission of the American Management Association.

[55] Charan, R., Drotter, S., & Noel, J. (2001). *The leadership pipeline: How to build the leadership-powered company*. San Francisco: Jossey-Bass.

[56] Hoppe, M. H. (2004). Cross-cultural issues in the development of leaders. In *The Center for Creative Leadership handbook*, pp. 331–360.

[57] Avolio, ch. 8.

Chapter 13

[1] Mitroff, I. I., & Anagnos, G. (2001). *Managing crises before they happen: What every executive and manager needs to know about crisis management*. New York: American Management Association; Schoenberg, A. (2005, Spring). Do crisis plans matter? A new perspective on leading during a crisis. *Public Relations Quarterly, 50*, 2–6; Perrow, C. (1999). *Normal accidents: Living with high-risk technologies*. Princeton, NJ: Princeton University Press.

[2] Fearn-Banks, K. (2002). *Crisis communications: A casebook approach* (2nd ed.). Mahwah, NJ: Lawrence Erlbaum.

[3] Harris, S., Smallen, J., Mitchell, C. (2006, February 18). Katrina report spreads blame. *National Journal*, p. 38. Retrieved April 22, 2006, from EBSCOhost; Marek, A. C. (2006, February 27). A post-Katrina public flaying. *U.S. News & World Report*, pp. 62–64. Retrieved April 22, 2006, from EBSCOhost.

[4] Fearn-Banks.

[5] Pauchant, T. C., & Mitroff, I. I. (1992). *Transforming the crisis-prone organization: Preventing individual, organization, and environmental tragedies*. San Francisco: Jossey-Bass.

[6] Coombs, W. T. (1999). *Ongoing crisis communication: Planning, managing, and responding*. Thousand Oaks, CA: Sage; Seeger, M. W., Sellnow, T. L., & Ulmer, R. R. (2003). *Communication and organizational crisis*. Westport, CT: Praeger.

[7] Mishra, R. (2003, August 27). Probe hits NASA in crash of shuttle. *The Boston Globe*, p. A1.

[8] Fink, S. (2000). *Crisis management: Planning for the inevitable*. New York: AMACOM.

[9] Bazerman, M. H., & Watkins, M. D. (2004). *Predictable surprises: The disasters you should have seen coming, and how to prevent them*. Boston: Harvard Business School Press.

[10] Bazerman & Watkins.

[11] Pauchant & Mitroff; Mitroff, I. I., & Pearson, C. M. (1993). *Crisis management: A diagnostic guide for improving your organization's crisis-preparedness*. San Francisco: Jossey-Bass.

[12] Coombs.

[13] Seeger et al.

[14] Mitroff, I. I., Pearson, C. M., & Harrington, L. K. (1996). *The essential guide to managing corporate crises: A step-by-step handbook for surviving major catastrophes.* New York: Oxford University Press, pp. 22–23. Copyright © 1996. By permission of Oxford University Press, Inc.

[15] Mitroff, I. I., & Alpsaian, M. C. (2003, April). Preparing for evil. *Harvard Business Review*, 109–115. See also: Mitroff, I. I. (2005). *Why some companies emerge stronger and better from a crisis.* New York: AMACOM.

[16] Coombs. See also: Fearn-Banks.

[17] Barton, L. (2001). *Crisis in organizations II.* Cincinnati: South-Western.

[18] Ray, S. J. (1999). *Strategic communication in crisis management: Lessons from the airline industry.* Westport, CT: Quorum Books.

[19] Coombs.

[20] Sturges, D. L. (1994). Communicating through crisis: A strategy for organizational survival. *Management Communication Quarterly, 7*, 297–316.

[21] Goldfarb, A. A. (2006, July 18). To agency insiders, cyber thefts and slow response are no surprise. *The Washington Post*, p. A17. Retrieved November 24, 2007, from LexisNexis Academic. Lee, C. (2006, May 24). Veterans angered by file scandal. *The Washington Post*, p. A21. Retrieved November 24, 2007, from LexisNexis Academic. Lee, C. (2006, May 27). VA knew early about data theft. *The Washington Post*, p. A04. Retrieved November 24, 2007, from LexisNexis Academic. Lee, C. (2006, July 12). Top VA officials criticized in data theft. *The Washington Post*, p. A13. Retrieved November 24, 2007, from LexisNexis Academic. Lee, C., & Brulliard, K. (2006, August 6). 2 Md. men arrested in theft of VA laptop. *The Washington Post*, p. C01. Retrieved November 24, 2007, from LexisNexis Academic. Neuman, J. (2006, July 12). Report faults VA on stolen laptop. *Los Angeles Times*, p. A20. Retrieved November 24, 2007, from LexisNexis Academic.

[22] Lee, VA knew early about data theft.

[23] Seeger, M. W., Sellnow, T. L., & Ulmer, R. R. (1998). Communication, organization, and crisis. In M. E. Roloff (Ed.), *Communication yearbook 21* (pp. 231–275). Thousand Oaks, CA: Sage.

[24] Gonzales, L. (2005). *Deep survival: Who lives, who dies and why.* New York: Norton.

[25] Simpson tells his story in the book *Touching the void* (Harper Perennial, 1998) and in the film of the same name.

[26] Olaniran, B. A., & Williams, D. D. (2001). Anticipatory model of crisis management: A vigilant response to technological crises. In R. L. Heath & G. Vazquez (Eds.), *Handbook of public relations* (pp. 487–500). Thousand Oaks, CA: Sage.

[27] Ray.

[28] Benoit, W. L. (1995). *Accounts, excuses and apologies.* Albany: State University of New York Press; Benoit, W. L. (2004). Image restoration discourse and crisis communication. In D. P. Millar & R. L. Heath (Eds.), *Responding to crisis: A rhetorical approach to crisis communication* (pp. 263–280). Mahwah, NJ: Lawrence Erlbaum. For an alternative list of image restoration strategies, see: Hearit, K. M. (2001). Corporate apologia: When an organization speaks in defense of itself. In R. L. Heath & G. Vazquez (Eds.), *Handbook of public relations* (pp. 487–500). Thousand Oaks, CA: Sage.

[29] Eisenberg, D., Szczesny, J. R., Forster, P., Larimer, T., Eskenazi, M., & Greenwald, J. (2000, September 18). Firestone's rough road. *Time*, pp. 38–40.

[30] Seeger et al., *Communication and organizational crisis.*

[31] Benoit, W. L., & Brinson, S. L. (1994). AT&T: Apologies are not enough. *Communication Quarterly, 42*, 75–88.

[32] Weick, K. E., & Sutcliffe, K. M. (2001). *Managing the unexpected: Assuring high performance in an age of complexity.* San Francisco: Jossey-Bass.

[33] Weick & Sutcliffe.

[34] Argenti, P. (2002, December). Crisis communication: Lessons from 9/11. *Harvard Business Review*, 103–109.

[35] Witt, J. L., & Morgan, J. (2002). *Stronger in the broken places: Nine lessons for turning crisis into triumph.* New York: Times Books/Henry Holt, p. 222.

[36] Mitroff & Anagnos; Pope, H. (1998, December 1). Angry Turks cast off Italian ties, whether they're genuine or not. *Wall Street Journal*, p. B1.

[37] Siemens Insight Consulting. (2006, September 22). *Communicating in a crisis: Which technologies can be relied on?* United Kingdom: Author.

Bibliography

Abrahams, J. (1995). *The mission statement book*. Berkeley, CA: Ten Speed Press.

Adams, J. L. (2001). *Conceptual blockbusting* (4th ed.). Cambridge, MA: Perseus Publishing.

Adams, J., Rice, R., & Instone, D. (1984). Follower attitudes toward women and judgments concerning performance by female and male leaders. *Academy of Management Journal, 27,* 636–643.

Adler, J. J. (1967). *The difference of man and the difference it makes*. New York: Holt, Rinehart and Winston.

Adler, N. J. (1991). *International dimensions of organizational behavior* (2nd ed.). Belmont, CA: Wadsworth.

Adler, N. J. (2002). *From Boston to Bejing: Managing with a world view*. Cincinnati, OH: South-Western.

Alavi, M. (2001). Review: Knowledge management and knowledge management systems: Conceptual foundations and research issues. *MIS Quarterly, 25,* 107–113.

Alderman, H. (1997). By virtue of a virtue. In D. Statman (Ed.), *Virtue Ethics* (pp. 145–164). Washington, DC: Georgetown University Press.

Alexander, J. A., Comfort, M. E., Weiner, B. J., & Bogue, R. (2001). Leadership in collaborative community health partnerships. *Nonprofit Management & Leadership, 12,* 159–175.

Alvesson, M. (2002). *Understanding organizational culture*. Thousand Oaks, CA: Sage.

Amour, S. (2002, February 5). Employees' new motto: Trust no one. *USA Today,* pp. 1A, 1B.

Anderson, P. A. (1998). Researching sex differences within sex similarities: The evolutionary consequences of reproductive behavior. In D. J. Canary & K. Dindia (Eds.), *Sex differences and similarities in communication* (pp. 83–100). Mahwah, NJ: Lawrence Erlbaum.

Andrews, P. (1984). Performance, self-esteem and perceptions of leadership emergence: A comparative study of men and women. *Western Journal of Speech Communication, 48,* 1–13.

Argyle, M., Gardner, G., & Ciofi, F. (1958). Supervisory methods related to productivity, absenteeism, and labor turnover. *Human Relations, 11,* 23–40.

Aries, E. (1998). Gender differences in interaction: A reexamination. In D. J. Canary & K. Dindia (Eds.), *Sex differences and similarities in communication* (pp. 65–81). Mahwah, NJ: Lawrence Erlbaum.

Asante, M. K., & Frye, J. K. (1977). *Contemporary public communication*. New York: Harper & Row.

Ashour, A. S. (1973). The contingency model of leadership effectiveness: An evaluation. *Organizational Behavior and Human Performance, 9,* 339–355.

Aspegren, R. E. (1963). A study of leadership behavior and its effects on morale and attitudes in selected elementary schools. *Dissertation Abstracts, 23,* 3708.

Atkin, C. K. (2001). Theory and principles of media health campaigns. In R. R. Rice & C. K. Atkin (Eds.), *Public communication campaigns* (3rd ed., pp. 49–68). Thousand Oaks, CA: Sage.

Auger, B. Y. (1972). *How to run better business meetings.* New York: AMACOM.

Autry, J. A., & Mitchell, S. (1998). *Real power: Business lessons from the Tao Te Ching.* New York: St. Martin's Press.

Avolio, B. J. (2005). *Leadership development in balance: Made/born.* Mahwah, NJ: Lawrence Erlbaum.

Avolio, B. J., & Bass, B. M. (2002). *Developing potential across a full range of leadership: Cases on transactional and transformational leadership.* Mahwah, NJ: Lawrence Erlbaum.

Avolio, B. J., & Gardner, W. L. (2005). Authentic leadership development: Getting to the root of positive forms of leadership. *Leadership Quarterly, 16,* 315–338.

Avolio, B. J, & Yammarino, F. J. (Eds.). (2002). *Transformational and charismatic leadership: The road ahead.* Boston: JAI.

Axelrod, R. (1984). *The evolution of cooperation.* New York: Basic Books.

Ayman, R., Adams, S., Fisher, B., & Hartman, E. (2003). Leadership development in higher education institutions: A present and future perspective. In S. E. Murphy & R. E. Riggio (Eds.), *The future of leadership development* (pp. 201–222). Mahwah, NJ: Lawrence Erlbaum.

Baird, J. E. (1977). Some nonverbal elements of leadership emergence. *Southern Speech Communication Journal, 42,* 352–361.

Baird, J., & Wieting, G. K. (1979, September). Nonverbal communication can be a motivational tool. *Personnel Journal,* 607–610.

Baldwin, D. A. (1971). The costs of power. *Journal of Conflict Resolution, 15,* 145–155.

Bales, R. F. (1970). *Personality and interpersonal behavior.* New York: Holt, Rinehart and Winston.

Bales, R. F., & Cohen, S. P. (1979). *Symlog: A system for the multiple level observation of groups.* London: Collier.

Bandura, A. (1977). Self-efficacy: Toward a unifying theory of behavioral change. *Psychological Review, 84,* 191–215.

Bandura, A., & Wood, R. (1989). Effect of perceived controllability and performance standards of self- regulation of complex decision making. *Journal of Personality and Social Psychology, 84,* 804–814.

Barad, E. (1993). Pygmalion–25 years after interpersonal expectations in the classroom. In P. D. Blanck (Ed.), *Interpersonal expectations: Theory, research, and applications* (pp. 125–153). Cambridge: Cambridge University Press.

Barnard, C. I. (1938). *The functions of the executive.* Cambridge: Harvard University Press.

Bartholomew, C. S., & Gustafson, S. B. (1998). Perceived Leader Integrity Scale: An instrument for assessing employee perceptions of leader integrity. *Leadership Quarterly, 9,* 127–145.

Barton, L. (2001). *Crisis in organizations II.* Cincinnati: South-Western Publishing.

Bass, B. (1985). *Leadership and performance beyond expectations.* New York: The Free Press.

Bass, B. M. (1960). *Leadership, psychology, and organizational behavior.* New York: Harper & Row.

Bass, B. M. (1990). From transactional to transformational leadership: Learning to share the vision. *Organizational Dynamics, 18,* 19–31

Bass, B. M. (1997). Does the transactional-transformational leadership paradigm transcend organizational and national boundaries? *American Psychologist, 52,* 130–139.

Bass, B. M. (Ed.). (1990). *Bass and Stogdill's handbook of leadership* (3rd ed.). New York: The Free Press.

Bass, B. M., & Avolio, B. J. (1993). Transformational leadership: A response to critiques. In M. M. Chemers & R. Ayman (Eds.), *Leadership theory and research: Perspectives and directions* (pp. 49–80). New York: Academic Press.

Bass, B. M., & Avolio, B. J. (1994). *Improving organizational effectiveness through transformational leadership.* Thousand Oaks, CA: Sage.

Bass, B. M., Burger, P. C., Doktor, R., & Barrett, G. V. (1979). *Assessment of managers: An international comparison.* New York: Free Press.

Bass, B.M., & Riggio, R.E. (2006). *Transformational leadership* (2nd ed.). Mahwah, NJ: Lawrence Erlbaum.

Batson, C. D., Van Lange, P. A. M., Ahmad, N., & Lishner, D. A. (2003). Altruism and helping behavior. In M. A. Hogg & J. Cooper (Eds.), *The Sage handbook of social psychology* (pp. 279–295). London: Sage.

Baum, R.J., Locke, E.A., & Kirkpatrick, S. (1998). A longitudinal study of the relations of vision and vision communication to venture growth in entrepreneurial firms. *Journal of Applied Psychology, 83,* 43–54.

Baumgartel, H. (1957). Leadership style as a variable in research administration. *Administrative Science Quarterly, 2,* 344–360.

Bazerman, M. H., & Neale, M. A. (1983). Heuristics in negotiation: Limitations to effective dispute resolution. In M. H. Bazerman & R. J. Lewecki (Eds.), *Negotiating in organizations* (pp. 51–67). Beverly Hills: Sage.

Bazerman, M. H., & Watkins, M. D. (2004). *Predictable surprises: The disasters you should have seen coming, and how to prevent them.* Boston: Harvard Business School Press.

Belasco, J. A., & Stayer, R. C. (1994). *Flight of the buffalo: Soaring to excellence, learning to let employees lead.* New York: Warner Books.

Belasen, A.T. (2008). *The theory and practice of corporate communication.* Los Angeles: Sage.

Bell, B. S. (2002). A typology of virtual teams: Implications for effective leadership. *Group & Organization Management, 27,* 14–49.

Benne, K. D., & Sheats, P. (1948). Functional roles of group members. *Journal of Social Issues, 4,* 41–49.

Bennet, D. & Bennet, A. (2003). The rise of the knowledge organization. In C. W. Holsapple (Ed.), *Handbook on knowledge management 1: Knowledge matters* (pp. 5–20). Berlin: Springer-Verlag.

Bennis, W. (1976). *The unconscious conspiracy: Why leaders can't lead.* New York: AMACOM Publishing.

Bennis, W., & Nanus, B. (1985). *Leaders: The strategies for taking charge.* New York: Harper & Row, pp. 17–18.

Bennis, W. G., & Nanus, B. (1997). *Leaders: The strategies for taking charge* (2nd ed.). New York: Harper & Row.

Bennis, W. G., & Thomas, R. J. (2002). *Geeks and geezers: How era, values and defining moments shape leaders.* Boston: Harvard Business School Press.

Bennis, W. G., & Thomas, R. J. (2004). Crucibles of leadership. In *Harvard Business Review on developing leaders* (pp. 151–170). Boston: Harvard Business School Publishing.

Benoit, W. L. (1995). *Accounts, excuses and apologies.* Albany, NY: State University of New York Press.

Benoit, W. L. (2004). Image restoration discourse and crisis communication. In D. P. Millar & R. L. Heath (Eds.), *Responding to crisis: A rhetorical approach to crisis communication* (263–280). Mahwah, NJ: Lawrence Erlbaum.

Benoit, W. L., & Brinson, S. L. (1994). AT & T: Apologies are not enough. *Communication Quarterly, 42,* 75–88.

Bentham, J. (1948). *An introduction to the principles of moral and legislation.* New York: Hafner Publishing.

Berlew, D., & Hall, D. (1966). The socialization of managers: Effects of expectations on performance. *Administrative Science Quarterly,* 208–223.

Berlo, D., Lemert, J., & Mertz, R. (1969). Dimensions for evaluation of the acceptability of message sources. *Public Opinion Quarterly, 33,* 563–576.

Bies, R., & Tripp, T. M. (1998). Two faces of the powerless: Coping with tyranny in organizations. In R. M. Kramer & M. A. Neale (Eds.), *Power and influence in organizations* (pp. 203–219). Thousand Oaks, CA: Sage.

Bingham, W.V. (1927). Leadership. In H.C. Metcalf, *The psychological foundations of management.* New York: Shaw.

Bird, F. B. (1996). *The muted conscience: Moral silence and the practice of ethics in business.* Westport, CT: Quarum Books.

Birsch, D., & Fielder, J. H. (Eds.). (1994). *The Ford Pinto case: A study in applied ethics, business, and technology.* Albany, NY: State University of New York Press.

Blake, R. R., & McCanse, A. A. (1991). *Leadership dilemmas—grid solutions.* Houston: Gulf Publishing.

Blake, R. R., & Mouton, J. S. (1985). *The managerial grid III: The key to leadership excellence.* Houston: Gulf Publishing.

Blake, R. R., Mouton, J. S., Barnes, L. B., & Greiner, L. E. (1964). Breakthrough in organization development. *Harvard Business Review, 42,* 133–155.

Block, P. (1993). *Stewardship: Choosing service over self-interest.* San Francisco: Berrett-Koehler.

Blum, L. A. (1988). Moral exemplars: Reflections on Schindler, the Trocmes, and others. *Midwest Studies in Philosophy, 13,* 196–221.

Bogardus, E.S. (1934). *Leaders and leadership.* New York: Appleton-Century.

Bok, S. (1999; updated edition). *Lying: Moral choice in public and private life.* New York: Random/Vintage Books.

Bormann, E. G. (1975). *Discussion and group methods* (2nd ed.). New York: Harper & Row.

Botkin, J. W., Elmandjra, M., & Malitza, M. (1979). *No limits to learning.* New York: Penguin Books.

Bowers, D. G., & Seashore, S. E. (1966). Predicting organizational effectiveness with a four-factor theory of leadership. *Administrative Science Quarterly, 2,* 238–263.

Boyatzis, R. E. (1982). *The competent manager.* New York: John Wiley.

Bradac, J., & Mulac, A. (1984). A molecular view of powerful and powerless speech styles: Attributional consequences of specific language features and communicator intentions. *Communication Monographs, 51,* 307–319.

Brembeck, W. L., & Howell, W. S. (1976). *Persuasion: A means of social influence* (2nd ed.). Englewood Cliffs, NJ: Prentice-Hall.

Bridges, J. A., & Nelson, R. A. (2000). Issues management: A relational approach. In J. A. Ledingham & S. D. Bruning (Eds.), *Public relations as relationship management: A relational approach to the study and practice of public relations* (pp. 95–115). Mahwah, NJ: Lawrence Erlbaum.

Brissett, D., & Edgley, C. (2005), The dramaturgical perspective. In D. Brissett & C. Edgley (Eds.), *Life as theater: A dramaturgical sourcebook* (2nd ed.). New York: Aldine de Gruyter.

Broverman, I., Broverman, D. M., Clarkson, F. E., Rosenkranz, P. S., & Vogel, S. R. (1970). Sex-role stereotypes and clinical judgments in mental health. *Journal of Counseling and Clinical Psychology, 34,* 1–7.

Brown, M. E., & Trevino, L. K. (2003, August). *The influence of leadership styles on unethical conduct in work groups: An empirical test.* Paper presented at the annual meeting of the Academy of Management, Seattle, WA.

Brown, P. T. (1999–2000, Winter). New directions in leadership development: A review of trends and best practices. *The Public Manager,* 37–41.

Brown, R. (1995). *Prejudice: Its social psychology.* Oxford, UK: Blackwell.

Bruhn, J. G. (2001). *Trust and the health of organizations.* New York: Kluwer/Plenum.

Burell, N. A., & Koper, R. J. (1994). The efficacy of power/powerless language on persuasiveness/ credibility: A meta-analytic review. In R. W. Preiss & M. Allen (Eds.), *Prospects and precautions in the use of meta-analysis* (pp. 235–255). Dubuque, IA: Brown & Benchmark.

Burke, K. (1968). *Language as a symbolic action.* Berkeley: University of California Press.

Burns, J. M. (1978). *Leadership.* New York: Harper & Row.

Burns, T., & Stalker, G. M. (1961). *The management of innovation.* Chicago: Quadrangle Books.

Cammalleri, J. A., Hendrick, H. W., Pittmen, W. C., Jr., Blout, H. D., & Prather, D. C. (1973). Effects of different leadership styles on group accuracy. *Journal of Applied Psychology, 57,* 32–37.

Capezio, P., & Morehouse, D. (1997). *Secrets of breakthrough leadership.* Franklin Lakes, NJ: Career Press.

Capodagli, B., & Jackson, L. (1999). *The Disney way.* New York: McGraw-Hill.

Carlisle, A. E. (2001). An Abilene defense: Commentary two. *Organizational Dynamics, 17,* 40–43.

Carlyle, T. (1907). *On heroes, hero-worship, and the heroic in history.* Boston: Houghton Mifflin. (Original work written in 1840).

Carlzon, J. (1987). *Moments of truth.* New York: Harper & Row.

Carroll, A. B., & Buchholtz, A. K. (2003). *Business & Society: Ethics and stakeholder management.* Mason, OH: Thomson/South-Western.

Carter, K., & Spitzack, C. (1990). Transformation and empowerment in gender and communication courses. *Women's Studies in Communication, 13,* 92–110.

Cartwright, D., & Zander, A. (1968). Leadership and performance of group functions: Introduction. In D. Cartwright and A. Zander (Eds.), *Group dynamics* (pp. 301–317). New York, Harper & Row.

Cascio, W. F. (2000). Managing a virtual workplace. *Academy of Management Executive, 14,* 81–90.

Cashman, K. (1998). *Leadership from the inside out.* Provo, UT: Executive Excellence Publishing.

Caudron, S. (1999, September). The looming leadership crisis. *Workforce,* 72–76.

Chaleff, I. (1995). *The courageous follower.* San Francisco: Berrett-Koehler.

Chang, M., & Gruner, C. R. (1981). Audience reaction to self-disparaging humor. *Southern Speech Communication Journal, 46,* 419–426.

Chang, R. (2001). *The passion plan at work.* San Francisco: Jossey Bass.

Chao, G. T., Walz, P. M., & Gardner, P. D. (1992). Formal and informal mentorships: A comparison on mentoring functions and contrast with nonmentored counterparts. *Personnel Psychology, 45,* 619–636.

Charan, R., Drotter, S., & Noel, J. (2001). *The leadership pipeline: How to build the leadership-powered company.* San Francisco: Jossey-Bass.

Chen, Z., Lawson, R. B., Gordon, L. R., & McIntosh, B. (1996). Groupthink: Deciding with the leader and the devil. *Psychological Record, 46,* 581–590.

Cherniss, C. (2000). Social and emotional competence in the workplace. In R. Bar-On & J. D. A. Parker (Eds.), *The handbook of emotional intelligence: Theory, development, assessment, and application at home, school, and in the workplace* (pp. 433–458). San Francisco: Jossey-Bass.

Cherniss, C., & Goleman, D. (Eds.). (2001). *The emotionally intelligent workplace: How to select for, measure, and improve emotional intelligence in individuals, groups and organizations.* San Francisco: Jossey-Bass.

Chhokar, J.S., Brodbeck, F.C., & House, R.J. (2007). *Culture and leadership across the world: The GLOBE book of in-depth studies of 25 societies.* Mahwah, NJ: Lawrence Erlbaum.

Chinese Culture Connection (1987). Chinese values and the search for culture-free dimensions of culture. *Journal of Cross-Cultural Psychology, 18,* 143–174.

Chouinard, Y. (2005). *Let my people go surfing.* New York: Penguin Press.

Chrislip, D. D., & Larson, C. E. (1994). *Collaborative leadership.* San Francisco: Jossey-Bass.

Cialdini, R. B. (2001). *Influence: Science and practice* (4th ed.). Boston: Allyn & Bacon.

Cialdini, R. B., Petrova, P. K., & Goldstein, N. J. (2004, Spring). The hidden costs of organizational dishonesty. *MIT Sloan Management Review,* 67–73.

Cialdini, R. B., Sagarin, B. J., & Rice, W. E. (2001). Training in ethical influence. In J. M. Darley, D. M. Messick, & T. R. Tyler (Eds.), *Social influences on ethical behavior in organizations* (pp. 137–153). Mahwah, NJ: Lawrence Erlbaum.

Cialdini, R., Vincent, J., Lewis, S., Catalan, J., Wheeler, D., & Darby, B. (1975). Reciprocal procedure for inducing compliance: The door-in-the-face technique. *Journal of Personality and Social Psychology, 31,* 206–213.

Clark, E. (2004). *Around the corporate campfire: How great leaders use stories to inspire success.* Sevierville, TN: Insight.

Collins, J. (2001). *Good to great.* New York: HarperBusiness.

Collins, J. C., & Porras, J. I. (2002). *Built to last.* New York: HarperBusiness.

Collins, J. C., & Porras, J. I. (1996, September–October). Building your company's vision. *Harvard Business Review,* 65–77.

Conger, J. A. (1989). Leadership: The art of empowering others. *The Academy of Management Executive, 3,* 17–24.

Conger, J. A. (1991). Inspiring others: The language of leadership. *Academy of Management Executive, 5,* 30–45.

Conger, J. A., & Benjamin, B. (1999). *Building leaders: How successful companies develop the next generation.* San Francisco: Jossey-Bass.

Conger, J. A., & Kanungo, R. N. (1987). Toward a behavioral theory of charismatic leadership in organizational settings. *Academy of Management Review, 12,* 637–647.

Conger, J. A., & Kanungo, R. N. (1988). The empowerment process: Integrating theory and practice. *Academy of Management Review, 13,* 471–482.

Conger, J. A., & Toegel, G. (2003). Action learning and multirater feedback: Pathways to leadership development? In S. E. Murphy & R. E. Riggio (Eds.), *The future of leadership development* (pp. 107–125). Mahwah, NJ: Lawrence Erlbaum.

Connaughton, S.L., & Ruben, B.D. (2005). Millennium leadership inc.: A case study of computer and internet-based communication in a simulated organization. In K. St. Amant & P. Zemliansky (Eds.), *Internet-based workplace communications* (pp. 40–67). Hershey, PA: Information SciencePublishing.

Coombs, W. T. (1999). *Ongoing crisis communication: Planning, managing, and responding.* Thousand Oaks, CA: Sage.

Cooper, R. K., & Sawat, A. (1996). *Executive EQ: Emotional intelligence in leadership and organizations.* New York: Grosset/Putnam.

Covey, S. R. (1989). *The seven habits of highly effective people.* New York: Simon and Schuster.

Cox, T. (1991). Managing cultural diversity: Implications for organizational competitiveness. *Academy of Management Executive, 5,* 45–56.

Cox, T. (1993). *Cultural diversity in organizations: Theory, research and practice.* San Francisco: Berrett-Koehler.

Cox. T. (2001). *Creating the multicultural organization: A strategy for capturing the power of diversity.* San Francisco: Jossey-Bass.

Cragan, J. F., & Wright, D. W. (1999). *Communication in small group discussion* (5th ed.). Belmont, CA: Wadsworth.

Craigie, F. C. (1999). The spirit and work: Observations about spirituality and organizational life. *Journal of Psychology and Christianity, 18,* 45–53.

Crawford, K. S., Thomas, E. D., & Fink, J. J. (1980). Pygmalion at sea: Improving the work effectiveness of low performers. *Journal of Applied Behavioral Science, 16,* 482–505.

Crosby, F. J. (1999). The developing literature on developmental relationships. In A. J. Murrell, F. J. Crosby, & R. J. Ely (Eds.), *Mentoring dilemmas: Developmental relationships within multicultural organizations* (pp. 3–20). Mahwah, NJ: Lawrence Erlbaum.

Daft, R. L. (2005). The *leadership experience.* Mason, OH: Thomson-Southwestern.

Daly, J. A., McCroskey, J. C., & Richmond, V. P. (1980). Relationship between vocal activity and perception of communication in small group interaction. *Western Journal of Speech Communication, 41,* 175–187.

Dance, F. E. X. (1982). A speech theory of human communication. In F. E. X. Dance (Ed.), *Human communication theory* (pp.120–146). New York: Harper & Row.

Daniels, J. L., & Daniels, N. C. (1993). *Global vision.* New York: McGraw-Hill.

Dansereau, F., Graen, G.G., & Haga, W. (1975). A vertical dyad linkage approach to leadership in formal organizations. *Organizational Behavior and Human Performance, 13,* 46–78.

Day, D. V., & Halpin, S. M. (2004). Growing leaders for tomorrow: An introduction. In D. Day, S. J. Zaccaro, & S. M. Halpin (Eds.), *Leader development for transforming organizations* (pp. 3–22). Mahwah, NJ: Lawrence Erlbaum.

Day, D. V., & O'Connor, P. M. (2003). Leadership development: Understanding the process. In S. E. Murphy & R. E. Riggio (Eds.), *The future of leadership development* (pp. 11–27). Mahwah, NJ: Lawrence Erlbaum.

Day, R. C., & Hamblin, R. L. (1964). Some effects of close and punitive styles of supervision. *American Journal of Sociology, 69,* 499–510.

DeFleur, M. L., Kearney, P., & Plax, T. G. (1993). *Mastering communication in contemporary America.* Mountain View, CA: Mayfield.

Den Hartog, D. N., House, R. J., Hanges, P. J., & Ruiz-Quintanilla, S. A. (1999). Culture specific and cross-culturally generalizable implicit leadership theories: Are attributes of charismatic/transformational leadership universally endorsed? *Leadership Quarterly, 10,* 219–256.

Denning, S. (2005). *The leader's guide to storytelling*. San Francisco: Jossey-Bass.

DePree, M. (1989). *Leadership is an art*. New York: Doubleday.

DePree, M. (1992). *Leadership jazz*. New York: Currency Doubleday.

Derr, C. B., Roussillon, S., & Bournois, F. (2002). Conclusion. In C. B. Derr, S. Roussillon, & F. Bournois (Eds.), *Cross-cultural approaches to leadership development* (pp. 289–303). Westport, CT: Quorum Books.

Deutsch, M. (1973). *The resolution of conflict*. New Haven, CT: Yale University Press.

Deveraux, M., & Johansen, R. (1994). *GlobalWork: Bridging distance, culture, and time*. San Francisco: Jossey-Bass.

Devito, J. (2000). *The elements of public speaking* (7th ed.). New York: Longman.

Dewey, J. (1910). *How we think*. Boston: D.C. Heath.

Dickerson-Jones, T. (1993). *50 activities for managing cultural diversity*. Amherst, MA: HRD Press.

Dirks, K. T. (1999). The effects of interpersonal trust on work group performance. *Journal of Applied Psychology, 84*, 445–455.

Dirks, K. T. (2000). Trust in leadership and team performance: Evidence from NCAA basketball, *Journal of Applied Psychology, 85*, 1004–1012.

Dirks, K. T., & Ferrin, D. L. (2002). Trust in leadership: Meta-analytic findings and implications for research and practice. *Journal of Applied Psychology, 87*, 611–628.

Dirks, K. T., & Skarlicki, D. P. (2004). Trust in leaders: Existing research and emerging issues. In R. M. Kramer & K. S. Cook (Eds.), *Trust and distrust in organizations: Dilemmas and approaches* (pp. 21–40). New York: Russell Sage Foundation.

Disney Institute. (2001). *Be our guest*. New York: Disney Enterprises.

Dow, T. (1969). The theory of charisma. *Sociological Quarterly, 10*, 306–318.

Dozier, D. M., Grunig, L. A., & Grunig, J. E. (1995). *Manager's guide to excellence in public relations and communication management*. Mahwah, NJ: Lawrence Erlbaum.

Dreher, D. (1995). *The Tao of personal leadership*. New York: HarperBusiness.

Dreyer, G. F., & Ash, R. A. (1990). A comparative study of mentoring among men and women in managerial, professional, and technological positions. *Journal of Applied Psychology, 75*, 539–546.

Driscoll, J. W. (1978). Trust and participation in organizational decision making as predictors of satisfaction. *Academy of Management Journal, 21*, 44–56.

Druskat, V. U., & Wolff, S. B. (2001, March). Building the emotional intelligence of groups. *Harvard Business Review*, 80–90.

DuBrin, A. J. (1995). *Leadership*. Boston: Houghton Mifflin.

DuBrin, A. J. (2007). *Leadership: research findings, practice, and skills*. Boston: Houghton Mifflin.

Duchon, D., Green, S. G. & Taber. T. D. (1988). Vertical dyad linkage: A longitudinal assessment of antecedents, measures, and consequences. *Journal of Applied Psychology, 71*, 56–60.

Duchon, D., & Plowman, D. A. (2005). Nurturing the spirit at work: Impact on work unit performance. *Leadership Quarterly, 16*, 807–833.

Dyer, W. G. (1985). The cycle of cultural evolution in organizations. In R. H. Killmann, M. J. Saxton, & R. Serpa (Eds.), *Gaining control of the corporate culture* (pp. 200–229). San Francisco: Jossey-Bass.

Eagly, A. H. (1987). *Sex differences in social behavior*. Hillsdale, NJ: Lawrence Erlbaum.

Eagly, A. H., & Carli, L.L. (2007). *Through the labyrinth: The truth about how women become leaders*. Boston: Harvard Business School Press.

Eagly, A. H., & Johnson, B. T. (1990). Gender and leadership style: A meta-analysis. *Psychological Bulletin, 108*, 233–256.

Eagly, A. J., & Karau, S. J. (1991). Gender and the emergence of leaders: A meta-analysis. *Journal of Personality and Social Psychology, 60*, 685–710.

Eden, D. (1984). Self-fulfilling prophecy as a management tool: Harnessing Pygmalion. *Academy of Management Review, 9*, 64–73.

Eden, D. (1990). *Pygmalion in management*. Lexington, MA: Lexington Books/D. C. Heath.

Eden, D. (1993). Interpersonal expectations in organizations. In P. D. Blanck (Ed.), *Interpersonal expectations: Theory, research, and applications* (pp. 154–178). Cambridge: Cambridge University Press.

Eden, D., & Ravid, G. (1982). Pygmalion vs. self-expectancy: Effects of instructor and self-expectancy on trainee performance. *Organizational Behavior and Human Performance, 30,* 351–364.

Eden, D., & Shani, A. B. (1982). Pygmalion goes to boot camp: Expectancy, leadership, and trainee performance. *Journal of Applied Psychology, 67,* 194–199.

Edmondson, A., & Moingeon, B. (1996). When to learn how and when to learn why: Appropriate organizational learning processes as a source of competitive advantage. In B. Moingeon & A. Edmondson (Eds.), *Organizational learning and competitive advantage* (pp. 17–37). London: Sage.

Eisenberg, E. M., & Riley, P. (2001). Organizational culture. In F. M. Jablin & L. L. Putnam (Eds.), *The new handbook of organizational communication advances in theory, research, and methods* (pp. 291– 322). Thousand Oaks, CA: Sage.

Eisenberg, N. (2000). Emotion, regulation, and moral development. *Annual Review of Psychology, 51,* 665–697.

Eisenberger, R., Fasolo, P., & Davis-LaMastro, C. (1990). Perceived organizational support and employee diligence, commitments, and innovation. *Journal of Applied Psychology, 75,* 57–59.

Elangovan, A. R., & Shapiro, D. L. (1998). Betrayal of trust in organizations. *Academy of Management Review, 23,* 547–566.

Elsbach, K. D. (2004). Managing images of trustworthiness in organizations. In R. M. Kramer & K. S. Cook (Eds.), *Trust and distrust in organizations: Dilemmas and approaches* (pp. 275–292). New York: Russell Sage Foundation.

Engleberg, I. N., & Wynn, D. R. (2003). *Working in groups: Communication principles and strategies* (3rd ed.). Boston: Houghton Mifflin.

Epstein, C. F. (1988). *Deceptive distinctions: Sex, gender, and the social order.* New Haven, CT: Yale University Press.

Erez, M., & Earley, P. C. (1993). *Culture, self-identity, and work.* New York: Oxford University Press.

Esser, J. K. (1998). Alive and well after 25 years: A review of groupthink research. *Organizational Behavior and Human Decision Processes, 73,* 116–141.

Etzioni, A. (1964). *Modern organizations.* Englewood Cliffs, NJ: Prentice-Hall.

Fagenson, E. A. (1989). The mentor advantage: Perceived career/job experiences of protégés versus non-proteges. *Journal of Organizational Behavior, 10,* 309–320.

Fairholm, G. W. (1996). Spiritual leadership: Fulfilling whole-self needs at work. *Leadership & Organization Development Journal, 17,* 11–17.

Fairhurst, G. T., & Sarr, R. A. (1996). *The art of framing: Managing the language of leadership.* San Francisco: Jossey-Bass.

Falbo, T. (1977). Multidimensional scaling of power strategies. *Journal of Personality and Social Psychology, 35,* 537–547.

Farris, G. F. (1972). The effect of individual roles on performance in innovative groups. *R & D Management, 3,* 23–28.

Fearn-Banks, K. (2002). *Crisis communications: A casebook approach* (2nd ed.). Mahwah, NJ: Lawrence Erlbaum.

Fiedler, F. E. (1967). *A theory of leadership effectiveness.* New York: McGraw-Hill.

Fiedler, F. E. (1972). Personality, motivational systems, and the behavior of high and low LPC scores. *Human Relations, 25,* 391–412.

Fiedler, F. E. (1978). The contingency model and the dynamics of the leadership process. In L. Berkowitz (Ed.), *Advances in experimental social psychology* (pp. 60–112). New York: Academic Press.

Fiedler, F. E., Chemers, M. M., & Mahar, L. (1976). *Improving leadership effectiveness: The leader match concept.* New York: John Wiley.

Fiedler, F. E., & Garcia, J. E. (1987). *New approaches to effective leadership: Cognitive resources and organizational performance.* New York: John Wiley.

Fink, S. (2000). *Crisis management: Planning for the inevitable.* New York: AMACOM.

Fisher, B. A. (1970). Decision emergence: Phases in group decision making. *Speech Monographs, 37,* 53–66.

Fisher, B. A., & Ellis, D. G. (1994). *Small group decision making* (4th ed.). New York: McGraw-Hill.

Fisher, K. (1993). *Leading self-directed work teams.* New York: McGraw-Hill.

Fisher, K., & Fisher, M.D. (2001). *The distance manager.* New York: McGraw-Hill.

Fisher, K.; Harper, B., & Harper, A. (1992). *Succeeding as a self-directed work team.* Mohegan Lake, NY: MW Corporation.

Fisher, R., & Ury, W. (1991). *Getting to yes* (2nd ed.). New York: Penguin Books.

Fiske, S. T. (1993, June). Controlling other people: The impact of power on stereotyping. *American Psychologist,* 621–628.

Fiske S. T. (1998). Stereotyping, prejudice, and discrimination. In D. T. Gilbert, S. T. Fiske, & G. Lindzey (Eds.), *The handbook of social psychology* (Vol. 2, pp. 357–411). Boston: McGraw-Hill.

Foster, D. A. (1992). *Bargaining across borders: How to negotiate business successfully anywhere in the world.* New York: McGraw-Hill.

Foster, R. J. (1998). *Celebration of discipline: The path to spiritual growth* (20th anniversary edition). San Francisco: HarperSanFrancisco.

Foti, R. J., Fraser, S. L., & Lord, R. G. (1982). Effects of leadership labels and prototypes on perceptions of political leaders. *Journal of Applied Psychology, 67,* 326–333.

Foulke, E. (1971). The perception of time compressed speech. In D. L. Horton & J. J. Jenkins (Eds.), *The perception of language* (pp. 79–107). Columbus, OH: Charles E. Merrill.

Fraker, A. (1996). Robert K. Greenleaf and business ethics: There is no code. In L. C. Spears (Ed.), *Reflections on leadership* (pp. 37–48). New York: John Wiley.

Freas, A. M. (2000). Coaching executives for business results. In M. Goldsmith, L. Lyons & A. Freas (Eds.), *Coaching for leadership: How the world's greatest coaches help leaders learn* (pp. 27–42). San Francisco: Jossey-Bass/Pfeiffer.

Freiberg, K., & Freiberg, J. (1996). *Nuts! Southwest Airlines crazy recipe for business and personal success.* New York: Broadway Books, p. 288.

Friedman, T. (2000). *The Lexus and the olive tree* (Expanded Version). New York: Anchor Books.

French, J. R. P., & Raven, B. (1959). The bases of social power. In D. Cartwright (Ed.), *Studies in social power* (pp. 150–167). Ann Arbor: University of Michigan, Institute for Social Research.

Fuller, B. J., Morrison, R., Jones, L., Bridger, D., & Brown, V. (1999). The effects of psychological empowerment on transformational leadership and job satisfaction. *Journal of Social Psychology, 139,* 389–391.

Gabarro, J. J. (1985, May–June). When a manager takes charge. *Harvard Business Review,* 110–123.

Gabarro, J. J. (1987). *The dynamics of taking charge.* Boston: Harvard University Press.

Gabarro, J. J. (1988). Executive leadership and succession: The process of taking charge. In D. C. Hambrick (Ed.), *The executive effect: Concepts and methods for studying top managers* (pp. 237–68). Greenwich, CT: JAI Press.

Gaines, J. (1993). "You don't necessarily have to be charismatic . . .": An interview with Anita Roddick and reflections on charismatic processes in the Body Shop International. *Leadership Quarterly, 4,* 347–359.

Gale, S. F. (2001, June). Bringing good leaders to light. *Training,* 38–42.

Galford, R., & Drapeau, A. S. (2003, February). The enemies of trust. *Harvard Business Review, 81,* 88–97.

Gardner, H. (1983). *Frames of mind.* New York: Basic Books.

Gardner, J. W. (1986). The tasks of leadership. (*Leadership Paper No. 2*). Washington, DC: Independent Sector.

Gardner, J. W. (1990). *On leadership.* New York, NY: Free Press.

Gardner, W. L. (1992). Lessons in organizational dramaturgy: The art of impression management. *Organizational Dynamics, 21,* 33–46.

Gardner, W. L., & Avolio, B. J. (1998). The charismatic relationship: A dramaturgical perspective. *Academy of Management Review, 23,* 32–58.

Gardner, W. L., Avolio, B. J., Luthans, F., May, D. R., & Walumbwa, F. (2005). "Can you see the real me?" A self-based model of authentic leader and follower development. *Leadership Quarterly, 16,* 343–372.

Gardner, W. L., & Cleavenger, D. (1998). The impression management strategies associated with transformational leadership at the world-class level: A psychological assessment. *Management Communication Quarterly, 12,* 3–41.

Gardner, W. L., & Martinko, M. J. (1988). Impression management in organizations. *Journal of Management, 14,* 321–338.

Garvin, D. A. (1993, July–August). Building a learning organization. *Harvard Business Review,* 86.

Garvin, D. A. (2000). *Learning in action: A guide to putting the learning organization to work.* Boston: Harvard Business School Press.

Geertz, C. (1977). Centers, kings, and charisma: Reflections on the symbolics of power. In J. Ben-David & T. Nichols (Eds.), *Culture and its creation: Essays in honor of Edward Shils* (pp. 150–171). Chicago: University of Chicago Press.

Geier, J. G. (1967). A trait approach to the study of leadership. *Journal of Communication, 17,* 316–323.

George, B. (2003). *Authentic leadership: Rediscovering the secrets to creating lasting value.* San Francisco: Jossey-Bass.

Gerber, R. (2002). *Leadership the Eleanor Roosevelt way: Timeless strategies from the first lady of courage.* New York: Prentice-Hall.

Gerstner, C. R., & Day, D. V. (1997). Meta-analytic review of leader-member exchange theory: Correlates and construct issues. *Journal of Applied Psychology, 82,* 827–844.

Getzels, J. W. (1973, November 21). Problem finding: The 343rd Convocation Address, the University of Chicago. *The University of Chicago Record, 9,* 281–283.

Getzels, J. W. (1975). Problem-finding and the inventiveness of solutions. *Journal of Creative Behavior, 9,* 12–18.

Giacalone, R. A., & Greenbergh, J. (Eds.), (1997). *Antisocial behavior in organizations.* Thousand Oaks, CA: Sage.

Giacalone, R. A., & Jurkiewicz, C. L. (2003). Toward a science of workplace spirituality. In R. A. Giacalone & Jurkiewicz (Eds.), *Handbook of workplace spirituality and organizational performance* (pp. 3–28). Armonk, NY: M. E. Sharpe.

Giambatista, R. C., Rowe, W. G., & Riaz, S. (2005). Nothing succeeds like succession: A critical review of leader succession literature since 1994. *Leadership Quarterly, 16,* 963–991.

Gilbert, J. A., & Tang, T. L (1998). An examination of organizational trust antecedents. *Public Personnel management, 27,* 321–338.

Giles, H., & Powesland, P. F. (1975). *Speech style and social evaluation.* London: Academic Press.

Gioia, D. A. (1992). Pinto fires and personal ethics: A script analysis of missed opportunities. *Journal of Business Ethics, 11,* 379–389.

Gladwell, M. (2002). *The tipping point: How little things can make a big difference.* Boston: Little Brown.

Goffman, E. (1959). *The presentation of self in everyday life.* Garden City, NY: Doubleday.

Goldberg, L.R. (1990). An alternative "description of personality": The big-five factor structure. *Journal of Personality and Social Psychology, 59,* 1216–1229.

Goleman, D. (1995). *Emotional intelligence: Why it can matter more than IQ.* New York: Bantam Books.

Goleman, D. (1998). *Working with emotional intelligence.* New York: Bantam Books.

Goleman, D., Boyatzis, R., & McKee, A. (2002). *Primal leadership: Realizing the power of emotional intelligence.* Boston: Harvard Business School Press.

Good, T., & Brophy, J. (1980). *Education psychology: A realistic approach.* New York: Holt, Rinehart and Winston.

Goodwin, D. K. (2005). *Team of rivals: The political genius of Abraham Lincoln.* New York: Simon & Schuster.

Goodwin, S. A. (2003). Power and prejudice: A social-cognitive perspective on power and leadership. In D. van Knippenberg & M. A. Hogg, *Leadership and power: Identity processes in groups and organizations* (pp. 138–152). London: Sage.

Gordon, G. E., & Rosen, N. (1981). Critical factors in leadership succession. *Organizational Behavior and Human Performance, 27,* 227–254.

Gordon, J. (1992, October). Work teams: How far have they come? *Training,* 59–65.

Gouran, D. S., & Hirokawa, R. Y. (1986). Counteractive functions of communication in effective group decision-making. In R. Y. Hirokawa & M. S. Poole (Eds.), *Communication and group decision-making* (pp. 81–90). Beverly Hills, CA: Sage.

Gouran, D. S., Hirokawa, R. Y., Julian, K. M., & Leatham, G. B. (1993). The evolution and current status of the functional perspective on communication in decision-making and problem-solving groups. In S. Deetz (Ed.), *Communication Yearbook 16* (pp. 573–600). Newbury Park, CA: Sage.

Gozdz, K., & Frager, R. (2003). Using everyday challenges of business to transform individuals and organizations. In R. A. Giacalone & C. L. Jurkiewicz (Eds.), *Handbook of workplace spirituality and organizational performance* (pp. 475–492). Armonk, NY: M. E. Sharpe.

Graen, G. (1976). Role-making processes within complex organizations. In M. D. Dunnette (Ed.), *Handbook of industrial organizational psychology* (pp. 1201–1246). Chicago: Rand-McNally.

Graen, G. B., & Cashman, J. F. (1975). A role-making of leadership in formal organizations: A developmental approach. In J. G. Hunt and L. L. Larson (Eds.), *Leadership frontiers* (pp. 143–165). Kent: Kent State University Press.

Graen, G. B., & Scandura, T. (1987). Toward a psychology of dyadic organizing. *Research in Organizational Behavior, 9,* 175–208.

Graen, G. B., & Uhl-Bien, M. (1998). Relationship-based approach to leadership. Development of leader-member exchange (LMX) theory of leadership over 25 years: Applying a multi-level multi- domain perspective. In F. Dansereau & F. J. Yammarino (Eds.), *Leadership: the multiple-level approaches* (pp. 103–158). Stamford, CT: JAI Press.

Graham, G. (2004). *Eight theories of ethics.* London: Routledge.

Grant, J. A., King, P. E., & Behnke, R. E. (1994). Compliance-gaining strategies, communication satisfaction, and willingness to comply. *Communication Reports, 7,* 99–108.

Greenleaf, R. K. (1977). *Servant leadership.* New York: Paulist Press.

Greguras, G. J., & Ford, J. M. (2006). An examination of the multidimensionality of supervisor and subordinate perceptions of leader-member exchange. *Journal of Occupational and Organizational Psychology, 79,* 433–465.

Griffin, E. (2009). *A first look at communication theory* (7th ed.). New York: McGraw-Hill.

Grover, S. L. (1997). Lying in organizations: Theory, research, and future directions. In R. A. Giacalone & J Greenberg (Eds.), *Antisocial behavior in organizations* (pp. 68–84). Thousand Oaks, CA: Sage.

Grunig, J. E., & Grunig, L. A. (1992). Models of public relations and communication. In J. E. Grunig, D. M. Dozier, W. I. Ehling, L. A. Grunig, F. C. Repper, & J. White (Eds.), *Excellence in public relations and communication management* (pp. 285–325). Hillsdale, NJ: Lawrence Erlbaum.

Grunig, L. A., Grunig, J. E., & Dozier, D. M. (2002). *Excellent public relations and effective organizations: A study of communication management in three countries.* Mahwah, NJ: Lawrence Erlbaum.

Guadine, A., & Thorne, L. (2001). Emotion and ethical decision-making in organizations. *Journal of Business Ethics, 31,* 175–187.

Guarrero, C. A. (1998, October). The leadership challenge. *Security Management,* 27–29.

Gudykunst, W. B., & Kim, Y. Y. (2003). *Communicating with strangers: An approach to intercultural communication* (4th ed.). New York: McGraw-Hill.

Guinness, O. (Ed.). (1999). *Character counts: Leadership qualities in Washington, Wilberforce, Lincoln, and Solzhenitsyn.* Grand Rapids, MI: Baker Books.

Hackman, M. Z. (1988). Audience reactions to the use of direct and personal disparaging humor in informative public address. *Communication Research Reports, 5,* 126–130.

Hackman, M. Z. (1988). Reactions to the use of self-disparaging humor by informative public speakers. *Southern Speech Communication Journal, 53,* 175–183.

Hackman, M. Z. (1989). The inner game of public speaking: Applying intrapersonal communication processes in the public speaking course. *Carolinas Speech Communication Annual, 5*, 41–47.

Hackman, M. Z., Furniss, A. H., Hills, M. J., & Paterson, T. J. (1992). Perceptions of gender-role characteristics and transformational leadership behaviours. *Perceptual and Motor Skills, 75*, 311–319.

Hackman, M. Z., & Johnson, C. (1994). *A cross-cultural investigation of innovativeness, willingness to communicate and need for cognition.* Paper presented at the Speech Communication Association convention, New Orleans, LA.

Haiman, F. S. (1949). An experimental study of the effects of ethos in public speaking. *Speech Monographs, 16*, 190–202.

Haire, M., Ghiselli, E. E., & Porter, L. W. (1966). *Managerial thinking: An international study.* New York: John Wiley.

Haleta, L. L. (1996). Student perceptions of teachers' use of language: The effects of powerful and powerless language on impression formation and uncertainty. *Communication Education, 45*, 16–28.

Hall, E. (1977). *Beyond culture.* Garden City, NY: Anchor.

Hample, D. (2003). Arguing skill. In J. O. Greene & B. R. Burleson (Eds.), *Handbook of communication and social interaction skills* (pp 439–477). Mahwah, NJ: Lawrence Erlbaum.

Harper, B., & Harper, A. (1992). *Succeeding as a self-directed work team.* Mohegan Lake, NY: MW Corporation.

Harris, P. R., & Moran, R. T. (1993). *Managing cultural differences* (4th ed.). Houston, TX: Gulf Publishing.

Hart, D. K. (1994). Administration and the ethics of virtue. In T. C. Cooper (Ed.). (1994). *The handbook of administrative ethics* (pp. 107–123). New York: Marcel Dakker.

Hart, R., Friedrich, G., & Brooks, W. (1975). *Public communication.* New York: Harper & Row.

Harvey, J. (1974, Summer). The Abilene Paradox: The mismanagement of agreement, *Organizational Dynamics*, 63–80.

Harvey, J. (1988). *The Abilene Paradox and other meditations on management.* New York: Simon & Schuster.

Harvey, M. (2006). Leadership and the human condition. In G. R. Goethals and G. L. J. Sorenson (Eds.), *The quest for a general theory of leadership* (pp. 39–45). Northampton, MA: Edward Elgar., p. 42.

Hauerwas, S. (1981). *A community of character.* Notre Dame, IN: University of Notre Dame Press.

Hawes, L. C. (1974). Social collectivities as communication: Perspectives of organizational behavior. *Quarterly Journal of Speech, 60*, 497–502.

Hays-Thomas, R. (2004). Why now? The contemporary focus on managing diversity. In M. S. Stockdale & F. J. Crosby, *The psychology and management of workplace diversity* (pp. 3–30). Malden, MA: Blackwell.

Hays-Thomas; Kossek, E. E., Lobel, S. A., & Brown, J. (2006). Human resource strategies to manage workplace diversity: Examining "the business case." In A. M. Konrad, P. Prasad, & J. K. Pringle (Eds.), *Handbook of workplace diversity* (pp. 53–74). London: Sage.

Hearit, K. M. (2001). Corporate apologia: When an organization speaks in defense of itself. In R. L. Heath & G. Vazquez (Eds.), *Handbook of public relations* (pp. 487–500). Thousand Oaks, CA: Sage.

Heath, R. L. (1997). *Strategic issues management: Organizations and public policy challenges.* Thousand Oaks, CA: Sage.

Heath, R. L. (2002). Issues management: Its past, present and future. *Journal of Public Affairs, 2*, 209–214.

Heenan, D. A., & Bennis, W. (1999). *Co-leaders: The power of great partnerships.* New York: John Wiley & Sons.

Heider, J. (1985). *The Tao of leadership.* New York: Bantam Books.

Hemphill, J. K., (1949). The leader and his group. *Journal of Educational Research, 28*, 225–229.

Hersey, P. (1984). *The situational leader.* Escondido, CA: Center for Leadership Studies.

Hersey, P., Blanchard, K. H., & Johnson, D. (2008). *Management of organizational behavior: Leading human resources* (9th ed.). Upper Saddle River, NJ: Prentice-Hall.

Hespe, G., & Wall, T. (1976). The demand for participation among employees. *Human Relations, 29*, 411–428.

Hill, N. (1976, August). Self-esteem: The key to effective leadership. *Administrative Management, 51*, 24–25.

Hill, T. A. (1976). An experimental study of the relationship between opinionated leadership and small group consensus. *Speech Monographs, 43*, 246–257.

Hinken, T. R., & Schriesheim, C. A. (1989). Development and application of new scales to measure the French and Raven (1959) bases of social power. *Journal of Applied Psychology, 74*, 561–567.

Hirokawa, R., & Pace, R. (1983). A descriptive investigation of the possible communication-based reasons for effective and ineffective group decision making. *Communication Monographs, 50*, 363–379.

Hirokawa, R. Y., & Scheerhorn, D. R. (1986). Communication in faulty group decision-making. In R. Y. Hirokawa & M. S. Poole (Eds.), *Communication and group decision-making* (pp. 63–80). Beverly Hills, CA: Sage.

Hise, R. T. (1968, Fall). The effect of close supervision on productivity of simulated managerial decision-making groups. *Business Studies, North Texas University,* pp. 96–104.

Hoefling, T. (2003). *Working virtually.* Sterling, VA: Stylus Publishing.

Hofling, C. K., Brotzman, E., Dalrymple, S., Graves, N., & Pierce, C. M. (1966). An experimental study of nurse-physician relationships. *Journal of Nervous and Mental Disease, 143*, 171–180.

Hofstede, G. (1980). Motivation, leadership and organization: Do American theories apply abroad? *Organizational Dynamics, 9*, 42–63.

Hofstede, G. (1984). The cultural relativity of the quality of life concept. *Academy of Management Review, 9*, 389–398.

Hofstede, G. (1991). *Cultures and organizations: Software of the mind.* London: McGraw-Hill.

Hofstede, G. (1993). Cultural constraints in management theories. *Academy of Management Executive, 7*, 81–94.

Hofstede, G. (2001). *Culture's consequences: Comparing values, behaviors, institutions, and organizations across nations* (2nd ed.). Thousand Oaks, CA: Sage.

Hofstede, G., & Bond, M. H. (1988). The Confucius connection: From cultural roots to economic growth. *Organizational Dynamics, 14*, 483–503.

Hollander, E. (1978). *Leadership dynamics: A practical guide to effective relationships.* New York: Free Press.

Hollander, E. P. (1992, April). The essential interdependence of leadership and followership. *Current Directions in Psychological Science,* 71–75.

Hopkins, S. A. (1997). Case #1: Downzing at Simtek. In W. E. Hopkins, *Ethical dimensions of diversity.* Thousand Oaks, CA: Sage.

Hoppe, M. H. (2004). Cross-cultural issues in the development of leaders. In C. C. McCauley, R. S. Moxley, & E. Van Velsor (Eds.), *The Center for Creative Leadership handbook of leadership development* (2nd ed., pp. 331–360). San Francisco: Jossey-Bass.

Hornstein, H. A. (1996). *Brutal bosses and their prey.* New York: Riverhead Books.

Hough, J., & Neuland, E. W. (2000). *Global business.* Oxford: Oxford University Press.

House, R. J. (1971). A path-goal theory of leadership effectiveness. *Administrative Science Quarterly, 16*, 321–338.

House, R. J. (1977). A 1976 theory of charismatic leadership. In J. G. Hunt & L. L. Larson (Eds.), *Leadership: The cutting edge* (pp. 189–207). Carbondale: Southern Illinois University Press.

House, R. J., Hanges, P. J., Javidan, M., Dorfman, P. W., & Gupta, V. (2004). *Culture, leadership, and organizations: The GLOBE study of 62 societies.* Thousand Oaks, CA: Sage.

House, R. J., & Mitchell, T. R. (1974). Path-goal theory of leadership. *Journal of Contemporary Business, 3*, 81–97.

House, R. J., & Singh, J. V. (1987). Organizational behavior: Some new directions for I/O psychology. In M. R. Rosenzweig & L. Porter (Eds.), *Annual Review of Psychology*, Vol. 38, (pp. 669–717). Palo Alto, CA: Annual Reviews.

Hovland, C. I., & Weiss, W. (1951). The influence of source credibility on communication effectiveness. *Public Opinion Quarterly, 15*, 635–650.

Hovland, C., Janis, I., & Kelley, H. H. (1953). *Communication and persuasion.* New Haven, CT: Yale University Press.

Howard, A., & Bray, D. W. (1988). *Managerial lives in transition: Advancing age and changing times.* New York: Guilford Press.

Howard, P. S., & Howard, J. M. (2001). *The owner's manual for personality at work.* Atlanta: Bard Press.

Howell, J. M., & Avolio, B. J. (1992). The ethics of charismatic leadership: Submission or liberation. *Academy of Management Executive, 6*, 43–54.

Huggins, N. (1987). Martin Luther King, Jr.: Charisma and leadership. *Journal of American History, 74*, 477–481.

Hughes, R.L., & Beatty, K.C. (2005). *Becoming a strategic leader.* San Francisco: Jossey-Bass.

Hult, G. T. M. (2003). An integration of thoughts on knowledge management. *Decision Sciences, 34*, 189–195.

Hunt, D. M., & Michael, C. (1983). Mentorship: A career training and development tool. *Academy of Management Review, 8*, 475–485.

Hunter, J. E., & Boster, F. J. (1987). A model of compliance-gaining message selection. *Communication Monographs, 54*, 63–84.

Ilies, R., Morgeson, F. P., & Nahrgang, J. D. (2005). Authentic leadership and eudaemonic well-being: Understanding leader-follower outcomes. *Leadership Quarterly, 16*, 373–394.

Inch, E. S. & Warnick, B., (2002). *Critical thinking and communication: The use of reason in argument* (4th ed.). Boston: Allyn & Bacon.

Infante, D. (1988). *Arguing constructively.* Long Grove, IL: Waveland Press.

Infante, D. A. (1995). Teaching students to understand and control verbal aggression. *Communication Education, 44*, 51–63.

Infante, D. A., & Gorden, W. I. (1985). Benefits versus bias: An investigation of argumentativeness, gender, and organizational outcomes. *Communication Research Reports, 2*, 196–201.

Infante, D. A., & Gorden, W. I. (1985). Superiors' argumentativeness and aggressiveness as predictors of subordinates' satisfaction. *Human Communication Research, 12*, 117–125.

Infante, D. A., & Gorden, W. I. (1989). Argumentativeness and affirming communicator style as predictors of satisfaction/dissatisfaction with subordinates. *Communication Quarterly, 31*, 81–90.

Infante, D. A., & Gorden, W. I. (1991). How employees see the boss: Test of an argumentative and affirming model of supervisors' communicative behavior. *Western Journal of Speech Communication, 55*, 294–304.

Infante, D. A., & Rancer, A. (1996). Argumentativeness and verbal aggressiveness: A review of recent theory and research. In B. Burleson (Ed.), *Communication Yearbook 19* (pp. 319–351). Thousand Oaks, CA: Sage.

Infante, D. A., & Rancer, A. S. (1982). A conceptualization and measure of argumentativeness. *Journal of Personality Assessment, 46*, 72–80.

Instone, D., Major, B., & Bunker, B. B. (1983). Gender, self-confidence, and social influence strategies: An organizational simulation. *Journal of Personality and Social Psychology, 44*, 322–333.

Isenhart, M. W., & Spangle, M. (2000). *Collaborative approaches to resolving conflict.* Thousand Oaks, CA: Sage.

Ives, W., Torry, B., & Gordon, C. (2002). Knowledge sharing is human behavior. In D. Morey, M. Maybury & B. Thuraisingham (Eds.), *Knowledge management: Classic and Contemporary works* (pp. 99–129). Cambridge, MA: MIT Press.

Jacobi, M. (1991). Mentoring and undergraduate academic success: A literature review. *Review of Educational Research, 61*(4), 505–532.

Jacobs, T. O. (1970). *Leadership and exchange in formal organizations.* Alexandria, VA: Human Resources Research Organization.

Jaffe, C. (2007). *Public speaking: Concepts and skills for a diverse society* (5th ed.). Belmont, CA: Wadsworth/Thomson.

Jamieson, K. H. (1995). *Beyond the double bind: Women and leadership.* New York: Oxford University Press.

Janis, I. (1971, November). Groupthink: The problems of conformity. *Psychology Today, 271–279.*

Janis, I. (1982). *Groupthink* (2nd ed.). Boston: Houghton Mifflin.

Janis, I. (1989). *Crucial decisions: Leadership in policymaking and crisis management.* New York: The Free Press.

Janis, I., & Mann, L. (1977). *Decision making.* New York: The Free Press.

Jarvenpaa, S. L., & Leidner, D. E. (1999). Communication and trust in global virtual teams. *Organization Science, 10,* 791–815.

Jenner, H. (1990). The Pygmalion Effect: The importance of expectancies. *Alcoholism Treatment Quarterly, 7,* 127–133.

Jennings, M. M. (2006). *The seven signs of ethical collapse: how to spot moral meltdowns in companies . . . before it's too late.* New York: St. Martin's Press.

Jensen, A. D., & Chilberg, J. G. (1991). *Small group communication.* Belmont, CA: Wadsworth.

Johannesen, R. L. (1991). Virtue ethics, character, and political communication. In R. E. Denton (Ed.), *Ethical dimensions of political communication* (pp. 69–90). New York: Praeger.

Johannesen, R. L. (2002). *Ethics in human communication* (5th ed). Long Grove, IL: Waveland Press.

Johnson, C. E. (1997, Spring). A leadership journey to the East. *Journal of Leadership Studies, 4,* 82–88.

Johnson, C. E. (2002). Evaluating the impact of emotional intelligence on leadership performance: Resonance or dissonance? *Selected Proceedings of the 2002 International Leadership Association convention* [online]. Available from http://www.academy.umd.edu/ILA.

Johnson, C. E. (2007). *Ethics in the workplace: Tools and tactics for organizational transformation.* Thousand Oaks, CA: Sage.

Johnson, C. E. (2009). *Meeting the ethical challenges of leadership: Casting light or shadow* (3rd ed.). Thousand Oaks, CA: Sage.

Johnson, C. E., Dixon, B., Hackman, M. Z., & Vinson, L. (1995). Willingness to communicate, the need for cognition and innovativeness: New Zealand students and professionals. In J. E. Aitken & L. J. Shedletsky (Eds.), *Intrapersonal communication processes* (pp. 376–381). Plymouth, MI: Midnight Oil and the Speech Communication Association.

Johnson, C. E., & Hackman, M. (1993). The status of leadership coursework in communication. *The Michigan Association of Speech Communication Journal, 28,* 1–13.

Johnson, C. E., & Hackman, M. (1995). *Creative communication: Principles and applications.* Long Grove, IL: Waveland Press.

Johnson, C. E., & Hackman, M. Z. (1998). *Public relations, collaborative leadership and community: A new vision for a new century.* Paper presented at the National Communication Association convention, New York, NY.

Johnson, C. E., & Vinson, L. (1987). Damned if you do, damned if you don't?: Status, powerful speech and evaluations of female witnesses. *Women's Studies in Communication, 10,* 37–44.

Johnson, C. E., Vinson, L., Hackman, M., & Hardin, T. (1989). The effects of an instructor's use of hesitation form on student ratings of quality, recommendations to hire, and lecture listening. *Journal of the International Listening Association, 3,* 32–43.

Jones, D. (2007, May 30). Do foreign executives balk at sports jargon? *USA Today,* pp. B1, B2.

Jones, L. B. (1996). *The path: Creating your mission statement for work and life.* New York: Hyperion.

Judge, T.A., Bono, J. E., Ilies, R., & Gerhardt, M.W. (2002). Personality and leadership: A qualitative and quantitative review. *Journal of Applied Psychology, 87,* 765–780.

Jussim, L., Madon, S., & Chatman, C. (1994), Teacher expectations and student achievement: Self-fulfilling prophecies, biases, and accuracy. In L. Heath et al. (Eds.), *Applications of heuristics and biases to social issues* (pp. 303–334). New York: Plenum Press.

Kahn, R. L. (1956). The prediction of productivity. *Journal of Social Issues, 12*, 41–49.

Kakabadse, A., Myers, A., McMahon, T., & Spony, G. (1995). Top management styles in Europe: Implications for business and cross-national teams. *European Business Journal, 7*, 17–27.

Kanungo, R. N., & Conger, J. A. (1990). The quest for altruism in organizations. In S. Srivastva & D. L. Cooperrider, and Associates (Eds.), *Appreciative management and leadership: The power of positive thought and action in organizations*. San Francisco: Jossey-Bass.

Kant, I. (1964). *Groundwork for the metaphysics of morals* (H. J. Ryan, Trans.). New York: Harper & Row.

Kanter, R. M. (1977). *Men and women of the corporation*. New York: Basic Books.

Kanter, R. M. (1977). Some effects of proportions on group life: Skewed sex rations and responses to token women. *American Journal of Sociology, 82*, 969–990.

Kanter, R. M. (1979, July–August). Power failure in management circuits. *Harvard Business Review, 57*, 65.

Kanter, R. M. (1983). *The change masters: Innovation for productivity in the American corporation*. New York: Simon and Schuster.

Kanter, R. M. (2001). An Abilene defense: Commentary one. *Organizational Dynamics, 17*, 37–39.

Kanungo, R. N., & Conger, J. A. (1990). The quest for altruism in organizations. In S. Srivastva and D. L. Cooperrider, and Associates (Eds.) *Appreciative management and leadership: The power of positive thought and action in organizations* (pp. 228–256). San Francisco: Jossey-Bass.

Kanungo, R. N., & Mendonica, M. (1996). *Ethical dimensions of leadership*. Thousand Oaks, CA: Sage.

Karsten, M. F. (1994). *Management and gender*. Westport, CT: Praeger.

Katz, D., Maccoby, N., & Morse, N. (1950). *Productivity, supervision, and morale in an office situation*. Ann Arbor: University of Michigan, Institute for Social Research.

Katz, D., Maccoby, N., Gurin, G., & Floor, L. (1951). *Productivity, supervision, and morale among railroad workers*. Ann Arbor: University of Michigan, Institute for Social Research.

Katzenbach, J. R. (1998). *Teams at the top: Unleashing the potential of both teams and individual leaders*. Boston: Harvard Business School Press.

Katzenbach, J. R. (2003). *Why pride matters more than money: The power of the world's greatest motivational force*. New York: Crown Business.

Katzenbach, J. R., & Smith, D. K. (1993). *The wisdom of teams*. Boston: Harvard Business School Press.

Katzenbach, J. R., & Smith, D. K. (1993, March–April). The discipline of teams. *Harvard Business Review*, 111–120.

Kayser, T. A. (1994). *Team power*. Burr Ridge, IL: Irwin.

Kayworth, T. R., & Leidner, D. E. (2001–2002). Leadership effectiveness in global virtual teams. *Journal of Management Information Systems, 18*, 7–40.

Kearney, P., Plax, T. G., Sorenson, G., & Smith, V. R. (1988). Experienced and prospective teachers' selections of compliance-gaining messages for "common" student misbehaviors. *Communication Education, 37*, 150–164.

Keegan, J. (1987). *The mask of command*. New York: Viking Penguin.

Keil, M. & Montealegre, R. (2000, Spring). Cutting your losses: Extracting your organization when a big project goes awry. *Sloan Management Review, 41*, 55–68.

Kellerman, B. (1999). Hitler's ghost: A manifesto. In, B. Kellerman & L. Matusak (Eds), *Cutting edge leadership 2000* (pp. 65–68). College Park, MD: Burns Academy of Leadership.

Kellerman, B. (2004). *Bad leadership*. Boston: Harvard University Press.

Kelley, R. (1992). *The power of followership: How to create leaders people want to follow and followers who lead themselves*. New York: Doubleday/Currency.

Kelley R. E. (1998). Followership in a leadership world. In L. C. Spears (Ed.), *Insights on leadership: Service, stewardship, spirit, and servant-leadership* (pp. 170–184). New York: John Wiley & Sons.

Kelman, H. C., & Hovland, C. I. (1953). "Reinstatement" of the communicator in delayed measurement of opinion change. *Journal of Abnormal and Social Psychology, 48*, 327–335.

Keltner, D., Langner, C. A., & Allison, M. L. (2006). Power and moral leadership. In D. L. Rhode (Ed.), *Moral leadership: The theory and practice of power, judgment and policy* (pp. 177–194). San Francisco: Jossey-Bass.

Kemp, K. F., & Smith, W. P. (1994). Information exchange, toughness, and integrative bargaining: The roles of explicit cues and perspective-take. *The International Journal of Conflict Management, 5,* 5–12.

Kenny, D. A., & Zaccaro, S. J. (1983). An estimate of variance due to traits in leadership. *Journal of Applied Psychology, 68,* 678–685.

Kerr, S., & Harlan, A. (1973). Predicting the effects of leadership training and experience from the contingency model: Some remaining problems. *Journal of Applied Psychology, 57,* 114–117.

Kidder, R. M. (1994). *Shared values for a troubled world: Conversations with men and women of conscience.* San Francisco: Jossey-Bass.

Kipnis, D., & Schmidt, S. M. (1988). Upward-influence styles: Relationship with performance evaluations, salary, and stress. *Administrative Science Quarterly, 33,* 528–542.

Kipnis, D., Schmidt, S. J., & Wilkinson, I. (1980). Intraorganizational influence tactics: Explorations in getting one's way. *Journal of Applied Psychology, 65,* 440–452.

Kipnis, D., Schmidt, S. M., Swaffin-Smith, C., & Wilkinson, I. (1984, Winter). Patterns of managerial influence: Shotgun managers, tacticians, and bystanders. *Organizational Dynamics,* 58–67.

Kirkman, B. L., Rosen, B., Gibson, C. B., Tesluk, P. E., & McPherson, S. O. (2002). Five challenges to virtual team success: Lessons from Sabre, Inc. *Academy of Management Executive, 16,* 67–79.

Kirkpatrick, S. A., & Locke, E. A. (1991). Leadership: Do traits matter? *The Executive, 5,* 48–60.

Kline, T. (1999). *Remaking teams: The revolutionary research-based guide that puts theory into practice.* San Francisco: Jossey-Bass.

Knittel, R. E. (1974). Essential and nonessential ritual programs of planned change. *Human Organization, 33,* 394–396.

Knutson, T. J., & Holdrige, W. E. (1975). Orientation behavior, leadership and consensus: A possible functional relationship. *Speech Monographs, 42,* 107–114.

Kogler Hill, S. E., Bahniuk, M. H., & Dobbs, J. (1989). The impact of mentoring and collegial support on faculty success: An analysis of support behavior information adequacy, and communication apprehension. *Communication Education, 38,* 15–33.

Konrad, A. M. (2006). Leveraging workplace diversity in organizations. *Organization Management Journal, 3,* 164–189.

Korba, R. J. (1986). *The rate of inner speech.* Unpublished doctoral dissertation, University of Denver.

Kotter, J. (1999). Leading change: The eight steps to transformation. In J. A. Conger, G. M. Spreitzer, & E. E. Lawler III (Eds.), *The leader's change handbook: An essential guide to setting direction and taking action* (pp. 87–99). San Francisco: Jossey-Bass.

Kotter, J. P. (1990). *A force for change: How leadership differs from management.* New York: Free Press.

Kotter, J. P. (1999). *On what leaders really do.* Boston: Harvard Business School Press.

Kouzes, J. M., & Posner, B. Z. (2002). *The leadership challenge: How to get extraordinary things done in organizations* (3rd ed.). San Francisco: Jossey-Bass.

Kouzes, J. M., & Posner, B. Z. (2003). *Credibility: How leaders gain and lose, why people demand it* (2nd ed.). San Francisco: Jossey-Bass.

Kouzes, J. M., & Posner, B. Z. (2007). *The leadership challenge: How to get extraordinary things done in organizations* (4th ed). San Francisco: Jossey-Bass.

Kram, K. E. (1985). *Mentoring at work: Developmental relationships in organizational life.* Glenview, IL: Scott, Foresman and Company.

Kram, K. E., & Bragar, M. C. (1992). Development through mentoring: A strategic approach. In D. H. Montross & C. J. Shinkman (Eds.), *Career development: Theory and practice.* Springfield, IL: Charles C. Thomas.

Kram, K. E., & Isabella, L. A. (1985). Mentoring alternatives: The role of peer relationships in career development. *Academy of Management Review, 28,* 110–132.

Kramer, R. M. (1999). Trust and distrust in organizations: Emerging perspectives, enduring questions. *Annual Review of Psychology, 50,* 569–598.

Kramer, R. M., & Tyler, T. R. (1996). *Trust in organizations: Frontiers of theory and research.* Thousand Oaks, CA: Sage.

Krech, D., & Crutchfield, R. (1948). *Theory and problems of social psychology.* New York, McGraw-Hill.

Kriegel, R., & Brandt, D. (1996). *Sacred cows make the best burgers: Paradigm-busting strategies for developing change-ready people and organizations.* New York: Warner Books.

Kriegel, R. J., & Patler, L. (1991*). If it ain't broke . . . break it!* New York: Warner Books.

Kruger, J., Epley, N., Parker, J., & Ng, Z. (2005). Egocentrism over e-mail: Can we communicate as well as we think? *Journal of Personality and Social Psychology, 89,* 925–936.

LaFasto, F., & Larson, C. (2001). *When teams work best.* Thousand Oaks, CA: Sage.

Landauer, T. J. (1962). Rate of implicit speech. *Perceptual and Motor Skills, 15,* 646.

Langer, E. J. (1989). *Mindfulness.* Reading MA: Addison-Wesley.

Larrabee, W. (1972). Paralinguistics, kinesics, and cultural anthropology. In L. Samovar & R. Porter (Eds.), *Intercultural communication: A reader* (pp. 172–180). Belmont, CA: Wadsworth.

Larson, C. E. (1969). Forms of analysis and small group problem-solving. *Speech Monographs, 36,* 452–455.

Larson, C. E., & LaFasto, F. M. J. (1989). *Teamwork: What must go right/What can go wrong.* Newbury Park, CA: Sage.

Lawrence, P. R., & Lorsch, J. W. (1967). *Organization and environment.* Cambridge: Harvard University Press.

Learman, L. A., Avorn, J., Everitt, D. E., & Rosenthal, R. (1990). Pygmalion in the nursing home: The effects of caregiver expectations on patient outcomes. *Journal* of *the American Geriatrics Society, 38,* 797–803.

Leathers, D. G. (1997). *Successful nonverbal communication: Principles and applications* (3rd ed.). New York: Macmillan.

Lee, O. (2002). Cultural differences in e-mail use of virtual teams: A critical social theory perspective. *CyberPsychology & Behavior, 5,* 227–232.

Levin, I. M. (2000). Vision revisited. *Journal of Applied Behavioral Science, 36,* 91–107.

Lewin, K., Lippitt, R., & White, R. K. (1939). Patterns of aggressive behavior in experimentally created "social climates." *Journal of Social Psychology, 10,* 271–299.

Ley, R. (1966). Labor turnover as a function of worker differences, work environment, and authoritarianism of foremen. *Journal of Applied Psychology, 50,* 497–500.

Lipman-Blumen, J. (2005). *The allure of toxic leaders.* New York: Oxford University Press.

Litzinger, W., & Schaefer, T. (1982, September–October). Leadership through followership. *Business Horizons,* 78–81.

Livingston, J. S. (1969). Pygmalion in management. *Harvard Business Review, 47,* 81–89.

Locke, E. A., & Latham, G. P. (1990). *A theory of goal setting & task performance.* Englewood Cliffs, NJ: Prentice-Hall.

Lombardo, M. M., & McCauley, C. D. (1988) *The dynamics of management derailment.* Technical Report No. 34. Greensboro, NC: Center for Creative Leadership.

Lord, R. G., De Vader, C. L., & Alliger, G. M. (1986). A meta-analysis of the relation between personality traits and leadership perceptions: An application of validity generalization procedures. *Journal of Applied Psychology, 71,* 402–410.

Lord, R. G., & Maher, K. J. (1991). *Leadership and information processing: Linking perceptions and performance.* Boston: Unwin Hyman.

Louw, D. J. (2001). *Ubuntu and the challenges of multiculturalism in post-apartheid South Africa* [online]. Available: http://www.phys.uu.nl/~unitwin/ubuntu.html.

Lucas, S. E. (2003). *The art of public speaking* (7th ed.). Boston: McGraw-Hill.

Luke, J. S. (1994). Character and conduct in the public service. In T. C. Cooper (Ed.), *The handbook of administrative ethic* (pp. 391–412). New York: Marcel Dakker.

Lundin, S. C., Paul, H., & Christensen, J. (2000). *Fish!* New York: Hyperion.

Lustig, M. W., & Koester, J. (2003). *Intercultural competence: Interpersonal competence across cultures* (4th ed.). New York: Longman.

Luthans, F., & Avolio, B. J. (2003). Authentic development: A positive developmental approach. In K. S. Cameron, J. E. Dutton, & R. E. Quinn (Eds.), *Positive organizational scholarship* (pp. 241–261). San Francisco: Barrett-Koehler.

Lutz, W. (1989). *Doublespeak*. New York: Harper & Row.

Lynam, D. R., & Milich, R. (1999). Project DARE: No effect at 10-year follow-up. *Journal of Consulting & Clinical Psychology, 67*, 590–594.

Maas, A., & Clark, R. D. (1984). Hidden impact of minorities: fifteen years of minority influence research. *Psychological Bulletin, 95*, 428–450.

MacIntyre, A. (1984). *After virtue: A study in moral theory* (2nd ed.). Notre Dame, IN: University of Notre Dame Press.

Mackworth, N. H. (1965). Originality. *American Psychologist, 20*, 51–66.

Madon, S., Jussim, L., & Eccles, J. (1997). In search of the powerful self-fulfilling prophecy. *Journal of Personality and Social Psychology, 72*, 791–809.

Magaziner, I. C., & Patinkin, M. (1989, March–April). Cold competition: GE wages the refrigerator war. *Harvard Business Review*, 114–124.

Magaziner, I. C., & Patinkin, M. (1989). *The silent war: Inside the global business battles shaping America's future*. New York: Random House.

Manning, G., & Curtis, K. (1988). *Leadership: Nine keys to success*. Cincinnati: South-Western.

Manz, C. C., & Neck, C. P. (1999). *Mastering self-leadership: Empowering yourself for personal excellence*. Upper Saddle River, NJ: Prentice-Hall.

Manz, C. C., & Peck, C. P. (1995). Teamthink: Beyond the groupthink syndrome in self-managing work teams. *Journal of Managerial Psychology, 10*, 7–15.

Manz, C. C., & Sims, H. P. (1989). *SuperLeadership: Leading others to lead themselves*. New York: Prentice-Hall.

Marquardt, M. (2005). *Leading with questions*. San Francisco: Jossey-Bass.

Marquardt, M. J., & Berger, N. O. (2000). *Global leaders for the 21st century*. Albany NY: State University of New York Press.

Marquardt, M. J., & Horvath, L. (2001). *Global teams*. Palo Alto, CA: Davies-Black Publishing.

Martin, F. (2002, April). So you failed . . . so what? *Unlimited*, 48.

Martin, J. (1992). *Cultures in organizations*. New York: Oxford University Press.

Martin, J. (2002). *Organizational culture: Mapping the terrain*. Thousand Oaks, CA: Sage.

Martin, J., & Powers, M. E. (1983). Truth or corporate propaganda: The value of a good story. In L. R. Pondy, P. J. Frost, G. Morgan, & T. C. Dandridge (Eds.), *Organizational symbolism* (pp. 93– 107). Greenwich, CT: JAI Press.

Marwell, G., & Schmitt, D. (1967). Dimensions of compliance-gaining behavior: An empirical analysis. *Sociometry, 30*, 350–364.

Maslow, A. H. (1970). *Motivation and personality*. New York: Harper & Row.

Maxwell, J. (2000). *Failing forward: Turning mistakes into stepping-stones for success*. Nashville: Thomas Nelson Publishers.

Mayer, J. D. (2001). A field guide to emotional intelligence. In J Ciarrochi, J. P. Forgas, & J. D. Mayer (Eds.), *Emotional intelligence in everyday life: A scientific inquiry* (pp. 3–24). Philadelphia: Psychology Press.

Mayer, R. C., & Gavin, M. B. (2005). Trust in management and performance: Who minds the shop while the employees watch the boss? *Academy of Management Journal, 48*, 874–888.

Mayo, A. J., & Nohira, N. (2005). *In their time: The greatest business leaders of the twentieth century*. Boston: Harvard Business School Press.

McCall, N. W., Jr., & Lombardo, M. M. (1983). *Off the track: Why and how successful executives get derailed*. Technical Report No. 21. Greensboro, NC: Center for Creative Leadership.

McCauley, C. D. (2001). Leader training and development. In S. J. Zaccaro & R. J. Klimoski (Eds.), *The nature of organizational leadership: Understanding the performance imperatives confronting today's leaders* (pp. 347–383). San Francisco: Jossey-Bass.

McCrae, R.R., & Costa, P.T. (1987). Validation of the five-factor model of personality across instruments and observers. *Journal of Personality and Social Psychology, 52*, 81–90.

McCroskey, J. C., & Richmond, C. P. (1990). Willingness to communicate: Differing cultural perspectives. *Southern Communication Journal, 56*, 72–77.

McCroskey, J. C., & Richmond, V. P. (1991). Willingness to communicate: A cognitive view. In M. Booth-Butterfield (Ed.), *Personality and interpersonal communication* (pp. 129–156). Newbury Park, CA: Sage.

McCroskey, J. C., & Richmond, V. P. (1996). *Fundamentals of human communication: An interpersonal perspective.* Long Grove, IL: Waveland Press.

McCroskey, J. C., & Richmond, V. P. (1998). Willingness to communicate. In J. C. McCroskey, J. A. Daly, M. M. Martin, & M. J. Beatty (Eds.), *Communication and personality: Trait perspectives* (pp. 119–131). Cresswell, NJ: Hampton Press.

McCroskey, J. C., & Young, T. J. (1981). Ethos and credibility: The construct and its measurement after three decades. *Central States Speech Journal, 32,* 24.

McGee-Cooper, A., & Trammell, D. (2002). From hero-as-leader to servant-as-leader. In L. C. Spears & M. Lawrence (Eds.), *Focus on leadership: Servant-leadership for the 21st century* (pp. 145–146). New York: John Wiley & Sons.

McGregor, D. (1960). *The human side of enterprise.* New York: McGraw-Hill.

McLain, D. L., & Hackman, K. (1999). Trust, risk, and decision-making in organizational change. *Public Administration Quarterly, 23,* 152–176.

McMahan, E. M. (1976). Nonverbal communication as a function of attribution in impression formation. *Communication Monographs, 43,* 287–294.

McNatt, D. B. (2000). Ancient Pygmalion joins contemporary management: A meta-analysis of the result. *Journal of Applied Psychology, 85,* 314–322.

Mednick, S. A. (1962). The associative basis of the creative process. *Psychological Review, 69,* 221.

Meilander, G. (1986). Virtue in contemporary religious thought. In R. J. Nehaus (Ed.), *Virtue: Public and private* (pp. 7–30). Grand Rapids, MI: Eerdmans.

Meindl, J. R. (1995). The romance of leadership as a follower-centric theory: A social constructionist approach. *Leadership Quarterly, 6,* 329–341.

Meindl, J. R., Ehrlich, S. B., & Dukerich, J. M. (1985). The romance of leadership. *Administrative Science Quarterly, 30,* 78–102.

Meltzer, L. (1956). Scientific productivity in organizational settings. *Journal of Social Issues, 12,* 32–40.

Messing, B. (1989). *The Tao of management.* New York: Bantam Books.

Meyer, H. H. (1968). Achievement motivation and industrial climates. In R. Tagiuri & G. H. Litwin (Eds.), *Organizational technology and organizational structure. Administrative Science Quarterly, 16,* 444–459.

Miller, A. N. (2002). An exploration of Kenyan public speaking patterns with implications for the American introductory public speaking course. *Communication Education, 51,* 168–182.

Miller, G. R. (1969). Contributions of communication research to the study of speech. In A. H. Monroe & D. Ehninger (Eds.), *Principles and types of speech communication* (6th brief ed., pp. 334–357). Glenview, IL: Scott, Foresman.

Mishra, A. K. (1996). Organizational responses to crisis: The centrality of trust. In R. M. Kramer & T. R. Tyler (Eds.), *Trust in organizations: Frontiers of theory and research* (pp. 261–287). Thousand Oaks, CA: Sage.

Mitroff, I., & Denton, E. A. (1999). *A spiritual audit of corporate America: A hard look at spirituality, religion, and values in the workplace.* San Francisco: Jossey-Bass.

Mitroff, I., & Denton, E. A. (1999, Summer). A study of spirituality in the workplace. *Sloan Management Review, 40,* 83–92.

Mitroff, I. I. (2005). *Why some companies emerge stronger and better from a crisis.* New York: AMACOM.

Mitroff, I. I., & Alpsaian, M. C. (2003, April). Preparing for evil. *Harvard Business Review,* 109–115.

Mitroff, I. I., & Anagnos, G. (2001). *Managing crises before they happen.* New York: American Management Association.

Mitroff, I. I., & Pearson, C. M. (1993). *Crisis management: A diagnostic guide for improving your organization's crisis-preparedness.* San Francisco: Jossey-Bass.

Mohr, L. B. (1971). Organizational technology and organizational structure. *Administrative Science Quarterly, 16,* 444–459.

Moorhead, G., Neck, C. P., & West, M. S. (1998). The tendency toward defective decision making within self-managing teams: The relevance of groupthink for the 21st century. *Organizational Behavior and Human Decision Processes, 73*, 327–351.

Mor Barak, M. E. (2005). *Managing diversity: Toward a globally inclusive workplace*. Thousand Oaks, CA: Sage.

Morrison, A. M. (1996). *The new leaders: Guidelines on leadership diversity in America*. San Francisco: Jossey-Bass.

Morrison, A. M., White, R. P., & Van Velsor, E. (1987). *Breaking the glass ceiling*. Reading, MA: Addison-Wesley.

Morrison, A. M., White, R. P., & Van Velsor, E. (1987, August). Executive women: Substance plus style. *Psychology Today*, 18–26.

Mortensen, C. D. (1966). Should the discussion group have an assigned leader? *The Speech Teacher, 15*, 34–41.

Moscovici, S., Mugny, G., & Van Avermaet, E. (Eds.). (1985). *Perspectives on minority influence*. Cambridge: Cambridge University Press.

Moxley, R. S., & Pulley, M. L. (2004). Hardships. In C. D. McCauley, R. S. Moxley, & E. Van Velsor (Eds.), *The Center for Creative Leadership handbook of leadership development* (2nd ed., pp. 183–203). San Francisco: Jossey-Bass.

Mueller, B. H., & Lee, J. (2002). Leader-member exchange and organizational communication satisfaction in multiple contexts. *Journal of Business Communication, 39*, 220–244.

Mullen, E. J. (1998). Vocational and psychosocial mentoring functions: Identifying mentors who serve both. *Human Resource Development Quarterly, 9*, 319–331.

Muringham, J. K., & Leung, T. K. (1976). The effects of leadership involvement and the importance of the task on subordinates' performance. *Organizational Behavior and Human Performance, 17*, 299–310.

Murray, M. (1991). *Beyond the myths and magic of mentoring*. San Francisco: Jossey-Bass.

Nahavandi, A. (2006). *The art and science of leadership* (4th ed.). Upper Saddle River, NJ: Pearson Prentice-Hall.

Nanus, B. (1992). *Visionary leadership*. San Francisco: Jossey-Bass.

Neale, M. A., & Bazerman, M. H. (1983). The role of perspective-taking ability in negotiating under different forms of arbitration. *Industrial and Labor Relations, 36*, 378–388.

Near, R., & Weckler, D. (1990, September). *Organizational and job characteristics related to self-managing teams*. Paper presented at the International Conference on Self-Managed Work Teams, Denton, TX.

Neck, C. P., & Houghton, J. D. (2006). Two decades of self-leadership theory and research: Past developments, present trends, and future possibilities. *Journal of Managerial Psychology, 21*, 270–295.

Neff, T. J., & Citrin, J. M. (1999). *Lessons from the top*. New York: Doubleday.

Newsom, D., Van Slyke turk, J., & Kruckeberg, D. (2004). *This is PR: The realities of public relations* (8th ed.) Stanford, CA: Wadsworth/Thompson Learning.

Nichols, R. G. (1961). Do we know how to listen? Practical helps in a modern age. *The Speech Teacher, 10*, 120–124.

Nielsen, R. P. (1998). Quaker foundations for Greenleaf's servant-leadership and "friendly disentangling" method. In L. Spears (Ed.), *Insights of leadership* (pp. 126–144). New York: Wiley.

Northouse, P. (2007). *Leadership: Theory and practice* (4th ed.). Thousand Oaks, CA: Sage.

O'Barr, W. (1984). Asking the right questions about language and power. In C. Kramarae, M. Schulz, & W. O'Barr (Eds.), *Language and power* (pp. 260–280). Beverly Hills: Sage.

O'Keefe, D. J. (1987). The persuasive effects of delaying identification of high and low-credibility communicators: A meta-analytic review. *Central States Speech Journal, 38*, 63–72.

O'Toole, J., Galbraith, J., Lawler, E. E. (2002). When two (or more) heads are better than one: The promise and pitfalls of shared leadership. *California Management Review, 44*, 65–83.

Offerman, L. R., & Hellmann, P. S. (1997). Culture's consequences for leadership behavior: National values in action. *Journal of Cross-Cultural Psychology, 28*, 342–351.

Ohlott, P. J. (2004). Job assignments. In C. D. McCauley, R. S. Moxley, & E. Van Velsor (Eds.), *The Center for Creative Leadership handbook of leadership development* (2nd ed., pp. 151–182). San Francisco: Jossey-Bass.

Olaniran, B. A., & Williams, D. D. (2001). Anticipatory model of crisis management: A vigilant response to technological crises. In R. L. Heath & G. Vazquez (Eds.), *Handbook of public relations* (pp. 487–500). Thousand Oaks, CA: Sage.

Opotow, S. (1990). Moral exclusion and injustice: An introduction. *Journal of Social Issues, 46,* 1–20.

Orsag Madigan, C., & Elwood, A. (1983). *Brainstorms and thunderbolts.* New York: Macmillan.

Otto, M. L. (1994). Mentoring: An adult developmental perspective. In M. A. Wunsch (Ed.), *Mentoring revisited: Making an impact on individuals and institutions.* San Francisco: Jossey-Bass.

Palast, G. (2003). *The best democracy money can buy* (rev. Am ed.). New York: Plume.

Palmer, P. (1998). Leading from within. In L. C. Spears (Ed.), *Insights on leadership: Service, stewardship, spirit, and servant-leadership* (pp. 197–208). New York: John Wiley.

Parnes, S. J. (1975). "Aha!" In I. A. Taylor & J. W. Getzels (Eds.), *Perspectives on creativity* (pp. 224– 248). Chicago: Aldine.

Parry, K.W., & Proctor-Thompson, S.B. (2002). Perceived integrity of transformational leaders in organisational settings. *Journal of Business Ethics, 35,* 75–96.

Pasternack, B. A., & O'Toole, J. (2002, second quarter). Yellow light leadership: How the world's best companies manage uncertainty. *Strategy + Business,* 74–83.

Patton, B. P., & Downs, T. M. (2003). *Decision-making group interaction: Achieving quality* (4th ed.). New York: Allyn & Bacon.

Pauchant, T. C., & Mitroff, I. I. (1992). *Transforming the crisis-prone organization: Preventing individual, organizational, and environmental tragedies.* San Francisco: Jossey-Bass.

Pearce, C. L. (2004). The future of leadership: Combining vertical and shared leadership to transform knowledge work. *Academy of Management Review, 18,* 47–57.

Pearce, C. L., & Conger, J. A. (2003). All those years ago: The historical underpinnings of shared leadership. In C. L. Pearce & J. A. Conger (Eds.), *Shared leadership: Reframing the hows and whys of leadership* (pp. 1–16). Thousand Oaks, CA: Sage.

Pearce, T. (2003). *Leading out loud: The authentic speaker, the credible leader.* San Francisco: Jossey-Bass.

Pearce, W. B. (1989). *Communication and the human condition.* Carbondale: Southern Illinois University Press.

Perrow, C. (1999). *Normal accidents: Living with high-risk technologies.* Princeton, NJ: Princeton University Press.

Peters, T. (1992). *Liberation management.* New York: Ballantine.

Peters, T. (1994). *The pursuit of wow!* New York: Vintage Books.

Peters, T., & Austin, N. (1985). *A passion for excellence: The leadership difference.* New York: Random House.

Peters, T. J., & Waterman, R. H., Jr. (1982). *In search of excellence.* New York: Harper & Row.

Petty, R. E., & Cacioppo, J. T. (1986). *Communication and persuasion: Central and peripheral routes to attitude change.* New York: Springer-Verlag.

Petty, R., & Wegener, D. (1999). The Elaboration Likelihood Model: Current status and controversies. In S. Chaiken & Y. Trope (Eds.), *Dual process theories in social psychology* (pp. 41–72). New York: Guildford.

Pfeffer, J. (1992, Winter). Understanding power in organizations. *California Management Review, 29–50.*

Phillips-Jones, L. (1983). *Mentors and proteges.* New York: Arbor House.

Piliavin, J. A., & Charng, H. W. (1990). Altruism: a review of recent theory and research. *Annual Review of Sociology, 16,* 27–65.

Ping, P. F., & Yukl, G. (2000). Perceived effectiveness of influence tactics in the United States and China. *Leadership Quarterly, 11,* 251–266.

Pittman, T. S., Rosenbach, W. E., & Potter, E. H. III. (2001). Followers as partners: Taking the initiative for action. In W. E. Rosenbach & R. L. Taylor (Eds.), *Contemporary issues in leadership* (5th ed., pp. 107–120). Boulder, CO: Westview Press.

Planalp, S. (1999). *Communicating emotion: Social, moral, and cultural processes.* Cambridge, UK: Cambridge University Press.

Poole, M. S. (1983). Decision development in small groups II: A study of multiple sequences in decision making. *Communication Monographs, 50,* 206–232.

Poole, M. S. (1983). Decision development in small groups III: A multiple sequence model of group decision development. *Communication Monographs, 50,* 321–341.

Post, S. G. (2002). The tradition of agape. In S. G. Post, L. G. Underwood, J. P. Schloss, & W. B. Hurlbut (Eds.), *Altruism & altruistic love: Science, philosophy, & religion in dialogue* (pp. 51–64). Oxford: Oxford University Press.

Powell, G. (1993). *Women and men in management* (2nd ed.). Newbury Park, CA: Sage.

Powell, G. (2003). *Women & men in management* (3rd ed.). Newbury Park, CA: Sage.

Pruitt, D. G., & Carnevale, P. J. (1993). *Negotiation in social conflict.* Pacific Grove, CA: Brooks/Cole.

Prusak, L., & Cohen, D. (2001, June). How to invest in social capital. *Harvard Business Review,* 86–93.

Pushkala, P., Pringle, J. K., & Konrad, A. M. (2006). Examining the contours of workplace diversity: Concepts, contexts and challenges. In A. M. Konrad, P. Prasad, & J. K. Pringle (Eds.), *Handbook of workplace diversity* (pp. 1–22). London: Sage.

Quinn, R. E., & Sprietzer, G. M. (1997). The road to empowerment: Seven questions every leader should ask. *Organizational Dynamics, 26,* 37–49.

Rafaeli, A., & Worline, M. (2000). Symbols in organizational culture. In N. M. Ashkanasy, C. P. M. Wilderom, & M. F. Peterson (Eds.), *Handbook of organizational culture and climate* (pp. 71–84). Thousand Oaks, CA: Sage.

Ramperstad, A. (1997). *Jackie Robinson.* New York: Knopf.

Rancer, A. S., & Avtgis, T. A. (2006). *Argumentative and aggressive communication: Theory, research, and application.* Thousand Oaks, CA: Sage.

Ray, D., & Bronstein, H. (1995). *Teaming up.* New York: McGraw-Hill.

Ray, S. J. (1999). *Strategic communication in crisis management: Lessons from the airline industry.* Westport, CT: Quorum Books.

Reardon, K. K. (1995). *They just don't get it, do they?* New York: Little Brown.

Reave, L. (2005). Spiritual values and practices related to leadership effectiveness. *Leadership Quarterly, 16,* 655–687.

Regula, C. R., & Julian, J. W. (1973). The impact of quality and frequency of task contributions on perceived ability. *Journal of Social Psychology, 89,* 115–122.

Renfro, W. L. (1993). *Issues management in strategic planning.* Westport, CT: Quorum Books.

Rest, J. (1986). *Moral development: Advances in research and theory.* New York: Praeger.

Rest, J. R. (1993). Research on moral judgment in college students. In A. Garrod (Ed.), *Approaches to moral development* (pp. 201–211). New York: Teachers College Press.

Rest, J. R. (1994). Background: Theory and research. In J. R. Rest & D. Narvaez (Eds.), *Moral development in the professions: Psychology and applied ethics* (pp. 1–25). Hillsdale, NJ: Lawrence Erlbaum.

Rhoads, K. V. L., & Cialdini, R. B. (2002). The business of influence: Principles that lead to success in commercial settings. In J. P. Dillard & M. Pfau (Eds.), *The persuasion handbook: Developments in theory and practice.* Thousand Oaks, CA: Sage.

Rice, R. R. (2001). Smokey Bear. In R. R. Rice & C. K. Atkins (Eds.), *Public communication campaigns* (3rd ed., pp. 276–279). Thousand Oaks, CA: Sage.

Richardson, R. J., & Thayer, S. K. (1993). *The charisma factor.* Englewood Cliffs, NJ: Prentice-Hall.

Richmond, V. P., & Roach, K. D. (1992). Willingness to communicate and employee success in U.S. organizations. *Journal of Applied Communication Research, 20,* 95–115.

Riecken, H. (1975). The effect of talkativeness on ability to influence group solutions of problems. In P. V. Crosbie (Ed.), *Interaction in small groups* (pp. 238–249). New York: Macmillan.

Riggio, R. E., Ciulla, J. B., & Sorenson, G. J. (2003). Leadership education at the undergraduate level: A liberal arts approach to leadership development. In S. E. Murphy & R. E. Riggio (Eds.), *The future of leadership development* (pp. 201–236). Mahwah, NJ: Lawrence Erlbaum.

Roberts, J. (2006). *A sense of the world: How a blind man became history's greatest traveler.* New York: HarperCollins.

Roddick, A. (1991). *Body and soul.* New York: Crown.

Rogers, E. M. (1995). *Diffusion of innovations* (4th ed.). New York: The Free Press.

Rogers, E. M., & Steinfatt, T. M. (1999). *Intercultural communication.* Long Grove, IL: Waveland Press.

Rogers, E. M., & Storey, J. D. (1987). Communication campaigns. In C. R. Berger & S. H. Chaffee (Eds.), *Handbook of Communication Science* (pp. 817–846). Newbury Park, CA: Sage.

Rokeach, M. (1973). *The nature of human values.* New York: Free Press.

Roloff, M. E., & Barnicott, E. F. (1978). The situational use of pro- and antisocial compliance-gaining strategies by high and low Machiavellians. In B. Ruben (Ed.), *Communication Yearbook 2* (pp. 193– 208). New Brunswick, NJ: Transaction Books.

Roloff, M. E., & Paulson, G. D. (2001). Confronting organizational transgressions. In J. M. Darley, D. M. Messick, & T. R. Tyler (Eds.,), *Social influences on ethical behavior in organizations* (pp. 53–68). Mahwah, NJ: Lawrence Erlbaum.

Roloff, M. E., Putnam, L. L., & Anastascou, L. (2003). Negotiation skills. In J. O. Greene & B. R. Burleson (Eds.), *Handbook of communication and social interaction skills* (pp. 801– 833). Mahwah, NJ: Lawrence Erlbaum.

Rosener, J. B. (1990, November–December). Ways women lead. *Harvard Business Review,* 119–125.

Rosenfeld, P., Giacalone, R. A., & Riordan, C. A. (1995*). Impression management in organizations: Theory, measurement, practice.* New York: Routledge.

Rosenthal, R. (1993). Interpersonal expectations: Some antecedents and some consequences. In P. D. Blanck (Ed.), *Interpersonal expectations: Theory, research and applications* (pp. 3–24) Cambridge: Cambridge University Press.

Rosenthal, R., & Jacobson, L. (1968). *Pygmalion in the classroom.* New York: Holt, Rinehart and Winston.

Ross, J., & Staw, B. M. (1993). Organizational escalation and exit: Lessons from the Shoreham nuclear power plant. *Academy of Management Journal, 36,* 701–732.

Rost, J. C. (1993; 1991). *Leadership for the twenty-first century.* New York: Praeger.

Rost, J. C. (1993). Leadership in the new millennium. *The Journal of Leadership Studies, 1,* 92–110.

Rothwell, J. D. (2001). *In mixed company: Small group communication* (4th ed.). Fort Worth: Harcourt Brace.

Rothwell, W. J. (2001). *Executive succession planning* (2nd ed.). New York: AMACOM.

Rubin, J. Z., & Brown, B. R. (1975). *The social psychology of bargaining and negotiation.* New York: Academic Press.

Rudin, S. A. (1964). Leadership as psychophysiological activation of group members: A case experimental study. *Psychological Reports, 15,* 577–578.

Ruschman, N. L. (2002). Servant-leadership and the best companies to work for in America. In L. C. Spears & M. Lawrence (Eds.), *Focus on leadership: Servant-leadership for the twenty-first century* (pp. 123–139). New York: Wiley & Sons.

Sadler, P. (2001). Leadership and organizational learning. In M. Dierkes, A. Berthoin Antal, J. Child, & I. Nonaka (Eds.), *Handbook of organizational learning and knowledge* (pp. 415– 427). Oxford: Oxford University Press.

Salovey, P., Bedwell, B. T., Detweiler, J. B., & Mayer, J. D. (2000). Current directions in emotional intelligence research. In M. Lewis & J. M. Haviland-Lewis, *Handbook of emotions* (2nd ed., pp. 504–520). New York: Guilford Press.

Sanders, D. A., & Sanders, J. A. (1984). *Teaching creativity through metaphor.* New York: Longman.

Sattler, W. M. (1947). Conceptions of ethos in ancient rhetoric. *Speech Monographs, 14,* 55–65.

Scheidel, T. M., & Crowell, L. (1964). Idea development in small discussion groups. *Quarterly Journal of Speech, 50,* 140–145.

Schein, E. H. (1983). The role of the founder in creating organizational culture. *Organizational Dynamics, 12,* 13–26.

Schein, E. H. (1992). *Organizational culture and leadership* (2nd ed.). San Francisco: Jossey-Bass.

Schermerhorn, R., & Bond, M. H. (1997). Cross-cultural leadership dynamics in collectivism and high power distance settings. *Leadership & Organization Development Journal, 18*, 187–193.

Schoenberg, A. (2005, Spring). Do crisis plans matter? A new perspective on leading during a crisis. *Public Relations Quarterly, 50*, 2–6.

Schriesheim, C. A., Castro, S. L., & Cogliser, C. C. (1999). Leader-member exchange (LMX) research: A comprehensive review of theory, measurement, and data-analytic practices. *Leadership Quarterly, 10*, 63–113.

Schriesheim, C. A., & Kerr, S. (1977). Theories and measures of leadership: A critical appraisal. In J. G. Hunt & L. L. Larson (Eds.), *Leadership: The cutting edge* (pp. 9–45). Carbondale: Southern Illinois University Press.

Schrodt, P., Cawyer, C. S., & Sanders, R. (2003). An examination of academic mentoring behaviors and new faculty members' satisfaction with socialization and tenure and promotion processes. *Communication Education, 52*, 17–29.

Schultz, B. (1979). Predicting emergent leaders: An exploratory study of the salience of communicative functions. *Small Group Behavior, 9*, 109–114.

Schultz, B. (1980). Communicative correlates of perceived leaders. *Small Group Behavior, 11*, 175–191.

Schultz, B. (1982). Argumentativeness: Its effect in group decision making and its role in leadership perception. *Communication Quarterly, 30*, 368–375.

Schultz, B. G. (1996). *Communicating in the small group: Theory and practice* (2nd ed.). New York: HarperCollins.

Sebeok, T. A., & Rosenthal, R. (Eds.). (1981). *The clever Hans phenomenon: Communication with horses, whales, apes, and people.* (Annals of the New York Academy of Sciences, Vol. 364.) New York: New York Academy of Sciences.

Sebeok, T. A., & Umiker-Sebeok, J. (1979). *Speaking of apes: A critical anthology of two-way communication with man.* New York: Plenum.

Seeger, M. W., Sellnow, T. L., & Ulmer, R. R. (1998). Communication, organization, and crisis. In M. E. Roloff (Ed.), *Communication yearbook 21* (pp. 231–275). Thousand Oaks, CA: Sage.

Seeger, M. W., Sellnow, T. L., & Ulmer, R. R. (2003). *Communication and organizational crisis.* Westport, CT: Praeger.

Seibert, S. C., Silver, S. R., & Randolph, R. W. (2004). Taking empowerment to the next level: A multiple-level model of empowerment, performance, and satisfaction. *Academy of Management Journal, 47*, 332–349.

Seifter, H., & Economy, P. (2001). *Leadership ensemble: Lessons in collaborative management from the world's only conductorless orchestra.* New York: Times Books.

Senge, P. M. (1990). *The fifth discipline: The art and practice of the learning organization.* New York: Doubleday/Currency.

Senge, P. M. (1990, Fall). The leader's new work: Building learning organizations. *Sloan Management Review*, 7–23.

Shamir, B., & Eilam, G. (2005). "What's your story?" A life-stories approach to authentic leadership development. *Leadership Quarterly, 16*, 395–417.

Shaw, M. E. (1955). A comparison of two types of leadership in various communication nets. *Journal of Abnormal and Social Psychology, 50*, 127–134.

Sherman, E. (2001, Fall). Women in political leadership: Reflections on larger social issues. *Leadership*, 4–5.

Sherwood, J. (1988). Creating work cultures with competitive advantage. *Organizational Dynamics, 16*, 4.

Shockley-Zalabak, P., & Burmester, S. B. (2001). *The power of networked teams.* New York: Oxford University Press.

Shockley-Zalabak, P., Ellis, K., & Cesaria, R. (2000). *Measuring organizational trust.* San Francisco: International Association of Business Communicators.

Shockley-Zalabak, P., Ellis, K. & Winograd, G. (2000). Organizational trust: What it means, why it matters. *Organization Development Journal, 18*, 35–47.

Simons, H. W., Morreale, J., & Gronbeck, B. (2003). *Persuasion in society.* Thousand Oaks, CA: Sage.

Simons T. (2000). Behavioral integrity: The perceived alignment between managers' words and deeds as a research focus. *Organization Science, 13,* 18–35.

Simons, T. (2002, September). The high cost of lost trust. *Harvard Business Review,* 18–19.

Sims, H. P., & Manz, C. C. (1996). *Company of heroes: Unleashing the power of self-leadership.* New York: John Wiley.

Singelis, T. M., Triandis, H. C., Bhawuk, D. S., & Gelfand, M. (1995). Horizontal and vertical dimensions of individualism and collectivism: A theoretical and measurement refinement. *Cross-Cultural Research, 29,* 240–275.

Singhal, A., & Rogers, E. (1999). *Entertainment-education: A communication strategy for social change.* Mahwah, NJ: Lawrence Erlbaum.

Skyrme, D. J. (2000). Developing a knowledge strategy: From management to leadership. In D. Morey, M. Maybury & B. Thuraisingham (Eds.), *Knowledge management: Classic and contemporary works* (pp. 61–83). Cambridge, MA: MIT Press.

Smith, A. E., Jussim, L., & Eccles, J. (1999). Do self-fulfilling prophecies accumulate, dissipate, or remain stable over time? *Journal of Personality and Social Psychology, 77,* 548–565.

Smith, T. W. (1990). *Ethnic images.* National Opinion Research Center, GSS Topical Report No. 19. Chicago: University of Chicago.

Snyder, N. H., & Graves, M. (1994). Leadership and vision. *Business Horizons, 37,* 1–7.

Solomon, R. (1988). Internal objections to virtue ethics. *Midwest Studies in Philosophy, 8,* 428–441.

Sorensen, R., & Pickett, T. (1986). A test of two teaching strategies designed to improve interview effectiveness: Rating behavior and videotaped feedback. *Communication Monographs, 35,* 13–22.

Sosi, J. J., Avolio, B. J., & Jung, D. I. (2002). Beneath the mask: Examining the relationship of self-presentation attributes and impression management to charismatic leadership. *Leadership Quarterly, 13,* 217–242.

Spears, L. (1998). Tracing the growing impact of servant-leadership. In L. Spears (Ed.), *Insights on leadership* (pp. 1–15). New York: Wiley & Sons.

Spencer, H. (1884). *The study of sociology.* New York: D. A. Appleton. (First published in 1873.)

Spitzack, C., & Carter, K. (1987). Women in communication studies: A typology for revision. *Quarterly Journal of Speech, 73,* 401–423.

Spreitzer, G. M. (1995). Psychological empowerment in the workplace: Dimensions, measurement, and validation. *Academy of Management Journal, 38,* 1422–1465.

Spreitzer, G. M. (1996). Social structural characteristics of psychological empowerment. *Academy of Management Journal, 39,* 483–504.

Spreitzer, G. M., Kizilos, M. A., & Nason, S. W. (1997). A dimensional analysis of the relationship between psychological empowerment and effectiveness, satisfaction, and strain. *Journal of Management, 23,* 679–704.

Stang, D. J. (1973). Effect of interaction rate on ratings of leadership and liking. *Journal of Personality and Social Psychology, 27,* 405–408.

Staw, B. M. (2001). The escalation of commitment to a course of action. *Academy of Management Review, 6,* 577–587.

Staw, B. M., & Sutton, R. (1993). Macro organizational psychology. In J. K. Murnighan (Ed.), *Social psychology in organizations: Advances in theory and research* (pp. 350–384). Englewood Cliffs, NJ: Prentice-Hall.

Stech, E. L. (1983). *Leadership communication.* Chicago: Nelson-Hall.

Stewart, C. J., Smith, C. A., & Denton, R. E. (2007). *Persuasion and social movements* (5th ed.). Long Grove, IL: Waveland Press.

Stewart, G.L., Manz, C.C., & Sims, H.P. (1999). *Team work and group dynamics.* New York: Wiley.

Stogdill, R. M. (1948). Personal factors associated with leadership: A survey of the literature. *Journal of Psychology, 25,* 35–71.

Stogdill, R. M. (1950). Leadership, membership and organization. *Psychological Bulletin, 47.*

Stogdill, R. M. (1965). *Managers, employees, organizations.* Columbus: Ohio State University, Bureau of Business Research.

Stogdill, R. M. (1974). *Handbook of leadership.* New York: The Free Press.

Stogdill, R. M., & Coons, A. E. (1957). *Leader behavior: Its description and measurement.* Columbus: Ohio State University, Bureau of Business Research.

Strong, S. R., & Dixon, D. N. (1971). Expertness, attractiveness, and influence in counseling. *Journal of Counseling Psychology, 18,* 562–570.

Strong, S. R., & Schmidt, L. D. (1970). Expertness and influence in counseling. *Journal of Counseling Psychology, 17,* 81–87.

Sturges, D. L. (1994). Communicating through crisis: A strategy for organizational survival. *Management Communication Quarterly, 7,* 297–316.

Susskind, L., & Field, P. (1996). *Dealing with an angry public: The mutual gains approach to resolving disputes.* New York: The Free Press.

Tannen, D. (1990). *You just don't understand: Women and men in conversation.* New York: Ballantine.

Tannen, D. (1994). *Talking from 9 to 5.* New York: William Morrow and Company.

Tannenbaum, R., & Schmidt, W. H. (1958). How to choose a leadership pattern. *Harvard Business Review, 36,* 95–101.

Tenbrusel, A. E., & Messick, D. M. (2001). Power asymmetries and the ethical atmosphere in negotiations. In J. M. Darley, D. M. Messick, & T. R. Tyler (Eds.), *Social influences on ethical behavior in organizations* (pp. 201–216). Mahwah, NJ: Lawrence Erlbaum.

Terrace, H. S., Pettito, L. A., Sanders, R. J., & Bever, T. G. (1979). Can an ape create a sentence? *Science, 206,* 891–902.

Terry, R. W. (1993). *Authentic leadership: Courage in action.* San Francisco: Jossey-Bass.

Thibault, J. W., & Kelley, H. H. (1978). *Interpersonal relations: A theory of interdependence.* New York: John Wiley.

Thomas, D. A. (2001, April–May). Race matters: The truth about mentoring minorities. *Harvard Business Review,* 99–107.

Thomas, D. A., & Ely, R. J. (1996, September–October). Making differences matter: A new paradigm for managing diversity. *Harvard Business Review,* 79–90.

Thomas, D. A., & Gabarro, J. J. (1999). *Breaking through: The making of minority executives in corporate America.* Boston: Harvard Business School Press.

Thomas, D. A. (2001, April–May). Race matters: The truth about mentoring minorities. *Harvard Business Review,* 99–107.

Thomas, K W., & Velthouse, B. A. (1990) Cognitive elements of empowerment: An "interpretive" model of intrinsic task motivation. *Academy of Management Review, 15,* 666–681.

Tichy, N. M. (1997). *The leadership engine.* New York: HarperBusiness.

Ting, S., & Hart, E. W. (2004). Formal coaching. In C. D. McCauley, & E. Van Velsor (Eds.), *The Center for Creative Leadership handbook of leadership development* (2nd ed., pp 116–150). San Francisco: Jossey-Bass.

Ting, S., & Scisco, P. (2006). *The CCL handbook of coaching: A guide for the leader coach.* San Francisco: Jossey-Bass.

Tompkins, P. K. (1982). *Communication as action: An introduction to rhetoric and communication.* Belmont, CA: Wadsworth.

Torricelli, R., & Carroll, A. (Eds.) (1999). *In our own words: Extraordinary speeches of the American century.* New York: Kodansha International.

Trevino, L. K., & Weaver, G. R. (2003). *Managing ethics in business organizations: Social scientific perspectives.* Stanford, CA: Stanford University Press.

Triandis, H. C. (1993). The contingency model in cross-cultural perspective. In M. M. Chemers & R. Ayman (Eds.), *Leadership theory and research: Perspectives and directions* (pp. 167–188). San Diego: Academic Press.

Trice, H. M., & Beyer, J. M. (1984). Studying organizational cultures through rites and ceremonials. *Academy of Management Review, 9,* 653–669.

Trice, H. M., & Beyer, J. M. (1985). Using six organizational rites to change culture. In R. H. Killmann, M. J. Saxton, & R. Serpa (Eds.), *Gaining control of the corporate culture* (pp. 370–399). San Francisco: Jossey-Bass.

Trice, H. M., & Beyer, J. M. (1993). *The cultures of work organizations.* Englewood Cliffs, NJ: Prentice-Hall.

Trist, E. L., & Bamforth, K. W. (1951). Some social and psychological consequences of the longwall method of coal-getting. *Human Relations, 4,* 3–38.

Tromprenaars, F. (1994). *Riding the waves of culture: Understanding diversity in global business.* Burr Ridge, IL: Irwin.

Tropman, J. (2003). *Making meetings work: Achieving high quality group decisions.* (2nd ed.). Thousand Oaks, CA: Sage.

Tucker, R. C. (1965). The dictator and totalitarianism. *World Politics, 17,* 565–573.

Turner, N., Barling, J., Epitropaki, O., Butcher, V., & Milner, C. (2002). Transformational leadership and moral reasoning. *Journal of Applied Psychology, 87,* 304–311.

Uhl-Bien, M. (2003). Relationship development as a key ingredient for leadership development. In S. E. Murphy & R. E. Riggo (Eds.), *The future of leadership development* (pp. 129–147). Mahwah, NJ: Erlbaum.

Ulrich, D., Von Glinow, M. A., & Todd, J. (1993). High-impact learning: Building and diffusing learning capability. *Organizational Dynamics, 22,* 52–66.

Useem, M. (1998). *The leadership moment.* New York: Times Books.

Useem, M. (2001). *Leading up: How to lead your boss so you both win.* New York: Crown Business.

Van der Merwe, W. L. (1996). Philosophy and the multi-cultural context of (post)apartheid South Africa. *Ethical Perspectives, 3,* 1–15.

Van Velsor, E., & McCauley, C. D. (2004). Introduction: Our view of leadership development. In *The Center for Creative Leadership handbook of leadership development* (2nd ed., pp. 1–22). San Francisco: Jossey-Bass.

Vinson, L. (1988, November). *An emotion-based model of compliance-gaining message selection.* Paper presented at the Speech Communication Association convention, New Orleans, LA.

Vinson, L., & Johnson, C. E. (1990). The relationship between the use of hesitations and/or hedges and listening: The role of perceived importance as a mediating variable. *Journal of the International Listening Association, 4,* 116–127.

Vinson, L., Johnson, C. E., & Hackman, M. (1992). *I like you just the way you are: Student evaluations of favorite and least favorite instructors using hesitant speech.* Paper presented at the Speech Communication Association convention, Chicago, IL.

von Oech, R. (1986). *A kick in the seat of the pants* (pp. 30, 32). New York: Harper & Row.

Vroom, V. H., & Mann, F. C. (1960). Leader authorization and employee attitudes. *Personnel Psychology, 13,* 125–140.

Walker, S. (1983). *Animal thought.* London: Routledge & Kegan Paul.

Wallas, G. (1926). *The art of thought.* New York: Harcourt.

Ward, C. D., & McGinnies, E. (1974). Persuasive effects of early and late mention of credible and non-credible sources. *Journal of Psychology, 86,* 17–23.

Warren, I. D. (1969). The effects of credibility in sources of testimony and audience attitudes toward speaker and topic. *Speech Monographs, 36,* 456–458.

Wasden, M., & Guzley, R. (2004, November). *Guided freedom leadership: Competent and capable individuals in the 21st century.* Paper presented at the International Leadership Association Conference, Washington, D.C.

Watson, D. (2003) *Death Sentences: How cliches, weasel words, and management-speak are strangling public language.* New York: Gotham Books.

Weatherall, A. (1998). Re-visioning gender and language research. *Women and language, 21,* 1–9.

Weaver, G. R., Trevino, L., & Cochran, P. L. (1999). Integrated and decoupled corporate social performance: Management commitments, external pressures, and corporate ethics practices. *Academy of Management Journal, 42,* 539–532.

Weaver, G. R., Trevino, L. K., & Cochran P. L. (1999). Corporate ethics practices in the mid-1990s: An empirical study of the Fortune 1000. *Journal of Business Ethics, 18,* 283–294.

Weber, M. (1947). *The theory of social and economic organization* (pp. 358–359). (A. M. Henderson & T. Parsons, Trans.) Glencoe, IL: The Free Press.

Weick, K. E., & Sutcliffe, K. M. (2001). *Managing the unexpected: Assuring high performance in an age of complexity*. San Francisco: Jossey-Bass.

Weisinger, H. (1998). *Emotional intelligence at work: The untapped edge for success*. San Francisco: Jossey-Bass.

Wellins, R. S., Byham, W. C., & Dixon, G. R. (1994). *Inside teams*. San Francisco: Jossey-Bass.

Wellins, R. S., Byham, W. C., & Wilson, J. M. (1991). *Empowered teams*. San Francisco: Jossey-Bass.

Weschler, I. R., Kahane, M., & Tannenbaum, R. (1952). Job satisfaction, productivity, and morale: A case study. *Occupational Psychology, 26*, 1–14.

White, L. A. (1949). *The science of culture*. New York: Farrar, Strauss and Cudahy.

White, R., & Lippitt, R. (1968). Leader behavior and member reaction in three "social climates." In D. Cartwright & A. Zander (Eds.), *Group dynamics* (pp. 318–335). New York: Harper & Row.

White, S. S., & Lock, E. A. (2000). Problems with the Pygmalion Effect and some proposed solutions. *Leadership Quarterly, 11*, 389–416.

Whitener, E. M. (1997). The impact of human resource activities on employee trust. *Human Resource Management Review, 7*, 380–405.

Whitener, E. M., Brodt, S. E., Korsgaard, J. A., & Werner, J. M. (1998). Managers as initiators of trust: An exchange relationship framework for understanding managerial trustworthy behavior. *Academy of Management Review, 23*, 513–530.

Whitman, R. F., & Foster, T. J. (1994). *Speaking in public*. New York: Macmillan.

Wilcox, D. L., Cameron, G. T., Ault, P. H., & Agee, W. K. (2003). *Public relations: Strategies and tactics* (7th ed.). New York: Longman.

Williams, G. R. (1993). Style and effectiveness in negotiation. In L. Hall (Ed.), *Negotiation: Strategies for mutual gain* (pp. 151–174). Newbury Park, CA: Sage.

Williams, V. (2002). *Virtual leadership*. Edison, NJ: Shadowbrook Publishing.

Winsten, J. A., & DeJong, W. (2001). The designated driver campaign. In R. R. Rice & C. K. Atkin (Eds.), *Public communication campaigns* (3rd ed., pp. 290–294). Thousand Oaks, CA: Sage.

Witherspoon, P. D. (1997). *Communicating Leadership: An organizational perspective*. Boston: Allyn & Bacon.

Witt, J. L., & Morgan, J. (2002). *Stronger in the broken places: Nine lessons for turning crisis into triumph*. New York: Times Books/Henry Holt.

Wood, J. T. (1999). *Gendered lives: Communication, gender and culture* (3rd ed.). Belmont, CA: Wadsworth.

Woodward, G. C., & Denton, R. E. (2004). *Persuasion & influence in American life* (5th ed.). Long Grove, IL: Waveland Press.

Woodward, J. (1965). *Industrial organization: Theory and practice*. Oxford: Oxford University Press.

Wyscoki, L. (1990, September). *Implementation of self-managed teams within a non-union manufacturing facility*. Paper presented at the International Conference on Self-Managed Work Teams, Denton, TX.

Yukl, G. (2006). *Leadership in organizations* (6th ed.). Upper Saddle River, NJ: Pearson Prentice-Hall.

Yukl, G., & Falbe, C. M. (1991). Importance of different power sources in downward and lateral relations. *Journal of Applied Psychology, 76*, 416–423.

Yukl, G., Falbe, C. M., & Youn, J. (1993). Patterns of influence behaviors for managers. *Group & Organization Management, 18*, 5–28.

Yukl, G., Guinan, P. J., & Sottolano, D. (1995). Influence tactics used for different objectives with subordinates, peers, and superiors. *Group & Organization Management, 20*, 272–296.

Zaccaro, S. J., Ardison, S. D., & Orvis, K. L. (2004). Leadership in virtual teams. In *Leadership development for transforming organizations: Growing leaders for tomorrow*. Mahwah, NJ: Lawrence Erlbaum.

Zaccaro, S. J., & Banks, D. J. (2001). Leadership, vision, and organizational effectiveness. In S. J. Zaccaro and R. K. Klimoski (Eds.), *The nature of organizational leadership* (pp. 181–218). San Francisco: Jossey Bass.

Zaccaro, S.J., Kemp, C., & Bader, P. (2004). Leader traits and attributes. In J. Antonakis, A.T. Cianciolo, R.J. Sternberg (Eds.) *The nature of leadership* (pp. 101–124). Thousand Oaks, CA: Sage.

Zachary, L. J. (2000). *The mentor's guide*. San Francisco: Jossey-Bass.

Zemke, R., Raines, C., & Filipczak, B. (2000). *Generations at work*. New York: AMACOM.

Ziller, R. C. (1954). Four techniques of group decision making under uncertainty. *American Psychologist, 9,* 498.

Zorn, T. E. (1991). Construct system development, transformational leadership and leadership messages. *Southern Communication Journal, 56,* 178–193.

Index